The State versus The People

The State versus The People

Revolutionary Justice in Russia's Civil War, 1917–1922

MATTHEW RENDLE

OXFORD
UNIVERSITY PRESS

OXFORD
UNIVERSITY PRESS

Great Clarendon Street, Oxford, OX2 6DP,
United Kingdom

Oxford University Press is a department of the University of Oxford.
It furthers the University's objective of excellence in research, scholarship,
and education by publishing worldwide. Oxford is a registered trade mark of
Oxford University Press in the UK and in certain other countries

First Edition published in 2020

Impression: 1

Published in the United States of America by Oxford University Press
198 Madison Avenue, New York, NY 10016, United States of America

British Library Cataloguing in Publication Data
Data available

Library of Congress Control Number: 2020930675

ISBN 978–0–19–884042–8

Printed and bound by
CPI Group (UK) Ltd, Croydon, CR0 4YY

Contents

List of Figures

List of Abbreviations and Glossary

BAR	Bakhmeteff Archive, Columbia University
Cheka	All-Russian Extraordinary Commission for the Struggle with Counter-Revolution and Sabotage
DSV	*Dekrety Sovetskoi vlasti* (18 volumes, Moscow, 1957–2009)
ESIu	*Ezhenedel'nik Sovetskoi iustitsii* (1922–9)
GARF	Gosudarstvennyi arkhiv Rossiiskoi Federatsii, Moscow
GPU	State Political Directorate (successor to the Cheka in 1922)
HIA	Hoover Institution Archives, Stanford
IZ	*Istoriia zakonodatel'stva SSSR i RSFSR po ugolovnomu protsessu i organizatsii suda i prokuratury, 1917–1954* (Moscow, 1955)
KT	Cassation Tribunal
Materialy	*Materialy Narodnogo Komissariata Iustitsii* (1918–22)
Narkomiust	Commissariat of Justice
Narkompros	Commissariat of Enlightenment
Narkomput	Commissariat of Paths and Communications
Narkomvnudel	Commissariat of Internal Affairs
Narkomvoen	Commissariat of War
NEP	New Economic Policy
OGPU	United State Political Directorate (successor to the GPU in 1923)
RGASPI	Rossiiskii gosudarstvennyi arkhiv sotsial'no-politicheskoi istorii, Moscow
RGVA	Rossiiskii gosudarstvennyi voennyi arkhiv, Moscow
RVTR	Revolutionary Military Tribunal of the Russian Republic
Sovnarkom	Council of People's Commissars
SR	Socialist Revolutionary/Revolutionaries
TsGAMO	Tsentral'nyi gosudarstvennyi arkhiv Moskovskoi oblasti, Moscow
uezd	district, subdivision of a province (pl. *uezdy*)
VOKhR	Internal Security Force of the Republic
volost'	parish, subdivision of an *uezd* (pl. *volosti*)
VTsIK	All-Russian Central Executive Committee of the Congress of Soviets
YIVO	YIVO Institute for Jewish Research, New York

Notes on the Text

When transliterating Russian, I have tried to use the Library of Congress system throughout to avoid confusion, retaining soft signs at the end of words.

I have preserved the dates used in Russia at the time. Therefore, all dates prior to 31 January 1918 are given according to the Julian calendar, which in the twentieth century ran thirteen days behind the new-style Gregorian calendar used by Western Europe. The Bolsheviks adopted the Gregorian calendar in February 1918, declaring that the day after 31 January would be 14 February.

Archival materials are referred to by their *fond* or collection number (f.), the *opis'* or section within the collection (op.), the actual file or *delo* number (d.), and the page number or *listok* (l.), or page numbers (ll.). I made extensive use of the microfilm collection 'The Archives of the Soviet Communist Party and Soviet State', which is available in various major libraries, especially the Hoover Institution. The documents from the archives of the Supreme Court (f. R-1005) and the Commissariat of Internal Affairs (f. R-393) were particularly valuable. However, I decided to use the Russian archival references throughout (rather than include reel numbers) as I also looked at files from these collections in Moscow, and I wish to avoid any confusion (finding aids make it possible to link the archival reference to the microfilm reel). The project to microfilm f. R-1005, in particular, was deliberately incomplete, missing one entire *opis'* and many case files.

Acknowledgements

This project has been over a decade in the making and I have racked up many debts during this period. For a start, the project would never have taken its current form without three developments. The British Academy funded a period of research in Moscow when I was finishing my previous study of tsarist elites and exploring their fate after the October Revolution, which inevitably led me to tribunals. I first examined the archival holdings of various tribunals during this trip and started to appreciate the wealth of material in them. The results, as well as feeding into my previous book, became an article in *Historical Research*, but the research may not have progressed further had it not been for a conference on 'Villains and Victims' at the University of Nottingham in 2010, where an enthusiastic reception convinced me to pursue the topic. I am grateful to Sarah Badcock for the invitation to attend and for organizing the publication of some of the papers in *Europe-Asia Studies*. The final step was the award of a Research Fellowship by the Leverhulme Trust in 2011–12, which provided a year's leave to really get this project started and to conduct research in Russia and the US. I am very grateful to Chris Read, David Saunders, Steve Smith, and Peter Waldron for acting as referees for these grant applications.

I am grateful to the British Academy for funding a further period of archival research in Russia once the project was underway, and to the College of Humanities at the University of Exeter for granting several periods of research leave that proved crucial to writing various chapters. Throughout, there were frequent visits to libraries and archives. In the UK, staff at the University of Birmingham, British Library, University of Glasgow, London School of Economics, and the School of Slavonic and East European Studies were particularly helpful, as were the inter-library loan staff at Exeter. In Moscow, staff at the State Archive of the Russian Federation, the Russian State Military Archive, and the Central State Archive of Moscow Region helped me access relevant materials, as did those in the Historical Library and the Russian State Library. In the US, individuals at various libraries at the universities of Berkeley, Chicago, Columbia, Harvard, Illinois at Urbana-Champaign, and Stanford were helpful in numerous ways, as was the New York Public Library and YIVO Institute for Jewish Research in New York. I am particularly grateful to the Hoover Institution at Stanford for access to their unparalleled collections on the revolutionary period during the Research Fellowship, especially the extensive microfilms of the archives of the Supreme Tribunal, which enabled me to explore the records in far more depth than I would have been able to otherwise and freed up time in Russia to concentrate on other materials. All the staff were incredibly helpful across two trips, and I would like to thank David Jacobs, in particular, for making my stays in Palo Alto extremely enjoyable.

The final stages of writing this book have been overshadowed by increasingly desperate attempts to obtain permissions for the various illustrations. I am very grateful to Allison Alsaker at East View Information Services, Andrea Felder at the New York Public Library, Anne Mar at Occidental College, Virginia Mokslaveskas at the Getty Research Institute, Sarah Patton at the Hoover Institution, and Diane Workman at the University of Exeter for facilitating permissions, providing high-quality versions of images, and answering complicated copyright queries. Earlier versions of parts of several chapters were published in *Europe-Asia Studies*, *Historical Research*, and *The Slavonic and East European Review*, and I thank various editors and reviewers for their valuable feedback. At Oxford University Press, Robert Faber first showed an interest in this project several years ago, and his comments, alongside the extensive reports of three initial reviewers, went a long way to shaping the final manuscript. Subsequently, Stephanie Ireland, Christina Wipf Perry, and Cathryn Steele have all helped shepherd the work from acceptance to publication, while additional reviews have continued to force me to think carefully about the book's central themes.

The field of Russian legal history has been a rapidly expanding one in recent years, and I have been fortunate to benefit from being on conference panels, holding conversations, and sharing work and resources with many of those involved. Grateful thanks are particularly due to Aaron Retish, who has been the source of many valuable ideas throughout and generously shared material as he has worked on his own parallel project on Soviet justice in the interwar period. I am also grateful to Lara Douds, Murray Frame, Chris Gilley, Tony Heywood, James Heinzen, George Levy, Dan Newman, Joe Nicholson, William Pomeranz, James Ryan, Francesca Silano, Yana Skorobogatov, Peter Solomon, Pavel Vasilyev, Jon Waterlow, and Elizabeth Wood, all of whom have either discussed conference papers, commented directly on my work, shared their own work, suggested sources, or simply helped me to explore important themes.

The length of this project has provided many different venues to try out various ideas and chapters, with the Association of Slavic, East European and Eurasian Studies, the British Association of Slavic and East European Studies, and the Study Group on the Russian Revolution deserving special mention. I would also like to thank audiences at the Historical Association in Exeter, the University of Glasgow, the University of Winchester, and the Russian Studies *kruzhok* at the University of Illinois Urbana-Champaign for their comments and queries, all of which invariably forced me to think again about key issues.

At Exeter, my biggest debt is to my fellow Russianist Claire McCallum, who has provided enthusiastic encouragement throughout, and who always took the time to read through my work and force me to think more clearly about key issues despite the fact that the topic was far removed from her own interests. During the final writing stage, our informal *kruzhok* also provided invaluable feedback—grateful thanks to Julia Leikin, Rachel Lin, and Claire McCallum! Elsewhere in the Department of History, although they probably will not realize it, Alex Fairfax-Cholmeley generously shared his knowledge of French revolutionary tribunals and his unpublished thesis, Stacey Hynd's penetrating questions early on forced me to read more widely across legal scholarship, and encouraging conversations with Tim Rees and Martin Thomas helped sharpen some ideas.

Finally, this book could not have been completed without the help of my family, particularly my wife, Laura; my parents, David and Susan; and my grandfather, Charles. I apologize for the length of time that you have all been forced to live with this project, as I know it has led to long absences abroad and too much time spent reading and writing when at home. Not only has Laura borne the brunt of this burden, but she rashly offered to help draw at short notice the line diagrams in the first and second chapters. As always, I will remain forever grateful!

Introduction

The challenges facing the new Bolshevik government after the October Revolution of 1917 were immense. Divided internally over tactics, their unilateral seizure of power came at a time when most Russians desired a coalition socialist government. The pressures of the First World War were ongoing and the weakness of the central state apparatus had fuelled local autonomy. Widespread strikes among civil servants paralysed official organs, and there were instances of armed resistance in Petrograd and Moscow, as well as other towns, with the threat of further organized resistance on the horizon. The Bolsheviks responded immediately in various ways, issuing popular decrees seeking peace and sanctioning land redistribution at the same time as restoring censorship and banning conservative and liberal political groups. Yet they continued to believe, with justification, that the threat of counter-revolution remained ever-present.

Many Bolshevik leaders increasingly felt they lacked a structured means to target this threat beyond individual acts of repression. On 22 November, a meeting of the Council of People's Commissars (Sovnarkom) agreed that the lack of a 'revolutionary court' placed the state in a 'desperate situation' and 'powerless' to deal with 'counter-revolutionary' crimes.[1] The resulting decree on courts created a two-pronged legal system. People's courts would deal with regular crimes, such as murder, theft, and disputes. Revolutionary tribunals would cover counter-revolutionary crimes—revolts, plots, sabotage, and the other abuses of class enemies. Both courts would reflect the 'will of the people' and were thus staffed by elected officials, not necessarily with a legal background, and guided by existing laws only insofar as these had not been overruled by decrees or socialist party programmes and did not contradict revolutionary conscience.[2] This was 'revolutionary justice', and the Bolsheviks expected it to play an important role in securing their authority. Tribunals, in particular, were the *revolutionary* element of this decree since they were designed to combat a counter-revolutionary threat that only existed because of the revolution.

For many commentators—then and now—the concept of revolutionary justice was an oxymoron; there was no justice in the violent revolutionary practices of the Bolsheviks. The establishment only a fortnight later of a new secret police, the

[1] *Protokoly zasedanii Soveta Narodnykh Komissarov RSFSR. Noiabr' 1917-mart 1918gg.* (Moscow, 2006), 44.

[2] *Dekrety Sovetskoi vlasti* (18 volumes, Moscow, 1957–2009), I, 124–6.

The State versus The People: Revolutionary Justice in Russia's Civil War, 1917–1922. Matthew Rendle, Oxford University Press (2020). © Matthew Rendle.
DOI: 10.1093/oso/9780198840428.001.0001

All-Russian Extraordinary Commission for the Struggle with Counter-Revolution and Sabotage (Cheka), reinforced the impression that law had quickly been superseded by revolutionary violence as the Bolsheviks struggled to hold on to power. Some scholars have charted a full-scale attack on law and 'legal nihilism'.[3] Others have agreed, describing revolutionary justice as 'legalised lawlessness' or 'legalised arbitrariness'; there were courts but no laws, only revolutionary consciousness, while people were punished arbitrarily for ill-defined crimes, with execution the only result.[4] Most have not been so blunt, but the assumption remains that tribunals at least were Bolshevik-controlled courts targeting the party's political and social enemies, inseparable from the Cheka and contributing to rising levels of violence. Often underpinning these negative assessments seems to be the belief that a system of law so different from those practised in the 'West', to quote a contemporary, particularly the idea of a legal system without law codes, cannot be considered a 'real judiciary' at all and instead was developed solely to subjugate the population to Bolshevik rule.[5]

There is much evidence to support these arguments. There are voluminous and graphic accounts of the Cheka's violent atrocities and, as this book describes, expanding definitions of counter-revolution came to encompass all sorts of crimes implicating ever more people. Tribunals spread across Russia from 1918, dispensing the death penalty for numerous, often seemingly trivial, crimes after short, incomplete trials. In short, as the civil rights society Memorial argued recently, the repressive policies of the Soviet Union were in evidence from its very first days, with many hundreds of arrests and frequent instances of lawlessness.[6]

A closer look at all the evidence, however, complicates this picture. There is no doubt that revolutionary justice was accompanied by a profusion of violence and violent rhetoric as the 'external language' in newspapers, propaganda, and public meetings preached a merciless attack on the revolution's enemies. The Bolsheviks' 'internal language' in classified reports and private meetings, though, was more nuanced, expressing a more complex view of the role of law during this period.[7] This language makes it clear that there was ongoing conflict between the Cheka

[3] E. Huskey, 'From Legal Nihilism to *Pravovoe Gosudarstvo*: Soviet Legal Development, 1917-1990', in D. Barry (ed.), *Toward the 'Rule of Law' in Russia? Political and Legal Reform in the Transitional Period* (Armonk, 1992), 24–5.

[4] For use of these terms, see I. Lapenna, 'Lenin, Law and Legality', in L. Schapiro and P. Reddaway (eds.), *Lenin. The Man, The Theorist, The Leader: A Reappraisal* (New York, 1967), 253; R. Pipes, *Legalised Lawlessness: Soviet Revolutionary Justice* (London, 1986), 10; J. Ryan, *Lenin's Terror: The Ideological Origins of Early Soviet State Violence* (London, 2012), 122; and A. Bosiacki, 'From Utopia to a Lawless State: Russian Marxism and Russian Revolutions as a Totalitarian Project', in Ł. Adamski and B. Gajos (eds.), *Circles of the Russian Revolution: Internal and International Consequences of the Year 1917 in Russia* (Abingdon, 2019), 52.

[5] A. Carter, 'The Bolshevist Substitute for a Judicial System', *Illinois Law Review*, 16, 5 (1922), 346.

[6] *Pervye aresty. 25 oktiabria 1917–4 ianvaria 1918* (Moscow, 2017).

[7] The idea of 'external' and 'internal' language is from D. Raleigh, *Experiencing Russia's Civil War: Politics, Society and Revolutionary Culture in Saratov, 1917–1922* (Princeton, 2002), esp. 44, 53, 60–2, 224–6, 409–10.

and legal organs over their respective roles and, indeed, within the party over the relative importance of revolutionary violence vis-à-vis revolutionary justice, some of which spilled out into the press. It is also clear that as the Commissariat of Justice (Narkomiust) contested the Cheka's arbitrary practices, it developed more complex forms of revolutionary justice, with regulations governing all stages of the legal process, culminating in new law codes in 1922. Caseloads increased and elements commonly associated with legal systems re-emerged, such as lawyers and appeals, while statistics indicate that executions only formed a small minority of sentences. All this suggests that revolutionary justice retained an important and distinct role for many Bolsheviks.

Few legal scholars now argue that law is autonomous—existing outside of society and its politics—or even that it is neutral, with no inequalities in how people experience the law. Equally, few would deny that it is functional, existing as a process of social control designed to maintain a perceived 'ideal' order in society across the whole spectrum of human relations. All societies, then, even revolutionary and authoritarian ones, need laws, and the Bolsheviks took law and legal organs seriously. They expended a significant amount of effort and scarce resources on congresses, newspapers, journals, and books debating the role of law in a revolutionary and socialist state, producing increasingly detailed and complex regulations. They did this not because they favoured law over violence or sought to rule 'by law' or to provide avenues for seeking 'justice'. Instead, they sought to use law alongside other methods to strengthen their authority, and promote and enforce revolutionary values. It might be better to think, as one historian has suggested, in terms of 'lawlessness legalized' rather than 'legalized lawlessness'; there may not have been law codes, but this 'lawlessness' was increasingly regulated by decrees and other orders, helping establish a new state infrastructure and promote the revolutionary values needed to create new Soviet citizens.[8]

This book explores the 'external' and 'internal' languages of revolutionary justice through a systematic study of tribunals, assessing their role in the revolutionary process and their contribution to Bolshevik victory in the civil war that followed the October Revolution. I do not deny the prevalence of violence during this period or that tribunals were repressive in many ways—there was often little 'justice' for those receiving a tribunal's verdict. At the same time, I analyse this new legal system on its own terms, exploring how the Bolsheviks understood the role of law and examining their expectations and experiences of revolutionary justice. Drawing insights from the scholarship on law produced by various disciplines, I argue that law became a valuable tool of government, facilitating the Bolsheviks' attempts to build a new revolutionary state and society.

[8] A. Retish, 'Poisk spravedlivosti v revoliutsii: mestnaia sudebnaia sistema Viatskoi gubernii v 1917-1922 gg.', in *Epokha voin i revoliutsii: 1914–1922* (St Petersburg, 2017), 160.

Law and Revolution

One reason why the role of law during the Russian Revolution has been unappreciated is because there is surprisingly little work on the role of law more generally in revolutions. Scholars have focused on the impact of revolution on law rather than the reverse, while many seem to assume that law is marginalized, even destroyed, during periods of severe upheaval.[9] Yet while a revolution may be an iconoclastic attack on the old, this destruction is enacted to create something new. Most revolutions act as the source of new laws, if only to defend, accelerate, or regulate the course of the revolution.[10] Law can also introduce the new (symbolic and *revolutionary* laws) and draw on the old (existing legal practices) to convey the authority and legitimacy of the new regime, and build new political and social structures.[11]

Writers from across the political spectrum argued in 1917 that the freedoms gained from the February Revolution should not mean an absence of law. On one level, this view was unrealistic; all countries need laws to maintain political and social order. Legality enabled society to live in unity. On another, the revolution provided an opportunity for legal reforms to enhance people's freedom. Liberals promoted the 'rule of law' and socialists championed a 'people's justice'—all believed law could help the revolution forge a better society. Furthermore, laws could also help bring about the end of revolution by re-establishing order, avoiding violence, and facilitating progress. In this sense, some authors argued, the February Revolution marked the 'triumph' of the law—a revolution favouring law and democracy over arbitrary, tyrannical power.[12] Indeed, despite increasing lawlessness as 1917 progressed, the Provisional Government made serious attempts between February and October to instigate civil rights and a 'law-based state'. It prepared for legal reform, and used law to promote its own revolutionary credentials, delegitimize the old regime, and target its enemies.[13] Similarly,

[9] See H. Berman, *Law and Revolution: The Formation of the Western Legal Tradition* (Cambridge, MA, 1983); and, on Russia, P. Beirne (ed.), *Revolution in Law: Contributions to the Development of Soviet Legal Theory, 1917–1938* (Armonk, 1990). It is notable that an extensive collection of political and sociological writings on revolution has no mention of law, courts, and justice in the index, but numerous references to violence; R. O'Kane (ed.), *Revolution: Critical Concepts in Political Science* (4 volumes, London and New York, 2000).

[10] H. Arendt, *On Revolution* (revised edition, London, 1965), 183.

[11] These points are explored in T. Borisova and J. Siro, 'Law between Revolution and Tradition: Russian and Finnish Revolutionary Legal Acts, 1917-18', *Comparative Legal History*, 2, 1 (2014), 84–113.

[12] For a range of views, see E. Chirikov, *Dushevnyi razgovor pro svobodu* (Petrograd, 1917), 13–14; M. Gernet, *Sud ili samosud* (Moscow, 1917); Ol'govich, *Velikaia rossiiskaia respublika* (2nd edition, Petrograd, 1917), 15–16; N. Polianskii, *Revoliutsiia-torzhestvo prava* (Moscow, 1917); M. Reisner, *Pravo i revoliutsiia* (Petrograd, 1917); and V. Rozenberg, *Svobodnyi narod* (2nd edition, Moscow, 1917), 8.

[13] See A. Demichev and R. Khachaturov (eds.), *Pamiatniki rossiiskogo prava. V 35 t. T. 21. Pamiatniki prava Vremennogo pravitel'stva* (Moscow, 2016); and W. Pomeranz, 'The Provisional Government and the Law-Based State', in C. Read, P. Waldron, and A. Lindenmeyr (eds.), *Russia's*

reflecting on five years of socialist law after the October Revolution, P. I. Stuchka, a former Commissar of Justice and the most influential Bolshevik legal theorist of the period, dismissed claims that revolution has nothing in common with law as 'bourgeois'. Legal reforms may have lagged behind the other dramatic changes during this period, he admitted, but law remained an inseparable part of creating a new state.[14]

The prevailing focus on the revolution's impact on law is partly because legal scholars have paid the most attention to revolutionary justice and partly due to limited archival access for many years. From the 1920s, those legal theorists involved in events started to write about them, combining reminiscences with the lessons learned from these formative years, usually with an eye on contemporaneous concerns and constrained politically by the need to articulate certain views.[15] These accounts are more informative than later formulaic Soviet studies,[16] but all prioritize how law was supposed to operate rather than how it actually did. The same focus on theory over practice dominated Western scholarship too, often because the lack of archival access forced a reliance on published documents.[17] Although some studies have continued this approach,[18] the post-1991 'archival revolution' has encouraged a greater focus on the practice of law, particularly how ordinary people experienced the justice system, although there has been more so far on the late imperial period than on Soviet Russia.[19]

Much the same trajectory is true of work specifically on revolutionary tribunals. Some of the earliest Soviet writers on law (Ia. L. Berman, N. V. Krylenko, and M. V. Kozhevnikov) had participated in tribunals, but Soviet studies still focused

Home Front in War and Revolution, 1914–22. Book 4: Reintegration—The Struggle for the State (Bloomington, 2018), 111–37.

[14] P. Stuchka, 'Five Years of Revolution in Law (1922)', in W. Rosenberg (ed.), *Bolshevik Visions* (2nd edition, 2 volumes, Ann Arbor, 1990), I, 190.

[15] For example, P. Maliantovich, *Revoliutsiia i pravosudie (Neskol'ko myslei i vospominanii)* (Moscow, 1918); N. Krylenko, *Sudoustroistvo RSFSR* (Moscow, 1923); Ia. Berman, *Ocherki po istorii sudoustroistva RSFSR* (Moscow, 1924); and M. Kozhevnikov, *Istoriia sovetskogo suda 1917–1956 gody* (Moscow, 1957).

[16] The most useful are V. Portnov and M. Slavin, *Pravovye osnovy stroitel'stva Krasnoi Armii, 1918–1920 gg.* (Moscow, 1985); and V. Portnov and M. Slavin , *Stanovlenie pravosudiia Sovetskoi Rossii (1917–1922 gg.)* (Moscow, 1990).

[17] For example, J. Hazard, *Settling Disputes in Soviet Society: The Formative Years of Legal Institutions* (New York, 1960); H. Berman, *Justice in the USSR* (Cambridge, MA., 1963); S. Kucherov, *The Organs of Soviet Administration of Justice: Their History and Operation* (Leiden, 1970); and P. Juviler, *Revolutionary Law and Order: Politics and Social Change in the USSR* (New York, 1976).

[18] For example, V. Bukov, *Ot Rossiiskogo suda prisiazhnykh k proletarskomu pravosudiiu* (Moscow, 1997); A. Bosiacki, *Utopia, Władza, Prawo. Doktryna i koncepcje prawne 'bolszewickiej' Rosji, 1917–1921* (Warsaw, 1999); S. Newton, *Law and the Making of the Soviet World* (Abingdon, 2015); and A. Demichev and R. Khachaturov (eds.), *Pamiatniki rossiiskogo prava. V 35 t. T. 23. Pervye dekrety sovetskoi vlasti* (Moscow, 2016).

[19] For a recent survey, see P. Solomon, 'Understanding the History of Soviet Criminal Justice: The Contribution of Archives and Other Sources', *The Russian Review*, 74, 2 (2015), 401–18.

more on the theory of tribunals than their practice.[20] More recent works have mined archives to partly rectify this imbalance, but they continue to demonstrate a limited sense of the role played by tribunals, focusing primarily on the building of institutional structures, official statistics, and personnel.[21] It is not that these areas are unimportant, but they are examined too narrowly: institutional building with reference only to the justice system rather than the state as a whole; statistics listed rather than analysed in the context of broader debates over what constituted counter-revolution, what happened in trials, and the objectives of particular punishments; personnel described rather than exploring how social background could influence practices, perceptions, and experiences. The first systematic study in English made some important arguments but was limited by restricted archival access and its anachronistic determination to judge tribunals by current legal standards.[22] It is only through explorations of specific trials,[23] or by focusing on how people experienced courts,[24] that broader issues concerning the role of law in the Russian Revolution have started to emerge.

By contrast, the study of law during the French Revolution has produced a greater sense of its importance.[25] Law helped destroy the old, promote the new, and define and defend revolutionary values. The justice system responded to official and popular pressures, encouraging radicalism prior to 1794 but helping to re-establish social stability afterwards through repression and persuasion. The state employed abstract values to enable it to target any perceived offence, but the proliferation of regulations on specific transgressions forged these acts into universal laws, facilitating the state's ambition to direct the revolutionary process, while maintaining the façade that law was the organized force of the people's

[20] See, especially, the three-volume study by Iu. Titov: *Sozdanie sistemy sovetskikh revoliutsionnykh tribunalov* (Moscow, 1983); *Razvitie sistemy sovetskikh revoliutsionnykh tribunalov* (Moscow, 1987); and *Sovetskie revoliutsionnye tribunaly v mirnye gody stroitel'stva sotsializma* (Moscow, 1988); as well as N. Smirnov, *Vysshie sudy revoliutsii (Tsentral'nye revoliutsionnye tribunaly, 1918–1922gg.)* (Moscow, 1990).

[21] Most recently, D. Gor'ev, *Deiatel'nost' revoliutsionnykh tribunalov na Kubani (1918–1922 gg.)* (Armavir, 2011); and A. Makutchev, '*Prigovor okonchatel'nyi, obzhalovaniiu ne podlezhit...*' *Revoliutsionnye tribunaly v Sovetskoi Rossii v gody Grazhdanskoi voiny* (Moscow, 2012).

[22] C. Story, 'In a Court of Law: The Revolutionary Tribunals in the Russian Civil War, 1917-1921' (PhD thesis, University of California Santa Cruz, 1998).

[23] See, in particular, A. Lindenmeyr, 'The First Soviet Political Trial: Countess Sofia Panina before the Petrograd Revolutionary Tribunal', *The Russian Review*, 60, 4 (2001), 505–25; and T. Penter, 'Öffentlichkeit und Rechtsprechung unter der frühen Sowjetmacht. Der Prozeß gegen den "Južnyj Rabočij" in Odessa 1918', *Jahrbücher für Geschichte Osteuropas*, 50, 4 (2002), 558–76.

[24] See especially the work of Aaron Retish: 'Controlling Revolution: Understandings of Violence through the Rural Soviet Courts, 1917-1923', *Europe-Asia Studies*, 65, 9 (2013), 1789–806; 'Poisk spravedlivosti v revoliutsii'; and 'Judicial Reforms and Revolutionary Justice: The Establishment of the Court System in Soviet Russia, 1917-22', in Read, Waldron, and Lindenmeyr, *Russia's Home Front in War and Revolution*, 371–401.

[25] For example, H. Brown, *Ending the French Revolution: Violence, Justice and Repression from the Terror to Napoleon* (Charlottesville, 2006); B. Shapiro, *Revolutionary Justice in Paris, 1789–1790* (Cambridge, 1993); D. Sutherland, *Murder in Aubagne: Lynching, Law and Justice during the French Revolution* (Cambridge, 2009); and A. Wills, *Criminal Life and Criminal Justice during the French Revolution* (Ann Arbor, 1979).

will.[26] Political trials, moreover, decided questions of ideology and political significance, helping to determine the revolution's direction.[27] Similarly, while early work on French revolutionary tribunals focused on their role as the leading agents of the terror,[28] recent studies have stressed greater complexity. The Paris tribunal only convicted a minority of defendants prior to 1794 while permitting a degree of agency for defendants as their ability to construct a defence through lawyers, witnesses, and petitions impacted on sentencing. Thus terror was contested; a system of repression was imposed, but people subjected it to debate, protest and reaction.[29]

All this reinforces the importance of law during revolution. Paraphrasing one study of the French Revolution, if we accept the premise of legalized lawlessness, then law does not only become uninteresting, it becomes irrelevant to the main process of any revolution and to understanding revolutionary politics. Yet the language of law (the *rights* of citizens, the desire for *justice*, the *crime* of counter-revolution) dominates the discourse of revolutions and is at the core of the disputes that shape the nature of revolutions.[30]

Ultimately, revolutions do not just appear, they are made, and they are defined by their relations to the past and their aspirations for the future. Law is central to this transition from old to new. The term 'transitional justice' is now a common one, but scholars invariably use the term to refer to countries moving from a repressive state to a democracy and the role that justice can play in this transition, dealing with a problematic past and establishing the organs and values required for the future, whether through institutions (commissions of inquiry or trials) or practices (prosecutions, apologies, reparations, or memorials).[31] Only rarely is there the appreciation that the 'tools' of transitional justice can be utilized by states other than democracies, but even then the same principles apply: transitional justice deals with the crimes of a former regime.[32] There was an element of this

[26] C. Hesse, 'The Law of the Terror', *Modern Language Notes*, 114, 4 (1999), 702–18.

[27] L. Winnie, 'The French Revolutionary Trials', in J. Meierhenrich and D. Pendas (eds.), *Political Trials in Theory and History* (Cambridge, 2017), 134–56.

[28] D. Greer, *The Incidence of Terror during the French Revolution* (Cambridge, MA, 1935); J. Godfrey, *Revolutionary Justice: A Study of the Organization, Personnel and Procedure of the Paris Tribunal, 1793–95* (Chapel Hill, 1951).

[29] See the work of Alex Fairfax-Cholmeley, especially 'Reassessing Revolutionary Justice: Suspects, the Paris Revolutionary Tribunal and the Terror in France, 1793-4' (PhD thesis, Queen Mary University of London, 2011); and 'Creating and Resisting the Terror: The Paris Revolutionary Tribunal, March-June 1793', *French History*, 32, 2 (2018), 203–25.

[30] M. Walzer, *Regicide and Revolution: Speeches at the Trial of Louis XVI* (new edition, New York, 1992), xi.

[31] N. Adler (ed.), *Understanding the Age of Transitional Justice* (New Brunswick, 2018); N. Palmer, P. Clark, and D. Granville (eds.), *Critical Perspectives in Transitional Justice* (Cambridge, 2012); L. Stan (ed.), *Transitional Justice in Eastern Europe and the Former Soviet Union* (Abingdon, 2009); R. Teitel, *Transitional Justice* (Oxford, 2000); and M. Williams, R. Nagy, and J. Elster (eds.), *Transitional Justice* (New York, 2012).

[32] For example, J. Elster, *Closing the Books: Transitional Justice in Historical Perspective* (Cambridge, 2004).

during the Russian Revolution, as the Provisional Government and the Bolsheviks investigated the abuses of former officials and targeted 'provocateurs' who had betrayed the revolutionary movement before 1917. But, for the Bolsheviks, the new proletarian law was 'transitional justice', guiding the revolution from the old regime to a future socialist state where law's necessity would wither away, and focusing more on those transgressing revolutionary ideals in the present than past offences. In this view, transitional justice is not just about solidifying the new by coming to terms with the past, but creating the new in the first place.

Considering revolutionary justice as a transitional form of justice—albeit not in the usual meaning of the term—and thinking functionally help us understand the multifaceted nature of the potential benefits of law to the Bolsheviks as they struggled to retain power. Authoritarian regimes invariably maintain legal systems, indicating that courts fulfil a range of functions for such states: they can be a means of social control alongside more repressive instruments, such as a secret police; a source of legitimacy by maintaining the façade of an independent overseer; a weapon for disciplining officials; a means of facilitating economic policy; and a potential scapegoat for controversial policies.[33] No state, it seems, is sufficiently authoritarian (or 'totalitarian') that it can dispense completely with such benefits.

Furthermore, all states use law for a multitude of purposes simultaneously, whether for maintaining social order, governing effectively, fostering public support, alleviating local conflict, or repressing threats.[34] Authoritarian states, in particular, often seek both repression and legitimacy in law.[35] Ostensibly, these are contradictory goals, but law can be used for political and conventional purposes at the same time, while it is too easy to dismiss the importance of creating even a façade of legitimacy through legal procedure. All societies struggle with the paradox that people believe courts should be impartial but realize courts often favour particular agendas or groups. This does not cause a crisis in many places, it has been argued, partly because the visual appearance of legitimacy helps sustain the paradox.[36] The more revolutionary justice, even tribunals, resembled accepted judicial procedure, the more it seemed to have a degree of legitimacy; the greater the levels of acceptance, the more effectively courts can enforce rulings and persuade the populace The revolution, moreover, changed the nature of legitimacy. The belief of lower social classes that democracy was for 'us' and not 'them',

[33] See T. Ginsburg and T. Moustafa (eds.), *Rule By Law: The Politics of Courts in Authoritarian Regimes* (Cambridge, 2008); and T. Moustafa, 'Law and Courts in Authoritarian Regimes', *Annual Review of Law and Social Science*, 10 (2014), 281–99.

[34] M. Shapiro, *Courts: A Comparative and Political Analysis* (Chicago, 1981), 22–4.

[35] H. Bækken, *Law and Power in Russia: Making Sense of Quasi-Legal Practices* (Abingdon, 2019), 3–4.

[36] See K. Bybee and A. Narasimhan, 'Courts and Judges: The Legitimacy Imperative and the Importance of Appearances', in A. Sarat and P. Ewick (eds.), *The Handbook of Law and Society* (Chichester, 2015), 118–33.

the privileged classes, combined with growing fears of imminent counter-revolution to generate widespread support for targeting threats to the revolution and a more partial, class-based form of justice.[37] This does not necessarily mean there was popular acceptance of the Bolsheviks' form of revolutionary justice, but it further emphasizes the relevance and potential influence of law during revolution.

In the end, as Lenin reputedly stated, law is a political instrument, even if the extent to which law is subject to direct intervention by politicians varies across time and place.[38] In this context, it is unsurprising that law is central to revolution: it defines and delegitimizes the old regime; it establishes the parameters of the new political and social order; it disseminates dramatic messages to those involved and the population at large to promote, teach, and enforce new ideologies, mentalities, and behaviours; it fosters criticism, self-discipline, and citizenship; and through all of this it strengthens the power and authority of the new state.

The Bolsheviks and the Law

Although it is frequently stated that the Bolsheviks had no master plan for reforming the legal system on assuming power,[39] this misses the key point: whilst the Bolsheviks did lack a clear plan on *exactly* how they would reform the legal system, as they lacked a plan for all areas of governance, they—guided by Marx and Engels—did have clear views on the role of law in society that appreciated the points above. Marx and Engels had not focused on law directly, but they had referred to it frequently and assigned it ideological, political, and economic functions.[40] Ideologically, law legitimated the existing social order by presenting it as normal, desirable, and fair, while divorcing the 'legal man', equal before the law, from the inequalities of the 'economic man', and while divorcing individuals from their class context. Politically, law was seen as an instrument classes used to improve their position vis-à-vis other classes, with the ruling classes usually enjoying greater access to law. Economically, law reinforced inequalities in property-holding, labour relations, and other spheres.[41]

The Bolsheviks read these writings in a very instrumentalist manner, placing greater stress on law's lack of impartiality. 'Society is not based on law,' Stuchka

[37] See various letters and petitions in M. Steinberg, *Voices of Revolution, 1917* (New Haven, 2001).

[38] J. Hazard, *Recollections of a Pioneering Sovietologist* (New York, 1987), 162–3.

[39] For example, J. Hazard, 'Soviet Law: The Bridge Years, 1917-1920', in W. Butler (ed.), *Russian Law: Historical and Political Perspectives* (Leyden, 1977), 238; P. Beirne, 'Editor's Introduction', in Beirne, *Revolution in Law*, ix; and Bosiacki, *Utopia, Władza, Prawo*, 383.

[40] M. Cain and A. Hunt, *Marx and Engels on Law* (London, 1979), ix. See also P. Hirst, 'Marx and Engels on Law, Crime and Morality', *Economy and Society*, 1, 1 (1972), 28–56.

[41] This discussion draws on the concise summary in K. Newman, *Law and Economic Organization: A Comparative Study of Preindustrial Societies* (Cambridge, 1983), 19–21.

stated, 'the law should be founded on society.'[42] Later the Bolsheviks defined law as a 'system or order of social relations corresponding to the interests of the ruling class and protected by the organized force of that class'.[43] To put it simply, whereas law had been used in bourgeois societies to defend the rule of the propertied classes, Bolshevik legal theorists believed it was inevitable and essential that law should help secure the interests of the new *proletarian* state.

Lenin agreed. Despite serving briefly as a lawyer, he also rarely wrote directly on law, but he did pen various polemical tracts on how tsarist law served the interests of the exploiting classes, tending to attribute greater direct control over law to the ruling classes than Marx. He also placed greater stress on law's repressive role and emphasized its educational capabilities, both of which anticipated the benefits of law after October 1917.[44] He argued that the public did not want to see courts as official institutions where functionaries applied various parts of the penal code but as public institutions that examined all of the political and social threads of the crime to expose the 'ulcers' of the present system in order to improve it. Judges needed to be more than officials, he argued; representatives of the public needed to be in court, and public opinion needed play a role when examining cases. There needed, in short, to be trials 'by the street'; not vigilante justice, but trials reflecting the will of the people.[45]

Not all of these arguments were confined to the Bolsheviks. Evidence suggests the tsarist legal system was commonly seen as unfair and out of touch with popular notions of justice.[46] Legal reform was, therefore, high on the agenda after the February Revolution, but there were fundamental disagreements; educated classes welcomed the opportunity to return to the principles of the 1864 legal reforms—an accessible legal process with independent judges and juries—which they felt had been eroded, but lower social classes favoured a more democratic legal system, with the election of judges and verdicts drawn from popular conceptions of justice rather than remote statutes. Temporary courts established in Petrograd implemented some of these ideas, but in the end there were few major reforms.[47] Tsarist courts continued in many places, but the

[42] Veteran [P. Stuchka], 'Na pochve zakona ili na pochve revoliutsii', *Pravda*, 11 (24) May 1917, 2–3.

[43] 'Guiding Principles of Criminal Law in the RSFSR (Dec. 1919)', in Rosenberg, *Bolshevik Visions*, I, 166.

[44] P. Beirne and A. Hunt, 'Law and the Constitution of Soviet Society: The Case of Comrade Lenin', in Beirne, *Revolution in Law*, 63–9; J. Burbank, 'Lenin and the Law in Revolutionary Russia', *Slavic Review*, 54, 1 (1995), 23–44; and Lapenna, 'Lenin, Law and Legality'.

[45] See the articles in V. Lenin, *Collected Works* (47 volumes, Moscow, 1960–70), IV, 387–402 (1901); V, 243–9 (1901); and XVIII, 304–6 (1912).

[46] J. Burbank, *Russian Peasants Go To Court: Legal Culture in the Countryside, 1905–1917* (Bloomington and Indianapolis, 2004); S. Frank, *Crime, Cultural Conflict, and Justice in Rural Russia, 1856–1914* (Berkeley, 1999); C. Gaudin, *Ruling Peasants: Village and State in Late Imperial Russia* (DeKalb, 2007); and L. McReynolds, *Murder Most Russian: True Crime and Punishment in Late Imperial Russia* (Ithaca, 2013).

[47] A. Nikolaev, 'Vremennye sudy v Petrograde (mart-iiul' 1917 g.): vzlet i padenie', in *Epokha voin i revoliutsii*, 87–99. See also Pomeranz, 'The Provisional Government', 117.

collapse of state authority removed their ability to enforce rulings; one lawyer recalled the foundations of law and order disintegrating under a weak government.[48] It was unsurprising that crime flourished, particularly in urban areas.[49] Together with popular sympathy for class-based action, noted above, this enabled the Bolsheviks to claim a degree of popular legitimacy for legal reform.

Therefore, while the Bolsheviks were not clear on exactly how law should play its role in building a new socialist state, their initial lack of action after the October Revolution was due more to other pressing priorities than a lack of interest. In an article written a fortnight after the revolution, Stuchka never doubted the value of law; the issue was simply how the legal system should be reformed, and the need to eliminate the repressive apparatus of the old regime in favour of democratically elected courts and judges. 'Every court', he argued, 'must be elected from top to bottom', creating a simpler and transparent legal system.[50] He later agreed with those party idealists who believed that if law was a bourgeois concept and crime the result of an exploitative society, law would wither away along with the state as socialism slowly eradicated exploitation. The move to socialism, though, required time and 'proletarian law'—the law of this transitional period—had a valuable role to play in removing the vestiges of the old order and inculcating new ideals.[51] The proletarian state needed to embrace law as a tool of government and wield its full force against bourgeois enemies. As D. I. Kurskii emphasized in November 1918 as Commissar of Justice, revolutionary justice was a means of forging discipline and order in the new state.[52]

Lenin's focus after October was also on law's practical significance.[53] Law was now the expression of the will of the proletariat state and thus served as a useful educational tool for disseminating the state's programme as well as a means of targeting the proletariat's enemies, maintaining discipline, and securing social order during this transitional period. This practical importance required flexibility; there was a need for statutes and regulation, but not for excessive formalism, while the state needed the ability to resort to extraordinary measures to defend the revolution if circumstances demanded. This was not 'legal nihilism' or 'legalized

[48] N. Karabchevskii, *Chto glaza moi videli* (2 volumes, Berlin, 1921), II, 154.

[49] See, most recently, T. Hasegawa, *Crime and Punishment in the Russian Revolution* (Cambridge, MA., 2017).

[50] P. Stuchka, 'Klassovoi ili demokraticheskii sud?', *Pravda*, 10 November 1917, 2. Similar points were made by the Commissar of the Enlightenment, A. V. Lunacharskii, in 'Revoliutsiia i sud', *Pravda*, 1 December 1917, 2.

[51] P. Stuchka, 'Proletarian Law (1919)', in Rosenberg, *Bolshevik Visions*, I, 162. On law under socialism, see E. Huskey, 'A Framework for the Analysis of Soviet Law', *The Russian Review*, 50, 1 (1991), 53–70.

[52] 'O revoliutsionnoi zakonnosti', in D. Kurskii, *Izbrannye stat'i i rechi* (2nd edition, Moscow, 1958), 45–6.

[53] Beirne and Hunt, 'Law and the Constitution of Soviet Society', 69–91; and their 'Lenin, Crime and Penal Politics, 1917-1924', in Beirne and Hunt, *Revolution in Law*, 99–135.

lawlessness', but a belief that law needed to serve the interests of the new state and the revolution, which were one and the same in the Bolsheviks' eyes.

The first public attempt to articulate a broader understanding of crime, the Guiding Principles of Criminal Law published in 1919, further stressed the social objectives of law. Crime was a 'socially harmful act', and a 'penalty' was preferred to punishment. Law was a practical process to assess the level of social harm inflicted and the penalty needed to defend society. The extent of the penalty depended on whether a crime was committed due to a lack of consciousness, material deprivation, or some other understandable motive, or because of persistent bourgeois values such as greed. Law facilitated social reconstruction as all criminals had the potential to be rehabilitated even if some would resist due to their social prejudices. Thus a proletarian court was interested in a wider range of factors than a bourgeois court, especially the social, economic, and political context of crime.[54] Revolutionary justice, therefore, not only promised a structured means of defending the revolution's political achievements, promoting order, and educating on behaviours and mentalities; it would also use a new approach to criminality to forge a new society and citizens.

In reality, not all of this was as revolutionary as the Bolsheviks argued. The political and educational role of law had long been recognized in Russia and elsewhere, and there was a long history of exceptional justice for political crimes along the lines of revolutionary tribunals, while the Bolsheviks' views on social harm emerged from existing debates across Europe. The allegedly simplified and revolutionary system of law became more complex over time as Russia was 're-legalized' during the civil war and, in any case, drew on existing customs and practices, not least to help attribute a sense of legitimacy and authority to revolutionary justice, as discussed above.[55]

The scale of Bolshevik ambitions should not be underplayed, however: revolutionary justice was nothing less than an attempt to forge a new legal culture in Russia. Legal culture is a contested concept, but its use reflects a desire to move the understanding of law away from a narrow focus on 'the set of rules or norms, written or unwritten, about right and wrong behaviour, duties and rights' to a broader 'social study' of law incorporating the social and legal forces that make law, the structures and rules of law itself, and the impact of law on wider

[54] 'Guiding Principles', in Rosenberg, *Bolshevik Visions*, I, 155–6.

[55] On continuities in practice, see T. Borisova and J. Burbank, 'Russia's Legal Trajectories', *Kritika*, 19, 3 (2018), 469–508; and M. Rendle, 'How Revolutionary was Revolutionary Justice? Legal Culture in Russia Across the Revolutionary Divide', in M. Neumann and A. Willimott (eds.), *Rethinking the Russian Revolution as Historical Divide: Tradition, Rupture, and Modernity* (Routledge, 2017), 46–66. On ideological continuities, see D. Beer, *Renovating Russia: The Human Sciences and the Fate of Liberal Modernity, 1880–1930* (Ithaca, 2008); and D. Hoffmann, *Cultivating the Masses: Modern State Practices and Soviet Socialism, 1914–1939* (Ithaca, 2011), 242–60. On re-legalization, see Hazard, *Settling Disputes*. For Hazard, these trends prevented 1917 from marking a break in the legal system; 'The Courts and the Legal System', in C. Black (ed.), *The Transformation of Russian Society: Aspects of Social Change since 1861* (Cambridge, MA., 1967), 145–64.

behaviour. This includes 'what people think about law, lawyers and the legal order', 'ideas, attitudes, opinions and expectations with regard to the legal system',[56] and assessing the 'general environment of thought, belief, practices and institutions' within which law exists.[57] These definitions encapsulate Bolshevik ambitions; they did not simply want to alter laws, they wanted to change the relationship between law and state, and how individuals thought about and interacted with the legal system.

Revolutionary Justice versus Revolutionary Violence

The problem for the Bolsheviks was that reforming law and legal culture took time, and they did not have time. Within weeks of the October Revolution, opponents were gathering in the south to form the Volunteer Army and the dissolution of the elected Constituent Assembly in January 1918 made civil war inevitable, heralding several years of intense struggle against an array of political and social forces.[58] The Bolsheviks controlled Russia's central industrial heartland, with better access to resources and transport infrastructure than their opponents, and they also acted quickly to rebuild the military. But enforcing discipline and rebuilding and exerting state control over the localities and the economy proved major challenges, as did dealing with growing opposition from within Bolshevik-held territory.

All these challenges led many Bolsheviks to doubt whether creating a revolutionary court would solve this 'desperate situation', as Sovnarkom had hoped on 22 November 1917. The alternative seemed a greater reliance on violence. Lenin made the intellectual argument for such a choice in *The Immediate Tasks of the Soviet Government*. In a draft written in late March 1918, he assigned an important role to courts; they would cement the principle of involving the exploited classes in state administration, while targeting exploiters trying to regain power and, more importantly, ensuring the strict self-discipline of workers. Coercion, he believed, was essential in the transition to socialism, and courts should be the organ enacting coercion, educating people in labour discipline and so on. But Lenin believed that law was currently lagging behind. In the final version of *The Immediate Tasks* in late April, he was clear: the lack of progress was due to

[56] L. Friedman, *The Legal System: A Social Science Perspective* (New York, 1975), 2–3; L. Friedman, 'The Place of Legal Culture in the Sociology of Law', in M. Freeman (ed.), *Law and Sociology* (Oxford, 2006), 189.

[57] R. Cotterell, *Law, Culture and Society: Legal Ideas in the Mirror of Social Theory* (Aldershot, 2006), 83, 88. See also D. Nelken, 'Defining and Using the Concept of Legal Culture', in E. Örücü and D. Nelken (eds.), *Comparative Law: A Handbook* (Oxford, 2007), 109–32; and S. Silbey, 'Legal Cultures and Cultures of Legality', in J. Hall, L. Grindstaff, and M-C. Lo (eds.), *Handbook of Cultural Sociology* (London, 2010), 470–9.

[58] For a recent survey, see J. Smele, *The 'Russian' Civil Wars, 1916–1926* (London, 2015).

insufficient ruthlessness. The level of coercion required depended on the development of the revolutionary class, the legacy of war, and the extent of the opposition; as government moves from military repression during civil war to administration, coercion shifts from on-the-spot shootings to trial by court. At that time, in his view, the need for repression was too strong and courts were too weak. Opposition needed to be dealt with more ruthlessly; party members taking bribes, workers involved in strikes, and political opponents engaged in armed struggle were all enemies of the working class.[59]

Lenin had always expected revolution to be defined by conflict and civil war, and he anticipated the extensive use of violence by the proletariat (represented by the Bolsheviks) to achieve victory. At the very least, the failures of earlier revolutions, especially the Paris Commune, made the need for violence seem self-evident. This is not to say that Lenin had a plan for violence but, rather, an intellectual rationale for why it was justified and to be expected, and how it could aid the revolution. It was the violence of the majority, not the exploiting minority as in the past, and it could make a symbolic impression and purge the population of enemies. It was also something quasi-sacred—a redemptive, purifying element of the transition from the old world to the new, expressing the hope and desire for a better life for humanity when wielded in the name of the revolution.[60]

Violence, therefore, may have already been present in Russia after decades of political turbulence converged with the impact of the First World War, but it became an integral part of government under the Bolsheviks and the default option for many officials rather than an exceptional wartime measure. For some, it also became a proactive tool for refashioning society. Here, though, there is a danger in accepting the Bolsheviks' external language at face value; violence was endemic, atrocities were frequent, and there were systematic attacks on certain groups, but local organs were not commonly instructed to 'cleanse', 'excise', or 'exterminate' elements of the body politic.[61] Most local organs seem to have been mainly responding to the ebb and flow of threats posed by particular groups at a given time, and they viewed violence prosaically: it was a means to project power and deal with fear, to attack and defend, while it could achieve material objectives and forge identities and communities.[62]

[59] Lenin, *Collected Works*, XXVII, 217–18, 264–8.

[60] See Ryan, *Lenin's Terror*, 9; as well as J. Ryan, 'The Sacralization of Violence: Bolshevik Justifications for Violence and Terror during the Civil War', *Slavic Review*, 74, 4 (2015), 808–31; and J. Ryan, '"War against War": The Significance of the Great War in the Thought of V. I. Lenin on Violence, 1914-21', in Read, Waldron, and Lindenmeyr, *Russia's Home Front in War and Revolution*, 257–78.

[61] P. Holquist, 'State Violence as Technique: The Logic of Violence in Soviet Totalitarianism', in A. Weiner (ed.), *Landscaping the Human Garden* (Stanford, 2003), 26–7; Hoffmann, *Cultivating the Masses*, 239–40.

[62] S. Smith, 'Violence in the Russian Revolution and Civil War, 1914-20', in Adamski and Gajos, *Circles of the Russian Revolution*, 25–39. For a comparable theoretical discussion, see the articles by

Yet violence was not the all-encompassing tool that many historians seem to assume. On the one hand, violence is paradoxically the response of weak states that need extraordinary organs, special commissions, and centrally appointed plenipotentiaries to enact policies in the absence of stronger, regular organs. Violence, it was assumed, would make the population too frightened to resist, but the evidence from across the civil war points to the contrary – there was growing resistance across society. Even the head of the Cheka, F. E. Dzerzhinskii, conceded in a circular to Cheka branches and tribunals in 1920 that constant severe repression was not as effective as matching the level of repression to the severity of the threat and using terror selectively.[63] In any case, the Bolsheviks lacked the ability to shoot every corrupt official, selfish deserter, recalcitrant worker, or peasant 'bandit'. And, despite their unreliability, the state needed these people to staff a rapidly expanding bureaucracy, reinforce a depleted army, keep industry working, and produce desperately needed supplies.

Many discussions of violence also assume a neat divide between violence and law; a society is based on law and order *or* it descends into violence and chaos.[64] The reality during Russia's civil war was less clear-cut. Lenin talked of the coercive role of law at the same time as urging the legalization of terror; that is, establishing clear parameters in which terror was justified and applied.[65] Lenin saw both as representing a distinct type and level of coercion, each required at different times to promote and enforce the state's policies.

Law, of course, can be seen as violent in any context. Individuals lose their freedom, their possessions, or their life as law imposes an imagined ideal on a present reality. Others enforce this violence, and offenders submit in fear of further violence.[66] Some scholars go further, describing how a society's narrative is ascribed on to the 'body' of another human and how the bodies of culprits are 'maimed' or 'flawed'.[67] Others talk about the 'terror' of the law enacted through the 'majesty', spectacle, and theatricality of the legal process, and sometimes through deliberately harsh sentences, even if they often turned out to be largely

I. Schröder, B. Schmidt, and G. Bowman in I. Schröder and B. Schmidt (eds.), *Anthropology of Violence and Conflict* (Abingdon, 2001).

[63] *F. E. Dzerzhinskii—predsedatel' VChK-OGPU. 1917–1926* (Moscow, 2007), 176–81 (17 April 1920).

[64] See, for example, L. Engelstein, *Russia in Flames: War, Revolution, and Civil War, 1917–1921* (New York, 2017), 270; and R. Suny, *Red Flag Unfurled: History, Historians and the Russian Revolution* (London, 2017), 251.

[65] Beirne and Hunt, 'Lenin, Crime and Penal Politics', 100, 122–4.

[66] R. Cover, 'Violence and the Word', *The Yale Law Journal*, 95, 8 (1986), 1601, 1604, 1608. See also A. Sarat and T. Kearns, 'A Journey Through Forgetting: Toward a Jurisprudence of Violence', in A. Sarat and T. Kearns (ed.), *The Fate of Law* (Ann Arbor, 1991), 209–74; A. Sarat and T. Kearns (eds.), *Law's Violence* (Ann Arbor, 1993); and A. Sarat (ed.), *Law, Violence and the Possibilities of Justice* (Princeton, 2001).

[67] J. Simonett, 'The Trial as One of the Performing Arts', *American Bar Association Journal*, 52, 12 (1966), 1145; M. Ball, 'All the Law's A Stage', *Law and Literature*, 11, 2 (1999), 218.

symbolic.[68] This violence is perpetuated as 'law's archive' preserves a record of offences for eternity.[69] Law, then, may act as a preferable counterbalance to (and contain) the destructive violence existing beyond the boundaries of law, but this should not disguise the fact that the boundaries between the two are more fluid than most admit.[70] At the very least, law is inseparable from issues of power and discipline, whether the power of states to exercise control, the power of citizens to pursue their interests, or social order when these powers are kept in balance.[71]

All this is particularly true of what some scholars have termed political justice—the use of judicial proceedings for political objectives.[72] If it is accepted that law cannot be divorced from its political, social, and cultural context, then all law is political to a certain extent. Yet there is no doubt that the 'quality of the politics pursued' varies across crimes and between trials, from the politics of persecution to the politics of legalism.[73] Overtly political forms of justice are more common in democracies than many concede, but the Bolsheviks' instrumentalist and Marxist understanding of the role of law clearly made law in early Soviet Russia far more political than in most legal systems.

Having said that, as noted, revolutionary justice was comprised of two strands—people's courts and revolutionary tribunals. As one historian who has studied both has noted, the two should not be seen as complete opposites; both were revolutionary organs with revolutionary goals, and both were political in the sense of acting as a means of extending state power, securing order, and promoting Bolshevik ideology.[74] Nevertheless, there were important differences. As courts dealing with 'regular' crimes, people's courts usually dealt with cases brought to them, adjudicating on conflicts and crimes that posed little direct political threat to the Bolsheviks. It is more reasonable to talk about justice and rights in this context, and to assess the interaction of state, law, and society in traditional ways.[75] Tribunals, however, were established specifically to combat counter-revolution and political threats, and they therefore engaged with the population very differently. Only a minority of cases were brought to them; the

[68] D. Hay, 'Property, Authority and the Criminal Law', in D. Hay et al., *Albion's Fatal Tree: Crime and Society in Eighteenth-Century England* (London, 1975), 18, 25–31.

[69] R. Mawani, 'Law's Archive', *Annual Review of Law and Social Science*, 8 (2012), 337–65.

[70] A. Sarat, 'Situating Law between the Realities of Violence and the Claims of Justice: An Introduction', in Sarat, *Law, Violence and the Possibilities of Justice*, 3–5.

[71] R. Cotterrell, *Law's Community: Legal Theory in Sociological Perspective* (Oxford, 1995), 4–7. For a broader theoretical discussion in this vein, see B. Golder and P. Fitzpatrick, *Foucault's Law* (Abingdon, 2009).

[72] O. Kirchheimer, 'Politics and Justice', in F. Burin and K. Shell (eds.), *Politics, Law and Social Change* (New York, 1969), 408–27; and O. Kirchheimer, *Political Justice: The Use of Legal Procedure for Political Ends* (Princeton, 1961).

[73] J. Shklar, *Legalism: Law, Morals, and Political Trials* (new edition, Cambridge, MA., 1986), 145, 220. See also J. Meierhenrich and D. Pendas, '"The Justice of My Cause is Clear, but There's Politics to Fear": Political Trials in Theory and History' in J. Meierhenrich and D. Pendas, *Political Trials in Theory and History*, 1–64.

[74] Retish, 'Poisk spravedlivosti v revoliutsii', 159.

[75] Berman, *Justice in the USSR*, 372–3.

vast majority saw the state imposing their concerns on the population. The Bolsheviks, of course, denied that tribunals were 'political'. In their eyes, these crimes were not crimes directed against them as a political party or even their form of politics, but were crimes against the people and the revolution, which were represented by the party.[76] Nonetheless, 'counter-revolution' was a political category, and the ability to use courts to enforce and promote political objectives no doubt attracted the Bolsheviks. The alleged threat posed by counter-revolution to the people, moreover, justified a harsher form of law.

Those involved in tribunals certainly viewed their role as straddling the boundaries between law and violence. Legal theorists saw tribunals as a 'weapon' of the proletariat in the same way as the Cheka or the Red Army.[77] Similarly, tribunal officials stressed that tribunals were not regular courts but 'fighting organs' of the revolution and did not shy away from using the term 'repression (*rasprava*)' to describe their activities. Tribunals were constantly engaged in 'battles' on various 'fronts'.[78] Yet these officials were also quick to distinguish the 'legal' repression of tribunals from the unrestrained violence of the Cheka. They saw tribunals as governed by rules that provided the source of their authority at the same time as constraining it, instructing them when and how to act. Regulations and procedure, in their view, were essential for managing repression and maximizing its potential. One official even underlined Dzerzhinskii's admission of the counterproductive nature of constant repression in the circular mentioned above, no doubt seeing it as justification.[79] Essentially, tribunals saw themselves as exceptional organs for exceptional times, operating between the regular law of people's courts and the arbitrary violence of the Cheka.

For leading Bolsheviks, then, it was not so much a question of revolutionary justice *or* revolutionary violence, but a mix of the two. Both had different objectives and impacts, and they complemented each other, even if the emphasis shifted from one to the other depending on the pressures of the conflict. Other combatants recognized this complementary role, such as the Volunteer Army in the south, who as well as conducting mass violence also established their own courts, as did some of the more organized peasant armies.[80] The Bolsheviks had neither the ability nor the desire to suppress all crimes violently, even

[76] P. Stuchka, 'Old and New Courts (4 January 1918)', reprinted in Rosenberg, *Bolshevik Visions*, I, 188.

[77] N. Bukharin and E. Preobrazhensky, *The ABC of Communism* (London, 1919), section 73, available at https://www.marxists.org/archive/bukharin/works/1920/abc/09.htm [accessed 13 June 2019].

[78] Krylenko, *Sudoustroistvo*, 15–17.

[79] GARF, f. R-1005, op. 1, d. 76, l. 361ob (circular, 18 April 1920). On the mutually reinforcing nature of order and violence, see S. Kalyvas, I. Shapiro, and T. Masoud, 'Introduction: Integrating the Study of Order, Conflict, and Violence', in S. Kalyvas, I. Shapiro, and T. Masoud (eds.), *Order, Conflict and Violence* (Cambridge, 2008), 1.

[80] V. Bortnevski, 'White Administration and White Terror (The Denikin Period)', *The Russian Review*, 52, 3 (1993), 354–66; and Holquist, 'Violent Russia', 648–9.

counter-revolutionary ones, but they could not condone these acts by doing nothing. Law enabled a more multifaceted response: it was inspired by revolutionary idealism but also utilized long-held legal customs and practices to enhance legitimacy and authority; it enacted the state's objectives yet retained a sense of separation from the state and the party; it preached a merciless response to criminal threats yet offered greater flexibility through a range of punitive measures and even discretion; and it sought to engage and educate through a variety of means rather than simply punish. Violence ebbed and flowed throughout the conflict. Law, in contrast, was increasingly stable and institutionalized, enabling a more constant and consistent means of fulfilling revolutionary objectives and targeting counter-revolutionary threats.

In some senses, moreover, tribunals promised more: not only could the Bolsheviks employ revolutionary justice *and* revolutionary violence, but tribunals formed a link between the 'regular' justice of people's courts and the violent practices of the Cheka. Tribunals permitted a more nuanced response to counter-revolution than the Cheka by enabling the use of those facets of law discussed above. Yet by applying greater and more prominent force than people's courts, they could send out a stronger message. Similarly, the political justice of tribunals was a form of violence that shared the same causes, functions, and meanings as other forms, from threatening and suppressing enemies to forging identities and communicating messages. Yet the use of legal procedure, the variety of sentences, and the prevalence of mercy clearly distinguished political justice from those forms of violence that inflicted much more brutal injuries.[81] Thus rather than assessing tribunals against 'normal' legal standards or dismissing them as no different from the Cheka, I see them as operating at the intersection of law and violence, and this book explores systematically the fluid boundaries between the two.[82] In doing so, I argue that tribunals merged aspects of law and violence to offer something distinct to the Bolsheviks that encapsulated the role of revolutionary justice more broadly during the civil war.

The State versus the People

This book, therefore, uses the title, *The State versus the People*, not to analyse exclusively, as another author has used a similar title to do, the 'iron fist' of the proletarian dictatorship and the repressive activities of the new Soviet state against

[81] As well as Smith, 'Violence', see S. Smith, 'Introduction: Reflections on Villains, Victims and Violence', *Europe-Asia Studies*, 65, 9 (2013), esp. 1691–3.

[82] It is worth noting that these arguments against drawing a sharp distinction between law and violence differ significantly from my earlier thoughts in M. Rendle, 'Revolutionary Tribunals and the Origins of Terror in Early Soviet Russia', *Historical Research*, 84, 226 (2011), 693–721.

its people.[83] Instead, the book explores the interaction between state and people, and how tribunals were used by the Bolsheviks as a means of solving the problems facing them during the civil war, distinct from pure violence, whether this was building an effective state, combating threats to this state, forging a new society, promoting ideology and correct behaviour, or regulating the relationship between state and society. The available sources mean the discussion is filtered through official expectations for tribunals, the records gathered on their operation, and the reports written on their performance. Questions concerning people's experiences and the impact of tribunals are addressed where possible but are often difficult to answer conclusively.

The first chapter provides the foundation for the rest of the book by charting the establishment of revolutionary justice. As noted above, although the Bolsheviks had a clear sense of the role of law in society and a clear desire to oversee legal reform, they did not have a coherent plan on exactly what they would do. Consequently, the new system emerged steadily through the year after October with the development of tribunals shaped by the Bolsheviks' experiences of early trials and the intensifying civil war. Chapter 1 examines the decrees that outlined the official role of tribunals, explores the experiences of the early trials, and looks at how tribunals started to operate in practice, both nationally and locally. From the start, tribunals were pitted against the Cheka, and this too shaped how tribunals took shape. By late 1918, however, tribunals were firmly in place, with a structure that only changed minimally thereafter and a distinct role alongside the Cheka.

The building of institutions like courts formed an important part of re-establishing central state authority during this period. The Bolsheviks inherited a shattered state, and their weaknesses, alongside widespread opposition, exacerbated the problem initially. As political courts targeting a wide variety of counter-revolutionary crimes, staffed by party members who proactively targeted criminals, tribunals were better placed to convey the authority and objectives of the state than other courts. Law really did become the 'emissary of the state', categorizing diverse human actions into a series of crimes and extending the state's reach across Russia.[84] Chapter 2 explores the steady expansion of tribunals as a means of exerting state authority from the end of 1918. By 1922, the Bolsheviks had re-established the state, and this achievement, the end of the civil war, and the publication of new law codes rendered many tribunals obsolete in a more stable Soviet Union.

[83] N. Werth, 'A State against its People: Violence, Repression, and Terror in the Soviet Union', in S. Courtois et al. (eds.), *The Black Book of Communism: Crimes, Terror, Repression* (Cambridge, MA, 1999), 33–268.

[84] See U. Baxi, '"The State's Emissary": The Place of the Law in Subaltern Studies', in P. Chatterjee and G. Panday (eds.), *Subaltern Studies VII: Writings on South Asian History and Society* (New Delhi, 1992), 247–64.

When this book considers the 'state', it focuses primarily on the Russian state, or Russian Soviet Federative Socialist Republic, with the majority of its evidence coming from European Russia and western Siberia. There is more evidence from these areas as the Bolsheviks controlled them more consistently across the civil war. Moreover, the other new republics formed their own commissariats of justice and issued their own decrees that, while generally following Moscow, differed in detail and timing. It seems wiser, particularly for official legislation, to focus on what emerged from Moscow. Finally, some areas of the former empire saw revolutionary justice compete with other forms of law, particularly religious law in Central Asia. Again, this book does use evidence from these areas, especially since tribunals tended to stand above customary forms of law, focusing on activities less affected by ethnic or religious concerns and controlled by local or Russian Bolsheviks, but it lacks the space to explore the specificities of these regions in depth.[85]

Chapter 3 examines how the Bolsheviks categorized counter-revolutionary crimes and, in doing so, exerted control over definitions of the revolution and sought to establish new 'norms'. Initial conceptions of counter-revolution revolved around revolts, plots, or sabotage conducted by obvious political and social enemies, but the Bolsheviks faced an increasing array of problems as the civil war intensified and more activities were soon included. The elasticity of the term provided tribunals with much of their power, but this did not inevitably mean 'lawlessness' or 'arbitrariness' – there may have been no formal law codes, but there were numerous decrees and tribunals targeted at specific threats based on the state's evolving fears and ambitions. Nevertheless, as the category of counter-revolution expanded, so too did the social backgrounds of counter-revolutionaries to encompass primarily lower-class 'criminals', which had significant implications for broader state–society relations.

The trial was the focal point of the legal process: it provided a forum for both sides to discuss their version of events; it produced the punitive sentence; and it also provided the basis for the educational message, whether in the courtroom or when publicized later. In doing so, it was the primary means by which tribunals projected the state's authority and ideology, and formed the main distinction between revolutionary justice and revolutionary violence. Chapter 4 pieces together the trial process, examining how cases were brought to trial, the individuals involved, the location, the trial procedure, and the sentences. Sentences were

[85] For the background, see various articles in S. Kirmse (ed.), *One Law for All? Western Models and Local Practices in (Post-)Imperial Contexts* (Frankfurt, 2012); S. Kirmse, *The Lawful Empire: Legal Change and Cultural Diversity in Late Imperial Russia* (Cambridge, 2019), 40-74; and M. Tissier, 'Local Laws and the Workings of Legal Knowledge in Late Imperial Russia', *Ab Imperio*, 4 (2012), 211–44. On post-1917, see P. Sartori, 'What Went Wrong? The Failure of Soviet Policy on *sharīʿa* Courts in Turkestan, 1917-1923', *Die Welt des Islams*, 50 (2010), 397–43. On tribunals, see the work of M. Sapargaliev and Kh. Sulaimanova listed in the bibliography.

far more varied than might be expected, or that Narkomiust encouraged, revealing differing conceptions of counter-revolution and the nature of revolutionary consciousness, and more broadly the flexibility of law over violence.

Many sentences were suspended, there were frequent national amnesties, and some offenders were released early—all termed 'mercy' by the Bolsheviks—which reiterated the flexibility of law. Bolshevik legal theorists argued that, if the danger posed by the crime changed, then so should the sentence, and there was no point incarcerating people who could be safely rehabilitated into society. But there were also other logical reasons, from reinforcing the image of the justice system as independent and the state as humane, to relieving pressure on overcrowded courts and prisons, to targeting social groups whose support or service was needed. Chapter 5 focuses on cassation, amnesties, and early release to examine how the Bolsheviks utilized mercy. It also explores the dialogue on justice that emerged in appeals, the strategies of appellants, and how their involuntary complicity in revolutionary justice may have reinforced its legitimacy and, in turn, the authority of the state.

All courts were, as officials liked to note, schoolrooms where people could learn about the revolution, the new proletarian state, and its ideals. Only a minority of people, however, were involved directly in tribunals or were able to watch trials in person. Chapter 6 analyses the wider publicity surrounding trials, making extensive use of national and local newspapers, images, and newsreels to examine how tribunals were portrayed, the language and images used, and how this fitted in with broader agitational attempts to mobilize people.

This book does not gloss over the problems, inconsistencies, and ineffectiveness often visible in the actions of tribunals in all these areas. Nor does it privilege tribunals over other state activities. But as one historian has reminded us, power was not lying on the ground after the October Revolution, ready to be picked up or 'seized'. It needed to be reconstructed, and while the Bolsheviks were the most successful at 'institutionalizing' the violence needed to win the civil war, they did not operate in 'one register'—a variety of tools enabled them to emerge victorious, including 'normal' state-building practices such as law.[86] By combining several tools, including law, violence, and agitation, tribunals played a significant role.

[86] Engelstein, *Russia in Flames*, xviii, xxiii, 264.

1
Creating Revolutionary Justice

Less than three weeks after the October Revolution, fighting armed resistance in many cities and facing extensive strikes from civil servants, the Council of People's Commissars (Sovnarkom) authorized work on the Decree on Courts. Led by the legal theorist and acting Commissar of Justice P. I. Stuchka, at least one draft was produced before a final version was agreed by Sovnarkom on 22 November 1917 and published two days later.[1] The absence of an official 'revolutionary court', Sovnarkom recorded, placed the state in a 'desperate situation', 'powerless' to deal with 'counter-revolutionary' crimes.[2] The new courts established in this decree, by implication, would solve this problem and help the Bolsheviks hold on to power. Beyond that, the decree outlined a role for law in building a new socialist state.

This decree, however, was not the beginning or end of creating revolutionary justice. On the one hand, its roots lay in earlier forms of justice, particularly developments since the February Revolution, and in the Bolsheviks' understanding of the role of law. On the other, the decree was brief and required elaboration, while the evolving nature of counter-revolution forced changes over subsequent months and years. This chapter charts the development of revolutionary justice as it responded and tried to enhance its effectiveness. As in other areas of governance, the Bolsheviks lacked a clear plan and consequently the new system emerged in stages, shaped by various decrees and regulations that reacted to specific challenges but whose content was also guided by a fundamental belief that law was a valuable tool for the new ruling proletariat. In the case of revolutionary tribunals, their evolution was also shaped by the experiences of high-profile national trials and everyday practices locally. By late 1918, when this chapter ends, not only had a structured hierarchy of tribunals emerged that reflected the new justice system more broadly, but legal officials had started to carve out a distinct role for law amid the violence of civil war, even if much work remained to be done.

Success was far from assured. As counter-revolution intensified, revolutionary justice had to combat a fundamental challenge to the very existence of law. From the moment a new secret police was established on 7 December 1917—the

[1] For a concise account of the process leading to this decree, see L. Antonova, 'Velikaia Oktiabr'skaia revoliutsiia i sozdanie narodnykh sudov, 1917-1918 gg.', *Iuridicheskaia Rossiia* (2008), 86–7, available at http://law.edu.ru/doc/document.asp?docID=1133185 [accessed 24 April 2019].

[2] *Protokoly zasedanii Soveta Narodnykh Komissarov RSFSR. Noiabr' 1917-mart 1918gg.* (Moscow, 2006), 44.

The State versus The People: Revolutionary Justice in Russia's Civil War, 1917–1922. Matthew Rendle, Oxford University Press (2020). © Matthew Rendle.
DOI: 10.1093/oso/9780198840428.001.0001

All-Russian Extraordinary Commission for the Struggle with Counter-Revolution and Sabotage (Cheka)—revolutionary justice was pitted against a different vision for combatting counter-revolution, one that championed a fast, violent, and often arbitrary response that offered a more obvious solution to the Bolsheviks' problems. Conflict between the Commissariat of Justice (Narkomiust) and the Cheka erupted immediately and continued intermittently throughout the civil war, but Narkomiust's initial fears that justice would be subsumed by violence had abated by late 1918 with the consolidation of the justice system.

For many, at the time and subsequently, the politicized nature of revolutionary justice meant that it was hardly distinguishable from revolutionary violence in any case, while the scale of violence during the civil war proved law's irrelevance in an increasingly authoritarian state. Disregarding law, however, avoids important questions. If law never exists outside of societies and their politics, what exactly made revolutionary justice more political than other forms of law? If revolutionary justice, particularly tribunals, was entirely political, then what role was it intended to play as the Bolsheviks established their new form of politics? How far did tribunals shape and reflect the changing nature of politics and power relations over the civil war? Ultimately, tribunals offered possibilities different from those of the Cheka and this became clearer across 1918. Trials could eliminate real or imagined enemies, pronounce on issues with political significance, and spread political messages.[3] Using trials rather than violence to achieve these aims promised to strengthen the Bolsheviks' legitimacy and authority, providing some degree of authentication for their political actions.[4] The need for violence remained, and tribunals intended to channel law's inherent violence, but tribunals were complementing the Cheka by late 1918 despite ongoing problems.

The Decree on Courts

The Decree on Courts abolished all existing courts, replacing them with local or people's courts. Judges would be elected by local soviets until they could be elected directly, and they would be joined by two jurors from a predetermined list. Prosecutors and defence counsels could now be 'moral citizens of both sexes enjoying civil rights', while the operation of justice locally would be overseen by commissars also appointed by local soviets. Courts would be guided by the existing laws of the tsarist government 'insofar as they had not been annulled by the revolution [decrees or socialist party programmes] and did not contradict

[3] J. Meierhenrich and D. Pendas, '"The Justice of My Cause is Clear, but There's Politics to Fear": Political Trials in Theory and History', in J. Meierhenrich and D. Pendas (eds.), *Political Trials in Theory and History* (Cambridge, 2017), 51–60.

[4] O. Kirchheimer, *Political Justice: The Use of Legal Procedure for Political Ends* (Princeton, 1961), 6.

revolutionary conscience [*sovest'*] or revolutionary legal consciousness [*pravosoznanie*]'. Finally, the decree ordered local soviets to establish revolutionary tribunals to deal with the threat of counter-revolution and target 'looting, exploitation, sabotage and the other abuses of merchants, industrialists, officials, and others'. A tribunal would consist of a chairman and six jurors elected by local soviets and a commission to investigate crimes.[5]

There is no doubt this decree initiated a legal system that deviated significantly from Western conceptions of law and was more unpredictable: electing untrained judges; permitting the public to act in the place of trained lawyers; challenging the pre-eminence of statutory law; and openly politicizing law by privileging revolutionary conscience. It is not surprising that tsarist legal officials recalled the 'colossal' (and, in their view, destructive) impact of the decree.[6] From the perspective of the Bolsheviks, though, the decree constituted a two-pronged attack on the lawlessness that challenged their hold on power.

First, regular crime had escalated since the February Revolution, and it was clear that the existing court system no longer had the means and authority to cope, especially in urban areas. It had also been clear since February that there was popular support for legal reform that prioritized popular conceptions of justice. In Petrograd, for instance, spontaneous courts had emerged with elected representatives from soldiers and workers acting as judges.[7] These were later disbanded by the Provisional Government, but re-emerged after October as district soviets formed revolutionary courts to combat widespread criminality. Workers and soldiers again served as judges, and there were no lawyers. They issued sentences not based on existing laws but focusing instead on the nature and circumstances of a crime, and the social background and age of the accused, often privileging the exploited and destitute over the propertied and wealthy. The audience offered opinions to ensure the court reflected the 'people's will'.[8] These courts spread quickly to Moscow and other towns, but there were plenty of inconsistencies and some areas lacked a court or were forced to rely on existing courts that were not sympathetic to the goals of the October Revolution. The new people's courts offered a more systematic approach and greater central control.

Second, the decree outlined a means of dealing with a crime—counter-revolution—that had only emerged since February and took on new forms after October, from armed revolts to sabotage, and posed the greatest threat to the Bolsheviks. Spontaneous local courts were ill-equipped to deal with such important and often

[5] *Dekrety Sovetskoi vlasti* [hereafter *DSV*] (18 volumes, Moscow, 1957–2009), I, 124–6.

[6] For example, S. Kobiakov, '"Krasnyi sud": Vpechatleniia zashchitnika v revoliutsionnykh tribunalakh', *Arkhiv Russkoi revoliutsii*, 7 (1922), 246; and N. Maier, 'Sluzhba v komissariate iustitsii i narodnom sude', *Arkhiv Russkoi revoloiutsii*, 8 (1923), 85–6.

[7] T. Hasegawa, *Crime and Punishment in the Russian Revolution* (Cambridge, MA, 2017), 86–92.

[8] *Izvestiia*, 8 November 1917, 2; 9 November, 7. See also 'Pervye narodnye revoliutsionnye sudy v Petrograde', *Istoricheskii arkhiv*, 1 (1957), 107–28; and V. Kayurov, 'The First People's Court', *Sputnik*, 7 (1967), 84–5.

large-scale crimes so, on 4 November, an investigative commission was established under the Military Revolutionary Committee of the Petrograd Soviet to arrest offenders (Moscow soon followed suit). But this commission was quickly overloaded; one participant described working day and night in a single room, writing on his knees as there was only one table.[9] The first draft of the Decree on Courts had envisaged all soviets creating these investigative commissions, but within days it became clear that a more substantial response was needed and the final version established special courts—tribunals—to create a systematic means of targeting counter-revolution.[10]

This response became clearer once the few lines on tribunals in the decree were supplemented by further 'guidance' a week later. Tribunals could form separate departments to focus on different crimes (allowing greater specialization than people's courts), trials would run for no more than a week (facilitating a quick response), and judges were selected by the local soviet (enhancing state control by removing the potential of the public electing judges directly). The sentences permitted were also listed (ensuring an appropriate punishment), including fines, public labour, imprisonment, public censure, and exile abroad.[11]

As the future chief prosecutor, N. V. Krylenko, recalled, the term 'revolutionary tribunal' was not used 'by chance': it was borrowed from the French Revolution.[12] This link was made in the first trial when the chairman, I. P. Zhukov, compared the tribunal to its French predecessors and declared it would be the 'fiercest defender of the rights and customs of the Russian Revolution' and would 'strictly judge all those who act against the will of the people'.[13] Otherwise, there were few open references to French tribunals, probably due to the latter's unsavoury association with terror, but also because, as Stuchka later insisted, the Bolsheviks only borrowed the name and the concept. Both revolutions, he noted, needed a means to struggle against their enemies, but the revolutions were different, the enemies were different, and thus tribunals would develop differently. Most notably, there was no terror immediately and a more diverse range of sentences. One tribunal official even argued that when Russia's tribunals did conduct terror, it was against clear enemies rather than what he saw as the indiscriminate terror of 1793–4.[14]

[9] 'Vospominaniia predsedatelia pervoi sledstvennoi komissii petrogradskogo soveta rabochikh i soldatskikh deputatov M. Iu. Kozlovskogo', *Sotsialisticheskaia zakonnost'*, 4 (1967), 17.

[10] The draft is in *Materialy Narodnogo Komissariata Iustitsii* [hereafter *Materialy*], 2 (1918), 103–4.

[11] *Izvestiia*, 28 November 1917, 7.

[12] N. Krylenko, 'Vozniknovenie i pervye mesiatsy raboty revoliutsionnykh tribunalov' in N. Krylenko (ed.), *Problemy ugolovnoi politiki* (4 volumes, Moscow, 1935–7), III, 30–1.

[13] GARF, f. R-1074, op. 1, d. 10, l. 20 (transcript, 10 December 1917). Zhukov referred to the French Revolution of 1848, but he appears to have had the tribunals of the 1790s in mind.

[14] P. Stuchka, 'Pervye revoliutsionnye tribunaly v Rossii', in *Piat' let Verkhovnogo suda, 1918–1923* (Moscow, 1923), no pag.; K. Danishevskii, *Revoliutsionnye voennye tribunaly* (Moscow, 1920), 59. See also N. Polianskii, 'Revoliutsionnye tribunaly', *Pravo i zhizn'*, 8–10 (1927), 76–9.

The Bolsheviks, unsurprisingly, did not see a problem with greater state control over law or its politicization. In their instrumentalist view, after all, law was always a tool used by the ruling classes to defend their interests, and it was imperative that law should be pressed into the service of the new proletarian state. Furthermore, all European countries prosecuted political crimes to a greater or lesser extent at this time, and Russia's laws prior to 1917 had tended to be harsher, more abundant, and vaguer, creating arbitrary and secret legal processes for those accused of crimes against the state and sovereign.[15] After the February Revolution, the Provisional Government abolished many of these laws to popular acclaim, but the concept of a political crime remained widespread, albeit increasingly articulated through the lens of counter-revolution, as demonstrated by the investigations into the Bolsheviks after the unrest in early July 1917 and into the Kornilov Revolt in late August.[16] After October, Stuchka rejected the idea of political crimes, focusing entirely on the struggle between revolution and counter-revolution. The former was now embodied by the Bolsheviks, representing the people's will, with the latter consisting of the people's class enemies. Tribunals targeted counter-revolution through a 'public inquiry', with the people participating in the 'public exposure' of their enemies.[17] Tribunals would, moreover, only be a temporary measure; once the revolution emerged victorious, counter-revolution, and thus the need for tribunals, would disappear.[18] I. N. Shteinberg, the Left Socialist Revolutionary (SR) Commissar of Justice after Stuchka from December 1917 to March 1918, added that tribunals served a transitional purpose, developing a revolutionary sense of justice and a socially moral self-consciousness, targeting specific activities and enemies rather than acting as organs of vengeance.[19]

The Bolsheviks, also unsurprisingly, did not believe the decree facilitated lawlessness. While the first draft had proposed abolishing all existing laws of 'overthrown' governments, Stuchka recalled how this was 'softened' in the face of opposition from Left SRs and some Bolsheviks who wanted new laws in place before old ones were abolished.[20] A sharp break from the past would leave courts

[15] J. Daly, 'Political Crime in Late Imperial Russia', *The Journal of Modern History*, 74, 1 (2002), 62–100.

[16] O. Ivantsova (ed.), *Sledstvennoe delo bol'shevikov: Materialy Predvaritel'nogo sledstviia o vooruzhennom vystuplenii 3–5 iiulia 1917 g. v g. Petrograde protiv gosudarstvennoi vlasti. Iiul'-oktiabr' 1917* (2 volumes, Moscow, 2012); and *Delo generala L. G. Kornilova; Avgust 1917g.-iiun' 1918g.* (2 volumes, Moscow, 2003).

[17] P. Stuchka, 'Old and New Courts (4 January 1918)', reprinted in W. Rosenberg (ed.), *Bolshevik Visions* (2nd edition, 2 volumes, Ann Arbor, 1990), I, 188.

[18] As noted in N. Krylenko, 'Revoliutsionnye tribunaly', *Vestnik zhizni*, 1 (1918), 81–7; and D. Kurskii, 'Osnovy revoliutsionnago suda', *Materialy*, 1 (1918), 60 (speech to a congress of justice officials, 21 April 1918).

[19] I. Shteinberg, *Nravstvennyi lik revoliutsii* (Berlin, 1923), 36.

[20] *Materialy*, 2 (1918), 103–4 (draft decree on courts); P. Stuchka, 'Five Years of Revolution in Law (December 1922)', reprinted in Rosenberg, *Bolshevik Visions*, I, 192–3.

lacking any form of guidance (and would possibly harm their legitimacy and authority), and Lenin, for one, apparently distrusted phrases without substance, such as 'revolutionary consciousness'.[21] Nevertheless, all socialists believed the pre-existing laws were exploitative relics of the old regime and a department in Narkomiust was devoted to preparing new codes. In the meantime the decrees, regulations, and orders issued by the government served as laws, just as they had done at various times for previous governments. To be sure, initially many gaps led to inconsistent practices on the part of all courts but, as the decrees multiplied and regulations governing courts became more complex, the 'lawlessness' became increasingly managed and controlled. And by the time the state did formally abolish all pre-October laws in November 1918, it was publishing its own collections of decrees and resolutions which essentially acted as law codes. The workers 'have no need for endless tomes of written laws', it was later pronounced, and 'when they [or their 'representatives', the Bolsheviks] have expressed their will in one of the fundamental decrees, they can leave the interpretation and application of these decrees . . . to the popular courts'.[22]

Legal officials and theorists also conveyed the sense they were creating a new, fairer form of law through their language. There was, for instance, a preference for *pravo* (law with connotations of truth, justice, and moral rights) over *zakon* (impersonal legal rights, written laws, and legalism), and *pravosudie* (justice) over *iustitsiia* (the system of justice, as reflected in 'Narkomiust'). Similarly, stress was placed on *spravedlivost'* (fairness or justice), always a subjective concept but which took on a class-based character during the revolution.[23] And *revoliutsionnaia sovest'* (revolutionary conscience) would ensure fairness (justice) if existing laws fell short of revolutionary ideals or written decrees were absent.

Indeed, it is semantics that provided tribunals with much of their power and menace, particularly the elasticity of 'counter-revolution'. Initially, most Bolsheviks held a narrow and class-based view – counter-revolutionaries were class enemies whose inevitable opposition the proletariat must overcome for the revolution to succeed. These enemies included capitalists (merchants, industrialists, and landowners), the political parties representing them (particularly the liberal Kadet party), and other privileged elements such as nobles, clergy, or officers. In an article published in 1918, Stuchka declared the need to remove their masks,[24] and few workers, soldiers, or peasants disputed the need to defend the revolution from these enemies. The problem was that this class-based view

[21] P. Stuchka, *Revoliutsionnaia rol' Sovetskogo prava* (3rd edition, Moscow, 1934), 91–2.

[22] N. Bukharin and E. Preobrazhensky, *The ABC of Communism* (London, 1919), available at https://www.marxists.org/archive/bukharin/works/1920/abc/09.htm [accessed 24 April 2019].

[23] See the discussion in M. Reisner, *Pravo i revoliutsiia* (Petrograd, 1917), 19–24. On considering legal language, see William Rosenberg's discussion comments in *Epokha voin i revoliutsii: 1914–1922* (St Petersburg, 2017), 149–50.

[24] P. Stuchka, 'Proletarskaia revoliutsiia i sud (1918)', reprinted in Stuchka, *Izbrannye proizvedeniia po Marksistsko-Leninskoi teorii prava* (Riga, 1964), 241.

quickly failed to explain the realities of the gathering opposition to the Bolsheviks (and thus threats to the revolution). As the Bolsheviks attacked other socialists, 'proletarians' became disillusioned with growing authoritarianism, while, as discussed below, officials tasked with operating tribunals locally made fewer distinctions between regular and counter-revolutionary crimes as they struggled for power. Many crimes reflected discontent with the new order or impacted on their ability to govern.

Narkomiust was taken over on 9 December 1917 by the Bolsheviks' new coalition partners in government, the Left SRs, who placed more emphasis on creating and adhering to legal procedure. Led by Shteinberg, they stressed that tribunals remained courts—new and revolutionary courts, serving a different purpose and based on different practices to tsarist courts, but still courts following some form of procedure. These views created some tensions with Bolsheviks (although not as many as later claimed) and also highlighted competing jurisdictions. Narkomiust regulated tribunals, but local soviets provided people and finance, while the Commissariat of Internal Affairs (Narkomvnudel) monitored their role in securing order. The creation of the Cheka further muddied the waters, as it was supposed to act as an investigative arm for tribunals but, as will be seen, developed into an autonomous institution with its own sentencing powers. These competing institutional interests remained even after the Left SRs had departed in March 1918.

Therefore, even Bolsheviks who subscribed to the view that the tribunal was not a 'normal' court founded on judicial subtlety and complexity, but an arm of political struggle directed at counter-revolution and dealing with crimes that did not exist in bourgeois laws, were forced to address key questions after the Decree on Courts. How does a court operate without established procedures? How does it deal with new, undefined crimes? How will 'revolutionary consciousness' guide sentencing? Can tribunals judge crimes as a 'court' *and* act as a 'political weapon'? In short, how will revolutionary justice work in practice?

The First Trials in Petrograd

The first tribunal was established in Petrograd on 3 December and held its first, highly anticipated trial on 10 December. Countess S. V. Panina, Deputy Minister of Education under the Provisional Government and a leading member of the liberal Kadet party, was accused of refusing to hand over 93,000 roubles belonging to the ministry to its new leaders. Panina stated that she would only deliver it to the legal authority, which in her view was the forthcoming, nationally elected Constituent Assembly. The Bolsheviks labelled this an act of sabotage and counter-revolution; it prevented their government from functioning effectively and thus, they argued, Panina was acting against the revolution that brought them to power.

This period was characterized by widespread strikes and acts of sabotage, so why was Panina selected for the first trial? Observers and historians have variously noted her political beliefs and the Bolsheviks' need for money in the face of uncooperative banks.[25] Panina's cousin claimed the Bolsheviks hoped to raise more money by obtaining bail or by allowing her to 'escape', permitting them to confiscate her property.[26] The Bolsheviks did offer bail for 180,000 roubles, twice as much as the missing sum.[27] Politically, her arrest came on the day her party was banned and the Constituent Assembly postponed. Panina later added a class dimension, claiming she had committed three sins; she was a Kadet, rich, and an aristocrat.[28] Coming after the abolition of social classes, this aristocratic background was a further crime. Either way, Panina represented several of the state's political and social enemies, and she must have seemed a safe choice for a high-profile first trial.

The trial, however, was not a success from the Bolsheviks' point of view.[29] It was delayed for several hours, partly due to turmoil in the courtroom caused by the hostility of Panina's supporters, which was only quashed when the chairman threatened to deploy force.[30] The belief that there was no need for an official prosecutor as the audience would act as one was challenged immediately as no one volunteered. Instead, the first two speakers defended Panina on the basis of her long history of educational and charitable work. The first speaker, Ia. Ia. Gurevich, who acted as Panina's defence counsel, also tried to undermine the rationale behind the trial. He argued that if the tribunal was a proper court, it had to proceed according to law or consciousness. According to law, she had not stolen the money, as she was willing to hand it over to the legal authority. According to consciousness, her history of charitable work hardly made her an enemy of the people. All that remained was to judge her as a political enemy, but this was not the job of a court.[31] When someone did finally press for Panina's conviction, it was on the basis of her social and political background as a member of a class and party opposed to the Bolsheviks, and the tribunal must defend the interests of

[25] F. Kamenskii, 'Pervyi tribunal v Petrograde. Zametki zhurnalista', *Sotsialisticheskaia zakonnost'*, 4 (1967), 23; E. Finn, 'Pervyi revoliutsionnyi tribunal', *Sovetskaia iustitsiia*, 8 (1967), 18; K. Kozlova and V. Orlov, 'Pervoe zasedanie narodnogo revtribunala', *Voprosy istorii*, 10 (1977), 212–13; E. Ershova, 'Pervyi protsess Petrogradskogo revtribunala v 1917 godu', in *Neizvestnye stranitsy istorii Verkhnevolzh'ia* (Tver', 1994), 91; A. Lindenmeyr, 'The First Soviet Political Trial: Countess Sofia Panina before the Petrograd Revolutionary Tribunal', *The Russian Review*, 60, 4 (2001), 513–14; and A. Lindenmeyr, *Citizen Countess: Sofia Panina and the Fate of Revolutionary Russia* (Madison, 2019), 204-17.

[26] 'A Bolshevist Trial', *The Times*, 31 January 1918, 5.

[27] Lindenmeyr, *Citizen Countess*, 202.

[28] BAR, S. V. Panina papers, box 14, 'Such is life', 3.

[29] The official transcript (GARF, f. R-1074, op. 1, d. 10. ll. 20–3) and report (*Izvestiia*, 12 December 1917, 6) do not always match other accounts of the trial (see the analysis in Lindenmeyr, 'First Soviet', 515–20).

[30] S. Ovsiankin, 'V pervom tribunale', *Sud idet!*, 21 (1927), 1216–17.

[31] For his own account, see Ia. Gurevich, 'Delo grafini S. V. Paninoi v revoliutsionnom tribunale', *Russkoe bogatstvo*, 11–12 (1917), 283–98.

workers and peasants. These accusations did little to dissuade observers that this was not a political court, particularly as the chairman, Zhukov, had been a Bolshevik party member since 1909. There were also allegations that Stuchka intervened to manipulate proceedings, which Zhukov later denied.[32] The tribunal found Panina guilty, publicly censured her, and ordered her to remain in prison until the sum of 93,000 roubles was turned over to the state, which it was within days.

Similar impressions emerged from the second major trial, of General V. G. Boldyrev.[33] A Junkers' revolt in Petrograd after the October Revolution had reinforced Bolshevik suspicions of officers as a reactionary group. They assumed, with some justification, that officers would form the backbone of any resistance. On 9 November, the Bolshevik's new Commander-in-Chief, Krylenko, who held this post prior to his involvement in tribunals, departed for military headquarters to assert his authority. On 11 November, he arrived at Pskov and asked to see the Commander of the Northern Front, General A. V. Cheremisov, to discuss his 'sociopolitical views'. Cheremisov refused. He later feigned illness, but Krylenko believed him to be healthy and an 'intriguer'. He was arrested and transferred to a Petrograd prison.[34] Krylenko met with a similar response a day later in Dvinsk, where the local commander, Boldyrev, also refused to cooperate and was arrested. As Cheremisov had at least expressed his discontent with the previous government by refusing to follow orders to suppress the October Revolution a fortnight earlier, Boldyrev was probably considered a better choice to place on trial in order to send out a message to other officers refusing to recognize Soviet power. At his trial on 14 December, Boldyrev claimed he was only following the orders of his army committee, which had not wanted to submit to a single-party authority. The committee had changed its mind, but Boldyrev feigned ignorance. But he admitted only recognizing the authority of the Constituent Assembly. Boldyrev, like Panina, made his trial political by denying that the Bolsheviks represented the people; only an elected assembly did, and by supporting it, he was not an enemy of the people, only of the Bolsheviks. However, despite favourable witness testimony, including from a soldier, he was sentenced

[32] BAR, Panina, 'Such', 6; A. Tyrkova-Williams, *From Liberty to Brest-Litovsk* (London, 1919), 388; I. Zhukov, 'Revoliutsionnyi tribunal (Vospominaniia pervogo predsedatelia tribunala)', *Rabochii sud*, 22 (1927), 1759–60.

[33] There were smaller trials between those of Panina and Boldyrev; *Novaia zhizn'*, 12 December 1917, 2; *Izvestiia*, 13 December 1917, 9–10, and 14 December 1917, 10. The official account of Boldyrev's trial is in *Izvestiia*, 15 December 1917, 15. See also E. Finn, 'Pervyi revoliutsionnyi tribunal', *Sovetskaia iustitsiia*, 10 (1967), 16–17. For foreign observations, see B. Beatty, *The Red Heart of Russia* (New York, 1918), 304–6; HIA, L. E. Browne papers, box 2, folder 9, untitled account, pp. 2–4; and Tyrkova-Williams, *Liberty*, 389–91. These accounts must be treated carefully as they are full of factual inaccuracies, but they agree on the gist and atmosphere of the trial.

[34] GARF, f. R-336, op. 1, d. 339, ll. 1 (accusations), 30–30ob, 45–45ob (testimonies, November 1918).

to three years in prison. This prompted turmoil in the court and his supporters had to be forcibly removed.[35]

These trials highlighted serious flaws. Tribunals were intended to send a decisive and unambiguous message to the state's enemies and the population at large. These trials did not. The public response, as reflected by the audience, was unexpected and mixed. Even if, as the Bolsheviks argued, the audiences were packed with bourgeois supporters of the accused, this still left the question of why the lower classes were not participating. The characterization of the accused as clear-cut enemies was challenged and was hardly reinforced by the sentences, which failed to send out a strong message to potential enemies. Both Panina and her counsel, for instance, felt they achieved the lightest sentence possible and had emerged victorious.[36] All this was perfect fodder for an opposition press whose scepticism towards tribunals turned to ridicule. What court, the Menshevik *Novaia zhizn'* asked, had no prosecution, no defence, and no real sentence?[37] It is hardly surprising, therefore, that reforms were mooted.

Only a few days before, seven Left SRs had formed a coalition government with the Bolsheviks and demanded the post of Commissar of Justice as one of the conditions of entry. This reflected their belief that justice was a means by which they could oversee policies and combat excesses. The new commissar, Shteinberg, aimed to prevent terror by ensuring that all prisoners were dealt with by courts; that all decrees were sanctioned by Narkomiust to ensure their legality; that the Decree on Courts was rewritten to place more emphasis on judges and lawyers; and that the operation of tribunals was better regulated to create 'just (*pravosudnyi*)' courts.[38] Shteinberg aimed to broaden the social base of support for the government and, in turn, reduce the need for violence to retain power. Rather than targeting entire parties or social classes, tribunals should focus on individuals who *had* committed crimes. These would be fully investigated and face socialist justice (*spravedlivost'*) in court.[39] Terror, he later claimed, was a mistake of the French Revolution he believed Russia could avoid.[40]

Under Shteinberg, Narkomiust quickly published two decrees on tribunals. The first, on 18 December, no doubt fuelled by the negative publicity surrounding the first trials, established a special tribunal for the press. This would target the publication of 'false or distorted information' on public events that harmed the

[35] Apparently other trials also ended in turmoil during this period; *Novaia zhizn'*, 21 December 1917, 3.

[36] BAR, Panina, 'Such', 7; Gurevich, 'Delo', 295–6.

[37] A. Goikhbarg, 'Kakoi eto sud?', *Novaia zhizn'*, 13 December 1917, 1 (also the parody on p. 2). See also Goikhbarg, 'Gde zhe sud?', *Novaia zhizn'*, 12 December 1917, 1.

[38] YIVO, RG 366, I. N. Steinberg papers, folder 967, 'Nakanune', 1–3 (statement of aims, 10 December 1917).

[39] *Partiia levykh sotsialistov-revoliutsionerov. Dokumenty i materialy. Tom I* (Moscow, 2000), 179 (telegram from Shteinberg to the Petrograd Soviet, February 1918).

[40] I. Steinberg, *In the Workshop of Revolution* (London, 1955), 59.

interests of the revolutionary people. Sentences could range from fines, public censure, or publishing a retraction, to the suppression of an organ and the confiscation of its printing press. The trial of a publication did not prevent the individuals involved from facing an ordinary tribunal.[41] The press was the main weapon of the Bolshevik opposition at this stage and, while the Decree on Press on 27 October had restored censorship, newspapers could rarely be silenced for long, usually reopening under a new name, and officials believed the number of hostile papers was increasing in late 1917.[42] The press tribunal, then, extended what constituted counter-revolution. It also added further potential for confusion with other tribunals over jurisdiction and it only consisted of three people, not seven as in other tribunals, encouraging accusations of inconsistent justice.

The second decree was published on the following day and provided instructions for all tribunals.[43] More extensive regulations, Shteinberg hoped, would reduce the impression that tribunals were arbitrary organs and increase their effectiveness. Five aspects are notable. First, the decree declared that tribunals would act against those organizing revolts or other resistance; those using official posts to undermine the state; economic saboteurs; and anyone violating government orders. While still vague, these instructions encouraged tribunals to look beyond obvious political and social enemies. The latter were likely to organize revolts or open sabotage, but failures in production, not fulfilling orders, or the misuse of authority were crimes likely to be committed by all types of individuals. Second, the decree confirmed the range of sentences, from fines, public censure, and the removal of political rights, to the confiscation of property, imprisonment, forced labour, and exile. Execution was not yet permitted. Third, information provided by individuals or institutions could form the basis of an inquiry, and the decision on whether to proceed to a trial had to be made within forty-eight hours of receiving information. Fourth, trials should be public, while defendants were entitled to a defence and could be assigned one if they did not provide their own. Finally, there was no right of appeal, although the Commissar of Justice could request a retrial if there were procedural violations or an obvious injustice.

In later years, Bolsheviks queued up to denounce the negative influence of the Left SRs on the development of tribunals. Stuchka was typical, calling them 'petty bourgeois liberals with radical-revolutionary phrases'. He condemned the weak stance on punishment—the absence of the death penalty—and noted the tribunals

[41] Reprinted in *Istoriia zakonodatel'stva SSSR i RSFSR po ugolovnomu protsessu i organizatsii suda i prokuratury, 1917–1954* [hereafter *IZ*] (Moscow, 1955), 34.

[42] E. Finn, 'Antisovetskaia pechat' na skam'e podsudimykh (zametki sovremennika o tribunalakh po delam pechati)', *Sovetskoe gosudarstvo i pravo*, 2 (1967), 72.

[43] *IZ*, 34–6 (19 December 1917).

of the French Revolution had only two results: innocence or death.[44] This image of Bolshevik radicalism versus Left SR insistence on the rule of law has proved remarkably persistent.[45] Yet as well as contradicting his earlier arguments that diverse punishments were a positive feature of Russian tribunals, Stuchka's criticisms are misleading. None of Shteinberg's actions with respect to tribunals aroused controversy at the time.[46] Many Bolsheviks still had doubts over the feasibility of the death penalty (its abolition had been a popular demand in 1917), while these decrees simply extended earlier regulations. Nothing was abolished after Shteinberg's departure either, while the development of the press tribunal and a more expansive conception of counter-revolution were in line with Bolshevik thinking. In all, as one historian has observed, the tribunal remained as far from a 'hardened' organ of terror at this stage as it was from a 'democratic' court, and there was still a sense of 'revolutionary romanticism' in how both sides viewed its role.[47] In their level of detail, though, these decrees did mark a step away from any 'legal nihilism' or 'legalized lawlessness' that may have existed.

The first test of these new regulations came with another high-profile trial at the turn of 1918. V. M. Purishkevich, a vocal monarchist, former deputy of the tsarist Duma and participant in Rasputin's murder, was accused, along with thirteen others, of armed conspiracy against the state. On 3 November 1917, Ensign E. V. Zelinskii was caught stealing forms from the staff of the Petrograd military region. Zelinskii claimed he was following Purishkevich's orders, who headed a counter-revolutionary organization. Premises connected to Purishkevich were searched, revealing a machine gun, revolvers, blank forms, a false passport, and cyanide. A letter to the Cossack general A. M. Kaledin was found, in which Purishkevich promised to organize armed support when Kaledin arrived in Petrograd as Purishkevich expected. Arrests were made. Interrogations established that some of the detained had participated in anti-revolutionary meetings and others in the Junkers' revolt against the Bolsheviks in Petrograd on 29 October, which had cost around 200 lives. Several had belonged to monarchist unions before 1917 and some wanted to restore the monarchy. The defendants

[44] Stuchka, 'Pervye revoliutsionnye tribunaly', no pag. Krylenko makes similar arguments in all of his later writings; see, for example, 'Revoliutsionnye tribunaly v praktike rossiiskoi proletarskoi revoliutsii', in *Oktiabr'skii perevorot i diktatura proletariata. Sbornik statei* (Moscow, 1919), 254.

[45] See, for example, P. Juviler, *Revolutionary Law and Order: Politics and Social Change in the USSR* (New York, 1976), 20–1; and A. Rabinowitch, *The Bolsheviks in Power: The First Year of Soviet Rule in Petrograd* (Bloomington and Indianapolis, 2007), 85–7.

[46] There were disagreements in January 1918 over other legal issues; see *Protokoly*, 212, 221, 223, 314, 459.

[47] O. P'ianova, 'Normativno-pravovye polozheniia organizatsii revoliutsionnykh tribunalov v pervyi period razvitiia sovetskogo gosudarstva i prava', in A. Kiselev (ed.), *Problemy istorii v stat'iakh i tezisakh molodykh uchenykh* (Omsk, 2002), 88.

were thus accused of various crimes, including participating in a revolt, plotting counter-revolution, and belonging to a counter-revolutionary organization.[48]

The tribunal convened on 22 December 1917, reconvened on 28 December, and sat several times over the following week. Unlike previous trials, it did not wait for the public to act as prosecutors but reverted to tsarist practices and appointed its own (as permitted by the new decree). Similarly, former tsarist lawyers were appointed as defence counsels.[49] The prosecution dominated far more than at previous trials, but Purishkevich still managed to deliver a three-hour speech proclaiming his innocence and attacking the court and the Bolsheviks.[50] The tribunal reached a verdict on 3 January. Purishkevich was sentenced to four years' forced labour in prison and three others to three years. All were eligible for release after a year, conditional on good behaviour. The remainder received lesser sentences, with a couple released on account of their young age.[51]

This trial represented a significant development for tribunals in several ways; it was the first trial of a group, it was a multi-day trial, and it was more carefully orchestrated, with no attempt to actively involve the public. It was also the first major trial where *intentions* were as important as *actions*. The prosecutors spent more time demonstrating that the defendants were the natural political and social enemies of the revolution than proving the existence of a plot. Indeed, the 'truth' of the allegations remains questionable. Purishkevich boasted of an organization in his letter to Kaledin and his testimony,[52] while none of the defendants denied its existence. But no concrete evidence was provided beyond some political meetings before October, and a few defendants denied even knowing Purishkevich. Given that all of them admitted hating the Bolsheviks, that some admitted to monarchist beliefs and others to procuring equipment and participating in the Junkers' revolt—all serious admissions in this context—there was no reason not to admit to participating in an organization.[53] Zelinskii, whose capture and evidence underpinned the trial, was accused of being a provocateur and mentally ill. His

[48] GARF, f. R-336, op. 1, d. 277, ll. 1–3ob (accusations and charges). Some defendants' testimonies were published in 'Zagovor monarkhicheskoi organizatsii V. M. Purishkevicha', *Krasnyi arkhiv*, 26 (1928), 169–85.

[49] V. Bobrishchev-Pushkin, 'Vospominaniia zashchitnika', *Sud idet!*, 21 (1927), 1231–3.

[50] *Izvestiia*, 4 January 1918, 3–4; 5 January, 4; 7 January, 3; 12 January, 6. Purishkevich's notes for his speech are in '"27-go fevralia my mogli stat' grazhdanami": Tiuremnye zapiski V. M. Purishkevicha. Dekabr' 1917-mart 1918g.', *Istoricheskii arkhiv*, 5–6 (1996), 118–49. Another defendant wrote sensationalist memoirs discussing the trial; F. Vinberg, *V plenu u 'obez'ian' (zapiski 'kontr-revoliutsionera')* (Kiev, 1918).

[51] GARF, f. R-336, op. 1, d. 277, ll. 6–6ob (sentence).

[52] GARF, f. R-336, op. 1, d. 277, ll. 20–20ob, 27 (letter and testimony).

[53] GARF, f. R-336, op. 1, d. 277, ll. 68–68ob, 86–87ob, 112, 117–17ob, 122–24, 131–2 (various testimonies).

testimony included wild accusations, such as a plot to murder Lenin and L. D. Trotskii, which even prosecutors dismissed.[54] The Bolshevik newspaper *Izvestiia* noted his abnormal behaviour during the trial and reported an escape attempt.[55] Another defendant was an SR who refused to sit alongside the monarchists. His only link to them was the Junkers' revolt. In sum, investigators constructed the accusations from various sources. The roots of Purishkevich's organization lay in a patriotic union he had headed during the First World War, which may or may not have still been active.[56] This union brought Purishkevich into contact with people who later participated in the Junkers' revolt unbeknown to him. This enabled investigators to draw a link between Purishkevich and the revolt, which was important as the Junkers' revolt had actually occurred. Otherwise, the accusations were all about Purishkevich's dreams.

There are signs, therefore, of greater care being taken over investigations and trials by early 1918. As opposition to Bolshevik rule grew, there were numerous plots of varying degrees of seriousness. The Bolsheviks believed the threat was real and they came to expect plots even where there were none. As a consequence, drawing tenuous links between defendants and making unsubstantiated allegations became more common. Various cases from this period see individuals accused of belonging to groups organizing armed uprisings, but there is rarely any solid evidence in the case files.[57] The unpredictability of early trials also threatened the punitive and educational objectives of tribunals, undermining their value to the state. The appointment of prosecutors, the marginalization of the audience, and a clearer set of allegations were all signs that the spontaneity of earlier trials was ending.

Press Tribunals

Despite these trends towards greater control, the experiences of press tribunals after their creation reflect tensions facing all tribunals, especially how to increase their effectiveness at the same time as expanding their activities. For a start, the press tribunal did not manage to hold any trials for a month after its formation on 18 December, although 117 newspapers were closed before the end of 1917,[58] newspapers were targeted by regular tribunals, and archives suggest investigations were launched into *Vremia* (a conservative paper), *Den'*, and *Volia naroda*

[54] GARF, f. R-336, op. 1, d. 277, l. 108 (testimony).

[55] *Izvestiia*, 4 January 1918, 3; 12 January 1918, 6.

[56] A. Ivanov suggests it was active; 'Konkurenty bol'shevikov sprava: Monarkhicheskaia organizatsiia V. M. Purishkevicha v 1917 g.', in *Velikaia rossiiskaia revoliutsiia 1917. 100 let izucheniia* (Moscow, 2017), 213–19.

[57] For example, GARF, f. R-336, op. 1, d. 19 (the case file of seventeen officers in a Finnish regiment in Mogilev); d. 249 (Count A. A. Olsuf'ev); and d. 334 (Colonel A. D. Khomutov).

[58] A. Okorokov, *Oktiabr' i krakh russkoi burzhuaznoi pressy* (Moscow, 1970), 249, 310.

(both socialist) by early January.[59] Some historians blamed internal disputes for the delay; others the restraining influence of the Left SRs.[60] None of this is convincing. After all, Shteinberg produced the initial decree, and the decree's main points were simply restated when the issue was reconsidered by Sovnarkom on 24 January. Equally, the second decree on the tribunal on 28 January only merged the decrees of 18–19 December.[61] Instead, the delay probably reflected organizational chaos across government, and the renewed efforts in January were possibly prompted by an increase in opposition following the dissolution of the long-awaited Constituent Assembly at the beginning of the month. Either way, A. A. Shreider, a Left SR, was appointed chairman by mid-January and trials followed soon afterwards.

Conservative, SR, and Jewish papers were among those first targeted, and a backlog of over twenty cases was awaiting trial in Petrograd by May.[62] Furthermore, although the decree only referred to a single press tribunal, Moscow followed suit, as did some provincial towns, such as Orenburg, Samara, and Tver'.[63] The press reported frequently on these trials. Initially, most papers were fined, censured, or temporarily closed, but measures soon became harsher. Papers were closed permanently, their editors tried by regular tribunals and imprisoned.[64] In essence, the state instructed tribunals to close opposition papers by any means.[65] The printed word, as the office for press affairs reportedly stated, must only serve the interests of the working classes and thus, by implication, the Bolsheviks.[66]

A particularly significant case was the action taken by the Commissar of Nationalities, I. V. Stalin, against one of the leaders of the Menshevik opposition, Iu. O. Martov. On 31 March, Martov condemned the recent peace treaty with the Germans in the party's newspaper, *Vpered!* While arguing that Russia's position in the Caucasus had been weakened by the treaty, Martov made a passing comment that Stalin had been expelled from the region's social democratic party in 1908 for

[59] GARF, f. R-337, op. 1, d. 6, ll. 1–3; d. 7 (case files).

[60] See A. Fraiman, 'Dekret Soveta Narodnykh Komissarov o revoliutsionnom tribunale pechati', *Vspomogatel'nye istoricheskie distsipliny*, 4 (1972), 20–1; T. Mironova, 'Revoliutsionnyi tribunal pechati petrogradskogo soveta', in G. Sobolev (ed.), *Piterskie rabochie v bor'be s kontrrevoliutsiei v 1917–1918gg.* (Moscow, 1986), 168; A. Resis, 'Lenin on Freedom of the Press', *The Russian Review*, 36, 3 (1977), 292–3; and Iu. Titov, *Sozdanie sistemy sovetskikh revoliutsionnykh tribunalov* (Moscow, 1983), 67–9.

[61] *Protokoly*, 290, 295; *DSV*, I, 432–4.

[62] *Pravda*, 28 January 1918, 4; V. Brovkin, *The Mensheviks after October* (Ithaca, 1987), 109.

[63] See A. D'iakonov, 'Posleoktiabr'skie eskizy', *Ezhenedel'nik sovetskoi iustitsii*, 44–45, 7 December 1922, 11; Orenburg soviet's *Izvestiia*, 26 April 1918, reprinted in D. Safonov, *Mezhdu imperiei i respublikoi sovetov: mestnye vlasti na iuzhnom Urale v 1917–1918 gg.* (Orenburg, 2008), 210; N. Gorokhovskii, *Stanovlenie i pravovoi status voennykh tribunalov v Srednem Povolzh'e (noiabr' 1917 g.–1922 g.)* (Tol'iatti, 2004), 11; and *Materialy*, 5 (1918), 51 (report from Tver' provincial department of justice, mid-October 1918).

[64] See the frequent reports in *Den'*, *Izvestiia*, *Novaia zhizn'*, and *Pravda* from February to April 1918.

[65] GARF, f. R-337, op. 1, d. 23, l. 3 (press commissariat to tribunal, 23 December 1917).

[66] *Novaia zhizn'*, 24 March 1918, 4.

organizing robberies.[67] Stalin accused Martov of libel the following day.[68] On 5 April, the case was heard by the press tribunal in Moscow. Taking place against a background of bitter disputes over the treaty and growing opposition from other socialist parties, the case initiated a lengthy debate that resulted in a stronger approach towards the press, other socialists, and opposition more generally.

It is clear from the trial transcript that Martov had significant support in the audience.[69] Martov questioned first whether his case should be tried by a tribunal: as a case of libel involving private individuals, it should be heard by the local people's court, not the 'political court' of the tribunal. Stalin disagreed, of course, stating that he was not acting as an individual but as a representative of a political party (and government) that Martov intended to harm by his allegations. The chairman agreed with Stalin and ordered the case to proceed, but Martov had immediately touched on procedural inconsistencies. Perhaps because Moscow's press tribunal operated under the auspices of the main tribunal, it circumvented the decree's stipulation that the press tribunal (referring to Petrograd) should target organs, not individuals. The question of punishing *Vpered!* was not raised, as it should have been if the information had been false. Equally, as Martov highlighted, tribunals did not appear to have dealt with libel against individuals previously, while the trial also focused on what an individual *said* rather than what s/he *had* done or *planned* to do.

Martov then raised the issue of witnesses. He would not accept that he had committed a 'crime against the people' and he wished to call witnesses to prove it, listing participants in the Georgian revolutionary movement. Stalin rejected this call, instead outlining his role in the revolutionary struggle, including prison and exile, before denying that he had been expelled or judged by his peers. The tribunal initially upheld Stalin's view. Martov protested again that such a case was not in the public interest, that it was politically motivated, and that the state was attacking him and his ideals without allowing him to defend himself. Rowdy applause from the audience led the chairman to clear the public from the hall. When the trial resumed, lawyers from both sides focused on whether it was practical to call Martov's witnesses. The transcript suggests that the defence counsels had the upper hand, delivering lengthy speeches, and eventually a compromise was reached. The tribunal would adjourn for a week to allow time to obtain witness statements.

Martov and his counsels questioned several times whether the tribunal was a 'court', asking whether it upheld parity and procedure for all involved or was merely a tool for the Bolsheviks to target their political enemies.[70] For Stalin, it was

[67] *Vpered!*, 31 March 1918, 1. [68] RGASPI, f. 558, op. 2, d. 3, l. 4 (letter, 1 April 1918).

[69] The transcript of the trial is in RGASPI, f. 558, op. 2, d. 3, ll. 7–37. Parts were published in Stalin, *Trudy. Tom 8 (aprel'-iiun' 1918)* (Moscow, 2016), 28–36. There are also accounts in the press, Bolshevik (*Izvestiia*, 6 April 1918, 3; *Pravda*, 6 April 1918, 3) and Menshevik (*Vpered!*, 6 April 1918, 2).

[70] RGASPI, f. 558, op. 2, d. 3, l. 29 (transcript).

the latter. His argument was basic: he denied the allegations and thus witnesses were irrelevant. What he said was true was a 'fact', and what his opponent alleged was a 'lie'.[71] In the end, though, the tribunal refused to submit completely to Stalin's demands after its initial wobble and it made an effort to contact the potential witnesses, sending telegrams to the authorities in Baku, Petrograd, and Tiflis, asking them to obtain statements.[72] But, as Martov feared, a week was far too short to overcome the distances and to locate people amid the revolutionary turmoil.

The debate over the jurisdiction of tribunals resumed when the trial restarted on 16 April, this time under Moscow's main tribunal as the press tribunal had been disbanded in the intervening period (see below).[73] Martov's lawyer read out the official decree stating that tribunals dealt with important political cases touching on the interests of the people. This was a private case of libel. Stalin's lawyer reiterated that Martov had not only referred to Stalin but talked about decisions made by other party members now in important state positions, thus undermining the government's authority. After a three-hour break for deliberation, the tribunal agreed with Martov that libel against individuals was not its concern, but it supported Stalin's arguments that the accusations were part of broader criticism of the government, and it proposed to judge Martov for this criticism. Martov asked furiously how the tribunal could act as a prosecutor, an investigator, and a court. Any criticisms, he argued, reflected his different political beliefs, and prosecution on this basis was purely political revenge. In this case, his lawyer added, all the Bolsheviks insulted should be present. This attempt to pit Menshevism against Bolshevism in court failed. The tribunal rejected Martov's protests, declared he was guilty of insulting the government with the aim of undermining its authority amongst the people, condemned this as 'thoughtless', and publicly censured him.[74]

This was far from a triumph for the Bolsheviks. This was made clear when *Izvestiia* failed to report that Martov's point about jurisdiction had been upheld, instead implying the sentence was for attacking Stalin *and* the government.[75] The next day saw a written cassation protest by Stalin to Narkomiust, and Narkomiust

[71] RGASPI, f. 558, op. 2, d. 3, l. 25 (transcript). There is evidence of his involvement in robberies; see S. Kotkin, *Stalin. Vol. I: Paradoxes of Power, 1878–1928* (London, 2014), 267–8; and R. Service, *Stalin* (London, 2004), 74–6.

[72] RGASPI, f. 558, op. 2, d. 3, ll. 42–9 (correspondence, undated). It was later claimed that a fellow Menshevik, B. I. Nikolaevskii, travelled to the Caucasus to gather evidence on Martov's behalf, but this was disregarded; B. Wolfe, *Three Who Made a Revolution* (2 volumes, New York, 1964), II, 173.

[73] There are brief handwritten notes in RGASPI, f. 558, op. 2, d. 3, ll. 62–63ob, but no transcript. See *Izvestiia*, 17 April 1918, 3 and *Pravda*, 17 April 1918, 3. There are accounts based on the Menshevik press in Brovkin, *Mensheviks*, 110–17; G. Aronson, 'Stalinskii protsess protiv Martova', *Sotsialisticheskii vestnik*, 7–8 (1939), 84–9; and 'Delo L. Martova v revoliutsionnom tribunale', *Obozrenie*, 15 (1985), 45–6, and 16 (1985), 43–6.

[74] The verdict is in GARF, f. R-1235, op. 93, d. 200, ll. 13–13ob.

[75] *Izvestiia*, 17 April 1918, 3. The distinction was made in *Pravda*, 17 April 1918, 3.

advised a retrial on 18 April.[76] The All-Russian Central Executive Committee of the Congress of Soviets (VTsIK) discussed the case on 25 April. Krylenko, by now chief prosecutor, restated the protests and proposed a new trial. The chairman, Ia. M. Sverdlov, did not allow Martov or other Mensheviks to speak and Krylenko's proposal was duly accepted by the Bolshevik majority. This prompted turmoil. Officially, Martov was expelled for protesting, along with a colleague. Unofficially, all Mensheviks walked out in support, while Latvian riflemen restored order.[77]

Martov's case was never retried. The Mensheviks claimed this reflected divisions in the Bolshevik leadership, many of whom were absent on 25 April when VTsIK took the decision under pressure from Stalin's supporters. While hardly sympathetic to Martov, Lenin and other senior Bolsheviks apparently felt Stalin was waging a personal vendetta.[78] At the very least, the trial was bad publicity. Martov took to the pages of *Vpered!* to condemn VTsIK and restate his arguments, while the paper carried out a vitriolic campaign highlighting the lack of political freedom.[79] Stalin's biographers have argued variously that the case was the reaction of a 'hypersensitive man', his growing political prominence, his political insecurity, his Georgian concern for honour, or his determination to politicize everything.[80] One historian, though, was correct to stress the wider implications: criticizing an individual Bolshevik now meant criticizing the party and the revolution.[81]

The press tribunal did manage to emphasize that written criticism was now considered to be as counter-revolutionary as sabotage or a revolt. As the chairman of a later trial of *Vpered!* noted, 'it is possible to prepare an uprising by arms or by preparing minds'.[82] Bolshevik prosecutors, such as Krylenko, refuted charges that they were attacking the freedom of speech. At the trial on 4 April 1918 of the editor of *Russkiia vedomosti*, who had published an interview with B. V. Savinkov, an SR and deputy minister in the Provisional Government, Krylenko argued it was not an interview but the promotion of a political agenda. This agenda, given Savinkov's proven links with counter-revolution and his open anti-Bolshevism, was an attack on the government. Such trials, therefore, were not about the

[76] GARF, f. R-1235, op. 93, d. 200, ll. 12, 14–15 (various correspondence, 17–18 April 1918).

[77] *Chetvertyi s"ezd sovetov rabochikh, krest'ianskikh, soldatskikh i kazach'ikh deputatov. Stenograficheskii otchet. Moskva, 1918g.* (Moscow, 1919), 194–6; I. Urilov, *Iu. O. Martov: Politik i istorik* (Moscow, 1997), 414.

[78] Aronson, 'Stalinskii', 87, 89.

[79] *Vpered!*, 26 April 1918, 2. Every issue of *Vpered!* from mid- to late April carried articles and readers' letters defending the freedom of speech, and trenchant accounts of Bolshevik attacks on the newspaper itself.

[80] Kotkin, *Stalin*, 267; H. Kuromiya, *Stalin* (Harlow, 2005), 38; Service, *Stalin*, 156.

[81] Brovkin, *Mensheviks*, 124.

[82] *Vpered!*, 21 April 1918, 3. For more details on the trial, see Brovkin, *Mensheviks*, 118–22.

freedom of speech but about targeting publications advocating counter-revolution.[83]

Nonetheless, concerns grew among Bolsheviks that press tribunals were ineffective, even counterproductive. In February, M. S. Gorelik resigned from Petrograd's press tribunal because it was causing 'great harm'. He disagreed with distinguishing crimes of 'words' from 'actions', and noted that press tribunals saw well-prepared defendants and witnesses, and a sympathetic audience (usually journalists, lawyers, or literary figures), combat an ill-prepared prosecution. The trials ended up judging the government, not the press. He advised disbanding the press tribunal and hearing cases in a regular tribunal. The investigations and prosecution had to be improved at least.[84] Similar concerns were raised by the chairman of Moscow's main tribunal, Ia. L. Berman, who stated bluntly in March 1918 that the press tribunal did not meet its objectives and noted similar problems. Separate sentences for the press reinforced the impression that the state was clamping down on free speech rather than actual crimes.[85] This was particularly true when dealing with other socialist parties at a time when their support was rising amid growing disillusionment with the Bolsheviks. Many of the sentences, moreover, were simply ineffective. Newspapers were forbidden to reopen under alternative names, and printing presses were confiscated, but many editors found alternatives.

Petrograd's authorities disbanded their press tribunal in mid-March, transferring cases to the city's main tribunal.[86] On 30 March, Stuchka (Commissar of Justice after Shteinberg's resignation in early March) suggested abolishing them to Sovnarkom, prompting Lenin to complain that press tribunals were being abandoned without a full discussion of their results.[87] If this discussion took place, it left no trace. Narkomiust sanctioned the disbandment of Moscow's press tribunal on 5 April, local Bolsheviks agreed on 8 April, and its cases (including Martov's) were also transferred to city's main tribunal.[88] Finally, the first Congress of Justice Officials recommended the disbandment of all press tribunals on 24 April,[89] and they were officially abolished as part of broader reforms on 4 May (see the section on defending revolutionary justice below).

[83] His speech was reprinted in N. Krylenko, *Za piat' let, 1918–1922 gg.* (Moscow–Petrograd, 1923), 22–7.

[84] The resignation letter was published later in *Novaia zhizn'*, 15 March 1918, 3. An unsigned and undated version containing the criticisms but not the resignation request is in Shteinberg's papers: YIVO, RG 366, Steinberg papers, folder 967. A contemporary recalled similar concerns; Finn, 'Antisovetskaia pechat', 73–5.

[85] GARF, f. A-353, op. 2, d. 11, l. 2 (correspondence from Narkomiust to Berman, 5 April 1918).

[86] *Novaia zhizn'*, 22 March 1918, 3. Mironova gives 9 March, but this seems too early ('Revoliutsionnyi tribunal pechati', 169), while Titov gives 23 March, which is a bit later than this report suggests (*Sozdanie*, 74).

[87] V. Lenin, *Collected Works* (47 volumes, Moscow, 1960–70), XXVII, 219.

[88] GARF, f. A-353, op. 2, d. 11, l. 3 (resolution of the commissars of Moscow region).

[89] *Materialy*, 1 (1918), 12 (resolution).

The Formation of Provincial Tribunals

At the same time as the Petrograd and press tribunals were experimenting with their first trials, tribunals were also spreading across Russia. At first they emerged independently of the centre, if driven by the same objectives. In Saratov, for instance, the provincial authorities proposed a 'revolutionary court' to enforce the 'fundamental laws' of the revolution on 20 November. A few days later, a further discussion revealed a desire to see various groups (the city's soviet, duma, and public) represented and the public act as prosecutors and defence counsels as well as deciding the verdict. There was a dispute over whether to harness existing legal expertise or not, with the majority seemingly deciding such expertise was irrelevant in revolutionary conditions. By the time a tribunal was actually created in early 1918 (with its first trial on 23 January), the authorities had received the decrees from Petrograd and established courts and investigative commissions along the same lines.[90]

This combination of local initiative followed by later conformity to official decrees broadly describes the process in other areas quick to organize, such as Kazan', where a tribunal was established on 27 November 1917,[91] and Moscow, which issued its own detailed instructions on 15 December before a first trial was held on 21 December.[92] An activist in Samara described how they decided to form a 'revolutionary' court in mid-November, which started sitting in early December. A month later, they received belated news of the Decree on Courts and took steps to establish a tribunal, which essentially meant renaming the existing court.[93] Most provincial towns, though, created tribunals later, from January to March 1918, following the principles laid down in the December decree.[94] In these instances, the impetus came from above. Provincial soviets were supposed to appoint a commissar of justice and establish their own commissariat or department of justice to oversee the creation and regulation of people's courts and tribunals within the province.[95] Where this worked to plan, as apparently in Iaroslavl', tribunals would become more organized and effective once regulated locally.[96] This process would be repeated in *uezdy* (districts), which would

[90] See the excerpts from official protocols in A. Kumakov and A. Simonov (eds.), *Proletarskaia revoliutsiia, kakoi my ee ne znaem* (2 volumes, Saratov, 2016), I, 126–7, 202, 286.

[91] *Znamia revoliutsii*, 6 December 1917, reprinted in *Kazanskaia gubernskaia chrezvychainaia komissiia (1917–1922). Sbornik dokumentov i materialov* (Kazan', 1989), 11.

[92] *Uprochenie sovetskoi vlasti v Moskve i Moskovskoi gubernii* (Moscow, 1958), 94–6.

[93] M. Martynov, 'Pervyi revoliutsionnyi sud', in *Oktiabr' v Samare: vospominaniia* (Kuibyshev, 1957), 210–11.

[94] For a useful survey, see Titov, *Sozdanie*, 36–63.

[95] For a good case study, see A. Abramovskii, 'Stanovlenie sovetskoi sudebnoi sistemy na Urale v 1917-18 gg.' (*kandidat* dissertation, Cheliabinsk Institute of the Ural Academy of State Service, 2004), 97–121.

[96] *Materialy*, 5 (1918), 22 (report on the activities of the provincial department of justice, 5 November 1918).

establish their own departments of justice and oversee the creation of courts in *volosti* (parishes). Reports sent in by many provinces, from Kazan' and Simbirsk to Pskov and Viatka, suggest that many *uezdy* and *volosti* had established tribunals by summer 1918.[97]

The picture was patchier elsewhere, though. In some places, such as Penza, tribunals were present in some *uezd* towns before one was established in the provincial capital.[98] Others had patchy coverage; in Ufa in May 1918, for example, only 11.1 per cent of *volosti* had a people's court and a tribunal, 25 per cent had only a tribunal, 27.8 per cent a people's court, and 41.7 per cent had neither.[99] In most places, it took time. Old courts persisted long into 1918 as authorities struggled for resources. In Moscow province, officials in some *uezdy* were advocating the importance of new courts in securing Bolshevik power by mid-December. But a meeting of the province's *uezd* commissars in early January revealed a provincial commissariat of justice was still being established, new courts were still needed in most places, and instructions were lacking. There was little progress a fortnight later. Some *uezdy* had their own justice officials, but all complained about the persistence of old courts and personnel while demanding new organs. To hasten the process, commissars focused on how existing courts and personnel could be adapted. To save resources, they also proposed having only a provincial tribunal, which was unusual at this stage. Yet even in April, a report described financial problems and estimated that only half of the province's *uezdy* had a complete court structure.[100]

The vague titles used to describe these courts, moreover, make it difficult to establish which type of court had been founded—a people's court or tribunal. Many localities report they have simply created 'revolutionary courts'. Petrozavodsk's assurance that it had formed a 'revolutionary court' to deal with uprisings suggests it had created a tribunal as envisaged by the state.[101] In Vyshnevolotskii *uezd* (Tver'), however, the 'people's revolutionary court' dealt with counter-revolution, sabotage, embezzlement, speculation, criminal cases, and divorce—that is, everything—while there is no evidence the 'revolutionary military tribunal' in Elatomskii *uezd* (Tambov) had anything to do with the military.[102]

[97] GARF, f. A-353, op. 2, d. 27, ll. 92ob, 127, 134ob-35; d. 84, ll. 2–2ob, 15–17ob (various reports, June 1918).

[98] V. Abramov, 'Sozdanie i deiatel'nost' mestnykh revoliutsionnykh tribunalov (1918–1922 gg.) (po materialam Penzenskoi gubernii)' (*kandidat* dissertation, Penza State Pedagogical University, 2004), 111–13.

[99] Abramovskii, 'Stanovlenie', 150.

[100] GARF, f. R-393, op. 3, d. 216, ll. 300–3 (protocols, 18 January 1918), 333–4 (report, after 2 April 1918); d. 217, ll. 65–65ob (protocols, 2–3 January 1918), 168ob-69 (protocols, 14 December 1917).

[101] *Vestnik Komissariata Vnutrennikh del*, 6 (22 February 1918), 13–14; 8 (8 March 1918), 4–5.

[102] GARF, f. R-393, op. 3, d. 415, ll. 6–8ob (report to provincial congress of justice officials, 10 March 1918); d. 410, l. 189 (protocol of *uezd* executive committee, 27 February 1918).

Partly, the issue is symbolic; it sounded good to have a 'revolutionary court' and even better to have a 'revolutionary military tribunal', and it is likely that local authorities believed such titles could enhance the authority of the new courts. Partly, it also indicates that tribunals served a different purpose locally than Narkomiust envisaged, as local officials saw them as a means of dealing with all their problems. Kolomenskii *uezd* (Moscow), for instance, noted that it was creating a tribunal for important political *and* civil cases, as well as 'normal' courts for other offences, thus seeing tribunals as a higher form of court.[103] Some officials held different conceptions of what constituted counter-revolution, seeing any challenge as a threat to their revolutionary authority. Partly, too, many local authorities struggled for finance and staff, and could only form a single new court. Some areas even argued there were not enough cases of counter-revolution. Officials in Omsk reported that, after their new tribunal had dealt with a former judge accused of sabotage, it had to move on to civil cases as there were insufficient instances of sabotage to fill its time.[104]

Either way, the activities of local tribunals were a concern for the First All-Russian Congress of Justice Officials, which was held in Moscow on 21–5 April 1918 and attended by twenty-three provincial representatives. The congress condemned the fact that many tribunals spent so much time investigating criminal cases. Prior to March 1918, for example, almost 30 per cent of the cases resolved by Ufa's tribunal concerned illicit brewing.[105] Reports sent to Narkomiust from this period reveal a worse situation in *uezdy*. Some *uezd* tribunals in Kazan' focused solely on illegal brewing, hooliganism, and looting.[106] In Demianskii *uezd* tribunal (Novgorod), 60 per cent of the cases investigated between 21 January and 17 May were crimes such as thefts, beatings, brawling, insults, arson, and drunkenness.[107] Less information exists for *volost'*-level tribunals, but the situation seems to have been worse still. Officials feared this focus on criminal cases was diverting tribunals from the crucial task of punishing counter-revolution (although the state soon came to regard activities such as illegal brewing as counter-revolutionary). Thus, the congress resolved that *uezd* and *volost'* tribunals should be abolished, with tribunals restricted to provincial capitals and other large towns. Too many tribunals placed a financial burden on local authorities and were difficult to control. It also reiterated that tribunals should deal with counter-revolutionary crimes.[108]

[103] GARF, f. R-393, op. 3, d. 217, ll. 168ob-69 (protocol of *uezd* soviet, 14 December 1917).
[104] *Materialy*, 1 (1918), 3–4 (report, 21 April 1918).
[105] *Materialy*, 1 (1918), 6 (report, 21 April 1918). This volume published the main reports from the congress.
[106] GARF, f. A-353, op. 2, d. 84, l. 15 (report, February 1918).
[107] GARF, f. A-353, op. 9, d. 45, ll. 90–90ob (Demianskii soviet to Narkomiust, 23 July 1918).
[108] *Materialy*, 1 (1918), 8–9, 12 (resolutions, 22 April and 24 April 1918).

This resolution was not binding, but it was another challenge facing Narkomiust. Concerns remained about the success of trials at the centre and pressure was growing to abolish press tribunals. Now officials were questioning the effectiveness of local tribunals. All this came within the context of increasing conflict. Armed opposition to the Bolsheviks had increased once the dissolution of the Constituent Assembly in early January had convinced many there was no other way of removing the Bolsheviks, while the coalition with the Left SRs had broken down in March over the controversial peace with Germany. Thus, as Bolshevik legal officials regained control of Narkomiust, they felt obliged to restate the *revolutionary* nature of justice as well as address the urgent need to make tribunals more effective. The problem was that practical pressures from expanding military operations were making an effective system even more difficult to achieve, while the leadership's 'external language' seemed to be prioritizing the use of revolutionary violence.

Defending Revolutionary Justice

The battle over whether revolutionary justice or revolutionary violence should guide the state's struggle against its enemies had raged from the start. Bolshevik legal theorists, as outlined in the Introduction, were clear on the distinction. Revolutionary justice may have sat somewhere on the spectrum between regular courts and the Cheka, but its targeted and regulated repression centred on a public trial. The Left SRs agreed, even if they tended to place more emphasis still on the importance of procedure. The Cheka, however, was founded on a different assumption. Its leader, F. E. Dzerzhinskii, apparently proclaimed he did not 'seek forms of revolutionary justice; we are not in need of justice. It is war now – face to face, a fight to the finish'.[109] These words encapsulated the Cheka's mentality: its officials were soldiers fighting a revolutionary war by any means. The Cheka was supposed to act as an investigative organ, searching out counter-revolution before passing cases to tribunals for judgement, but it soon enacted its own arbitrary and usually violent form of justice.

Shteinberg and the Cheka clashed from the start. On 18 December, the Cheka arrested socialists supporting the forthcoming Constituent Assembly, in which the Bolsheviks were a minority. Shteinberg was outraged. If some deserved arrest, Narkomiust should issue specific warrants. Otherwise, these arrests were purely a political action and Shteinberg helped release the prisoners. Dzerzhinskii com-

[109] G. Leggett, *The Cheka: Lenin's Political Police* (revised edition, Oxford, 1986), 17.

plained to Sovnarkom, asserting the Cheka's independence, asking how it can conduct 'judicial tricks' (warrants) in the 'war' with counter-revolution.[110] Sovnarkom reprimanded Shteinberg and confirmed that only it could revise the Cheka's orders. Shteinberg responded by trying to ensure that Narkomiust could oversee the Cheka's activities and sanction future arrests. A few days later, Sovnarkom agreed that Narkomiust should be informed of sensitive arrests, but restated the Cheka's independence. Sovnarkom also permitted five Left SRs to join the Cheka's leadership on 7 January and stipulated that anyone arrested should be charged within forty-eight hours or released.[111] But, as Shteinberg later confessed, he lacked any real power.[112]

Nevertheless, many Bolshevik legal officials supported Left SR complaints. On 29 January, the new chairman of Petrograd's tribunal, S. S. Zorin, complained to Sovnarkom that the legal process was 'completely disorganized' because of the Cheka, which conducted its own investigations and dispensed its own 'justice'. This wasted resources and the resulting confusion undermined the state authority. Prisons were overflowing, yet the tribunal was not overloaded. Most prisoners came from the Cheka, and the tribunal had no idea who the Cheka arrested or what was done with them. Zorin asked Sovnarkom to confirm tribunals as the sole organ for investigating and sentencing offenders for counter-revolutionary crimes. Officially, Sovnarkom agreed: the Cheka would search out, curtail, and prevent crimes, but further investigations would be conducted by tribunals.[113] Unofficially, neither the presence of Left SRs in the Cheka nor the complaints of Bolsheviks made any real difference.

Ultimately, Shteinberg argued that Lenin supported terror over justice, believing it impossible to make a revolution without executions. There was more to it than this, however. The problem for many Bolshevik leaders was not the concept of revolutionary justice but its results. Most sentences, in their view, were too lenient, especially as the civil war intensified, and sent out the wrong message. One of the judges, A. V. Galkin, defended the sentences, arguing they demonstrated the 'humanitarianism' of the workers and the objectivity of tribunals that rejected draconian 'bourgeois' laws.[114] But—worryingly for the Bolsheviks—their opponents were confused. To be sure, plenty condemned the harsh political nature of

[110] YIVO, RG 366, Steinberg papers, folder 963A, 'When I Was a People's Commissar. Lenin and Dzerzhinsky at Work', 16. This English-language draft was published in German as I. Steinberg, *Als ich Volkskommissar war. Episoden aus der russischen Oktoberrevolution* (Munich, 1929), 32. Curiously, however, this account is not in Steinberg's published English-language memoirs, *Workshop*.

[111] *Protokoly*, 129, 149, 192–3, 453–4.

[112] *Partiia levykh sotsialistov-revoliutsionerov. Tom I*, 344–8 (speech, party's second congress, 19 April 1918).

[113] *Protokoly*, 324 (Sovnarkom meeting, 31 January 1918), 326 (Zorin's complaint).

[114] A. Galkin, 'O revoliutsionnom tribunale', *Pravda*, 20 January 1918, 2. Later he placed blame on the Left SRs, arguing that they bombarded tribunals with procedural formalities when forms were unimportant in the struggle against enemies; 'Pervyi tribunal (Vospominaniia)', *Rabochii sud*, 21 (1927), 1655–6.

tribunals, but some believed sentences reflected an arbitrary and desperate response rather than a focused weapon.[115] Some, such as the Kadets in the case of Panina, saw the sentences as victories. They indicated a state too weak to do anything else.[116] A few felt sentences were pointless. N. P. Okunev, a Moscow businessman, recorded that a former provocateur was sentenced to the removal of his civil rights and public confidence, and exiled. But he doubted 'public confidence' existed and felt exile from material hardship was not a punishment.[117] Others pointed to disparity between the severe allegations and the sentences. *Vremia* argued that if the monarchist Purishkevich had organized a plot, the sentence was far too lax. If, as the defendants claimed, the tribunal was a party court, it was also merciful, as Purishkevich was a vocal critic. And if the defendants were tried as political opponents, all such opponents should be arrested. In short, there was no obvious logic behind the sentence.[118]

These interpretations bothered Bolshevik leaders, and Lenin pressed for greater ruthlessness. On 14 January, he demanded extrajudicial executions to deal with speculators and bandits causing food shortages. On 21 February, despite Left SR protests, Sovnarkom's decree 'The Socialist Fatherland is in Danger' urged that all speculators, spies, hooligans, and counter-revolutionaries be shot on the spot. The Cheka then issued similar instructions.[119] Coercion, Lenin argued, was essential in the transition to socialism. But while he still believed courts should be the organ that carried out coercion, targeting exploiters, educating people in labour discipline, and so on, too little had been achieved so far. There was simply insufficient ruthlessness. The extent of opposition and the weakness of the revolutionary class meant the need for violence was too strong.[120] Yet Lenin did not abandon courts but pressed for greater ruthlessness on their part too. On 30 March, he argued there was too much focus on 'petty reform' and not enough on creating a 'truly revolutionary court that is rapid and mercilessly severe' with its enemies. On 15 April, he asked Narkomiust leaders to report on what they had done so far to publish a collection of laws; to ensure speedier and more ruthless court action against counter-revolutionaries; to spread judicial propaganda among the people; and to involve lower classes in the work of courts.[121] He reacted angrily when Moscow's tribunal on 2 May sentenced several of its investigators, who had accepted bribes to free prisoners, to six months in prison and a ban on holding

[115] See, for example, the cartoon in *Baraban* where the blindfolded, impartial figure of justice is transformed under the Bolsheviks to a blinded tribunal that can no longer differentiate between villains and victims [1 (1918), 16] or the discussion of the 'senseless sadism' of tribunals in the Mensheviks' *Den'* [2 April 1918, 5].

[116] Tyrkova-Williams, *Liberty*, 385–9.

[117] N. Okunev, *Dnevnik Moskvicha (1917–1924)* (Paris, 1990), 147 (31 January 1918).

[118] *Vremia*, 5 January 1918, 1 (a copy is in GARF, f. R-337, op. 1, d. 6, l. 12).

[119] Lenin, *Collected Works*, XXVI, 501; XXVII, 33; *Pravda*, 23 February 1918, 1.

[120] See the draft and final version of 'The Immediate Tasks of the Soviet Government (March-April 1918)', in Lenin, *Collected Works*, XXVII, 217–18, 264–8.

[121] Lenin, *Collected Works*, XXVII, 219–20; XLIV, 76–7.

public office for five years, despite Krylenko stressing the case was crucial to the tribunal's integrity.[122] 'To award bribe-takers such derisively weak and mild sentences instead of shooting is disgraceful behaviour for a Communist and a revolutionary,' he argued.[123] Sovnarkom also attacked this 'exceptional leniency' and asked Narkomiust to establish minimum sentences for bribery.[124]

Furthermore, the authorities pressed Narkomiust to reform tribunals. On 30 March, Sovnarkom proposed creating a new tribunal, with authority over all others, which would act quickly and ruthlessly. Several days later, echoing Lenin, it urged Narkomiust to concentrate on results, not petty changes, and tasked it with producing a new decree on tribunals.[125] In response, post-Shteinberg, Narkomiust defended its revolutionary credentials rigorously, and its vision for the future of tribunals resulted in four decrees.[126] First, on 4 May, tribunals were restricted to provincial capitals, large industrial centres (later defined as having over 200,000 inhabitants), and major railway junctions. All other tribunals were abolished, including the press tribunal. Tribunals were instructed to pay more attention to pogroms, hooliganism, espionage, forgery, and bribery. Second, on 29 May, a supreme tribunal was established under VTsIK to judge serious cases from across Russia.[127] It would be a focal point, uniting tribunals and acting as a role model for procedure and sentencing. The Deputy Commissar of Justice, D. I. Kurskii, in a speech on the same day, noted that some cases were too serious for local tribunals to judge as they had broader significance for the state. He admitted that some local tribunals had not always reached the highest standards and there needed to be a stronger defence of the revolution's achievements.[128] In *Izvestiia* on the same day, his superior, Stuchka, agreed; tribunals had already aided the 'political struggle', but this new tribunal would strengthen the state's response to counter-revolution.[129] Third, on 11 June, a cassation department was created under VTsIK to process complaints made against tribunals. But rather than rectifying miscarriages of justice, cassation was seen as a means to regulate tribunals and enhance central control. Finally, on 16 June, tribunals were permitted to impose the death penalty, thereby dramatically increasing their sentencing powers.[130]

These reforms did not pass without futile opposition from other socialists. After Kurskii's speech, delivered to the Fourth Congress of Soviets, one SR argued that the nature of tribunals had changed, reducing the people's role, and this should be

[122] Krylenko, *Za piat'*, 492–506 (prosecutor's speech).
[123] Lenin, *Collected Works*, XXVII, 322.
[124] *DSV*, II, 236–7. These attacks and Krylenko's appeal resulted in a new sentence of ten years forced labour.
[125] GARF, f. A-353, op. 2, d. 11, l. 7 (telegram, 2 April 1918).
[126] P. Stuchka, 'Revoliutsionnyia zadachi komissariata iustitsii', *Izvestiia*, 16 April 1918, 4.
[127] *DSV*, II, 231–4, 335–9. *Uezd* departments of justice were also abolished in July.
[128] *Chetvertyi*, 345. [129] P. Stuchka, 'Revoliutsionnye tribunaly', *Izvestiia*, 29 May 1918, 1.
[130] *DSV*, II, 420–1; *IZ*, 46–7.

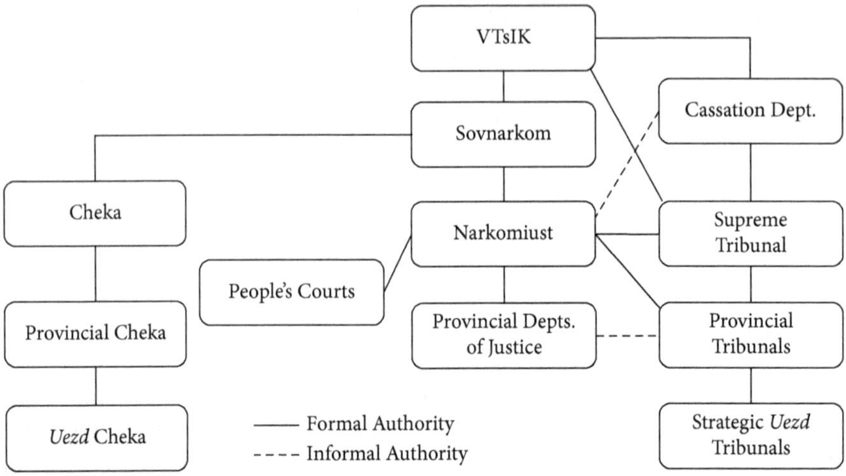

Figure 1.1 The tribunal system, May 1918.

reinstated as a major achievement of the revolution. Martov agreed, accusing the state of not trusting workers. Tribunals no longer served workers' interests, undermining the state's ability to enforce laws. Another believed the new tribunal was an attempt to remove more powers from local soviets.[131] A similar debate on 11 June about cassation raised further points: enhancing VTsIK's role in the legal process meant little given the Bolsheviks' domination, while new decrees had no point if the autonomous Cheka remained pre-eminent.[132] Finally, there were vitriolic debates over the death penalty that almost split the Left SRs.[133]

These accusations held some truth: much was about asserting central control. Before May, tribunals remained decentralized and unevenly distributed. Through streamlining their numbers, Narkomiust hoped to improve its ability to exert control and sharpen the focus on counter-revolution (see Figure 1.1). The following decrees on the Supreme Tribunal and cassation enhanced central control further, with the latter in particular proving a valuable means of ensuring conformity to official regulations (see Chapter 5). It may also not be coincidental that the biggest threat yet, the revolt of the Czech Legion in May 1918, which essentially ended Bolshevik control over large swathes of territory from the Volga to Siberia, came before the last three decrees. The creation of the Supreme Tribunal promised a much more visible forum to judge counter-revolutionary threats from across Russia, while the death penalty reflected the

[131] *Chetvertyi*, 346–54. [132] *Chetvertyi*, 415–16.

[133] *Partiia levykh sotsialistov-revoliutsionerov. Dokumenty i materialy. Tom II. Chast' I* (Moscow, 2010), 90–3, 175, 405–6, 672–3 (various meetings, speeches, and resolutions, June 1918); *Izvestiia*, 6 July 1918, 4 (Left SR report to the All-Russian Congress of Soviets).

scale of this threat. Overall, as one contemporary later remarked, the tribunal system was still not yet complete, but it was becoming more structured.[134]

The Supreme Tribunal

The Supreme Tribunal had an immediate impact. Its first case was Captain A. M. Shchastnyi, Commander of the Baltic Fleet, who was arrested on 27 May after clashing with Trotskii, Commissar of War, over the extent of the German threat.[135] Shchastnyi's desire to preserve the Baltic Fleet and local fortifications, even at the risk of renewed conflict with Germany, was opposed by Sovnarkom. His background as a noble officer fuelled suspicions, and he was accused of exploiting Russia's perilous situation to ferment counter-revolution.[136] These allegations against a popular commander prompted protests among sailors, but Trotskii was determined to use Shchastnyi as an example to other serving former tsarist officers and assert control over an independent-minded navy.[137] The investigation was rushed and uncovered contradictory evidence, but the trial went ahead on 20–1 June, by which time tribunals were permitted to issue the death penalty. There is no evidence this was introduced for this case, but it reinforced the sense of the trial as a landmark – a former senior officer in a new tribunal granted extended powers. In retrospect, the outcome was inevitable.

The trial was tightly controlled and public access restricted.[138] Shchastnyi was allowed one lawyer (he requested two), who was only given the evidence half an hour before the trial. The only witness permitted in court was Trotskii. His long testimony accused Shchastnyi of undermining the government and fostering discontent among sailors in preparation for a revolt. Trotskii suggested he had political ambitions and wanted to become the dictator of the Baltic fleet and assume a national role. This was counter-revolution.[139] Shchastnyi's lawyer dismantled the charges one by one, an easy task given their tenuous nature, and Shchastnyi proclaimed his innocence. But after lengthy deliberations the tribunal convicted him and, to universal surprise, pronounced the death penalty.

[134] Ia. Berman, *Ocherki po istorii sudoustroistva RSFSR* (Moscow, 1924), 16–17.

[135] For background, see A. Rabinowitch, 'The Shchastny File: Trotsky and the Case of the Hero of the Baltic Fleet', *The Russian Review*, 58, 4 (1999), 615–34. The protocol of the trial and other official documents are in *Delo komanduiushchego Baltiiskim flotom A. M. Shchastnogo* (Moscow, 2013).

[136] *Izvestiia*, 16 June 1918, 6. The charges are elaborated in Trotskii's deposition to the investigation on 4 June; L. Trotskii, *Sochineniia* (21 volumes, Moscow-Leningrad, 1925–7), t. 17, ch. 1, 317–22.

[137] K. Nazarenko, *Flot, revoliutsiia i vlast' v Rossii: 1917–1921* (Moscow, 2011), 244–5.

[138] Later accounts declared the trial was closed to the public, but a contemporary report noted the audience was removed after Trotskii's testimony following a request by the defence, because Shchastnyi wished to discuss 'secret' information (presumably confidential military details); *Krasnaia armiia*, 22 June 1918, 4.

[139] Trotskii, *Sochineniia*, t. 17, ch. 1, 322–9. This is reprinted in *The Military Writings and Speeches of Leon Trotsky: How the Revolution Armed*, trans. B. Pearce (5 volumes, London, 1979–81), I, 173–82.

Shchastnyi's lawyer appealed against the obvious procedural violations, particularly restricted access to evidence and the lack of witnesses, but this was dismissed.[140] After a heated debate in VTsIK, the sentence was confirmed on 22 June and Shchastnyi executed.[141]

This sentence was significant. The Cheka had shot plenty of people, but courts had not.[142] Sailors protested, contemporaries feared it signalled the onset of terror, and socialists launched furious attacks on the trial and the death penalty. Martov argued that Trotskii acted as a prosecutor, not a witness, and that the tribunal was 'a joke of a court'.[143] Another Menshevik urged popular protests against this 'bloody senselessness'.[144] And, as the Left SRs noted, the death penalty marked the return of the institutional violence of tsarism and the loss of one of the great achievements of the revolution.[145]

The Bolshevik press went on the defensive. *Izvestiia* emphasized the accusations by assigning most space to the prosecution. The defence was dealt with quickly, conveying the sense of an unconvincing response, before the accusations were reiterated in the form of the sentence.[146] More unusual was the defence of the death penalty offered by Krylenko in an interview. He argued that the main goals of tribunals had not been reached prior to this case because of the interference of Left SRs and lawyers. The struggle against counter-revolution must be reflected in tribunals' decisions as well as investigations. The only measure that could protect the revolution was the death penalty. The tribunal was doing its duty.[147] They were at 'war', *Krasnaia armiia* reminded readers, and all was fair in love and war (*na voine, kak na voine*).[148] This reaction reaffirmed that this trial was a milestone. The state had always investigated any suspicions that those working for them were disloyal or had concealed aspects of their past that undermined their professed support, but this trial was different.

A month earlier, the former Commissar for Naval Affairs, P. E. Dybenko, had been judged by Moscow's tribunal. A popular leader of the sailors in 1917, Dybenko had disagreed with the proposed peace treaty with Germany and had launched an unauthorized and failed counterattack in response to German

[140] *Delo komanduiushchego*, 62–4.

[141] GARF, f. R-1235, op. 93, d. 215, l. 2. An account of VTsIK's meeting is in *Novaia zhizn'*, 29 June 1918, 1.

[142] Irkutsk's tribunal dispensed the death penalty on 5 January 1918 not knowing it was illegal and wishing to send out a clear message in its first trial; L. Muller, 'Deiatel'nost' revoliutsionnogo tribunala', in G. Vendrikh (ed.), *Kak my borolis' za vlast' sovetov v Irkutskoi gubernii* (Irkutsk, 1957), 143–4. Other cases surely existed.

[143] Iu. Martov, 'Doloi smertnuiu kazn'! (1918)', reprinted in Martov, *Izbrannoe* (Moscow, 2000), 376–7.

[144] V. Stroev [Desnitskii], 'Doloi smertnuiu kazn'!', *Novaia zhizn'*, 23 June 1918, 1.

[145] *Partiia levykh sotsialistov-revoliutsionerov. Tom I*, 72–3.

[146] *Izvestiia*, 21 June 1918, 5; 22 June 1918, 6.

[147] *Izvestiia*, 23 June 1918, 3.

[148] *Krasnaia armiia*, 26 June 1918, 1. It offered further justification on 3 July 1918, 1.

advances towards Petrograd in February 1918.[149] Dybenko's determination to keep fighting threatened the peace talks and he was arrested. Ten charges were levelled against him relating to the defeat, his subsequent 'cowardly and dishonourable' flight, drunkenness among the troops, and the unauthorized shooting of two soldiers.[150] The week-long trial started on 9 May.[151] Key witnesses were ignored, while Dybenko saw the process as a political trial designed to remove him from power and discredit his political standing, as well as opposition to the peace treaty. The judge refused to discuss wider political circumstances or call political figures as witnesses. Instead, the trial descended into impenetrable military detail as carefully vetted witnesses testified to Dybenko's military mistakes. As prosecutor, Krylenko demanded imprisonment and that Dybenko should be prevented from holding public or political office in future. The tribunal, however, acquitted him of all charges. The state may have done all it dared. The sailors may not have accepted the death penalty, while Dybenko's personal relationship with fellow commissar A. M. Kollontai made it difficult to condemn him without harming her. As it was, Krylenko still felt forced to give an interview justifying the allegations.[152]

A month later, Shchastnyi was less fortunate. The fragile peace with Germany was in even more danger and the civil war had worsened with the Czech Revolt. The creation of the Supreme Tribunal itself reflected a changed political atmosphere that demanded a greater show of ruthlessness. Shchastnyi lacked official influence (as provided by Kollontai) and was from a harmful social class (noble not peasant). This time, as Sverdlov noted in early July to the Fifth All-Russian Congress of Soviets, the tribunal truly considered the seriousness of the current moment.[153] The Supreme Tribunal did so again in its next case, which investigated fifteen former tsarist secret-police provocateurs and resulted in eight executions. According to a former defence lawyer, executions became the only sentence passed by this tribunal.[154] This was not true, but the powers of tribunals had been extended, and this new tribunal marked a significant step in creating a unified, hierarchical, and higher-profile tribunal system. One diarist may have dismissed Dybenko's trial as material for an operetta, farce, or vaudeville, but the mere fact he was reflecting on the war of words between Krylenko and Dybenko revealed the greater publicity garnered by such trials.[155]

149 E. Mawdsley, *The Russian Revolution and the Baltic Fleet* (Basingstoke, 1978), 144–5.

150 The accusations were summarized in *Izvestiia*, 3 May 1918, 5. In an unprecedented step, an extensive description of events then appeared in *Izvestiia*, 4 May 1918, 5; and 10 May 1918, 5.

151 Incomplete transcripts are in TsGAMO, f. 4613, op. 2, d. 10. Reports are in most issues of *Izvestiia*, 10–21 May 1918, always on p. 5. See also *Novaia zhizn'*, 1 May, 1, and various 10–18 May, always p. 3.

152 *Rabochaia i krest'ianskaia krasnaia armiia i flot*, 20 April 1918, 3.

153 Cited in Titov, *Sozdanie*, 87.

154 Kobiakov, 'Krasnyi sud', 246, 261.

155 Okunev, *Dnevnik*, 180 (entry, 19 May 1918).

Streamlining Provincial Tribunals

Beyond the Supreme Tribunal, the May reforms took many months to implement, primarily because the restriction of tribunals to provincial capitals, industrial centres, and significant railway junctions came just as they were expanding rapidly, especially into *uezdy*. The tribunal in Kotel'nicheskii *uezd* (Viatka), for example, was only established on 26 April and had heard just three cases before the reforms led to its abolition on 18 May.[156] Moreover, the delays as news of the reforms slowly spread meant that many tribunals were still being created (now illegally) after 4 May; at least one *uezd* in Orenburg province was creating *volost'* tribunals in late May.[157] A list from this period named forty tribunals, mainly at provincial level, while a later report believed forty-eight tribunals existed on 11 June 1918.[158] Unless Narkomiust was completely ill-informed, these numbers represented their aspirations. The real number at this stage was much higher as most provinces had tribunals in several or more *uezdy* and many *volosti*. Streamlining this structure would take time.

Most areas complied without question, even if it took months, but some questioned the wisdom of removing all *uezd* tribunals, citing concerns over workload and strategic location, particularly as the conflict expanded. Both these issues were evident in a long-running dispute with the authorities in Viatka province. Local justice officials argued first that, if all *uezd* tribunals were abolished, then the provincial tribunal would be unable to cope with the workload – it already had 150 cases, which was too many.[159] Then, in late August 1918, they highlighted the presence of martial law, military conflict, and counter-revolutionary activity (including the Czech Revolt in neighbouring provinces). All this required active courts. Removing *uezd* tribunals left some villages 300–400 *versty* (with no railways) from the provincial capital. Narkomiust eventually relented, allowing tribunals in Kotel'nich and Sarapul alongside the provincial tribunal in Viatka. Malmyzh, however, then started pleading for a tribunal on the basis of the size of its *uezd*, its dark 'alien' population (the *Votiaki*, who were apparently controlled by 'bourgeoisie'), and the prevalence of counter-revolution (after a nearby revolt in Izhevsk in August). It had steamer ports and railway stations that needed defending. These pleas were rejected as its *uezd* was close enough to Sarapul.[160] Other provinces raised similar concerns, making clear that some tribunals were dealing with what local authorities viewed as significant

[156] GARF, f. A-353, op. 9, d. 45, l. 54 (report to Viatka provincial commissar of justice, 23 June 1918).

[157] Abramovskii, 'Stanovlenie', 187.

[158] GARF, f. A-353, op. 1, d. 1, ll. 19–19ob (undated list); op. 2, d. 23, ll. 39gob (report, December 1919).

[159] GARF, f. A-353, op. 2, d. 27, l. 17ob (report to national congress of commissars of justice, late June 1918).

[160] GARF, f. R-1005, op. 2, d. 7, ll. 1–1ob, 34–38ob (correspondence, August–November 1918).

caseloads in strategic locations, and these tribunals were considered valuable weapons in the increasing struggle against opposition.

In the end Narkomiust bowed to pressure and sanctioned the continuation of about a dozen *uezd* tribunals in towns and railway junctions with economic or military importance that were not covered in the original decree, such as Briansk (Orel province), Ekaterinburg (Perm'), Kronstadt (Petrograd), Kozlov (Tambov), and Rybinsk (Iaroslavl'). But the picture was complicated by some local authorities circumventing the reforms by declaring local tribunals subsidiary 'branches' of their provincial tribunal or by other ruses. Increasingly, Narkomiust relied on the cassation department to control recalcitrant localities by upholding appeals made by defendants. The May decree was published in *Izvestiia* on 14 May and Narkomiust allowed local authorities until 24 May to comply.[161] After that, the department abolished sentences issued by *uezd* tribunals on the basis that these tribunals were illegal.

Yet this could open a new can of worms. Kurganskii *uezd* tribunal (Tobol'sk) was rebuked for sentencing crimes after 4 May, but there were still no other courts in the *uezd*.[162] Narkomiust estimated that two-thirds of Russia under Bolshevik control had implemented the Decree on Courts by mid-July 1918, but ongoing gaps hindered tribunal reform.[163] Moreover, some provincial tribunals were incapable of taking cases from *uezd* tribunals. Penza's provincial tribunal, for instance, was not functioning in June 1918 as it did not have a chair and 'criminal' elements flourished.[164] The tribunal in Tambov was also dormant, primarily because a revolt in June had destroyed records, the investigative commission, and the tribunal's premises.[165] Other tribunals reported a lack of workers or other practical problems, many of which resulted from the growing pressures of civil war.

Even in the new capital, Moscow, concerns were raised on 27 July as the tribunal lacked a chairman and members. The chairman was on leave, one of his deputies had left, and the other was overworked. The position was 'desperate'. The situation had worsened within a fortnight. A meeting of the provincial justice department stressed how many workers had been lost and questioned whether the tribunal should continue to exist. It ended up avoiding such a drastic move, noting astutely that it was a 'political' question beyond their jurisdiction, but the issue returned a week later. The tribunal was so short-staffed that it had lost almost every 'responsible' worker and its investigative process was in tatters. Again,

161 Iu. Titov, *Razvitie sistemy sovetskikh revoliutsionnykh tribunalov* (Moscow, 1987), 5.

162 GARF, f. R-1005, op. 2, d. 1, l. 11 (cassation department to Narkomiust, 22 July 1918).

163 GARF, f. A-353, op. 1, d. 1, l. 23 (report to congress of local commissars of justice, 15 July 1918).

164 GARF, f. A-353, op. 2, d. 27, l. 54ob (report to congress of local commissars of justice, 28 June 1918).

165 GARF, f. A-353, op. 2, d. 27, l. 127 (report to congress of local commissars of justice, late June 1918).

closure was avoided in favour of major restructuring. It is not clear what was done, but a new chairman was appointed in September. Yet the problems resurfaced in late November. First, the tribunal requested that all officials with a legal education working for Moscow's soviet be transferred to it.[166] Second, a report noted it still lacked leadership, prosecutors, and a complete investigative department, which was headed illegally by the chairman, a different person from September's appointee. Tribunal members also acted as prosecutors. These irregularities had resulted in appeals, while the lack of prosecutors had halted progress on cases. The tribunal was not influential—how could it be? The report took a swipe at the provincial judicial department, noting that its head, L. A. Savrasov, was part of Narkomiust's leadership, headed its prison department, and spent only an hour a day at best on provincial matters. The proposed solutions were obvious: appoint additional staff and more capable people to key posts. The soviet later rejected a proposal by the city's tribunal to merge with its provincial counterpart.[167] In the end the tribunal survived, but its precarious position despite its prominence in the capital emphasized the practical problems still facing the tribunal system in late 1918.

Attacking Revolutionary Terror

By the late summer of 1918, therefore, the position of tribunals remained in flux in many ways. The May reforms had promised to create a more effective system, but if the Supreme Tribunal had provided an indication of what this might look like, then the ongoing problems of local tribunals highlighted the challenges, particularly as the threat of counter-revolution seemed to be forever increasing. The revolt of the Czech legion had facilitated the emergence of alternative socialist governments in the Volga region and Siberia, while July saw a series of short-lived but still threatening revolts by the Bolsheviks' former allies, the Left SRs. Throughout, the threat from the Volunteer Army in the south was also steadily increasing. This meant that the fundamental challenge—the battle between supporters of revolutionary justice and those supporting violence—remained in the foreground.

In this respect the May reforms unexpectedly left tribunals in a weaker position, as it turned out tribunals were retreating from *uezdy* to become more efficient at the same time as the Cheka was expanding into them, as well as into frontier zones

[166] TsGAMO, f. 4998, op. 1, d. 13, ll. 5ob, 12ob-13, 16ob, 28ob, 51 (protocols of meetings of the judicial department, 27 July, 7 August, 14 August, 4 September, 29 November 1918).

[167] GARF, f. R-393, op. 5, d. 836, ll. 39, 42 (protocol of meeting of Soviet, 30 November 1918, and report). The tribunal's restructuring lasted well into 1919; V. Klimenko, *Moskva. Revoliutsiia. Pravoporiadok. Stolichnaia pravookhranitel'naia sistema: vozniknovenie, razvitie, bor'ba v kontse 1917–1920 gg.* (Moscow, 2010), 48–9.

and communication hubs. The problems this caused were highlighted at the Second All-Russian Congress of Justice Officials in Moscow on 2–6 July 1918, attended by thirty-four local representatives. Speaker after speaker voiced concerns over the activities of these branches, most of which mirrored those made earlier in the year. They complained that the Cheka was unaccountable; it acted beyond its official remit, interfering with tribunals and limiting their effectiveness; and it left prisoners languishing in jails indefinitely and overused the death penalty. The Cheka acted as state within a state, and its activities should be curtailed and controlled. As long as it retained its current form, one speaker argued, justice would always take second place. The congress resolved that provincial executive committees should exert 'direct' control over the Cheka, and it should focus on the most significant forms of counter-revolution.[168] Much of the language was measured, but it was clear the conflict between justice organs and the Cheka, apparent from the start, was gathering pace, and Narkomiust and VTsIK (through the cassation department) received numerous complaints throughout 1918.

What annoyed officials most was that, rather than acting as an investigative organ that transferred cases to the tribunal for judgement, as stipulated in official decrees, the Cheka increasingly dealt with them itself. In some cases, even when a case was transferred, the Cheka informed the tribunal of its desired verdict. All this undermined tribunals. The department of justice in Nizhnii Novgorod, for example, reported that its tribunal judged relatively few cases because of 'abnormal' relations with the local Cheka, which only passed on minor cases. If this could be changed, its tribunal could play a significant role locally.[169]

The Cheka did not always deny these charges. On 26 July 1918, Stuchka wrote to the Cheka complaining that chaos reigned in its activities. Cases were not being passed to courts, people freed by Narkomiust were still in prison, and Narkomiust had not received information on others arrested. He demanded information as justice officials were supposed to be 'custodians of the law'. On 1 August, the Cheka replied, agreeing that Narkomiust had the right to information, and blaming the problems on insufficient personnel, complex work, and poor conditions. It suggested Narkomiust appoint a representative to liaise with them and facilitate the flow of information, something that slowly developed.[170] Yet as 1918 ended, Narkomiust was still working out who had been arrested, still noting the negative impact on courts, and still trying to find a resolution.[171] Despite some prominent tribunal officials transferring to the Cheka, including Galkin and

[168] *Materialy*, 3 (1918), 13–17 (discussion and resolution, 4 July 1918).

[169] GARF, f. R-1005, op. 2, d. 30, l. 9 (report to the cassation department, 22 October 1918).

[170] GARF, f. A-353, op. 2, d. 12, ll. 35–6 (correspondence).

[171] GARF, f. R-393, op. 2, d. 1, ll. 298, 310 (protocols of meetings of Narkomiust, August–September 1918); f. A-353, op. 2, d. 14, ll. 102–05ob, 127 (November–December) and d. 835, ll. 151–51ob (18 November).

Zhukov, its legality did not improve; instead, paradoxically, it seemed to encourage the belief that tribunals were an unnecessary formality in most cases.

These tensions were exacerbated by the official onset of terror in autumn 1918. An attempt on Lenin's life and the murder of the head of the Petrograd Cheka, M. S. Uritskii, prompted Sovnarkom to declare on 5 September that securing the rear through terror was essential, the Cheka's activities should be strengthened, and there should be greater emphasis on shooting active opponents and publicizing these activities.[172] This initiated what became known as the Red Terror. To a certain extent, this decree simply sanctioned existing Cheka activities, but arbitrary violence reached new levels under state sponsorship over subsequent months. Unlike the French Revolution, however, when revolutionary tribunals were an inseparable part of the terror, the Red Terror was directed and enacted by the Cheka. Indeed, the focus on terror actually threatened to further marginalize tribunals.

Consequently, a congress of tribunal officials in Moscow on 29 October–3 November was less measured in its language than the July congress of justice officials. They admitted that extreme measures were essential to combat growing counter-revolution, accepted that there were problems with tribunals, and recognized the importance of the Cheka as an investigative organ. However, they protested vigorously at the transformation of the Cheka, accelerated by the terror, from an investigative organ to a court of law, enacting its own judgements on the accused. Moreover, there was no openness in its processes or activities and no possibility of questioning them. Tribunal officials accused the Cheka of violating its authority, intruding into their jurisdiction, and failing to recognize their rights or respond to their queries. When the Cheka did transfer cases, the files were usually incomplete, with key documents unsigned or absent, such as witness statements. The congress demanded new decrees on the jurisdiction of the Cheka and on the conditions under which acting outside of the legal framework was permissible. It also pressed for independent regulation of the Cheka's activities, and (again) for the primacy of tribunals in judging and sentencing criminals.[173]

These demands were reported verbatim in *Izvestiia* and *Pravda*, which, while noting that tribunals needed further reform, were sympathetic to arguments that they were weakened by the Cheka's actions. Both papers reiterated the call to curtail Cheka activities.[174] All this reflected gathering opposition to the Cheka across the state apparatus. Prominent Bolsheviks criticized the Cheka publicly, while soviets and their parent organ, Narkomvnudel, were particularly vocal. They were ordered to establish and finance local branches of the Cheka, but had no

[172] GARF, f. A-353, op. 2, d. 8, l. 75 (Sovnarkom resolution, 5 September 1918).
[173] N. Krylenko, *Sudoustroistvo RSFSR* (Moscow, 1923), 322–5.
[174] *Izvestiia*, 10 November 1918, 3, and *Pravda*, 21 November 1918, 3.

control over them. Many Chekists were corrupt and inefficient, and arbitrary violence was counterproductive.[175] The onset of terror exacerbated these tensions, prompting debates at all levels. In Riazan', for instance, the presidium of the provincial soviet saw an argument with the Cheka on 11 September over the latter's autonomy and concealment of information. The same points were raised in a meeting of the executive committee the following day.[176] At the same time, the soviet in Borisoglebskii *uezd* in the province resolved that the Cheka must be controlled by the *uezd* executive committee. The autonomy of the Cheka was creating dual power locally.[177] A survey of soviets in October 1918 saw around 85 per cent of those polled (nearly 150) demand that local soviets be given greater control over the Cheka,[178] while a congress of chairmen of provincial executive committees insisted the Cheka's separatism contravened the fundamental goal of government unity.[179] This all led Narkomvnudel to reach out to Narkomiust and seek greater cooperation between all those fighting counter-revolution.[180]

Sovnarkom was forced to act after an article was published in the Cheka's weekly newspaper in September 1918 advocating the use of torture. It condemned the article, closed the paper, and created the first of several commissions to investigate the Cheka.[181] The Cheka, though, defended its purpose vigorously and, when it came to the crunch, received official backing. While Lenin admitted in a speech to Cheka staff on 7 November that there had been mistakes, he argued this was inevitable and these were individual mistakes. The bigger picture was of a drastic struggle against the bourgeoisie: the harder the Bolsheviks pressed, the more the bourgeoisie resisted, and the Cheka was vital in this fight.[182]

The fact that these arguments rumbled on into 1919, as discussed in Chapter 2, and failed to restrict the Cheka's autonomy or ability to dispense arbitrary justice, and the fact that violence and terror only escalated as the civil war worsened in 1919, might seem to signal, at best, that the subordinate position of revolutionary justice had been confirmed by this stage and, at worst, that the legal system was little more than a subsidiary of the Cheka. Yet, returning to the questions posed at the start, these arguments revealed several important points.

[175] For discussions of criticism, see L. Gerson, *The Secret Police in Lenin's Russia* (Philadelphia, 1976), 191–200; Leggett, *Cheka*, 123–9; M. Melancon, 'Revolutionary Culture in the Early Soviet Republic: Communist Executive Committees versus the Cheka, Fall 1918', *Jahrbücher für Geschichte Osteuropas*, 57, 1 (2009), 1–22; and J. Ryan, 'The Sacralization of Violence: Bolshevik Justifications for Violence and Terror during the Civil War', *Slavic Review*, 74, 4 (2015), 814–18.

[176] GARF, f. R-393, op. 3, d. 305, ll. 123–4, 184–5ob (protocols, 11–12 September 1918).

[177] GARF, f. R-393, op. 3, d. 382, l. 164 (protocols, 20 September 1918).

[178] Melancon, 'Revolutionary Culture', 13.

[179] GARF, f. R-393, op. 2, d. 56, l. 427 (protocols, November 1918).

[180] GARF, f. R-393, op. 1, d. 6v, ll. 127–8 (protocol of the college of Narkomvnudel, 14 November 1918).

[181] E. Acton and T. Stableford, *The Soviet Union: A Documentary History. Vol. I, 1917–40* (Exeter, 2005), 120–2.

[182] Lenin, *Collected Works*, XXVIII, 169–70.

First, it is notable how far justice officials were committed to revolutionary justice—that is, to a reformed legal system and a degree of order and procedure in investigations and sentencing. They did not deny the Cheka a role in searching out counter-revolution and they knew a harsh response to counter-revolution was required under the circumstances. Indeed, as politics determined what constituted counter-revolution at any given time, tribunals were as political an organ as the Cheka. But their conception of the role of law led them to believe the best way to combat these threats (and educate the population) remained the controlled and focused use of repression guided by regulations and open to public scrutiny. Thus justice may have been political and repressive, but it remained distinct from uncontrolled violence. It was clear, moreover, that many others in government shared the same view for various reasons, from local soviets fearful for their own authority and the counterproductive impact of the Cheka to senior Bolsheviks sceptical of the effectiveness of unrestrained violence. The Cheka, then, had secured official backing but not an unconditional victory.

Second, the practical experiences of tribunals since November had resulted in a clearer sense of what revolutionary justice should look like in practice and the role it could play in building a socialist state. This was particularly true if additional developments are also considered: the legislative activities of the government; the increasingly structured activities of Narkomiust; new family and labour law codes, and a new constitution; growing numbers of legal publications; expanding theoretical discussions of legal matters; and, of course, the experiences of people's courts. Against this background, Narkomiust continued to believe the revolution could build a better legal system than ever seen before – it needed only to overcome the shortcomings evident during the debates with the Cheka. Furthermore, local officials provided guidance on what still needed to be done at the congress in late October–early November. Passionate debates over personnel shortages and 'cumbersome' structures resulted in calls for reducing the size of tribunals and uniting all of their regulations into a single accessible decree.[183] It was no coincidence that Narkomiust started planning further reform soon after this congress.

Narkomiust's main priority was to establish its own authority so that it could lead the reforms and ensure conformity, and there were signs it was moving closer to doing so by late 1918. Further instructions issued by the cassation department were a key step in this respect. On the basis of over 300 appeals submitted to it since its creation, the department provided the clearest outline yet of what constituted counter-revolution and reiterated, with greater clarity, the regulations on investigative commissions, lawyers, sentences, and cassation.[184] On the one

[183] Krylenko, *Sudoustroistvo*, 93–101 (discussion of congress), 310–25 (resolutions). See also *Izvestiia*, 31 October 1918, 5; and Titov, *Razvitie*, 11–13.
[184] *IZ*, 58–63.

hand, the instructions implied ongoing problems; too many incorrectly formed tribunals were still judging inappropriate crimes in unsanctioned ways, leading to undesirable and ineffective sentences. On the other, the instructions represented the cassation department exerting its authority—and central authority more generally—with greater clarity and force than before, and this had a steady impact over subsequent months.

Finally, despite the seeming supremacy of the Cheka and ongoing problems with their effectiveness, no one ever suggested abolishing tribunals. At some level, then, the Bolshevik leadership agreed with justice officials that tribunals had a distinct role to play. Indeed, their workload was expanding as the conflict intensified, despite their complaints that they were being marginalized by the Cheka. Therefore, by the end of 1918, a year on from the Decree on Courts, tribunals had managed to develop from a sentence in a decree into a comprehensive system, and had carved out a niche for themselves amid arguments over the relevance and effectiveness of revolutionary justice. These arguments had not disappeared, however, and Narkomiust still had to prove the importance of law for the Bolshevik state. If law offered a more multifaceted approach to combatting counter-revolution than violence, alongside the possibility of strengthening Bolshevik authority and authenticating their political actions, this still needed to be demonstrated in practice.

2
Extending State Authority

Courts help all states maintain political and social order, but the ability of law to help the state exert power is its principal attraction for authoritarian states.[1] Certainly, the importance of law for the Bolsheviks centred on its ability to strengthen and defend the new proletarian state just as it had, in their opinion, the bourgeois state before. This was particularly true given the nature of the state after October 1917. Centrifugal tendencies prior to the February Revolution had developed into full-scale localism as central state control broke down in 1917 and localities—provincial, *uezd*, and *volost'*—enacted their own revolutions.[2] The Bolsheviks not only had to defeat their political enemies, they also had to rebuild the state apparatus.

A key part of re-establishing state authority was rebuilding state institutions locally. The Bolsheviks needed a physical presence across Russia, both to be *able* to act and to be *seen* acting, and to bring the revolution and its ideas directly to the people. There were, of course, a multitude of governing organs already present, from local soviets and party organs to the innumerable committees overseeing various important areas, and the Bolsheviks sought to take control of these in the months after October. There was also the blunt force offered by the Cheka as it spread across the provinces in 1918. But courts provided something different. They too asserted the state's presence, its political and social values, and its ambitions.[3] But they were also a punitive tool for local officials to maintain order and a means to regulate these same officials. They were an interactive forum where people could engage with the state to address wrongs and seek 'justice'. And although there was often little pomp or ceremony, courts still brought the 'majesty' of the law—authority in procedure and ceremony—to the localities; in short, law was a multifaceted 'emissary' of the state.[4]

[1] M. Shapiro, *Courts: A Comparative and Political Analysis* (Chicago, 1981), 22–4; T. Moustafa, 'Law and Courts in Authoritarian Regimes', *Annual Review of Law and Social Science*, 10 (2014), 283.

[2] For more on this theme, see M. Rendle, 'The Problem of the "Local" in Revolutionary Russia: Moscow Province, 1914-1922', in S. Badcock, L. Novikova, and A. Retish (eds.), *Russia's Home Front in War and Revolution, 1914–22. Book 1. Russia's Revolution in Regional Perspective* (Bloomington, 2015), 19–44.

[3] A point also made in A. Retish, 'Judicial Reforms and Revolutionary Justice: The Establishment of the Court System in Soviet Russia, 1917-22', in C. Read, P. Waldron, and A. Lindenmeyr (eds.), *Russia's Home Front in War and Revolution, 1914–22. Book 4: Reintegration—The Struggle for the State* (Bloomington, 2018), 371–401.

[4] On the 'majesty' of law, see D. Hay, 'Property, Authority and the Criminal Law', in D. Hay et al., *Albion's Fatal Tree: Crime and Society in Eighteenth-Century England* (London, 1975), 27. On law as

The State versus The People: Revolutionary Justice in Russia's Civil War, 1917–1922. Matthew Rendle, Oxford University Press (2020). © Matthew Rendle.
DOI: 10.1093/oso/9780198840428.001.0001

Revolutionary tribunals, as state-led prosecutorial courts bringing the state's political concerns to the people, were better placed to convey the authority and ideology of the state than people's courts. Tribunal officials may have been 'local', but they did not see themselves as embedded in the locality in the same way as other local officials; they were part of one of the 'fighting' organs at the front line of the revolution, using law as a revolutionary weapon against the revolution's enemies. Yet the Bolsheviks were still struggling to fulfil the potential of tribunals by late 1918. They had targeted political enemies and their publications, uncovering numerous counter-revolutionary activities while also promoting the Bolsheviks' conception of the revolution. The arguments of legal theorists, the increasingly regulated legal process, and the public nature of trials promoted the Bolsheviks as defending the revolution (and the people), enhancing their legitimacy. Nevertheless, many Bolsheviks perceived inadequacies: there was too much opposition, it was too determined, and tribunals were not sufficiently efficient and harsh to act effectively as a deterrent, leaving many to look for a solution in the revolutionary violence of the Cheka. The reforms in May 1918 had tried to create a more effective system by streamlining tribunals, restricting them to significant centres to focus scarce resources and foster consistency, but it became clear this had restricted their reach at the same time as the gathering conflict required a greater presence across Russia. In November 1918 the socialist-led opposition east of the Volga fell to a military dictatorship led by Admiral A. V. Kolchak, which launched a major offensive in spring 1919. The Volunteer Army in the south started its own offensive later in the year, while other anti-Bolshevik forces were active in the north and west. Meanwhile, support for other socialists remained significant in many Bolshevik-held territories.

To prove their value, tribunals had to reach beyond abstract spaces to reach the places that held meaning in people's everyday lives.[5] When distinguishing between space and place, the importance of experience, intimacy, and feeling has been stressed in transforming an abstract space into a place where people work and live; a place is made up of experiences, often fleeting and undramatic, repeated daily over years, with a unique blend of sights, sounds, and smells, all of which provide meaning and stability to those living there.[6] For tribunals to be effective,

the state's emissary, see U. Baxi, '"The State's Emissary": The Place of the Law in Subaltern Studies', in P. Chatterjee and G. Panday (eds.), *Subaltern Studies VII: Writings on South Asian History and Society* (New Delhi, 1992), 247–64.

[5] This draws on comments on agitation made in R. Argenbright, 'Vanguard of "Socialist Colonization"? The Krasnyi Vostok Expedition of 1920', *Central Asian Survey*, 30, 3–4 (2011), 438–40. See also his 'Soviet Agitational Vehicles: Bolsheviks in Strange Places', in M. Bassin, C. Ely, and M. Stockdale (eds.), *Space, Place and Power in Modern Russia: Essays in the New Spatial History* (DeKalb, 2010), 142–63.

[6] Y. Tuan, *Space and Place: The Perspective of Experience* (London, 1977), 6, 136–48, 179, 183–4.

they had to invade these places, whether the military barracks, the railway carriage, the river steamer, or the village square.

This chapter charts how tribunals responded to this challenge, expanding into the military and transport networks, both crucial areas during the civil war, as well as organizing travelling sessions to reach into remoter areas. At the height of their activities in 1920, hundreds of tribunals judged hundreds of thousands of cases involving many more people given the prevalence of mass crimes. Expansion, though, exacerbated the challenges facing tribunals. The Commissariat of Justice (Narkomiust) was already preparing reforms in autumn 1918 to deal with concerns over efficiency, consistency, and unity, all seen as crucial if tribunals were to garner respect for their activities. Yet expansion was driven by local initiative and facilitated by other bodies, particularly the Commissariats of War (Narkomvoen) and Paths and Communications (Narkomput), fuelling inconsistency and disunity as tribunals developed into a three-pronged system where civilian, military, and transport tribunals acted independently of each other. Thus Narkomiust was simultaneously trying to help the state extend its authority while also attempting to exert its own across the tribunal system. As this chapter explores, it did the latter primarily through a profusion of decrees that sought, gradually and repetitively, to encourage consistency and unity across different types of tribunals. It also sought information on what was happening on the ground, even conducting inspections, to help it intervene where anomalies were discovered. These efforts eventually resulted in the unification of all three types of tribunals in June 1921.

Yet just as unity was being achieved, another problem re-emerged—the broader role of revolutionary justice. By 1921, the nature of the civil war was changing as the conflict with obvious political and social enemies on the periphery of Bolshevik-held territory declined. Even legal officials started feeling that, if the revolution was finally emerging victorious (and, by implication, the threat of counter-revolution receding), there was less need for exceptional forms of justice. Tribunals continued to justify their importance as the Bolsheviks switched attention to rising internal dissent from peasants and workers, but even this slowly receded in 1922 after the concessions of the New Economic Policy (NEP) in spring 1921. For some legal officials, this marked an opportunity to unite the two strands of revolutionary justice—people's courts and revolutionary tribunals—into a reformed legal system that would not only defend the revolution but also help to build socialism. After much debate, most tribunals were duly abolished in late 1922 as part of major legal reforms. The ability for occasional recourse to exceptional forms of justice remained, but the revolutionary consciousness that characterized the civil war was transformed into a more predictable revolutionary legality that signalled a new role for law in the foundation of a socialist state.

Military Tribunals

The most obvious area for tribunals to expand into was the military. The spread of conflict led to the creation of the Red Army in January 1918, but there was little enthusiasm on the part of the population and it became a struggle to maintain the fighting capabilities of the new army. Initially, there were no plans to use courts to enforce discipline. The Decree on Courts had disbanded existing military courts in November 1917, while Narkomiust opposed military courts in its May 1918 decrees on tribunals as it feared losing control over the new court system.[7] However, it could not prevent military officials from looking to courts as a solution to their problems. Old courts persisted illegally to deal with indiscipline, and these were joined by unofficial 'revolutionary' courts.[8] As with civilian courts at this time, it is difficult to clarify what a 'revolutionary' court meant. One 'military tribunal' in the 5th Army in December 1917 had military and civilian members dealing with counter-revolution, while a 'comrade' court focused on indiscipline.[9] Elsewhere, it is not clear whether some 'military' tribunals dealt exclusively with either the military or counter-revolution.

The first official courts in the Red Army came when front-line regimental courts and company comrade courts were permitted in July 1918.[10] The former would resolve regular criminal cases; the latter covered lesser crimes, such as violations of non-military orders and duties, minor military property crimes, drinking, gambling, late return from leave, and violations of 'comradeship' (such as insults). At this stage, serious cases of counter-revolution were still referred to civilian tribunals. As the fighting spread, however, and the Bolsheviks' position became more precarious, almost any crime was seen as a breach of discipline and as amounting to counter-revolution. The tense military situation demanded that such crimes were dealt with swiftly and harshly, and military officials felt that civilian tribunals were slow, far from the action, unsure of military regulations, and ignorant of military concerns.[11]

With these issues in mind, military courts expanded spontaneously, most notably with the courts initiated by local commanders on the front line against the Czech Revolt in July–August in places such as Kazan', Perm', Simbirsk, and Ufa. The 1st Army was the first in mid-July, followed by the 3rd and 5th Armies in early August.[12] Contemporaries highlight these courts as the first military

[7] *Materialy Narodnogo Komissariata Iustitsii* [hereafter *Materialy*], 3 (1918), 13.

[8] M. Kozhevnikov, *Istoriia sovetskogo suda 1917–1956 gody* (Moscow, 1957), 49–51.

[9] E. Gorodetskii, *Rozhdenie sovetskogo gosudarstva 1917–1918* (Moscow, 1987), 209–11.

[10] *Istoriia zakonodatel'stva SSSR i RSFSR po ugolovnomu protsessu i organizatsii suda i prokuratury, 1917–1954* [hereafter *IZ*] (Moscow, 1955), 55–6 (23 July 1918).

[11] L. Gusev, *Sovetskaia voennaia iustitsiia v gody inostrannoi voennoi interventsii i grazhdanskoi voiny (1918–1920 gg.)* (Avtoreferat dissertatsii, Moscow, 1950), 9.

[12] Only vague information is available, as is evident in three later reports by V. V. Ul'rikh, head of the military tribunal system from 1921, which all cover the same developments but differ on detail:

tribunals; one described the 'first' court being held in the station at Inza (Simbirsk province) to deal with desertion, while another attributed the 'first' tribunal to a court in Perm' that dealt with a fire in the garrison.[13] But most were called 'military field courts' or 'exceptional troikas' and varied in their activities, even if they may have been modelled on tribunals. The 3rd Army in Perm', for instance, established a military–revolutionary field court in August 1918 before creating similar courts in each division.[14]

These courts remained unofficial, but a proposal by military authorities on 15 September to form a Revolutionary Military Tribunal of the Russian Republic (RVTR) was finally realized on 14 October.[15] Chaired by K. Kh. Danishevskii, it made military tribunals official and created a means of controlling them. Although the RVTR did not meet in earnest until early December, tribunals spread across the military and were present on all three fronts and in all eleven armies by the end of the year, with the navy soon following. When the RVTR did meet, it focused on the structure of these tribunals, ensuring that each front tribunal exercised authority over each army tribunal, with the latter having branches at divisional level. It also started to provide guidance on procedures and sentences, and it formed its own investigative branch to oversee all military tribunals and examine serious cases.[16]

As Danishevskii made clear in an interview in *Izvestiia* in January 1919, military tribunals were a response to the escalating military threat, especially the Czech Revolt, and were not guided by legal norms but political expediency (*tselesoobraznost'*), with fair but unlimited sentencing (he detailed three outcomes: innocence, imprisonment, and execution).[17] Later he noted that tribunals attached to armies and divisions had the capability to move around with these units, providing rapid justice with full knowledge of the military situation, rather than waiting for civilian tribunals based many miles away to deliver a verdict based on a limited awareness of events.[18]

'Voennye tribunaly', in *Piat' let Verkhovnogo suda, 1918–1923* (Moscow, 1923), no pag.; 'Voennye tribunaly (1918-1928 g.)', *Vestnik Verkhovnogo Suda SSSR i Prokuratury Verkhovnogo Suda SSSR*, 5–6 (1928), 7–15; and 'K desiatiletiiu voennykh tribunalov', *Ezhenedel'nik Sovetskoi iustitsii* [hereafter *ESIu*], 51–2, 31 December 1928, 1269.

[13] A. Upel'kin, 'Pervyi tribunal (k desiatiletiiu voennykh tribunalov)', *Sud idet!*, 21 (1928), 1167–72; A. Chuvatin, 'Pervye tribunaly', in *Voennye tribunaly—organy sotsialisticheskogo pravosudiia* (Moscow, 1958), 53–62. See also V. Sorokin, 'Stranichki proshlogo', in *Voennye tribunaly*, 63–9. Soviet historians agree: V. Portnov and M. Slavin, *Pravovye osnovy stroitel'stva Krasnoi Armii, 1918–20gg.* (Moscow, 1985), 196–212.

[14] GARF, f. R-1005, op. 3, d. 21, l. 3 (report by the military tribunal in Ekaterinburg, 20 January 1922).

[15] *Revvoensovet Respubliki. Protokoly. 1918–1919 gg.* (Moscow, 1997), 30–1, 40, 66.

[16] RGVA, f. 33987, op. 2, d. 53, ll. 131–2 (report by Danishevskii, 31 January 1919).

[17] *Izvestiia*, 3 January 1919, 2.

[18] K. Danishevskii, *Revoliutsionnye voennye tribunaly* (Moscow, 1920), 6, 15–16, 22.

The first detailed regulations were circulated to military tribunals on 8 January 1919 and an official decree published on 14 February.[19] Generally, military tribunals mirrored their civilian counterparts, but several features distinguished them beyond their focus on crimes committed in the sphere of military activities by military personnel or prisoners of war. First, military tribunals were only composed of three people, as opposed to the seven in civilian tribunals at this stage. These were appointed (and financed) by front or army revolutionary military councils, ensuring Narkomvoen's control, and should be 'political worker-communists', a more precise wording than instructions for civilian tribunals. Second, the decree did not reference tsarist laws, reflecting their final rejection in November 1918. Sentences should reflect the interests of the Soviet republic and its defence, the class war being waged by the proletariat, and revolutionary legal consciousness and conscience. The explicit emphasis on class war was again specific to military tribunals. Third, the sentences of military tribunals were not subject to cassation and had to be enacted within twenty-four hours, facilitating the rapid justice considered necessary in military conditions. Sentences could be altered on the initiative of a superior tribunal if circumstances, information, or the political situation changed. Later regulations clarified jurisdiction and procedure.[20] There was also restructuring over time as the army's structure changed; most notably, tribunals were formed in military regions (*okrugi*) with the same powers as front tribunals.[21]

Military tribunals were, therefore, considered exceptional organs for the military aspect of the civil war, distinct from other tribunals, with some measures designed to ensure legal repression was harsher in this strategic area. These tribunals were capable of reaching into the heart of everyday military operations, from the decision-making organs to operations on the ground. The branches of army tribunals in divisions, in particular, were part of the active military. They were constantly on the move, travelling with their divisions as the front ebbed and flowed, while their members were often called upon to fight and they suffered losses like other parts of the division. This had an impact on their work. Reports were often more concerned about general matters—the military position, the political mood of the population, supplies, and sanitary conditions—than legal activities.[22] The constant movement made it difficult to maintain regular contact with their parent tribunal, and frequent fighting disrupted investigations and trials, and exacerbated general problems with personnel and resources.

[19] Danishevskii, *Revoliutsionnye voennye tribunaly*, 13. I have only found a copy sent on 14 January; RGVA, f. 33987, op. 2, d. 53, ll. 133–6ob. The decree is in *IZ*, 79–80.

[20] *Dekrety Sovetskoi vlasti* [hereafter *DSV*] (18 volumes, Moscow, 1957–2009), VI, 286–97; *IZ*, 119–20, 138–43.

[21] Danishevskii, *Revoliutsionnye voennye tribunaly*, 18–19.

[22] GARF, f. R-1005, op. 1, d. 52, ll. 60–1 (report, 16th Cavalry Division's military tribunal, North Caucasus, 12 August 1921); d. 53, ll. 26–30 (report, military tribunal in the Caucasian army, August–September 1921).

Divisional tribunals were supposed to be the lowest level of military tribunal, but odd references note tribunals at regimental and garrison level, either to deal with relatively minor cases that were clogging up other tribunals or to ensure that punishment was swift, thereby increasing the tribunal's impact locally.[23] Other evidence reveals short-lived local tribunals to deal with particular problems. In Petrograd, for instance, military tribunals were established in each of its ten districts on 20 October 1919 to deal with cases directly relating to the defence of the city when it was besieged by the forces of General N. N. Iudenich. They worked more quickly than normal, with those arrested judged within a day. Officials worked through the night gathering evidence and trials were held twice daily, often taking less than a few hours. Tribunals heard up to forty cases a day in some districts and dealt with hundreds in the first few days, usually involving desertion, but also other disruptive actions, such as several Chinese sentenced for manufacturing opium. Some pronounced the death penalty, but forced labour was more common. These tribunals only lasted a matter of weeks and were disbanded officially on 12 November as the military threat receded.[24]

Statistics produced later stated that 18 military tribunals were created by the end of 1918, with another 96 in 1919, 133 in 1920, and 13 in 1921—numbers that parallel the rise and fall of military engagements in the civil war.[25] Not all tribunals endured amid the frequent reorganizations of the Red Army, while rapidly fluctuating events quickly made any information held centrally obsolete. Statistics from 15 May 1921 suggest the existence of 193 military tribunals, including 43 focusing on railways.[26] Other statistics from the same period provide similar numbers. This suggests that around 150 tribunals existed within the military itself at this time. This was several times more than the number of civilian tribunals, and this was the bare minimum; archival files exist for at least 540 tribunals that operated at some stage during the civil war, including in the rear, even if the number active at any one time was much smaller.[27]

Military tribunals extended their reach into the rear in 1920. Armed forces had existed under the Cheka and other organs since 1918 to target revolts, secure transport, and facilitate food requisitioning. On 28 May 1919, these united into the military-run Internal Security Force of the Republic (*Voisk vnutrennei okhrany respubliki* or VOKhR), which lasted until February 1922 and established a

[23] RGVA, f. 33987, op. 1, d. 196, l. 321 (14th Army tribunal to Trotskii, 13 August 1919).

[24] *Krasnaia gazeta*, 24 October 1919, 4; 29 October, 4; 31 October, 2; 1 November, 4; 12 November, 2.

[25] GARF, f. R-1005, op. 1, d. 145, ll. 1–8 (report, undated, 1923).

[26] GARF, f. R-1005, op. 1, d. 57, ll. 2–3ob (list of tribunals).

[27] I was denied access to these records in RGVA in 2012, but I did view the relevant catalogue of the archive's holdings, *Fondovye knigi po grazhdanskoi voine*, which provided this figure. One Soviet study gave a figure of 422; V. Portnov and G. Smirnova, *Sovetskaia voennaia iustitsiia (1918–1920 gg.)* (Moscow, 1960), 6.

formal military presence in the rear.[28] On 11 January 1920, a tribunal under VOKhR was created, later renamed the Main Tribunal, which was subordinate to the RVTR and oversaw the establishment of local VOKhR tribunals.[29] These had jurisdiction over military personnel working for VOKhR in areas without an existing military tribunal and enjoyed the same powers as military tribunals. One report gave a total of forty-five of these tribunals in 1920, another fifty-two in 1920–1, while a historian noted nine district (*okrug*) VOKhR tribunals with thirty-nine branches, most starting in July–September 1920.[30] Essentially, these constituted 'rear' military tribunals, and initial distinctions between VOKhR and military tribunals broke down when the two were merged in November 1920.[31] As a result, there were military tribunals at the front and the rear by early 1921, with huge swathes of strategically important territory subject to military control, and this meant civilian and military tribunals coexisted in many cities, albeit with different jurisdictions.

The rapid development of military tribunals came with problems. As early as July 1919, a meeting of representatives of military tribunals on the Eastern Front highlighted the disunited and amateurish nature of much of their work, and pushed for more open trials (and greater publicity) to create a more powerful educational message.[32] Numerous inconsistencies and poor practices led Danishevskii (like Narkomiust earlier) to appreciate that the cassation process could be a means of strengthening central control, uniformity, and consistency.[33] The First All-Russian Congress of Military Tribunal Officials on 17–20 February 1920 agreed, apart from when the punishment was execution, which should remain the preserve of the RVTR to ensure a quick response, so the RVTR became a member of the Cassation Tribunal (along with transport tribunals) on 4 May 1920.[34] It now submitted reports and sentences for scrutiny by civilians, thereby taking the first step towards unifying all tribunals (see Unifying the Tribunal System section, below).

Nevertheless, the RVTR was keen to ensure that military tribunals retained a distinct role. By late 1920, various party and government figures were questioning whether military tribunals were necessary now that several fronts in the civil war had been liquidated. One RVTR member pointed to the continued fighting on

[28] *Vnutrennie voiska sovetskoi respubliki (1917–1922 gg.)* (Moscow, 1972), 4–10. See also G. Leggett, *The Cheka: Lenin's Political Police* (revised edition, Oxford, 1986), 209–13.

[29] *Vnutrennie voiska*, 144–5 (decree); GARF, f. R-1005, op. 1, d. 145, l. 8 (report on tribunals, c.1923).

[30] GARF, f. R-1005, op. 1, d. 145, l. 8; d. 6, ll. 32–34; V. Abramov, 'Sozdanie i deiatel'nost' mestnykh revoliutsionnykh tribunalov (1918–1922 gg.) (po materialam Penzenskoi gubernii)' (*kandidat* dissertation, Penza State Pedagogical University, 2004), 171.

[31] *IZ*, 158–9 (25 November 1920).

[32] Portnov and Smirnova, *Sovetskaia voennaia iustitsiia*, 27.

[33] Danishevskii, *Revoliutsionnye voennye tribunaly*, 47–50.

[34] GARF, f. A-353, op. 4, d. 23, l. 4 (excerpt from meeting, 19 February 1920); *DSV*, V, 15–16; *IZ*, 143.

other fronts. Another argued that the general counter-revolutionary threat required severe repression and doubted that civilian tribunals were sufficient on their own (primarily because of cassation and a lack of knowledge of military conditions), with the alternative being a return to the 'obsolete' methods of the Cheka. The RVTR commissioned a report on the work of military tribunals, which emphasized the ongoing threats to the state and the importance of military tribunals in fighting them.[35]

The belief that the war was not over and that the prevalence of banditry, desertion, and counter-revolution in the military required a level of 'exceptional repression' only military tribunals could provide was shared locally. A conference of tribunal officials in Sevastopol' declared that desertion, corruption, banditry, espionage, and counter-revolutionary plots abounded in the military, and organs of a 'military character' were needed to eradicate them. Civilian courts were 'weak' and 'inexperienced', and concentrated on 'judging' when there was need 'to punish', and 'to punish in the military way (*karat' po voennomu*)'.[36] Others also questioned the ability of the Cheka and the party to deal with threats.[37] Within military tribunals, then, a conception of a distinct military form of revolutionary justice had emerged—situated somewhere between civilian tribunals and the Cheka—and its future became central to debates surrounding a unified tribunal system in 1921.

Transport Tribunals

Alongside the military, another obvious area for tribunals to target was the transport network. Railways, in particular, had played a central role in the revolution from the start and they were a magnet for crime; wagons of scarce supplies proved irresistible to bandits, thieves, corrupt officials, and enemy forces. As early as July 1917, the authorities in Viatka had proposed special courts to deal with such crimes, and similar ideas were raised in a national congress of railway workers.[38] These problems worsened with the onset of civil war as tracks, bridges, and wagons were destroyed, telegraph apparatus sabotaged, fuel stolen, and so on.

Narkomiust, though, in line with its response to early proposals for military courts, initially resisted establishing special transport courts outside of its own

[35] GARF, f. R-1005, op. 1, d. 57, ll. 75–6 (protocol of meeting, 14 December 1920), 77–81ob (report).

[36] *Krasnyi Chernomorskom-Azovskii flot*, 12 March 1921, 3–4 (in GARF, f. R-1005, op. 1, d. 56, ll. 32–32ob).

[37] GARF, f. R-1005, op. 1, d. 56, l. 148 (report, chairman of Novorossiisk military tribunal, 4 August 1921).

[38] GARF, f. 1790, op. 2, d. 14, ll. 1–1ob (Provincial Commissar to the Ministry of Justice, 1 July 1917).

authority.[39] However, as in the military, comrade courts emerged alongside local proposals for tribunals. Narkomput and the All-Russian Railway Congress sanctioned a tribunal in Voronezh on the Moscow–Kiev–Voronezh railway on 12 May, much to the ire of nearby Kursk's civilian tribunal, which called it illegal, incompetent, and criminal.[40] The Commissar of War, L. D. Trotskii, sanctioned a military tribunal with authority over the Moscow–Kazan' railway in early August 1918 to help combat the Czech Revolt and supported similar moves elsewhere.[41] Narkomiust agreed to Trotskii's actions (it had little choice), but opposed other initiatives.[42] In arguments made in November against a tribunal in Petrozavodsk covering the Murmansk railway, Narkomiust claimed such a tribunal would deal with too many general crimes and its work could easily be handled by extra sessions of the civilian tribunal.[43]

Nevertheless, arguments made by supporters of the Petrozavodsk tribunal—that its central location enabled the tribunal to deal more effectively with crimes (gathering evidence and interviewing witnesses) on a railway traversing three provinces than individual civilian tribunals—became a powerful element of a broader argument not just for military tribunals devoted to railways but for independent railway tribunals. After all, railways were governed independently, subject to specific regulations like the military, faced unique challenges, and required a court staffed with specialists. Officials pointed out the crucial role of transport, the importance of political education for its workers, and the need to enforce discipline.

In the end, civil war pressures prevailed. On 28 November 1918, the Council of People's Commissars (Sovnarkom) declared martial law on all railways at the front. All railway personnel were now under Narkomvoen rather than Narkomput, and all military tribunals should include representatives from railways and extend their scope accordingly.[44] Railway tribunals were also mentioned in passing in the decree on tribunals on 12 April 1919, thereby acknowledging their existence officially even if there were few other details.[45]

Later in 1919, as the threat from the east and south receded, the authorities assessed the role of the transport system systematically.[46] On 12 November,

[39] On the arguments and the emergence of unofficial railway tribunals, see S. Charnyi, 'Revoliutsionnye voennye tribunaly na transporte. 1918–1923' (2014) at http://polit.ru/article/2014/05/11/revtrib/ [accessed 9 May 2019].

[40] GARF, f. A-353, op. 2, d. 31, ll. 119–19ob (notes of a trial by a railway tribunal in Voronezh, 5 August 1918); d. 37, ll. 2–5 (correspondence between Kursk's tribunal and Narkomiust, September 1918).

[41] *The Military Writings and Speeches of Leon Trotsky: How the Revolution Armed*, trans. B. Pearce (5 volumes, London, 1979–81), I, 309–10 (order published in *Izvestiia*, 11 August 1918).

[42] GARF, f. A-353, op. 2, d. 835, l. 97 (protocol of meeting, 8 August 1918).

[43] GARF, f. A-353, op. 3, d. 46, ll. 1–4 (various correspondence, November 1918–January 1919).

[44] Iu. Titov, *Razvitie sistemy sovetskikh revoliutsionnykh tribunalov* (Moscow, 1987), 59, 63.

[45] *DSV*, V, 12.

[46] Iu. Mezhin, 'Revoliutsionnyi sud na transporte', in *Piat' let Verkhovnogo suda*, no pag.

special legal organs were permitted to enforce martial law as it was extended across the railway network.[47] The decree on military tribunals on 20 November declared that tribunals responsible for railways had the right to sentence people for intentional destruction or damage to railway lines, bridges, and other edifices, including telegraph and telephone lines and stores of state property.[48] These tribunals either focused on particular railway lines or were based at strategic junctions, but they remained a branch of the military tribunal system. On 15 December, new railway tribunals were created in Moscow, Petrograd, Ruzaevka, and Gomel'. Apparently some existing military tribunals overseeing railways were simply renamed as railway tribunals at this point. These were to focus on railway personnel committing crimes rather than general crimes on the railway. It was also stated that, while railway tribunals remained within the military tribunal system, Narkomput could voice its views and observe investigations.[49] This new role explains why later accounts dated the birth of railway tribunals to December, as this provided the basis for their future independence.

This independence arrived on 18 March 1920. Railway tribunals were referenced repeatedly in a wide-ranging decree on tribunals before the first decree solely concerning them was published on the same day.[50] This brought railway tribunals out from under the military, with the creation of their own overseeing tribunal, the Main Revolutionary Military Railway Tribunal (chaired by Iu. Iu. Mezhin), appointed by and responsible to Narkomput.[51] Narkomput also now approved the chairmen and deputy chairmen of all railway tribunals, bringing another set of institutional concerns to bear on the tribunal system. Otherwise, the decree tasked railway tribunals with judging all crimes of railway personnel linked to the disruption of the railways or the normal passage of transport, damage to railway property, carelessness, and non-fulfilment of duties—essentially the majority of crimes. Sentences were not subject to cassation: railway tribunals were supervised by the Cassation Tribunal but, as with military tribunals, the initiative for cassation rested with the overseeing tribunal rather than the defendants as in civilian tribunals (see Chapter 5).

The March 1920 decree focused on railways, despite a few passing comments on transport as a whole, but at some stage that year the state realized that railways were not the only important means of transportation. Similar crimes were also

[47] V. Abramov, 'Formirovanie i deiatel'nost' revoliutsionnykh voennykh zheleznodorozhnykh tribunalov na territorii Penzenskoi gubernii na pervom etape svoego sushchestvovaniia (1920–1921 gg.)', in O. Petrunina (ed.), *XXI vek: itogi proshlogo i problemy nastoiashchego. Vyp. 4. Ch. 1* (Penza, 2003), 135.

[48] *DSV*, VI, 287.

[49] *Revvoensovet Respubliki. Protokoly. 1918–1919 gg.*, 532; Abramov, 'Formirovanie', 136.

[50] *IZ*, 126–36.

[51] Apparently, the Main Tribunal had existed unofficially since late February and had started organizing railway tribunals; GARF, f. R-1005, op. 2, d. 83, l. 88 (report on railway tribunals up to 1 July 1920, undated).

present on important water links, particularly along the Volga, and in the south around the Black and Caspian seas. One report noted that the establishment of martial law on the water network on 12 May brought it under the purview of railway tribunals, and by mid-1920 all water networks apart from those in Siberia were covered.[52] The two sets of tribunals—railway and water—later became officially known as revolutionary military tribunals of railway and water transport.

As railway tribunals were initially synonymous with military tribunals, it is difficult to trace their precise development and, as with other tribunals, numbers fluctuated as 'branches' came and went. They also faced the same practical problems; indeed, overcoming shortages in personnel was more problematic as ideally staff needed to be experienced in party, tribunal, and military work, while also having knowledge of railways. Other tribunals struggled to find people matching two of these criteria, so it is unsurprising that it was 'almost impossible' to find people who met all four. In the end, party work was prioritized.[53] Nonetheless, a report in mid-1920 listed twenty-four railway tribunals (including the Main Tribunal, four branches in smaller towns, four military tribunals with the powers of railway tribunals, and six water transport tribunals).[54] Another list in late July 1920 detailed thirty-four tribunals. Several had existed from December 1919, but the vast majority were formed after the March 1920 decree.[55] Other statistics suggest forty-three by May 1921, while an undated list from this period covered fifty tribunals, including eleven for water transport.[56] Either way, these numbers indicate that a further step had been taken in expanding the scope of tribunals, as they had now entered riverside towns and seaports as well as railway stations and junctions.

Travelling Sessions

The final step in extending the reach of tribunals came with the development of travelling sessions. The intensifying civil war in 1919 saw the Bolsheviks facing military threats from all directions by the middle of the year, and the resultant growth in mass crimes such as desertion or banditry saw more attention devoted to reaching the remoter parts of Russia. Civilian tribunals, for instance, were now restricted to major towns that could be many hundreds of miles away from the villages that harboured deserters, bandits, or those resisting food quotas. Transport tribunals faced the same problem and even though military tribunals were more flexible, moving with their divisions, they still found themselves miles

[52] GARF, f. R-1005, op. 2, d. 83, l. 88 (report on railway tribunals up to 1 July 1920, undated).
[53] GARF, f. R-1005, op. 2, d. 83, l. 88 ob (report on railway tribunals up to 1 July 1920, undated).
[54] GARF, f. R-1005, op. 2, d. 83, ll. 88–88ob (report on railway tribunals up to 1 July 1920, undated).
[55] GARF, f. R-3042, op. 1, d. 6, ll. 41–43ob (report, 24 July 1920).
[56] GARF, f. R-1005, op. 1, d. 57, ll. 2–3ob (list of tribunals, 15 May 1921), 87–8 (list, undated).

away from many crimes and criminals. As one report noted, speed was of the essence if a tribunal was to dispense effective justice; a desertion case, for instance, lost significance with each day that passed as the absence of severe retribution suggested to the perpetrator and those watching that the state was powerless to respond.[57] Commissions for desertion and food supply were granted legal powers to investigate and sentence crimes, even at *uezd* level, but their procedures, consistency, and effectiveness were doubted by justice officials who did not want to see their monopoly over sentencing eroded further.

All tribunals, therefore, started looking at ways of projecting their authority beyond their main base, and most decided to form temporary 'travelling sessions'.[58] These would see members of the tribunal's staff tour towns and villages, or areas where troops were stationed, or railways stations and ports, to investigate crimes, hold trials, and sentence perpetrators. Some tribunals, such as Nizhnii Novgorod, organized such sessions as early as autumn 1918, and these were sanctioned by the First Congress of Tribunal Officials in October–November.[59] Most, though, acted in 1919. The initiative came from below as decrees only mention sessions in passing; the January 1919 decree on military tribunals, for instance, permitted sessions if tribunals needed to visit the locations of crimes, while the April decree on all tribunals also acknowledged the possibility.[60] Yet the central authorities soon became more enthusiastic. By June, the Commissar of Justice, D. I. Kurskii, was suggesting weekly trips by sessions into *uezdy* and *volosti* to deal with deserters, while tribunals were being urged to use sessions to deal with desertion and food requisitioning violations a year later.[61]

Some sessions were little more than the provincial tribunal continuing or resurrecting former *uezd* tribunals as a 'branch' of the tribunal in one or two significant towns. They had permanent premises and staff.[62] Some provinces did something similar, but on a temporary basis: they sent out a group of people every few months to the same town to judge cases, but they would return afterwards. By

[57] GARF, f. R-1005, op. 1, d. 49, l. 72 (inspection report on the Urals regional military tribunal, 8 May 1921).

[58] The *vyezdnaia sessiia* of a tribunal. I have used 'travelling sessions' to convey how tribunals appointed several members to form a session of the court that travelled on a pre-planned route from place to place. No doubt some officials were influenced by similar trips made before 1917 to increase the scope, speed, and accessibility of the justice system; see E. Krestiannikov, 'Along the Routes of Justice: Judicial Circuit Riding in Western Siberia during the Late Imperial Period', *Kritika*, 20, 2 (2019), 315–44.

[59] O. Kostrova, 'Sudebnye preobrazovaniia v Rossii v 1917–1922 gg. (na primere Nizhegorodskoi gubernii) (*kandidat* dissertation, Moscow Humanitarian-Economics Institute—Nizhnii Novgorod Branch, 2008), 133–4; N. Krylenko, *Sudoustroistvo RSFSR* (Moscow, 1923), 316.

[60] RGVA, f. 33987, op. 2, d. 53, l. 135ob (14 February 1919); *DSV*, V, 12 (12 April 1920).

[61] A. Makutchev, '*Prigovor okonchatel'nyi, obzhalovaniiu ne podlezhit*... ' *Revoliutsionnye tribunaly v Sovetskoi Rossii v gody Grazhdanskoi voiny* (Moscow, 2012), 60; GARF, f. R-1005, op. 2, d. 1, l. 168aob (Narkomiust correspondence, 21 July 1920), 275, 284 (cassation tribunal correspondence, 16 December 1920).

[62] For example, the 'permanent' session underneath Petrograd's provincial tribunal in Kronstadt; GARF, f. R-1005, op. 1, d. 47, l. 46 (correspondence, mid-July 1921).

1921, for instance, there seemed to be a tribunal in Sarapul, not Izhevsk as originally decided, but counter-revolutionary crime had become so common in Izhevsk that Sarapul's officials felt forced to create a presence there. As the chairman noted, they wanted the time between committing the crime and being punished for it to be 'almost instant', and observing cases at the scene of the crime was the best solution.[63]

Most tribunals, however, established new itineraries for each session. They appointed a chairman, two additional judges, several administrative staff, and soldiers for security. The session stopped in various towns and villages to investigate cases, set up a court, dispense justice, and project the authority of their parent tribunal. Some of these trips lasted a week or two; others traversed large distances for several months. In April 1921, the travelling session of the railway tribunal based in Kiev embarked on an eleven-day trip, covering over 500 miles and five towns to the west and south-west of the city. They judged thirty-six cases, dismissing another eighteen before trial as unjustified. The crimes included stealing firewood earmarked for trains, oppositional agitation, mechanical sabotage, undermining discipline, desertion, speculation, illegal brewing, delaying trains without reason, horse theft, drunkenness, and forgery—a typical roster. The session punished ineffective and corrupt officials, and in doing so—it claimed—educated people and projected greater authority than local courts because it knew official policies and represented the highest legal organs.[64]

Sessions of military tribunals often served a more focused role, dispatched to areas of intense military action to punish 'panic', indiscipline, desertion, and ineffective leadership. Some actually found themselves involved in the fighting, and it was hoped that such sessions would not only punish instantly any crimes committed—thereby mitigating their negative impact on the fighting—but also prevent retreat and reinforce discipline through their physical presence. Sessions were also sent to investigate military defeats, seeking those responsible for the 'crimes' of retreat or the advance of the enemy. One chairman, who later recalled all these experiences, reprinted a mandate provided to one of his sessions: it outlined the session's composition, itinerary, objectives, and powers, ordering all soviets, party organs, and military authorities to assist it, and emphasized its right to use telegraphs and telephones.[65]

Other sessions performed a variety of roles. A session of Voronezh's tribunal spent 1–15 March 1919 dealing with an overcrowded prison in Pavlovskii *uezd*

[63] GARF, f. R-1005, op. 1, d. 40, l. 43ob (report from Sarapul tribunal, undated, early 1921).

[64] GARF, f. R-1005, op. 1, d. 116, ll. 90–2 (report by chairman of the South-Western Railway Tribunal in Kiev to the Main Railway Tribunal, 7 May 1921).

[65] A. Chuvatin, 'Pervye tribunaly' and 'Delo uchastnikov belogvardeiskogo desantnogo otriada', in *Voennye tribunaly—organy sotsialisticheskogo pravosudiia* (Moscow, 1958), 53–62, 242–6. These are memoirs from the Western and Caucasian Fronts in 1919–20. The mandate is reprinted on pp. 242–3.

where inmates had been waiting months for a trial.[66] On 14 May 1922, a session of the local transport tribunal left Nizhnii Novgorod for Astrakhan on a steamer. Its aim was not only to hold trials but to establish better relations with local authorities and inspect prisons to check they were meeting official regulations. The session spent four months on the Volga, visiting Vladimirovka, Tsaritsyn, Saratov, Samara, Simbirsk, and Kazan'. The report noted that 88 cases were judged (involving 404 people), several prisons visited, and meetings held with local justice officials, investigators, and other tribunals.[67]

Some tribunals managed, despite staff shortages, to send out several sessions simultaneously. Moscow's regional transport tribunal, for instance, sent out sessions on 14, 18, and 22 December with different chairmen and personnel, all of which took several weeks to complete. One went towards Kursk and then up to Viaz'ma. Another went on a circuit of Riazan', Ruzaevka, Syzran', Kuznetsk, Penza, and Morshansk. A final one went to Murom, Arzamask, Kazan', Nizhnii Novgorod, and Vladimir. Many of the crimes judged—from the patchy details available—appear typical, usually thefts from wagons and passengers, some of which involved forged documents.[68]

Sessions also varied widely in the scale of their operations. Some dealt with a single defendant over a matter of days, while others dealt with hundreds of individuals in a single day, even sentencing dozens in single trials. Sometimes this was a logical means of dealing with cases of mass desertion or village unrest, but just as often such trials encompassed numerous people accused of very different crimes. One trial in Mozhga (Viatka province), for instance, tried sixteen people over two days for a range of apparently unconnected crimes: a counter-revolutionary plot; banditry; desertion; speculation; dereliction of duty; drunkenness; gambling; and hiding deserters and bandits.[69] By contrast, the session of the military tribunal of the Northern Caucasus region lasted a week (23–9 July 1921), but only dealt with the crimes of a few senior military personnel.[70] Such trials, through their length and publicity, acted as 'model' trials locally, mirroring prominent national trials of obvious enemies. This was particularly true of the sessions organized by the Supreme Tribunal, which involved senior personnel and dealt with issues of national prominence.[71]

[66] V. Pertsev, '"Imenem revoliutsii!": Iz istorii sozdaniia i deiatel'nosti Voronezhskogo gubernskogo revoliutsionnogo tribunala v 1917-1923 gg.', *Vestnik Voronezhskogo gosudarstvennogo universiteta. Seriia: Istoriia, politologiia, sotsiologiia*, 1 (2008), 35.

[67] GARF, f. R-3042, op. 1, d. 96, ll. 59–67 (chairman's report, 12 September 1922). This was the tenth session organized by this tribunal and it was abnormally long. Others lasted no longer than a month and a half (l. 78).

[68] TsGAMO, f. 4762, op. 1, d. 1, ll. 69, 74, 79 (itineraries); op. 2, d. 1 (sentences).

[69] GARF, f. R-1005, op. 2, d. 104, l. 562 (trial transcript, 16–17 July 1921).

[70] *Znamia truda*, 2 August 1921, 2 (a copy is in GARF, f. R-1005, op. 1, d. 52, l. 122).

[71] For example, the session held in Ivanovo-Voznesensk on 21–5 April 1922 related to the ongoing investigations surrounding Patriarch Tikhon; GARF, f. R-1005, op. 1a, d. 377, ll. 94ob-96.

Taken together, these sessions became a very significant aspect of tribunals' activities. In January–March 1923, incomplete statistics indicate thirteen to eighteen sessions of military and transport tribunals in any one month, ranging from two days to over two months in duration, with an average of three to four weeks.[72] This was the case in 1921–2 as well. The military tribunal in Novorossiisk recorded twenty-eight sessions between September 1920 and July 1921, which dealt with an average of four cases each time, usually significant ones with 'large public-educational significance', while Tula's provincial tribunal organized over 350 sessions in 1918–21.[73] Cheliabinsk's military tribunal organized six in the first four months of 1921, which apparently formed most of its workload.[74] This was likely not the case everywhere. Most were probably closer to the experiences of the military tribunal of the Western Front, where sessions seem to have dealt with roughly 10 per cent of the cases of the parent tribunal.[75] But there is the sense that this commitment was increasing steadily in many places. The Perm' railway tribunal, for instance, noted that sessions were running for 12–14 days monthly prior to August 1922, but it expected this to increase. Sure enough, its next report in December recorded sessions lasting for 2–3 weeks each month.[76]

Sessions did face numerous problems.[77] Amid personnel shortages, it was difficult to find people to staff lengthy sessions. Trips cost money (also scarce), while transport over long distances was slow and problematic. Participants suffered illnesses and faced adverse weather, while sessions found themselves helping with local problems, from fighting and firefighting to solving murders. It was also dangerous work, particularly when dealing with desperate deserters and violent rural insurgencies.

Yet holding trials locally (often at the scene of the crime) not only allowed cases to be judged relatively quickly but also reached out to the intended audience: those who knew the criminal, knew a crime had been committed, were potential criminals, and those who were waiting to see what the state would or could do. Moreover, while most tribunals held public trials, a trial in a small town or village was very different from one in a large and busy city. Whereas tribunals in the latter complained that workers were not as interested as they hoped and that attendance was poor amid competing demands on workers' time, a village session became the centre of attention. Although trials were often rushed affairs, the sessions still brought some of the 'majesty of the law' to villages and were probably the most

[72] GARF, f. R-1005, op. 1, d. 62, ll. 102–4 (information gathered by the Supreme Court, 16 May 1923).

[73] GARF, f. R-1005, op. 1, d. 56, l. 148ob (report by chairman, 4 August 1921); Makutchev, *Prigovor*, 60.

[74] GARF, f. R-1005, op. 1, d. 49, ll. 67, 95ob (inspection, 11 and 30 May 1921).

[75] GARF, f. R-3042, op. 1, d. 77, ll. 9–11ob (various reports, March–June 1922).

[76] GARF, f. R-3042, op. 1, d. 84, ll. 19 (report, 5 August 1922), 33 (report, 1 December 1922).

[77] These were predictable given pre-1917 experiences of trips; Krestiannikov, 'Along the Routes of Justice'.

visible manifestation of state power seen by many for years. Their outsider status and focus on state concerns, alongside their willingness to take local officials to task, distinguished the sessions from other local state organs embedded in the locality. The novelty of the spectacle also constituted entertainment, and venues were often overflowing. Reports note that some trials were apparently seen by 5,000 people a day, with many coming and going.[78]

Lacking a permanent building, sessions took over various spaces. Some used 'official' spaces, usually a room in the building of the local authorities. Most, however, preferred 'unofficial' places, no doubt to challenge those in authority locally and also to bring the revolution closer to people's everyday lives. Many held meetings in the open air, with one describing judges sitting on tables as there were no chairs.[79] The railway tribunal in the Baikal region of Siberia used workshops and depots for meetings of its session.[80] The session at Perm' used third-class halls at stations, factories, local theatres, and even railway wagons, while the session travelling the Volga frequently used clubs for water-transport workers.[81] Another water-transport tribunal extolled the benefits of holding trials on the steamer itself; it was quick, avoided searching for a local building, and was close to where the target audience worked.[82] These places had meaning in people's everyday lives—where they lived, worked, and relaxed—thereby enhancing the visibility, accessibility, and impact of tribunals.

Tribunal officials were in no doubt about the effectiveness of travelling sessions. Time and again, they reported that bringing tribunals closer to the people was the most effective form of deterrence. The chairman of Orel's provincial tribunal declared that sentencing deserters locally in Livny, a small town to the south-east, had led directly to 3,000 more deserters voluntarily handing themselves in.[83] Others made similarly expansive claims. They were, in part, justifying their activities to the central authorities and claiming successes. But given that they frequently highlighted problems in other areas, and sessions involved expenses, hardships, and dangers that were surely unwelcome if not seen as valuable, it seems likely that most believed these sessions helped project tribunals and state authority.

Unifying the Tribunal System

It was clear, however, that the development of military and transport tribunals, as well as the growing prevalence of travelling sessions, departed significantly from

[78] GARF, f. R-3042, op. 1, d. 73 (report from Bugul'ma, 20 June 1920); d. 23, l. 37 (anon. report, early 1921).

[79] Petrov, 'Iz proshlogo', 42.

[80] GARF, f. R-1005, op. 1, d. 116, l. 216 (report, 12 July 1921).

[81] GARF, f. R-3042, op. 1, d. 84, ll. 8, 13, 16ob (reports from Perm', November 1920, 2 April 1921, and 13 March 1922); d. 96, ll. 59–67 (report from Volga tribunal, 12 September 1922).

[82] GARF, f. R-3042, op. 1, d. 95, l. 17 (report from the Baltic-Mariinskii tribunal, 3 December 1920).

[83] GARF, f. R-1005, op. 2, d. 54, l. 1 (report, 7 September 1920).

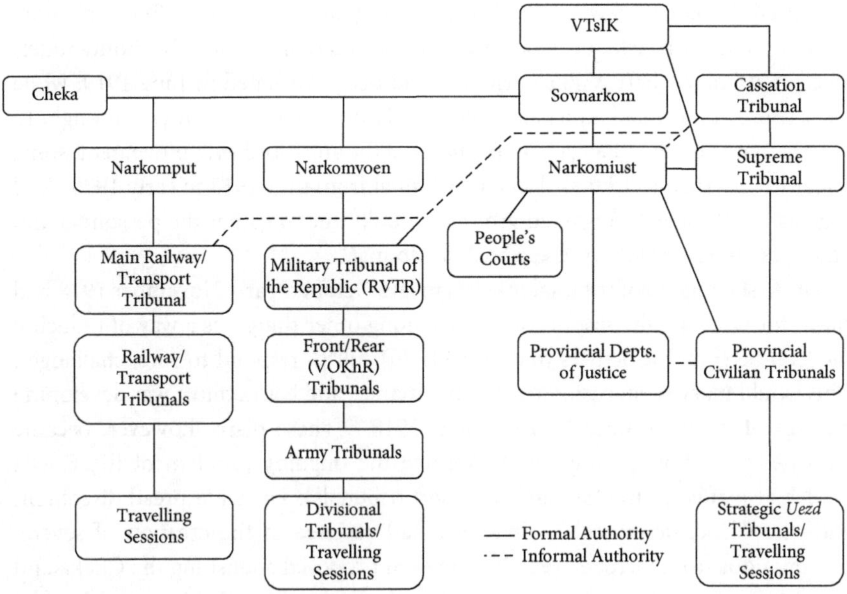

Figure 2.1 The tribunal system, 1919–June 1921.

the simple tribunals envisaged in November 1917 to a complex system of three parallel, largely independent, often overlapping and conflicting, elements (civilian, military, and transport), with numerous tribunals challenging attempts to foster consistency and uniformity (see Figure 2.1). Furthermore, more authorities were now involved alongside Narkomiust and local soviets, including Narkomvoen, Narkomput, military councils, and railway commissars. Given that issues of consistency and uniformity had been paramount at the end of 1918, it was hardly surprising that these concerns increased in parallel with this additional complexity.

At first, Narkomiust only had the authority to focus on civilian tribunals and these faced sufficient problems in 1919. Nominally, there should have been around fifty tribunals in European Russia—one per province and a few others in strategic and significant towns. The reality was different. On the one hand, Narkomiust was still arguing with some provinces over permitted *uezd* tribunals, such as Viatka, where the tribunal in Sarapul was still operating despite official condemnation.[84] There were still too many tribunals in these areas. On the other hand, heightened military conflict led to attacks on tribunals and to their staff being conscripted or evacuated. In some places tribunals ceased to function at times during 1919, as happened in Gomel', Novgorod, Orel, Orenburg, Perm', and

[84] GARF, f. R-1005, op. 2, d. 1, l. 39 (provincial tribunal to Narkomiust, April 1919); d. 4, ll. 55–55ob (Sarapul department of justice to Viatka provincial executive committee, March 1919).

Petrograd, to name a few.[85] Sometimes, Narkomiust struggled to find out information. It had to ask the Commissariat of Internal Affairs (Narkomvnudel) whether it knew where Vil'na's tribunal had been evacuated in June 1919, while Ufa's tribunal was finally tracked down to Balashov after it was initially thought to be in Samara and then Penza.[86] In the heart of the anti-Bolshevik movement, some major towns, such as Irkutsk, lacked a tribunal from mid-1918 to early 1920. And even as the Bolsheviks regained ground, it took time to gather the personnel and other resources needed to re-establish a tribunal.

The first congress of tribunal officials in late October–early November 1918 had called for reducing the size of tribunals, among other things, as a way of reducing the 'cumbersome' structures that made it difficult to respond to such challenges. This would make them easier to staff and finance, and Narkomiust was developing reforms along these lines by December 1918.[87] These plans, however, became entwined with further attempts to resolve the ongoing problem of the Cheka (which also affected military and transport tribunals). The widespread discontent with the Cheka described in Chapter 1 had resulted in the creation of several commissions from October 1918.[88] One even proposed abolishing the Cheka and transferring its powers to revamped tribunals, but nothing had been resolved by the turn of 1919.[89]

The clash of views at a party conference in Moscow on 30 January 1919 with over 300 delegates present clarified the position of both sides. For N. V. Krylenko—prosecutor, legal theorist, and author of Narkomiust's plans to reform tribunals—the Cheka did not operate under any kind of law, leading to numerous mistakes and abuses of power. Tribunals may be slower, but they conducted proper investigations. For F. E. Dzerzhinskii, head of the Cheka, the attacks on the Cheka were playing into the hands of the state's enemies. All state organs had their problems, but circumstances were against mass paperwork and endless procedures. The subsequent debate was divided, but speakers were clear that unity between the Cheka and tribunals was essential and that both required reform. The final resolution reaffirmed that, first, the Cheka should only act as an investigative organ and, second, tribunals enjoyed sentencing powers, but they

[85] See correspondence with Narkomiust; GARF, f. A-353, op. 3, d. 156, ll. 27–8 (Gomel'), 67 (Novgorod), 71 (Orenburg), 78–78ob (Orel), 86 (Perm'), 89 (Petrograd).

[86] GARF, f. R-393, op. 10, d. 110, l. 67 (Narkomiust to NKVD, 26 June 1919); f. A-353, op. 3, d. 14, l. 27 (correspondence between Narkomiust and Samara's provincial department of justice, April 1919).

[87] GARF, f. A-353, op. 2, d. 2, ll. 163–4 (protocols of Narkomiust college meetings, 11 and 13 December 1918). See also Titov, *Razvitie*, 18–25.

[88] Leggett, *Cheka*, 128–46; D. Novoselov, 'Krizis VChK v kontse 1918-nachale 1919 godov', *Otechestvennaia istoriia*, 6 (2005), 66–77.

[89] D. Novoselov, '"Pristupit' nemedlenno k likvidatsii VChK..." Proekt L. B. Kameneva o reformirovanii VChK i sistemy revtribunalov', *Voenno-istoricheskii zhurnal*, 12 (2006), 51–5; D. Novoselov, 'Nesostoiavshaiasia reforma: proekt L'va Kameneva o reformirovanii VChK i sistemy revtribunalov', *Voenno-istoricheskii arkhiv*, 3 (2010), 29–43.

must reduce formalities and increase speed.[90] A leading article on the debate in *Izvestiia* agreed, adding that, while tribunals were political courts, their sentences remained too lenient and failed to correspond to the political threat.[91]

A final commission created by the party's central committee led to a decree on 17 February, which ordered the Cheka to relinquish all powers of sentencing to 'restructured' tribunals, and it retained the right to enact 'immediate reprisals' to curb revolts by bandits and counter-revolutionaries and in areas under martial law. A restructured tribunal consisted of three people, towns of over 200,000 inhabitants (as well as provincial capitals) could establish a city tribunal as well as a provincial one, and tribunals could decide whether witnesses or lawyers were needed. Tribunals could inspect Cheka investigations and visit prisons to check on the condition of prisoners.[92] In a speech on the same day, Dzerzhinskii supported these reforms, arguing that reducing the size of tribunals ended unnecessary formalities and created a more decisive organ.[93] These reforms were confirmed in a longer decree on tribunals published on 12 April 1919.[94]

These changes were significant for civilian tribunals. It had not only been difficult to find seven suitable individuals but, as one local official highlighted, it was then difficult to get them all in the same place at the same time, as most held other posts.[95] Civilian tribunals were now brought in line with military and transport tribunals, increasing consistency across the system. It must have also speeded up trials, reducing the discussion, as did the new powers to dispense with lawyers and witnesses, usually utilized for routine cases (see Chapter 4). The April decree also saw the cassation department renamed as a tribunal. Although ostensibly designed to adjudicate on procedural complaints, Narkomiust had realized that cassation was not only a means to remind tribunals about procedure (enhancing uniformity), but its ability to declare sentences void required it to investigate tribunal activities, providing justification for central interference. Thus, the Cassation Tribunal may not have been empowered officially to instruct on procedure until 18 March 1920, but it had long become the primary means by which the central authorities exerted control over local tribunals (see Chapter 5).

These reforms, though, did not end the conflict with the Cheka. The abolition of *uezd* branches of the Cheka, often the perpetrators of the worst atrocities, in January 1919 represented a worthwhile gain, but the Cheka retained the right to conduct 'immediate reprisals' against revolts by bandits and 'counter-

[90] 'Iz istorii vzaimootnoshenii chrezvychainykh komissii i revoliutsionnykh tribunalov', *Voprosy istorii*, 7 (1990), 155–63.

[91] G. Damberg, 'K reorganizatsii Revoliutsionnykh tribunalov i Chrezv. komissii', *Izvestiia*, 31 January 1919, 1.

[92] *DSV*, IV, 400–2.

[93] 'F. E. Dzerzhinskii o revoliutsionnoi zakonnosti', *Istoricheskii arkhiv*, 1 (1958), 10–11.

[94] *DSV*, V, 11–17.

[95] GARF, f. R-1005, op. 2, d. 95, ll. 82–82ob (Vitebsk's commissar of justice to Narkomiust, 18 November 1918).

revolutionaries'. It was also permitted greater powers in areas under martial law—large swathes of Russia during the civil war. In these areas, the Cheka could act against counter-revolutionary organizations and activities (not just revolts): treachery; espionage; those concealing arms, conducting arson, and harming communication, infrastructure, and supplies; banditry (including murder, robbery and theft, breaking into supply depots and shops); and others.[96] Essentially, it had a free rein to act as before.

Moreover, the Cheka was permitted to create its own 'special revolutionary tribunal' on 21 October 1919 to sentence large-scale speculation by officials, including embezzlement, bribery, and forgery. Meetings were supposedly public, but this tribunal was not restricted by any kind of legal processes or subject to cassation.[97] It lasted until 18 March 1920, when it was abolished as part of a broader decree on tribunals. Even then, the Cheka could still form special military tribunals (with two Cheka representatives and one from the local military authorities) in areas that lacked a VOKhR tribunal.[98]

Other organs also seized sentencing powers from tribunals. On 13 December 1919, all provincial commissions for the struggle with desertion were temporarily granted the rights of tribunals and able to sentence deserters as long as a representative of the provincial tribunal was present. Similarly, *uezd* commissions were permitted to dispense sentences to deserters, which were subject to appeal to the provincial commission.[99] Justice officials made concerted attempts to restrict the sentences that commissions could dispense to fines and have them transfer serious cases to tribunals, and their powers were restricted and largely transferred on 8 April 1920.[100] Nevertheless, commissions sentenced thousands of deserters, provoking the ire of tribunals with their inconsistency, while the transfer of their cases back to tribunals in 1920 overloaded many civilian tribunals.[101]

It is hardly surprising, therefore, that the search for greater effectiveness continued with a further decree on tribunals on 18 March 1920 that focused again on the same two issues—the Cheka and uniformity.[102] On the first issue, a Cheka representative was now to be present in every civilian, military, and transport tribunal (including the Supreme Tribunal) to forge closer links

[96] *IZ*, 88–9 (20 June 1919).

[97] *DSV*, VI, 216–18. The first meeting was on 14 November, chaired by Dzerzhinskii; Leggett, *Cheka*, 216.

[98] *Vnutrennie voiska*, 164 (order from the presidium of the Cheka, 17 March 1920).

[99] *IZ*, 119.

[100] GARF, f. R-1005, op. 2, d. 1, l. 52ob (minutes of the college of Narkomiust, 25 February 1920); *IZ*, 136–7.

[101] The chairman of Orel's tribunal complained that the cases inherited from the provincial commission revealed numerous illegalities, from incomplete transcripts and illegal sentences to evidence that cases had been resolved out of court or the chair had acted as the prosecutor; GARF, f. R-1005, op. 2, d. 54, l. 1ob (7 September 1920).

[102] *IZ*, 126–33. It was published in *Izvestiia* on 27 March 1920, and contemporaries usually refer to this date.

(Narkomiust failed to obtain reciprocal rights for its own representatives to participate in Cheka meetings).[103] Instructions signed by Dzerzhinskii and Krylenko were sent to all Cheka branches ordering them to select representatives, prevent 'antagonism', and create a 'united organ' of struggle, while urging them to follow the 'spirit (*po dukhu*)' of the law. The instructions recognized that constant, severe repression was not as effective as altering the level of repression to match the severity of the crime—the 'epoch' of Red Terror, the authors noted, was over.[104] In short, this was the most determined attempt yet to regulate the relationship between revolutionary justice and revolutionary violence.

On the second issue of uniformity, the Cassation Tribunal was given the authority to approve the appointment of tribunal chairmen, reducing local influence over personnel, while all three types of tribunal were subject to the same cassation process and had to send their sentences to the Cassation Tribunal, which now included a representative from the RVTR. This enabled intervention in the case of anomalies and the nature of cassation—assessing whether correct procedure had been followed—empowered the Cassation Tribunal to examine all aspects of a tribunal, including composition, administrative structure, investigations, trials, and sentences. All this marked a sizable step forward in the exertion of central control and mirrored developments across the state apparatus as a whole.

Yet the obvious next step—the unification of the three types of tribunals—had not been taken, no doubt because those commissariats that stood to lose the most, Narkomvoen and Narkomput, were keen to retain their authority and felt that Narkomiust did not understand the problems facing their particular areas. Nevertheless, continued pressure on tribunals from outside to maximize their effectiveness, combined with the evolving nature of the civil war, brought unity on to the agenda in 1921. By this stage, the military conflict with external enemies was receding and the focus was turning to rising levels of internal dissent, especially the widespread unrest in the countryside impacting on food quotas and seen as fuelling urban strikes and even underpinning the high-profile revolt of the sailors in Kronstadt. To combat this, the party congress in March launched the NEP, which introduced a fixed tax in kind on agricultural produce, encouraging peasants to sell any surplus for profit and fostering small-scale trade with the aim of reviving the economy. Although not immediate, this shift had a significant impact on tribunals. It was not quite the shift from 'war to peace' that one report noted optimistically, no doubt echoing official proclamations, but tribunals changed 'sharply' from focusing primarily on military discipline and desertion to enforcing the new tax, protecting property and raw materials, and targeting inefficiency and corruption—or, in the Cassation Tribunal's words, from the military front to the

[103] GARF, f. R-1005, op. 2, d. 1, l. 52 (minutes of the college of Narkomiust, 25 February 1920).

[104] GARF, f. R-1005, op. 1, d. 76, ll. 361–62ob (17 April 1920). This has been published in *F. E. Dzerzhinskii—predsedatel' VChK-OGPU. 1917–1926* (Moscow, 2007), 176–81.

'economic' front.[105] To be sure, tribunals had been focusing on these crimes for some time, while issues of desertion and military discipline did not disappear, but the need in particular to secure food supplies as famine spread across huge swathes of the country became the primary focus of tribunals.

With the military threat receding, there seemed little sense in cities hosting more than one tribunal, particularly given the struggle for resources. By May 1921, for instance, four tribunals operated out of Omsk: a civilian tribunal; a military tribunal covering Siberia; a branch of the military tribunal responsible for the Omsk region; and a tribunal for Siberia's railways.[106] Omsk was far from unique and these tribunals operated independently of each other, despite now dealing with similar crimes. Therefore, somewhat inevitably, a decree on 23 June 1921 unified all tribunals.[107] It created a single Supreme Tribunal under the All-Russian Central Executive Committee of the Congress of Soviets (VTsIK) with four colleges: cassation, legal, military, and military transport. The last two would replace the RVTR and Main Railway Tribunal respectively. There would be branches of the Supreme Tribunal in federal republics and autonomous regions. VTsIK controlled staffing, although Narkomvoen and Narkomput would have representatives in their respective colleges; indeed, the chairmen of the RVTR (Ul'rikh) and the Main Railway Tribunal (Mezhin) transferred to head their colleges.[108] Military tribunals would be abolished where military activities had ceased if local conditions were acceptable, and civilian tribunals would establish a department to oversee military crimes with military representatives. Military tribunals could be created to deal with specific cases of banditry or counter-revolutionary revolts. Transport tribunals were restricted to one per railway and water region, with the decree finally abandoning the term 'railway tribunals' in favour of 'military transport tribunals'.

This decree took time to filter down to the provinces, with some places not hearing about it until August and taking another month or two to implement the changes.[109] Some regional branches of the Supreme Tribunal were not active until well into 1922.[110] There were also opponents within the military who still distrusted civilian tribunals. Yet military tribunals did disappear from all but the

[105] GARF, f. R-1005, op. 3, d. 84, ll. 30–30ob (inspection, Tatar tribunal, autumn 1921); op. 2, d. 75, ll. 221–21ob (cassation tribunal to the party's central committee, March 1921).

[106] GARF, f. R-1005, op. 1, d. 49, ll. 129–30ob (inspection, 13 May 1921).

[107] *DSV*, XVI, 145–53. These proposals had been under discussion since 28 March 1921.

[108] *DSV*, XVII, 316.

[109] GARF, f. R-1005, op. 3, d. 46, l. 47 (report, Samara, 12 November 1921); d. 227, l. 11ob (report, Kalmytskii republic, 22 August 1921); d. 118, l. 70 (report, Viatka, October 1922).

[110] O. P'ianova, 'Revoliutsionnye tribunaly Zapadnoi Sibiri (konets 1917 – nachalo 1923 gg.)' (*kandidat* dissertation, Omsk State Pedagogical University, 2002), 172–86; T. Sudakova, 'Sozdanie i deiatel'nost' Otdeleniia Verkhovnogo tribunala VTsIK v Gorskoi ASSR (1921–1923 gg.): Istoricheskii aspekt' (*kandidat* dissertation, North Ossetian State University, 2009), 68–80.

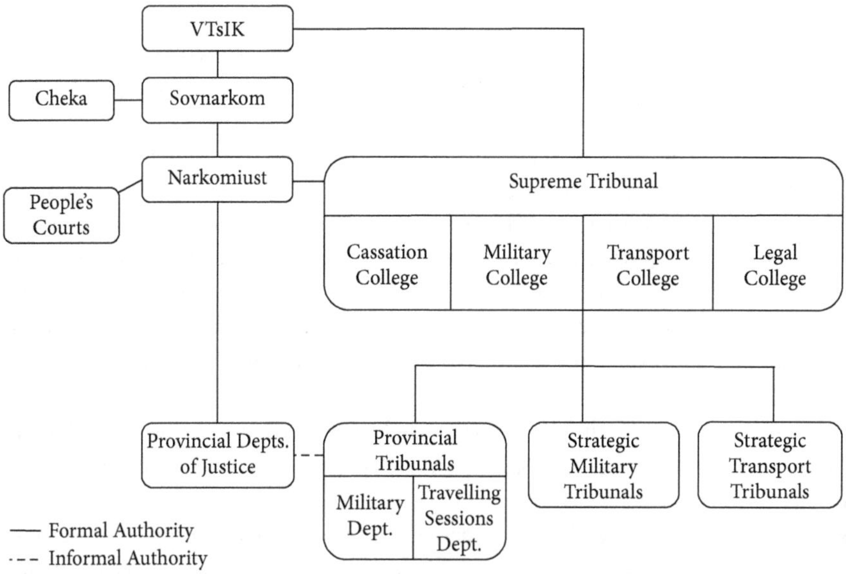

Figure 2.2 The tribunal system, June 1921–1922.

major fronts, with Ul'rikh noting that only four remained.[111] The number of transport tribunals also fell, with one report noting a decline to twenty-four in the first half of 1922 and another citing only nineteen after June 1921.[112] By late 1921, most provinces had a tribunal organized into four main departments: investigative or general; military; tax or food supplies; and travelling sessions.[113] As one contemporary noted, the decree heralded a new epoch with a unified and centrally controlled tribunal system (Figure 2.2).[114]

Inspecting Tribunals

Narkomiust was aware, however, that its attempts to foster uniformity and consistency—whether issuing decrees, streamlining tribunals and procedures, or interfering in sentencing through cassation—were rarely completely successful. Some problems caused by the civil war were unavoidable; some, like the Cheka,

[111] V. Ul'rikh, 'Voennye tribunaly', *Rabochii sud*, 21 (1927), 1658; Ul'rikh, 'Voennye tribunaly', in *Piat' let*.

[112] GARF, f. R-3042, op. 1, d. 38, l. 2 (25 November 1922); *ESIu*, 39–40, 27 October–4 November 1922, 36–7.

[113] See the instructions from June to July (*DSV*, XVI, 385–7; GARF, f. R-1005, op. 1, d. 1, l. 4). There were inevitable anomalies. Kursk's tribunal included a department for railways as well as the others (op. 3, d. 136, l. 96).

[114] Ia. Berman, *Ocherki po istorii sudoustroistva RSFSR* (Moscow, 1924), 31–2.

beyond the scope of individual tribunals. Others, though, remained stubbornly persistent, from officials defending local concerns against national interests to simple ignorance on the part of officials. Narkomiust's means of finding out about these anomalies were initially not particularly reliable. All tribunals were required to submit regular reports, but these were a carefully managed portrayal of a tribunal's activities; they highlighted challenges but underplayed the extent to which tribunals deviated from decrees or faced problems of their own making. Authors viewed reports as an opportunity to press for action from Narkomiust, and there was little way of assessing whether tribunals had responded to Narkomiust's own suggestions. Cassation enabled forceful intervention, but only after the fact and usually in relation to specific cases rather than addressing any bigger issues.

Therefore, the Cassation Tribunal started organizing inspections of tribunals from late 1919. A typical tour saw an inspector visit military tribunals in Viatka, Perm', Ekaterinburg, Cheliabinsk, Ufa, Samara, and Saratov.[115] These inspections were rarely lengthy, often lasting a matter of hours and seldom more than a day, and they focused on procedural issues. Thus inspectors commented on a tribunal's structure, staffing (quantity and quality), record-keeping, investigative procedures, finances, agitational activities, and adherence to central decrees rather than examining investigations, trials, or cases. They then produced reports with instructions on remedying any problems. Similar terminology was used, partly because there were relatively few inspectors. Tribunals functioned 'correctly (*pravil'no*)', 'thoroughly (*akkuratno*)', or 'satisfactorily (*udovletvoritel'no*)' if they followed regulations. If not, there were 'deficiencies (*nedostatki*)' or 'defects (*defekty*)', and 'instructions (*ukazaniia*)' were provided to rectify these problems.

Few tribunals escaped criticism. Inspectors probably felt obliged to raise something to emphasize their own value. But inspections did detail strengths and weaknesses as set against the state's priorities and expectations. This information was unique to a certain extent, reflecting the author's priorities and that particular moment in time. The fluctuating conflict meant that tribunals could be functioning smoothly one month only to face insurmountable problems the next. Taken together, however, core issues emerged that affected all tribunals, constant across the civil war and the country, although worse nearer the fighting.

Every inspection focused on personnel. At one level, there was the *quantity* of people available, from an extreme in Omsk in 1921, where the railway tribunal turned out to lack any staff and exist only on paper, to most other tribunals, which were short-staffed on investigative or administrative personnel, either because of a shortage of qualified people, conscription, or other demands.[116] Some tribunals

[115] GARF, f. R-1005, op. 1, d. 49 (various reports, April–May 1921).
[116] GARF, f. R-1005, op. 1, d. 49, ll. 129–30ob (13 May 1921).

had less than half of their required workforce at times.[117] At another level, there was the *quality* of personnel. All central authorities believed that the correct person in a post could solve any problem and there was constant concern over this area.[118] Inspectors sometimes condemned the lack of judicial education,[119] but usually focused on inexperienced leadership, non-party backgrounds, or poor character. An inspection of Siberia's railway tribunals concluded that Baikal's tribunal was 'weak', as officials waited for cases to come to them, rather than proactively investigating crimes, and were 'weak', 'spineless', and 'inactive'; the same was true to a lesser extent in Tomsk, where officials lacked 'initiative' and were insufficiently politically literate; and, finally, the chairman of Omsk's tribunal was 'impressionistic', with a criminal past, and should be prosecuted for his inactivity.[120] As one military tribunal chairman noted, a sufficient quantity of 'energetic' and 'conscientious' party workers was the main requirement for a successful tribunal.[121]

Tribunals themselves were keen to emphasize that this was part of a broader struggle for resources, especially financial. The tribunal in Vladikavkaz, for instance, lacked 'political' and 'technical' workers. Staff held multiple official posts in the local administration due to personnel shortages and they lacked time for tribunal work, and often knowledge of laws and regulations. Vladikavkaz noted various reasons for its problems, including its distance from Moscow, the resultant lack of instructions, the tribal and 'dark' population, local nationalist and separatist tendencies, and the prominence of sharia law. Primarily, though, its problems were financial, as the local department of justice failed to provide sufficient funds.[122] Other tribunals reported they lacked money for wages, transport, building repairs, telephones, and even paper and pens. One tribunal was forced to acquire land to grow food to eat.[123] All this was exacerbated by excessive workloads and tribunals complained repeatedly about too many cases. In June 1921, for example, the military tribunal in Tambov reported that liquidating a revolt had created a 'colossal' number of cases. Staff worked every evening and investigators worked ten-hour days. On top of this, there were plans to transfer 3,000 further cases from the provincial committee on desertion that had 'chaotic' and 'incomplete' records, and that had been left so long they had almost lost significance. In short, the tribunal could not cope.[124]

[117] For example, GARF, f. R-1005, op. 3, d. 108, l. 9 (Vitebsk, 35% of workforce, January 1922); d. 118, l. 10 (Viatka, 48% of workforce, 31 January 1922); d. 196, l. 18ob (Tiumen', 31% of workforce, 7 November 1922).

[118] Some inspections focused exclusively on the background of personnel; for example, GARF, f. R-1005, op. 1, d. 49, ll. 46–46ob (Western Front, 1 April 1921), 66–67ob (Urals, 30 May 1921).

[119] GARF, f. R-1005, op. 3, d. 37, l. 54 (Penza, 16 August 1920); d. 224, l. 16 (Bashkiria, mid-1922).

[120] GARF, f. R-1005, op. 1, d. 116, ll. 216–19 (12 July 1921).

[121] GARF, f. R-1005, op. 1, d. 52, l. 61 (report from 16th Cavalry Division, North Caucasus, 12 August 1921).

[122] GARF, f. R-1005, op. 3, d. 233, ll. 68–70ob (report, 30 August 1922).

[123] GARF, f. R-1005, op. 1, d. 56, l. 148a (report from Black Sea military tribunal, 12 August 1920).

[124] GARF, f. R-1005, op. 1, d. 51, l. 63 (letter from tribunal, 12 June 1921).

Inspectors were sympathetic to personnel shortages, huge workloads, and calls for more funding, but their reports reveal deep concerns about the quality of the work conducted, particularly shortcomings in investigations. From compiling evidence to processing cases, inspectors were rarely satisfied. Ufa's military tribunal was unusual in the level of criticism it received in 1921. With over a hundred unresolved cases, the inspection claimed this was the worst in the region, possibly the country, with double the average. Non-party investigators, including former officials from Kolchak's regime, had failed to grasp the scale of the problem and there was indiscipline. The inspector advised removing these officials within twenty-four hours and disciplining staff. The inspector did recognize that the general work of the tribunal was 'satisfactory' and accepted the difficulties of finding investigators in Ufa who were party members. The fundamental problem in Ufa, the inspector concluded, was that the military tribunal should not be dealing with most of the unresolved cases: civilian counter-revolutionary cases should go to the civilian tribunal; petty thievery among soldiers to regimental courts; and petty civilian thievery to people's courts.[125] Tribunals had been criticized from the start for not focusing solely on 'counter-revolutionary' crimes and becoming bogged down with petty crimes, and this problem clearly persisted. Too many civilian cases in military tribunals, in particular, meant the tribunal lost its character as an organ for *military* justice.

Inspectors were also critical of poor record-keeping, most commonly incomplete case files, not least because they relied on such records for their inspections. Sometimes it was a matter of failing to note the beginning and end dates of the investigation, or even to sign and date documents. Unsigned documents, as the Cassation Tribunal pointed out to Moscow's tribunal, lacked legal force and enabled a successful appeal under cassation.[126] Inspectors constantly provided guidance on what papers should be included and their format. There was often no inventory of files or disordered files. Most tribunals had their archives criticized; those in Ekaterinburg's military tribunal, for instance, were described as 'slovenly', and this was common.[127] One chairman was criticized for putting case files in his pocket, forgetting about them, and only passing them on several months later.[128]

It is difficult to assess the impact of inspectors. Their reports certainly provided the central authorities with another valuable source of information, distinct from tribunals' own reports or cassation appeals, and distinct in their approach, measuring tribunals against the ideal model laid out in decrees. Inspectors were also diligent in recommending improvements and some tribunals at least were assessed on their response. Yet, ultimately, the same problems persisted; the

[125] GARF, f. R-1005, op. 1, d. 49, l. 107–07ob (15 May 1921).
[126] GARF, f. R-1005, op. 2, d. 50, l. 24 (correspondence, 16 March 1920).
[127] GARF, f. R-1005, op. 1, d. 49, l. 73ob (6–7 May 1921).
[128] RGASPI, f. 17, op. 109, d. 201, l. 1ob (inspection, military tribunal in 8th Army, August 1919).

reduction in military conflict alleviated some problems, especially finance, but caseloads (and the associated challenges) remained high as the focus shifted from desertion and revolts to corruption and economic crimes.

From Revolutionary Consciousness to Revolutionary Legality

Any further responses to these ongoing problems, however, became subsumed within a wider debate over the role of revolutionary justice as the nature of the civil war changed. This debate was significantly different from one that had plagued tribunals in 1917–18. For a start, there were signs that the compromise hammered out with the Cheka in March 1920 was achieving results. To be sure, there were still complaints. The chair of Tambov's provincial tribunal, for example, claimed the decree had brought 'huge relief and satisfaction' to 'the hearts of tribunal workers'. Tribunals had a lawful place in the revolution and, in turn, provided law and order to the revolution. But, he despaired, nothing had changed. The Cheka continued to act autonomously and secretly to investigate and sentence all types of criminals, and to maintain its own separate prison system.[129] Others complained that local branches of the Cheka failed to send representatives to tribunals, rendering tribunals illegal as they then failed to meet regulations.[130] Yet the complaints were slowly matched by more positive reports. In Omsk, the provincial tribunal included a Cheka representative who attended all its meetings, while the tribunal's chairman was also the deputy chairman of the local Cheka. This forged 'firm' links between the two in the city.[131] Many others reported at least one Cheka representative in their meetings and noted improved cooperation and reduced conflict. Equally, a questionnaire circulated to local Cheka branches in June 1920 elicited an overwhelmingly positive response to the question on relations with tribunals; most reported 'normal' or 'satisfactory' relations, with a couple noting 'better' relations than before.[132]

Instead, tribunals found themselves facing the same accusations from local organs that they had levelled against the Cheka. All provincial executive committees, departments of justice, and local party cells were struggling for a share of scarce personnel, finances, and material resources. Executive committees and military councils, influenced by party officials, directed the staffing of tribunals (even if this power had been diluted) and their finances. Consequently, many committees and councils felt they had the right to interfere in the activities of

[129] GARF, f. R-1005, op. 2, d. 60, ll. 8–10ob (report, September 1920).

[130] For example, see the complaint from the chairman of Altai provincial tribunal, '*Rukovodstvuias' revoliutsionnoi sovest'iu…' Sbornik dokumentov po istorii Altaiskoi gubChK 1919–1922* (Barnaul, 2006), 30–1.

[131] GARF, f. R-1005, op. 1, d. 49, l. 129 (report on Omsk's tribunals, 13 May 1921).

[132] GARF, f. R-1005, op. 2, d. 20, ll. 238–38ob (23 June 1920).

tribunals, particularly if their own staff were accused, as increasingly occurred once tribunals prioritized prosecuting corruption. Such conflicts became particularly sensitive when involving party members. On the one hand, members were not immune from prosecution, although tribunals had to follow stricter procedures, informing local party organs within a day when members were arrested and providing details. On the other, senior tribunal officials were all members, ensuring a degree of party influence within tribunals. Tribunals, therefore, operated amid a minefield of local power struggles. This was particularly true of military and transport tribunals, which were independent of local civilian organs but established in areas where the fighting and pressure on resources were more intense, and they struggled to integrate into local civilian power structures.[133]

The chairman of the military tribunal in Sarapul described a fairly typical scenario. Created in May 1920 as a branch of the military tribunal in Viatka, it acted—in his words—as a military, railway, and civilian tribunal rolled into one. It had 'strained' relations with the existing authorities from the start, as they refused assistance in finding premises, equipment, and arranging lighting, among other issues. The tribunal managed to establish itself and slowly convinced the *uezd* authorities to value it as a revolutionary organ by attacking local crimes. But the tribunal then targeted drunkenness among several *uezd* officials, which led the *uezd* executive committee to accuse it of interference, agitate against it, and discredit its workers. There was no foundation to any of these accusations apparently, but the dispute reached up to the central authorities in Moscow.[134]

A serious conflict, such as that in Voronezh in 1919, could paralyse a tribunal. In this case, the civilian tribunal had already investigated the actions of the provincial executive committee, various food supply committees, the housing department, the militia, and other bodies during 1918–19, before accusing the leader of the provincial committee of the party of exceeding his authority. This may have been the final straw, as the local organs clearly resented the imprisonment of much-needed staff for what they saw as petty cases of corruption. In any case, it prompted a wholesale attack by Voronezh party officials: tribunal officials were 'counter-revolutionaries' who had exceeded their authority and they were excluded from the party. Attempts were made to remove them from the civilian tribunal and prosecute them in a military tribunal. By late August, the tribunal was inactive; its members expected arrest at any minute and requested central support. The Cassation Tribunal contacted the party's central committee, asking for 'urgent' measures to resolve the conflict, defending the tribunal, and condemning party interference, while highlighting legal pathways for complaints. The order

[133] On civil–military conflict, see Abramov, 'Sozdanie', 209–16; P. Fedorenko, 'Revoliutsionnye tribunaly Smolenskoi gubernii (dekabr' 1917–1922 gg.)' (*kandidat* dissertation, Smolensk State University, 2006), 160–72; Makutchev, *Prigovor okonchatel'nyi*, 65–74; and V. Portnov and M. Slavin, *Stanovlenie pravosudiia Sovetskoi Rossii (1917–1922 gg.)* (Moscow, 1990), 129.

[134] GARF, f. R-1005, op. 1, d. 40, ll. 43–44ob (report from Sarapul, undated, early 1921).

dismissing tribunal workers was a 'criminal' abuse of their powers by local party officials: it weakened the tribunal—a 'military organ'—during a period of acute military danger. Despite several attempts to resolve the conflict, the central committee finally agreed to stop targeting tribunal staff only if cases were dropped against its own officials.[135]

Some of these conflicts involved clearly illegal actions on the part of other organs and reflected tribunal (and state) concerns to use revolutionary justice to exercise control over the state apparatus. Other instances, though, reflected local authorities wishing to have a say in a powerful organ they appointed and funded, and held some powers over, such as confirming death sentences. Moreover, as Tula's committee pointed out, if tribunals were not responsible to executive committees through local departments of justice, they could only be responsible to their own revolutionary consciousness, official decrees, and the Cassation Tribunal—the implication being that, like the Cheka, none of this was 'democratic'.[136] Indeed, one *uezd* executive committee argued that the local tribunal 'terrorizes not only the population, but also soviet institutions'—language not dissimilar to that used against the Cheka.[137]

In response, tribunals—ironically also using the same language as the Cheka used to respond to criticism—saw themselves as distinct from other local organs of power. As the cassation authorities explained to Tambov's provincial tribunal after a query in late 1918 about whether the tribunal was independent or subordinate to the local department of justice, the tribunal was a 'special organ' to combat counter-revolution. It acted independently and was subordinate only economically to the department, which had the right to supervise it and complain about it, but not to issue orders or to interfere.[138] Party organs had the same rights for those cases that involved their members; they could receive information and act as defence counsels, but not interfere.[139] For individual tribunals, local organs provided inadequate funding and support anyway, while the Cassation Tribunal was responsible to the same 'democratic' VTsIK as the executive committees.

These conflicts reached new levels by 1920, and two congresses laid out opposing viewpoints. The Second Congress of Tribunal Officials on 26–8 April 1920 was dominated by debates over how to maintain the independence and authority of tribunals: first, from interference from executive committees (particularly over personnel); second, from interference from local departments of justice despite their role as financiers (over personnel, again, as well as broader activities); and, third, defending them against the Cheka (debates reiterated

[135] GARF, f. R-1005, d. 3, ll. 91–91ob (correspondence, 16 May and 25 July 1919); op. 2, d. 27, ll. 3–6ob, 9, 14–15, 26, 31 (correspondence, August–September 1919).

[136] GARF, f. A-353, op. 2, d. 78b, ll. 114, 116 (letters to Narkomiust, 30 May and 28 June 1919).

[137] GARF, f. R-3042, op. 1, d. 73, l. 5 (Bugul'minskii *uezd* committee, undated, 1920).

[138] GARF, f. R-1005, op. 2, d. 17, ll. 8–9 (9 January 1919).

[139] GARF, f. R-1005, op. 2, d. 81, ll. 121–3 (report produced by the RVTR, January 1921).

complaints and points made in the first congress in 1918). In the end, however, the congress could only urge the wider publication of regulations on the rights of tribunals vis-à-vis local organs, and suggest using the new links with the Cheka as a means of influencing the Cheka and exerting tribunal authority.[140]

The second and more important forum was the Third All-Russian Congress of Justice Officials on 25–9 June. Here, on 28 June, Krylenko led a debate on the relationship between Narkomiust and tribunals, and between tribunals and the Cheka.[141] He defended tribunals as legal organs and argued against any kind of interference from local departments of justice. The Cassation Tribunal supervised tribunals, and any authority given to local organs represented the decentralization of power and threatened to make local departments a law unto themselves. Departments could only observe the finances of tribunals, their statistics, and questions surrounding amnesties. Krylenko then restated existing arguments concerning tribunals' rights regarding the Cheka. Few objected to Krylenko's attacks on the Cheka, but his trenchant defence of the autonomy of tribunals prompted a vigorous response. His opponents argued that departments of justice were part of the local soviet, the supreme local authority, and that they should enjoy rights over tribunals and receive weekly reports on their activities. Krylenko lost the argument, but the congress lacked authority and could only push for the rights of departments and resolve that the conflict harmed the impact of revolutionary justice.[142]

The onset of the NEP reinvigorated the debate, however, with some justice officials at the highest levels, including the Commissar of Justice, Kurskii, feeling that the NEP and the reduction of military operations offered an opportunity to move beyond exceptional forms of repression and normalize Soviet justice.[143] The very existence of tribunals was now under threat. Provincial congresses of justice officials in Moscow and Penza in mid-January 1922, for example, renewed criticisms of tribunals and called for greater restrictions on their activities. Participants also asked whether conditions were now favourable to unifying the two parallel strands of the legal system—people's courts and tribunals.[144]

This debate dominated the Fourth All-Russian Congress of Justice Officials on 26–30 January 1922.[145] Kurskii's opening address acknowledged the calls for greater unity between tribunals and people's courts, and challenged the congress

[140] GARF, f. A-353, op. 4, d. 23, ll. 16–18ob (report by Krylenko on organizational questions). See also Krylenko, *Sudoustroistvo*, 121–6 (discussion), 373–81 (transcript of resolutions).

[141] This debate is in the published minutes from the congress; *Materialy*, XI–XII (1921), 82–96.

[142] The resolutions are in *Materialy*, XI–XII (1921), prilozhenie, 3, 5–10.

[143] *Materialy*, XVI–XVII (1922), 7 (speech, Fourth All-Russian Congress of Justice Officials, 26 January 1922). Also Ia. Brandenburgskii, 'Novaia ekonomicheskaia politika i sovetskaia iustitsiia', *ESIu*, 9, 2 March 1922, 1–2.

[144] *ESIu*, 3, 15 January 1922, 12 (Moscow congress report); Abramov, 'Sozdanie', 222 (Penza).

[145] The minutes are in *Materialy*, XVI–XVII (1922). The coverage below is from 10, 32–61, and prilozhenie, 5.

to come to a resolution. The debate was then launched by a delegate who argued that tribunals were not courts in the strict sense of the word, but 'fighting (*boevoi*)' organs of the class dictatorship. This was not a problem, but tribunals were interfering in the work of other courts, seizing petty cases. Tribunals had an important role in the economic campaigns, so should not be abolished, but they must operate according to clearer principles and not take precedence over other forms of justice. This argument reiterated those from the previous congress, but the response of Krylenko, usually a staunch defender of tribunals, was unusual. He admitted he did not see the need for parallel forms of justice in principle, even if tribunals were not yet ready to be abolished, and he talked of the need for fundamental legal reform. A. M. D'iakonov, former chairman of Moscow's tribunal, agreed on the need for major reform, prompted if nothing else by the changing circumstances of the NEP, and he also noted the overlapping jurisdictions of people's courts and tribunals, which led to red tape, arguments, and weakened legal organs. He suggested uniting around people's courts, which could hold special sessions utilizing experts to deal with important political crimes. Some agreed, emphasizing red tape and the need for greater legality; some disagreed, questioning whether the civil war was over and the state could afford to disband tribunals. One delegate argued that the state still required a level of terror and, if tribunals did not administer this exceptional justice, who would? Neither the Cheka nor people's courts were desirable in his view.

The divides bridged the usual interest groups, which in itself demonstrated the importance of the issues involved, questioning as they did the very basis of the revolutionary justice formulated after the October Revolution. Krylenko, a tribunal official, questioned their purpose, some from people's courts defended tribunals, while some provincial officials were apparently unaware of the concerns until this debate.[146] The congress did not vote on the discussion immediately, instead tasking a commission to explore the question further. In the end, the congress resolved to call for greater unity between people's courts and tribunals, and restrictions on tribunals rather than their abolition. The new law codes expected soon would have clearer definitions of crimes, helping to clarify respective jurisdictions.

For the moment, therefore, tribunals continued unaffected. Senior figures continued to promote their role, with Lenin talking in February 1922 ahead of the major trial of the Socialist Revolutionaries about the need for decisive revolutionary justice and the importance of the 'tremendous' educational role of tribunals when dealing with political enemies. He urged Narkomiust to create more 'model (*obraztsovyi*)' trials to serve as examples to the population and to become more proactive, even militant.[147] Tribunals also took on more cases as the

[146] I. Slavin, 'Na s"ezde', *ESIu*, 5, 29 January 1922, 2–3.
[147] V. Lenin, *Polnoe sobranie sochinenii* (5th edition, 55 volumes, Moscow, 1971–5), XLIV, 396–9.

Cheka was reorganized into the State Political Directorate (GPU) on 6 February 1922, with the loss of many of its extrajudicial sentencing powers, although it regained most of these powers within a month.[148] Even so, reports make it clear that many tribunals faced an increase in workload as they took over responsibility for many of the Cheka's cases, most incomplete. Moscow's tribunal was typical in complaining about the level of this increase, especially as it involved difficult investigations. It requested more staff to conduct these investigations and the mundane tasks of searches and arrests.[149]

The long-awaited criminal law codes—to replace the tsarist laws abolished in November 1918—were finally published in 1922. Despite claims by some Bolsheviks that the new state did not require law codes and decrees were sufficient, Narkomiust started preparations from spring 1918, arguing that the absence of codes exacerbated diversity and inconsistency.[150] At the Third All-Russian Congress of Justice Officials in June 1920, Narkomiust's representative was exasperated that harmful crimes, like speculation, were punished by a small fine in one place and a prison sentence in another: 'in the interests of the centralization of power,' he went on, 'we must publish law codes.' Some attendees demurred, but, as Krylenko argued, it did not mean resurrecting old laws but refining legal consciousness, which should not mean 'the consciousness of one or another judge, but also the cumulative experience' as expressed by various norms.[151] Lenin made a similar case: law should be uniform and not pander to 'the long-standing Russian view and semi-barbarous habits that desire to preserve Kaluga law as distinct from Kazan' law'. Legal consciousness required greater central control.[152]

At the Fourth All-Russian Congress of Justice Officials in January 1922, the language changed, even if the substance of the argument did not. Kurskii argued that Russia needed revolutionary legality (*zakonnost'*) based on written laws so that it could be understood by a wide mass of workers and peasants.[153] This was not the first time the term 'legality' had been used, but it was being used systematically by 1922 to contrast with consciousness (*soznanie*), which had dominated legal discourse since October. Consciousness had reflected the improvisation of a state struggling to survive; or, as one theorist later put it, Russia had been governed by expediency (*tselesoobraznost'*), with laws having only one aim—to defend Soviet power. Now legality was required to help construct the Soviet

[148] See the documents in D. Shearer and V. Khaustov, *Stalin and the Lubianka: A Documentary History of the Political Police and Security Organs in the Soviet Union,1922–1953* (New Haven, 2015), 19–23.

[149] GARF, f. R-1005, op. 3, d. 141, l. 12 (report, early June 1922). More broadly, see A. Lisitsyn, 'K uprazdneniiu VChK', *ESIu*, 7, 12 February 1922, 2–3.

[150] See D. Chistiakov, 'Organizatsiia kodifikatsionnykh rabot v pervye gody sovetskoi vlasti (1917-1923)', *Sovetskoe gosudarstvo i pravo*, 5 (1956), 10–22.

[151] The debate is in *Materialy*, XI–XII, 73–81. Quotes from 73–4, 77.

[152] Lenin, *Polnoe*, XLV, 198–9 (20 May 1922).

[153] *Materialy*, XVI–XVII (1922), 9. Also P. Stuchka, 'Revoliutsionnaia zakonnost'', *Izvestiia*, 25 March 1922.

state.[154] Laws had multiple aims under the NEP and legality was founded in statutory law, standing for order and uniformity over arbitrariness, and should thus inspire greater respect.[155]

The code relevant to tribunals—the criminal code—was published on 1 June, with a code on procedure in criminal cases coming into force on 1 July to ensure that laws were enacted correctly.[156] These defined crimes, procedures, and punishments in unprecedented detail, but they were not intended to restrict tribunals, simply to enhance consistency and thus effectiveness. The code confirmed the elasticity of the term 'counter-revolution', and people could also be convicted of acts that were not defined as crimes but were analogous to acts that were, providing tribunals with some leeway. Elements of revolutionary consciousness also remained, with judges permitted to sentence within a range of punishments depending on circumstances and even demonstrate leniency in 'exceptional circumstances'.[157] Indeed, Lenin ordered the codes not to abolish 'terror' but to provide it with a legal foundation and create a uniform legal consciousness that could be applied where needed.[158]

As always, the codes took time to filter down to tribunals, with some taking months to hear about them. And they were not always received sympathetically. A congress of military tribunal officials in the North Caucasus on 2–4 August 1922, for instance, saw speakers bemoan both the perceived loss of some of the powers of military tribunals and the continual attempts of the authorities to centralize power at the expense of local autonomy.[159] Otherwise, the codes had various impacts. On the one hand, they increased workload as they demanded adherence to a stricter and more extensive set of procedures and regulations than before. Saratov's tribunal moaned that the codes had increased their work by half.[160] On the other hand, the codes became a welcome means of legitimizing tribunal activities, and they were increasingly referenced, if not always correctly, in inspections, reports, sentences, and appeals.

The law codes did, however, provide fresh momentum to arguments that tribunals and people's courts should be merged, as they provided further evidence

[154] I. Emel'ianov, *Chto takoe revoliutsionnaia zakonnost' i zachem ona nuzhna* (Moscow, 1926), 13, 22.

[155] For example, Ia. Brandenburgskii, 'Revoliutsionnaia zakonnost', prokuratura i advokatura', *Sovetskoe pravo*, 2 (1922), 3–16; A. Trainin, 'O revoliutsionnoi zakonnosti', *Pravo i zhizn'*, 1 (1922), 5–8; A. Zhivopostsev, 'Chto zhe takoe "zakonnost"', *Vestnik proletarskogo prava i iuridicheskikh norm* [Tambov], 3–4 (1922), 1–4.

[156] On their creation, see O. Maksimova, *Zakonotvorchestvo v sovetskoi Rossii v 1917–1922 godakh* (Moscow, 2011), 282–345. Otherwise, see *Ugolovno-protsessual'nyi kodeks RSFSR* (Moscow, 1922); and *Ugolovnyi kodeks RSFSR* (Moscow, 1922).

[157] A. Piontkovskii, 'Kontr-revoliutsionnye prestupleniia v Ugolovnom Kodekse RSFSR', *Sovetskoe pravo*, 2 (1924), 7–40; and *Ugolovnyi kodeks*, 6 (article 28).

[158] V. Lenin, *Collected Works* (47 volumes, Moscow, 1960–70), III, 358–9 (17 May 1922).

[159] GARF, f. R-1005, op. 1, d. 110, ll. 166aob–168 (minutes).

[160] GARF, f. R-1005, op. 3, d. 245, l. 3 (report, August 1922).

that Russia was moving from exceptional forms of justice governed by civil war conditions to justice regulated by written laws and procedures. In a leading article in Narkomiust's journal, A. S. Lisitsyn, who had supported tribunals at the Fourth All-Russian Congress of Justice Officials, admitted that the codes removed the need for exceptional forms of justice and that Narkomiust had essentially decided to abolish tribunals. Tribunals were organs that conducted 'terror' against enemies and were rendered obsolete by the new codes. He outlined proposals for a united court. A. Ia. Estrin made a similar argument soon afterwards in the same journal, albeit from a more theoretical standpoint, concluding the civil war was over, the codes had already moderated tribunals, and exceptional courts (apart from military tribunals) no longer made sense.[161]

Sure enough, a decree published on 11 November 1922 (effective from 1 January 1923) abolished all civilian tribunals, leaving only people's courts. Military and transport tribunals remained to deal with serious military and economic crimes, on the basis that the military in many countries have separate courts. The whole system was now overseen by a supreme court, which continued to have military and transport colleges. Special sessions of people's courts would deal with workers, land issues, and property disputes between state organs.[162] Afterwards, Lisitsyn argued that the disappearance of civilian tribunals removed the fundamental error (in retrospect) of two parallel courts created by the decree in 1917.[163] Another activist, Ia. L. Berman, reflected that, while the reform was not complete as special courts remained, 90 per cent of the system was now united. Revolutionary legality was strengthened and personal and property rights guaranteed.[164] Such appraisals were to be expected, but the reforms did mark the end of the transitional period of revolutionary justice – the new system, by and large, survived with few major changes until 1991.[165]

The Persistence of Exceptional Justice

The abolition of civilian tribunals did not happen overnight. Most continued into 1923 as news of the reforms spread and they dealt with their backlog of cases. Transport tribunals continued legally, but the November 1922 decree stipulated there should only be seven (Moscow, Petrograd, Khar'kov, Rostov na Donu, Omsk, Tashkent, and Smolensk).[166] One report, though, charted a reduction to

161 A. Lisitsyn, 'Sliianie narodnykh sudov i revoliutsionnykh tribunalov', *ESIu*, 26–27, 17–24 July 1922, 1–2; A. Estrin, 'Edinaia sudebnaia sistema i marksistskaia teoriia prava', *ESIu*, 29–30, 10–17 August 1922, 4–7.

162 *IZ*, 238–47.

163 A. Lisitsyn, 'Itogi i perspektivy', *ESIu*, 44–5, 7 December 1922, 18–19.

164 Berman, *Ocherki*, 71.

165 For a recent overview, see J. Daly, *Crime and Punishment in Russia* (London, 2018).

166 *IZ*, 247 (st. 86–91).

eight regional transport tribunals (Moscow, Petrograd, West, South-East, North-East, Siberia, Caucasus, and Turkestan), a change initiated prior to the decree.[167] Two further regional tribunals (South and Far East) were formed in February 1923.[168] Either way, these tribunals were also increasingly seen as unnecessary as the NEP stabilized the economy and they were abolished on 23 November 1923.

This left military tribunals as the sole survivor, and these courts continued for the rest of the Soviet Union. Their survival reflected the ability of the military to distinguish military justice from civilian justice, even after the end of the civil war, and the state's willingness to accept this distinction as not abnormal in any legal system. An increasingly vocal contingent within the military, led by prominent officers such as S. M. Budennyi, M. N. Tukhachevskii, and K. E. Voroshilov, had been pressing for the revival of separate military tribunals from late 1921, not long after the decree unifying tribunals. They employed the usual arguments that civilian tribunals lacked specialist knowledge, processed cases too slowly, and dispensed inappropriate sentences, and VTsIK seemed to agree that the abolition of so many military tribunals after June 1921 was premature, given persistent unrest. Their numbers rose again steadily in 1922 as they were re-established in major regions, with one report listing forty-five in October and a later account forty-eight in 1923.[169]

The demise of civilian tribunals seems sudden. One minute they were playing a leading role in crucial campaigns against banditry, food tax violations, and corruption; the next, they were deemed surplus to requirements. And this seems particularly surprising as these crimes did not disappear. It does not seem to have been a question of effectiveness in the same manner as earlier arguments against tribunals. They may have suffered persistent problems, but they had been an increasingly active and visible arm of the state as the civil war progressed, acting alongside other government organs to rebuild central state authority. As courts, they had offered something different, providing a discursive forum (unlike local organs of government or the Cheka) to discuss the state's view of the revolution and its objectives, wielding harsher punitive force than regular courts, but permitting greater flexibility than the Cheka (as discussed further in subsequent chapters). They had also penetrated a wide range of key places, whether front lines, railway stations, ports, or villages, even if many areas remained untouched. Their development employed the practices (decrees and information gathering) by which all central organs gradually exerted authority over localities, while also

[167] GARF, f. R-3042, op. 1, d. 39, ll. 2–2ob (report, undated). The reform was apparently enacted on 5 October 1922 and orders sent to existing transport tribunals on 13 October; TsGAMO, f. 4762, op. 1, d. 1, ll. 13–13ob.

[168] GARF, f. R-1005, op. 1, d. 145, ll. 9–9ob (report, undated, 1923).

[169] GARF, f. R-1005, op. 1, d. 27, ll. 103–03ob (order of the Supreme Tribunal, 9 October 1922); and Ul'rikh's accounts: 'Voennye tribunaly', no pag.; 'K desiatiletiiu', 1270; and 'Voennye tribunaly (1918-1928 g.)', 12–13.

facilitating this process by enabling the state to regulate its own officials, targeting abuses of power and corruption even if, again, more needed to be done. In doing so, tribunals, and revolutionary justice more broadly, had helped extend the authority of the state.

Ultimately, tribunals fell victim to broader decisions about the nature of the state and the role of law. Tribunals had emerged amid a desperate struggle for survival in the aftermath of the October Revolution. By 1922, the Bolsheviks had survived a brutal civil war and were more confident in their authority despite ongoing social unrest. They had rebuilt the state apparatus to an acceptable level and they believed their focus needed to shift to rebuilding the economy to quell the remaining dissent. They were also keen to draw a line under the civil war. Taking the emphasis away from counter-revolution, even if economic crimes had previously been categorized as counter-revolutionary, was important politically to stress the revolution's victory. In this narrative, abolishing tribunals was a symbolic statement that counter-revolution had been defeated. Law still needed to be *revolutionary*, officials argued, but in a different way, with greater legalism and transparency to facilitate the NEP. Unifying the legal system around people's courts offered a 'regular' and more cost-effective way to use law to build a new state than the 'fighting' organs of the revolution.

Yet the exceptional justice embodied by tribunals did not disappear. The Bolsheviks still recognized the value of a form of coercion sitting between people's courts and the new GPU. Most crimes were no longer considered sufficiently threatening to the state, but some areas remained sensitive and some crimes too large and politically important to ignore. The continuation of tribunals in the military represented one sensitive area. But when it came to civilian cases, the Bolsheviks now felt that exceptional justice could be employed through individual trials rather than a formal system of courts. From the start, high-profile trials had served as focal points for important political messages and, as the civil war progressed, Lenin and others urged greater use of such 'model' trials to educate and mobilize. These focused more on conveying the general crime and the resulting educational message effectively than the specifics of individual cases. By 1922, the greater levels of organization surrounding some of these trials had started to transform them into 'show' trials in that all aspects were managed by local and national authorities, including predetermining the trial process and the sentence. This left less room for spontaneity in the courtroom and for any type of 'justice' other than that decided by the state. The largest such trial—of the Socialist Revolutionaries—was held by the Supreme Tribunal in June–August 1922, only months before its abolition.

This transformation and this particular trial are discussed further in Chapter 4, but suffice to say that, although the Bolsheviks did not view this trial as an unmitigated success, it was felt that its failings could be remedied in the future. More fundamentally, it no longer seemed to matter whether important trials were conducted as part of an organized court system or not. Indeed, isolated trials emphasized the exceptional and uncommon nature of the threat after 1922 rather than the mass trials of the tribunal system, which implied more widespread opposition and undermined claims of victory and growing stability. Most tribunals may have been abolished in 1922–3, therefore, but show trials continued the role of exceptional justice in extending state authority after the 1922 reforms.

3

Categorizing Counter-Revolution

As increasingly active and visible 'emissaries of the state', revolutionary tribunals helped other organs rebuild central state authority by offering a more discursive and flexible means of influencing people's beliefs and behaviours. Law categorizes adverse human actions into a series of predefined crimes, and these categories, in turn, are intended to influence thoughts and actions, with people either responding directly or having to adjust because of others who have responded.[1] For the Bolsheviks, categorization was also bound up with establishing control over revolutionary discourse and the power that flowed from this dominance—that is, establishing what were *revolutionary* beliefs and actions, and thus what constituted counter-revolution and a crime. Painting actions as revolutionary gave them legitimacy as representing the will of the people; condemning actions as counter-revolutionary labelled the perpetrators as enemies of the people. This enabled the Bolsheviks to target threats to their authority and—they hoped—focus popular anger, and politicize and mobilize people, while disguising the gap between rhetoric and reality in the new state by blaming enemies for shortcomings.[2] In the longer term, the Bolsheviks hoped law could help forge new, Soviet citizens and build a socialist society. Here, the role of law in defining new, post-revolutionary norms was as important as its ability to target abnormality: normalization, after all, is an important instrument of power.[3]

The trouble during revolutions and civil wars is that understandings of revolution and counter-revolution are constantly evolving, making it difficult to construct stable categories of normality and criminality. This was exacerbated in Russia by the rapid growth in criminal activity as defined prior to 1917 and the repudiation of pre-revolutionary laws by late 1918. State and society largely agreed that regular crimes, such as theft and murder, remained crimes, but discord surrounded counter-revolution amid divergent political views and varying assessments of what was sufficient to harm the revolution. There were also new crimes that needed categorizing, while regular crimes could be counter-revolutionary

[1] See U. Baxi, '"The State's Emissary": The Place of the Law in Subaltern Studies', in P. Chatterjee and G. Panday (eds.), *Subaltern Studies VII* (New Delhi, 1992), 249–50; and M. Feeley, 'The Concept of Law in Social Science: A Critique and Notes on an Expanded View', *Law and Society Review*, 10, 4 (1976), 515.

[2] The last point is also made in D. Raleigh, *Experiencing Russia's Civil War: Politics, Society and Revolutionary Culture in Saratov, 1917–1922* (Princeton, 2002), 410.

[3] M. Foucault, *Discipline and Punish: The Birth of the Prison* (London, 1977), 178, 183–4.

The State versus The People: Revolutionary Justice in Russia's Civil War, 1917–1922. Matthew Rendle, Oxford University Press (2020). © Matthew Rendle.
DOI: 10.1093/oso/9780198840428.001.0001

depending on the timing, the motives of the criminal, the identity of the victim, and their impact on the state.

General discussions of criminality rarely helped categorization, as their definitions remained traditional, albeit couched in the now ubiquitous language of class. One columnist wrote that a crime was an act directed against the objectives established by peasants and workers, and organized by their state.[4] Official guidelines declared that, if criminal law is the legal measures by which the system of social relations of a given class society protects itself from violations (crimes) by repression (punishment), then Soviet criminal law protected the system of social relations reflecting the interests of the labouring masses. Crime was any act violating this system, defined by official decrees in the absence of law codes.[5] Given that a crime in any state is essentially an action violating the political and social order as decided by the dominant group(s) within that state, none of this was particularly informative.

Moreover, technically all crime could be seen as counter-revolutionary in the sense that crime represents a form of dissent against the political and social order (and, in this case, the revolution). This elasticity has underpinned the arguments of those historians who argue this was a period of 'legalized lawlessness' or those who uncritically equate law with violence—in the absence of written laws, any act could be designated counter-revolutionary and punished arbitrarily. Certainly, this elasticity provided tribunals with much of their threat and power as it provided them with the potential to target all crimes. In practice, though, the Bolsheviks exempted most crimes from the counter-revolutionary category by blaming them on the exploitative legacy of the old regime, expecting them to disappear once the equality promised by the revolution took effect or, in other words, once socialism had been achieved.

Some crimes, of course, could not be exempted; they were conscious acts against the Bolshevik state with the aim of damaging or overthrowing it (and thus the revolution). And, just as had happened during the French Revolution, the state employed an abstract and elastic value—counter-revolution—to enable it to target any perceived offence at the same time as issuing ever more detailed regulations on precise acts that constituted counter-revolutionary activity at any given time.[6] Doing this, just as it did for their predecessors, facilitated Bolshevik ambitions to exert control, while maintaining a defence against unforeseen circumstances. To be sure, definitions remained ambiguous, instructions were ignored at times, and anomalies were always present, but, rather than acting arbitrarily, the evidence reveals tribunals usually focused on specific, defined

[4] P. K., 'Prestuplenie i nakazanie v Sovetskoi Respublike', *Izvestiia*, 5 August 1919, 1.

[5] 'Guiding Principles of Criminal Law in the RSFSR (12 December 1919)', reprinted in W. Rosenberg (ed.), *Bolshevik Visions* (2nd edition, 2 volumes, Ann Arbor, 1990), I, 166.

[6] C. Hesse, 'The Law of the Terror', *Modern Language Notes*, 114, 4 (1999), 702–18.

activities and expressed clear priorities at various times. The problem was, on the one hand, keeping abreast of the latest threats to the revolution and, on the other, determining what was a 'conscious' act of counter-revolution as opposed to an 'unconscious' act by someone still suffering from the exploitative legacy of the old regime, or determining whether a criminal had intended to damage the revolution or was simply acting for material gain, since the latter often caused the former.

This chapter examines the crimes targeted by tribunals, shifting conceptions of the counter-revolutionary threat and the implications for the state. When defending the revolution in the immediate aftermath of October, counter-revolution was categorized in relatively narrow terms: the plots and sabotage conducted by obvious 'bourgeois' enemies. With the onset of a brutal civil war, however, and a desperate struggle to survive, it became clear that a much broader range of activities threatened the new state (and the revolution): speculation, corruption, desertion, and banditry were all more common and harmful than 'bourgeois' plots. As military conflict declined and the focus switched to internal unrest and the economic reforms of the New Economic Policy (NEP), tribunals became a key weapon in the battle to maintain discipline within the state apparatus and to regulate the economy, both areas where authoritarian states have commonly seen value in employing law.[7] The numerous regulations defining crimes culminated in 1922 in criminal law codes which were supposed to confirm stable categories of criminality and normality.

The changing nature of counter-revolution led to a comparable transformation in the counter-revolutionary, from the 'bourgeoisie' who organized revolts and conducted anti-Soviet agitation to the 'ordinary' people who bought and sold goods (speculated), resisted food quotas (banditry), fled from the Red Army (deserted), or misused any official power they enjoyed (crimes of office), often simply in a desperate attempt to survive the civil war. The Bolsheviks were not keen to highlight this change, using class-based categories (kulaks), pejorative labels (bandits), or visual portrayals of 'traditional' bourgeois figures to mask the problematic fact that many of their supposedly natural supporters were acting against them. The Bolsheviks also manipulated the concept of counter-revolution to paint events in a more favourable light. As this chapter details, tribunals remained focused on counter-revolution, but a decreasing proportion of their cases were actually officially classified as counter-revolution as opposed to economic crimes or crimes of office. By keeping their external language and the official category focused on plots and revolts, the Bolsheviks could still portray 'counter-revolutionaries' as acceptable class enemies and, as these crimes declined, use this to reinforce a politically acceptable narrative that depicted the Bolsheviks (and the revolution) as emerging victorious over counter-revolutionary forces. All

[7] T. Moustafa, 'Law and Courts in Authoritarian Regimes', *Annual Review of Law and Social Science*, 10 (2014), 283–5.

this masked deep contradictions, of course, and this chapter explores these, but it reinforces the centrality of tribunals in the struggle to define and target the counter-revolutionary threat, and thus shape people's beliefs and behaviours.

The Emergence of Counter-Revolution

Fears of counter-revolution had dominated political discourse since the February Revolution, fuelled by constant comparisons with 1789. For the Bolsheviks, however, counter-revolution was not something that *might* occur – it was inevitable. To succeed, their revolution had to target the bourgeoisie, who would inevitably fight back, and the harder the revolution pressed, the more desperate this fight would become. Events immediately after October only served to prove this; the Junkers' revolt in Petrograd, extensive fighting in Moscow, and the widespread strikes of civil servants that persisted for weeks, to name just a few.

The Decree on Courts in November 1917, therefore, distinguished between civil, criminal, and counter-revolutionary offences. The first two would be the focus of people's courts, while the latter would be dealt with by tribunals. Counter-revolution was itself a crime, and tribunals would also judge the sabotage, looting (*maroderstvo*), embezzlement (*khishchnichestvo*), and other abuses (*zloupotrebleniia*) conducted by industrialists, traders (*torgovtsy*), officers, and others.[8] Although brief, the decree established the two assumptions that underpinned revolutionary justice: first, the revolution had created a new type of crime—counter-revolution—conducted by the bourgeois enemies of the revolutionary proletariat; and, second, a special court with distinct powers was required to deal with this threat. Highlighting and categorizing counter-revolution as a crime also served to legitimize the actions taken by the Bolsheviks (as representatives of the revolution) against this threat.

Within weeks, official language started to focus more on crimes than perpetrators. The decree on tribunals on 19 December simply listed seven counter-revolutionary crimes: organizing, participating in or not preventing revolts or active opposition; using a position in state or public life to harm the activities of institutions and businesses (including sabotage, and concealing or destroying documents and property); preventing the production of consumer goods without justification; purchasing, concealing, damaging, or destroying consumer goods, preventing them from going on the market or increasing their price (speculation); violating the decrees, orders, and published instructions of government; abuses of authority by those in public or administrative positions (crimes of office); and, finally, crimes committed against the people through the press. The last went to

[8] *Dekrety Sovetskoi vlasti* [hereafter *DSV*] (18 volumes, Moscow, 1957–2009), I, 124–6 (22 November 1917).

the press tribunal, established a day earlier to target the publication of false or selective information about public affairs and those publications acting against the interests of the people.[9]

This list provided the basis for tribunals' activities for the rest of their existence, with the addition of pogroms, hooliganism, espionage, bribery, forgery, and the illegal use of documents in May 1918.[10] It is worth noting that none of these were unusual crimes for a state to target – the concept of a political crime was well developed in Russia and Europe before 1917, and could include a range of activities from treason and conspiracies to economic crimes and the spoken and written word, all grouped under loose terminology. It was also not unusual to have a special court to deal with such crimes.[11] Here, though, the objectives were more sinister, with the crimes designed not just to protect the 'state' but to strengthen the authority of a particular party. And it was also a constantly evolving list that mixed growing precision with ongoing elasticity, expanding on what constituted counter-revolution while retaining the term 'counter-revolution' as a catch-all to cover any other threatening acts.

The class element was also distinct. Although the wording became less precise on expected criminals, views remained traditional initially. In early 1918, P. I. Stuchka, deputy Commissar of Justice, referenced counter-revolutionaries, such as V. M. Purishkevich (a monarchist leader), General L. G. Kornilov (who headed a revolt in August 1917), P. N. Miliukov (the liberal leader), and N. D. Avksent'ev (a right-wing Socialist Revolutionary).[12] Other leading Bolsheviks also expected tribunals to focus on obvious political and social enemies. According to Stuchka, these people were not targeted as political opponents but as the revolution's (class) enemies. The two, of course, were one and the same.

These expectations were reflected in the initial activities of Petrograd's tribunal and its investigative commission. The latter's archives contain 417 files on cases from October (and before) to May 1918.[13] The first files concentrated on resistance to the October Revolution by Junkers and officers in Petrograd and, in all, 11 per cent of files concerned similar revolts or plans for them. A further 44 per cent

[9] Reprinted in *Istoriia zakonodatel'stva SSSR i RSFSR po ugolovnomu protsessu i organizatsii suda i prokuratury, 1917–1954* [hereafter *IZ*] (Moscow, 1955), 34–5.

[10] *DSV*, II, 231–4 (4 May 1918).

[11] J. Daly, 'Political Crime in Late Imperial Russia', *The Journal of Modern History*, 74, 1 (2002), 62–100; and B. Ingraham, *Political Crime in Europe: A Comparative Study of France, Germany, and England* (Berkeley, 1979), 20–2, 30–1.

[12] P. Stuchka, 'Old and New Courts (4 January 1918)', reprinted in Rosenberg, *Bolshevik Visions*, I, 188.

[13] GARF, f. R-336. Some cases have more than one file. Documents from these files and the biographies of those involved are included in B. Belenkin (ed.), *Pervye aresty. 25 oktiabria 1917–4 ianvaria 1918* (Moscow, 2017) and his 'Repressivnye praktiki bol'shevistskoi vlasti na rannem etape (25 oktiabria 1917 – 4 ianvaria 1918)', in *Uroki Oktiabria i praktiki sovetskoi sistemy 1920–1950-e gody* (Moscow, 2018), 712–27.

Figure 3.1 The Last Supper (1917).
Source: *Pravda*, 8 November 1917, 3.

of files concerned activities such as agitation against Soviet power, spreading propaganda or false rumours, membership of counter-revolutionary groups, or simply not recognizing Soviet power.

Almost all those involved qualified as obvious political and social enemies. As noted in Chapter 1, the first high-profile trials involved a liberal noble, an officer, and a group of monarchists and officers. The rhetoric surrounding these trials painted a picture of former elites pitted against a workers' state. A report on the initial arrests in the Purishkevich Affair, for instance, was published alongside a cartoon of bourgeois figures, fat and well dressed, toasting a portrait of Nicholas II (Figure 3.1). The scene had religious overtones and included a priest, even though none were involved in the plot. Prosecutors spent as much time in the trial proving that all were *natural* social and political opponents (as nobles and officers) as they did the existence of a plot. What the defendants represented was as important as what they had done; as a judge noted, the 'new world judges the old world'.[14] Similar cases saw the former prime minister of the Provisional

[14] *Izvestiia*, 4 January 1918, 3–4.

Government, Prince G. E. L'vov, and the president of Moscow-Kazan' railway, Count N. K. fon Mekk, arrested in spring–summer 1918 for alleged involvement in 'plots'.[15] The tribunal expected such individuals to oppose the October Revolution and spent huge amounts of time investigating such cases, despite the absence of concrete evidence or a significant threat.

A more potent threat came from the sabotage of civil servants. As the Bolsheviks tried to establish control over ministries and other crucial institutions (such as banks), they met with passive resistance and strikes from officials that persisted for months. Similarly, as the Bolsheviks struggled to constrain rising economic chaos, they clamped down on 'economic saboteurs' and speculators who undermined their policies. Dozens of cases of sabotage were investigated—22 per cent of the files in Petrograd's tribunal. Many files lack detail beyond the broad accusation, which often boiled down to a simple dereliction of duties or petty theft, but some involved active agitation for political alternatives and damage to factory machinery.[16] Those targeted were generally pre-October officials who remained in post for their expertise but whose loyalty was doubted, especially if they were also from suspect social backgrounds.

A prominent case in point was V. I. Krivosh, who offered to work for the state and was assigned to the Commissariat of Foreign Affairs as he could decipher cryptograms and knew languages. However, rumours about his past prompted an investigation. He was arrested on 25 January 1918 after a former Okhrana official testified against him. Apparently he had passed information on Russian émigrés to the Okhrana when he worked as a censor and translator for the tsarist government, as well as informing on opposition parties. He was also accused of spying for the Germans during the First World War. Above all else, the Bolsheviks highlighted his attempt to conceal his past and viewed his offer to serve them as a deliberate ploy to discredit the new state. An investigation also revealed that Krivosh was a noble, born in Austria–Hungary (fuelling accusations of spying). His past was traced in minute detail, files were unearthed in archives, and a suspicious sum of money was discovered in his flat. He was found guilty on 14 March and sentenced to a year in prison.[17]

The espionage elements of the case lent it similarities to some of the 11 per cent of crimes in Petrograd's case files that concerned espionage, forgery, and petty crimes such as illegal searches, brawling, and theft.[18] The state also systematically targeted provocateurs who had informed on revolutionaries prior to 1917.

[15] On L'vov, see *Pravda*, 9 March 1918, 1, and 'Kniaz' G. E. L'vov v Ekaterinburgskoi tiur'me', *Istoricheskii arkhiv*, 3 (2002), 140–70. On Mekk, see GARF, f. R-543, op. 1, d. 7 (case file, June 1918).

[16] GARF, f. R-336, op. 1, dd. 73, 246–8, 359–60 (various case files).

[17] GARF, f. R-1074, op. 1, d. 6, ll. 1–2, 11, 16a–19ob. His case received wide press coverage (for the most useful articles, see *Izvestiia*, 27 February 1918, 5; *Novaia zhizn'*, 15 March 1918, 4; and *Pravda*, 17 March 1918, 4).

[18] The remaining 12% of files concerned arrests for unspecified crimes or appeals.

The early case files of the Supreme Tribunal were dominated by such cases, with some going back to the 1890s.[19] One prominent trial was that of R. V. Malinovskii, the former Bolshevik spokesman in the tsarist Duma, who had been an agent of the Okhrana, and was sentenced to death in November 1918.[20]

By this stage the Bolsheviks had recognized that political threats were emerging not just from monarchists and liberals but from other socialists and even dissenting Bolsheviks, as demonstrated by the trials of Iu. O. Martov, P. E. Dybenko, and Captain A. M. Shchastnyi (covered in Chapter 1). The trial of Martov, a Menshevik leader, was a prelude to a sustained attack on the Mensheviks as the party's popularity rose amid growing social unrest. It was also the trial of their Moscow newspaper, *Vpered!*, in which the tribunal ruled that 'it is possible to prepare an uprising by arms or by preparing minds', which emphasized that verbal opposition was now categorized as counter-revolution.[21] The high-profile trials of senior military officials—Dybenko, former Commissar of Naval Affairs, in May, and Shchastnyi, former Commander of the Baltic Fleet, in June—represented a growing determination to focus on misbehaving officials. These trials were driven by the specific political context, but the underlying accusation of crimes of office was one taken ever more seriously.

A broader range of crimes (including planning or inciting crime) and criminals was also steadily emerging through these cases. In late 1917, Lenin argued the Bolsheviks did not just have political enemies but enemies in 'everyday economic life', and idlers, shirkers, and rogues constituted as great a threat to the revolution as the bourgeoisie.[22] There was no immediate impact on the caseload of Petrograd's tribunal, but whereas *Izvestiia* and *Pravda*, for instance, reported solely on trials concerning provocateurs, sabotage, plots, and oppositional newspapers before spring 1918, afterwards articles started to cover a wider range of crimes, from unauthorized searches to illicit brewing (both sabotage through ill discipline), involving more and more criminals from lower social groups.

The activities of local tribunals had always been more diverse. Some adopted central definitions of crimes and some used similar language to emphasize certain aspects, such as Iziumskii *uezd* (Khar'kov), which targeted crimes belittling the dignity and power of the revolutionary organs as well as the amoral acts of officials that undermined the authority of these organs. Others, though, had their own concerns. Stavropol' added violations to property and person, the unauthorized concealing of arms and cartridges, and targeted the spreading of lies and rumours.[23] Perm' added the non-payment of tax 'contributions', an essential

[19] GARF, f. R-1005, op. 1a. For an example of one stretching back to the 1890s, see d. 49 (G. M. Terian).

[20] See *Delo provokatora Malinovskogo* (Moscow, 1992).

[21] *Vpered!*, 21 April 1918, 3.

[22] V. Lenin, *Collected Works* (47 volumes, Moscow, 1960–70), XXVI, 411, 414 (24–7 December 1917).

[23] *Materialy narodnogo komissariata iustitsii* [hereafter *Materialy*], II (1918), 37–8 (Iziumskii *uezd* regulations, 20 December 1917), 48–9 (Stavropol' regulations, n.d.).

source of income for most local authorities.[24] Some covered a wide variety of crimes in the absence of alternative courts or because tribunals were seen as more 'revolutionary' and potent. This diversity reflected differing objectives and threats. Fewer monarchists, industrialists, landowners, and other 'bourgeois' figures were plotting to overthrow Soviet power locally than in the centre, but there were corrupt officials, illegal economic activities preventing control over production and the receipt of crucial taxes, and a plethora of crimes generally, all of which undermined the legitimacy of the new state and reduced public support. Some tribunals, such as in Ukraine, did not even bother to use the term 'counter-revolution' in their focus on illegal traders, hidden food reserves, and corrupt officials.[25]

In this sense, the localities were ahead of the centre. Within a year or so, lesser economic crimes, such as illegal brewing, were targeted relentlessly as a national problem, but such concerns were still on the horizon in mid-1918. In the meantime, the Commissariat of Justice (Narkomiust) felt local tribunals were bogged down in petty cases, reducing their ability to deal effectively with important threats. Some provincial authorities also issued warnings. The department of justice in Perm' instructed courts that simply not recognizing Soviet power was not sufficient for prosecution—it would take all their time. The revolution, in any case, did not need to be recognized by the bourgeoisie. Equally, basic criticism of the state was also not a crime and should only be prosecuted if critics falsified or manipulated facts to set the population against the state.[26]

The same fear of overwhelming tribunals lay behind debates over scale. On 20 July, for example, a decree stated that speculators should go to people's courts as long as the sentence was not expected to exceed five years' imprisonment or a fine of 10,000 roubles. Two days later, another decree specified that the crime should be judged by tribunals. A further day later, a decree on people's courts restated the first decree![27] Contradictory decrees were not unusual, but this example reveals emerging problems: certain crimes—such as speculation—were inherently counter-revolutionary, but tribunals needed to focus on the most important crimes. Petty speculation posed an insignificant threat, was too common, and people's courts were sufficient in these instances. Much early confusion, therefore, reflected disagreements over the scale required for crimes to pose a serious counter-revolutionary threat.

The battle to ensure conformity culminated in a circular from the cassation department on 6 October 1918.[28] It had received over 300 appeals since its

[24] *Grazhdanskaia voina v Prikam'e. Mai 1918 – ianvar' 1920 gg.* (Perm', 2008), 124–5 (circular, 13 June 1918).

[25] *Velikaia oktiabr'skaia sotsialisticheskaia revoliutsiia na Ukraine. Fevral' 1917-aprel' 1918* (3 volumes, Kiev, 1957), III, 311–12, 361, 453–5 (various resolutions, January–February 1918).

[26] *Grazhdanskaia voina v Prikam'e*, 124–5 (circular, 13 June 1918).

[27] *IZ*, 47–8, 50.

[28] *IZ*, 58–61.

inception and felt obliged to clarify what constituted counter-revolution, categorizing crimes in eight groups: counter-revolutionary plots; sabotage; discrediting authority; forgery; crimes of office; espionage; hooliganism (creating disorder when enacting official instructions, insulting moral feelings or political convictions, and those harming the revolution prior to October, such as provocateurs and the tsarist secret police); and speculation. Tribunals were encouraged to focus more on intention when combating counter-revolutionary plots; what was *intended* was as dangerous as what actually *happened.* Conversely, tribunals were urged to be more selective for other crimes. The circular repeatedly stressed the issue of scale; simple non-fulfilment of orders, basic insubordination, or petty complaints, for example, should be heard by people's courts. As a later decree on people's courts stated, if in doubt, assess the 'political significance' of a case.[29] All this, of course, was as subjective as assessing counter-revolution in the first place, but clearly tribunals were being urged to make judgements about what *really* mattered.

Legal theorists used this circular to try to impose their broader understanding of crime on local officials. In their eyes, crime resulted from the remnants of bourgeois practices and mentalities, of exploitation and social conflict, of a primitive consciousness, and of not just a criminal's personality but their socio-economic background. Some theorists did not even use the word 'crime', preferring to talk of a 'socially harmful' act, while securing society's defence was about removing broader harmful social factors. As the revolution strengthened, exploitation and conflict would disappear, thereby removing the causes of crime.[30] These ideas were rooted in the scientific debates conducted before 1917.[31] Counter-revolution was situated within this framework; it was a unique crime brought into existence by the revolution, and the revolution's inevitable triumph would render it obsolete.

The practical message for local courts was that they needed to know the relationship between individual criminals and their socio-economic environment.[32] They also needed to examine all the circumstances surrounding a case,

[29] *IZ*, 66 (30 November 1918).

[30] For example, see M. Kozlovskii, 'Proletarskaia revoliutsiia i ugolovnoe pravo', *Proletarskaia revoliutsiia i pravo*, 1 (1918), 26–7. There is a useful discussion of the views of key figures in A. Gertsenzon, *Ugolovnoe pravo i sotsiologiia (Problemy sotsiologii ugolovnogo prava i ugolovnoi politiki)* (Moscow, 1970), 222–58, 271–81.

[31] See Z. Bialkowski, 'The Transformation of Academic Criminal Jurisprudence into Criminology in Late Imperial Russia' (PhD dissertation, University of California, Berkeley, 2007); D. Beer, *Renovating Russia: The Human Sciences and the Fate of Liberal Modernity, 1880–1930* (Ithaca, 2008), 194–5; D. Hoffmann, *Cultivating the Masses: Modern State Practices and Soviet Socialism, 1914–1939* (Ithaca, 2011), 240–8; and S. Kowalsky, *Deviant Women: Female Crime and Criminality in Revolutionary Russia, 1880–1930* (DeKalb, 2009), 9, 61–5.

[32] This was the focus of the professional study of criminology that emerged during the civil war and peaked in the 1920s with innovative research, new organizations, and several journals; Kowalsky, *Deviant Women*, 50–76.

from the background and beliefs of the criminal to the nature and impact of the crime. These ideas were extended in the 'Guiding Principles on Criminal Law' in December 1919. The Principles also made it clear that crime covered both action and inaction, where a failure to act enabled a crime to occur. A crime could be committed, attempted, or intended—there was no distinction between the three—by perpetrators (those who took part), initiators (those who incited crime), or accomplices (those who aided the crime or concealed criminals).[33]

There were contradictions here, not least over the issue of individual agency, where theorists often underplayed the role of the individual in favour of the importance of the socio-economic environment without appreciating that individuals reacted to this environment in different ways, making it difficult to use such criteria when assessing whether someone was a 'conscious' counter-revolutionary or not.[34] Equally, it is difficult to see the idealistic thinking of legal theorists reflected in the pragmatic concerns of local officials or the arguments of defendants where, for the most part, crime comes across as viewed uncritically, even if there were debates over intention and scale when deciding whether to pursue a case, and beliefs and backgrounds were certainly considered when passing sentences (see Chapter 4).

By late 1918, therefore, a much clearer sense of counter-revolution and what it entailed had emerged. A large part of this, as the Bolsheviks continually reiterated, was driven by the contingencies of civil war and the potency of the threats facing the new state. Yet their theoretical conception of crime also urged flexibility, teaching that crimes would match the threats facing society at any given time and tribunals should act accordingly. An act could be threatening one minute, requiring a harsh response, but less harmful another and perhaps not worthy of a response. Provocateurs were a case in point: they embodied the hidden enemy in the months immediately after October, concealing counter-revolution behind a mask of support, but their threat was dissipating by late 1918, to be replaced by more urgent challenges, and many were released by later amnesties. Legal theorists, in short, expected counter-revolution to be a constantly evolving category driven by circumstances.

The Expansion of Counter-Revolution

The civil war saw the most intense fighting throughout 1919, and it is no surprise that the transformation in crimes and criminals is more evident during this

[33] 'Guiding Principles', 166–8 (12 December 1919).

[34] For an interesting discussion, see J. Ryan, '"They know not what they do?" Bolshevik Understandings of the Agency of the Perpetrator, 1918-1930', *Historical Research*, 90, 247 (2017), 151–71.

period. Officially, little changed. A discussion of criminal laws by D. I. Kurskii, the Commissar of Justice, in spring 1919 made it clear that the state's external language continued to focus on open opposition, counter-revolutionary agitation, violations of duty, not fulfilling regulations, and various actions in between.[35] The relative severity of these actions fluctuated as the position of the Bolsheviks evolved, but lists of counter-revolutionary crimes in decrees remained stable. In practice, however, the growing intensity of the conflict fuelled the rapid growth of military tribunals. Even more than other tribunals, they regarded themselves as 'fighting organs' of the soviet state, and these tribunals brought a different perspective on crime.

Most military tribunals were established on the initiative of particular regiments and armies to deal with all types of crimes committed by soldiers, some of which were harmful to the military but rarely consisted of any openly counter-revolutionary revolts. Later accounts of early trials recall a fire caused by undisciplined soldiers, armed robbery, embezzlement, desertion, fleeing from the battlefield, speculation, robbery, hooliganism, brawls, illegal brewing, and drunkenness.[36] The first chairman of the Military Tribunal of the Republic, K. Kh. Danishevskii, admitted that military tribunals had been forced to judge regular crimes and even civil cases as there were rarely any other courts; soviets were weak at the front and had failed to organize courts, and regimental courts were missing in many places.[37]

The first circular on military tribunals in January 1919 tried to categorize military crimes as those concerning civilian tribunals but committed by military personnel or within the scope of military activities. The stress on treachery, forged documents and money, and imposture highlighted crimes prevalent at the front. But the further emphasis on incomplete, careless, or negligent service duties, as well as stealing classified plans or revealing military secrets, reflected distinct concerns, as did attacks on infrastructure and communications. Equally, crimes like arson, brawling (*buistvo*), rape, and violent attacks reflected fears of military indiscipline. All demonstrated that military tribunals faced a slightly different set of threats from those targeted by civilian tribunals.[38]

Indeed, Danishevskii stressed the huge challenges from the start.[39] At a time when Narkomiust was urging civilian tribunals to focus on the most threatening counter-revolutionary crimes, leaving regular crimes (*obshcheugolovnye dela*) to people's courts, he argued that Narkomiust focused excessively on counter-

[35] D. Kurskii, 'Novoe ugolovnoe pravo', *Proletarskoe revoliutsiia i pravo*, 2–4 (February–April 1919), 24.

[36] A. Chuvatin, 'Pervye tribunaly', in *Voennye tribunaly—organy sotsialisticheskogo pravosudiia* (Moscow, 1958), 54–6.

[37] K. Danishevskii, *Revoliutsionnye voennye tribunaly* (Moscow, 1920), 21–2.

[38] RGVA, f. 33987, op. 2, d. 53, ll. 133ob-34ob (regulations, 14 January 1919).

[39] *Izvestiia*, 3 January 1919, 2 (interview with Danishevskii).

revolution: every crime committed at or near the front, whether by civilians or military personnel, damaged the fighting capabilities of the army, particularly in active areas of the front lacking alternative courts. Danishevskii still made a distinction between counter-revolutionary and other crimes, but recognized that both had the same impact—weakening state authority. He listed ten crimes that military tribunals covered: crimes against Soviet power (counter-revolution); military crimes; large-scale speculation; crimes against public property; desertion; crimes against workers' discipline, organizations, production, and distribution; large-scale crimes of office and bribery; the malicious discrediting of workers' and peasants' authority; banditry; and general crimes where no other courts existed. At the same time, he accepted the need for special departments for criminal cases and for insignificant crimes to transfer to people's courts where possible.[40] Targeting all crimes, therefore, was desirable in the military, but, for all his bluster, Danishevskii was constrained by limited resources and rising levels of crime.

Nonetheless, official decrees on military tribunals remained distinct from those on civilian tribunals. A decree on 20 November 1919, for instance, talked about general crimes (such as looting, infringements on a person's life, rape, violence, forgery, and the illegal adoption of unearned ranks and uniforms) alongside military crimes (such as not fulfilling military orders, transferring to the other side, voluntarily being taken prisoner, leaving the field of battle, violating the rules of service, desertion, destroying or stealing military equipment, arms, uniforms and property, brawling, and gambling).[41] Regulations from 1920 on transport tribunals followed this lead, with an extra emphasis on anything affecting the normal operation of transport, and on thefts, embezzlement, expropriation, and speculation.[42] By comparison, a decree on civilian tribunals on the same day continued to talk about similar crimes as those covered by the cassation department in late 1918.[43]

The most important crimes, however, were identical to those covered by civilian tribunals, and this exacerbated existing problems of jurisdiction. It was already unclear in some instances whether a case should go to a tribunal or a people's court, and now there was the issue of which tribunal. Plenty of cases were transferred between courts, and their fate depended on the perceptions of decision makers. On 19 November 1918, a commission under the All-Russian Central Executive Committee (VTsIK) discussed the murder of a member of the Cheka (and official of the local soviet) and two Red Army men who had travelled to a village in Riazan' province to arrest a priest. Villagers had gathered in protest and, incited by aggressive orators, had beaten the visitors to death. The commission did not believe there was evidence of counter-revolutionary motives; it was a case of the crowd being provoked into a typical case of vigilante justice (*samosud*), and

[40] Danishevskii, *Revoliutsionnye*, 23–9. [41] *DSV*, VI, 286–9.
[42] *IZ*, 134–5 (18 March 1920). [43] *IZ*, 127 (18 March 1920).

such murders were dealt with by people's courts. Yet the commission did note that the event reflected the harmful relations between the villagers and soviet power (and its agents), and many similar cases were kept by tribunals without hesitation, even if VTsIK agreed with the commission's decision.[44]

As Stuchka admitted bluntly, expediency often governed whether cases ended up in a tribunal or people's court.[45] Desertion, for instance, should be dealt with by military tribunals, as Narkomiust was keen to remind civilian tribunals, but the physical location of deserters in villages far from the front meant that all courts, not just tribunals, dealt with cases.[46] Nevertheless, tribunals steadily placed more emphasis on several existing criteria as the civil war progressed to assess whether a criminal act came under their jurisdiction.

Tribunals assessed more systematically the 'political' nature of a crime alongside its 'counter-revolutionary' character. Most files lack sufficient detail to understand decisions, but verdicts went both ways. From September to November 1918, the provincial tribunal in Iaroslavl' met frequently (from twice a day to every few days) to decide whether cases should be prosecuted, transferred elsewhere, or curtailed.[47] 'Abuses' of power and crimes of office were frequently assessed as not political or counter-revolutionary, despite regulations demanding that tribunals deal with these crimes. Theft was often classed as 'simply' theft and not political. This reflects the fact that most crimes of office must have been petty infringements and more suitable for people's courts. By contrast, revolts, desertion, sabotage, and agitation were usually considered political acts. Even then some decisions seem unusual without context; for example, deciding in one case that anti-Soviet agitation was not counter-revolutionary.[48] The basic point, though, is that case-by-case decisions were made and criteria utilized, even if the answer was subjective and often inconsistent.

Another consideration was intent. Tribunals were under no illusion about the growth in criminality. Railway tribunals talked of the 'hungry mood' of the population fuelling thefts from wagons. Military tribunals reported the desperate lack of necessities behind speculation by soldiers. Saratov's tribunal emphasized how the deteriorating material position of peasants (insufficient seeds, supplies, and livestock) fuelled a range of crimes, from speculation and property crimes to crimes of office, banditry, and desertion. Crimea's tribunal simply noted that the 'catastrophically difficult situation' had prompted 'the colossal and systematic

[44] GARF, f. R-1235, op. 93, d. 214, ll. 91–91ob, 100, 102 (case details, November 1918).

[45] P. Stuchka, 'Revoliutsionnaia bor'ba ili bor'ba s kontrrevoliutsiei (1919)', reprinted in P. Stuchka, *Za sovetskuiu vlast' v Latvii, 1918–1920* (Riga, 1964), 479.

[46] GARF, f. A-353, op. 2, d. 78b, l. 55 (telegram from Narkomiust to Tula's executive committee, 5 June 1919).

[47] GARF, f. R-393, op. 13, dd. 540, 542. The only detail is usually a few words on the crime and the decision.

[48] GARF, f. R-393, op. 13, d. 542, l. 59 (protocol, 15 October 1919).

growth in a whole series of crimes'.[49] Much crime, then, was not political as such: crimes were committed to survive, not to make a political statement, even if they had political consequences. Tribunals began to recognize this in their decisions, prompted partly by urgings to examine socio-economic backgrounds, partly by the need to reduce a workload growing out of control, and partly through the determination to deal only with the most threatening crimes.

The two key words were 'malicious (*zlostnyi*)' and 'selfish (*korystnyi*)'. In a meeting on 25 April 1919, the provincial tribunal in Tver' bemoaned that desertion was growing to 'incredible' levels, and the tribunal needed to focus its energies on malicious deserters.[50] Official decrees also used similar terminology from this period: had someone, for instance, deserted on the spur of the moment or been forced by hardships at home, or was it a selfish, planned action, occurring at a crucial time or when the individual held an important position, or were they a repeat offender? An attempt to define this in April 1919 categorized malicious desertion as when an individual had been absent for over two weeks, had left with army property, had deliberately concealed themselves at the time of their call-up, had resisted arrest, or had deserted more than once.[51] Another tribunal defined malicious desertion as when someone had deserted twice or more; just once reflected a 'weakness of will (*po slabosti voli*)'.[52] Other assessments were clear-cut. In December 1918, the tribunal in Orel reported on two members of the Cheka arrested for speculation: this was a 'particularly malicious' case since the two had gathered 50,000 roubles and a similar amount in jewels, and were about to flee to Ukraine.[53] Similarly, Tashkent's railway tribunal sentenced seventeen people to death for systematically attacking wagons and stores in Orenburg station. They had conducted planned attacks over nine months from January to September 1920, stealing thousands of *puds* of grain.[54] These were not the acts of individuals desperate to survive or provide for their family, but acts designed to make a larger profit.

Not all cases, of course, were decided on the basis of reasoned criteria. L. D. Trotskii, Commissar for War, apparently sent a guard to a tribunal for simply allowing an official into a meeting without permission.[55] He admitted that the guard was honourable and conscientious, and that he had performed acts of

[49] GARF, f. R-3042, op. 1, d. 2, l. 45 (circular to railway tribunals, 13 November 1920); RGVA, f. 33988, op. 2, d. 245, l. 2ob (report of the Western Front's military tribunal for 1921, early 1922); GARF, f. R-1005, op. 3, d. 245, ll. 1aob (report by Saratov tribunal, late August 1922), 6 (report by Crimea's tribunal, 10 April 1922).

[50] GARF, f. A-353, op. 3, d. 125, l. 2 (records of a plenary meeting).

[51] S. Olikov, *Dezertirstvo v krasnoi armii i bor'ba s nim* (Moscow, 1926), 27.

[52] A. Makutchev, *"Prigovor okonchatel'nyi, obzhalovaniiu ne podlezhit..." Revoliutsionnye tribunaly v Sovetskoi Rossii v gody Grazhdanskoi voiny* (Moscow, 2012), 140.

[53] GARF, f. A-353, op. 9, d. 101, ll. 1–2 (report to Narkomiust, 2 December 1918).

[54] GARF, f. R-1005, op. 1, d. 8, ll. 60–1 (sentence, 4 January 1921).

[55] *The Military Writings and Speeches of Leon Trotsky: How the Revolution Armed*, trans. B. Pearce (5 volumes, London, 1979–81), IV, 238–9 (resolution, 13 September 1921).

bravery in the past, but condemned his slackness towards everyday responsibilities. It was the result of a lack of inner discipline—apparently a widespread problem in the military—and this case, Trotskii argued, should serve as an example for all. Such severe and arbitrary reactions were no doubt far from unusual as tribunals sought to make symbolic statements about particular activities or simply flaunted their power.

Equally, it is clear that—reasoned criteria or not—a huge range of activities continued to occupy tribunals throughout the civil war. On 1 June 1921 the military tribunal on the Volga, for instance, was investigating 128 people who had committed a vast array of crimes: brewing samogon, self-harm, desertion, agitation, theft (from property to alcohol), banditry, counter-revolution, forgery, concealing conspirators, sabotage, drunkenness, seizing wood, negligence, arson, murder, bribery, hooliganism, conducting illegal searches, fleeing from duty, harmful relations with peasants, opposing soviet power, concealing arms, speculation, and false declarations. Desertion, theft, and forgery were the most common, as always.[56] Even the cases making it to trial could be diverse. Moscow's provincial tribunal sentenced people in May–June 1919 for agitating against Soviet power, stealing food, desertion, using forged documents, abuse of authority, financial corruption, murder, drunkenness, requisitioning, possessing a counter-revolutionary brochure, and dealing with the former tsarist police, among other things, with misusing or exceeding authority the most common crime.[57]

It is unsurprising, therefore, that these activities involved more and more people from a wider range of social backgrounds as the civil war unfolded. To take another example from Trotskii: in early 1920, the train he used to travel around the front derailed in a snowdrift, lost a carriage, and was delayed for nineteen hours. Another train on a special mission was also delayed. Trotskii was furious. Why had the previous station not informed him of the dangers? Why had no one cleared the line? Why had it taken so long for anyone to come to look for the train, which was expected and had derailed not far from a small station? It was all criminal negligence, from the railway officials guilty of assuming the train would get through, to the local village and its soviet, which had not bothered to clear the line properly, to the regional soviet for not allocating sufficient resources to railways, to the local Cheka for not forcing people to clear the snow. It smacked of slackness and sabotage. And this was a special train. What happened to normal trains carrying vital food and goods? The country (and Bolshevik success) depended on transport.[58] In short, this one incident brought a variety of people, from officials at various levels to ordinary peasants, in front of a military tribunal for a crime that was not consciously counter-revolutionary. Indeed, by 1920–1

[56] GARF, f. R-1005, op. 1, d. 48, ll. 207–8 (list of cases).
[57] TsGAMO, f. 4612, op. 2, d. 4, ll. 11–48 (sentences, May–June 1919).
[58] *Military Writings*, III, 74–7 (resolution, 9 February 1920).

most 'counter-revolutionaries' were peasants, given that most officials had peasant backgrounds, as did most soldiers. The adoption of the NEP in March 1921, which introduced capitalist elements into the economy and a fixed tax on grain, only exacerbated this trend as it pushed economic crimes up the agenda, particularly in the countryside.

As traced in Chapter 2, 1921 also saw the unification of the tribunal system. As part of this, officials tried to bring greater clarity to the diverse range of crimes by grouping them into a smaller number of categories, each with several subcategories. Initially, five categories were common: crimes against the state (counter-revolution, plots, revolts, pogroms, murder of officials, destroying property, agitation, spreading rumours, treachery, espionage, discrediting the authority of officials, and crimes against the constitution); crimes against the established order of government (violating the rules of production and distribution, forging money and documents, speculation, evading state duties, and violating other norms); military crimes (desertion, looting, and not fulfilling, negligently fulfilling, or violating orders); crimes of office (exceeding, abusing, or ineffective authority, bribery and extortion, forgery, appropriation and embezzlement, sabotage, and negligent relations to official duties); and general crimes (acting against the life, health, and property of individuals, non-political banditry, robbery, theft, fleeing from arrest, and other crimes).[59]

The interesting element here is the position of counter-revolution as a subcategory. Tribunals were still judging crimes that threatened the state (and thus the revolution) and were therefore 'counter-revolutionary', and the external and internal language of tribunals said as much. Yet when it came to categorization, counter-revolution remained associated with acts such as plots or revolts and was even slightly distinct from these, perhaps signifying something similar but on a greater scale. The cause for this is unclear. Certainly, such activities were becoming less common and less threatening, and the Bolsheviks wanted to focus on those crimes affecting their ability to govern (including economic crimes and crimes of office). Creating distinct categories provided their message on these crimes with greater prominence. Equally, with the fighting receding, it was politically convenient to imply a corresponding reduction in counter-revolution, supported by the statistics discussed below (Figure 3.3). The revolution truly was emerging victorious over counter-revolution.

Nevertheless, tribunals were clearly conducting a balancing act by the end of the civil war. On the one hand, they considered a vast range of cases, seemingly justifying accusations that they targeted everyone and everything. Some

[59] GARF, f. R-1005, op. 1, d. 76, ll. 59ob–62ob (instructions to tribunals, 7 September 1921). In 1922, tribunal statistics were categorized into six groups of crimes: against soviet power; against government order; against the person; against property; crimes of office; and military crimes (GARF, f. A-353, op. 5, d. 72b, ll. 103–03ob).

Bolsheviks boasted that tribunals enjoyed the authority to assess any crime for its counter-revolutionary threat.[60] On the other hand, regulations, changing circumstances, and the decision-making process meant that tribunals did not believe they acted arbitrarily. They felt they targeted the most dangerous crimes as befitted the circumstances and considered cases systematically. As military tribunals were reminded in early 1921, proletarian law was a 'practical method' not led by general norms, but ever-changing 'revolutionary goals driven by the national and international situation at the current time'.[61] Nonetheless, these trends and tensions—and the resulting problems—become even clearer when counter-revolution is examined quantitatively, as the Bolsheviks also did.

Quantifying Counter-Revolution

Statistics were important for the Bolsheviks from the start. Narkomiust had a 'department of statistics' by June 1918 and was collecting statistics on crimes systematically by the end of the year.[62] These formed a central part of its published reports and articles as well as internal discussions. Statistics were seen to provide 'scientific' proof of the threat facing the state, and thus the importance of Narkomiust, its activities, and law more generally. In the knowledge–power nexus, statistics also provided information on local trends and activities, enabling Narkomiust to identify problems and justify its frequent exhortations to speed up processes and dispense particular sentences, all of which extended central state authority.

Some legal theorists in Narkomiust were also interested in statistics for what they suggested about broader trends in criminality, thereby continuing pre-revolutionary practices. Several of these individuals, such as M. N. Gernet, E. N. Tarnovskii, and A. N. Trainin, had been active participants in the so-called 'left wing' of the sociological school of pre-1917 criminologists, seeing the causes of crime as a product of contemporary social conditions (much like Marxists) and employing a psychiatric approach to understand how criminals reacted to this environment. Some took the next natural step of considering socio-economic factors, and some, such as Gernet, participated in revolutionary circles. For them, statistics enabled an objective, scientific discussion of crime and criminals.[63]

[60] Ia. Berman, *Ocherki po istorii sudoustroistva RSFSR* (Moscow, 1924), 28.

[61] GARF, f. R-1005, op. 1, d. 44, l. 41 (circular to all military tribunals, 5 February 1921).

[62] GARF, f. A-353, op. 1, d. 1, ll. 14–15 (correspondence to local departments and soviets, 21 and 26 June 1918).

[63] See Bialkowski, 'Transformation', 172–85; Kowalsky, *Deviant Women*, 37–40, 213; and L. Shelley, 'Soviet Criminology: Its Birth and Demise, 1917-1936', *Slavic Review*, 38, 4 (1979), 614–28.

The statistics are more problematic, of course, than Narkomiust admitted. They were rarely complete, for a start. The first attempt to gather systematic information on tribunals was made in November 1918 with a request for statistics for the previous year. A questionnaire was sent to the forty-one tribunals known to exist, but some local tribunals were operating without Narkomiust's knowledge and not all responded. Information from thirty-two tribunals was received. Not all of these answered the entire questionnaire, while some tribunals had been established by December 1917, others not until summer 1918, resulting in statistics covering various periods.[64] These problems persisted. Narkomiust sent another request in September 1919. Tribunals took months to respond, recorded information in various ways, and provided conflicting figures, and the number of tribunals was continually fluctuating.

There were also differences in how tribunals interpreted the questions. As noted, terms such as counter-revolution were elastic and open to multiple interpretations, and the same was true of the social background of criminals. Social identities were fluid during this period as workers moved to the countryside in search of food, peasants were conscripted into the Red Army, and former privileged groups undertook manual work to survive. Some statistics distinguished between occupations pre- and post-October, but not all. Some officials categorized people in simplistic Marxist terms, ascribing backgrounds, such as rich, middle-income, and poor peasants, to fit in with their own expectations of class divides.

It is also possible that tribunals falsified information, but there was little reason to do so; there were no quotas to fulfil or specified targets, although most tribunals wanted to convey to Narkomiust the scale of the challenges facing them. Some were criticized heavily for having large numbers of unresolved cases and for excessively mild sentences, yet tribunals continued to provide clear evidence of delays and report a wide range of punishments, which suggests the deliberate manipulation of statistics was rare at this stage.

The biggest problem was simply inaccurate record-keeping. The Second All-Russian Congress of Tribunal Officials in April 1920 declared that tribunals should submit an account of their activities every three months, along with statistics on crimes and criminals.[65] But few reported this regularly, probably due to the practicalities of civil war. Many blamed fighting, personnel losses, or evacuation for gaps in their statistics.[66] Otherwise, reports frequently have figures revised or crossed out, sometimes entire categories. With mass crimes such as desertion or banditry, and the increasing prevalence of travelling sessions, it must have been very difficult for understaffed and underfunded tribunals to keep an

[64] These problems are discussed prior to an analysis of the results in Ia. Berman, 'O revoliutsionnykh tribunalakh', *Proletarskaia revoliutsiia i pravo*, 1 (January 1919), 47.

[65] GARF, f. A-353, op. 4, d. 23, l. 21 (26–8 April 1920).

[66] See, for example, various letters in GARF, A-353, op. 3, d. 156, ll. 19 (Voronezh), 27 (Gomel'), 86 (Perm'), 89 (Petrograd), 126 (Tambov), 135 (Tula) (correspondence, October–December 1919).

accurate track of their activities. Sometimes, the numbers simply do not add up. Voronezh's tribunal blamed their inconsistent statistics in 1920 on their inability to hire a statistician until December (others experienced similar problems), remarking optimistically that their statistics were now precise and accurate.[67] Greater accuracy was sometimes claimed in later reports as some tribunals provided updated figures for earlier periods. But even some published statistics do not add up, while different reports use statistics from different numbers of tribunals over different timescales, making comparisons difficult.

When looking for information on particular crimes, moreover, tribunals were only part of the justice system. Clearly many 'counter-revolutionary' crimes ended up in people's courts and, while Narkomiust gathered statistics on them in the same way, the problems were magnified as thousands of them existed. Similarly, various organs beyond the justice system held sentencing powers at times during the civil war. The most obvious was the Cheka, but there were others, such as commissions for desertion, banditry, and food supply. These organs made less effort to record their activities or, in the case of the Cheka, may have never recorded many victims. Tribunal statistics, therefore, only provide part of the picture of revolutionary justice and the struggle against counter-revolution.

All statistics, however, are problematic and only ever provide a guide to the real picture, and those on tribunals are far from valueless. On the one hand, better central control and working practices, and a steadily improving working environment, mean these statistics are likely to be more reliable as the civil war progressed; they are certainly sent to Narkomiust more regularly and provide more detail. As such, the broad trends displayed in the statistics likely reflect real trends (they reinforce themes from the decrees discussed above), even if the unreliability of precise numbers must be stressed. On the other hand, it might not be clear—beyond their use in reports and articles (by both Narkomiust and local tribunals), usually to justify in some way—whether statistics influenced policy, but they did inform how the state viewed and responded to counter-revolution, while gathering and processing this information formed an important part of the extension and exercise of state power.

The first statistics on tribunals were published in early 1919.[68] Thirty-two tribunals had responded, investigating 12,223 cases in the year prior to October 1918—an average of 381 each. Numbers varied from the 49 cases covered by tribunals in Tula and Northern Dvinsk to the 1,697 in Elets and 1,132 in Rybinsk (neither a provincial capital). This diversity was blamed on the lack of people's courts in these areas, confusion over jurisdiction, and the slow dissolution of *uezd*

[67] GARF, f. A-353, op. 4, d. 58, l. 59ob (report, January 1921).

[68] I focus here on statistics gathered centrally. Russian historians often differ in precise numbers when they draw on provincial archives. None, however, appear to challenge the main trends discussed here.

tribunals.[69] This total must be lower than the true figure, as not all tribunals responded and cases dealt with by disbanded *uezd* tribunals were often ignored. These usually dealt with more crimes than their provincial counterparts, such as Rzhev (Tver' province), which investigated over 500 cases but was not included.[70] Confusion was endemic. Orel's department of justice reported on four tribunals in its territory; the provincial tribunal had dealt with 61 cases, while *uezd* tribunals in Livny and Briansk had investigated 267 and 659 respectively, although the former had now closed. Another *uezd* tribunal in Elets had closed and the department had no statistics from it.[71] Yet the published results, as noted, did have statistics from Elets, higher figures from Briansk and Orel, but nothing on Livny. Even in the centre, the published figure for Moscow's tribunal was 404, yet other sources cited over 2,000 cases for a comparable period.[72]

The statistics for subsequent years are outlined in Figure 3.2. The figures for 1919 are also particularly problematic, as over half of the thirty-six tribunals responding provided statistics for only half the year and many others had gaps due to the pressures of the civil war. Figures become more comprehensive for 1920–2, but there remains a disparity between the archival and published records, as the latter only used tribunals with complete statistics.[73] Transport tribunals were also not distinguished from military tribunals initially.

These statistics indicate, unsurprisingly, an increase in caseloads as conflict escalated, although probably more gradual than portrayed, given the problems with the 1918–19 figures. In part, this reflected the expanding nature of counter-revolution. In part, it also reflected the growth in the number of tribunals. But the average number of cases in each civilian tribunal in 1920 was 858, compared to 381 in 1918. Sizeable differences did remain, with a tribunal at the heart of the fighting in the Kuban recording 2,779 cases compared to 208 in Olonets in the north. Crime levels then declined significantly in military tribunals as the fighting died down, but remained constant in civilian tribunals as the focus shifted to violations of the NEP or corrupt officials. Transport tribunals actually became busier, with the emphasis on rebuilding the transport and economic infrastructure under the NEP.[74]

[69] Berman, 'O revoliutsionnykh tribunalakh', 48–9.

[70] GARF, f. A-353, op. 9, d. 45, l. 153 (there are numerous other examples in this *delo*).

[71] GARF, f. R-1005, op. 2, d. 13, ll. 3–3ob (correspondence to cassation department, 8 November 1918).

[72] *Proletarskoe revoliutsiia i pravo*, 5–6, 1–15 October 1918, 78; D. Kurskii, 'Narodnyi sud', *Vestnik zhizni*, 2 (1918), 73. *Izvestiia* (16 July 1918, 6) cites 1,708 cases in Moscow for only 21 December 1917 to 1 June 1918.

[73] The report on military tribunals for 1921 admitted excluding about 10% of returns from tribunals as they were illegally completed or delayed, but claimed this only involved 1.5% of cases.

[74] This contradicts a recent argument that railway tribunals experienced a reduction from February 1922, from a peak of over 1,000 cases per month in 1921; S. Charnyi, 'Revoliutsionnye voennye tribunaly na transporte. 1918-1923' (2014), available at http://polit.ru/article/2014/05/11/revtrib/ [last accessed on 9 October 2017].

	Civilian tribunals	Military tribunals	Transport tribunals
1918	12,223 (published)[75]	-	-
1919	17,501 (archive)[76]	25,643 (archive/published)[77]	-
1920	41,206 (archive)[78]	167,162 (archive/published)[79]	9,596 (archive)[80]
1921	44,944 (archive)[81]	91,830 (published)[82]	9,958 (published)[83]
1922	45,811 (published)[84]	45,540 (published)[85]	27,200 (archive)[86]

Figure 3.2 Cases investigated by tribunals, 1918–22.[87]

To put these figures in context, the tsarist state punished 10,931 people for political crimes from 1894 to 1903 and 35,000 from 1906 to 1912, possibly around 60,000 in total if military courts are included.[88] Similarly, a survey in 1920 recorded 1,377,778 investigated crimes: 86 per cent by people's courts, 12 per cent by military tribunals, and 2 per cent by civilian tribunals.[89] The 2,022 cases recorded in Moscow's tribunal in the first half of 1918 were dwarfed by 44,924 cases

[75] Berman, 'O revoliutsionnykh tribunalakh', 48–9.

[76] GARF, f. A-353, op. 3, d. 156. These figures are from 36 tribunals; most supplied incomplete information. My calculations incorporate clear corrections to printed statistics in reports and correct obvious errors.

[77] GARF, f. A-353, op. 4, d. 111, l. 2. This report admits that statistics were only gathered from late 1919. Trudy tsentral'nyi statisticheskogo upravleniia. Tom VIII. Vypusk 2. Statisticheskii ezhegodnik 1918-1920 gg. Vypusk vtoroi [hereafter Trudy 1] (Moscow, 1922), 91.

[78] GARF, f. A-353, op. 4, d. 112. These figures come from 48 tribunals; 8 provided incomplete information. This compares to published figures of 36,903 from 45 tribunals (Trudy 1, 88) and Narkomiust's reported figures of 33,097 (RSFSR. Narodnyi Komissariat Iustitsii. Otchet IX Vserossiiskomu s"ezdu sovetov (Moscow, 1921), 21).

[79] GARF, f. A-353, op. 4, d. 111, l. 179. This included 3,785 railway cases. The same figure is in D. Rodin, 'Revoliutsionnye tribunaly v 1920-1922 gg.', Vestnik statistiki, 8, 1-3 (1923), 161. Another report stated 160,576 (RGVA, f. 33988, op. 3a, d. 16, l. 4ob).

[80] GARF, f. R-1005, op. 1, d. 57, ll. 82, 84 (figures from RVTR). Published figures gave 9,562 (Trudy 1, 94).

[81] GARF, f. A-353, op. 5, dd. 75, 83. This covers 50 tribunals; 8 provided incomplete information. A report on legal institutions in 1921–2 noted 35,111 cases (GARF, f. A-353, op. 5, d. 72b, l. 185).

[82] Rodin, 'Revoliutsionnye tribunaly', 161; 74,246 were recorded in the first half and 17,584 in the second.

[83] Rodin, 'Revoliutsionnye tribunaly', 161. This figure only covers the second half of 1921.

[84] Trudy tsentral'nyi statisticheskogo upravleniia. Tom VIII. Vypusk 6. Statisticheskii ezhegodnik 1922 i 1923 g. Vypusk vtoroi [hereafter Trudy 2] (Moscow, 1925), 67. Based on information from 62 tribunals.

[85] Trudy 2, 68. Based on information from 12 tribunals.

[86] GARF, f. R-3042, op. 1, d. 38, l. 2 (first half of 1922); d. 39, l. 2ob (second half).

[87] 'Archive' signifies figures taken from the original, unpublished reports from local tribunals or unpublished Narkomiust reports. 'Published' signifies figures published in statistical surveys. Conflicting figures often exist in different published accounts. In this case, the most comprehensive is used (in terms of tribunals counted).

[88] Daly, 'Political Crime', 82–6.

[89] E. Tarnovskii, 'Dvizhenie prestupnosti v predelakh R.S.F.S.R. po svedeniiam mestnykh sudov za 1919-20 gg.', *Proletarskaia revoliutsiia i pravo*, 15 (1921), 3, 12. His absolute totals for tribunals are far too low, but this is also likely to be true of people's courts, so the percentages are probably more accurate.

in the city's people courts, as were the 6,543 cases in Samara's tribunal from February 1919 to April 1921 compared to 107,180 in the province's people's courts in 1919–20.[90] Tribunals also usually dealt with fewer cases than the Cheka. The most recent figures suggest the security police investigated 200,271 new cases in 1921 and 119,329 in 1922,[91] while in Perm' the tribunal's total of 420 cases in the second half of 1919 was much less than the 2,616 in local Cheka branches.[92] All this confirms that tribunals were an exceptional court compared to people's courts, and while they were more active than political courts under tsarism (albeit operating during revolution and civil war), they were more focused than the Cheka.

The statistics also emphasize the huge role played by military tribunals at the height of the civil war. They were far busier than civilian tribunals, boasting an average of 6,283 cases each in 1920, with the tribunal on the Western Front recording 29,058 cases. It is clear, though, that the caseload of military tribunals was more closely linked to the fighting. In 1920, for instance, the authorities noted the war with Poland led to almost twice as many cases in June than January. Another surge in cases in July was followed by a steady increase to the end of year as the Polish conflict was joined by an offensive in the south by General P. N. Vrangel' and then by peasant revolts led by A. S. Antonov and N. I. Makhno.[93] There was a sharp fall across 1921, from 74,246 cases in the first half to 17,584 in the second half, as fighting ceased on several fronts, although the emergence of distinct railway tribunals also contributed to this fall as they took on a growing caseload. In three and a half months from their official creation on 18 March 1920 to 1 July, railway tribunals resolved 1,795 cases, but this rose to 7,801 in the next five months and increased further as these tribunals spread into water transport.

What is hidden in Figure 3.2 is that the numbers of people investigated also increased rapidly as tribunals judged mass crimes such as banditry, desertion, and food-tax violations, where cases involved groups rather than individuals. Incomplete figures record that 47,311 people were involved in 41,629 cases investigated in 1921, rising to 106,818 people in 1922 at a time when Figure 3.2 suggests caseloads decreased.[94] Cherepovets tribunal recorded 399 cases in 1921 involving 3,890 people, while a newspaper cited 289 cases in Moscow in the same period involving 1,214.[95] The mass character of crimes was particularly evident in

[90] D. Kurskii, 'Narodnye sudy', in *Oktiabr'skii perevorot i diktatura proletariata. Sbornik statei* (Moscow, 1919), 244–5; Sh. Gizatulin, *Prestupnost' v Rossiiskoi provintsii i bor'ba s nei v Oktiabre 1917–1922 gg. (na materialakh Samarskoi gubernii)* (Samara, 2012), 108, 115. For a useful comparative survey, see A. Gertsenzon, 'Gubernskie revoliutsionnye tribunaly, narodnye sudy i tovarishcheskie sudy v 1918-1920 gg. (Materialy k istorii sovetskoi ugolovnoi politiki)', *Sovetskoe gosudarstvo*, 6 (1933), 57–72.

[91] O. Mozokhin, *Pravo na represii: Vnesudebnye polnomochiia organov gosudarstvennoi bezopasnosti (1918–1953)* (Moscow, 2006), 246–52.

[92] *Grazhdanskaia voina v Prikam'e*, 429 (report from local Cheka, December 1919).

[93] RGVA, f. 33988, op. 3a, d. 16, l. 4ob (report on military tribunals in 1920, n.d.).

[94] Gertsenzon, 'Gubernskie revoliutsionnye tribunaly', 69.

[95] GARF, f. A-353, op. 5, d. 18, l. 217 (report, 20 January 1922); *Rabochaia Moskva*, 26 February 1922, 4.

travelling sessions, which often dealt with desertion, banditry, and mass rural resistance. A report from Voronezh in January 1921 talked of a session investigating 14,700 people in one trip, but the tribunal reported just 2,422 cases across the entire year.[96] Individual trials in Enesei province and Irkutsk in December 1920 accused 190 and 261 respectively.[97] Tribunals, then, had an even greater impact than simply studying caseloads suggests.

Examining the types of crimes committed, only 5,420 of the 12,223 cases recorded in 1918 (44 per cent) were cases that civilian tribunals were supposed to investigate (the rest should have gone to people's courts), as tribunals struggled to focus on counter-revolutionary crimes during their first year. As discussed in Chapter 1, *uezd* tribunals were the main culprits, but even provincial tribunals struggled for focus: 416 of 593 cases in Kursk (70 per cent) between 18 June and 30 September 1918 dealt with general crimes.[98] This diversity continued throughout the civil war as many tribunals tried to avoid official sanction by placing significant numbers of crimes in a vague 'other' category: Samara recorded 601 of 850 cases between 1 January and 15 June 1921 (70 per cent) in this category, and it was far from alone in this practice.[99]

The 5,420 counter-revolutionary crimes in 1918 consisted of six categories: 1,915 counter-revolutionary actions (35 per cent); 1,722 cases of speculation (32 per cent); 1,037 instances of bribery, forgery, and illegal use of documents (19 per cent); 399 pogroms (7 per cent); 324 cases of sabotage (6 per cent); and 23 cases of espionage (under 1 per cent). Again, tribunals varied widely. There were 191 cases of counter-revolution in Smolensk and 173 in Vladimir, accounting for 77 per cent and 72 per cent of their caseload respectively. There were 124 in Tambov (34 per cent of its caseload), but only 3 cases in Morshansk (2 per cent) and 13 in Kirsanov (7 per cent), both *uezdy* in Tambov. Instead, there were 78 cases of speculation in Morshansk (52 per cent) and 139 in Kirsanov (76 per cent), while only 49 in Tambov (14 per cent).[100] Plots and revolts, of course, were more likely in urban areas at this time, but these differences also reflect differing perceptions of the counter-revolutionary threat, with rural areas quicker to feel the corrosive impact of everyday acts of disobedience.

The obvious changes over the civil war (Figure 3.3) were the steady fall in counter-revolution and speculation, the rise in crimes of office, and the emergence of a new category—crimes against the order of government (*prestupleniia protiv poriadka upravleniia*). A catch-all term in some respects, this category encompassed a range of criminal activities, from avoiding state service (including

[96] GARF, f. R-1005, op. 3, d. 45, l. 150 (report, 20 June 1921).

[97] M. Pivovarov, 'Revoliutsionnye tribunaly v Sibiri (noiabr' 1919 - ianvar' 1923 g.)' (*kandidat* dissertation, Novosibirsk State University, 2007), 104.

[98] GARF, f. R-1005, op. 2, d. 10, l. 1ob (report to cassation department, n.d.).

[99] GARF, f. R-1005, op. 3, d. 45, l. 150 (report, 20 June 1921).

[100] Berman, 'O revoliutsionnykh tribunalakh', esp. 48–9, 53–6.

Year	Counter-revolution	Speculation	Crimes of office	Against public order	Other	Total
1918	35	32	19[101]	–	14	100
1920	18	6	28	48[102]	–	100
1921	11	6	29	54	–	100
1922 (first half)	7	–	21	59	13	100

Figure 3.3 Types of crimes in civilian tribunals, 1920–2 (in per cent).[103]
Source: Berman, 'O revoliutsionnykh tribunalakh', 48–9, 53–6; Rodin, 'Revoliutsionnye tribunaly', 158.

desertion) to some economic crimes (including speculation, thereby explaining its demise as an individual category) and crimes against public order. The term obscures some of the points raised by various statistics in the archives. One survey of civilian tribunals in the second half of 1920, for instance, noted that almost 21 per cent of prosecutions involved desertion, emphasizing that this crime remained a major focus for all tribunals.[104] Otherwise, the decrease in counter-revolutionary crime reinforces the points above; namely that it remained associated with traditional counter-revolutionary acts (revolts and plots) and that it was politically convenient by 1921–2 to be able to report a decline.

As before, these figures mask geographical diversity. According to Narkomiust, some provinces, particularly those around Moscow (such as Kaluga, Tula, Tver', and Riazan'), saw less than 5 per cent of their cases classified as counter-revolutionary in 1921; others, particularly in the north and east (such as Arkhangel'sk, Simbirsk, Viatka, and most of Siberia) placed over 20 per cent of their cases in this category. Much reflected the geographical spread of the fighting, with crimes of office more common in those provinces at the heart of the Bolshevik state (over 40 per cent in Moscow, Kaluga, Tula, Tambov, and others) and far more counter-revolutionary revolts and plots around the periphery.[105] Remoter provinces, though, had a tendency to classify more activities as counter-revolutionary than those at the centre.

These categories also mask the sheer diversity of crime still investigated by tribunals. The military tribunal on the southern front, for example, compiled a list of around a hundred individuals convicted in August 1919. There were the expected crimes: theft; speculation; espionage; desertion; agitation; sabotage; selling state property; ill-discipline; not fulfilling orders; forgery; organizing plots; and

[101] Crimes of office were not categorized as such in the 1918 statistics, but this figure includes bribery, forgery, and the illegal use of documents—all crimes usually committed by people in official posts.
[102] Other published statistics suggest this figure should belong in the 'other' category; Trudy 1, 88.
[103] Archives and official reports reveal similar trends. There are no published figures for 1919 and archives are too incomplete.
[104] GARF, f. A-353, op. 4, d. 111, l. 206 (list of crimes for the second half of 1920, n.d.).
[105] *RSFSR. Narodnyi Komissariat Iustitsii. Otchet*, 52; GARF, f. A-353, op. 5, d. 72b, l. 79a (report, n.d.).

Year	Political	Military	Crimes of office	Criminal	Other	Total
1920 (second half)	13	25	21	38	3	100
1921 (first half)	14	27	25	34	–	100
1921 (second half)	15	20	35	22	8	100
1922 (first half)	6	22	45	22	5	100

Figure 3.4 Types of crimes in military tribunals, 1920–2 (in per cent).
Source: Rodin, 'Revoliutsionnye tribunaly', 158.

Year	Political	Crimes of office	Against public order	Criminal	Other	Total
1920 (Mar.–Dec.)	6	46	19	29	–	100
1921 (second half)	3	68	9	17	3	100
1922 (first half)	1	81	4	13	1	100

Figure 3.5 Types of crimes in transport tribunals, 1920–2 (in per cent).
Source: Rodin, 'Revoliutsionnye tribunaly', 159.[106]

so on. In addition, a political worker did not pay for his room at a hotel; another man for a meal at a canteen; and another for his use of a car. One commissar was convicted of negligence on duty for acquiring worthless typewriters for prohibitively high prices. One doctor had illegally convened a meeting to raise funds for a gift and had illegally imposed a contribution on everyone for this purpose. Another doctor was caught drunk in a public place. A commander was convicted of illegally keeping a saddle and harness, while a soldier had been illegally exchanging herrings and potatoes.[107]

Many of these acts were 'crimes of office', and the rise in these crimes was far more evident in military and, especially, transport tribunals (see Figures 3.4 and 3.5). Within this category, other statistics for 1922 reveal the prominence of theft from state stores (44–49 per cent of all crimes over the two halves of 1922) and bribery, extortion, sabotage, and negligent relations to duties.[108] Transport was extremely susceptible to robbery and theft of state goods, while transport tribunals also dealt with cases relating to underperformance, crashes, or other mishaps (variously tasked as sabotage, not fulfilling duties, or violations of regulations). That said, only 7–9 per cent of cases in transport tribunals in 1920–2 was classified by the authorities as crimes specific to railways, with the rest being political, military, or general crimes.[109]

[106] A more detailed breakdown of crimes in 1920 is in *Trudy 1*, 94–5.
[107] RGASPI, f. 17, op. 109, d. 201, ll. 235ob-248 (report, n.d.).
[108] GARF, f. R-3042, op. 1, d. 38, l. 16ob (first half of 1922); d. 39, l. 16ob (second half).
[109] GARF, f. R-1005, op. 1, d. 57, ll. 83, 85 (figures produced by RVTR).

Overall, it is worth reiterating the 'decline' in counter-revolutionary and political crimes. The state did not abandon counter-revolution as a category. All these crimes were still counter-revolutionary in that they harmed the state and the revolution, and, more specifically, the term retained political value for particularly threatening crimes and 'model' trials. But it is clear the state no longer wanted to stress counter-revolution as it emerged victorious from the civil war. After all, the Bolsheviks could hardly claim victory if there remained high levels of counter-revolution, and it suited the political narrative if statistics could provide 'scientific' proof of a fall. It also became evident that different categories might help combat more urgent threats. Economic crimes, for instance, were seen by the state as counter-revolutionary but not by ordinary people, and distinguishing them allowed the state to stress the damage they caused without becoming bogged down in whether the acts were consciously counter-revolutionary or not. In other words, counter-revolutionary activities continued, but organized counter-revolution was disappearing.

Quantifying Counter-Revolutionaries

The shifting nature of counter-revolution and the increasingly broad range of crimes targeted led to a corresponding shift in the backgrounds of those investigated and convicted. The statistics on 'counter-revolutionaries' are patchy and usually from the later period of the civil war when information was gathered more consistently. But several points stand out. The vast majority of those convicted were men (96.5 per cent in 1920–2) and young to middle-aged, with only a quarter over 40 years old.[110] These basic characteristics are unsurprising: young male soldiers in the Red Army fed into desertion statistics, while peasant 'bandits' were usually also male, as were most officials at this stage.

The prevalence of these crimes meant that tribunals had to abandon their initial expectation that counter-revolutionaries would be obvious political and social enemies. Instead, they were focusing overwhelmingly on people who had been peasants before the October Revolution (Figure 3.6) even if the increasingly fluid social structure amid the turmoil of civil war meant that many of these 'peasants' were now soldiers, officials, or in positions of responsibility in the party, state, or military (Figure 3.7). This picture is reinforced when examining educational (Figure 3.8) or party backgrounds (Figure 3.9).

A report on military tribunals in the second half of 1920 also noted that the majority of all crimes were committed by people with peasant backgrounds, especially desertion (83.3 per cent). Those with working-class backgrounds were more likely to be involved in crimes of office (not fulfilling orders, incorrect use of

[110] Rodin, 'Revoliutsionnye tribunaly', 177. Juveniles (under 18 years) were supposedly judged separately, even if they had been involved in counter-revolutionary crimes, although it is hard to know if this happened in reality.

	State crimes	Crimes against public order	Military crimes	Crimes of office	General
Workers and craftsmen	10	2	9	25	21
Peasants	71	97	81	52	62
Intelligentsia	9	–	6	8	3
People using hired labour	1	–	–	1	–
Other	9	1	4	14	14
Total	100	100	100	100	100

Figure 3.6 Social position of convicted criminals in tribunals in late 1921–early 1922 on the eve of October 1917 (in per cent).
Source: Rodin, 'Revoliutsionnye tribunaly', 173, 178, 181, 183, 185.

	State Crimes	Crimes against public order	Military crimes	Crimes of office	General
Command Structure	7	–	9	7	4
Soldier or Sailor	11	1	73	16	32
Responsible Worker	5	1	2	21	4
Rank-and-file Official	7	1	3	25	9
Workers and Craftsmen	6	1	2	13	16
Peasants	56	94	10	13	25
Other	8	2	1	5	10
Total	100	100	100	100	100

Figure 3.7 Occupation of convicted criminals in tribunals in late 1921–early 1922 when crime committed (in per cent).
Source: Rodin, 'Revoliutsionnye tribunaly', 173, 178, 181, 183, 185.

	State crimes	Crimes against public order	Military crimes	Crimes of office	General
Higher	2	–	–	2	–
Middle	9	–	7	9	4
Lower and domestic	69	51	82	80	81
Illiterate	20	49	11	9	15
Total	100	100	100	100	100

Figure 3.8 Education of convicted criminals in tribunals in late 1921–early 1922 (in per cent).
Source: Rodin, 'Revoliutsionnye tribunaly', 174, 178, 181, 183, 185.

	State crimes	Crimes against public order	Military crimes	Crimes of office	General
Communist Party member	6	–	6	11	7
Member of another party	1	–	–	–	–
Non-party	93	100	94	89	93
Total	100	100	100	100	100

Figure 3.9 Party background of convicted criminals in tribunals in late 1921–early 1922 (in per cent).
Source: Rodin, 'Revoliutsionnye tribunaly', 174, 179, 181, 183, 185.

authority, and so on), reflecting that many from such backgrounds had been promoted over recent peasant recruits. The report also linked crimes with rank. Soldiers, as might be expected, formed the majority of most crimes, especially desertion and not fulfilling orders (both over 70 per cent). But political crimes (plots, revolts, and so on) were as likely to be carried out by people who were neither soldiers nor in the command structure, presumably administrators, while this group was more likely to be engaged in espionage. People in the command structure were responsible for almost a third of all cases of abuses of power, or excessive or ineffective use of authority, as might be expected, but were also commonly not fulfilling orders, enacting other duties or involved in general crimes.[111]

There were, as always, anomalies in the statistics. Transport tribunals classified 20 per cent of those convicted in an 'other' category in 1920, rather than workers, peasants, intelligentsia, or people using hired labour.[112] The railway tribunal in Samara claimed that an unusually high 63 per cent (505 of 796) of those convicted from January to June 1922 were not peasants, workers, or intelligentsia, but had hired labour or were from another social background.[113] In Orel, 53 per cent of the 1,283 cases investigated between April 1920 and early 1921 were committed by peasants, 7.4 per cent by workers, and a high 39.6 per cent by the intelligentsia and bourgeoisie.[114] Clearly tribunals were classifying criminals in different ways, with some seemingly conditioned into seeing all enemies as bourgeois (they opposed the revolution and thus must be bourgeois) or trying to apply Marxist categories to criminals. From 1 January to 1 July 1921, the provincial tribunal in Arkhangel'sk prosecuted 256 peasants (out of 313 overall convictions), noting that 88 were classified as rich peasants (kulaks), 137 as middle-income peasants (*sredniaki*), and 31 as poor peasants (*bedniaki*).[115]

[111] GARF, f. A-353, op. 4, d. 111, l. 206 (report, n.d.).
[112] GARF, f. R-3042, op. 1, d. 38, ll. 16ob-17 (first half of 1922); d. 39, l. 16ob (second half).
[113] GARF, f. R-3042, op. 1, d. 86, ll. 11ob, 14ob (successive reports, n.d.).
[114] GARF, f. R-1005, op. 3, d. 35, l. 17ob (report, 10 February 1921).
[115] GARF, f. R-1005, op. 3, d. 10, l. 26 (report, 23 November 1921).

Statistics from particular localities again provide nuance to the broad categories used to compile national averages. As well as 256 peasants in Arkhangel'sk, 41 townspeople, 4 honourable citizens, 3 nobles, 3 priests, 2 foreigners, and 4 others were also convicted. A total of 303 were males over 18 years old and 9 were women, while one male was under 18. Similarly, in Kazan' 521 were convicted from January to March 1920, of which 427 (82 per cent) were peasants, 63 workers, 18 officials, 5 engineers, 2 teachers, 1 a trader, and 1 a lawyer.[116] The military tribunal on the Southern Front in August 1919 saw crimes committed by people employed in all the jobs needed to enable the military to function: commissars, doctors, supply managers, porters, orderlies, clerks, caretakers, office boys, forest rangers, butchers, grooms, and so on.[117] Similarly, a typical rural trial on 16 July 1921 in Votskaia autonomous region sentenced sixteen people for involvement in a range of criminal activities from plots, banditry and desertion, to speculation, crimes of office, and drunkenness. All but two were male, all were in court for the first time, and most had served in the tsarist military but not the Red Army. Most were married (some with children) and had a basic education. Some owned a little land, and one apparently had a cow and a horse. Others worked as carpenters, millers, or locksmiths. Only a few were party members and these had joined in 1918–19. If anyone had served in an official post, it was only in a parish organ.[118]

Local reports also reveal the extent to which crimes of office involved officials at all levels. The transport tribunal for the Baltic Sea noted that of the 506 people prosecuted, 59 had been heads of departments and sections, 57 agents of various organs, and 37 responsible workers.[119] Similarly, a report by the transport department of the Supreme Tribunal and the Cheka to VTsIK noted that 3,798 people had been arrested for theft, embezzling stores, breaking into wagons, and other such crimes in June–August 1921. While 60 per cent were peasants, 33 per cent workers, and 7 per cent from other social backgrounds, 860 (23 per cent) had been officials in the railway militia, 536 (14 per cent) in the general militia, 152 (4 per cent) railway personnel, 26 in the criminal-investigative department of the militia, and 16 in the Cheka.[120] Twenty-eight per cent of those sentenced by the travelling session of the South-west Front in autumn 1920 were from the command structure. They were found guilty of various crimes, from illegal arrests, bribery, and expropriating state property to panicked flight, drunkenness, and anti-Soviet agitation.[121]

116 GARF, f. A-353, op. 4, d. 112, l. 88 (report, n.d.). The backgrounds of the other four were not given.

117 RGASPI, f. 17, op. 109, d. 201, ll. 235ob-48 (report, n.d.).

118 GARF, f. R-1005, op. 2, d. 104, ll. 562–64ob (trial protocol, 16 July 1921).

119 GARF, f. R-3042, op. 1, d. 95, l. 34 (annual report, 20 May 1921).

120 GARF, f. A-353, op. 4, d. 28, ll. 148–9 (report, 22 October 1921); 88% were literate and 5% party members.

121 RGASPI, f. 17, op. 109, d. 245, ll. 1–2 (report on activities between 31 July and 3 September 1920, n.d.).

In short, the statistics indicate that counter-revolutionaries could and did come from all social backgrounds serving in any type of post. This again reflects the elasticity of the term and the power of tribunals to investigate any individual, reinforcing the coercive role of law and tribunals. This could also be seen to reflect their seeming arbitrariness, but these statistics are not particularly surprising (or arbitrary) for the crimes investigated. The focus of tribunals on particular crimes (especially desertion, banditry, and crimes of office) as the civil war progressed is clearly reflected. Nevertheless, even if predictable, the variety of social backgrounds of counter-revolutionaries was a concerning development and a source of tension for the Bolsheviks that only escalated with the growing prevalence of mass crimes and the shock campaigns launched to target them.

Mass Crimes and Shock Campaigns

By 1920–1 tribunals were dealing with crimes on a mass scale. One historian noted that Viatka's tribunal held the 'Trial of the 256' in June 1920, all accused of crimes of office, and argued that many tribunals faced 'organized' crime—organizations operating in cities capable of providing false documents to deserters and other criminal services for a fee.[122] This was not the case in most places, but all tribunals did face mass crimes and they responded by relying increasingly on 'shock campaigns (*udarnye zadanii*)'. One participant recalled how tribunals were wholly occupied by these campaigns by 1921, citing campaigns to target crimes of office, collect the new food tax, and so on; others referred to the 'shock nature (*udarnost'*)' of their work to convey the scale of the threat.[123] The stress on these 'new' campaigns is a bit misleading; tribunals still investigated a wide range of crimes, while they had targeted the crimes involved in these campaigns for several years. But the state did start to devote special attention to targeting urgent issues, especially crimes committed on a mass scale—desertion, banditry, violations of food taxes, crimes of office, and religious activity—and tribunals took a central role.[124] This role, moreover, was increasingly militarized as tribunals undertook 'campaigns' on the food or church 'front', 'fighting' the revolution's enemies.

[122] I. Narskii, *Zhizn' v katastrofe: Budni naseleniia Urala v 1917–1922 gg.* (Moscow, 2001), 449.

[123] P. Alimov, 'Tri goda Sovetskoi iustitsii v Sibiri', *Zhizn' Sibiri*, 6–7 (1923), 79; D. Gor'ev, *Deiatel'nost' revoliutsionnykh tribunalov na Kubani (1918–1922 gg.)* (Armavir, 2011), 108.

[124] The prominence of these campaigns is clear from local studies of tribunals; P. Fedorenko, 'Revoliutsionnye tribunaly Smolenskoi gubernii (dekabr' 1917–1922 gg.)' (*kandidat* dissertation, Smolensk State University, 2006), 79–98, 116–37; N. Gorokhovskii, *Stanovlenie i pravovoi status voennykh tribunalov v Srednem Povolzh'e (noiabr' 1917 g. – 1922 g.)* (Tol'iatti, 2004), 75–85; I. Malykh, 'Sozdanie i deiatel'nost' revoliutsionnykh tribunalov na Iuzhnom Urale v 1919–1921 godakh (istoricheskii aspekt)' (*kandidat* dissertation, Cheliabinsk Institute of the Ural's Academy of State Service, 2010), 78–113, 184–96; and T. Sudakova, 'Sozdanie i deiatel'nost' Otdeleniia Verkhovnogo tribunala VTsIK v Gorskoi ASSR (1921-1923 gg.): Istoricheskii aspekt' (*kandidat* dissertation, North Ossetian State University, 2009), 119–75.

These campaigns reinforced the ongoing expansion in how the state understood counter-revolution. This was certainly the case with the campaign against food-tax violations. Tribunals had targeted those resisting food requisitioning since 1918, but they were at the forefront of the food 'front', as many called it, after the introduction of the NEP in March 1921, ensuring the new tax-in-kind was collected. A legacy of forced requisitions, where officials had essentially seized as much grain as possible rather than just the prescribed quotas, had left a suspicious peasantry resistant to state intervention. Entire *volosti* in some *uezdy* refused to pay.[125] When this became apparent across summer 1921, frequent decrees were issued, all allocating tribunals a central role. In early July, one of these outlined the two-pronged role of tribunals. On the one hand, tribunals reinforced the authority of food supply organs, punishing anyone who disobeyed their orders. On the other, tribunals regulated these organs, targeting ineffective or corrupt officials, thereby making them stronger.[126]

From June 1921, tribunals established special departments to oversee the campaign, and on 12 July they were told to create 'permanent' travelling sessions to deal with the huge number of cases, which were to include local food supply and soviet officials. They were easier to organize than usual sessions, since they required fewer officials and were funded by provincial food committees.[127] A report from the first half of 1922 highlighted tribunals—Vitebsk, Kaluga, Riazan', Tver' Iaroslavl', and Cherepovets among them—where over 85 per cent of cases involved food-tax crimes, although others remained under 10 per cent.[128] Over 100 travelling sessions were sent out over all the *uezdy* in Siberia in 1921,[129] and 155 of 162 cases (1,869 of 1,883 people involved) observed in 8 sessions of the Tiumen' tribunal in November 1921–January 1922 involved non-payment.[130] Large swathes of the peasantry were involved. One of the few reports to comment on the background of those convicted (from the Crimea) noted that 47 per cent were large households (over 50 *desiatiny*), 40 per cent middle households (20–50 *desiatiny*), 12 per cent small households (under 20 *desiatiny*), and 1 per cent landless.[131]

As the new sowing season approached and amid fears of widespread famine, Narkomiust supported these activities through a frequent 'struggle with hunger' section in its weekly journal from February 1922, arguing that it was a civic duty to pay the tax, not just to fulfil the state's needs but those of people dying from

[125] GARF, f. R-1005, op. 3, d. 16, ll. 25–25ob (report from Vologda, October 1921).

[126] *DSV*, XVII, 256–60 (2 July 1921).

[127] *IZ*, 175–8 (3 October 1921, citing decree on 12 July).

[128] GARF, f. A-353, op. 5, d. 72b, l. 185ob (report on legal institutions, 1921–2).

[129] O. P'ianova, 'Revoliutsionnye tribunaly Zapadnoi Sibiri (konets 1917 – nachalo 1923 gg.)' (*kandidat* dissertation, Omsk State Pedagogical University, 2002), 205. See also Pivovarov, 'Revoliutsionnye tribunaly', 68–71, 152–82, and M. Pivovarov, 'Uchastie revoliutsionnykh tribunalov Sibiri v prodovol'stvennoi kampanii 1920-1921 gg.', *Gumanitarnye nauki v Sibiri*, 2 (2005), 88–91.

[130] GARF, f. R-1005, op. 3, d. 196, l. 20 (report, 7 February 1922).

[131] GARF, f. R-1005, op. 3, d. 211, ll. 2ob-3 (report from the food tax department of the Crimean tribunal from 1 September 1921 to 1 January 1922, 15 January 1922).

hunger.[132] This language was also adopted by the authorities in at least one province, Kursk, which issued appeals stressing the difficult economic position and worsening hunger when urging officials and sessions to act decisively and severely, demonstrating 'revolutionary energy' when dealing with offenders.[133]

The food 'front' became part of a broader economic 'front' as tribunals were urged to target other economic issues under the NEP. Tribunals had always been involved with economic crimes, especially speculation, which had involved various activities, from illegal brewing to those peasants in Penza province sentenced to five years' forced labour and imprisonment for opening an oil press, processing oil seeds, and selling them to the public.[134] But as the civil war transformed into an internal economic war, tribunals enforced decrees on everything from the production of peat to enforcing the salt monopoly.[135] As with other categories, economic crimes became broader, particularly as the Bolsheviks belatedly appreciated the interrelated nature of the economy and how economic concerns underpinned criminal activity. As the tribunal for Kuban' and the Black Sea noted, much banditry rested on economic matters, and political banditry (actions prompted by political opposition) turned into the banditry of hunger (acting through a need to survive) as harvests deteriorated.[136]

The campaign against religion also demonstrated that categories become ever broader. Religious groups had also been targeted from the start, particularly the Orthodox Church, as its formal privileges under tsarism made clergy obvious counter-revolutionaries alongside other class enemies. The Church lost its position as the state-sponsored religion in January 1918 and attacks on clergy and high-profile trials followed. Priests were prosecuted for various crimes, from counter-revolution, exploitation, and extortion to agitation, speculation, and publishing offences. These crimes were easily applied to clergy, but some tribunals were more enterprising. One priest, I. A. Skvortsov, complained that he had been accused of extortion, despotic relations with the local school (including torturing children and criticizing teachers), illegal use of land, selling church wine, fostering arguments among peasants, illegal use of the church press, and counter-revolutionary agitation.[137]

By 1922, however, a more sustained campaign had started.[138] Fewer military operations, the desire to eradicate a class enemy once and for all, the need for

[132] *ESIu*, 12 February 1922, 1. See also many subsequent issues in March–June 1922.

[133] GARF, f. R-1005, op. 3, d. 137, ll.36–36ob (appeal, n.d.). See also other appeals on ll. 37–9.

[134] J. Daly and L. Trofimov (eds.), *Russia in War and Revolution, 1914–1922. A Documentary History* (Indianapolis, 2009), 166–7 (trial resolution, 17 January 1921).

[135] *DSV*, XIV, 102–3, 239 (12 and 20 April 1921); XVIII, 277–8 (29 August 1921).

[136] GARF, f. R-1005, op. 3, d. 209, l. 49 (report, 6 March 1922).

[137] *'Prispelo vremia podviga . . .' Dokumenty Sviashchennogo Sobora Pravoslavnoi Rossiiskoi Tserkvi 1917–1918 gg. o nachale gonenii na Tserkov'* (Moscow, 2012), 316–23 (appeal to Patriarch Tikhon, 14 April 1918).

[138] As well as the studies cited below, see Iu. Titov, 'Revoliutsionnye tribunaly v bor'be s tserkovnoi kontrrevoliutsiei', in I. Isaev and O. Omel'chenko (eds.), *Istoriko-pravovye voprosy vzaimootnoshenii*

wealth, and the recognition of an opportune time came together. Lenin argued in March 1922 that starvation would make people less sympathetic towards the Church, while an article in Narkomiust's journal noted the valuables held in the 'cathedrals' of various 'cults' (churches, mosques, and synagogues) should be used to purchase bread.[139] Indeed, opposition to the seizures of church valuables now became the most common crime. Since valuables would contribute to the state's funds (and thus the revolution), any opposition was a direct attack on the people, contributing to their hunger and their harsh material conditions. Across 55 tribunals, at least 231 cases involving 732 people were heard, resulting in 44 executions and 346 prison sentences.[140] Many trials included laity, especially those active in religious societies, thereby attacking belief more generally.[141]

The ongoing campaign against desertion also saw a steady expansion in definitions of criminality. Tribunals were swamped in desertion cases by 1919 and special commissions were created. At provincial level, these held the same powers as tribunals as long as a tribunal member was present, while those in *uezdy* could issue lesser sentences for minor offences. These commissions provided a permanent local presence, but tribunals were also urged to create departments for desertion to include representatives from local committees.[142] Yet combatting desertion remained extremely difficult as deserters easily fled into the countryside once the authorities arrived in their village. Thus the state came to see concealing deserters or withholding information on them as equally serious. Moreover, targeting relatives of deserters—usually under the pretext of 'concealing' the whereabouts of the perpetrators—was the only conceivable action available in the absence of the offenders. And it was considered effective. One official described participating in a session that spent two months in various *volosti* in Aleksinskii *uezd* in Tula province in May 1919. They liaised with local officials, using local knowledge to issue threats against their families, confiscate livestock, or worse. Apparently these threats, more than anything else, had an impact. Another official reported that such sessions forced a passive population to assist the authorities.[143]

gosudarstva i tserkvi v istorii Rossii (Moscow, 1988), 147–68; and J. Ryan, 'Cleansing NEP Russia: State Violence against the Russian Orthodox Church in 1922', *Europe-Asia Studies*, 65, 9 (2013), 1807–26.

[139] R. Pipes (ed.), *The Unknown Lenin* (New Haven, 1996), 152–5 (letter to Molotov for the politburo, 19 March 1922); and Ia. Brandenburgskii, 'Organy iustitsii v bor'be s golodom', *ESIu*, 23 March 1922, 1–2.

[140] J. Daly, '"Storming the Last Citadel": The Bolshevik Assault on the Church, 1922', in V. Brovkin (ed.), *The Bolsheviks in Russian Society* (New Haven, 1997), 257.

[141] M. Kail', *Vlast' i pravoslavnye veruiushchie v Rossiiskoi provintsii nachala 1920-x godov* (Smolensk, 2008), 224. For accounts of trials in Smolensk, see M. Kail', *Pravoslavnaia tserkov' i veruiushchie Smolenskoi eparkhii v gody revoliutsii i grazhdanskoi voiny* (Moscow, 2010), 97–114.

[142] *IZ*, 119 (13 December 1919), 136 (8 April 1920).

[143] N. Nemtsov, 'Sud bez formal'nostei', *Rabochii sud*, 21 (1927), 1659–62; GARF, f. R-1005, op. 67, d. 13, l. 3ob (report on Vologda's provincial tribunal June–October 1920, 7 October 1920). On the

The campaign was slowing down by 1921. Desertion was still serious, but regulations eased as fighting receded. Amnesties began to cover convicted deserters, less serious cases went to people's courts (those not involving important military situations, people in important posts, banditry or gangs, or forged documents), and desertion departments in tribunals closed.[144] Instead, similar tactics were employed against banditry—a crime that encompassed everything from organized peasant armies to attacks on official buildings, food requisitioning squads, trains and supply depots by individuals, gangs or entire villages.[145] In March 1921, commissions were formed to unite 'military' (force) and 'political' (agitation) methods. These did not have legal powers like their desertion counterparts, but coordinated all the relevant organs.[146] Otherwise, the military tribunal on the Western Front recorded twenty travelling sessions in 1921 devoted to banditry, some lasting over a month. 'Destructive' punishments were the most effective, such as confiscating the property of family or helpers.[147]

These campaigns brought crimes of office to the fore, since tribunals found themselves targeting officials as frequently as the general population. The rapid expansion of state organs after October had brought many unsuitable people into service, and the shift to the civil war's 'internal' front meant a greater focus on their activities and performance, even those involved in law enforcement itself.[148] From 1921 to 1922, decrees prioritized the campaign against embezzlement (*khishchenie*) from the state and other abuses of authority, including bribe-taking. The scale of the problem was not in doubt, as the statistics above make clear. Viatka's tribunal reported that half of its cases in the year before October 1922 involved crimes of office. Of these, 35 per cent involved abusing, exceeding, or ineffectively using their authority; 25 per cent expropriating stores; 25 per cent bribery and extortion; and 15 per cent sabotage and negligence.[149] Tribunals conducting food campaigns reported chaotic and poorly prepared supply organs, with some officials setting their own levels of tax.[150] The Bolsheviks believed that,

overwhelming challenge and the role of tribunals, see K. Levshin, *Dezertirstvo v Krasnoi armii v gody Grazhdanskoi voiny (po materialam Severo-Zapada Rossii)* (St Petersburg, 2016), esp. 88–90, 143–4.

[144] *DSV*, XIII, 10–12 (2 February 1921).

[145] See, for example, *'Antonovshchina'. Krest'ianskoe vosstanie v Tambovskoi oblasti v 1920–1921 gg.: Dokumenty, materialy, vospominaniia* (Tambov, 2007), 266 (RVTR to the military tribunal in Tambov, 21 January 1921).

[146] *DSV*, XIII, 514–15 (31 March 1921); XVIII, 200–2 (18 August 1921).

[147] RGVA, f. 33988, op. 2, d. 245, ll. 6ob-10ob (report, early 1922).

[148] A. Pozdniakova, 'Dolzhnostnye prestupleniia sotrudnikov pravookhranitel'nykh organov v 1918-1919 gg. (po materialam Viatskogo gubernskogo revoliutsionnogo tribunala)', *Vestnik Viatskogo gosudarstvennogo gumanitarnogo universiteta*, 4 (5) (2012), 79–84; and M. Chigrin, 'Dolzhnostnye prestupleniia sotrudnikov pravookhranitel'nykh organov v 1918-1919 gg. (po materialam Simbirskogo gubernskogo revoliutsionnogo tribunala)',*Izvestiia Samarskogo nauchnogo tsentra Rossiiskoi akademii nauk*, 20, 3 (2) (2018), 315-20.

[149] GARF, f. R-1005, op. 3, d. 118, ll. 71–71ob (report, n.d.).

[150] GARF, f. R-1005, op. 3, d. 16, ll. 25–25ob (report, Vologda, October 1921).

if the correct people were appointed with sufficient political consciousness (meaning they used their powers effectively and followed orders), then policies would be successful. Instead, offenders forgot their duty, harmed hungry workers and peasants, and discredited Soviet power.[151]

A specific campaign against bribe-taking (*vziatochnichestvo*) was operating by 1921, but there remained an 'epidemic' of bribery a year later.[152] This fuelled an escalation of the campaign, with a special effort starting—initially for a month—from 10 October 1922. It was, in the words of one commentator, the end of the civil war and the struggle with class enemies, and the beginning of the war against disorganization and hunger. Everyone needed to fight.[153] Subsequent articles in Narkomiust's journal charted progress in this 'war' through copious statistics. An initial, incomplete report noted 817 cases in all courts over the month, and the campaign's perceived success saw it extended into 1923, when numbers rose to 4,763 cases by May.[154] This campaign gathered pace alongside a similar one on red tape (*volokita*), another crime present throughout the civil war but with a lower profile despite contributing to impressions of the government as ineffective and inefficient.[155]

Historians have drawn links between these mass campaigns and the 'mass operations' of later years as campaigns against speculators and bribe-takers turned seamlessly into campaigns against NEP men, kulaks, and others in the 1920s to 1930s.[156] It was not so much that this transformation was inevitable, but rather that the practices and mechanisms were in place by the end of the civil war. Tribunals were a case in point; the targeted approach, fluid definitions, flood of decrees, threats, and use of special commissions and inter-institutional cooperation all represented practices later extended in scale. The main element missing at this stage was intensity as despite the pressures of civil war, practices remained far more flexible and lenient than the mass operations of later years.[157]

[151] *IZ*, 163–4 (26 February 1921).

[152] *DSV*, XVIII, 148–9 (16 August 1921); *Brianskii rabochii*, 16 September 1922, 1 (in GARF, f. R-1005, op. 3, d. 106, l. 3). See also I. Orlov and G. Markosian, *Vziatka i bor'ba s nei v gody nepa* (Moscow, 2011).

[153] See, for example, I. Slavin, 'Voina so vziatochnichestvom', *ESIu*, 6 October 1922, 1–2.

[154] A. Estrin, 'Vziatochnichestvo i ugolovnaia repressiia', *ESIu*, 27 October–4 November 1922, 6–10, and 11 November 1922, 3–6; 'Itogi udarnoi kampanii po bor'be so vziatochnichestvom', *ESIu*, 30 December 1922, 22–3; V. Zen'kovich, 'K itogam bor'by so vziatochnichestvom', *ESIu*, 13 March 1923, 219–20; V. Zen'kovich, 'K itogam bor'by so vziatochnichestvom', *ESIu*, 31 May 1923, 492.

[155] A. Lisitsyn, 'Pora perestroit'sia po-boevomu', *ESIu*, 9 March 1922, 1–3; M. Grodzinskii, 'Sabotazh, biurokratizm i volokita', *ESIu*, 20 May 1922, 2–3.

[156] See P. Hagenloh, '"Mass Operations under Lenin and Stalin', in J. Harris (ed.), *The Anatomy of Terror: Political Violence under Stalin* (Oxford, 2013), 163–75; J. Harris, *The Great Fear: Stalin's Terror of the 1930s* (Oxford, 2016), 31–5; and P. Holquist, 'State Violence as Technique: The Logic of Violence in Soviet Totalitarianism', in A. Weiner (ed.), *Landscaping the Human Garden* (Stanford, 2003), 31.

[157] This is discussed in respect to punishment and mercy in Chapters 4 and 5 respectively.

The Search for Stable Categories

It should be clear by now that the idea of 'lawlessness' in early Soviet Russia is more complex than many commentators imply: there were elastic categories, numerous crimes, and much arbitrariness, but increasingly there were also detailed regulations, clear priorities, and attempts to foster consistency. There were no written codes, but there were countless decrees that essentially acted as codes. Moreover, despite the bravado of theorists like Stuchka and Krylenko, the Bolsheviks were not against issuing their own set of codes. As noted in Chapter 2, Narkomiust had been harbouring plans since 1918, Lenin was keen, and other Bolsheviks felt it might be beneficial. Many courts lacked complete sets of decrees and demonstrated little grasp of specifics even if they understood the main tenets of official policy. Now Soviet Russia was increasingly stable, promoting revolutionary legality (*zakonnost'*), of which written law codes were a central element, over revolutionary consciousness (*soznanie*), offered order and uniformity over improvisation and arbitrariness. Written laws, in other words, might help increase consistency and broaden knowledge of the law, and help create stable and easily accessible definitions of criminal behaviour and the new social order.

The criminal code was active from 1 June 1922 and gathered together the decrees discussed above. Guided by the experience of civil war, the preamble eschewed assumptions that counter-revolution consisted of specific actions committed by certain types of class enemies; instead, it defined crime as consisting of all socially dangerous actions or inaction committed by all types of dangerous people. The codes also declared that people could be convicted of acts that were not yet defined as crimes but were analogous to acts that were, in case further developments created new crimes.[158] After that, eight categories of crime were outlined: counter-revolution; crimes against government order; crimes of office; violations in the laws governing the separation of Church and state; economic crimes; crimes against life, person, and property; military crimes; and crimes against public security and order.

The code brought together definitions in one place and provided the first guidance on punishments for each crime (see Chapter 4), but there was nothing on jurisdiction. Crimes against government order, for instance, ranged from armed bands and attacks on infrastructure (dealt with by tribunals) and non-payment of taxes (by tribunals if it involved food taxes), to trying to leave or enter the country without a passport or participating illegally in elections (not dealt with by tribunals). Other categories were a similar mix. This no doubt reflected the continued importance placed on circumstances, scale, motivation, and the background of the criminal in determining whether certain crimes went to tribunals or

[158] *Ugolovnyi kodeks R.S.F.S.R.* (Moscow, 1922), 3 (articles 5–7, 10).

not, but, in the short term, it required clarification and a new procedural code came into force on 1 July detailing how courts should implement the code. This stated that tribunals dealt with five of the eight categories: counter-revolutionary 'state' crimes; crimes against government order; crimes of office; 'special' economic and property crimes; and military crimes.[159] Later categorization cited the specific articles relevant to tribunals.[160] Nevertheless, all this must have contributed to existing confusion and fuelled the arguments (discussed in Chapter 2) of those pressing for a unified court system now that the civil war had ended.

The codes were heavily promoted and a pamphlet commemorating the fifth anniversary of the Supreme Court even published a double page of images depicting eight key crimes and their punishments. The first page (Figure 3.10, clockwise from top left) covered involvement in the organizations of the international bourgeoisie, espionage, abuses of authority, and participation in armed bands, with the other page highlighting bribery, religious crimes, expropriations, and desertion. And there is evidence that greater consistency was emerging steadily prior to the abolition of tribunals. Certainly some tribunals took months to hear about the codes, and there is plenty of evidence of ongoing diversity and provincial idiosyncrasies, but one article believed the chaos and exceptionalism of civil war were turning into security and norms.[161] Another author reported that officials had a better grasp of crimes and processes due to the codes.[162] More and more tribunals cited the code in their activities and used the standardized categories in their discussions, statistics, and reporting.

The prominence of counter-revolution, along with economic crimes and crimes of office, was one of the few elements distinguishing this code from its tsarist predecessors.[163] Similarly, the first major trial after the code—that of the Socialist Revolutionaries—revolved around 'traditional' counter-revolution: attacking the October Revolution; planning armed revolt; creating a military organization; links with the international bourgeoisie; links with the White opposition; and so on.[164] Yet many things had changed over the civil war. Definitions of counter-revolution had expanded far beyond the activities envisaged in November 1917, and this spawned new categories of crime threatening to the state and the revolution. On the one hand, this meant tribunals became ever busier, particularly once they expanded into the military, and this reaffirms the civil war as a period of

[159] *Ugolovno-protsessual'nyi kodeks R. S. F. S. R. utv. V. Ts. I. K. 25 Maia 1922g. s alfavitno-postateinym ukazetelam i oglavleniem* (Moscow, 1922), 11–12 (article 28).

[160] GARF, f. R-1005, op. 1, d. 140, l. 1a (statistics on military crimes, November 1922).

[161] A. Zhivopostsev, 'Chto zhe takoe zakonnost'?', *Vestnik proletarskogo prava i iuridicheskikh norm* [Tambov], 3–4 (1922), 1–4.

[162] GARF, f. R-3042, op. 1, d. 84, l. 19ob (report from Perm' transport tribunal, 5 August 1922).

[163] See A. Piontkovskii, 'Kontr-revoliutsionnye prestupleniia v Ugolovnom Kodekse RSFSR', *Sovetskoe pravo*, 2 (1924), 7–40. Also P. Solomon, *Soviet Criminal Justice under Stalin* (Cambridge, 1996), 28–30.

[164] *Protsess P. S.-R.: Prigovor Verkhovnogo revoliutsionnogo tribunala postanovlenie prizidiuma V. Ts.I.K. i vozzvanie Kominterna* (Moscow, 1922), 4.

Figure 3.10 Who is punished and how in Soviet Russia (1923).
Source: *Piat' let Verkhovnogo suda, 1918–1923* (Moscow, 1923).

increasing social unrest and the role of exceptional justice and legal coercion in maintaining order. On the other, the growing precision in the categorization of crime formed part of the extension of state control and, more generally, the state-(re)building project of the Bolsheviks. This may have lacked impact initially amid the rapid growth in opposition and unrest, but categorizing crime was central to the Bolsheviks' vision for a new social order—defining acceptable and normal behaviour, while condemning the unacceptable and abnormal—and tribunals also played a key role in realizing this vision, as their prominence in the mass campaigns proved.

The changing nature of counter-revolution, however, revealed some of the tensions and contradictions facing the Bolsheviks during the civil war that historians have highlighted through studies of other areas. The most worrying development was the shifting nature of the criminal. Pushed to its furthest extent, theory suggested there was no such person as a criminal, merely people forced to commit criminal acts because of the circumstances in which they found themselves. Realists in Narkomiust had always scoffed at this idealism, and the realities of the civil war demanded that people conducting serious criminal acts were found, punished, and treated as criminals, to serve as examples for everyone else. This was easy to justify, ideologically and practically, for the expected class enemy—the irredeemable bourgeoisie, whether noble, officer, industrialist, or clergy. It was far more problematic when it became apparent that most counter-revolutionary crimes were committed by proletarians—workers and peasants—who were supposed to support the revolution.

Traditional enemies were still there, of course, and they continued to dominate the Bolsheviks' external language. Numerous state-sponsored posters, in particular, cement the presence of monarchists, landowners, officers, and wealthy businessmen as the revolution's enemies throughout the civil war, with one in 1919 portraying them on the receiving end of popular justice (Figure 3.11). Such posters

Figure 3.11 The People's Court (1919).

Source: Poster RU/SU 63, Poster collection, Hoover Institution Archives.

were visually impressive, politically acceptable, and allegorical rather than depicting real trials. But it was hard to ignore that this poster appeared at a time when the internal language of tribunals was dominated by deserters, recalcitrant peasants, and misbehaving officials. Apart from posters castigating deserters, it was difficult to admit this contradiction publicly. One tactic was to use class terms to mask popular discontent (such as kulak for a rich, exploitative peasant) or pejorative terms (such as bandit) to convey social and cultural condemnation.[165] Another tactic, as discussed, was to soften the hard categories of counter-revolution as they clashed in the courtroom with the realities of everyday life by exploring socio-economic backgrounds, politics, and intent. This was much easier to do in courts—one of the benefits of revolutionary justice—than elsewhere, as cases could be explored, defendants interrogated and assessed, and witnesses quizzed to obtain a more detailed picture.

Contradictory language was nothing new,[166] but there were similar contradictions in the effect this had on revolutionary justice. If the violence of law categorized certain acts as counter-revolutionary, then, in legal officials' eyes, categorization marked law's control over violence and the first step to achieving justice for the people and the revolution over the counter-revolutionary threat.[167] Law's role in managing and defining acceptable levels of violence can also be seen in the numerous trials of officials for abusing their authority.[168] Yet the elastic nature of counter-revolution undoubtedly accelerated the increasing polarization of society. Here, law was fuelling violence rather than restraining or containing it.

All this exacerbated divisions between society and the new state, and created a lasting legacy, not least with respect to the peasantry. Lenin and other leading Bolsheviks had always been suspicious of the peasantry's revolutionary credentials, and the increasing resistance in the countryside confirmed these doubts. Law—in its contradictory role—both contributed to this emerging conflict and served as one of the main weapons in it. None of this was comparable to the systematic, planned violence against the peasantry in the later 1920s, but the categorization of various forms of rural crime as counter-revolutionary, the perception of the peasant as inherently counter-revolutionary, as proven by their activities during this period, and the belief that this threat persisted no doubt laid the roots of future developments.

165 O. Figes, *Peasant Russia, Civil War* (Oxford, 1989), 340–53.
166 Raleigh, *Experiencing Russia's Civil War*, 410.
167 For this idea, see Baxi, 'The State's Emissary', 249.
168 A. Retish, 'Judicial Reforms and Revolutionary Justice: The Establishment of the Court System in Soviet Russia, 1917-22', in C. Read, P. Waldron, and A. Lindenmeyr (eds.), *Russia's Home Front in War and Revolution, 1914–22. Book 4: Reintegration—The Struggle for the State* (Bloomington, 2018), 397.

4
The Trial

The distinct role of revolutionary tribunals has been asserted in several contexts so far in this book. Standing between people's courts and the Cheka, tribunals offered a more forceful approach to combatting counter-revolution than regular organs of justice, but a more flexible one than unregulated violence. Categories of counter-revolution could be articulated, enforced, and publicized in the courtroom, helping to establish the parameters of the new political and social order. But at the same time these seemingly unyielding categories could be softened to recognize the limitations of state power during the civil war (not every counter-revolutionary could be shot or imprisoned) and the realities of everyday life (most counter-revolutionary activities emerged from a struggle to survive). Exploring politics, intent, and socio-economic backgrounds in the courtroom allowed the state to condemn counter-revolution publicly, while providing a rationale for a range of responses depending on contingencies.

The focal part of this process, therefore, was the trial. It allowed both sides to discuss their version of events in public; it formed the basis of the educational message, whether in the actual courtroom or when publicized later; and it produced the state's response in the form of punishment. If law was to compel people to act in certain ways and forge model Soviet citizens, and if it was to deter, rehabilitate, and punish, then the trial was crucial, and it was the primary means by which tribunals projected the state's authority and ideology, and the main distinction between revolutionary justice and violence.

Studies are often keen to distinguish between trial and punishment. As one argued, it is important to hold a trial even if there is no punishment: it is where 'wrongs' are formally recognized, attributed, and condemned—it establishes the 'truth' of wrongdoing. This can be a form of punishment itself, as those found guilty are condemned in public.[1] The Bolsheviks also made this distinction. Trials indicated that certain behaviour was unacceptable and *why*; as one official noted, the legal process was a 'school'.[2] It was not just deciding guilt or innocence but establishing the validity of the state's ideas and values. It was important to punish dangerous crimes, but it was equally important to convey *why* these crimes were dangerous and to do so repeatedly across Russia. Thus, particularly during the first

[1] A. Duff, L. Farmer, S. Marshall, and V. Tadros, *The Trial on Trial: Volume 3. Towards a Normative Theory of the Criminal Trial* (Oxford and Portland, 2007), 81–3.

[2] GARF, f. R-3042, op. 1, d. 23, l. 37 (report on railway tribunals, spring 1921).

The State versus The People: Revolutionary Justice in Russia's Civil War, 1917–1922. Matthew Rendle, Oxford University Press (2020). © Matthew Rendle.
DOI: 10.1093/oso/9780198840428.001.0001

year, the Bolsheviks saw public condemnation as a suitable punishment, and many officials continued to believe that lesser punishments or even mercy were appropriate as long as the severity of the crime had been proven. For mass crimes, the individual on trial was less important than the bigger picture, with the trial more an ideological lesson than a legal forum. The Deputy Commissar of Justice, P. I. Stuchka, wrote that the *public* exposure of crimes would 'remove the masks' from the counter-revolution's heroes, and proving the existence of these enemies justified the Bolsheviks' actions.[3] Tribunal trials were not a search for the 'truth' in the conventional sense, then, but the 'truth' was not completely absent: the Bolsheviks needed to determine what threatened their authority, establish a framework for this threat, and convince people of its validity in order to justify their actions and mobilize support.[4]

Many legal scholars also contend that trials allow public scrutiny of the legal process, facilitating justice.[5] Tribunals were not concerned with justice as we would understand it, but the public nature of trials could be harnessed to help legitimate political trials.[6] Trials are not the quickest or most certain means of sentencing and punishing, and alternatives existed (the Cheka), but 'destroying the enemy', as noted, is not the sole purpose of political trials.[7] A public trial—however imperfect—contributed to an image of order and authority with some independence from politics, and the impression of a verdict in the people's interests. Although there were plenty of flaws, as will be seen, a level of procedure was adhered to, evidence presented, witnesses questioned, and the allegations countered. All this made tribunals, in the words of one official, look better in the eyes of the people than those organs that administered sentences without trials. Their relative openness, in his view, enabled tribunals to garner more public confidence, even if the use of the death penalty fostered suspicion.[8] The trial became an interactive discourse between the state and the people, each stating their views and responding to their opponents' arguments, with the audience influencing proceedings (shouting or applauding) and even legitimizing them (their presence supported the official line that trials represented the people's will). Legitimacy was enhanced because, as outlined in this chapter, trials were not a foregone conclusion; insufficient evidence and ineffective prosecutors led to dismissed cases and acquittals, while arguments in the trial did influence the

[3] P. Stuchka, 'Old and New Courts (1918)', reprinted in W. Rosenberg (ed.), *Bolshevik Visions* (2nd edition, 2 volumes, Ann Arbor, 1990), I, 188.

[4] These arguments are informed by J. Meierhenrich and D. Pendas, '"The Justice of My Cause is Clear, but There's Politics to Fear": Political Trials in Theory and History', in J. Meierhenrich and D. Pendas (eds.), *Political Trials in Theory and History* (Cambridge, 2017), 35, 40–2.

[5] Duff, Farmer, Marshall, and Tadros, *The Trial on Trial*, 259–85.

[6] Using law as a source of legitimacy is common in authoritarian states; T. Moustafa, 'Law and Courts in Authoritarian Regimes', *Annual Review of Law and Social Science*, 10 (2014), 286–7.

[7] O. Kirchheimer, *Political Justice: The Use of Legal Procedure for Political Ends* (Princeton, 1961), 6.

[8] GARF, f. R-3042, op. 1, d. 84, l. 4ob (report from the railway tribunal in Perm', November 1920).

sentence. This uncertainty also made trials appear more objective and thus more effective, even if inadvertently; as has been noted, the didactic element of the trial is blunted if its outcome is predictable—a drama must be uncertain to be completely effective.[9]

And all trials can be powerful dramatic events where the performances of participants are central to persuading, understanding, and judging.[10] The interaction of state and society in the form of judges, defendants, and (sometimes) witnesses and lawyers provided an often compelling mix of power, ideology, and personal tragedy. A. V. Peshekhonov, a socialist critic and observer, compared 'strolling' into Petrograd's tribunal during its early days—where a 'new and merry farce' was always playing—with visiting the theatre.[11] Few defendants would have been as flippant with their lives at stake, but there was a performative element to trials that was particularly important in a largely illiterate society, and trials appropriated verbal, visual, and structural elements from the theatre.[12] All sides put on a performance, whether to justify the allegation, claim innocence, or convince of the authority of the court. All sides used emotional rhetoric, and hyperbole and superlatives abounded, whether describing the heinous nature of the threat or the wretched circumstances behind a crime. Trials were even sometimes advertised in the press in a format similar to theatre plays, where the crime constituted the plot, the prosecutors were in large print as the stars, and the defendants in smaller type as the supporting cast.[13] In many places, particularly smaller towns and villages, crowds attended because it was entertaining, appealing to their curiosity and base instincts.

Nonetheless, trials cannot be completely distinguished from punishment; the 'majesty' and 'terror' of law reinforce a court's authority and lend weight to its message.[14] Lenin argued that punishment had to be 'sufficiently impressive' to act as a deterrent, and officials repeated this mantra.[15] The chairman of the Main Railway Tribunal, Iu. Iu. Mezhin, felt sentences should be severe, especially in the early months of a tribunal, so it could establish its authority as a 'formidable' weapon. Sentences, he also noted, were publicized afterwards so needed to send a

[9] L. Farmer, 'Trials', in A. Sarat, M. Anderson, and C. Frank (eds.), *Law and the Humanities: An Introduction* (Cambridge, 2010), 469.

[10] R. Burns, *A Theory of the Trial* (Princeton, 1999), 133, 136–7; M. Damaška, *The Faces of Justice and State Authority: A Comparative Approach to the Legal Process* (New Haven, 1986), 51, 62.

[11] A. Peshekhonov, *Pochemu ia ne emigriroval?* (Berlin, 1923), 53.

[12] R. Stites, 'Trial as Theatre in the Russian Revolution', *Theatre Research International*, 23, 1 (1998), 7–13. More generally, see M. Ball, 'The Play's the Thing: An Unscientific Reflection on Courts Under the Rubric of Theater', *Stanford Law Review*, 28, 1 (1975), 81–115; and J. Simonett, 'The Trial as One of the Performing Arts', *American Bar Association Journal*, 52, 12 (1966), 1145–7.

[13] For example, *Kommunisticheskii trud*, 15 December 1921, 3.

[14] For these terms, see D. Hay, 'Property, Authority and the Criminal Law', in D. Hay et al., *Albion's Fatal Tree: Crime and Society in Eighteenth-Century England* (London, 1975), 26–31.

[15] V. Lenin, *Collected Works* (47 volumes, Moscow, 1960–70), XLV, 348 (order, 20 October 1921).

clear message to the wider population.[16] They must deter some, wrote L. D. Trotskii, Commissar of War, while fostering confidence in others; that is, they must frighten some into behaving correctly and reassure others that correct behaviour was worthwhile.[17] Other reports cited the famous French proverb, 'à la guerre comme à la guerre', either in French or its Russian equivalent (*na voine, kak na voine*)—all actions are justified in war.[18]

Yet, as this chapter will demonstrate, the 'external language' of harsh sentences and mercilessness differed from the wide range of sentences dispensed in practice. This was partly explained by disparities between central and local authorities, and the struggle of the former to impose their authority. But behind the rhetoric central organs also sought alternative and more nuanced responses to counter-revolution than those offered by the Cheka. And when tribunals did impose the death sentence, officials believed their procedural authority and public nature made this acceptable violence on the part of the state.

None of this is meant to imply that trials ran smoothly for the Bolsheviks. Individual tribunals ran trials differently and dispensed vastly different sentences for similar crimes. This made it difficult to convey a clear and consistent message. Central authorities exacerbated diversity by preaching mercilessness while tacitly encouraging moderation. An immense effort went into the relatively few high-profile trials, leaving the majority short and functional with insufficiently clear messages as tribunals struggled to deal with their workload. Tribunals also had an ambiguous relationship with the audience from the start. Legal theorists envisaged a court driven by ordinary people acting as prosecutors, advocates, witnesses, and even offering guidance on sentences. Thus tribunals would truly dispense popular justice. This relied on the assumption that the audience would act in accordance with Bolshevik ideals—naïve, perhaps, but one made nevertheless. There was genuine surprise after the first trials when the audience failed to condemn the defendants in the manner expected. This threatened the purpose of tribunals and corrupted their political message.

This chapter pieces together the trial process, examining how cases were brought to court, the legal personnel, location, procedures, and sentences. As the civil war progressed, the pressures of conflict and high caseloads meant most trials were cursory affairs, permitting little exploration of the crime, even if they did discuss evidence and interrogate witnesses. From the start, however, some cases were considered sufficiently important to warrant a more high-profile trial in a prominent location, using lawyers and surrounded by greater publicity. Over time, Lenin urged more of these 'model (*obraztsovyi*)' trials to use particular cases

16 GARF, f. R-3042, op. 1, d. 2, ll. 2, 12 (circulars to railway tribunals, n.d. and 3 May 1920).

17 *The Military Writings and Speeches of Leon Trotsky: How the Revolution Armed*, trans. B. Pearce (5 volumes, London, 1979–81), II, 200–3 (article, 23 April 1919).

18 GARF, f. A-353, op. 2, d. 26, l. 10 (report, western region tribunals, n.d.); *Krasnaia armiia*, 26 June 1918, 1.

to throw a spotlight on common threats. In some senses, these were 'show (*pokazatel'nyi*)' trials in that the verdict was preordained to a greater extent than 'everyday' trials, charges and evidence were more likely to be prefabricated, and the trial was focused on demonizing the defendants and educating the audience.[19] But this term is more suited to those trials that started appearing in 1922. By then the Bolsheviks were not only drawing on their experiences of holding trials to exert even greater control over the process but using major trials to deal with more exceptional crimes, culminating in the trial of the Socialist Revolutionaries. All trials, though, remained as problematic as they were valuable: the dialogue was never as tightly controlled as in trials in the late 1920s to 1930s, the educational message far from clear in many cases, and the sentences far more varied and inconsistent than the authorities expected.

The Pre-Trial Process

The first problem lay in the pre-trial investigation. Nothing was said about procedure initially. Key figures behind tribunals, such as Stuchka, probably felt that much was self-evident (the need to gather evidence and formulate a case) and the most important step was establishing the new court. But the first chairman of Petrograd's tribunal complained he had no experience of legal matters, received no guidance, and had no laws to guide him.[20] The state's case in the first trial, discussed in Chapter 1, suffered accordingly from an incoherent prosecution. Other early trials revealed incomplete investigations, weak evidence, and unclear accusations. Memoirs describe defendants reading about the allegations against them in newspapers and mingling together in prison.[21] These problems persisted. A member of a military tribunal recalled that they had no idea of legal work initially. When the defendant arrived from a military unit with details of his crime, they simply judged him and wrote the sentence in a book. It was often difficult to judge without research, so they created an investigative commission and also acquired a clerk who had worked in courts prior to 1917 to guide them on procedure.[22] Many of his suggestions, though, were deemed 'unacceptable', highlighting initial tensions between a *revolutionary* legal system and an *effective* system.

[19] For definitions of a 'show' trial, see A. Allo, 'The 'Show' in the 'Show Trial': Contextualizing the Politicization of the Courtroom', *Barry Law Review*, 15 (2010), esp. 52–3, 64.

[20] I. Zhukov, 'Revoliutsionnyi tribunal (Vospominaniia pervogo predsedatelia tribunala)', *Rabochii sud*, 22 (1927), 1759.

[21] S. Ovsiankin, 'V pervom tribunale', *Sud idet!*, 21 (1927), 1208–14; V. Pavlov, 'Moi vospominaniia o "Krestakh"', *Krasnaia letopis'*, 2–3 (1922), 144–9; and F. Vinberg, *V plenu u 'obez'ian' (zapiski 'kontr-revoliutsionera')* (Kiev, 1918), 8–9, 13–14, 20, 34–5.

[22] A. Ustiuzhaninov, 'V voennye gody', in *Voennye tribunaly—organy sotsialisticheskogo pravosudiia* (Moscow, 1958), 90–1.

The People's Commissariat of Justice (Narkomiust) decided quickly that there was no point in having a revolutionary system if it was not effective. The first two chapters detailed how tribunals became embedded within an increasingly regulated and centralized legal system, with the aim of ensuring they operated more consistently and effectively. Successive decrees on tribunals became more comprehensive and internal regulations still more so, covering all aspects of the legal process and culminating in the criminal–procedural code (effective from 1 July 1922). Tribunals, therefore, increasingly operated within prescribed parameters. Critics, then and now, would argue this was a veneer of a legal process that did not disguise the Bolsheviks' control over courts and arbitrary practices on the ground. This is true, but the emerging legal process was heavily influenced by Western models (hardly surprising given that most Bolshevik theorists were former lawyers or educated in the law), and, while procedural safeguards were designed more to enhance consistency than ensure justice, the result often had positive results for defendants, meaning only a minority of cases investigated by tribunals went to court (see Figure 4.1) and providing the basis for cassation (see Chapter 5).

Cases came to tribunals from various sources: the Cheka, people's courts, militia, civil and military organs, denunciations, or individuals' own initiative. Viatka's provincial tribunal noted that 37 per cent of its cases from January to September 1919 came from the Cheka, 3 per cent from the local militia, 2 per cent from citizens' denunciations, 1 per cent from people's courts, and the rest from elsewhere. From July to September 1920, Arkhangel'sk's provincial tribunal received cases from thirty different sources, including various branches of the Cheka (again 37 per cent), the militia (25 per cent), people's courts (16 per cent), other tribunals (7 per cent), and various local organs (14 per cent).[23] Figures vary, but the Cheka was the most important source for most tribunals.

	Sent to trial	Dismissed	Transferred to another court
1919	35	38	27
1920	28	37	35
1921	32	26	42

Figure 4.1 The destination of cases investigated by provincial tribunals (in per cent).
Source: GARF, f. A-353, op. 3, d. 156; op. 4, d. 112; and op. 5, dd. 75, 83.

[23] GARF, f. A-353, op. 3, d. 156, l. 23 (report, Viatka); f. R-1005, op. 67, d. 12, l. 53 (report, Arkhangel'sk).

All tribunals were obliged to assess cases within forty-eight hours. Almost all required further investigation before a decision was made.[24] This was done by a tribunal's investigative commission, by an administrative (*rasporiaditel'nyi*) meeting of the judges (as opposed to a legal meeting or trial), or in a meeting of the leading members (college) of the tribunal. There were usually three outcomes: a case was brought to trial, closed, or transferred to a people's court if not sufficiently counter-revolutionary. Moscow's tribunal weeded out unsuitable cases as soon as they arrived before making decisions on the remainder after an investigation. As the caseload increased, meetings were almost daily and usually discussed six to eight cases a day, although this number rose to thirty-five one day.[25] It became impossible to assess all but the most clear-cut cases within forty-eight hours; too many complex cases, too few personnel, huge territories, and difficult conditions meant that some tribunals took months to find evidence and witnesses. Officials pointed this out repeatedly and it was debated at the highest levels, but the timescale remained on paper if not in reality.

There is not much evidence available to explore the decision-making process, but a report on the activities of Tsaritsyn's provincial tribunal in Nikolaevskii *uezd* from December 1920 to March 1921 provides some idea. In December, eighteen cases were discussed in an administrative meeting: twelve concerned a refusal to pay the grain quota; three concealed bread; one illegal testimony on the amount of land sown; one speculation in salt; and one the expenditure involved in grain collection. All were dismissed: in two cases, the quota had now been fulfilled; there was one mitigating case of illness; ten cases benefitted from an amnesty; three cases lacked evidence; one was dismissed due to the advanced age of the defendant; and one person did not have any grain. Subsequent months saw the same process elsewhere in the province as cases were dismissed for lack of evidence or because the original crime (usually not fulfilling the quota) had now been rectified or was considered unimportant. Even accusations of seemingly obvious counter--revolution—revolt, sabotage, crimes of office, and desertion—were dismissed as lacking evidence or importance. Similar cases, though, did make it to trial on other occasions, so clearly the tribunal was assessing each individually.[26]

Statistics mask a great deal of variation between tribunals, but reports sent to Narkomiust (Figure 4.1) suggest that only 35 per cent of cases made it to trial in a provincial tribunal in 1919, 28 per cent in 1920, and 32 per cent in 1921. Comparable figures exist elsewhere; in December 1919, Narkomiust reported

[24] On changes in investigative structures over time, see V. Lomov and N. Lomov, *Organy predvaritel'nogo sledstviia Sovetskoi Rossii v period grazhdanskoi voiny (seredina 1918 g.-1920 g.)* (Volgograd, 2003).

[25] TsGAMO, f. 4612, op. 1, d. 280, ll. 64–64ob (protocol of the inspection committee, 3 December 1918); op. 2, d. 2 (protocols of the presidium, 3 February to 16 December 1919); op. 2, d. 3 (protocols of the investigative commission, 20 February to 27 September 1919).

[26] GARF, f. A-353, op. 5, d. 84, ll. 2–12ob (various statistics, December 1920 to March 1921).

that 32 per cent of cases were tried, while a later report noted 27 per cent in the first half of 1921.[27] Other reports recorded 31 per cent in 1920 in military tribunals and 41 per cent in the first half of 1922, and 45 per cent in transport tribunals from March to June 1920 and 27 per cent in 1922.[28]

None of this is meant to imply that procedures were perfect; too many inspections (see Chapter 2) or appeals (Chapter 5) suggest otherwise. But the point is that, as tribunals developed, so too did a legal process—however imperfect—that attempted to ensure that by the time a tribunal brought a case to court, it was convinced a crime had occurred, there was sufficient evidence, and the crime was sufficiently counter-revolutionary to be worthy of a tribunal. Much rested, of course, on what was considered 'sufficient' evidence and a 'crime', but being investigated by a tribunal did not inevitably lead to a trial.

The Revolutionary Judge

The composition of tribunals was another problem facing the authorities. Tsarist-era legal officials, while not banned, were expected to oppose the revolution as they were believed to have colluded in the oppression of the proletariat. Moreover, revolutionary justice needed to be inclusive if it was to represent the people's will. Indeed, the emphasis on revolutionary consciousness over statutory law marginalized legal training, and it was believed that those without legal education would be less likely to subscribe to pre-existing prejudices and be more attuned to popular opinion. The broader objectives of trials, furthermore, meant that tribunal workers had to be revolutionary fighters and political agitators as well as legal officials. Legislation, therefore, stressed that anyone could be a judge who was appointed by the local soviet. In reality, Bolshevik domination of the soviets meant that Narkomiust expected judges to be party members, who were considered the most capable of defending the interests of the revolution and demonstrating revolutionary consciousness.

The numbers required, however, quickly grew beyond initial expectations as caseloads grew and the legal process became more complex. In the provincial tribunal in Viatka in June 1919, for example, there were forty-six people and they required more: twenty-one in the tribunal, twenty-one in its investigative commission, and four in the college of prosecutors. The tribunal consisted of a

[27] GARF, f. A-353, op. 5, d. 72b, l. 79a (report on tribunals, 1920–1, n.d.).

[28] GARF, f. A-353, op. 4, d. 111, l. 179 (report on military tribunals, n.d.); op. 3, d. 40. l. 131 (report on railway tribunals up to 1 July 1920, n.d.); RGVA, f. 33988, op. 2, d. 454, l. 7 (report on military tribunals, mid-1922); GARF, f. R-3042, op. 1, d. 38, l. 6; d. 39, l. 5 (reports on transport tribunals in 1922, n.d.). One set of published figures suggests that 63–5 % of cases in military tribunals went to trial, but these were based on a restricted sample; *Trudy tsentral'nyi statisticheskogo upravleniia. Tom VIII. Vypusk 2. Statisticheskii ezhegodnik 1918–1920 gg. Vypusk vtoroi* [hereafter *Trudy 1*] (Moscow, 1922), 90–2.

chairman, two members (judges), ten candidate members, three secretaries, two typists, and a clerk, a watchman, and a messenger. The investigative commission was formed of a chairman, five members, seven workers, two secretaries, two clerks, two typists, a watchman, and a messenger. Finally, the college of prosecutors included three members and an office worker. There was a wage structure (a judge earned twice as much as a typist) and opportunities to progress (from candidate members to members).[29] Viatka was about average at this time for a civilian tribunal, although some employed stenographers, statisticians, security personnel, and others. Numbers increased further as workloads peaked in 1920–1. Moscow's tribunal recorded ninety-six people in 1921, rising from fifty-eight in 1920.[30] Some military and transport tribunals were even larger, sometimes over 150.[31]

Tribunals complained repeatedly about staff shortages, particularly investigators and judges. There was a shortage of conscientious party members across the state, rations and pay were often better elsewhere, and posts involved directly in the fighting or the economy were considered more crucial. And then there were illnesses, absences, and arrests. In 1918–19, Moscow tribunal faced never-ending queries over appointments, transfers, holidays, and wages.[32] From late 1917 to early 1923, it had seven chairman and its composition completely changed three times as it lost 341 people to other posts.[33] Riazan' recorded twelve changes in June 1922, eleven in July, seven in September, and nine in November.[34] Throughout the civil war, tribunals reported being only a half to two-thirds complete, although their intended size remains unclear. Reports suggested thirty-three in April 1920, including six judges and five investigators, rising to eighty-eight by autumn 1921, including nine judges and ten investigators.[35] Nothing, though, was confirmed officially.

Staffing pressures were a factor in the decision in February 1919 to reduce the number of judges required in a trial by a civilian tribunal from seven to three in common with military and transport tribunals. Yet these tribunals also had problems, as ideally their judges required specialist knowledge of these areas. A report on railway tribunals stated that judges should have party, tribunal, and

[29] GARF, f. A-353, op. 3, d. 141, ll. 63–4 (correspondence to Narkomiust, 7 June 1919).

[30] TsGAMO, f. 4613, op. 2, d. 90, ll. 38, 209–10 (various records on personnel).

[31] M. Pivovarov, 'Struktura i kadrovyi sostav revoliutsionnykh tribunalov v Sibiri (konets 1919 – nachalo 1923 g.)', in I. Kuznetsov (ed.), *Sibir': problemy istorii povsednevnosti XVII-XX vv.* (Novosibirsk, 2005), 114–25.

[32] TsGAMO, f. 4613, op. 2, d. 6 (protocols, 21 September 1918 to 2 September 1919).

[33] See D. Pavlov's introduction to '"Rukovodstvuias' obstoiatel'stvami dela i veleniiami revoliutsionnoi sovesti": Dokumenty Tsentral'nogo gosudarstvennogo arkhiva Moskovskoi oblasti o deiatel'nosti Moskovskogo revoliutsionnogo tribunala. 1917-1922 gg.', in *Almanakh 'Rossiia. XX vek'*, available at https://www.alexanderyakovlev.org/almanah/inside/almanah-intro/72272 accessed 12 June 2019.

[34] GARF, f. R-1005, op. 5, d. 79, ll. 30, 38, 45, 62 (reports to the Supreme Tribunal, July–December 1922).

[35] GARF, f. A-353, op. 4, d. 23, ll. 16–16ob (2nd Congress of Chairmen of Tribunals, 26–8 April 1920); f. R-1005, op. 3, d. 3, ll. 91–91ob (composition of provincial tribunals, autumn 1921).

military experience (mainly understanding military discipline and structure), as well as a knowledge of railways. It was almost impossible to meet all these criteria, although the first—party experience—was deemed the most important. With this in mind, officials specified that chairmen of railway tribunals should have at least three years' party membership, something that was not said explicitly for other tribunals. Only two tribunals failed to meet this condition.[36]

Tribunal judges were from lower social backgrounds and more party-orientated than judges in other courts, thus representing a sharper break from the old legal system. In 1918, 90 per cent of fifty judges in twenty-nine civilian tribunals were party members, 42 per cent were workers, 60 per cent had low levels of education, 26 per cent middling levels, and 14 per cent high.[37] By 1922, over 99 per cent of 265 tribunal officials surveyed were party members. Another survey of a hundred recorded that 50 per cent were workers, 19 per cent civil servants, 10 per cent peasants, 2 per cent had previous legal experience, 83 per cent had low levels of education, 10 per cent middling, and 4 per cent high.[38] In the military, statistics on over 650 judges in 135 tribunals in 1920 noted that 38 per cent had joined the party before October 1917 and another 33 per cent in 1918, 6 per cent had higher education and 26 per cent middle, and 86 per cent were between 20 and 35 years old. Chairmen were usually older and longer-term party members.[39] Archived personnel records tend to agree, although they suggest more strongly that most had joined the party after October or at least after February 1917.[40] These records confirm that judges were male and usually Russian. Moscow's tribunal stood out in 1921 for employing six women (three as investigators), as did the military tribunal in Saratov for employing Germans, a Pole, and a Greek in 1922.[41]

People who had been party members since 1917 and worked in tribunals from the start were described as 'experienced' and were in demand, especially if they had a 'capacity for work'.[42] Tribunals asked repeatedly for anyone with legal

[36] GARF, f. A-353, op. 3, d. 40, l. 130ob (report on railway tribunals up to 1 July 1920).

[37] M. Kozhevnikov, *Istoriia sovetskogo suda 1917–1956 gody* (Moscow, 1957), 40.

[38] E. Tarnovskii, 'Lichnyi sostav i repressiia revtribunalov', *Ezhenedel'nik Sovetskoi iustitsii* [hereafter *ESIu*], 11, 16 March 1922, 6–7. These figures were later disputed, with the suggestion that all judges belonged to the party and greater numbers had higher (6%) and middling (17%) levels of education as well as legal backgrounds (8%); T. Roginskii, 'K voprosu o lichnom sostave i repressiiakh revtribunalov', *ESIu*, 13, 1 April 1922, 6–7.

[39] RGVA, f. 33988, op. 3a, d. 16, l. 179 (annual report on military tribunals in 1920).

[40] GARF, f. R-1005, op. 5, dd. 47 (Arkhangel'sk), 50 (Vitebsk), 54 (Viatka), 64 (Moscow), 75 (Petrograd), 79 (Riazan'), 81 (Saratov), 89 (Tambov), 93 (Tiumen'), 140 (military tribunals on the Western Front), 146 (Volga military tribunals), 150 (Moscow military tribunal), 177 (Baltic military tribunals) (personnel folders, 1920–1). For a series of short biographies of local officials, see M. Pivovarov, 'Revoliutsionnye tribunaly v Sibiri (noiabr' 1919 - ianvar' 1923 g.)' (*kandidat* dissertation, Novosibirsk State University, 2007), 188–239.

[41] GARF, f. R-1005, op. 5, d. 64, l. 2 (report, 11 August 1921); d. 146, l. 256 (report, 1 June 1922).

[42] GARF, f. R-1005, op. 5, d. 47, ll. 53, 60 (comments on I. K. Gorbunov, chair of Arkhangel'sk tribunal, September–November 1922); d. 54, ll. 8, 47 (comments on I. A. Farfonov, chair of Viatka tribunal, August 1922); f. R-3042, op. 1, d. 387, ll. 9–9ob (comments on Comrade Blokhin, 14 June 1920).

knowledge serving elsewhere to be transferred to them, suggesting a legal background was valued despite rhetoric to the contrary.[43] Otherwise, testimonials make it clear that a good worker knew the job, was interested in it, and was politically aware. Such workers were disciplined and diligent, capable of initiative, leadership, dealing with subordinates effectively, and acting as a 'good' comrade. Conversely, people were criticized for lacking initiative, acting weakly and slowly, or being politically unreliable.[44]

Investigators were more likely to have a higher level of education than judges, including legal education or experience, and less likely to be party members. The struggle for competent investigators was worse still, as the post required greater technical skills. Tribunals sent frequent appeals to Narkomiust and were often forced to employ tsarist-era officials. Arkhangel'sk's tribunal even described how, after going almost a month in March 1921 without a single investigator, it had poached a 'legal specialist' from a labour camp where he was serving a five-year sentence from the Cheka for a crime of office.[45] One chairman complained of the 'anti-political' (non-party) composition of his chancellery (including investigators) and felt isolated, while others moaned that investigations were in the hands of 'specialists' who could not be fully trusted.[46]

Personnel records also highlight increasing interference in appointments by the central authorities. Initially, judges were to be re-elected or changed every few months; there was a fear that a new caste of legal workers would emerge otherwise, isolated from the people as before 1917.[47] Moreover, since elections were conducted by local soviets, this demonstrated the 'democratic' nature of the new courts since soviets were, in theory, elected bodies. But this practice meant a constant flow of inexperienced people and provided local soviets with too much influence. Thus, as part of Narkomiust's push for central control, legislation extended the period between elections and permitted the Supreme Tribunal to approve appointments, thus mirroring the steady centralization of all state appointments during this period. By 1922, Narkomiust was appointing individuals, transferring others, and dealing with complaints, illnesses, or requests to work elsewhere. It focused particularly on chairmen and their deputies—the senior positions—and soviets were relegated to approving its choice.

What did all this mean? Individuals mattered in the absence of clear definitions of crimes and punishments, and judges mattered more as they wielded huge

[43] TsGAMO, f. 4613, op. 2, d. 6, ll. 15ob–16 (protocols of Moscow tribunal's presidium, 26 October 1918); GARF, f. R-3042, op. 1, d. 23, ll. 28–28ob (report from main railway tribunal, spring 1921).

[44] GARF, f. R-1005, op. 5, d. 179, ll. 2ob–10, 13 (various testimonies, early 1923).

[45] GARF, f. R-1005, op. 3, d. 10, ll. 23ob, 24ob (report on Arkhangel'sk tribunal, 23 November 1921).

[46] GARF, f. R-1005, op. 2, d. 59, l. 22 (former chairman of Stavropol' tribunal to the cassation tribunal, 27 November 1920); f. A-353, op. 3, d. 125, l. 1 (plenary meeting of Tver' tribunal, 19 March 1919); d. 40, l. 134 (report on railway tribunals up to 1 July 1920).

[47] See the speech of M. A. Reisner at the First Congress of Justice Officials on 22 April 1918; *Materialy Narodnogo Komissariata Iustitsii* [hereafter *Materialy*], 1 (1918), 49–50.

influence over all stages of the process. The statistician E. N. Tarnovskii argued that the less educated the judges, the harsher the sentence.[48] Most anti-Bolshevik critics simply assumed that party membership alone indicated the harsh, politicized nature of tribunals. But judges were recent recruits to the party. The vast majority had no knowledge of law, and no one had experience of tribunals initially. Whereas some rectified this as the months passed, constant personnel changes meant there remained a degree of inexperience at any given time and expertise often amounted to little more than working in a court for a few months. It would be surprising if these judges shared the same understanding of revolutionary justice as Narkomiust, especially since little guidance was provided beyond using their 'revolutionary conscience'.

And what was this 'conscience' when applied to law? Revolts and plots by obvious political or social enemies were straightforward, but how would these people approach crimes committed by workers and peasants from similar backgrounds to themselves? There were proposals to run training courses, but nothing systematic emerged. With limited resources, Narkomiust believed party membership alongside instructions and journals made tribunals less of a concern than more diverse and dispersed people's courts.[49] Some provincial organs agreed, citing the wider range of cases in those courts and the different types of law involved, while hinting that those involved were less capable of mastering political questions.[50] Reflecting later, however, tribunal judges recall being thrown in at the deep end and forced to cope, but developing a 'class feeling (*klassovoe chut'e*)', often through observing others or reading what materials were available.[51] Nevertheless, it is unsurprising, as discussed below (Figures 4.4 and 4.5), that sentences were more diverse than the state anticipated and often exhibited signs of greater continuity with existing popular concepts of justice than anything revolutionary.

The Revolutionary Lawyer

The other important figures in trials were lawyers.[52] As with judges, initial sentiment opposed the idea of professional lawyers, and the first decree on courts

[48] Tarnovskii, 'Lichnyi sostav'. This was contested in Roginskii, 'K voprosu o lichnom sostave'.

[49] GARF, f. A-353, op. 5, d. 17, ll. 91–92ob (report on training, 4th Congress of Justice Officials, January 1922).

[50] GARF, f. A-353, op. 2, d. 26, l. 5ob (report from Astrakhan's department of justice, late 1918).

[51] The quote is from P. Lavrov, 'Vospominaniia', *Proletarskii sud*, 4–5 (1924), 25. See also A. Chuvatin, 'Pervye tribunaly', in *Voennye tribunaly*, 57; and Beliakov in *Rabochii sud*, 21 (1927), 1720–1.

[52] Various terms for lawyers were used. For consistency, I use prosecutors (*obviniteli* or *prokuratury*), advocates (*advokatury, prisiazhnye poverennye*, and *zashchitniki*), and, for both, lawyers (*pravozastupniki*).

in November 1917 declared that anyone could act for the prosecution or defence. The initial conception of trials envisaged a scenario with no formal appointments on either side, but members of the audience standing up to attack or defend the accused. In the trial of Countess S. V Panina (Chapter 1), the state did not appoint a prosecution, expecting volunteers from the public to argue the case against an obvious social and political enemy. This did not occur and when a speaker did emerge, he expressed a broad hatred of the exploiting classes but nothing specifically on Panina, leaving an uninspiring bureaucrat to outline the details of the crime. By contrast, Panina appointed an advocate and audience members were willing to speak up for her, creating a seemingly spontaneous, popular defence. The accused in other early trials appointed former tsarist advocates. These traditional practices were more effective than revolutionary innovations and, unsurprisingly, the Bolsheviks followed suit for the first large trial—the Purishkevich affair—and appointed prosecutors to pursue the case systematically.

Lawyers, especially advocates, were equally suspicious of the Bolsheviks. Some did serve, especially socialist sympathizers, but a heated debate erupted after the Decree on Courts on whether advocates should participate in 'politicized' courts. B. L. Gershun, an advocate since 1895, believed the new courts were a 'parody' of a court.[53] This view enjoyed support in professional bodies initially, with an assembly of Petrograd's advocates, chaired by I. V. Gessen, a vocal liberal opponent of the Bolsheviks, voting 200 to 4 not to participate.[54] Within two months, however, material need and realization of Bolshevik supremacy softened views.[55] A debate in the assembly in January saw a shift towards compromise, and on 31 January participants voted 146 to 79 to participate and then in June overwhelmingly (324 votes to 4) to join the Bolsheviks' new college of legal representatives.[56] Gershun implied that supporters were mostly younger and one such individual, B. S. Utevskii, who was 31 years old at the time, recalled they served not only as advocates but across the state apparatus. Utevskii only remained an advocate briefly, citing difficulties in coming to terms with the fledgling nature of the new courts and in adapting old thoughts, experiences, and practices to new approaches. Instead, he helped create courts in Minsk, Vilnius, and Kiev.[57] Some senior figures participated; V. M. Bobrishchev-Pushkin, an advocate since 1874, argued he had even more of a duty to participate given the problems surrounding the new courts.[58]

[53] B. Gershun, 'Vospominaniia advokata', *Novyi zhurnal*, 43 (1955), 149–50.

[54] V. Bobrishchev-Pushkin, 'Vospominaniia zashchitnika', *Sud idet!*, 21 (1927), 1229–31.

[55] N. Maier, 'Sluzhba v komissariate iustitsii i narodnom sude', *Arkhiv Russkoi revoloiutsii*, 8 (1923), 56–7.

[56] *Novaia zhizn'*, 25 January 1918, 3; 14 February 1918, 3; and 8 June 1918, 3. Similar debates occurred in other cities; see E. Huskey, *Russian Lawyers and the Soviet State: The Origins and Development of the Soviet Bar, 1917–1939* (Princeton, 1986), 39–44; and M. Shalamov, *Istoriia sovetskoi advokatury* (Moscow, 1939), 17.

[57] B. Utevskii, *Vospominaniia iurista* (Moscow, 1989), 211–17.

[58] Bobrishchev-Pushkin, 'Vospominaniia', 1231–2.

For the Bolsheviks, if lawyers were to be involved in the legal process, their role had to be regulated to ensure their commitment to the new system. With the abolition of the tsarist bar, tribunals were instructed in December 1917 to form local colleges of legal representatives (*pravozastupniki*) from those who wished to act as lawyers and were approved by soviets. Trials would appoint a prosecutor from the college and, if the accused lacked one, an advocate. This did not preclude audience members from speaking on either side. A decree in March 1918 ruled that only members of a college should receive payment for their work, placing material obstacles in front of non-approved advocates, while colleges of prosecutors were established under tribunals in May 1918 to participate in investigations. Finally, all advocates had to be members of a college of legal representatives in April 1919,[59] although some practised unofficially in the manner of the underground advocates of the tsarist era.[60]

This is the broad picture: names of institutions changed, legislation was inconsistent, and variations persisted between different types of tribunals.[61] The main points, however, are fivefold. First, lawyers continued to play a role in trials, even of counter-revolutionary crimes. Second, the desire to create a reliable means of prosecution to ensure an effective trial drove early legislation, and most tribunals were quicker to introduce prosecutors than advocates. Third, creating colleges of prosecutors under tribunals meant prosecutors became part of the tribunal staff—some acted interchangeably as prosecutors and judges—meaning the more independent colleges of legal representatives equated to advocates in many places. Fourth, state control over advocates increased steadily, and making their continued appointment (and livelihood) dependent on official approval removed their independence and limited their influence. Numbers fell accordingly, with one estimate suggesting a fall from 12,000–13,000 in Russia prior to 1917 to around 2,800 by 1923.[62] Finally, the rapidly increasing workload made it difficult to find enough lawyers and allocate them sufficient time in trials. Consequently, legislation started to stress that tribunals had the right to decide whether to use lawyers at all; if they decided to use prosecutors, they had to use advocates, but if

[59] *Istoriia zakonodatel'stva SSSR i RSFSR po ugolovnomu protsessu i organizatsii suda i prokuratury, 1917–1954* [hereafter *IZ*] (Moscow, 1955), 36, 43–5, 84. See also *Prokuratura i advokatura* (Moscow, 1922).

[60] One article condemned the 'dark personalities' of the 'underground advocates' misleading tribunal defendants in Kursk; *Izvestiia Kurskago ob"edinennago soveta raboch., soldatsk., i krest'iansk. deputatov*, 5 April 1918, 4. See also Huskey, *Russian Lawyers*, 65; and E. Rivlin, *Sovetskaia advokatura* (Moscow, 1926), 42–7.

[61] For more, see N. Cherkasova, 'Stanovlenie instituta zashchity v sovetskom sude (1917–1921 gg.), in *Iz istorii sovetskogo gosudarstva i prava* (Moscow, 1989), 77–95; Huskey, *Russian Lawyers*, 44–76; M. Kozhevnikov, 'Organy, vypolniavshie funktsii sovetskoi prokuratury do ee uchrezhdeniia (1917-22 gg.)', *Uchenye zapiski. Trudy Iuridicheskogo fakul'teta*, 144 (1949), 37–84; Rivlin, *Sovetskaia advokatura*, 18–26; Shalamov, *Istoriia*, 14–45; and A. Tager, 'O prokurature i advokature, obvinenii i zashchite', *Pravo i zhizn'*, 8–10 (1927), 55–67.

[62] A. Klevtsov, 'Ob otnoshenii kommunistov k advokature v 1920-e gody', in Iu. Pilipenko and S. Volodina (eds.), *Advokatura. Gosudarstvo. Obshchestvo* (Moscow, 2006), 371.

they thought the case did not require a prosecution, it did not need a defence. The procedural codes in 1922 confirmed that this decision rested on the importance and complexity of the case, and whether there was special political or public interest in it.[63]

Nevertheless, there remained tension over the role of lawyers. Some officials, including a senior member of Narkomiust, believed that even prosecutors were unnecessary as an unwelcome flashback to oppressive tsarist courts. Instead, the chairman could outline the allegations against the defendant.[64] Most disagreed, arguing that, if the tribunal was a weapon, then it needed to be in capable hands, and experienced prosecutors committed to the revolution would ensure this.[65] Prosecutors also had an educational role, publicizing the law and explaining violations.[66] Advocates were far more contentious. Supporters believed they ensured procedure was followed, provided information to enable judges to exercise revolutionary consciousness, and helped defendants understand the law and the legal process, which was particularly important given poor levels of literacy and political consciousness.[67] In short, they were to aid the court as much as their client. Many officials, though, doubted those acting as advocates were sufficiently reliable. Advocates were far more likely to be from a non-proletarian, non-party background, and have higher legal education and legal experience, than any other group in the new justice system. The fact that most served due to material need, and local authorities were forced to use them in the absence of alternatives, also did not engender trust. As the authorities in Astrakhan concluded, they may have vetted these 'old' lawyers, but it was crucial to create an experienced cadre of new lawyers from workers and peasants.[68]

Similar criticisms persisted throughout the civil war. The first steps to create a new professional class came when, in July 1922, Moscow's soviet advertised for a new college of advocates. Applicants needed two years' experience as judges, investigators, or lawyers, or needed to possess legal knowledge. The names of over 850 applicants were published, and readers were invited to comment on their suitability. This was deemed the best way to exercise workers' control and weed out those not suited politically or practically to the new work.[69] Even then, there was a debate on the front pages of *Pravda* questioning whether party members should participate in the new college or not.[70]

[63] *IZ*, 221 (codes, article 415).

[64] TsGAMO, f. 4998, op. 1, d. 13, l. 15 (N. A. Cherliunchakevich in a meeting of Moscow's Department of Justice, 10 August 1918).

[65] GARF, f. A-353, op. 2, d. 27, l. 136 (report from Tver', mid 1918).

[66] M. Kozhevnikov and N. Lagovier, *Obshchestvennyi obvinitel'* (Moscow, 1925), 9–13.

[67] Rivlin, *Sovetskaia advokatura*, 9–17, 61–6.

[68] GARF, f. A-353, op. 2, d. 26, l. 4ob-5 (report, late 1918).

[69] *Rabochaia Moskva*, 13 July 1922, 1; 2 August, 2, 7; 23 August, 3.

[70] *Pravda*, 8 August 1922, 1; 13 August, 1; 24 August, 1.

All this made it difficult for advocates to influence proceedings. Bobrishchev-Pushkin described how advocates lacked administrative support and had to walk miles across towns, hungry and cold, to gather information. It was difficult to obtain files and access defendants and witnesses. They had to portray themselves as loyal co-workers of the state, yet defending counter-revolutionary crimes risked condoning counter-revolution. Some were arrested for pointing out procedural errors in court. Bolsheviks moaned to Bobrishchev-Pushkin about the behaviour of advocates and advocates complained to him about their position. Despite this, he argued that advocates were never more important than in such primitive courts.[71] But their influence was limited. Trial transcripts suggest that many were passive, unwilling, or unable to make their voice heard, rarely criticizing and often pleading for mercy rather than arguing for innocence. It has been suggested that their presence provided a slight advantage in people's courts when it came to acquittals, reduced sentences, and appeals.[72] In tribunals, at the very least, their presence did not harm defendants and may have kept them better informed.

In Court

When it came to the actual trial, the first decision was location. The early trials in Petrograd intended to make a symbolic statement about the new court and required a suitably prominent location. The former palace of the tsar's uncle, Grand Duke Nikolai Nikolaevich, was chosen, and it proved memorable as it is mentioned in most accounts. The 'ducal music room' was used, which was spacious, with 'walls panelled in rare woods'.[73] This projected formality alongside a symbolic message that the new state had taken over the spaces of former elites. It was also similar to 'a modern stage set', enhancing its value as an instructive forum.[74] A trial of Mensheviks in Odessa in 1918 was held in the city's theatre, with the judges prominent on stage, the defendants in the orchestra pit, and several thousand spectators in the stalls.[75] The use of prominent buildings for major trials continued in subsequent years as it enhanced a trial's visibility and enabled more people to experience it directly. The trial of Metropolitan Veniamin in Petrograd in 1922 took place in the former noble assembly, with its imposing

[71] Bobrishchev-Pushkin, 'Vospominaniia', 1234.
[72] J. Hazard, *Settling Disputes in Soviet Society* (New York, 1960), 35–6.
[73] A. Williams, *Journey into Revolution: Petrograd, 1917–1918* (Chicago, 1969), 163. See also B. Beatty, *The Red Heart of Russia* (New York, 1918), 295.
[74] L. Bryant, *Six Red Months in Russia* (London and West Nyack, 1982), 194.
[75] T. Penter, 'Öffentlichkeit und Rechtsprechung unter der frühen Sowjetmacht. Der Prozeß gegen den "Južnyj Rabočij" in Odessa 1918', *Jahrbücher für Geschichte Osteuropas*, 50, 4 (2002), 564. A similar location was used for a trial of Saratov's clergy in 1918; A. Mramornov (ed.), *Sudebnyi protsess protiv Saratovskogo dukhovenstva v 1918–1919 gg.* (Saratov, 2013), 51 (the photo is also on the cover).

columns and chandeliers, prominent stage for the judges, and expansive space for a large audience visible in photographs.[76] Amid the chaos of civil war, though, it could be difficult to find something suitable. The military tribunal in Novorossiisk reported triumphantly when it acquired a building in the city's centre; there were large numbers interested in revolutionary justice, it noted, and the tribunal could now fulfil its moral and educational objectives.[77]

The proliferation of mass crimes soon made prominent buildings impractical, even unsuitable, for all but the largest trials. When Petrograd's tribunal complained it was forced to hold trials in a small hall in 1921 without an audience, the authorities advised strengthening links with workers by holding trials in factories and living quarters.[78] This approach was deliberately taken by travelling sessions, discussed in Chapter 2, as they attempted to reach less accessible audiences. Smaller towns and villages, railway junctions, or temporary regimental bases did not have such prominent spaces, but something less formal—village square, station, factory, or even a railway wagon or steamer—could prove to be a more effective way of reaching the intended audience. It had to be functional, though; a court in Siberia was declared in 'chaos' and accused of discrediting tribunals as it was located in a corridor, held trials in a nearby room, and thus lacked any agitational-political influence.[79]

A prominent building in a city was suitable for major trials designed to spread a broader message, as it provided greater visibility for audiences and reporters. It also served as a clear reminder of the presence of Bolshevik authority in a larger urban environment. By contrast, the intended audience was smaller outside provincial cities and the message more focused. Here, using everyday locations served as a softer, subtler expression of Bolshevik power, revealing the pervasive reach of law and power. The location undoubtedly affected how justice was performed, with major venues lending themselves to greater formality, stage-managed drama, and excessive theatricality, all no doubt intimidating most defendants. Smaller spaces restricted formality but could surely be equally dramatic and intimidating in their own way as they disrupted the normality and stability of everyday life.

Many educated observers stressed what one scholar has termed the 'anti-theatrical theatricality' of the new trials; the new judges self-consciously dressed plainly, spoke simply, and did not follow legal conventions to emphasize the extent of the break with the tsarist legal system.[80] While this is partly true, it

[76] https://humus.livejournal.com/6581735.html [accessed 16 October 2019]. For details of the location, see *'Delo' Mitropolita Veniamina (Petrograd, 1922 g.)* (Moscow, 1991), 7.

[77] GARF, f. R-1005, op. 1, d. 56, l. 148 (report from the Black Sea military tribunal, 12 August 1920).

[78] GARF, f. R-1005, op. 3, d. 39, l. 92 (instructions to Petrograd tribunal after June 1921, when an earlier report on the tribunal noted the lack of a permanent building, l. 40).

[79] GARF, f. R-1005, op. 1, d. 116, ll. 218–18ob (inspection report, 12 July 1921).

[80] J. Cassiday, *The Enemy on Trial: Early Soviet Courts on Stage and Screen* (DeKalb, 2000), 37.

Figure 4.2 Petrograd's revolutionary tribunal, late 1917.
Source: Courtesy of Occidental College Special Collections and College Archives and the Beatty Family, *Bessie Beatty Papers*.

does not tell the entire story. Some images do appear revolutionary; self-conscious judges pose amid simple surroundings (usually a long table) in front of revolutionary banners and portraits of Lenin or Marx.[81] More images, though, portray relatively well-dressed figures, such as those in the first trials in Petrograd, where four of the seven judges wear 'bourgeois' suits and ties, and there is less evidence of revolutionary accompaniments (see Figure 4.2). Most photographs, indeed, place papers, books, and bells to the fore, no doubt to stress the formality and authority of the court.[82] It is probably more accurate, then, to see tribunals conducting a balancing act, trying to appear distinct from repressive 'bourgeois' justice and representative of the people's will, but projecting sufficient continuity and formality to convey legitimacy and authority.

In terms of how people experienced the courtroom, this balance comes out clearly in the trial of former commissar, P. E. Dybenko, in May 1918. Despite being a prominent trial—the first of a leading Bolshevik official—it is in a more functional location, which better reflects most trials. In Figure 4.3, the judges can just be seen behind a table on a dais at the front, with the chairman occupying an ornate chair. The prosecutor, N. V. Krylenko, is visible at a lectern on the right (see Figure 6.1 for greater detail); other photos show the defendants at the front around tables on the left. Members of the audience, though, are seated informally on stools, squashed into the room, and are now standing, having pushed forward through the barrier separating them from the judges to hear the verdict. For those

[81] See, for example, an undated photograph of the military tribunal at the Turkestan front, available at http://polit.ru/article/2014/05/11/revtrib/ accessed 13 June 2019.
[82] GARF, f. A-353, op. 5, d. 18, ll. 203–4 (photograph of college of Cherepovets department of justice in 1921); and the judges at Veniamin's trial, https://humus.livejournal.com/6581735.html accessed 16 October 2019.

Figure 4.3 The verdict at the trial of P. E. Dybenko, May 1918.
Source: Getty Research Institute, Los Angeles (97.R.36).

brought before tribunals, therefore, locations have changed, but layouts are clearly recognizable as courts—and remain distinct from any other scenario likely to be encountered in daily life—even if some elements are far from traditional.

This balancing act stretched to trial procedure. Initially, judges lacked legal experience and received no guidance on organizing effective trials. Consequently, early trials vacillated between revolutionary idealism and perceptions of traditional legal norms. This tended to lead to the inconsistent presentation of evidence and interrogation of witnesses; prosecutors and advocates speaking out of turn; and lengthy speeches from defendants, such as the three-hour, virulently anti-Bolshevik rant delivered by the monarchist V. M. Purishkevich at his trial. This was uncomfortably close to echoing the Bolsheviks' own tactics in trials prior to 1917, using them as a stage from which to attack the regime. In 1918, instructions appeared on how to run a trial and these mirrored 'normal' legal procedure, from outlining the case, introducing the defendants and presenting accusations, to hearing pleas, examining the evidence, and hearing lawyers' arguments, before the tribunal retired for discussion prior to pronouncing a sentence.[83] As with pre-trial

[83] *Materialy*, 2 (1918), 67–8; GARF, f. R-1005, op. 3, d. 92, ll. 24–5 (instructions published by the Supreme Tribunal in 1922). The description of other courts in Hazard, *Settling Disputes*, 321–7, is also relevant.

procedures, these undoubtedly made trials more effective in fulfilling their objectives and added to the veneer of legal objectivity.

The chairs of tribunals often tried to frame the case and influence the narrative from the start. In the first trial, the chair declared the tribunal would be the 'fiercest' defender of the rights and customs of the revolution, thereby attempting to place the tribunal above politics, as it was harder to oppose the revolution openly.[84] A tribunal in Kungur (Perm' province) opened with a similarly emotive and mobilizing message—the history of the 'struggle of the oppressed with the enslavers'—before discussing old courts, new proletarian courts, and the goals of tribunals as extraordinary punitive organs and part of the workers' 'front'.[85] Here the agitational role of the court came to the fore, but it was also emotional, appealing to people to move beyond individual crimes to consider the bigger picture, revolutionary achievements, threats, and the future, and to view themselves as participants in a national struggle.

Initially, though, trials struggled to create a convincing narrative. Of those cases discussed in Chapter 1, the absence of a prosecution in the first trial meant observers were unclear on whether Panina was being tried for stealing state funds, her politics, or her class origins. Her history of charitable work then allowed her to create a strong counter-narrative; even if she had acted against the Bolsheviks, she could hardly be against the people. The Purishkevich trial, a few weeks later, went smoother as appointed prosecutors produced a clearer set of accusations, but testimonies were revoked in court, evidence was unconvincing, a key witness collapsed in hysterics with a mental breakdown, and the accused spoke openly of their hatred of the Bolsheviks. The trial of Iu. O. Martov saw him try to transform I. V. Stalin's allegations into a political dispute with the Bolsheviks, and the trial had to be stopped when the audience started to respond to his points. The spectators were removed and only readmitted after their tickets (and likely allegiance) was rechecked.[86]

In the trials of political opponents, in particular, defendants were never as compliant throughout this period as in later trials and anti-Bolshevik speeches were never eradicated. Nevertheless, tribunals became more adept at dealing with these challenges. The cases of Dybenko and Shchastnyi, also discussed in Chapter 1, saw smoother trials with clearly presented (if selective) evidence, marginalized defences, vetted and passive audiences, and careful coverage in the increasingly Bolshevik-controlled press.[87] Narratives became more coherent and

[84] GARF, f. R-1074, op. 1, d. 10, ll. 20–22ob (transcript, 10 December 1917).

[85] GARF, f. R-3042, op. 1, d. 84, ll. 8ob (report, November 1922).

[86] See Chapter 1 for references. The audience of a trial was removed as early as December 1917 when a journalist used a libel trial to compare repressive measures with tsarism; *Odesskii listok*, 24 December 1917, 3.

[87] A detailed list was compiled of those entitled to tickets for a trial of clergy in Saratov in October 1918, including members of professional unions, state officials, party members, intellectual or

better aligned with key political, social, and cultural themes. This gave trials a better chance of fulfilling their brief to change beliefs and behaviour.

All this led to the emergence of a clear distinction between those 'everyday' trials that dominated tribunals as caseloads increased and trials of major political enemies or 'model' trials of significant threats that required more careful planning and, often, guidance from party officials. A trial in May 1920 of ministers in the White government in Siberia under Admiral A. V. Kolchak took almost three months to prepare, with local party officials leading all elements of the process, including the sentence, as guilt was preordained.[88] Similarly, on 16 February 1921 the chairman of the Siberian Revolutionary Committee ordered the military tribunal to organize a 'large' trial in Ishim (Tiumen' province) to respond to kulak revolts, murders of communists, and criminal acts by officials. The tribunal should select suitable cases and gather materials. The aim, he stated, was to strengthen state policies and food supply. The resulting trial on 22–8 February of ninety-three people and six food-supply officials saw the former accused of armed revolt (resisting food-tax quotas) and the latter of crimes of office. Forty-six were sentenced to death (one later commuted), forty-five to prison, and eight released. The sentence was prefaced with the achievements and challenges of the revolution, making it clear that these local crimes, unconnected and probably resulting from material hardship, constituted an example of a clear threat to the revolution nationally.[89]

As more formal events, these major trials left more detailed transcripts of proceedings, and it is clear that, for all involved, the narrative and counter-narrative played on emotive and binary characteristics. Panina's advocate, for instance, emphasized that her charitable work meant she could not be an 'enemy' of the people, but must be a 'friend'. A beneficiary of her charity described how the education she funded provided 'light and joy' during the 'black days' of despotism. Do not give the world a bad impression of the revolution, he pleaded, but demonstrate that the revolution values its friends. By contrast, her accuser argued that Panina was not an individual but a representative of an 'exploiting' class and member of a party opposing Soviet power. The tribunal needed to defend the 'great' ideals of the revolution against the exploiting class. A Bolshevik official

conscious workers (*intelligentnye truzheniki*), students, residents, clergyman, workers, and soldiers; Mramornov, *Sudebnyi protsess*, 139–56.

[88] V. Poznanskii, 'Sud nad ministrami Kolchaka', *Izvestiia Sibirskogo otdeleniia akademii nauk SSSR. Seriia istorii, filologii i filosofii*, 1 (1990), 44–51. See also the detailed preparations for various trials of clergy in spring–summer 1922; *Arkhivy Kremlia. Politbiuro i tserkov' 1922–1925 gg.* (2 volumes, Moscow, 1997–8), I, 197–304.

[89] *Sibirskaia vandeia. Dokumenty* (2 volumes, Moscow, 2000–1), II, 198, 304–8. A detailed account is in V. Shishkin, 'Ishimskii sudebnyi protsess (22-28 fevralia 1921 g.)', in I. Kuryshev (ed.), *Krest'ianstvo vostochnykh regionov Rossii i Kazakhstana v revoliutsiiakh i grazhdanskoi voine (1905–1921gg.)* (Ishim, 2006), 187–201.

stressed the human cost of the money she withheld, noting how the wives of those in military service, the injured, and the hungry needed to eat. How was it possible, he asked, to deem a person 'noble (*blagorodstvo*)' in their behaviour when they were causing such suffering.[90]

Many trials of former elites like Panina focused on class. From Purishkevich in early 1918, to the former procurator of the Holy Synod and president of the United Nobility, A. D. Samarin, in 1920, to officer and warlord Baron R. F. Ungern-Shternberg in 1921, the Bolsheviks sought to frame such trials as the inevitable struggle between the revolution and its enemies. In these trials, there were as many questions on the defendants' backgrounds, political views, and pre-1917 social injustices as there were on specific crimes. Samarin faced questions about his social origins, wealth, landownership, and ministerial position.[91] By the time the prosecutor, Krylenko, moved on to the accusations, he hoped no doubt to have convinced observers that Samarin was the antithesis of everything the revolution stood for, an inveterate political and social opponent, and thus someone who must have committed the alleged crimes. Here, what defendants represented was as important as their actions; as the judge stated to Purishkevich, the 'new world judges the old world'.[92] All this undoubtedly increased the drama and, the Bolsheviks hoped, emphasized that enemies existed, were dangerous, and that only force could defend the revolution.

Most 'everyday' trials, however, were prepared without outside interference and were over quickly with little fanfare. The chairman played a central role, considering whether to hear witnesses, deciding whether the accused had answered a question satisfactorily, and, given that most trials lacked the time for lawyers, acting as the surrogate prosecutor, asking the questions and setting the tone. The defendant could face no more than a dozen questions, sometimes a handful, and the same was true of witnesses if present.[93] In the trial of I. V. Kiselev, who faced three accusations relating to his alleged opposition to the Bolsheviks' nationalization of the local merchant fleet in Arkhangel'sk and his relationship to local opposition forces, the transcript records four questions—one on each accusation and one on an appearance in a court held by the Whites. Two witnesses were asked a question each.[94] This transcript may be a summary rather than a verbatim record—some transcripts include timings that are longer than the content

[90] GARF, f. R-1074, op. 1, d. 10, ll. 20–22ob (transcript, 10 December 1917). This official transcript does not always match other accounts, something highlighted in A. Lindenmeyr, 'The First Soviet Political Trial: Countess Sofia Panina before the Petrograd Revolutionary Tribunal', *The Russian Review*, 60, 4 (2001), 515–20.

[91] GARF, f. A-353, op. 2, d. 837b, ll. 1–20ob, 51 (transcript, 11 January 1920).

[92] *Izvestiia*, 4 January 1918, 3–4.

[93] This discussion is based on samples of transcripts from Moscow's tribunal (1918–21) [TsGAMO, f. 4613, op. 2, dd. 12, 31, 56, 62], the transport tribunal of the northern region (1920) [GARF, f. R-3042, op. 1, d. 392, ll. 1–23], and various transcripts from local tribunals preserved centrally (1918–22) GARF, f. R-1005, op. 7.

[94] GARF, f. R-3042, op. 1, d. 392, ll. 7–7ob (14 August 1920).

requires—but trials were concise. Moscow's trials varied in duration from 25–40 minutes to 4–5 hours. Its travelling sessions were shorter, with few longer than two hours and most under an hour, enabling several trials per day. The tribunal seemed to expect trials to last no more than two hours, as they scheduled several per day, commonly at 10 a.m., midday, and 2 p.m.[95] This brevity must have restricted the educational value of trials.

The outcome of these trials was not preordained, particularly if witnesses were present. Almost every trial recorded missing witnesses—either people feared coming to court or could not be bothered—and trials continued regardless. When witnesses were convinced a crime had been committed, using firm language, a guilty verdict was usually assured, even if witnesses remained hazy on the details. In the case of M. G. Afanas'ev, accused of unauthorized absences from service, both witnesses confirmed several but were uncertain on dates. This was sufficient to result in a guilty verdict.[96] In contrast, where witnesses were vague, using language such as 'they say' or 'rumours say', the decision often went to the defendant. D. G. Terletskii was accused of counter-revolution and speculation, but both witnesses knew nothing for certain, citing only general talk and rumours. The case was dismissed.[97] Oral testimony dominated. It was quicker to prepare, encouraged emotion and drama, facilitated equality, and overcame problems caused by illiteracy. It was also assigned a greater legal weight, overturning the 'bourgeois' emphasis on written testimony to permit trials to assess the true reliability and sincerity of defendants and witnesses.[98]

All trials disliked hearsay or ambiguity as it complicated their attempts to establish a clear narrative. When asked his political views, A. M. Ustinov (accused of desertion) declared he recognized the authorities that 'exist at the present time'. Dissatisfied with this unconvincing response, the tribunal asked what he would do if there was another authority tomorrow, to which he replied he would go with 'the Reds'.[99] A. E. Val'kov accepted he had destroyed property but disputed the court's proposed reason, denying he was an active opponent of Soviet power. He may have been 'bourgeois' by social background, but not in conviction or upbringing; that is, he worked and had not harmed the new state.[100] In another example, when Simonenko, a union official accused of theft, was asked if he pleaded guilty, he answered, 'as far as I am able to recognize'. When pressed to

[95] TsGAMO, f. 4613, op. 2, d. 6, ll. 172ob, 180–81ob (minutes of college meetings, 18 April and 26 May 1919).

[96] GARF, f. R-3042, op. 1, d. 392, ll. 1–1ob (23 July 1920).

[97] GARF, f. R-3042, op. 1, d. 392, ll. 9–9ob (17 August 1920).

[98] For relevant discussions, see L. Mason, 'The "Burden of Proof": Criminal Justice and the Renewal of Oral Culture during the French Revolution', *The Journal of Modern History*, 76, 1 (2004), 29–61; and A. Portelli, 'The Oral Shape of the Law: The "April 7 Case"', in A. Portelli, *The Death of Luigi Trastulli and Other Stories: Form and Meaning in Oral History* (Albany, 1991), 241–69.

[99] GARF, f. R-3042, op. 1, d. 392, ll. 13–13ob (24 August 1920).

[100] GARF, f. R-3042, op. 1, d. 392, ll. 22–3 (13 September 1920).

be precise, he said 'no', he believed himself to be not guilty as his actions were due to his inexperience.[101]

To combat ambiguity, prosecutors invariably stressed the 'facts (*fakty*)' and stressed the threats to the revolution. The chief prosecutor, Krylenko, epitomized these tactics. His speeches often started with the class struggle of workers and peasants, the victory of the October Revolution, and a reminder to the audience and judges that tribunals should defend this victory. He used the terms 'fact' and 'counter-revolution' frequently, usually to establish the mentality and intention of the defendant, and drew links to indisputable acts of counter-revolution. He often finished by challenging tribunals to demonstrate their ability to protect the revolution, stressing it was their 'duty' to impose a strict penalty.[102] Other prosecutors used similar language—'let's move to the facts' or 'I observe a series of facts'—to establish and control the narrative.[103]

Even where present, advocates had few opportunities to challenge – contesting 'facts' might leave them accused of counter-revolution too. Most seemed resigned to fulfilling their envisaged role and focused on procedural irregularities. Defendants questioned witnesses more than advocates, as it was safer for them to do so. In their summaries, advocates tried to subvert the narrative by providing alternative 'facts' or different interpretations, but it was hard to do this successfully. It was more productive to stress mitigating contextual evidence, whether naïvety or material position. This also fulfilled their official role of providing all the information needed for the tribunal to assess the crime.

Defendants also took this approach in their closing speeches, combatting facts with emotion. Kogan, accused of speculation, proclaimed he had already been punished terribly, his life and career were ruined, as was his family, he had tuberculosis, and he implored the tribunal to spare his life.[104] P. M. Klochkov, accused of theft, pleaded with judges to send him to the front to serve with blood for his crimes,[105] a plea often made by deserters, while others asked to be treated lightly (*miagko*) or with mercy (*pomilovat'*). Kiselev provided, in his words, a 'complete biography' of his life, emphasizing his difficult material position (he had five children) and how he had raised himself from the lowest levels of society (*iz nizov*) through hard work. Glukhovskii, accused of a crime of office, stressed peasant roots, family, poor literacy, and support for the Bolsheviks.[106] If possible, defendants highlighted their involvement in the revolutionary movement before 1917 to prove they could not be counter-revolutionaries. These speeches tried to

[101] TsGAMO, f. 4613, op. 2, d. 12, ll. 12–14ob (3 April 1919).

[102] N. Krylenko, *Za piat' let, 1918–1922gg. Obvinitel'nye rechi po naibolee krupnym protsessam, zaslushannym v Moskovskom i verkhovnom revoliutsionnykh tribunalakh* (Moscow–Petrograd, 1923).

[103] GARF, f. R-1005, op. 8, d. 7, ll. 647–8 (trial of B. M. Dymenko, 5–6 May 1920).

[104] TsGAMO, f. 4613, op. 2, d. 11, l. 93 (23 April 1918).

[105] TsGAMO, f. 4613, op. 2, d. 31, ll. 74–97 (17 May 1919).

[106] TsGAMO, f. 4613, op. 2, d. 114, ll. 100–100ob (23–6 April 1921).

individualize mass crimes and usually reflected traditional views of justice, placing circumstances to the fore and viewing crimes committed inadvertently or through material need as hardly crimes at all. These approaches could yield positive results since they partly aligned with official views on criminality.

Punishment and Revolutionary Consciousness

The final act of the trial, of course, is the verdict, which reinforces the varied objectives of trials. The level of the penalty might emphasize or distort the intended message to offenders, potential offenders, and the wider public. Punishment also has its own objectives: to remove dangerous elements from society, punish them for their actions, rehabilitate if possible, and discourage others from committing similar acts.[107]

In theory, the Bolsheviks were clear: punishment was not about retribution or atoning for guilt but defending society from those who commit crimes or attempt to, and from the future possible crimes of these individuals and others.[108] To achieve this, a person could be 'socialized' (rehabilitated), 'isolated' if they refuse, or 'physically eliminated' in 'exceptional' circumstances. Selecting a punishment meant evaluating the degree of danger for society of the criminal *and* the act, and required assessing all the circumstances of a case, including the personality of the criminal, social background, intent, material need, personal gain, consciousness, and previous criminal background. All criminals were capable of rehabilitation through a mix of labour and cultural–educational work, but the likelihood of success depended on social background.[109] One official argued that proletarian justice should not be repression. Criminals were ill and talk should be of hospitals, clinics, correction, and treatment rather than prisons, punishment, and revenge. He described shooting not as a punishment but as a precise operation to cure society from a particular ill.[110] Another talked not of prisons but of correctional facilities (*ispravdom*) to act as schools of physical work for the intelligentsia and for the development of character (consciousness) for others.[111] These theories

[107] D. Garland, *Punishment and Modern Society: A Study in Social Theory* (Oxford, 1990), 250–7, 265–7.

[108] On penal policy, see P. Solomon, 'Soviet Penal Policy, 1917-1934: A Reinterpretation', *Slavic Review*, 39, 2 (1980), 195–217; E. Wimberg, '"Replacing the Shackles": Soviet Penal Theory, Policy and Practice, 1917-1930' (PhD dissertation, University of Pittsburgh, 1996); and A. Retish, 'Breaking Free from the Prison Walls: Penal Reforms and Prison Life in Revolutionary Russia', *Historical Research*, 90, 247 (2017), 134–50.

[109] 'Guiding Principles', 166–7. On criminal theory, see J. Ryan, 'The Sacralization of Violence: Bolshevik Justifications for Violence and Terror during the Civil War', *Slavic Review*, 74, 4 (2015), 827–9.

[110] GARF, f. R-3042, op. 1, d. 23, ll. 48–48ob, 49ob (report by the chairman of the transport tribunal in the Baltic region to the Second Congress of Tribunal Chairmen in March–April 1921).

[111] GARF, f. R-3042, op. 1, d. 23, ll. 33–4 (anonymous report, spring 1921).

could justify anything from acquittal (no longer posing a social danger) to death (irredeemable), depending on the individual case. This emphasis on rehabilitation was another point distinguishing tribunals from the repressive language and actions of the Cheka.

In practice, though, amid a brutal civil war and faced with the expanding nature of counter-revolution, officials had to ensure that the punitive role of tribunals had an immediate impact while working within practical restraints. Personnel shortages meant the state still needed corrupt officials and deserters, and recalcitrant peasants were essential for food supply, while the authorities lacked the capacity to shoot and imprison all those sentenced, let alone re-educate and rehabilitate them. The result was a progressive penal policy in some respects, particularly the use of non-custodial sentences of various types, but one tempered by frequent instances of arbitrary violence and driven on the ground by practical demands rather than a coherent sense of the purpose and objectives of various types of punishment.

Tribunals were permitted from December 1917 to issue fines, prison sentences, public censure, and exile. They could also declare someone an enemy of the people, remove their political rights, confiscate their property, and compel community work. After the addition of the death penalty in June 1918, this list remained stable, although exile was removed, compulsory labour and suspended sentences were prioritized at times, and penal battalions were introduced. But decrees provided no guidance on the penalties suitable for particular crimes; tribunals were told to make a judgement based on circumstances and revolutionary conscience (*sovest'*). Later decrees elaborated on procedures and crimes, but only added that tribunals should be guided by the interests of the socialist republic (and defending it from its enemies), the interests of the proletarian class war, and should utilize communist legal consciousness or sense of justice (*pravosoznanie*) alongside revolutionary conscience.[112]

The Bolsheviks never defined 'revolutionary conscience' or 'legal consciousness', and it was often simply employed as shorthand for a new, simpler, and fairer legal system.[113] It seemed to mean the experiences, views, and intuition of the ordinary 'class-conscious' workers and peasants who made the revolution and now staffed the judicial system. These groups were supposedly aware of the interests of their class and the revolution. Apparently Lenin believed these phrases were vague, and Stuchka, as one of the authors of this early legislation, belatedly agreed. He noted that the Bolsheviks had not provided sufficient instructions and, whereas class consciousness was a relatively clear concept, legal consciousness was

[112] *IZ*, 34–6, 46–7, 79–80. The short-lived press tribunal had a few additional measures, such as publishing a denial, closing a publication, or seizing a printing press.

[113] For example, S. B., 'Revoliutsionnoe pravosoznanie', *Izvestiia*, 12 December 1918, 1.

not. He admitted it had roots in the theories of the pre-revolutionary, liberal lawyer L. I. Petrazhitskii, who promoted law as a tool for social engineering and argued it could be positive (based on decrees or customs) or intuitive (based on an individual's experiences and sense of ethics, rights, and duties). Intuition, Stuchka believed, was required by the unique conditions of the revolution, but he bemoaned that legal consciousness remained infused with old traditions and prejudices.[114] People's experiences and views, inevitably, and the understanding of justice emerging from them, did not change overnight with the revolution.[115]

Later attempts to provide further clarification were only partly successful. G. M. Portugalov traced the history of the idea of conscience from Rome and the Holy Inquisition to the Enlightenment and the French Revolution. Although distinguishing 'socialist' conscience from its predecessors, he presumably intended to counter accusations that it was a vacuous term used to disguise arbitrariness by historicizing the concept. But in doing so, he minimized its revolutionary nature and repeated basic assumptions. Enacting revolutionary conscience meant investigating the circumstances of a case (causes, evidence, beliefs, and personalities), conducting objective logical work (using scientific methods to research the crimes and the people) and utilizing lived experiences. For this, courts of workers judging workers provided the best guarantee of a mutual understanding of life, world view, customs, and lifestyles. Finally, a common Marxist understanding of law, knowledge of decrees, and training ensured a uniform 'mass' legal consciousness rather than numerous individual interpretations.[116]

Much of this would have been familiar. Prior to 1917, juries had reached verdicts on the basis of accepted 'norms' of behaviour (influenced by custom, personal circumstances and experiences, press accounts of crime, and even crime fiction), sympathy for the accused, and suspicion of the legal system, and lawyers often urged them to follow their consciences.[117] The similarities with rural courts were more striking. In these, verdicts were dispensed by several elected peasant

[114] P. Stuchka, 'Proletarian Law (1919)', 'The Marxist Concept of Law (1922)', 'Lenin and the Revolutionary Decree (1925)', and 'Legal Consciousness (1925-7)', in P. Stuchka, *Selected Writings on Soviet Law and Marxism*, ed. R. Sharlet, P. Maggs, and P. Beirne (Armonk and London, 1988), 20, 35, 90, 160–1. See also J. Gorecki, 'Leon Petrazycki', in J. Gorecki (ed.), *Sociology and Jurisprudence of Leon Petrażycki* (Urbana, 1975), 1–15; and, for broader European influences on the role of feeling in law, P. Vasilyev, 'Beyond Dispassion: Emotions and Judicial Decision-Making in Modern Europe', *Rechtsgeschichte—Legal History*, 25 (2017), 277–85.

[115] J. Hazard, 'Law and Tradition in the New Russia', *Oxford Slavonic Papers*, 4 (1953), 137.

[116] G. Portugalov, *Revoliutsionnaia sovest' i sotsialisticheskoe pravosoznanie* (Petrograd, 1922). For a detailed discussion of this work, see P. Vasilyev, 'Revolutionary Conscience, Remorse and Resentment: Emotions and Early Soviet Criminal Law, 1917-22', *Historical Research*, 90, 247 (2017), 117–33.

[117] J. Atwell, 'The Russian Jury', *Slavonic and East European Review*, 53, 130 (1975), 55–7; A. Afanas'ev, 'Jurors and Jury Trials in Imperial Russia, 1866-1885', in B. Eklof, J. Bushnell, and L. Zakharova (eds.), *Russia's Great Reforms, 1855–1881* (Bloomington, 1994), 214–30; and L. McReynolds, *Murder Most Russian: True Crime and Punishment in Late Imperial Russia* (Ithaca, 2013).

judges (who, as in tribunals, did not require previous legal experience). No lawyers or jury were present, but peasants saw this panel, usually local figures, as a quasi-jury. Judges were instructed to decide cases 'according to conscience, on the basis of evidence contained in the case'. They took the character and reputation of those involved seriously, including witnesses, assigning greater weight to those deemed law-abiding and hard-working, with village observations, opinions, and rumours, and the remorse of the defendant, all influential. Thus different outcomes were possible for similar crimes.[118]

Both pre- and post-1917, therefore, crime was inseparable from the personality and life of the accused. This was something all tribunal officials could understand and, on the ground, a narrower concept of consciousness was practised, with tribunals assessing the extent to which individuals and groups had consciously (*soznatel'no*) committed crimes; that is, how far they realized their acts were not only illegal, but had broader repercussions for the revolution, and whether they had intended to harm the revolution.[119] Someone's low level of culture (*nizkii kul'turnyi uroven'*) may mean they were not conscious (*nesoznatel'nyi*) of the repercussions of their actions or had committed an act unintentionally (*neumyshlenno*). With this in mind, the authorities stressed it was crucial to discuss all the circumstances, even if the defendant pleaded guilty in a straightforward case.[120]

Transcripts reveal trials exploring these issues. A travelling session in Volokolamsk in August 1920 did not believe the protests of Skorokhodov, accused of 'malicious' desertion, and claimed he was a 'conscious' enemy of the workers, a 'coward', and a 'careerist', who 'consciously' hid from service during a period of difficult struggle for workers and peasants. Nonetheless, his 'low cultural level' warranted a commutation of the initial death penalty to fifteen years in prison with forced labour. This verdict contrasted with that of Garanov, whose trial started five minutes later. A party member and an officer, also convicted of malicious desertion, and whose 'careerism' had discredited the party and the pride of the officer corps, Garanov was shot.[121] Neither officers nor party members, by definition, had a low cultural level. In other cases, the tribunal decided that some, including repeat offenders, did not want to become useful citizens, while deserters who did not voluntarily come forward when first requested revealed their true character.[122] Elsewhere, three of four people accused of serving in Kolchak's government in Siberia, seizing property, and murdering communists, received prison terms instead of death sentences due to their low cultural level,

[118] J. Burbank, *Russian Peasants Go To Court: Legal Culture in the Countryside, 1905–1917* (Bloomington and Indianapolis, 2004); C. Gaudin, *Ruling Peasants: Village and State in Late Imperial Russia* (DeKalb, 2007); and S. Frank, *Crime, Cultural Conflict, and Justice in Rural Russia, 1856–1914* (Berkeley, 1999).

[119] P. K., 'Prestuplenie i nakazanie v Sovetskoi Respublike', *Izvestiia*, 5 August 1919, 1.

[120] GARF, f. R-1005, op. 3, d. 92, ll. 24–5 (instructions on the order of legal meetings, 1922).

[121] TsGAMO, f. 4613, op. 2, d. 62, ll. 1–4 (transcripts, 18 August 1920).

[122] TsGAMO, f. 4613, op. 2, d. 62, ll. 5–7, 13, 22–4, 42–4 (transcripts, 18, 21, and 23 August 1920).

and another was freed as being faint-hearted, presumably indicating his inability to resist the pressure to serve.[123]

A sincere confession (*chistoserdechnoe priznanie*) was also important, usually leading to a reduced prison term or suspended sentence, especially if combined with a lower social background.[124] Even F. I. Dolin, a former informer for the tsarist police, was found 'sincere', as he had acted to redeem his father's crimes, his children served in the Red Army and he did not pose a threat to the new state.[125] A. V. Golyshev pleaded guilty to stealing a passenger's money on a steamer. When asked why, Golyshev claimed not to know and could not recall if he had needed the money. The chairman asked whether he had 'consciously' stolen the money, to which Golyshev said 'yes' and added that he was very repentant. The chairman noted reports that he had performed cultural–educational work in the village. Golyshev replied that he had simply helped clarify some matters for the peasants. The final sentence was reduced by two-thirds for his 'sincere' repentance, peasant background, favourable character statements from his village, and his promise to repay the money (another sign of sincerity).[126] Conversely, 'insincere' explanations were treated harshly. Judges in Moscow's tribunal, for instance, did not appreciate a Red Army officer, who should have been a 'conscious', responsible citizen, behaving insincerely like an 'unconscious' one, or when a soldier claimed he had deserted to help with work on the farm when it was the middle of winter and there could be no urgent work.[127] Sincerity, of course, was a subjective assessment and relied on a defendant's ability to appear remorseful and forge a rapport with the judges.

Occasionally, judges called on experts to help them decide. The finances of some tribunals reveal ongoing payments for expertise (*ekspertiza*). This could range from technical expertise, such as confirming forged signatures or documents, elaborating on the information contained in tsarist police files, or adjudicating on matters of theology when considering whether Orthodox churches should be voluntarily donating their valuables to aid the hungry. It could also include medical expertise, especially psychiatric opinion on whether a defendant was fit to stand trial or posed a threat to society; those deemed to be mentally ill were not supposed to be punished, as they were unaware of their actions.[128]

[123] *Grazhdanskaia voina v Prikam'e. Mai 1918 – ianvar' 1920 gg.* (Perm', 2008), 400–1 (trial of I. Negodiaev and others in Perm' provincial tribunal, 15 August 1919).

[124] This was true of people's courts as well; P. Vasilyev, 'Sex and Drugs and Revolutionary Justice: Negotiating "Female Criminality" in the Early Soviet Courtroom', *Journal of Social Policy Studies*, 16, 2 (2018), 349.

[125] TsGAMO, f. 4612, op. 2, d. 4, l. 48 (sentence, 6 June 1919).

[126] GARF, f. R-3042, op. 1, d. 392, l. 3 (sentence, 26 July 1920).

[127] TsGAMO, f. 4613, op. 2, d. 62, ll. 3, 5–6 (sentence, 18 August 1920).

[128] TsGAMO, f. 4612, op. 2, d. 6, ll. 173ob, 187ob, 191 (protocols of meetings, 18 April, 23 May, and 10 July 1919; f. 4613, op. 2, d. 62, ll. 94, 105, 111 (protocols, 8, 15, and 18 September 1920). For background, see D. Healey, *Bolshevik Sexual Forensics: Diagnosing Disorder in the Clinic and*

There remained fundamental problems, though. It was possible to accept theoretically that an individual's agency was constrained by their social context, and crimes were a product of 'bourgeois' oppression and a lack of awareness about the new world, but it did not disguise the fact that individuals reacted to the same contexts in different ways.[129] It was very difficult, then, for tribunals to determine levels of intention, agency, and sincerity. All this, together with ignorance of the permitted punishments, led to a wide range of sentences for similar crimes.

Quantifying Punishment

This diversity is revealed in the statistics gathered by Narkomiust. On the surface, these portrayed a tribunal system which found the vast majority of defendants guilty—convictions rose from 81 per cent in 1919 to 86 per cent in 1921 and 89 per cent in the first half of 1922—and sentenced them to one of a handful of punishments.[130] A deeper probe into the figures, however, reveals that sentences remained stubbornly varied despite the best efforts of the authorities.

The obvious starting point is particularly problematic. Reports indicate that the death penalty rose to 18 per cent of sentences in 1919, before falling to 3 per cent in 1920–1 (Figure 4.4).[131] But there are three immediate problems. First, the 1919 figure is misleading. Nizhnii Novgorod, Samara, and Ufa provided abnormally high figures (41–70 per cent), but 90–94 per cent of their sentences were suspended. Here the death sentence seems to have been wielded symbolically, with tribunals rarely intending to uphold it. Indeed, the majority of death sentences for 1919 across all tribunals were suspended, reducing those that remained beyond the end of the trial to 6 per cent. This practice was soon prohibited as counterproductive. Second, Narkomiust did not request information on

Courtroom, 1917–1939 (DeKalb, 2009), 18–26; and I. Krylov, *Sudebnaia ekspertiza v ugolovnom protsesse* (Leningrad, 1963), 135–57.

[129] For a thought-provoking discussion of agency, see J. Ryan, '"They know not what they do?" Bolshevik Understandings of the Agency of Perpetrators, 1918-1930', *Historical Research*, 90, 247 (2017), 151–71.

[130] In the following discussion, the figures for civilian tribunals in 1919–21 are based on statistics submitted by local tribunals in GARF, f. A-353, op. 3, d. 156 (1919); op. 4, d. 112 (1920); and op. 5, dd. 75, 83 (1921). These cover thirty-five tribunals in 1919, forty-eight in 1920, and forty-nine in 1921, more than published reports. Other tribunals are referenced separately. The problems with the statistics are discussed in Chapter 3. For the 1922 figure, see GARF, f. A-353, op. 5, d. 72b, l. 185 (report on legal institutions, 1921–2). These conviction figures are comparable with military tribunals (90% in the first half of 1922) but higher than transport tribunals (81%): RGVA, f. 33988, op. 2, d. 454, l. 14 (report on military tribunals, 1922); and GARF, f. R-3042, op. 1, d. 38, ll. 18ob-19; d. 39, l. 3 (reports on transport tribunals, 1922).

[131] It was apparently 0.3% in 1918 (prison formed 38% of sentences and fines 33%); Ia. Berman, 'O revoliutsionnykh tribunalakh', *Proletarskaia revoliutsiia i pravo*, 11 (1919), 60–1.

	Shot	Prison	Compulsory Labour	Fine	Public Censure	Other	% Sentences Suspended
1919	18	41	7	5	6	23	33
1920	3	65	12	3	3	14	32
1921	3	63	6	5	2	21	31

Figure 4.4 Archival reports on sentences in civilian tribunals, 1919–21 (in per cent).
Source: GARF, f. A-353, op. 3, d. 156; op. 4, d. 112; and op. 5, dd. 75, 83.

death sentences in 1920.[132] Some tribunals added the information, enabling the percentage provided in Figure 4.5, but since 74 per cent of tribunals reported shootings in 1919 and 87 per cent in 1921, and only 33 per cent in 1920, this is clearly too low. Finally, many death sentences remaining beyond the end of the trial were later appealed or amnestied (see Chapter 5).

Relatively low percentages are comparable with other statistics. Figure 4.5, for instance, is from a widely cited official report. Other reports record death sentences as 6 per cent of sentences in military tribunals in 1920 and transport tribunals in 1921–2, falling to 5 per cent in the first half of 1922 for the former and 1 per cent in the second half of 1922 for the latter.[133] With the rhetoric of mercilessness, there was no reason to underreport shootings. If anything, officials at all levels revealed a growing aversion to the death penalty. To be sure, tribunals could act severely. By 1922, more crimes could be punished by death than before and death rates were far higher than pre-1917 and European norms.[134] Military tribunals dispensed death sentences during the last fortnight in December 1919 for crimes ranging from desertion, revolt, aiding the Whites, and speculation, to drunkenness, robbery, and organizing a card game,[135] and its use increased during periods of heavy fighting.[136] But as the state attempted to appease social unrest, the Commissar of Justice stated in September 1920 that shooting should only be used when tribunals were convinced that it was pointless trying to reform the guilty through other punishments.[137] In addition, Bolshevik leaders talked of restricting shootings for desertion to those 'exceptionally malicious (*iskliuchitel'no*

[132] The death penalty was officially abolished for civilian tribunals on 17 January 1920 after the defeat of various White forces [*DSV*, VII, 104–5], but it was reinstated in areas under martial law on 22 May (24 provinces) and in all areas on 4 November (S. Zhil'tsov, *Smertnaia kazn' v istorii Rossii* (Moscow, 2002), 262–6).

[133] GARF, f. A-353, op. 4, d. 111, l. 179 (military tribunals, 1920); f. R-3042, op. 1, d. 38, l. 4ob; d. 39, l. 3ob (transport tribunals, 1921–2); RGVA, f. 33988, op. 2, d. 454, l. 14 (military tribunals, 1922).

[134] W. Adams, 'Capital Punishment in Imperial and Soviet Law', *The American Journal of Comparative Law*, 18, 3 (1970), 575–94; J. Daly, 'Criminal Punishment and Europeanization in Late Imperial Russia', *Jahrbücher für Geschichte Osteuropas*, 47, 3 (2000), 341–62.

[135] GARF, f. A-353, op. 3, d. 140, ll. 4–6 (report on military tribunals, 17–29 December 1919).

[136] GARF, f. A-353, op. 4, d. 111, ll. 46ob-47 (statistics for military tribunals, 1920).

[137] GARF, f. R-1005, op. 2, d. 20, l. 37 (Narkomiust to the Cassation Tribunal, 13 September 1920).

Year (1st/ 2ndhalf)	Shot	Prison	Forced labour	Property seizures	Public censure	Other	% Prison sentences suspended
1920 (1st)	11	62	8	6	3	10	40
1920 (2nd)	7	74	7	2	2	8	48
1921 (1st)	5	78	6	1	4	6	45
1921 (2nd)	2	58	6	6	1	27	51
1922 (1st)	1	32	2	49	1	15	60

Figure 4.5 Official report on sentences in civilian tribunals, 1920–2 (in per cent).
Source: GARF, f. A-353, op. 5, d. 72b, ll. 182, 185ob.[138]

zlostnyi)' deserters involved in banditry, counter-revolution plots, or inciting others to desert.[139]

Most sentences involved a prison term: 41 per cent in 1919, rising to 65 per cent in 1920 and 63 per cent in 1921 (Figure 4.4). Official reports provide comparable statistics (Figure 4.5), with the number falling in 1922 as civilian tribunals confiscated property instead to enforce new food taxes resulting from the New Economic Policy (NEP). The length of sentences initially varied widely. Participants recalled indeterminate sentences, such as the end of the civil war or the victory of world revolution, while trials in Voronezh dispensed everything from a week to twenty-five years, life, and the cessation of civil war.[140] Narkomiust soon demanded precise lengths and most were relatively short, especially after 21 March 1921 when all courts were instructed to limit terms to no longer than five years. In Kaluga in 1921, 33 per cent of prison sentences were under six months, 32 per cent for six–twelve months, 16 per cent for one–two years, 11 per cent for two–three years, and 8 per cent for three–five years. In Cherepovets, the figures were 19 per cent, 26 per cent, 20 per cent, 16 per cent, and 19 per cent respectively.[141] Unaffected by the NEP, prison formed the majority of sentences throughout in military and transport tribunals. They used different categories. In the former, almost 8 per cent of all sentences in 1920 involved a prison term under six months, 27 per cent over six months, and 17 per cent were sent to a concentration camp or penal battalion.[142] The latter sentenced 29 per cent of all those convicted to less than two years in prison and 39 per cent to a longer term in the first half of 1922.[143]

[138] These figures from a report on the activities of legal organs in 1921–2 were based on thirty-five tribunals. An article using these statistics provides figures for the first half of 1919 with 14 % shot, 50% imprisoned, 8% forced labour, 8% property seizures, 8% public censure, 12% other, and 27% suspended; E. Tarnovskii, 'Sudebnaia repressiia v tsifrakh za 1919-1922gg.', ESIu, 44–45, 7 December 1922, 44.

[139] GARF, f. R-1005, op. 2, d. 2, l. 457 (meeting of the party's central committee, 6 August 1920).

[140] Chuvatin, 'Pervye tribunaly', 55; Ustiuzhaninov, 'V voennye gody', 91; GARF, f. A-353, op. 4, d. 58, l. 60 (report, 7 February 1921).

[141] GARF, f. A-353, op. 5, d. 83, l. 93 (Kaluga); op. 5, d. 18, ll. 217–18 (Cherepovets).

[142] GARF, f. A-353, op. 4, d. 111, l. 179 (statistics for military tribunals in 1920).

[143] GARF, f. R-3042, op. 1, d. 38, l. 5ob; d. 39, l. 3ob (reports on transport tribunals in 1922).

Military tribunals often distinguished between a prison (*tiur'ma*) and a concentration camp (*kontsentratsionnyi lager'*), as did other tribunals occasionally. Others referred to correctional facilities (*ispravitel'nyi dom*) and forced labour camps (*lager' prinuditel'nykh rabot*).[144] It is hard to discern any consistency, probably reflecting different understandings of prison, different names used for similar institutions, and the type of facilities available locally. Judges never state what they hope different prisons will achieve—rehabilitation or punishment. In Arkhangel'sk, correctional facilities were for rehabilitation, as they included skilled work alongside a library, theatre, and sometimes school, music, and sports facilities. Forced labour camps here, where most were sent, probably focused on punishment.[145]

Almost all prison sentences ostensibly involved labour; it was seen as essential to teach the value of labour to forge conscientious Soviet citizens, while imprisonment without labour amounted to 'enforced parasitism'.[146] Equally, deserters dispatched to penal battalions were able to redeem themselves through dangerous work. Some officials, however, including the head of the Cheka, F. E. Dzerzhinskii, felt that too many from the lower classes were imprisoned. In his view, prison was for the bourgeoisie and the lower classes should face 'comradely influence (*tovarishcheskie vozdeistvie*)'.[147] Such sentiments may have been behind periodic attempts to push for labour without imprisonment, such as in 1920 (Figure 4.4). This could involve actual labour or paying 25–50 per cent of one's salary to the state.[148] One tribunal urged tactical use of this labour, using people with specialist knowledge in state organs as long as they did not pose a danger or could be supervised, and using others for manual labour. All labour, though, should be made to feel like compulsory labour, even outside prison.[149]

Other punishments accounted for smaller percentages. Public censure epitomized the revolutionary idealism that imbued tribunals in their initial months. One

[144] As well as Retish and Wimberg, see S. Brazevich, 'Istoricheskaia sotsiologiia revoliutsionnogo nasiliia: kontsentratsionnye lageria kak organizovannaia forma politicheskikh repressii v sovetskoi Rossii v 1918-1922 gg.', in *Uroki Oktiabria i praktiki sovetskoi sistemy 1920–1950-e gody* (Moscow, 2018), 728–37; A. Demichev and R. Khachaturov (eds.), *Pamiatniki rossiiskogo prava. T. 23. Pervye dekrety sovetskoi vlasti* (Moscow, 2016), 363–457; and M. Jakobson, *Origins of the Gulag: The Soviet Prison Camp System, 1917–34* (Lexington, 1993).

[145] GARF, f. R-1005, op. 3, d. 10, l. 84ob, 85ob-86 (reports, 29 September and 18 December 1920). See also the reports delivered to the First Congress of Provincial Prison Departments on 20–3 September 1920 in *Materialy*, 8 (1920); and V. Iakubson, 'Kul'turno-prosvetitel'naia rabota v tiur'me', *ESIu*, 19–20, 31 May 1922, 11–13.

[146] N. Bukharin and E. Preobrazhensky, *The ABC of Communism* (London, 1919), section 74, available at https://www.marxists.org/archive/bukharin/works/1920/abc/09.htm [accessed 13 June 2019]. Practical restraints, though, meant that many did not actually end up working; Jakobson, *Origins*, 36, 59, 64.

[147] *F. E. Dzerzhinskii—predsedatel' VChK-OGPU. 1917-1926* (Moscow, 2007), 238, 244 (8, 13 January 1921).

[148] Jakobson, *Origins*, 25, 44.

[149] GARF, f. R-3042, op. 1, d. 371, l. 17 (instructions from Vitebsk tribunal to city authorities, 12 June 1920).

Bolshevik described it later, in the context of a trial of Mensheviks in Saratov, as the worst of all punishments, as it expelled them from their own class—the workers—and was a terrible blow.[150] Others argued it enhanced social consciousness and a sense of public responsibility.[151] Indeed, experiencing the legal process was a deterrent for some, with the Menshevik F. I. Dan recalling vividly that anyone in prison was taking part in 'a kind of lottery' where the stake was their life and the nervous atmosphere weighed heavily on people's minds.[152] Nevertheless, it is hard to see censure wielding significant impact during a civil war. Some tribunals, particularly in the military, declared people to be 'outside of the law' (0.4 per cent of sentences in 1920),[153] thereby losing political and civil rights (affecting rations, housing, and so on), and preventing them from holding responsible posts. However, bureaucracies must have struggled to enforce this amid the turmoil. The same questionable impact was true of fines, if only because people lacked the ability to pay anything substantial as material conditions worsened. As a circular to people's courts explained—where fines formed 50–60 per cent of punishments—it only worked if people paid and if the amount was commensurate with the wealth of the criminal.[154] Debtors were threatened with labour, but this too required an efficient bureaucracy to enforce.

The most ambiguous category is, of course, the 'other' column in Figure 4.5. It is this column that emphasizes the diversity of tribunal activities, as one in five sentences fell into it at times. For some tribunals, it was much more: 73 per cent of sentences in Penza and Petrograd in 1919, 86 per cent in Ekaterinburg in 1921, and 60 per cent in Cherepovets and Riazan' in the same year. By placing so many sentences in this bracket, tribunals concealed the wide diversity in their practices that helps appreciate their flexibility. Everything from sending people to the front to arbitrary 'contributions' fell into this category. One tribunal imposed a 'contribution' for the use of poor families of Red Army soldiers of 850 horses, 750 cows, 2,500 sheep, 1,000 sheepskin coats, 1,000 pairs of felt boots, 5,000 pairs of socks, and 5,000 pairs of woollen mittens on a village found guilty of concealing deserters.[155]

Also key to understanding the flexibility of revolutionary justice is the prevalence of suspended (*uslovnyi*) sentences across this period—almost a third of sentences in civilian and military tribunals, if less in transport tribunals.[156] These, moreover, are underestimated. Narkomiust asked tribunals to record

[150] V. Antonov-Saratovskii, 'Sud idet! (Vospominaniia)', *Sud idet!*, 21 (1927), 1182.

[151] Bukharin and Preobrazhensky, *ABC*, section 74.

[152] F. Dan, *Two Years of Wandering. A Menshevik Leader in Lenin's Russia* (London, 2016), 142.

[153] GARF, f. A-353, op. 4, d. 111, l. 179 (statistics for military tribunals in 1920).

[154] GARF, f. R-1005, op. 2, d. 1, l. 50 (circular to local authorities, 20 January 1920).

[155] GARF, f. R-3042, op. 1, d. 84, l. 9ob (report on Perm' railway tribunal in October 1920).

[156] GARF, f. A-353, op. 4, d. 111, l. 179 (statistics, 1920); RGVA, f. 33988, op. 2, d. 454, l. 14 (report, 1922).

suspended prison sentences, but all types of sentences could be suspended, particularly for first offences if there were exceptional circumstances or the person did not pose a threat.[157] One official argued that suspended sentences applied psychological pressure suitable for lesser crimes, forcing someone to correct their behaviour without a prison sentence.[158] Other instructions stated that, if the sole purpose of a sentence was for 'social–educational' punishment and the offender was not 'bourgeois', a suspended sentence, compulsory labour without imprisonment, refusal of rights, or public censure was more appropriate than prison.[159] This must have been attractive to local authorities, as these sentences were cheaper, relieved overloaded prisons, and projected an image of mercy.

There are few systematic statistics on whether certain sentences were more common for particular crimes. Tula's tribunal shot a higher percentage of people in 1918–23 for banditry and anti-Soviet agitation than for rural unrest, not paying taxes, or crimes of office.[160] In military tribunals in the second half of 1920, individuals were eleven times more likely to be sentenced to death for traditional counter-revolutionary crimes and espionage than for misuse of authority, with other crimes in between. People were also far more likely to be sentenced to a short prison term (less than six months) for not following orders or misusing authority (as well as crimes in the 'other' category), suggesting leniency towards officials for lesser, redeemable crimes. Deserters were likely to receive longer terms or be sent to penal battalions. Suspended sentences were divided fairly equally, although deserters were slightly less likely to receive them, presumably due to pressing needs at the front.[161]

Tribunals do not appear to have kept systematic records on whether punishments were enforced, perhaps unsurprisingly given the conditions. Scattered reports indicate that some defendants were tried in their absence and were never tracked down; death sentences were not enacted for various reasons; prisons were too overcrowded to take more prisoners or organize forced labour; and fines became worthless amid rampant inflation or could not be paid. It is also easy to imagine an understaffed and overstretched bureaucracy struggling to keep tabs on criminals and their crimes. Yet is also clear that many hundreds were executed, thousands imprisoned, and many others forced to complete their punishment. The power of the tribunal, then, must have seemed real, particularly as the state grew stronger, even if there remained a chance that any punishment could be evaded.

Narkomiust and the Cassation Tribunal continued their centralizing efforts throughout, with, as is clear, a mixed impact on consistency. The authorities were trying to find a balance. Some tribunals did not act with 'proletarian firmness', but

[157] 'Guiding Principles', 169. [158] GARF, f. R-3042, op. 1, d. 23, ll. 53ob-54 (report, n.d.).

[159] GARF, f. R-1005, op. 1, d. 44, l. 41ob (circular to military tribunals, 5 February 1921).

[160] A. Makutchev, *'Prigovor okonchatel'nyi, obzhalovaniiu ne podlezhit...' Revoliutsionnye tribunaly v Sovetskoi Rossii v gody Grazhdanskoi voiny* (Moscow, 2012), 116, 130, 143.

[161] GARF, f. A-353, op. 4, d. 111, l. 207 (statistics for military tribunals in 1920).

some were far too severe.[162] The idealistic sentences of the early period disappeared, and it is possible to see decrees limiting the length of prison sentences take effect. The criminal law codes in June 1922 represented another attempt to forge consistency, but while they clarified what constituted a crime, they stipulated a range of suitable sentences for each crime. Revolutionary consciousness (and diversity) was retained, therefore, as judges still had to decide on a precise sentence within this range and could even display greater leniency in 'exceptional circumstances'.[163]

Yet this diversity reinforces the distinction between revolutionary justice and violence. One tribunal official later recalled a constant struggle to balance when it was best to be severe and apply repression, and conversely when it was appropriate to be more lenient (or, in his words, merciful). He recognized the value of both. Tribunals were not only 'weapons' of repression, but also of discipline, education, and even 'communist assistance'.[164] Certain crimes, such as clear and deliberate opposition, were treated harshly by all tribunals. Other crimes were treated harshly at particular places and times as changing official policies interacted with the evolving fears and concerns of local officials. But flexibility was always present, centrally and locally, providing tribunals with a wider range of options to respond to changing threats and practical realities than the more limited scope of the Cheka.

From 'Model' Trial to 'Show' Trial

The ongoing balancing act over sentences, though, reflected a broader sense among leading Bolsheviks as the civil war progressed that major trials were still not fulfilling their potential. Take, for example, the trial in May 1919 of V. F. Dzhunkovskii, former deputy Minister of the Interior and head of the tsarist secret police. Planned in advance and widely advertised, it seemed to have a convincing narrative of an oppressive tsarist functionary. Yet many in the audience supported Dzhunkovskii on the basis of his earlier stint as governor of Moscow, his charitable work, and his 'humane' character. Witnesses presented more evidence in favour than against, and Dzhunkovskii defended himself systematically. The narrative struggled to gain traction, and the sentence of imprisonment until the end of the civil war was seen as a minor victory by his supporters.[165] Not much, it appeared, had been learned since Panina's trial in

[162] GARF, f. A-353, op. 3, d. 56, l. 111 (correspondence, Vitebsk, 1 August 1919); f. R-1005, op. 3, d. 196, ll. 14ob, 22–22ob (correspondence, Tiumen', March 1922); d. 211, ll. 2–3 (report, Crimea, 15 January 1922).

[163] *Ugolovnyi kodeks RSFSR* (Moscow, 1922), 6 (article 28).

[164] G. Segal, 'Iz raboty voennykh tribunalov epokhi grazhdanskoi voiny', *Rabochii sud*, 21 (1927), 1668.

[165] R. Robbins, *Overtaken by the Night: One Russian's Journey Through Peace, War, Revolution, and Terror* (Pittsburgh, 2017), 422–32.

late 1917, and although other trials went more smoothly, the authorities struggled constantly with the difficulties of running an effective major trial.

One problem with this type of political trial was that such individuals no longer posed a real threat to the Bolsheviks, making it difficult to justify the role of tribunals in defending the revolution and combatting urgent threats. This explained the shift in major trials towards 'model (*obraztsovyi*)' trials designed to spotlight particular crimes rather than individuals. Tribunals selected cases that served as the best examples of current threats and held trials in locations (such as theatres and cinemas) or on days (Sundays or holidays) when the widest range of people could attend.[166] Most tribunals, as noted above, staged them. Yet while these trials demonstrated some leadership from outside the tribunal, usually local soviets or party organs, they were not completely managed. The narrative was rarely agreed in advance and there was little attempt to control proceedings. In a trial of 138 peasants in Irkutsk on 14–23 January 1921 for an armed revolt, for instance, the prosecutor's closing speech lasted six hours and two advocates spoke for five and a half hours and three hours respectively—lengths of time that could hardly have engaged an audience of apparently over 700 people, mostly peasants. Forty-seven defendants, moreover, were freed due to a lack of evidence.[167]

It was not until 1922 that the Bolsheviks' experiments with trials reached a 'synthesis' with the trial of the Socialist Revolutionaries (SRs), their long-standing socialist opponents.[168] This trial saw far greater management of the entire process than witnessed before, no doubt prompted by the SRs' enduring support among workers. The decision to hold a trial was taken by 28 December 1921, and various commissions were established involving senior figures such as N. I. Bukharin, Dzerzhinskii, L. B. Kamenev, Stalin, and Trotskii. These discussed all aspects of the trial, from the narrative and timescale to agitation and publicity, but it took six months of planning at the highest levels of government to produce a 'workable script'.[169]

The accusations were based on the testimony of a former SR and subsequent Cheka agent, G. I. Semenov, who admitted to various terrorist activities against Soviet power, most prominently the attempted murder of Lenin in 1918. Semenov alleged that senior SR leaders sanctioned these attacks, and he named ninety-three others involved. This prompted months of interrogations and the Bolsheviks had

[166] GARF, f. R-1005, op. 3, d. 80, l. 35 (report from Gorskii tribunal, October 1921).

[167] *Vlast' truda*, 12 February 1921, in *Sibirskaia vandeia*, I, 583.

[168] Cassiday, *Enemy on Trial*, 43. Many of the church trials that ran concurrently with this trial displayed similar features but were not given the same prominence; see, for example, the documents in *Arkhivy Kremlia*, I, 197–304.

[169] S. Smith, *Captives of Revolution: The Socialist Revolutionaries and the Bolshevik Dictatorship, 1918–1923* (Pittsburgh, 2011), 245. The level of central control throughout is obvious from the documents collected in *Sudebnyi protsess nad sotsialistami-revoliutsionerami (iiun'-avgust 1922 g.)* (Moscow, 2002). For a survey, see K. Morozov, *Sudebnyi protsess sotsialistov-revoliutsionerov i tiuremnoe protivostoianie (1922–1926)* (Moscow, 2005), 171–85. The educational elements of the trial are discussed in detail in Chapter 6.

produced a clear narrative by the summer; namely, the SRs had joined the bourgeoisie in fighting the workers and peasants after the October Revolution and conducted terrorist attacks on the government in 1918 before collaborating with the Whites and 'bourgeois' allies abroad. In doing all this, the SR leadership had betrayed the revolution, the people, and their party. As with all trials, the Bolsheviks aimed to impose their narrative on the revolutionary discourse, but this was the most sophisticated attempt yet. It sought not just to delegitimize the SRs and undermine its support but to split the party, turning its rank and file against the leaders, offering redemption to the former as long as they joined the Bolsheviks, while condemning, punishing, and removing the latter's threat. With this in mind, thirty-four people stood trial in two groups. There were twenty-two 'leaders' in the first group and twelve members in the second group (including Semenov) who had agreed to testify against their erstwhile comrades as part of their redemptive process.[170]

The organizers took no chances with the judges, appointing a senior party member, G. L. Piatakov, as chairman. One experienced tribunal official, A. V. Galkin, refused to serve as a judge, however, protesting at Piatakov's lack of legal experience, but political reliability was deemed more important for such a trial.[171] Thus Bukharin and other senior communists, M. N. Pokrovskii and M. P. Tomskii, helped defend the second group of SRs, while the advocates for the first group were constantly monitored and harassed. This was particularly true of several foreign advocates who came on behalf of the international socialist movement, including Theodor Liebknecht and Emil Vandervelde. Few chances were taken with the witnesses also, with only half of the defence's requests granted.[172]

The trial was held in the ballroom of Moscow's former noble club, with its imposing marble columns and grand chandeliers. Foreign observers described a 'symphony of red' as the judges on the dais sat behind benches draped in red, with revolutionary slogans on banners behind them.[173] The location combined elements of the major trials discussed. Formality (and authority) mixed with informality (*revolutionary* justice), with the judges taking centre stage, the prosecution and defence on either side, and the audience in front, but with haphazard procedure, lengthy and impassioned arguments, and—in some accounts—a vocal crowd.

Around 1,200 tickets were distributed each day, with 60 per cent apparently going to the local party committee for members and workers, and 40 per cent to

[170] Morozov, *Sudebnyi protsess*, 167, 186–207. See also M. Jansen, *A Show Trial under Lenin* (The Hague, 1982), 23–9, 48–9, 53–4; and Smith, *Captives*, 241–5.

[171] *Sudebnyi protsess*, 405–7 (letter from Galkin to Krylenko, 17 May 1922).

[172] Jansen, *Show Trial*, 76–8.

[173] F. Mackenzie, *Russia before Dawn* (London, 1923), 284. See also W. Duranty, 'Defy Soviet Court in Treason Trial', *The New York Times*, 10 June 1922, 1; and P. Hibben, 'Moscow's Treason Trial', *The Nation*, 27 September 1922, 300.

the secret police, to include defendants' families, press correspondents, and tribunal and government personnel. The audience was carefully vetted, tickets checked on entry and exit, and police agents sat among them to monitor and guide responses. There was also a well-organized security presence in the streets around the court.[174] A further demonstration of public support was organized on 20 June, the second anniversary of the death of one of the Bolsheviks supposedly murdered by the SRs, when apparently 300,000 people took to the streets. Piatakov, Krylenko, Bukharin, and others spoke to the crowds, while a group of workers was permitted into the court to harangue the defendants and call for the death penalty. As the advocates for the first group protested, this was a huge violation of procedure and destroyed any image of impartiality.[175]

The prosecutors employed tested strategies. Starting with the historical struggle of the proletariat, their case linked the SRs to proven examples of counter-revolutionary opposition before outlining their crimes. The accusations were linked to the new law codes to project an image of legality. While their guilt was preordained, there was doubt over the sentence. In an attempt to appease foreign socialists, a leading Bolshevik had promised prior to the trial that the death penalty would not be an option. He did not have the authority to make this promise, though, and other Bolsheviks reacted furiously while being aware of the potential backlash of acting too harshly. The Commissar of Justice, D. I. Kurskii, provided the first sign of a compromise when he declared that an independent court could not be bound by any promises, but that the All-Russian Central Executive Committee of the Congress of Soviets (VTsIK) could grant clemency in the event of a death sentence.[176] Sure enough, the tribunal sentenced twelve of the first group of twenty-two to death on 7 August, and the rest were given prison sentences. It also pronounced death on three of the second group of twelve collaborators, but requested a pardon as they had acknowledged and repudiated their crimes. Discussions at the highest levels of government revealed splits among the Bolshevik leadership, but the majority favoured compromise, with the death sentences suspended on condition that no further SR opposition emerged. These Bolsheviks seemed mindful of the need to retain influence among the international socialist movement and to not further alienate Russia diplomatically.[177]

The trial was massive. It lasted 48 days; investigated 177 people (rising to 188); brought 34 to trial; and resulted in 113 volumes of testimonies, trial transcripts, and other documents in the secret police's archive alone, as well as numerous files

[174] *Sudebnyi protsess*, 73; Morozov, *Sudebnyi protsess*, 288–301, 314–18, 443–52.

[175] *Sudebnyi protsess*, 75–7 (introduction); Jansen, *Show Trial*, 67–73.

[176] *Pravda*, 19 April 1922, 3. The chair reiterated the court's independence; *Pravoeserovskii politicheskii protsess v Moskve. 8 iiunia-4 avgusta 1922 g. Stenogrammy sudebnykh zasedanii* (Moscow, 2011), 84.

[177] For the split, see the minutes of meetings on 7 August in *Sudebnyi protsess*, 322–4. On the sentences, see Jansen, *Show Trial*, 39–41, 127–40; Smith, *Captives*, 259–60; and *Sudebnyi protsess*, 83–7.

elsewhere.[178] It demonstrated the Bolsheviks bringing together all their experiences from previous years. It also revealed some new strategies, not least making some of the defendants part of the state's narrative, so it was not just the Bolsheviks against the SRs but the SRs divided, while the willingness (even if forced) of some SRs to collaborate served, in theory, to reinforce the allegations.[179] More complex strategies were, of course, developed in later years, but all this marked a distinct change from partly organized 'model' trials to carefully stage-managed 'show (*pokazatel'nyi*)' trials. That this trial was intended to serve as an example comes across in Narkomiust's journal, where articles focused more on procedure, with various innovations classed as 'interesting moments', rather than providing a dramatic account of crimes.[180]

Yet even if this helped convince the Bolsheviks that trials rather than an entire tribunal system were sufficient to enact exceptional justice after the civil war (see Chapter 2), it still highlighted the pitfalls. The length—six days a week for two months—led to an inevitable loss of public interest. The Politburo ordered a quick end to the trial as early as 22 June, but the judges could not deliver.[181] They could not control what the defendants said, and the trial descended into a political contest with long and impenetrable testimonies. In the tradition of revolutionaries before 1917, the SRs used the trial to showcase resistance, and both sides ended up accusing each other of betraying the revolution. Such accusations against the Bolsheviks tapped into popular dissatisfaction and reminded people of the revolution's original democratic ideals. Procedurally, it was difficult to reconcile the trial's many objectives. Tight control helped the Bolsheviks' narrative to dominate but harmed attempts to convey the trial as independent, while engaging with the crowds on 20 June portrayed the trial as reflecting the will of the people but again harmed its legitimacy. All this heralded a renewed attack on the SRs that removed them as a political threat, but its precise influence as opposed to the other means of repression and persuasion used remains unclear.[182]

The audience also remained a problem in trials. It is not certain that even the hand-picked audience in the trial of the SRs was completely convinced. Foreign observers seemed unsure. One correspondent described an audience moving from rapt intensity and roaring support to fatigued silence and disinterest as the trial progressed.[183] Others reported a shift from a 'seething' audience pushing closer to the platform at the start to one wearied long before the end or even one largely

[178] *Pravoeserovskii politicheskii protsess*, 7, 19–20.

[179] This integration of narratives is typical of well-developed political trials, which seek to do more than simply pit one political ideology against another; Kirchheimer, *Political Justice*, 97–9.

[180] Seven articles were published in *ESIu* from 16 June to 31 August 1922.

[181] *Sudebnyi protsess*, 282–3 (Politburo resolution).

[182] Jansen, *Show Trial*, 174–7; Smith, *Captives*, 261–6.

[183] W. Duranty, 'Defy Soviet Court', 1; 'Goad Communists to Fury in Moscow', *The New York Times*, 12 June 1922, 3; 'Spare 14 Socialists; Hold 12 Hostages', *The New York Times*, 10 August 1922, 4.

passive throughout.[184] One person's intensity, no doubt, is another's passivity. But mixed reports exist for the entire period. Accounts of mass applause after each sentence or huge interest in trials that forced tribunals to move to bigger premises may misrepresent politeness or curiosity for support.[185] The same may be true of travelling sessions that reported thousands turning up and trials transforming previously suspicious observers.[186] Certainly, other accounts indicate audiences disagreeing with the sentence for being too harsh (such as the death penalty for an 'audacious' theft that was reduced later after a crowd descended on the prison) or too lenient (a year in prison for a naval commander who abused his position).[187] Audiences were also threatened for applauding defendants. Some audiences even regarded the tribunal not as an organ of justice but as a 'bloodthirsty monster (*krovozhadnoe chudovishche*)'.[188] In the end, tribunals targeted issues at the root of popular discontent, and controlling audiences was always going to be difficult.

Punishment also remained problematic. The compromise for the SRs satisfied few and did not match the allegedly heinous crimes. Elsewhere, sentences were dispensed with an eye on their external reception, but differing interpretations of this context often led to indecision or conflict. The trial of Kolchak's former ministers in May 1920 saw disputes among local party bosses over whether to shoot them all or a certain percentage, and about what either action said about the image of the court. They then resisted calls for mercy from central party organs, believing there was popular pressure for severity. During the church trials, even the Politburo was split on the desirability of death sentences.[189] In other cases, officials reported that severe sentences provoked local resistance so tribunals avoided them, or that reactions changed from village to village, with a severe sentence needed to force one village to comply, while the same sentence provoked a conflict in another.[190]

Nonetheless, trials were the focal point and distinctive feature of revolutionary justice. They offered a discursive public forum where the state articulated its vision of the revolution, attacked alternative visions, categorized crimes, and used coercion and persuasion to punish and change harmful beliefs and behaviours. They projected state authority and ideology, while their public nature and degree of unpredictability conveyed a sense of legitimacy. Some people were forced,

[184] Mackenzie, *Russia before Dawn*, 237–8, 243; Hibben, 'Moscow's Treason Trial', 299–300.

[185] GARF, f. R-3042, op. 1, d. 84, l. 9ob (report, Perm' railway tribunal, November 1920); f. R-1005, op. 2, d. 54, l. 1 (report, Orel tribunal, 7 September 1920); *Zaria* [Simbirsk], 3 March 1920, 3.

[186] RGVA, f. 33988, op. 2, d. 245, ll. 4ob-5ob (report on military tribunals on the Western Front, March 1922); GARF, f. R-1005, op. 67, d. 13, l. 3ob (report, Vologda tribunal, 7 October 1920).

[187] *Rabochaia i krest'ianskaia krasnaia armiia i flot*, 27 January 1918, 3; GARF, f. R-3042, op. 1, d. 97, l. 1ob (report, Caspian Sea tribunal, autumn 1921).

[188] GARF, f. R-1005, op. 3, d. 10, ll. 28--28ob (report, Arkhangel'sk tribunal, 23 November 1921).

[189] Poznanskii, 'Sud', 47–50; *Arkhivy Kremlia*, I, 197–8, 213–14, 217 (church trials in May 1922).

[190] A. Zvezdov, 'V period podgotovki Oktiabr'skoi revoliutsii', in *V boiakh za vlast' sovetov (vospominanii uchastnikov sotsialisticheskii revoliutsii i grazhdanskoi voine v Omske i Omskoi oblasti)* (Omsk, 1957), 42.

frightened, or persuaded to change their behaviour by being judged or through observing trials, helping tribunals forge Soviet citizens. Still others pretended to change. But the Bolsheviks were under no illusions that trials were completely effective. They were always intended—and this is how the Bolsheviks probably viewed the trial of the SRs—to be one of several means of coercion and persuasion. The benefit of the trial as opposed to, say, just violence or agitation alone lay in its mix of punitive force, agitational (and emotional) power, drama, and flexibility. It allowed the Bolsheviks to categorize and condemn—to establish the 'truth' of wrongdoing—while still permitting a range of responses depending on the strength of state power, the realities of everyday life, and the nature of the threat at a particular time and place.

5
The Logic of Mercy

The external language of the Bolsheviks portrayed tribunals as a merciless weapon, and fluid definitions of crimes and frequent harsh punishments—not least dispensing the death penalty for seemingly insignificant crimes—offer plenty of supporting evidence. As the previous chapters have demonstrated, however, a range of evidence suggests a more complicated picture. Chapters 1 and 2 noted in passing the emergence of a formal cassation process from 1918 that, while not granting an automatic right to appeal, permitted defendants to complain if they felt procedures had been violated. Chapter 4 also explored the wide range of sentences dispensed. High levels of suspended sentences, in particular, reveal the greater flexibility of tribunals as organs practising a mix of coercion and persuasion. To reiterate from the last chapter the point made by one judge, G. M. Segal, tribunals struggled constantly to balance severity and leniency (or, in his words, to decide when to be 'merciful'), as tribunals were 'weapons' not only of repression but also of discipline, education, and even 'assistance'.[1]

Yet mercy is not a term that should be used lightly when discussing revolutionary justice. In some instances, the practices above constitute standard procedure in most legal systems. In other cases, they may enable the correction of mistakes—that is, achieve 'justice' rather than demonstrate mercy. Nevertheless, the Bolsheviks reserved the right of courts to dispense 'mercy (*pomilovanie*)' from the first Decree on Courts onwards and portrayed these actions as such. They believed people were committing crimes against the revolution and felt anything less than the severest penalty did represent mercy. Suspended or light sentences, appeals, early release, and amnesties were all framed as proving the 'lenient (*miagkii*)' or 'humanitarian (*gumanitarnyi*)' nature of the proletarian state, delivering mercy to those who had committed crimes through a lack of consciousness, material hardship, or pressure from anti-Bolshevik forces. As the legal system developed, particularly after the reforms of 1922, these practices were also portrayed as providing a guarantee of legality, ensuring the new laws were followed.[2] As crime, moreover, was considered a socially dangerous act and punishment corresponded to the level of that danger, if that level fell through changes in a person's character or sociopolitical circumstances, then punishment

[1] G. Segal, 'Iz raboty voennykh tribunalov epokhi grazhdanskoi voiny', *Rabochii sud*, 21 (1927), 1668.
[2] E. Kutsova, *Sovetskaia kassatsiia kak garantiia zakonnosti i pravosudii* (Moscow, 1957), 3–29.

The State versus The People: Revolutionary Justice in Russia's Civil War, 1917–1922. Matthew Rendle,
Oxford University Press (2020). © Matthew Rendle.
DOI: 10.1093/oso/9780198840428.001.0001

should also be reduced. In these cases, these acts of mercy were logical, permitting people who were no longer dangerous to return to socially useful work.[3]

There was, however, even more logic to mercy; as Segal realized, if the violence inherent in revolutionary justice constituted a powerful weapon in some scenarios, the ability to demonstrate mercy was an equally important weapon at other times. Or in other words, if punishment is instrumental, serving a political and social purpose, so too is mercy.[4] Excessive violence can be counterproductive—as F. E. Dzerzhinskii, head of the Cheka, admitted—fostering more resistance than it can quell.[5] The value of revolutionary justice, therefore, was not just providing a means for more nuanced punitive approaches than the Cheka, as already argued, but also permitting non-punitive approaches backed up with punitive force. An unrelentingly brutal justice system, furthermore, undermines the system's authority and legitimacy. By contrast, a more flexible system sustains the impression that law stands above the state and acts impartially, and helps to legitimize the system as people acknowledge its authority by working within it. Cassation was also a means of central supervision, providing a flow of information to the top while projecting central power down to the localities.[6] At the very least, mercy permitted the state to intervene periodically in a paternalist manner, wielding power and humanity, while blending violence and discretion.

The Bolsheviks appreciated more of these benefits as the civil war progressed, but they were far from the first Russian rulers to do so. Tsars had preached merciless punishment in their laws, only to cast themselves as benevolent overseers, ensuring that the judicious use of mercy became central to the state's justice system. Mercy was, as one historian observed, a strategy of governance from Muscovy onwards and, as another noted, it could project the image of a strong state.[7] The challenges faced by the Bolsheviks made these potential benefits attractive. Revolutionary justice grappled with vast variations in procedure, understandings of crimes, and sentencing. It also struggled to track down

[3] S Fainblit, *Amnistiia i sudebnyi prigovor* (Moscow–Leningrad, 1927); N. Popov, 'Amnistiia v oznamenovanie obrazovaniia SSSR osnovnye zadachi organov sovetskoi iustitsii v bor'be s prestupnost'iu', *Ezhenedel'nik sovetskoi iustitsii* [hereafter *ESIu*], 36, 13 September 1923, 817–19; and B. Utevskii, *Dosrochnoe osvobozhdenie i amnistiia* (Moscow, 1927). See also the later accounts by N. Durmanov, *Osvobozhdenie ot nakazaniia po sovetskomu pravu* (Moscow, 1957); and V. Kvashis, *Gumanizm sovetskogo ugolovnogo prava* (Moscow, 1969).

[4] The following discussion is influenced by D. Hay, 'Property, Authority and the Criminal Law', in D. Hay (ed.), *Albion's Fatal Tree: Crime and Society in Eighteenth-Century England* (London, 1975), 17–63, esp. 48–49, 55–6; and C. Strange, 'Introduction', in C. Strange (ed.), *Qualities of Mercy: Justice, Punishment and Discretion* (Vancouver, 1996), 3–20.

[5] *F. E. Dzerzhinskii—predsedatel' VChK-OGPU. 1917–1926* (Moscow, 2007), 176–81 (17 April 1920).

[6] M. Shapiro, *Courts: A Comparative and Political Analysis* (Chicago, 1981), 38–9, 49–55; M. Damaška, *The Faces of Justice and State Authority: A Comparative Approach to the Legal Process* (New Haven, 1986), 48–50.

[7] N. Kollmann, 'The Quality of Mercy in Early Modern Legal Practice', *Kritika*, 7, 1 (2006), 5–22; J. Burbank, 'Mercy, Punishment and the Law: The Qualities of Justice at Township Courts', *Kritika*, 7, 1 (2006), 23–60.

witnesses and enforce sentences when faced with shortages in manpower, mass crimes, and overcrowded prisons. Dispensing mercy could help conceal impotence, disguising the system's flaws rather than risk undermining it. The state was in the awkward position of needing the skills of many 'criminals', whether requiring peasant 'bandits' to continue farming, convincing deserters to rejoin a depleted Red Army, or re-employing corrupt officials in a rapidly expanding bureaucracy. Punishment is always important at some level to demonstrate that states have the will and ability to act, but in many cases, it has been argued, *what* is said about punishment, and *how* it is said, may be just as important as whether it is implemented.[8] Mercy enabled discretion: crimes could be condemned, targeted, and hopefully reduced, but the state's needs still be met. For the Bolsheviks, the sentence was the rule, but mercy could be a justified exception.

In this way, mercy helped regulate relations between state and society. It moderated the threat posed by the state and suggested it understood the pressures faced by people in everyday life. It promoted the image that law could be about compassion as well as terror, and recognized factors that law could not, including the coercive influence of the Bolsheviks' enemies. At the same time, people were forced to engage and identify with the official categories and characteristics of counter-revolution by participating in the various practices of mercy, thus further imposing the state's objectives and ideas on to people. Consciously or not, this fostered deference and a tacit acceptance of the broader basis of the new social order.

In this context, therefore, mercy is not about the Bolsheviks being genuinely merciful or compassionate, even if it did provide concrete benefits to people. Instead, it is about mercy as a 'coldly logical' act.[9] This chapter discusses three practices in detail—cassation appeals, amnesties, and early release—to explore in detail how the Bolsheviks used mercy. It should be noted, though, that mercy was not without its dangers. If it became too widespread, then it was hard to frame it as an exception to the rule of law; it became regular practice and was considered as such by potential criminals. Equally, if mercy was seen as revealing weakness rather than projecting strength, this too threatened the state's authority. This chapter charts this balancing act as mercy developed into an integral part of revolutionary justice.

The Nature of Cassation

The first Decree on Courts in November 1917 permitted cassation only for certain cases in people's courts, but tribunals soon followed suit. Regulations on 19

[8] D. Garland, *Punishment and Modern Society: A Study in Social Theory* (Oxford, 1990), 257.
[9] Strange, 'Introduction', 5.

December declared that sentences were final, but the Commissariat of Justice (Narkomiust) could suggest holding a second and final trial to the presidium of the All-Russian Executive Committee of the Congress of Soviets (VTsIK) in the case of procedural violations or unjust verdicts. A proper cassation department was established in Narkomiust on 25 January 1918 to examine complaints against tribunals.[10] According to procedures clarified on 5 March, a complaint had to be made within two weeks of the sentence to the tribunal concerned. If eligible, the tribunal had to transfer it, along with the case file, to the cassation department within three days. The department had a week to assess the case; they either rejected the appeal or accepted it and transferred it to the legal department of VTsIK for confirmation. VTsIK had a fortnight to reject the department's decision or confirm it, and then the case would be referred for a second and final trial under the original tribunal, albeit with different judges.[11]

The debates surrounding inconsistent procedures and sentences in the first few trials probably encouraged Narkomiust to introduce this measure of oversight. The use of cassation in Europe derived from the cassation tribunal created during the French Revolution to quash judicial decisions based on an incorrect interpretation of legislation. The tribunal did not provide guidance or alter sentences, but simply ordered a retrial.[12] The legal reforms in 1864 introduced cassation into Russia, where it evolved over time to enforce statutory over customary law (and with it central authority) and provide guidance to local courts.[13] By continuing this rather than introducing an automatic right to appeal, the Bolsheviks argued that a revolutionary court saw a defendant judged by a popularly elected court with the involvement of the public. They doubted that an appeals court could offer a better judgement, and it would undermine the original court. Instead, cassation focused on the 'quality of the legal work', avoiding a lengthy appeals process that revisited the circumstances of every case. But there were also political benefits: cassation encouraged consistency, justified central intervention, and could 'raise' local officials to the 'correct' level.[14]

In practice, however, there was confusion. On the one hand, tribunals were not clear on cassation. On 10 March 1918, for example, the chairman of the tribunal in

[10] *Istoriia zakonodatel'stva SSSR i RSFSR po ugolovnomu protsessu i organizatsii suda i prokuratury, 1917–1954* [hereafter *IZ*] (Moscow, 1955), 34–6, 38.

[11] *Gazeta rabochego i krest'ianskogo pravitel'stva*, 5 March 1918 (in GARF, f. A-353, op. 2, d. 123, ll. 1–3).

[12] J. Merryman, *The Civil Law Tradition: An Introduction to the Legal Systems of Western Europe and Latin America* (2nd edition, Stanford, 1985), 39–40.

[13] G. Bhat, 'The Rule of *Zakon*: The Criminal Cassation Department and Legality in Late Imperial Russia, 1866-94', *The Russian Review*, 72, 4 (2013), 622–46; B. Levin-Stankevich, 'Cassation, Judicial Interpretation and the Development of Civil and Criminal Law in Russia, 1864-1917: The Institutional Consequences of the 1864 Court Reform in Russia' (PhD dissertation, State University of New York, Buffalo, 1984).

[14] A. Tager, 'Osnovyne problemy kassatsii v sovetskom ugolovnom protsesse', in N. Krylenko (ed.), *Problemy ugolovnoi politiki* (4 volumes, Moscow, 1935–7), IV, 67–71.

Tver' declared incorrectly that there were neither appeals nor cassation, and he was not alone in believing that sentences were final.[15] Stavropol', in contrast, operated an appeals process, allowing three days to lodge appeals.[16] On the other hand, defendants submitted 'appeals' irrespective of official legislation.[17] These detailed all manner of grievances and were addressed to a wide range of institutions and individuals, including Narkomiust, VTsIK, local soviets, local departments of justice, and leading Bolsheviks. Indeed, authorities often received multiple appeals from defendants, relatives, lawyers, and friends about the same case. Most found their way to Narkomiust eventually, yet officials usually lacked sufficient information to make a decision or cases were passed between organs. All this led Narkomiust to doubt the value of its cassation department as early as April 1918.[18]

A solution came with the creation of a cassation department under VTsIK on 11 June. It consisted of three people: a chairman (appointed by Narkomiust and confirmed by VTsIK) and two members (one each from Narkomiust and VTsIK). The basis for cassation remained the same, and appeals had to be submitted within a fortnight of the sentence to the sentencing tribunal. Tribunals had three days to forward them on (with case files), members of the College of Prosecutors under the Supreme Tribunal (established on 29 May) would prepare a report, and the new cassation department had two weeks to decide. If upheld, the case would be subjected to a retrial, usually by the same tribunal with different personnel. If the sentence was adjudged not to match the crime or the appellant was clearly innocent, the case would go to VTsIK, which could change the sentence or dismiss the case without a retrial.[19]

According to N. V. Krylenko, the state prosecutor, this step created a clearer decision-making process, and ensured the 'popularly elected' VTsIK decided the most important and complex cases. The Bolsheviks' political opponents were quick to query what constituted an unfair sentence when there was no guidance on sentencing, while observing that supervision by VTsIK meant nothing if it was dominated by the Bolsheviks.[20] These points were true, but the ability of VTsIK to

[15] GARF, f. R-393, op. 3, d. 415, l. 6ob (report to a congress of *uezd* commissars of justice).

[16] *Materialy Narodnogo Komissariata Iustitsii* [hereafter *Materialy*], 1 (1918), 35 (report by the provincial commissar of justice to a congress of local justice officials, 20 April 1918), and 2 (1918), 49 (undated resolution).

[17] I have used 'appeal' in lieu of several Russian words used. The common and official term was *zhaloba*, which is better translated as 'complaint'. *Proshenie* was fairly common, reflecting a sense of requesting pardon or mercy, while *obzhalovanie* became more common later. *Zaiavlenie* was used (and more rarely *ob"iasnenie*), conveying a more factual approach—a statement, request, or explanation. The content was similar irrespective of the title.

[18] GARF, f. A-353, op. 2, d. 835, ll. 10 (protocols of meeting, 4 April 1918).

[19] *Dekrety sovetskoi vlasti* [hereafter *DSV*] (18 volumes, Moscow, 1957–2009), II, 420–1. Cases originating in the Supreme Tribunal went directly to VTsIK, and those involving the death penalty were reviewed automatically.

[20] The debate is in *Chetvertyi Vserossiiskii s"ezd sovetov rabochikh, krest'ianskikh, soldatskikh i kazach'ikh deputatov. Stenograficheskii otchet. Moskva, 1918g.* (Moscow, 1919), 412–16.

dismiss cases and change sentences is notable as, strictly speaking, this was no longer cassation, and it marked a move—as political opposition grew—to use cassation to assert greater central authority over revolutionary justice.

Reforms in April 1919 and March 1920 developed this move further. On 4 April 1919, the department was renamed the Cassation Tribunal (KT). Defendants now had only twenty-four hours to appeal. A member of the KT (*chlen-dokladchik*), who was also a member of the College of Prosecutors, wrote a resolution (*zakliuchenie*) on the appeal to inform the final decision, which had to be made within a week. Cases where a sentence needed to be changed were still submitted to VTsIK.[21] On 18 March 1920, the KT was permitted to supervise procedural and related questions, as well as cassation, to ensure the activities of tribunals were united. In addition, all sentences, not just those subject to a cassation appeal, and including those from military and railroad tribunals, were now transferred to the KT.[22] The KT did not confirm every one before it was enacted, but it was able to intervene when obvious anomalies were spotted. This ability to supervise *all* the activities of *all* tribunals marked a significant expansion in the KT's powers, which now covered everything from legislating on procedures and conducting inspections to examining the composition, finances, and administrative structures of tribunals. All this greatly enhanced the level of central control.

Initially, military tribunals were clear they were not subject to appeals or cassation.[23] According to K. Kh. Danishevskii, chairman of the Revolutionary Military Tribunal of the Republic (RVTR), which held authority over all military tribunals, cassation was rejected as impossible practically. Military tribunals worked in difficult conditions and needed to enact sentences quickly and decisively to project their authority and maximize impact.[24] In reality, the system was more flexible, and earlier instructions to military tribunals stressed that, while they were not subject to appellation or cassation, if there was new information, or changing circumstances and political considerations, revolutionary military councils could review sentences and order a retrial.[25] A later decree added that the sentences of each military tribunal could be reviewed by the tribunal immediately above it as well as the relevant military council, while the RVTR oversaw all sentences.[26] When railway tribunals emerged from the shadows of military tribunals in 1920, they adopted a similar system.[27] After the March 1920 decree, however, a further decree on military tribunals on 4 May 1920, while still refusing to explicitly state that cassation was applicable, noted that the chairman of RVTR was now a member of the KT, and confirmed that reports and sentences of all

[21] *DSV*, V, 15–16. [22] *IZ*, 131–3. [23] *IZ*, 79–80 (14 February 1919).
[24] K. Danishevskii, *Revoliutsionnye voennye tribunaly* (Moscow, 1920), 46, 50.
[25] RGVA, f. 33987, op. 2, d. 53, l. 136 (from Revolutionary Military Council of the Republic, 19 January 1919).
[26] *DSV*, 295–6 (20 November 1919). [27] *IZ*, 135 (18 March 1920).

military tribunals were to be submitted to the KT for examination (railway tribunals were to do the same).[28] Again, it was not so much that the KT *would* check each sentence, but rather that it *could*. Now, as Danishevskii admitted, military tribunals were essentially subjected to cassation, and most military tribunals responded to appeals in the same way as their civilian counterparts. He admitted that removing inconsistencies strengthened military tribunals, as it did all tribunals.[29] These powers of central oversight culminated in June 1921 with the official unification of all tribunals, discussed in Chapter 2, into a single tribunal consisting of four colleges, including cassation.[30]

The growing regulation of the cassation process on paper should not disguise ongoing variations on the ground. Some tribunals continued to declare that the sentence was effective immediately and no appeals were permitted, which, while technically true, conveyed the sense that no further options were available to those convicted.[31] By contrast, Moscow's tribunal in 1919–20 finished every trial by stating that the sentence was final but subject to appeal to the cassation process within forty-eight hours.[32] Appeals had to be directed to the KT by the same tribunals whose decisions were being contested, and some appellants complained that they were refused the right to appeal, and this must have been the easiest route for tribunals.[33] There was also the fundamental problem of judging procedural errors without comprehensive procedural or law codes. Decrees and regulations helped, but there remained room for confusion.

Yet the system was more flexible in practice than on paper. Regulations stipulated strict avenues for appeal, but there were plenty of instances of positive results outside of these. Appeals sent to the wrong place were usually forwarded on, while unofficial channels could reap rewards in a patrimonial state.[34] L. D. Trotskii received appeals from military personnel in his capacity as Commissar of War.[35] G. K. Ordzhonikidze, as chairman of the North Caucasus Revolutionary Committee and on the Revolutionary Council of the Red Caucasus Army, received appeals from officials, organizations, and military personnel.[36] Leading Bolsheviks often acted outside official channels, asking for information or

[28] *IZ*, 143. [29] Danishevskii, *Revoliutsionnye*, 47–50.

[30] *DSV*, XVI, 145–52 (23 June 1921).

[31] GARF, f. R-3042, op. 1, d. 392, ll. 1–3ob, 7–7ob (trial transcripts, Water Transport Tribunal, Northern Region, July–August 1920).

[32] TsGAMO, f. 4613, op. 2, dd. 31, 64 (trial transcripts, May–August 1919 and May–December 1920).

[33] GARF, f. R-1005, op. 2, d. 9, l. 3 (appeal, M. I. Kamenskii, 18 June 1919). On 1 April 1919, Moscow's tribunal rejected seven appeals with no reasons provided; TsGAMO, f. 4613, op. 2, d. 6, l. 161ob (minutes). Iaroslavl' tribunal was the same; GARF, f. R-393, op. 13, d. 542, ll. 43, 57 (protocols, 8 and 14 October 1919).

[34] D. Newman, 'Criminal Strategies and Institutional Concerns in the Soviet Legal System: An Analysis of Criminal Appeals in Moscow Province, 1921-1928' (PhD thesis, University of California Los Angeles, 2013), 241–76.

[35] RGVA, f. 33987, op. 1, dd. 196, 225 (both 1919).

[36] RGASPI, f. 85, op. 8, d. 333, ll. 5, 24–29ob; d. 338, ll. 2–2ob (1920–1).

a favourable resolution. Few appeals kept to the official timescale, with some taking weeks to appeal and waiting months for a resolution. This prolonged imprisonment and uncertainty, but was not cause for dismissal, even if cases were dismissed for numerous other reasons.

It is also apparent that the two bases for cassation on paper—procedural violations and an unfair sentence—could be fluid. Violations could be anything from an incorrectly established tribunal (too few members or too many) to ignoring evidence or an abuse of powers (usually the tribunal had considered a case that should have been tried by a people's court). Equally, assessing whether a sentence was unfair remained subjective, with differences of opinion between central and local authorities, while the latter often misapplied laws on sentencing once these became clearer. Given that tribunals operated in turbulent conditions and were understaffed, poorly financed, and administratively disorganized, and given that assessments of the danger of certain crimes fluctuated widely (influencing assessments of the fairness of a sentence), this left plenty of room for appellants.

Furthermore, once an appeal was made, the KT examined all the materials submitted for irregularities and did not rule simply on the basis of the points made in the appeal. This meant appellants only had to get their appeal examined to have a chance that something might be picked up. It also reinforced the fact that, in practice, the cassation process operated more like an appeals process, as it proved difficult to divorce questions of procedure from those of evidence. To make judgements about whether investigations had followed procedure or sentences were unjust required assessment of all the circumstances surrounding a case. This was reinforced by small changes made to cassation in the criminal code, published on 22 May 1922, which noted that a sentence could be annulled if the investigation had failed to disclose all the facts relevant to the sentence, as well as if there had been violations in procedure, interpreting the new code, or if the sentence was obviously unjust. This provided the KT with further authority to delve into all aspects of a case.[37]

All this, then, provides a mixed picture on whether cassation reaped concrete benefits for those who appealed, and official statistics on the process, incomplete as usual, reinforce this uncertainty. As noted in Figure 5.1, appeals rose across 1919–20 as, on the one hand, the caseload of tribunals increased and, on the other, the KT steadily extended its authority. By November 1919, the KT complained to Narkomiust that they were holding two meetings a week and more would be needed soon, and they required additional workers.[38] Protocols of meetings in

[37] *Ugolovno-protsessual'nyi kodeks R. S. F. S. R. utv. V. Ts. I. K. 25 Maia 1922g. s alfavitno-postateinym ukazetelam i oglavleniem* (Moscow, 1922), st. 359–63 (cassation), 433–47 (on cassation and tribunals).

[38] GARF, f. A-353, op. 3, d. 29, ll. 81–81ob (20 November 1919).

Year	Meetings	Cases	Sentences annulled	Sentences changed	Sentences unchanged
1919	54	559	98 (17.5%)	103 (18.4%)	358 (64.1%)
1920[204]	57	1430	268 (18.7%)	77 (5.4%)	1085 (75.9%)

Figure 5.1 Official statistics on the Cassation Tribunal, 1919–20.

Source: *Trudy tsentral'nyi statisticheskogo upravleniia. Tom VIII. Vypusk 2. Statisticheskii ezhegodnik 1918–1920 gg. Vypusk vtoroi* [hereafter *Trudy 1*] (Moscow, 1922), 84 (Figures cover appeals dealt with by the KT and not those submitted to local tribunals and dismissed as unfounded).

Year	Sentences annulled	Procedural violations	Outside jurisdiction
1919	98	77 (78.6%)	21 (21.4%)
1920[205]	268	248 (92.5%)	20 (7.5%)

Figure 5.2 Reasons for annulling a sentence, 1919–20.

Source: *Trudy 1*, 84.

1919 indicate that the number of cases per meeting, usually five to twelve, could range from a single case to as many as thirty-eight.[39] Meetings grew in size and number in 1920–1, but even so less than 1 per cent of all tribunal cases in 1920 was entering into the cassation system (contrast Figure 5.1 with Figure 3.2). Although most sentences were annulled due to procedural errors (see Figure 5.2), there must have been many more errors than this given the disorganization surrounding the system at the height of the civil war. Most annulled sentences also simply meant a case was sent back to a tribunal for retrial, and the vast majority of these individuals were probably reconvicted, while some statistics on changed sentences from 1920 suggest 77 per cent were actually increased.[40]

Nevertheless, the scope of cassation was broader than it initially appeared, and even Krylenko recognized that the term 'cassation' was a misnomer as sentences were changed and cases dismissed without retrials.[41] This was to be expected. In France and Germany, cassation systems evolved across the nineteenth century from quashing incorrect decisions to suggesting the correct interpretation, to 'revising' sentences to save cases from returning to lower courts, and to reconcile legislative gaps.[42] The Bolsheviks may not have envisaged any need for cassation initially, but its rapid evolution into a wider-ranging organ enabled central bodies,

[39] GARF, f. R-1005, op. 2, dd. 22–5.

[40] GARF, f. R-1005, op. 2, d. 1, l. 284ob (report of the KT to the 8th Congress of Soviets, December 1920).

[41] N. Krylenko, *Sudoustroistvo RSFSR* (Moscow, 1923), 56. For later assessments, see S. Kucherov, *The Organs of Soviet Administration of Justice: Their History and Operation* (Leiden, 1970), 622, 641–2; and P. Solomon, *Criminal Justice under Stalin* (Cambridge, 1996), 52–3.

[42] Merryman, *Civil Law*, 40–3.

facing growing threats and needing an efficient justice system, to obtain information about local practices and exert authority (far from perfectly but improving over time). For much of the time, whether people gained justice from an appeal was of little interest to most Bolsheviks compared with their desire to see tribunals become more consistent and effective. Yet some did benefit from appeals, usually in terms of a reduced sentence. Equally, cassation aided the state's ability to implement decisions that did benefit people, whether capping the length of prison sentences to five years (see Chapter 4), a growing desire to avoid the death penalty, or, as discussed below, implementing wide-ranging amnesties. As one contemporary noted, it was a means of 'reducing repression' without needing a retrial.[43]

A Dialogue on Justice

The cassation process was driven by appeals, and these provide insights into the continuation of largely traditional 'popular' conceptions of justice, demonstrating how people tried to fit these views into the language of revolutionary justice. Appeals do not convey the unmediated voice of appellants, of course. A scribe—whether a clerk, teacher, priest, or lawyer—was often involved, since most people remained illiterate. Most appeals indicate knowledge of the legal regulations from somewhere, with a few written explicitly by lawyers.[44] Appellants were also guided by what they thought the state wanted to hear and what would achieve success. Appeals, then, were 'public transcripts' rather than a genuine reflection of an individual's thoughts, but appellants must have endorsed their content and helped determine content and tone.[45] All this, as with petitions prior to 1917, led to a 'schizophrenic' effect; a mix of personal information, formal references to decrees, and attempts to embrace the perceived priorities of the state in a 'shotgun' approach that hoped to ensure something in the petition would hit home.[46] This made sense: the KT assessed all aspects of a case once something had prompted a review. Yet appeals rarely simply begged for mercy. One historian noted how late imperial petitions lacked the 'ritual lament' element—a portrayal of the petitioner as powerless and living in misery—apparent in earlier and later petitions.[47] The same is true here. Appellants had a subject (their sentence) and

[43] Tager, 'Osnovyne problemy kassatsii', 71.

[44] Narkomiust reported in 1921 that 53.5 of appeals seemed literate, 26.9 were judicial in nature, 2.6 were written by jurists, while 17 appeared illiterate; *RSFSR. Narodnyi Komissariat Iustitsii. Otchet IX Vserossiiskomu s"ezdu sovetov* (Moscow, 1921), 10. Some were typed, which required help for most, although officials did type up some appeals later for the record.

[45] G. Freeze, *From Supplication to Revolution* (Oxford, 1988), 8.

[46] C. Gaudin, *Ruling Peasants: Village and State in Late Imperial Russia* (DeKalb, 2007), 126–8.

[47] Gaudin, *Ruling Peasants*, 237. On 'ritual lament', see H. Dewey and A. Kleimola, 'The Petition (*čelobitnaja*) as an Old Russian Literary Genre', *The Slavic and East European Journal*, 14, 3 (1970), 284–301; M. Palat, 'Regulating Conflict through the Petition', in Palat (ed.), *Social Identities in Revolutionary Russia* (Basingstoke, 2001), 86–112; Newman, 'Criminal Strategies', 166–211; and

objective (reducing or overturning it). They requested justice or mercy, but, rather than begging for it (even if they highlighted material hardships), most asserted their right to a trial that abided by regulations or, as they saw it, a fair sentence, which usually involved considering material circumstances.

Similarly, the state's resolutions on appeals provide another insight into official views, but are also restricted. Records of decisions are often brief, descriptive, and fragmentary; decisions are not explained, there are gaps, or the various players speak with different voices. It is, for instance, the resolution of the *chlen-dokladchik* to the rest of the KT on whether to accept or reject an appeal that usually survives. These resolutions provide a valuable summary of the case, the original sentence, and the main points of the appeal, and they reveal why *this* official thinks an appeal should be upheld or rejected. But it is not always clear whether the resolution was accepted by the KT or, afterwards, by VTsIK. Evidence suggests the vast majority were, but there were also instances of disagreements.[48]

Early appeals tended to claim that the allegations were inaccurate and the authorities mistaken or corrupt, or witnesses unreliable. Some claimed they had been unfairly treated compared to others who had committed similar crimes, or excused their actions on account of naïvety or a genuine mistake, sometimes stressing their previous unblemished history or good character.[49] As the basis for cassation—procedural violations and unfair sentences—became established, more appellants focused on these issues. Appeals claimed investigations were incomplete, tribunals inadequately staffed, and witnesses had not been called or interrogated thoroughly, and so on, alongside questioning whether a crime had actually occurred. There were plenty of procedural violations at this time, of course, but the growing emphasis on this area suggests growing awareness of the cassation process, either directly or through lawyers or other officials. It also indicates certain assumptions about what *should* be part of the legal process, particularly the frequent complaints that witnesses were disregarded or not called, or that the allegations were unclear or not presented to them on time.

Officials took these complaints seriously, using all the documents available, from trial records to witness statements, to reach a decision. Their decisions were not always consistent, but they seem to have been determined to enforce correct procedures where possible. Clearly, some issues mattered more than others or

G. Alexopoulos, 'The Ritual Lament: A Narrative of Appeal in the 1920s and 1930s', *Russian History*, 24 (1997), 117–29. The appeals here, with demands to uphold procedural norms sitting alongside personal hardships, seem akin to those discussed in V. Kivelson, 'Muscovite "Citizenship": Rights without Freedom', *The Journal of Modern History*, 74, 3 (2002), 479–82.

[48] As records do seem to exist on disagreements, the sole presence of a resolution in the files seems to indicate that it was accepted, and this section generally works on this assumption.

[49] GARF, f. R-336, op. 1, d. 271, ll. 5–5ob (appeal, N. I. Pokrovskii, 8 November 1917); d. 334, l. 20 (appeal, A. D. Khomutov, 28 February 1918); f. A-353, op. 2, d. 251, ll. 1–2 (appeal, P. G. L'vov, March 1918).

were seen as more achievable. It was crucial that tribunals were of the correct size and type; this fed into the desire of the authorities to enforce central control and ensure consistency. Appeals were upheld because there were too few people on the tribunal, with tribunals rebuked and told to conduct the trial properly next time. A common basis for a successful appeal in mid to late 1918 was that a sentence had been dispensed by a *uezd* tribunal after these had been abolished on 4 May. A. V. Aref'eva was a typical case. She was accused of counter-revolutionary activities and insulting Soviet power, and had been sentenced by Kamyshlovskii *uezd* tribunal (Ekaterinburg province) to having her property and capital confiscated and exile, the latter commuted later due to ill health. Aref'eva appealed on the basis of absent witnesses and an inappropriate sentence, but officials were only interested in the fact that the sentence had been dispensed by a *uezd* tribunal on 25 May. The 4 May decree had been published in *Izvestiia* on 14 May, the tribunal should not have existed, and the case was transferred to the provincial tribunal for retrial.[50]

Other procedural violations—harder to enforce—were treated more inconsistently, but officials became stricter over time. Some early resolutions noted that tribunals had been 'exceptionally careless' but argued that there had been no serious procedural violations or that these had been insufficient to distort the legal process given the defendant's 'obvious guilt'.[51] But from 1919 the KT was more likely to recognize that a sentence may be correct, but to resolve it had no legal basis and a retrial was needed due to 'fundamental' violations (such as problems with statements or incorrectly defined crimes).[52] By the early 1920s, the KT condemned tribunals for failing to provide details of the allegations in sufficient time for the defendant to respond, or to provide enough evidence to prove a crime had been committed, or for not having sentences signed by all the judges. It demanded the elimination of these obvious abuses.[53]

Arguments surrounding evidence, witnesses, and lawyers were particularly unclear, in part due to the flexibility of official legislation (tribunals, for example, were allowed to decide whether lawyers were needed) and in part due to the KT's reliance on the materials sent to it. The KT did not carry out additional investigations, so if there was no evidence of problems in the records, there was no basis for an appeal, even if records were incomplete.[54] It was damning of appeals

[50] GARF, f. R-1005, op. 7, d. 4, ll. 7–7ob (resolution, undated).

[51] GARF, f. R-1005, op. 7, d. 20, ll. 1–3 (appeal and resolution, V. G. Zhukovskii and M. V. Verizhskii, April–July 1918); d. 30, ll. 2–5 (appeal and resolution, N. D. Konanykin, August 1918).

[52] GARF, f. R-1005, op. 7, d. 80, ll. 18–19ob (resolutions, various, 31 December 1918); d. 140, ll. 3–4, 11–12 (appeal and resolution, P. M. Mileant, April–May 1919).

[53] GARF, f. R-1005, op. 7, d. 640, l. 3 (resolution, K. Malysh, October 1920); d. 900, ll. 6–6ob (resolutions, various, October–November 1921); d. 1580, ll. 4–4ob (resolutions, various, February 1922).

[54] Most obviously, few complete trial transcripts exist in the files despite official requirements, likely because of the scarcity and cost of stenographers. The KT acknowledged that this absence was a

containing complaints that it thought should have been raised in the trial but had not been according to the records. In one case, it dismissed a complaint that the appellant had not been permitted a lawyer as 'fictitious', since the transcript gave no indication he had requested one, even after the chairman had asked about lawyers.[55] Similarly, tribunals were free to decide how much of the testimony of any witnesses should be used; a complaint that Voronezh's tribunal had only considered 10 per cent of the evidence (along with very selective use of witnesses) was quickly dismissed.[56] Otherwise, inconsistencies abound; the KT could be unsympathetic to arguments that witnesses for the defence had not appeared,[57] but then uphold claims that defendants had been refused a chance to interrogate witnesses.[58] And there were instances where the KT felt that guilt had been 'completely established', however incomplete the legal process,[59] and sentences were fair as they were based on 'circumstances' and 'revolutionary consciousness' as required.[60]

These judgements demonstrate the rapid expansion of cassation beyond assessing whether legislation had been followed to making judgements about the case, especially about the nature of the crime and levels of guilt. B. S. Bel'skii was convicted on 5 June 1918 by the tribunal in Iur'evskii *uezd* in Kostroma province for counter-revolution, sabotage, and not recognizing Soviet power, all resulting from a long-standing dispute with the local *volost'* land committee. Bel'skii's lengthy appeal on 7 June made eight points noting numerous procedural violations, including that the *uezd* tribunal should not exist after May. He alleged it was the land committee that was counter-revolutionary as he had been trying to get it to enforce central decrees, but it had refused. The KT accepted the violations, even spotting one not mentioned by Bel'skii—the tribunal had only consisted of three people not seven. But the KT also resolved there was no evidence of a crime. Sabotage was when an individual used their position in state or public service to harm the republic, but Bel'skii was a private individual with no evidence that he did not recognize Soviet power. The sentence was annulled and the case closed.[61] Later, A. A. Mikhaleiskii was sentenced to forced labour for five years by Kursk's tribunal on 20 January 1921 for discrediting Soviet power. He was a party member who fled his militia post as White forces approached. Yet the KT argued it was ill

procedural violation, but was forced to accept the trial protocol (a briefer summary of the main arguments) as sufficient in most cases.

[55] GARF, f. R-1005, op. 7, d. 45, ll. 4–4ob (resolution, A. Podmorin, November 1918).
[56] GARF, f. R-1005, op. 7, d. 11, ll. 6–6ob (resolution, I. Vasil'ev, July 1918).
[57] GARF, f. R-1005, op. 7, d. 5, l. 9 (resolution, M. Baikus, 21 October 1918).
[58] GARF, f. R-1005, op. 7, d. 6, l. 9 (resolution, Father Berezovskii, 13 August 1918).
[59] TsGAMO, f. 4612, op. 1, d. 300a, ll. 6–7ob (resolution, B. L. Kozliakovskii, May 1919).
[60] GARF, f. R-1005, op. 7, d. 11, l. 6 (resolution, I. Vasil'ev, July 1918); d. 130, ll. 12–12ob (resolution, E. Korolev, May–July 1919); d. 1140, ll. 11–11ob (resolution, A. D. Goriachev, September 1921).
[61] GARF, f. R-1005, op. 7, d. 10, ll. 3–4ob, 14–16, 47–47ob (appeals and resolutions, June 1918).

discipline, not a crime (despite plenty of cases when ill discipline was considered a serious crime), and Mikhaleiskii had already been disciplined through his exclusion from the party. The sentence was annulled.[62] Another unusual case was that of N. D. Konanykin, who was sentenced by Kaluga's tribunal to six years in prison with forced labour for agitation against Soviet power, essentially inciting a crowd to unrest. His appeal, written by a legal aide, revolved around procedural errors and that he was not politically minded. He was a young (21-year-old), poor, excitable, and nervous worker who was drunk at the time. The advice of the *chlen-dokladchik* was that procedural problems did not distort the legal process – this was not a drunken accident but a deliberate crime. However, the KT, supported by VTsIK, believed it was not deliberate and decreed that the sentence was too harsh, reducing it to three years in prison with forced labour and exile from the province upon release.[63] These sorts of decisions exceeded the KT's authority and placed it on a par with an appeals court rather than a cassation court.

Returning to the content of appeals, most did not prioritize personal factors, seemingly appreciating that complaining about legal procedure and definitions of crimes had more chance of success. There were exceptions. On 2 April 1918, A. O. Aleksandrov was convicted by the tribunal in Kungur (Perm' province) for illegally preparing and selling spirits, and was sentenced to six months in prison or a fine of 1,000 roubles. He denied selling spirits, attributing such stories to malicious rumours, but admitted manufacturing them. The harsh penalty, he argued, would have a massive impact on his family as he had six mouths to feed. He could not afford the fine and the prison sentence would affect his family's ability to find bread. He noted that he had spilt blood for the bourgeoisie by losing a hand fighting in the tsarist army during the Russo-Japanese War, and he was only a poor proletarian who never expected such punishment. Narkomiust was unforgiving. On 30 April, it ruled the act illegal, the guilt obvious, and the sentence legal.[64] M. Baikus was convicted of counter-revolutionary agitation by Vladimir's tribunal. The first part of his appeal focused on the fact that he had worked for the 'poor' people since the start of the revolution, emphasizing what he claimed was his revolutionary background and that he was not a class enemy. His appeal was also rejected.[65] Others contested the possibility that individuals could be from the working classes *and* counter-revolutionary – the two categories were seen by many as mutually exclusive.[66] But these points were usually made as part of a broader set of arguments.

[62] GARF, f. R-1005, op. 7, d. 940, ll. 8–8ob (resolution, January 1921).

[63] GARF, f. R-1005, op. 7, d. 30, ll. 2–5, 11 (appeal, resolution, and presidium decision, August–September 1918).

[64] GARF, f. A-353, op. 2, d. 214, ll. 3–4, 6–6ob (appeal and resolution, April 1918).

[65] GARF, f. R-1005, op. 7, d. 5, l. 9 (resolution, 21 October 1918).

[66] GARF, f. R-1005, op. 7, d. 65, l. 6 (resolution, M.Kharlampiev, 11 October 1918); d. 70, ll. 1–3 (appeal and resolution, M. F. Shertov, November 1918).

After mid-1919, however, the KT's resolutions start noting 'mitigating circumstances' as a possible basis for cassation. The source of this change is unclear. Several resolutions cite the Decree on Tribunals in April 1919, but this says nothing explicitly. Instead, it is probably linked to the difficulties associated with growing instances of mass crimes and distinguishing 'malicious' offenders (see Chapter 3). In any case, this introduced further subjectivity into cassation and appellants were sufficiently aware to adapt their appeals accordingly. Assertions became more common that workers or poor peasants could not be counter-revolutionaries by definition, as did attempts to portray the appellant as sincere, apolitical, or struggling to cope with material conditions (usually young, with a large, dependent family).[67] A. V. Kocherev was typical in arguing he had 'sincerely (*chistoserdechno*)' described how he had become 'involuntarily (*nevol'no*)' involved in armed unrest. He was forced to participate because 'of course, I would sooner die than allow myself to raise a hand against the power of workers and peasants'.[68] The appeals of relatives were particularly emotional, with extensive detail provided on social background, education, occupation, family, material conditions, and the character of the accused.[69] Other appeals claimed their relative had been led astray or, simply, others had done worse.[70] These appeals also contain the starkest language, such as the father who stated that he and his wife faced starvation and death without their son.[71]

Sincerity and the level of political consciousness counted for more than mitigating circumstances when deciding the original sentence, and this often remained the case in cassation.[72] M. O. Kheif and M. I. Babadzhan, for instance, were sentenced to death by the Kazan' tribunal on 20 December 1918 for blackmail, deception, and other abuses. The *chlen-dokladchik* advised the KT that their appeal had no official grounds but suggested the sentence be reduced to a long prison term on the grounds of 'benevolence' and 'humanity'. The KT and VTsIK disagreed: the crimes were 'selfish' and 'harmful', and the sentence was 'completely fair'.[73] In another case from Kazan', A. P. Shiliaev was sentenced to death, but the *chlen-dokladchik* accepted pleas that Shiliaev was mentally ill,

[67] GARF, f. R-1005, op. 7, d. 130, ll. 12–12ob (resolution, E. Korolev, May–July 1919); d. 440, ll. 8ob–9 (appeal, G. V. Shamanov, 27 June 1919).

[68] GARF, f. R-1005, op. 2, d. 3, ll. 229–29ob (appeal, 21 August 1919).

[69] GARF, f. R-1005, op. 7, d. 260, ll. 9–9ob (appeal, brother of A. Betshev, July–August 1919); d. 380, ll. 4–4ob (appeal, sister of V. V. Fomin, 23 August 1919); d. 524, ll 8–8ob (appeal, son of I. I. Evropin, August 1919).

[70] GARF, f. R-1235, op. 56, d. 16, l. 589 (mother of N. Morkovin, 22 November 1920); op. 58, d. 49, ll. 167–67ob (appeal, I. P. Abramov for son, n.d.).

[71] RGASPI, f. 85, op. 8, d. 333, ll. 24–24ob (appeal, father of P. G. Bebutov, 12 August 1921).

[72] Social background was less significant for the KT than procedure throughout this period. The vast majority of defendants, after all, were from lower social classes. This contrasts with Newman's view that it played a more significant role in the early 1920s; 'Criminal Strategies', 170–1, 176, 184, 189, 193–200, 204–5.

[73] GARF, f. R-1005, op. 7, d. 85, ll. 5–6, 9–9ob, 12 (resolutions and decisions, December 1918–January 1919).

suggesting he should be examined by an expert and, if true, sent to a special hospital. Again, the KT and VTsIK disagreed, transferring the case to a people's court with no mention of an evaluation.[74] Indeed, circumstances were just as likely to be cited when officials wanted to send a harsh message. There are numerous examples where the KT stressed that the appellant held a responsible post, usually as a local official or party member, and thus their crimes discredited Soviet power more broadly.[75] Mitigating circumstances, then, were as much about distinguishing 'malicious' criminals as dispensing mercy.

Few appellants, moreover, raise the theme of redemption during this period compared to later years, and fewer still attempt to portray themselves as an ideal Soviet citizen.[76] Several used the verbs 'to atone (*zagladit'*)' or 'to erase (*izgladit'*)'. P. Tsymbal talked about having made a 'huge mistake' in deserting, which harmed the proletariat, and desired to be sent back to the front so he could 'erase the shameful brand of a deserter'. He swore he would not desert again because he wanted to 'erase' his guilt and be useful to the country alongside his brother comrades rather than languishing in prison.[77] M. F. Lagutin and P. V. Kriukov talked of a desire 'to atone' for the mistakes of their youth and to be sent to the front, where they would serve until the 'last drops of their blood' if necessary.[78] V. V. Lapurko was more assertive, arguing that he had the 'right (*pravo*)' to atone for his crime through labour.[79] A few expressed similar sentiments in passing. A. P. Kulichev, sentenced to death, asked instead to be sent to the front, 'where I would be able to redeem my guilt'.[80] Some mentioned they could be socially useful through their labour or skills, and noted their determination to work if given the chance.[81] Occasionally, appellants noted the state's obvious need for specialized workers directly.[82] The majority, however, clearly did not feel they had to promise acts of redemption or paint an image of themselves as productive members of society to aid their appeal, and there is little sense such promises influenced the cassation process anyway (even if, as noted in the Other Acts of Mercy section below, the state did consider early release for specialists).

[74] GARF, f. R-1005, op. 7, d. 390, ll. 1–2, 17–18, 20 (appeal and resolution, July–November 1919).

[75] GARF, f. R-1005, op. 7, d. 120, l. 32 (resolution, L. Daianov, 27 August 1919); d. 143, ll. 11–12 (resolution, V. I. Ogladin, June–July 1919). d. 190, ll. 12–13 (resolution, M. Zharov, June 1919).

[76] It became more common in the 1920s, possibly as what constituted an 'ideal' citizen became better known and more stable; Newman, 'Criminal Strategies', 171, 191–2; and D. Newman, 'Cassation of Criminal Cases from Moscow Province Courts and Tribunals, 1921-1928', *The Soviet and Post-Soviet Review*, 41, 2 (2014), 146–68.

[77] GARF, f. R-1005, op. 2, d. 11, l. 6 (appeal, 1919).

[78] GARF, f. R-1005, op. 2, d. 55, ll. 20–1 (appeal, 19 August 1920).

[79] GARF, f. R-1005, op. 2, d. 20, ll. 251–51ob (appeal, 30 June 1920).

[80] GARF, f. R-1005, op. 7, d. 200, l. 2 (appeal, 6 June 1919).

[81] GARF, f. R-1235, op. 94, d. 68, ll. 195–6 (appeal, A. V. Salov, 21 February 1919); f. R-1005, op. 7, d. 180, l. 3 (resolution, I. I. Brokht, June 1919); d. 500, l. 8 (resolution, K. M. Stakhov, July–October 1919).

[82] GARF, f. R-1235, op. 56, d. 16, ll. 250–1 (appeal, relative of D. A. Davidov, 25 August 1920).

All these appeals provide a sense of popular conceptions of justice. Social background and material position mattered for people and a *just* sentence considered them.[83] This emerges from N. P. Sokolova's appeal in defence of her husband, who was sentenced to death in Voronezh in April 1922 for forging money and documents. Sokolova did not deny a crime had been committed according to the *law*, but argued forcefully that *circumstances* would have forced anyone into this 'crime'. Her peasant husband supported a family amid widespread hunger and no food reserves. He had never been in trouble before, he had held responsible official posts since the October Revolution, and he had always acted in the interests of the proletariat and its state. The KT rejected her pleas, but VTsIK commuted the sentence to ten years in prison, although it did not say why and imprisonment did not alleviate the family's material needs.[84] For Sokolova, circumstances not only reduced the crime's seriousness but explained why this case was an exception. Like most petitioners, she did not challenge official definitions but asked for an exception to be made.

This failure to challenge the official narrative surrounding revolutionary justice is the most ambiguous point to emerge from this dialogue. It would have been natural, of course, for appellants to fear that outright challenges or hostility would harm their case, and this may have been true, confirming them as counter-revolutionaries in the eyes of officials. Nevertheless, many people probably did believe that counter-revolutionaries existed and that political courts were a justified means of targeting them. After all, there is plenty of evidence of people's propensity to divide society into 'us' and 'them' after the February Revolution and of the radicalization of the popular mood caused by fears of counter-revolution.[85] These fears were stoked by the relentless propaganda produced by the Bolsheviks after the October Revolution. In this context, the problem with revolutionary justice, as expressed by Sokolova, was not that official definitions or priorities were mistaken but that they had been wrongly applied in certain cases. Cassation and other acts of mercy offered a route to highlight and rectify mistakes for those wrongly caught up in the process, but taking this path legitimized the fundamental rationale for tribunals. It was, then, in the interests of the state to foster these beliefs, admitting some mistakes to reinforce the vast majority of 'correct' decisions.

Nevertheless, the mixed success of cassation (see Figure 5.1) and the small percentage of cases going to cassation were not just due to the increasing efficiency of the system (as argued by Bolshevik legal theorists) or the growing harshness of the state (as critics argued), but also reflected the emergence of an alternative and more widespread act of mercy—amnesties. By the 1920s, appeals were

[83] As was the case before 1917; see C. Frierson, 'Crime and Punishment in the Russian Village: Rural Concepts of Criminality at the end of the Nineteenth Century', *Slavic Review*, 46, 1 (1987), 55–69.

[84] GARF, f. R-1005, op. 7, d. 2420, ll. 2, 8, 13–14 (appeal and resolution, April–August 1922).

[85] See, for example, O. Figes and B. Kolonitskii, *Interpreting the Russian Revolution: The Language and Symbols of 1917* (New Haven, 1999); and M. Steinberg, *Voices of Revolution, 1917* (New Haven, 2001).

abandoning the subjective 'mitigating circumstances' approach to return to the more objective approach of 1918 and early 1919. This time, though, appellants included a section on why they were eligible for an amnesty or why an amnesty had been ignored or wrongly applied in their case. Resolutions, in turn, concluded by confirming eligibility or not. Amnesties, it was becoming clear, offered more concrete results than cassation for both sides.

The Prevalence of Amnesties

Given the overwhelming focus of contemporaries and historians on violence, it might come as a surprise to realize that the civil war experienced one of the greatest frequencies of amnesties in Russia's history. One of the first acts of the Provisional Government after the February Revolution was to issue a celebratory amnesty for political prisoners.[86] While the Bolsheviks did not issue a comparable amnesty on taking power, one study has noted eleven amnesties between 1918 and 1921 in Russia.[87] In reality, there were more, especially if the territory of the former Russian Empire is included. Some released entire categories of criminals, while others targeted particular social or political groups, or focused on specific crimes or localities. The most frequent and wide-ranging were 'hybrid amnesties'; they released certain types of criminals and reduced punishment for others.[88]

The first amnesties came when at least two local authorities felt it would be a suitable way of celebrating the first anniversary of the February Revolution. Bezhetskii *uezd* soviet (Tver') amnestied those imprisoned for 'unimportant' crimes (mainly theft), entrusting the task to its investigative commission. Twenty-four people were released, ten of whom had been in prison from before the October Revolution. The local prison authorities were uneasy, informing the national board for prisons which, in turn, asked Narkomiust whether it was legal for local authorities to release those guilty of what it felt were 'important' crimes. Narkomiust replied that it was not and ordered the prosecution of the commission, but the matter was dropped once it became clear that various local organs were complicit.[89] A similar amnesty in Timskii *uezd* (Kursk) prompted the same reaction from Narkomiust.[90]

[86] For details and subsequent amnesties, see P. Iakobi, *Amnistii 1917 goda* (Petrograd, 1917). This continued a long tradition of amnesties: H. Dewey and A. Kleimola, 'Old Muscovite Amnesties: Theory and Practice', *Russian History*, 3, 1 (1976), 49–60; Burbank, 'Mercy', 23–60; and R. Wortman, *Scenarios of Power: Myth and Ceremony in Russian Monarchy* (2 volumes, Princeton, 1995–2000), II, 457–8.

[87] M. Jakobson, *Origins of the Gulag: The Soviet Prison Camp System, 1917–1934* (Lexington, 1993), 20.

[88] M. Freeman, *Necessary Evils: Amnesties and the Search for Justice* (Cambridge, 2009), 12–17. Most of the relevant decrees are reprinted in P. Romashkin, *Amnistiia i pomilovanie v SSSR* (Moscow, 1959).

[89] GARF, f. A-353, op. 2, d. 207, ll. 1–11 (various correspondence, March–June 1918).

[90] 'Kratkaia zapiska o sudakh revoliutsionnogo vremeni v Timskom uezde', *Materialy*, 5 (1918), 15–16.

More significant was the amnesty issued in Petrograd during the May Day celebrations in 1918. The circumstances remain vague. City officials seem to have wanted to regain public support and ease overcrowded prisons, which were causing problems with food, housing, and disease as well as antagonizing Kronstadt sailors, whose base was used as an overflow. The situation was so desperate by January 1918 that Lenin recommended that a third to a half of all prisoners should be transferred to provincial prisons where food supplies were better.[91] This did not occur and officials considered alternatives, deciding on an amnesty on 27 April. At the Congress of Soviets of the Northern Region (which included Petrograd) on 29 April, the city's party leader, G. E. Zinov'ev, argued that Bolshevik power had strengthened, individual opponents no longer posed a threat, and workers and peasants no longer wished to treat their enemies in the same manner as bourgeois states.[92] Eighty-four delegates voted for an amnesty, seventeen voted against, and fifteen abstained. The proposal was then passed by Petrograd's soviet.[93] The amnesty freed all prisoners with less than six months of their sentence left, those who had committed 'political' crimes, and those over 70 years old, and it halved the sentences of serious cases. It excluded bribe-takers, traitors, and speculators, and had several other caveats. It covered all crimes committed before 1 May, even if not yet resolved.[94]

Narkomiust was dismayed, fearing that the last few months' work would be undone, and demanded that obvious counter-revolutionaries be excluded. Petrograd officials were defensive, claiming the initiative had come from local legal organs and the amnesty would free no more than fifteen people, mainly those involved in the plot led by V. M. Purishkevich, none of whom had more than two months left on their sentences.[95] In truth, these individuals had years left and the amnesty freed many more. A Menshevik newspaper estimated around 200 benefitted, many of whom were high-profile enemies who deserved imprisonment, like Purishkevich.[96] The amnesty was indeed widely invoked. Broad definitions of what constituted a 'political' crime enabled many to claim eligibility. Some stopped contesting their case, instead noting that the accusations, even if incorrect, fell within the amnesty's terms.[97] The numbers were sufficient for Petrograd's tribunal to produce a pre-printed release form to ease the process, with a gap for

[91] Jakobson, *Origins*, 29.

[92] The speech is summarized in *Za svobodu!* [Samara], 30 April 1918, 2; and *Izvestiia Shuiskago soveta*, 1 May 1918, 3. See also A. Rabinowitch, *The Bolsheviks in Power* (Bloomington and Indianapolis, 2007), 221–2.

[93] *Izvestiia*, 1 May 1918, 5; *Vpered!*, 1 May 1918, 3.

[94] *Izvestiia*, 3 May 1918, 3.

[95] GARF, f. A-353, op. 2, d. 2, ll. 38, 42 (protocols of the meetings of the college, 10 and 14 May 1918).

[96] *Vpered!*, 3 May 1918, 3; 4 May 1918, 2. Similar Menshevik fears were expressed in *Den'*, 1 May 1918, 2.

[97] GARF, f. R-336, op. 1, d. 334, ll. 9–11 (various documents, A. D. Khomutov, May 1918).

the defendant's name above a generic statement that the defendant should be released under the amnesty.[98]

Rumours spread that the amnesty would be extended to the whole country.[99] It was not, but it was reported in local papers and some authorities followed Petrograd's lead. In early June, officials in Penza proposed publishing Petrograd's amnesty verbatim, arguing it would lead to a 'significant reduction' in their workload, but they faced 'mass opposition' led by the local Cheka. Instead, the officials asked the government to extend the amnesty.[100] The same occurred in Siberia, while the authorities in Arkhangel'sk did adopt Petrograd's amnesty.[101] Narkomiust was livid: a dubious amnesty was spreading and local authorities were acting independently just as the state was trying to strengthen central control. On 6 June, responding to the Siberian proposal, Narkomiust stated that only the central authorities could issue amnesties.[102] This was restated by P. I. Stuchka as Commissar of Justice at a congress of local justice officials on 6 July, when he declared that the state was focused on expediency, not mercy. Petrograd's amnesty had freed 'undesirables' who should be in prison, while others had released robbers. There must be no more local amnesties.[103] A few days later, the new constitution reiterated that only the Congress of Soviets and VTsIK could issue amnesties.[104]

This power was exercised on 6 November 1918. At the Sixth All-Russian Exceptional Congress of Soviets, L. B. Kamenev, a senior party figure, proposed a national amnesty to coincide with the anniversary of the October Revolution. The proletarian state was strong enough, he argued, to show 'mercy' to those prepared to lay down their arms and recognize its authority.[105] All those arrested on suspicion of being involved with plots or oppositional groups would be released if their guilt was not proven within two weeks. All hostages would be freed except where they were held in response to hostages seized by opponents. Finally, all courts would re-examine all cases with a view to releasing those who did not endanger the state. The scale of the struggle was emphasized and the need for harsh measures, but the Red Army's success permitted mercy. The word 'amnesty' was not used in the decree, but it was in *Izvestiia* and *Pravda*, which both printed the text in full.[106]

The Bolsheviks may have been trying to diffuse the criticism surrounding their policy of Red Terror after 5 September following an attempt on Lenin's life.

[98] GARF, f. R-336, op. 1, d. 73, l. 1ob; d. 75, l. 1 (preprinted forms).

[99] *Vpered!*, 4 May 1918, 3.

[100] GARF, f. A-353, op. 2, d. 27, ll. 55ob-56 (report of Penza's provincial commissar of justice to a congress of local commissars of justice in Moscow, 28 June 1918).

[101] Iu. Titov, *Sozdanie sistemy sovetskikh revoliutsionnykh tribunalov* (Moscow, 1983), 35–6.

[102] GARF, f. A-353, op. 2, d. 2, l. 61 (protocols, 6 June 1918).

[103] 'Zhurnal soedinennogo zasedaniia sektsii Vtorogo Vserossiiskogo S"ezda Oblastnykh i Gubernskikh Komissarov Iustitsii. 4-go Iiulia 1918 g.', *Materialy*, 3 (1918), 33–4.

[104] Romashkin, *Amnistiia*, 80.

[105] *Shestoi vserossiiskii chrezvychainyi s"ezd sovetov rab., kr., kaz. i krasnoarm. deput. Stenograficheskii otchet. 6–9 noiabria 1918 g.* (Moscow, 1919), 37–8.

[106] Romashkin, *Amnistiia*, 82–3; *Izvestiia*, 9 November 1918, 2; and *Pravda*, 9 November 1918, 3.

Kamenev stated that an amnesty would combat the 'lies and libel' spreading in Russia and the Western press about the Cheka's activities and methods.[107] Cheka leaders themselves noted later in a private meeting that the amnesty would help convince those wavering in their support.[108] Tensions between state and society had grown throughout 1918; there was opposition to the reintroduction of the death penalty in June, rising support for rival socialist parties, frequent revolts, and more arrests from a wider range of social groups. The state probably felt the need to ease these tensions, while the text promised that the amnesty would regulate judicial organs to ensure they worked in a rational and fair manner, targeting only real enemies.

Yet this decree was not as generous on paper as the Petrograd amnesty. Most prisoners had their guilt proven within a fortnight, the categories of eligible crimes were vague, and terror continued. Moreover, on 15 November the presidium of the Cheka demanded that provocateurs, former tsarist police and officials, Black Hundred activists, spies, saboteurs, counter-revolutionary agitators (particularly priests, officials, and those in the Red Army), and those convicted for stealing explosives and arms were excluded. VTsIK agreed.[109]

Nonetheless, amnesties became a regular act after November 1918 for the rest of the civil war; one formed a central part of the anniversary celebrations of the October Revolution, while another was issued around April–May each year, although not always tied to the May Day celebrations. Additional amnesties focused on specific crimes. Broadly speaking, several trends are visible. First, amnesties became more generous, possibly as the various bodies involved became used to them and less fearful of their consequences. Second, Narkomiust took responsibility for them as part of the greater centralization of legal affairs and state matters more generally, leading to greater regulation and the production of instructions on their implementation. Finally, some groups fared better than others in each amnesty, indicating the state's shifting concerns across this period.

These trends are visible in three amnesties issued in 1919. On 23 February 1919, an amnesty celebrated the first anniversary of the creation of the Red Army. It released all those involved in disorder and mass crimes as long as these did not have a 'White Guard' character or involve robbery, rape, or arson; all those imprisoned for first-time desertion; all those guilty of ill discipline (if not part of a White Guard plot); and all those imprisoned for military crimes who agreed to return to service in the Red Army.[110] On 25 April, another amnesty urged courts to re-examine cases and release those no longer posing a danger. This decree was

[107] *Shestoi*, 38.

[108] *Arkhiv VChK: Sbornik dokumentov* (Moscow, 2007), 295 (Cheka presidium meeting, 15 November 1918).

[109] *Arkhiv VChK*, 295 (Cheka presidium meeting); *Iz istorii Vserossiiskoi chrezvychainoi komissii (1917–1921 gg.)* (Moscow, 1958), 217 (VTsIK presidium meeting, 18 November 1918).

[110] *Izvestiia*, 23 February 1919, 3.

directed at workers and peasants caught up in the escalating unrest. All those who were not organizers, instigators, or leaders but were involved through a lack of 'consciousness' should be released, as should those involved in unorganized unrest.[111] Finally, on 5 November, there was an extensive two-part amnesty marking the second anniversary of the October Revolution. The main decree released all prisoners except those involved in plots or armed struggle, or who had committed 'selfish' crimes for personal gain. Those ineligible but with sentences of over five years' imprisonment would see them reduced to five years. Deserters sentenced to death would have this reduced to five years in prison. Deserters with lesser sentences were given the option, if repentant, to accept a fine and return to the front, while those on the run would be pardoned if they returned by 25 November. Another decree on the same day amnestied imprisoned members of rival political parties if they were willing to defend the state, unless they had actively participated in counter-revolution.[112]

As amnesties became more complex, local officials struggled to enact them correctly, and Narkomiust produced instructions from November 1919 to clear up misunderstandings. These clarified that 'selfish' crimes included speculation and the dereliction of duties, and provided guidance on altering prison sentences. They also outlined a timescale: commissions enacting the amnesty should finish by December, while courts had another month to re-examine cases.[113] Confusion continued, though. The fact that local courts issued a wider range of sentences than Narkomiust expected or condoned created categories of prisoners whose status under various amnesties was unclear. Successive decrees were forced to become more explicit, structuring instructions around lists of crimes or the various stages in the legal process, detailing the required action in each case.[114] In November 1922, 10,000 copies were printed of a booklet containing the amnesty, instructions, and relevant information.[115]

The November 1919 amnesty set the example for the future in its content and tone. The blanket reduction of sentences, irrespective of the seriousness of the crime, was extended in future amnesties. Policies on deserters were repeated, betraying continued concern over staffing the Red Army. Along with the focus on workers and peasants, this was designed to convince people that the state remained their 'proletarian' government despite repressive supply and conscription policies. The olive branch to political opponents aimed to undermine support for rival parties as internal debates grew within them over how they should act as the civil war intensified. All this represented the use of amnesties to help tackle

[111] Romashkin, *Amnistiia*, 83. [112] Romashkin, *Amnistiia*, 84–6.

[113] Romashkin, *Amnistiia*, 302. Instructions were later published in national newspapers; for example, *Pravda*, 6 November 1920, 8; and 9 November 1922, 5.

[114] GARF, f. R-3042, op. 1, d. 2, ll. 10–11 (circular to railway tribunals, November 1920); TsGAMO, f. 4762, op. 1, d. 1, ll. 45, 49–49ob (orders to local tribunals, 24 and 29 November 1922).

[115] *Amnistiia 1922 goda k V-i godovshchine Oktiabr'skoi revoliutsii* (Moscow, 1922).

immediate political problems. At the same time, the authorities were keen to stress that the mercy of the state was a sign of strength not weakness, and those who remained dangerous were not eligible; as one paper entitled its coverage, 'he who is strong is also merciful (*kto silen, tot i milostiv*)'.[116]

Amnesties in 1920–2 were variations on the 1919 model.[117] Counter-revolutionaries (active opponents) remained excluded, alongside bandits, professional thieves, and repeat offenders. The theme of redemption appears more frequently, especially for potentially productive individuals; the amnesty on 1 May 1920, for example, urged the release of all those willing to participate in the economic struggle to redeem their crimes. Recidivists, by contrast, were unproductive and irredeemable. In May 1920, 'harmful' speculators were excluded, but a year later, after the start of the NEP, an amnesty on 29 April focused exclusively on those sentenced for not fulfilling food quotas or paying taxes, and for trading (speculating) in food, raw materials, and fodder. This aimed to demonstrate that the Bolsheviks were serious about the NEP by offering mercy to those convicted under former policies. Moreover, as the November 1922 amnesty clarified, the state now distinguished between crimes motivated by material need, as much speculation had been, and crimes committed for profit—the illegal production, sale, and trade of alcohol was firmly excluded, for instance.

By 1921, victory in the civil war was assured and amnesties reflected the need to come to terms with other legacies of the war.[118] An amnesty was offered on 3 November 1921 for workers and peasants who fought in the White armies and were now in prison or exile. A day later, an amnesty was offered to workers and peasants involved in the Kronstadt Revolt. Views of banditry also became more flexible, with a focus on leaders or organizers rather than the masses involved: people who had been 'deceived' into fighting for the Whites, or those whose 'lack of consciousness' led to their involvement in revolts, would be shown mercy. The end result was a desire to ease growing conflict between state and society.[119] This was also evident in the November 1922 amnesty. These highlighted twenty-five areas affected by famine in 1921–2 and encouraged officials there to release those

[116] *Krasnaia znamia* [Penza], 7 November 1919, 1. The same phrase is in *Nabat* [Orsha], 15 November 1919, 1.

[117] There were general amnesties on 1 May 1920, 6 November 1920, 29 April 1921, 3–4 November 1921, 27 February 1922, and 2 November 1922, as well as several specific ones; Romashkin, *Amnistiia*, 86–100, 302–21.

[118] Peace treaties provided amnesties for Estonians, Finns, Latvians, Lithuanians, and Poles imprisoned in Russia for political crimes. On 10 February 1921, an interdepartmental committee with provincial branches was created to implement them; GARF, f. R-5209, op. 1, d. 1, l. 202 (report of the chair to the Cheka, 19 April 1921).

[119] A newspaper in Odessa argued that an amnesty for those who fought with the Ukrainian leader, S. V. Petliura, against the Bolsheviks would reconcile past local conflict; *Pravda*, 5 June 1921, 1. Such an amnesty was part of the decree on 3 November 1921 and was later extended by the Ukrainian authorities; C. Gilley, *The 'Change of Signposts' in the Ukrainian Emigration* (Stuttgart, 2009), 232–42.

convicted of crimes such as theft and speculation, irrespective of their sentences.[120]

Later amnesties were also more precise. The November 1921 amnesty was typical, releasing all those with less than a year remaining in prison, halving the sentences of those with one–three years remaining, reducing by a third those with three–five years left, and capping the maximum sentence at five years. The death penalty was often changed to five years in prison. Narkomiust was attempting to make implementing amnesties an objective process, leaving no room for local initiative and thus inconsistencies.

All the above amnesties were issued in Moscow, but amnesties were also issued by fledgling soviet governments in newly established autonomous regions from 1919.[121] These followed a similar template, although there were always slight differences. Some regions saw amnesties as an opportunity to assert independence and facilitate the state-building process. In Georgia, a May Day amnesty in 1921 pardoning former oppositionists was entitled 'Decree No. 1', suggesting it was seen as the foundation stone of the new Soviet republic.[122] Similarly, the timing of Ukrainian amnesties—October to coincide with its annual congress of soviets, not November—emphasized that amnesties served their concerns not Moscow's.[123] Moscow reacted differently to these amnesties. It was happy to publish Ukrainian amnesties in newspapers and help enact them,[124] but a dispute erupted when Turkestan published an amnesty in November 1921 without the authorization of VTsIK. VTsIK wanted to preserve its authority across all republics, and the Supreme Tribunal also wanted to sanction it, as they did other amnesties.[125] Moscow also asserted the primacy of Russia when areas of confusion emerged, particularly in military and railway tribunals, whose jurisdiction often crossed borders. After the Ukrainian amnesty in May 1920, the main railway tribunal asked whether this affected railways running into Ukraine.[126] In November 1921, Orenburg military tribunal, whose jurisdiction crossed the Kirgiz border, asked which amnesty to apply.[127] Moscow asserted its authority both times, but was powerless to do so within republics once they established their own legal system.

[120] *Amnistiia 1922*, 9, 17–18. [121] Romashkin, *Amnistiia*, 137–54, 274–88, 302–17.

[122] GARF, f. R-1005, op. 1, d. 85, l. 282 (excerpt from *Izvestiia Narkomvnudela Sotsialisticheskoi Sovetskoi Respubliki Gruzii*, 23 April 1921).

[123] V. Vasilenko, 'Bil'shovits'ki amnistii pochatku 1920-x rr. iak zasib borot'bi proti povstans'kogo rukhu', *Z arkhiviv VUChK-GPU-NKVD-KGB*, 1 (2011), 89–155, at http://history.org.ua/JournALL/gpu/gpu_2011_1/5.pdf [accessed 12 March 2020].

[124] Romashkin, *Amnistiia*, 90; *Izvestiia*, 9 November 1920, 3; *Pravda*, 9 November 1920, 2.

[125] GARF, f. R-1005, op. 3, d. 1, ll. 78 (meeting of the supreme tribunal's plenum, 19 November 1921), 79–83 (telegram to VTsIK, 14 November 1921), 88–89ob (regulations on amnesties in republics and regions, undated).

[126] GARF, f. A-353, op. 4, d. 30, ll. 1–2 (correspondence, June 1920).

[127] GARF, f. R-1005, op. 1, d. 86, ll. 421–3 (correspondence, March 1921).

The Importance of Amnesties

Amnesties only mattered, of course, if they were actually implemented, and many historians assume that Soviet amnesties, overshadowed as they were by violence and repression, were largely symbolic acts. It is true that there do not appear to be systematic statistics on how many benefitted.[128] However, Narkomiust requested information on amnesties from local officials, so there are statistics on the impact of certain amnesties in particular provinces. A sense of scale can also be gained from the incomplete lists gathered by the Supreme Tribunal. Ultimately, though, the impact of each amnesty varied across Russia for no discernible reason, although local efficiency (both in implementing amnesties and keeping records) and local crime rates no doubt played a role. Provinces close to the military fronts of the civil war, for instance, faced greater pressures from desertion, food-supply revolts, and speculation, sentenced more people for these crimes, and thus found that more people were eligible for amnesties.

What is clear is that tribunals were quick to implement amnesties after some initial reluctance. The justice department in Moscow province, for example, rejected on 24 October 1918 a proposal by local courts for an amnesty to celebrate the forthcoming anniversary of the October Revolution, no doubt influenced by Narkomiust's reluctance to sanction amnesties at this stage.[129] However, it quickly implemented the November amnesty a fortnight later. Over seventy-six people convicted of counter-revolutionary activities benefitted, including misuse of official power, undermining authority, drunkenness, and hooliganism. A few, including speculators, murderers, and saboteurs, benefitted from the section in the decree permitting the release of those who no longer posed any danger to the state, which might have been easy to dismiss as purely symbolic.[130]

A year later, Tula's officials played out a by then typical scenario. The amnesty of 5 November 1919 was discussed by justice officials in the provincial soviet on 12 November. As instructed by Narkomiust, a temporary commission was formed ten days later to enact the amnesty. It asked for clarification on certain points, but by the end of the month, as required officially, it claimed to have re-examined the cases of most inmates in the provincial prison to determine eligibility.[131] By 1920–1, provinces routinely established commissions involving all relevant bodies—local departments of justice, tribunals, people's courts, the Cheka, prison officials—to implement amnesties and review cases.[132] Amnesties were published

[128] The same problem has been noted recently for Ukraine; Vasilenko, 'Bil'shovits'ki', 91–2.

[129] TsGAMO, f. 4998, op. 1, d. 13, l. 44ob (protocol of meeting).

[130] TsGAMO, f. 66, op. 25, d. 8, ll. 8–40 (protocols of Moscow tribunal, 13–29 November 1918). Seventy-six people are noted in the records, plus an unspecified number of factory 'officials'.

[131] GARF, f. A-353, op. 2, d. 78b, ll. 189–89ob (report to Narkomiust, 29 November 1919).

[132] GARF, f. A-353, op. 4, d. 46, l. 490 (Smolensk, November 1920); op. 5, d. 17, l. 72ob (Omsk, November 1921); op. 4, d. 45, l. 14 (Orel, November 1921).

in local newspapers and provincial organs often reissued key elements, such as the reductions in sentences, for distribution within the province.[133] Many tribunals implemented them at the end of a trial for current cases, after guilt had been pronounced and a sentence passed. As a final step, the Cassation Tribunal reviewed the results of each tribunal's decisions, which took the form of long lists of individuals, crimes, and resolutions. If anything seemed irregular, the Tribunal asked for the decision to be reviewed or altered.

Variations in impact were clear in reports on the November 1919 amnesty. In Perm', 613 of 1,022 prisoners (60 per cent) were freed, while 39 had their sentences reduced and 10 were refused amnesty because they still posed a danger to the state. In Kazan', 462 were released, 55 received shorter sentences, and 10 were refused. In Riazan', the figures were 221, 17 and 18 respectively. In Ekaterinburg, the tribunal freed 25, eased the sentences of 8, refused amnesty to 143, and ended 138 investigations. In Orel, 77 of 93 (83 per cent) imprisoned by tribunals were freed, 5 had their sentences reduced, and 11 were refused. In Briansk, 39 from 50 imprisoned by tribunals were freed (78 per cent), with 8 reduced sentences and 3 refused.[134] Numerous comparable reports from across Russia exist for every amnesty, and these suggest authorities did reconsider every case, as instructed, and that thousands benefitted.

These figures, moreover, are just from tribunals: many more were amnestied by people's courts and the Cheka. One contemporary claimed the Cheka preferred to execute people on the eve of an amnesty rather than release them.[135] Other evidence, though, suggests the Cheka also released hundreds either incarcerated or under investigation. Moscow's soviet, for instance, established a commission involving its own representative alongside those from the local department of justice, tribunal, and Cheka branch that reviewed 1,040 cases after the November 1920 amnesty, most of which involved the Cheka's cases. Around 58 per cent were freed (602 cases), mostly involving cases of counter-revolution or speculation.[136]

It is also clear that amnesties were applied to a wide range of crimes. Arkhangel'sk's provincial camp for forced labour, for example, compiled a list of twenty-four individuals eligible for amnesty in November 1920. Their crimes included sympathizing with the Whites, desertion, theft, banditry, illegal brewing, corruption, speculation, and being a 'harmful element'. All had their sentences reduced.[137] Banditry, in particular, was condemned across this period, yet those

[133] GARF, f. R-1005, op. 2, d. 63, ll. 47–47ob (circular from Tula's department of justice to local organs, 13 May 1920); op. 3, d. 137, l. 25 (circular from Kursk's tribunal to travelling sessions, 26 November 1921).

[134] GARF, f. A-353, op. 3, d. 211, ll. 2 (Perm', 23 December 1919), 7–10 (Riazan', 31 December 1919), 57 (Ekaterinburg, 31 January 1920), 58 (Kazan', n.d.), 77 (Orel and Briansk, undated).

[135] S. Melgounov, *The Red Terror in Russia* (Westport, 1975), 54.

[136] TsGAMO, f. 66, op. 1, d. 453, ll. 298–99ob (report, January 1921). See also the report on Cheka releases in *Krasnaia gazeta* [Petrograd], 12 November 1919, 2.

[137] GARF, f. R-1005, op. 1, d. 73, ll. 230–30ob (list of prisoners).

convicted of it were amnestied. Here there were disparities. Some tribunals refused to discuss amnesty in cases of banditry, or even crimes such as desertion or murder; others applied amnesties to all crimes. Officials had to be careful. In July 1922, the Kalmytskii region was allowed to offer an amnesty for bandits to encourage people to return to 'peaceful' work after large-scale unrest, but Moscow prosecuted several officials for exceeding the terms of this amnesty by releasing known leaders.[138]

The most comprehensive statistics chart the impact of the November 1920 amnesty on ninety military tribunals. In all, 23,669 people benefitted, 71.8 per cent of whom had been sentenced, with the rest still under investigation. A total of 61.3 per cent were freed completely, 11.6 per cent received conditional freedom, and 27.1 per cent had their sentences reduced. Of the latter, most (36.6 per cent) received a reduced sentence of five years (although 7.5 per cent remained with higher sentences), while of the 55.9 per cent with lower sentences the majority were reduced by a half or two-thirds. Most of these decisions (77.8 per cent) were made in procedural rather than legal meetings of the tribunal, and it was the first time 96.5 per cent of cases had been submitted for amnesty.[139]

These figures reveal two notable parts of the process. First, for 3.5 per cent of individuals it was the second time (or more) their case had been considered. Cases were re-examined under successive amnesties. Those initially refused were often declared eligible for a subsequent amnesty as terms and the state's concerns changed over time. Most obviously, tsarist-era provocateurs were pursued relentlessly immediately after the October Revolution and were refused amnesty, but, as the civil war intensified, they appeared less threatening and were often released.[140] Equally, although some amnesties stipulated whether or not someone was eligible who had already received a reduced sentence from a previous amnesty, others did not, and individuals had their sentences reduced in stages by successive amnesties, often prompted by the Supreme Tribunal.[141] It was even possible to apply multiple amnesties at the same time. P. V. Platonov was sentenced belatedly to two years in prison on 29 December 1922 for a crime committed on 14 January 1921. This sentence was halved using the November 1921 amnesty as the crime had been committed beforehand. This left less than a year's sentence, which made Platonov eligible for release under the November 1922 amnesty.[142]

The second notable point is that most cases were reviewed by procedural meetings. As noted, the instructions issued alongside amnesties reflected

[138] GARF, f. R-1005, op. 1a, d. 511, ll. 18–21, 24, 31–31ob (various appeals and resolutions, 1922). These officials were themselves amnestied in November 1922.

[139] GARF, f. A-353, op. 4, d. 111, l. 210 (report on military tribunals in the first half of 1920, undated).

[140] GARF, f. R-1005, op. 1a, d. 28, ll. 64–74 (case of A. N. Nikolaev, various documents, 1919–20).

[141] GARF, f. R-1005, op. 7, d. 560, l. 9 (case of E. G. Voloskov, resolution of VTsIK, 20 January 1921).

[142] TsGAMO, f. 4762, op. 1, d. 14, l. 36 (sentence).

Narkomiust's desire to remove arbitrariness on the part of local courts, turning amnesties into an administrative process where cases were assessed for their eligibility depending on the crime committed, rather than analysing the particulars of individual cases. Thus, amnesty records are often terse, providing little evidence of any discussion about the relative threats posed by different crimes or the role of different types of sentences. On 23 December 1918, a prosecutor wrote in his rebuttal to a defendant's appeal that it was 'strange' the tribunal had granted amnesty in a case of blackmail and corruption by an official without considering whether the individual posed a danger to the revolution.[143] As time passed, however, such comments disappeared and it became clear to all concerned that the amnesty process was largely administrative.

Later amnesties did offer scope for judgement when deciding what was a 'conscious' action or what constituted a 'selfish' crime. Only occasionally, though, do records reveal the decision-making process. On 18 May 1920, Penza's provincial tribunal heard the case of eight peasants accused of seizing livestock from poorer peasants and other crimes. All had their sentences reduced under the amnesties of November 1919 and May 1920 apart from one—the person who initiated the crimes. His actions were deemed deliberate and more serious.[144] When asked to reconsider a case by VTsIK in May 1920, Novgorod's tribunal again rejected an amnesty due to the 'malicious' character of the defendants, who had engaged in systematic speculation.[145] On 21 November 1922, the military tribunal in Tashkent sentenced a man to death for illegally purchasing cartridges from soldiers. He was ineligible for amnesty, it stated, as a 'professional' purchaser of weapons for criminal use.[146] A debate over the fate of seventeen deserters in the organizational–instructional department of the military college of the Supreme Court on 20 April 1923 questioned the November 1922 amnesty's lenient stance on deserters. Leniency was proclaimed, but only after a long debate on the nature of desertion indicated unease; the euphoria of military victory, officials noted, could not conceal the seriousness of desertion as a crime.[147] Yet ultimately, as with most cases, the only judgement open to them was assigning a crime to a category in the amnesty and then implementing the instructions assigned to that category, even if they disagreed.

The key point is that all courts were expected to enact amnesties and instructions often read primarily as exhortations to act. Instructions in November 1920, for instance, urged local officials to view crimes that did not lead to personal gain more favourably, even suggesting granting complete freedom, leaving reduced sentences for 'selfish' crimes, including common crimes such as drunkenness and

[143] GARF, f. R-1005, op. 7, d. 85, l. 5ob.
[144] GARF, f. R-1005, op. 2, d. 21, ll. 122–22ob (case report from the secretary of the tribunal).
[145] GARF, f. R-1235, op. 56, d. 13, l. 37 (resolution of Novgorod's tribunal, 8 May 1920).
[146] GARF, f. R-1005, op. 1, d. 25, l. 100 (telegram to the military college of VTsIK).
[147] GARF, f. R-1005, op. 1, d. 59, ll. 73–73ob (report).

murder. The instructions implied that officials should err on the side of leniency if possible.[148] The RVTR circulated a note on 25 February 1921 complaining that too many military tribunals were pronouncing sentences 'without the right to amnesty', contradicting amnesty decrees and the sentiment behind them.[149] Yet the authorities remained quick to admonish tribunals acting illegally, such as Iaroslavl', which lowered a sentence from one year to six months before changing it illegally to a one-million-roubles fine due to the defendant's 'old age', or Moscow, whose tribunal reduced a sentence from five to three years in November 1920. In the latter case, Narkomiust noted that the decree stipulated sentences had to be reduced by two-thirds, a half, or a third. It then suggested the sentence be reduced by two-thirds to one year and eight months.[150]

As noted, amnesties also became a central part of the cassation process. Some appeals referred to particular points of an amnesty and related it to their case. Some simply noted that amnesties had benefitted all types of criminals, implying it was unfair they had not benefitted, or noted that those sentenced with them had benefitted but they had not. Some engaged with a perceived notion of the meaning of amnesty, claiming, for example, that an amnesty was an act of mercy and no one can be denied mercy.[151] In 1921, 21 per cent of complaints (931) to Narkomiust concerned the incorrect application of amnesties and mercy, equalling the scale of complaints against the Cheka and only exceeded by complaints directed at people's courts.[152] As with all appeals, the authorities usually acted when procedural error was proved, a crime wrongly classified, a sentence incorrectly reduced, or a case incorrectly rejected for amnesty.

Amnesties, therefore, were not purely symbolic. As the Supreme Tribunal reminded the Don regional tribunal, they were created by the highest state organs and courts could not refuse to implement them.[153] A similar message was conveyed to Saratov's provincial tribunal when it refused amnesty for two brothers on the grounds that they were 'enemies of the people'. Amnesties, the tribunal was told, were not concerned with whether defendants were 'enemies of the people' if their crimes were eligible under the terms dictated by the state. Saratov was ordered to review the case with a view to reducing the punishment.[154] Indeed, the impact of amnesties was such that the Riazan' tribunal complained in April 1920, after being warned it had not considered enough cases for amnesty, that a

[148] GARF, f. R-1005, op. 1, d. 44, ll. 7–7ob (circular from the RVTR to all military tribunals, 13 January 1921).

[149] GARF, f. R-1005, op. 1, d. 44, l. 59 (circular from the RVTR to all military tribunals).

[150] GARF, f. R-1005, op. 3, d. 205, l. 3 (report on the Iaroslavl' tribunal from an inspection on 12–14 February 1922); f. A-353, op. 5, d. 355, ll. 42–3 (correspondence with Moscow, April 1921).

[151] GARF, f. R-1005, op. 1a, d. 28, l. 29; op. 1a, d. 1409, ll. 195, 225ob; op. 2, d. 1, ll. 398–98ob; op. 2, d. 20, ll. 251–51ob; op. 7, d. 125, l. 2ob (various appeals).

[152] *RSFSR. Narodnyi Komissariat Iustitsii*, 9.

[153] GARF, f. R-1005, op. 3, d. 206, ll. 175–75ob (correspondence, December 1922).

[154] GARF, f. R-1005, op. 7, d. 700, l. 2 (resolution on the appeal from 13 July 1920, undated).

false understanding of the state's mercy was leading all criminals to expect an amnesty.[155] If true, this would have undermined the value of amnesties to the state; if criminals begin to count on amnesties, it undermines the seriousness of committing crimes. Riazan' may have been exaggerating, but defendants must have realized the concrete benefits granted by these frequent amnesties.

Other Acts of Mercy

Cassation and amnesties dominate the evidence from tribunals, but there were other acts of mercy that may have been more common in other courts. In February 1918, for instance, local courts in Kamyshevskoe were told they could consider mercy for juveniles and those suffering from nervous breakdowns (after confirmation by medical personnel).[156] Both these issues were much discussed in judicial publications, but they rarely appear in tribunal cases. A report to the Congress of Soviets in December 1919 also mentioned that twenty-two appeals sent to VTsIK had simply asked for mercy, of which eleven were successful.[157] It is not clear why mercy was requested or why some were successful and others not, or whether any related to tribunals, and there is little evidence on other cases of 'pure' mercy, but these cases may well have concerned private amnesties independent of mass amnesty decrees. This avenue appears to have been relatively limited in both numbers involved and success during the civil war, probably because of the prevalence of mass amnesties. It did, though, become more common and successful afterwards; in 1921, 81.5 per cent of applicants were rejected, 11.4 per cent released, and 7.1 per cent had their sentence eased, but in 1922, the figures were 64 per cent, 18.6 per cent, and 17.2 per cent respectively, and success rates improved further over the next couple of years.[158]

A more wide-ranging act was the rare official decree on a related matter. On 21 March 1921, for instance, the Council of People's Commissars (Sovnarkom) limited the maximum prison sentence to five years.[159] This led to the reduction of thousands of sentences. The military college of the Supreme Tribunal was still rubber-stamping decisions in October which reduced the sentences of thousands of individuals convicted of crimes in military tribunals, ranging from desertion, banditry, dereliction of duties, and speculation, to forgery, agitation, and drunkenness. Most had originally been sentenced to between ten and twenty years.[160]

[155] GARF, f. R-1005, op. 2, d. 2, l. 290 (Riazan' tribunal to VTsIK, 18 April 1920).
[156] *Materialy*, 2 (1918), 51 (regulations, 4 February 1918).
[157] GARF, f. R-1005, op. 2, d. 20, l. 244 (report to the 7th All-Russian Congress of Soviets, December 1919).
[158] Fainblit, *Amnistiia*, 32. [159] *IZ*, 165.
[160] See the numerous lists in GARF, f. R-1005, op. 1, dd. 73–4. Some contain over 2,000 names.

In terms of a systematic policy, however, the next most comprehensive act of mercy after cassation and mass amnesty was early release or parole. Debates over introducing parole in Russia emerged in the late nineteenth century before a bill was passed in 1909. Supporters championed it as progressive and humane, allowing reformed prisoners to serve some of their sentence in the community and providing a stimulus for good behaviour. This rationale enabled early release to slot easily into Soviet conceptions of criminality. But, of course, it also had more practical benefits, providing a means to manipulate behaviour in prison and another 'release valve' for overcrowded prisons.[161]

In May 1918, a congress of commissars of justice in Siberia, the Urals, and Turkestan produced an extensive resolution on conditional early release. It could apply to those who had served half of their sentence (or over five years if the sentence was indeterminate) as long as there was evidence the prisoner would live honestly upon release (as recommended by officials or responsible personnel, such as doctors). Each town would create a commission composing of justice, prison, and other relevant officials to oversee the process. If a crime was committed during a period of conditional release, the individual would be rearrested.[162]

This resolution was published in Narkomiust's official journal, presumably indicating official support, and foreshadowed national policies later in 1918. Narkomiust was working on a draft decree by 9 October, with a final version agreed on 25 November.[163] This decree noted that prisoners may be released early on the basis of their appeals, or those by relatives or the authorities, if they had served at least half of their sentence. The court made its decision in an open meeting, could call on experts to testify (such as those involved in educational activities in the prison), and release was conditional on not reoffending.[164] These conditions were modified in March 1921 when it was decreed that no prison sentence could be longer than five years and that 'conditional' release meant either a prisoner's complete release from punishment or their transfer to forced labour without imprisonment for the remainder of their sentence. Either should still only occur after half the sentence had been served, although some provincial organs did gain the ability to release a prisoner earlier than this.[165]

Like other aspects of revolutionary justice, meetings on early release rarely followed official instructions to the letter. The circular in June 1921 specified that

[161] M. Elie and J. Hardy, '"Letting the Beasts out of the Cage": Parole in the Post-Soviet Gulag, 1953-1973', *Europe-Asia Studies*, 67, 4 (2015), 579–605.

[162] *Materialy*, 2 (1918), 64–6 (resolution, 25 May 1918). Viatka province also had a commission for early release which started work in late June 1918; GARF, f. A-353, op. 2, d. 27, l. 18 (report, provincial commissar of justice to the All-Russian Congress of Commissars of Justice, n.d.).

[163] GARF, f. A-353, op. 2, d. 2, ll. 138, 156–7 (protocols).

[164] *IZ*, 65–6. For an outline of the development of Soviet policy, see M. Grodzinskii, 'Sudebnoe osvobozhdenie ot nakazaniia i ego evoliutsiia v sovetskom prave', *Vestnik sovetskoi iustitsii*, 4 (1923), 87–9.

[165] *IZ*, 165 (decree, 21 March 1921).

cases were to be heard at open meetings. The appellant was to be invited, along with representatives of the petitioning organ (the decree implied that most appeals would be made by an institution), representatives of the provincial committee for early release, and, if needed, lawyers. The meeting would first hear the petitioner and advocate (if present), then the provincial representative, before giving the last word to the appellant and reaching a decision.[166]

The rare transcripts of such meetings reveal less formality but clear intentions. In July 1921 the Supreme Tribunal examined the case of A. S. Chagodaev, who had appealed in late 1920 to have his sentence reduced to forced labour without imprisonment. Chagodaev declared he wanted to become a 'free citizen', and work honourably and conscientiously, as he had done throughout his prison sentence. An official confirmed his 'energetic work' and that he had organized orchestras in prison, meaning the prison authorities had full confidence in him. The result is unclear from the file, but the focus of the meeting—the productivity and sincerity of Chagodaev—is clear.[167] The same concerns are evident in two cases overseen by Moscow's tribunal. The chairman spent most of the time asking about the background of the two prisoners (education, occupation, family, activities before October and before the First World War, and relationship to the Communist Party), before allowing a brief word to the provincial representative. This was even more informal, but the meeting still probed into the potential value of the prisoners and their work (one was noted to be a 'good worker').[168] Conversely, Tula's tribunal confirmed it was not willing to release anyone still considered 'dangerous', even if they had completed half of their sentence or more.[169]

In 1921, there were 47,129 applications for early release across the legal system, of which 32,888 (69.8 per cent) were accepted (only 11,030 were in prison, with others released from labour sentences without imprisonment). These statistics do not distinguish between courts, but figures on categories of crime suggest that crimes usually dealt with by tribunals formed a comparable percentage; the success rates of those convicted of counter-revolution (63.8 per cent) and crimes of office (67.7 per cent) were only slightly below the average above, while desertion (78.7 per cent) was higher. For those convicted of counter-revolution, women were more likely to be freed completely (71.1 per cent) than men (58.5 per cent). Women formed 12.1 per cent of all successful appeals, 11.9 per cent of appeals submitted, and 7 per cent of prisoners.[170]

The involvement of prison officers, especially prison educational departments, suggests that good behaviour and evidence of a conscientious attempt to reform

166 TsGAMO, f. 4613, op. 2, d. 56, ll. 58–58ob (circular from the KT to all tribunals, 9 June 1921).
167 GARF, f. R-1005, op. 1a, d. 52, ll. 350–50ob (transcript of meeting, 8 July 1921).
168 TsGAMO, f. 4613, op. 2, d. 56, ll. 59–60 (transcript of meeting, 15 June 1921).
169 GARF, f. R-1005, op. 3, d. 194, l. 29 (telegram, 28 April 1922).
170 V. Iakubson, 'Dosrochnoe osvobozhdenie v RSFSR za 1921 god', *ESIu*, 46–47, 30 December 1922, 7–10.

their character were clear criteria for an individual's release, as was the authorities' belief that they no longer posed a threat to the state. The decree of March 1921 restated that prison served two purposes: to remove dangers to the state and to rehabilitate individuals to a working life.[171] The theoretical literature supported this. One article claimed early release was practised in Russia to a greater extent than elsewhere because Russia was not interested in the crime committed but only in whether the authorities had confidence in a criminal's ability to act to the benefit of society and the state in future. It rejected criticism that early release undermined the punitive force of legal sentences.[172] Another article talked about early release as mercy and a means of reconciling the inevitable 'collision between law and life'. Punishment, moreover, was a form of 'social defence', and applying it when society did not need defending was pointless and perverted the very essence of justice.[173] A later work boasted that early release was a 'clear' expression of the humanism of Soviet law and commented—more convincingly—that it provided a stimulus for prisoners to re-educate themselves into ideal citizens.[174]

Ultimately, there were two clear benefits for the state. First, early release was another means, along with amnesties, to deal with the changing nature of crime at a time when rapidly fluctuating events quickly rendered some crimes relatively harmless while increasing the danger posed by others. The pressures on courts and prisons meant the state could not afford to maintain punishment for relatively harmless crimes when far more dangerous individuals existed. Unlike amnesties, though, early release operated behind the scenes. Second, the concept of rehabilitating prisoners into useful working lives became increasingly important for local authorities facing a multitude of personnel problems and a perennial shortage of skilled labour. Various local institutions proposed individuals for early release, as they were legally entitled to do, and courts often released these people into the care of these institutions. A circular to tribunals in 1921 noted that courts could make the petitioning institution responsible for the prisoner, thereby granting them control over the individual, or specify the nature of the work that a prisoner could do or their place of work.[175] Some tribunals, such as the water transport tribunal of the northern region, noted explicitly that they were happy to agree to the early release of a prisoner, as requested by the local authorities, because there was a high demand for skilled workers. This tribunal also acted to ensure prisoners could conduct specialist work for official bodies as part of the labour element of their sentences.[176] Thus, again unlike amnesties, early release enabled mercy for specific individuals irrespective of their crime.

[171] *IZ*, 165. [172] Iakubson, 'Dosrochnoe', 7–10. [173] Grodzinskii, 'Sudebnoe', 87, 89.
[174] Durmanov, *Osvobozhdenie*, 44.
[175] TsGAMO, f. 4613, op. 2, d. 56, ll. 58–58ob (circular from the KT, 9 June 1921).
[176] GARF, f. R-3042, op. 1, d. 392, ll. 14, 19 (meetings, 5 and 11 September 1920).

The Logic of Mercy

The Bolsheviks never outlined a coherent set of objectives for the activities described in this chapter beyond championing the various circumstances permitting them to be merciful. At one end of the scale there were occasional signs of genuine mercy, even if tinged with a belief in the rightness of the Bolsheviks' revolutionary path; to paraphrase a contemporary, these activities helped rectify the 'tragically' inevitable mistakes made by punitive forces facing an immense task.[177] At the other end of the scale there was an element of pure symbolism, projecting an image of benevolence and strength during periods when little of either existed. Continuing, moreover, to dispense harsh sentences for crimes while following them with acts of mercy may have left prisoners with the impression that they had been released due to the state's humanity.[178] The same was true of rare individual acts of mercy, such as when the chairman of VTsIK, M. I. Kalinin, visited Nizhnii Novgorod in October 1922 and sanctioned the release of several hundred peasants and workers convicted of petty crimes who promised to become productive workers. His representative also intervened in a case two weeks later to urge mercy.[179] Yet if these practices were primarily about mercy or symbolism, one might expect them to be widely promoted. They were not: even the coverage of amnesties was muted in all newspapers. Penza's local newspaper stood out by publishing lists of hundreds of cases considered for the November 1919 amnesty over half a dozen issues. These involved all types of crimes, and the paper noted whether they had been accepted or not.[180] As far as it is possible to tell, the vast majority of newspapers restricted themselves to reprinting the decrees with the odd editorial. The Bolsheviks may have feared revealing weakness by exposing the frequency of amnesties or the central role of cassation, preferring instead to ensure that mercy was less obvious, always serving as the exception to the rule.

Similarly, theoretical explanations also only have an element of truth. By viewing crime as a 'social danger', it is easy to see the nature of any danger to society changing over time, and mercy did often reflect the rapidly changing conditions of civil war that rendered some former crimes harmless or framed them as mistakes stemming from a lack of consciousness. But these arguments were not made systematically, publicly or privately, until after 1922, and do not explain why the state continued to sentence people for committing the same crimes as mentioned in acts of mercy. The 'ideology' of mercy, then, is better

[177] Fainblit, *Amnistiia*, 17, 36–7.

[178] Vasilenko argued that the Ukrainian authorities deliberately dispensed excessive sentences for minor crimes in order to reduce them and demonstrate humanity and generosity; 'Bil'shovits'ki', 112.

[179] GARF, f. R-1235, op. 58, d. 18, ll. 190–1, 281 (correspondence, 27 October and 13 November 1922).

[180] *Krasnoe znamia*, 18–21 November 1919 (pp. 3 or 4), 25–26 November (pp. 2 or 3).

viewed as a convenient framework to explain and justify mercy rather than as its main motivator.

In reality, mercy served a number of purposes, most of which were 'coldly logical', to return to the phrase introduced at the start of this chapter. It was a useful means of relieving state–society conflict (the use of amnesties, for example, to deal with rural unrest or seek post-conflict reconciliation) or solving the state's problems (amnesties enabling the return of deserters to the military or early release targeting valuable specialists). Moreover, embedding mercy in the form of cassation into the system of revolutionary justice helped exert central state control and distinguished the legal system from the Cheka, hopefully serving to prevent the inherent violence of law from undermining entirely people's perception of it as something distinct from the state and its other punitive arms. Overall, mercy acted as a crucial 'safety valve',[181] relieving pressure on an overstretched system of revolutionary justice, reducing resistance to the state, and, by targeting lower social groups, providing substance to the state's claims to be a workers' and peasants' government.

These 'coldly logical' benefits are hard to quantify. One exception is the impact of mercy on prisons. As early as August 1918, Sovnarkom complained to Narkomvnudel that it was impossible to find space in Moscow's prisons; there were two to four people for every place, mentally ill prisoners alongside others, numerous diseases, and no one transferred to hospital. Disease had spread to the surrounding urban population.[182] Similar situations existed across Russia. By late 1921, there were officially 73,194 prisoners in 60,468 places (1.21 per place), but reports admitted much worse overcrowding in major cities,[183] while prisons only had 55 per cent of their quota of staff.[184] Amnesties, in particular, were intended to alleviate overcrowding. A Narkomiust circular on the May 1920 amnesty admitted a basic aim was to transfer prisoners to forced labour without imprisonment rather than complete freedom,[185] while the main railway tribunal thought (incorrectly) the amnesty applied 'exclusively' to those sentenced to imprisonment and not to other punishments.[186] And amnesties made a difference. Most prisoners were serving short sentences and amnesties were generous to them. A report to the

[181] I borrow this term from B. McKnight, *The Quality of Mercy: Amnesties and Traditional Chinese Justice* (Honolulu, 1981), 117, who argues amnesties played a similar role in pre-modern China.

[182] GARF, f. R-393, op. 1, d. 29, l. 69 (Sovnarkom to the NKVD, undated); op. 3, d. 510, ll. 353–353ob, 356 (NKVD report on prisons, undated); op. 3, d. 216, l. 196ob (protocol of an emergency meeting of Moscow's provincial executive committee, 11 December 1918).

[183] *RSFSR. Tiuremnoe delo v 1921 godu. Otchet Narodnogo Komissariata Iustitsii po Tsentral'nomu Ispravitel'no-Trudovomu Otdelu IX-mu Vserossiiskomu S"ezdu Sovetov R., Kr., i K. D.* (Moscow, 1921), 8. Three organs (Narkomiust, Narkomvnudel, and the Cheka) oversaw prisoners during this period, often in the same prison. These numbers are from Narkomiust, but similar numbers existed for the NKVD; Jakobson, *Origins*, 24.

[184] *Materialy*, 11–12 (1921), 47, 59 (minutes, 25–9 June 1920).

[185] GARF, f. R-3042, op. 1, d. 15, l. 11 (instructions, undated).

[186] GARF, f. R-3042, op. 1, d. 15, ll. 13–13ob (instructions, 8 May 1920).

First All-Russian Congress of Provincial Prison Departments in September 1920 highlighted that the November 1919 amnesty and victories on some fronts of the civil war had combined to reduce the prison population by 30 per cent. In terms of those serving sentences rather than awaiting trial, the impact was more dramatic, with 75–80 per cent released in some places and 46 per cent across Russia.[187] Equally, the monthly statistics on prison capacity in 1920–1 reveal that prisons were emptier in December–January and in June after the usual amnesties, even if numbers quickly grew again.[188]

Similar impacts can be discerned elsewhere. Deserters swamped courts, especially tribunals: one estimate suggested that 1.7 million people deserted in 1919 alone.[189] Amnesties formed part of an evolving policy of incentives and punishments designed to combat the problem and could have a significant impact as long as they were introduced when deserters were receptive, were not too frequent, and were applied alongside repression.[190] Entire 'amnesty weeks' were offered in 1919–20. One of the most successful was in 3–9 June 1919, when 98,183 deserters returned, and it was extended for a month, raising the total to 436,398.[191] The same was true when dealing with thousands of peasants involved in 'banditry' or armed resistance. One observer implied that a special amnesty directed at entire units of the Antonov revolt in Tambov enjoyed some success.[192] It is true, as one historian has noted, that for amnesties to work peasant rebels had to know about them, desire one, and trust the Bolsheviks to honour it, all of which were doubtful.[193] But there was a difference between a revolt's leaders and its foot soldiers. Most 'bandits' were forcibly mobilized by local leaders, avoiding military conscription, or were reacting to (or seeking revenge for) seizures of food and property. Most soon tired of fighting, feared for their families, and were tempted by an amnesty. Even the more committed were convinced that the tide was turning by 1921 and amnesties provided an exit route and a basis for tentative reconciliation.[194] Amnesties militate against the 'possibly disastrous consequences of a wrong political choice', and plenty of such choices were made by the Bolsheviks throughout the civil war.[195]

[187] 'Doklad po Administrativno-Raspredelitel'nomu Otdelu TsKO', *Materialy*, 8 (1920), 30.

[188] *Materialy*, 8 (1920), 120 (protocols, 1st Congress of Provincial Prison Departments, 20–3 September 1920).

[189] S. Olikov, *Dezertirstvo v Krasnoi armii i bor'ba s nim* (Moscow, 1926), 30–1.

[190] Olikov, *Dezertirstvo*, 51. See also K. Levshin, *Dezertirstvo v Krasnoi armii v gody Grazhdanskoi voiny (po materialam Severo-Zapada Rossii)* (St Petersburg, 2016), 143–51; J. Sanborn, *Drafting the Russian Nation* (DeKalb, 2003), 50–5; and A. Wright, 'Stemming the Flow: The Red Army Anti-Desertion Campaign in Soviet Karelia (1919)', *Revolutionary Russia*, 25, 2 (2012), 154–5.

[191] Olikov, *Dezertirstvo*, 40–2, 100–2.

[192] D. Smirnov, *Zapiski chekista* (2nd edition, Minsk, 1972), 73.

[193] E. Landis, *Bandits and Partisans: The Antonov Movement in the Russian Civil War* (Pittsburgh, 2008), 111–12, 208–9, 256, 343.

[194] Vasilenko, 'Bil'shovits'ki', 102, 109–11.

[195] O. Kirchheimer, *Political Justice: The Use of Legal Procedure for Political Ends* (Princeton, 1961), 410.

The logic of mercy was not restricted solely to these practical crises but also fed into even bigger issues. Cassation, for instance, offered valuable information about conditions and practices across Russia. As well as helping establish a more consistent legal system, this formed part of broader state efforts by the end of the civil war to listen to all types of appeals, with the aim of aiding its centralizing, state-building project and monitoring a sense of popular moods. The latter, as historians have increasingly recognized, was important not only to assess popularity and resistance but to provide the knowledge required to transform the population. The Bolsheviks were not unique in this ambition, and other methods of assessing moods took precedence over cassation, but this nevertheless fitted into, and reinforced, these broader state-building objectives as they developed across the civil war.[196]

Central control was not achieved overnight. Inconsistent resolutions reveal a state that fluctuated in its interpretations of its own laws and in its objectives, while local tribunals fought central control. Even as the latter prevailed, it left a sour taste in many places. A later account by an official in Kazan' listed various cases when the local tribunal's sentence was overturned. Apparently, the tribunal had judged the cases correctly, but its sentences had not corresponded to the crime. The author remained baffled years later, resenting the lack of trust from the centre and believing that reducing sentences for no clear reason had undermined the tribunal.[197] Similar resentments, ironically, existed higher up. Iu. Iu. Mezhin, the chairman of the Main Railroad Tribunal, complained to Trotskii (as head of the railways) in May 1920 that his tribunal had sentenced a Cheka official to death for abuse of authority, embezzling property and money, drunkenness, and other crimes. A day later, VTsIK had postponed the sentence until the case was re-examined without giving a reason. Mezhin asked whether it was possible to have mercy irrespective of the degree of proof and the seriousness of the crime, and he believed re-examining a case implied the sentence was not considered appropriate or legal, which represented a vote of no confidence in the court.[198]

For 'model' and 'show' trials, central interference became the norm. Just as various organs beyond the tribunal decided on the need to organize these major trials, influenced the process, and managed the sentence, so too did they decide whether mercy was suitable. Take, for example, the trial of Red Army commander and Cossack leader, F. K. Mironov, in October 1919 for insubordination. Immediately after demanding and receiving the death penalty, the lead

[196] See P. Holquist, '"Information is the Alpha and Omega of Our Work": Bolshevik Surveillance in its Pan-European Context', *The Journal of Modern History*, 96, 3 (1997), 415–50.

[197] Kamenskii, 'Neskol'ko slov o deiatel'nosti Revtribunala, Sovnarsuda i Obsuda ATSSR za tri goda ikh sushchestvovaniia', *Vestnik Sovetskoi Iustitsii*, 4 (1923), 16–18.

[198] GARF, f. R-3042, op. 1, d. 7, ll. 38–9 (letter, 5 May 1920). The dispute rumbled on into June; ll. 74, 131, 135, 144 (correspondence, May–June, 1920). There are other materials in d. 12, ll. 1–2 (May 1920).

prosecutor, I. T. Smilga, suggested that the higher authorities show mercy; the death penalty, he argued, was 'not useful' in this case. The original sentence, it seemed, made the required symbolic point, but in reality there were fears that a harsh sentence might harm the relations of the state with the Cossacks. Mironov and his lawyer also appealed to senior figures, including Lenin, before the Politburo agreed to suspend the sentence.[199] Similar high-level decisions can be seen in the trial of Metropolitan Veniamin and leading Petrograd clergy in July 1922. Death sentences were initially dispensed to ten priests, but after appeals a special commission of leading Bolsheviks decided to reduce the sentence for six of them. Four remained 'leaders' and 'fully conscious' of their counter-revolutionary activities. The Politburo agreed. Further appeals from the remaining four led VTsIK to ask for directives from the Politburo, which again rejected them.[200] The four were shot soon afterwards. In these major trials, then, the usual channels of cassation and mercy did not apply, just as other elements of these trials were more tightly controlled by the state.

From another perspective, mercy forced further engagement with the state, its organs and its objectives. Appellants acquired a better understanding of the legal process (even if they received advice from others), about the role of law and courts and, more broadly, about the objectives of the new state. To hope to achieve any kind of success, they had to play by the state's rules (create a certain narrative and utilize certain categorizations, for example), and in doing so they reinforced the basis of revolutionary justice and enhanced the power and legitimacy of the state. Thus, appeals may be 'narratives of self-justification' keen to tell a good story through the circumstances surrounding their case,[201] but they forced individuals to engage with the state's objectives, discuss meanings of criminality and good character, debate procedure, and address larger public narratives about what makes a good Soviet citizen. There was no standard template, as the public narrative of what constituted correct behaviour was in flux – different actions were crimes one year and ignored the next. Few attacked the system and understandably so; it was easier and safer to demonstrate how the system had been misapplied in their case, how their act was not actually a crime, or how the legal process was flawed in this instance. But this all implied that certain crimes and a correct process did exist. Thus appellants engaged in the 'involuntary complicity' that scholars have noted in later periods, in other contexts, and in other

[199] *Filipp Mironov (Tikhii Don v 1917–1921 gg.). Dokumenty i materialy* (Moscow, 1997), 430–6 (various documents around 7 October 1919). The chair of the tribunal, D. V. Poluian, justified mercy as fair for someone who was not a 'class enemy' but had made a 'mistake'; *Krasnoe znamia* [Penza], 14 December 1919, 2.

[200] *Arkhivy Kremlia. Politbiuro i tserkov' 1922–1925 gg.* (2 volumes, Moscow, 1997–8), I, 232–43 (various documents, 5 July–2 August 1922).

[201] L. Siegelbaum, 'Narratives of Appeal and the Appeal of Narratives: Labor Discipline and its Contestation in the Early Soviet Period', *Russian History*, 24, 1 (1997), 67–8.

countries.[202] Even if superficial, this apparent acceptance of the system may have still served to strengthen and extend it.

Sending petitions could also be seen as a form of resistance—a means by which a subordinate group can defend its interests in an acceptable manner.[203] By agreeing there were accepted norms of behaviour, punishable crimes, and suitable punishments, but by claiming it was tribunals that had deviated from accepted ways of interpreting these, appellants were taking a moral stance that it was hard for the state to condemn. Moreover, while 'accepting' the system made it easier for the authorities to uphold their appeal without losing authority, by standing up for a greater emphasis on circumstances, and popular interpretations of crime and punishment, appellants agreed the revolution needed a new form of revolutionary justice and were trying to influence this new system, consciously or subconsciously.

Ultimately, it is worth stressing that mercy, even if only modifying or correcting the obvious abuses of revolutionary justice, could have a real impact on people's lives. Inconsistent legislation and implementation meant it was arbitrary in many instances, most upheld appeals simply led to a retrial, and it was certainly more likely to benefit some people than others in any case (whether the lower social classes or certain categories of criminal). Nevertheless, mercy did provide tangible benefits for many in the form of release or reduced sentences, and a concrete avenue to challenge the punitive power of the state.

[202] G. Alexopoulos, 'Victim Talk: Defense Testimony and Denunciation under Stalin', *Law & Social Inquiry*, 24, 3 (1999), 639.

[203] This argument is influenced by J. Scott, *Domination and the Arts of Resistance: Hidden Transcripts* (New Haven, 1990), 94–5, 101.

6
Publicizing Revolutionary Justice

The central purpose of law in any society is to guide behaviour and beliefs: to discourage and punish certain actions while encouraging others, thereby acting as a key means of social control.[1] The educational role of law, therefore, is inseparable from its punitive role, and every legal ruling sends out a message to the perpetrator and to wider society. There are two stages to this process: the educational message of each decision *and* its dissemination so people know, even if only at a basic level, how they should act, why, and the consequences of not doing so. This educational role is usually even stronger in the legal systems of authoritarian regimes, where the desire to send clear political and social messages often takes priority over the search for truth and justice.[2] Whether people respond in the intended manner is another matter, of course, as various factors guide behaviour, not just law, while laws can also have unintended consequences.[3] Yet a state's ability to compose and publicize the required message is the first step in ensuring law's effectiveness.

Revolutionary justice was no exception. Bolsheviks at all levels, from Lenin to local officials, promoted the court as a schoolroom where people could learn about the revolution, the new proletarian state, and acceptable behaviour as new Soviet citizens. Indeed, in some types of trials, most notably those involving the clergy, the desire to educate people about the dangers of the broader crime often pushed the actual activities of the defendants into the background.[4] Rather than courts defending the rights of 'conscious' citizens, then, they often focused explicitly on transforming the 'unconscious' citizen into a 'conscious' one, and this emphasis remained throughout the Soviet period in what one scholar has termed the 'parental' element of Soviet law.[5] In this sense, law was part of the wider project

[1] L. Friedman, *The Legal System: A Social Science Perspective* (New York, 1975), esp. 2, 16–18, 56, 61; and M. Shapiro, *Courts: A Comparative and Political Analysis* (Chicago, 1981), 17–28.

[2] P. Solomon, 'Judicial Power in Authoritarian States: The Russian Experience', in T. Ginsburg and T. Moustafa (eds.), *Rule By Law: The Politics of Courts in Authoritarian Regimes* (Cambridge, 2008), 261–82.

[3] M. Feeley, 'The Concept of Laws in Social Science: A Critique and Notes on an Expanded View', *Law and Society Review*, 10, 4 (1976), 497–523.

[4] See R. Greene, *Bodies Like Bright Stars: Saints and Relics in Orthodox Russia* (DeKalb, 2010), 135–7.

[5] H. Berman, *Justice in the USSR* (Cambridge, MA, 1963), 282–4.

The State versus The People: Revolutionary Justice in Russia's Civil War, 1917–1922. Matthew Rendle,
Oxford University Press (2020). © Matthew Rendle.
DOI: 10.1093/oso/9780198840428.001.0001

of mass political enlightenment and mobilization that engulfed Russia after the October Revolution.[6]

Yet despite the growing reach of tribunals and ever-increasing numbers of people drawn into revolutionary justice as defendants or witnesses, the formal legal system—investigations, trials, appeals—only involved a small proportion of the population directly. Family, friends, and acquaintances could get caught up in the process, while some chose to attend trials, but this was still insufficient for law to shape the thoughts and actions of wider society. Officials realized this, and many commented on the importance of publicity. The drama of trials can form a powerful educational tool with competing narratives, intriguing plots, compelling characters, and tough moral choices.[7] As revolutionaries before 1917, the Bolsheviks had used trials to spread their ideas and mobilize people against tsarism; it was now a question of using the same forum to mobilize people behind the new revolutionary state. They believed, somewhat naïvely, that, if trials could provide suitable role models, then the audience would replicate this revolutionary behaviour in their own lives.[8]

In this case, the Bolsheviks needed to expand the audience to capture as much of the country as possible. And as the civil war progressed, they could use the extensive propaganda apparatus that was emerging as they poured immense energy and resources into developing an array of textual, visual, and oral means of communicating with the population, from pamphlets, posters, cinema, and theatre, to networks of agitators, reading rooms and agitational trains, ships and carts. The growth in the number of newspapers, advances in photographic technology, and the development of film as a powerful visual medium all provided the Bolsheviks with unprecedented opportunities to spread their message.

Yet the difficulties in ensuring trials, sentences, and practices of mercy formed clear, consistent, and 'correct' messages, which have been explored in earlier chapters, hindered dissemination. It is difficult to publicize clearly a legal judgement that appeared confused, inconsistent, and irrational in the first place. This judgement, moreover, had to serve as propaganda *and* agitation; that is, in the Bolsheviks' conceptions of the terms, it had to help educate in the broader political and economic processes beneath events (propaganda) as well as mobilize people to act (agitation). In other spheres, these elements often worked separately,

[6] See V. Kerzhentsev, *Kul'tura i sovetskaia vlast'* (Moscow, 1919), esp. 12–22; P. Kenez, *The Birth of the Propaganda State: Soviet Methods of Mass Mobilization, 1917–1929* (Cambridge, 1985); and D. Hoffmann, *Cultivating the Masses: Modern State Practices and Soviet Socialism, 1914–1939* (Ithaca, 2011), 211–21.

[7] For more on these topics, see L. Farmer, 'Trials', in A. Sarat, M. Anderson, and C. Frank (eds.), *Law and the Humanities: An Introduction* (Cambridge, 2010), 455–77; and C. Clover, 'Law and the Order of Popular Culture', in A. Sarat and T. Kearns (eds.), *Law in the Domains of Culture* (Ann Arbor, 1998), 97–119.

[8] This sentiment extended across revolutionary society and culture to encompass theatre, art, and literature; see J. Cassiday, *The Enemy on Trial: Early Soviet Courts on Stage and Screen* (DeKalb, 2000), 17.

requiring as they did different timescales, techniques, languages, and levels of education on the part of their audiences.[9]

The civil war was also a period of competing priorities, and law was only one means of educating the population. How much space in congested newspapers was needed to represent a trial effectively? Which of the hundreds of trials would convey a message most effectively? Which aspects of trials should be stressed? How could photographs be used at a time when few newspapers or journals were capable of publishing them? How could the drama and educational message of the trial be conveyed through silent films? Then there were more fundamental problems. For all the educational potential in the dramatic and theatrical elements of the trial, for instance, if the outcome was predetermined—as it often seemed to be in major trials—or if justice seemed absent, the inevitability of an unjust sentence could only undermine the educational role of revolutionary justice.[10] And how could the state assess whether the publicity was effective and whether law was educating people? The Bolsheviks' answers evolved but, as elsewhere, remained far from consistent and effective.

This chapter makes extensive use of newspapers (national and local), images, and newsreels to examine how tribunals were portrayed, the language used, the messages conveyed, and how this fitted into broader attempts to mobilize people. Effective or not, what does remain clear from the Bolsheviks' struggles with the questions above and others is that they envisaged legal organs serving as a central means of communication between state and society. Revolutionary justice provided better material for education than the Cheka, and the authorities were constantly concerned by their fear that it was not fulfilling its educational role as effectively as they had hoped.

The Educational Role of Law

Investing hope in the educational role of law was not new in Russia. After legal reforms in 1864, the tsarist state and its legal officials hoped law would play a prominent role in developing people into conscious citizens. The peasants' *volost'* courts, for instance, aimed to provide a forum where peasants engaged with the state beyond conscription and taxes; they would act as citizens by participating in official organs that regulated behaviour and defended rights. Urban peace courts and jury service were to have the same effect.[11] Increasing efforts were also made

[9] For more, see M. Lenoe, *Closer to the Masses: Stalinist Culture, Social Revolution, and Soviet Newspapers* (Cambridge, MA, 2004), 26–8.

[10] As pointed out in a different context in M. Ball, 'The Play's the Thing: An Unscientific Reflection on Courts Under the Rubric of Theater', *Stanford Law Review*, 28, 1 (1975), 99.

[11] J. Burbank, 'Legal Culture, Citizenship, and Peasant Jurisprudence: Perspectives from the Early Twentieth Century', in P. Solomon (ed.), *Reforming Justice in Russia, 1864–1996* (Armonk, 1997), 99;

to educate people in the law with the production of pamphlets, textbooks, and other materials to explain laws and legal terms, and to help teach law in schools, prompting extensive debates on the best techniques for popularizing law.[12]

The extent to which all this was successful is questionable.[13] On the one hand, Russians were using courts in increasing numbers in the years before the First World War, meaning they must have seen value in them and were exposed to the legal process and its values. More generally, elements of law and the legal process were part of more and more people's lives in late imperial Russia, whether through going to court with cases, serving on juries, simply reading about cases in newspapers, or the 'staggering popularity' of crime fiction among the lower and middle classes.[14] On the other hand, this did not necessarily make them citizens. Many people probably used courts as a last resort, while peasants tended to use courts for smaller disputes or particular crimes, not trusting them to deal with more serious conflicts. Courts retained a strong element of traditional community justice, while attempts by peace courts to marry statutory law with custom often only emphasized the differences between the two. Attempts to popularize law struggled amid arguments over strategy and abstract notions of the intended reader. Nevertheless, despite these problems, there seems little doubt that law had more potential to mould the actions and beliefs of Russians on the eve of the Russian Revolution than ever before.

Bolshevik legal theorists tended to take this potential for granted, focusing their efforts on the mechanics of building a new legal system, with its educational role implicit in some of their assertions, such as their stress on the importance of public trials or their idealized notion of the public acting as the prosecution and

J. Neuberger, 'Popular Legal Cultures: The St Petersburg *Mirovoi sud*', in B. Eklof, J. Bushnell, and L. Zakharova (eds.), *Russia's Great Reforms, 1855–1881* (Bloomington, 1994), 231–46; J. Attwell, 'The Russian Jury', *Slavonic and East European Review*, 53, 130 (1975), 44–61; and S. Kirmse, *The Lawful Empire: Legal Change and Cultural Diversity in Late Imperial Russia* (Cambridge, 2019), 148-72.

[12] M. Tissier, 'Legal Literature 'for the People' and the Use of Language (Late Nineteenth and Early Twentieth Century)', in N. Vakhtin and B. Firsov (eds.), *Public Debate in Russia: Matters of (Dis)order* (Edinburgh, 2016), 85–100.

[13] Historians are divided on this issue. For cautious views, see C. Gaudin, *Ruling Peasants: Village and State in Late Imperial Russia* (DeKalb, 2007), 130–1; Neuberger, 'Popular Legal Cultures', 234–5, 240–2; V. Bezgin, *Pravovaia kul'tura russkogo sela (vtoraia polovina XIX—nachalo XX veka)* (Tambov, 2012), 71–7; and Kirmse, *Lawful Empire*, 210-13, 276-8, 282-3. A more positive view is in J. Burbank, *Russian Peasants Go To Court: Legal Culture in the Countryside, 1905–1917* (Bloomington and Indianapolis, 2004), 268–71, while more negative views are in J. Baberowski, 'Law, the Judicial System and the Legal Profession', in D. Lieven (ed.), *The Cambridge History of Russia. Volume II: Imperial Russia, 1689–1917* (Cambridge, 2006), 344–68; S. Frank, *Crime, Cultural Conflict, and Justice in Rural Russia, 1856–1914* (Berkeley, 1999), 95–103, 113–14, 297–312; and T. Shatkovskaia, *Pravovaia mental'nost' Rossiiskikh krest'ian vtoroi poloviny XIX veka* (Rostov-na-Donu, 2000), 119–20, 207–8.

[14] For the prominent position of law and crime in popular culture, see J. Brooks, *When Russia Learned to Read: Literacy and Popular Literature, 1861–1917* (Princeton, 1985), 200–8; B. Dralyuk, *Western Crime Fiction Goes East: The Russian Pinkerton Craze, 1907–1934* (Leiden, 2012); and L. McReynolds, *Murder Most Russian: True Crime and Punishment in Late Imperial Russia* (Ithaca, 2013).

the defence.[15] It was the Bolshevik leadership, less vested in the minutiae of legal procedure and more interested in the wider contribution of law to building a new state and winning the civil war, who talked explicitly of the importance of the educational role of law. They were, though, primarily focused on counter-revolutionary crimes and their political agenda. To be sure, as the new state consolidated, statistics indicate the numbers of cases brought to people's courts—comparable to tsarist-era *volost'* and peace courts—had resumed pre-1917 trends by the early 1920s; there were rising numbers of civil cases, falling numbers of criminal cases, and a steady growth in cases overall.[16] But this was the softer political agenda of law. The prosecution of counter-revolutionary crimes, particularly in tribunals, saw the state seek to impose a harder political agenda on the people, compelling them to engage with the legal system over acts that fewer people saw as crimes than, say, murder or theft. The pressures of civil war, moreover, demanded quicker results from revolutionary justice than earlier attempts to foster citizenship through law.

The Bolsheviks, Lenin argued, should not be utopians and assume people would act immediately as model citizens – law was the form of coercion needed to 'educate' people in discipline and behaviour in key areas.[17] What happened in trials remained central, formulating the message to be disseminated (hence, as noted in earlier chapters, his criticism of lenient sentences sending out the wrong message about the state's intentions), but Lenin's focus on dissemination was clear from the start. In April 1918, he chased the Commissariat of Justice (Narkomiust) for information on judicial propaganda amongst the population, particularly the lower classes in the form of printed material, lectures, or classes.[18] His subsequent berating of Narkomiust for not organizing enough 'model' trials revealed his ongoing concern that messages were not being disseminated effectively. Indeed, it has been argued that his demand for 'model (*obraztsovyi*)' trials rather than 'show (*pokazatel'nyi*)' trials reflected his focus on education rather than simply repression.[19] More than once, the word 'educational' (or an equivalent) is italicized in his explanations for why model trials were important; such trials provided better publicity, particularly in the press, and there needed to be 'noise' about the trials for the 'educational role of the courts is tremendous'.[20]

[15] See, for example, A. Lunacharskii, 'Revoliutsiia i sud', *Pravda*, 1 December 1917, 2; and the later survey in P. Liublinskii, 'O publichnosti sudebnykh zasedanii', *Vestnik Sovetskoi iustitsii*, 3 (13) (1924), 74–7.

[16] See, for example, *Otchet plenumu Moskovskogo soveta R. K. i K. D. o rabote Moskovskogo gubernskogo suda za 1924 god* (Moscow, 1925), 10–11.

[17] Draft of the 'Immediate Tasks of the Soviet Government', 28 March 1918, in V. Lenin, *Collected Works* (47 volumes, Moscow, 1960–70), XXVII, 217–18.

[18] Lenin, *Collected Works*, XLIV, 76–7 (letter to Narkomiust, 15 April 1918).

[19] P. Beirne and A. Hunt, 'Lenin, Crime and Penal Politics, 1917-1924' in P. Beirne (ed.), *Revolution in Law: Contributions to the Development of Soviet Legal Theory, 1917–1938* (Armonk, 1990), 116–17.

[20] Lenin, *Collected Works*, XXXVI, 560–5 (letter to D. I. Kurskii, 20 February 1922). See also letters to Moscow's tribunal and Kurskii on 20 October and 4 November 1921 respectively (XLV, 348, 369).

L. D. Trotskii, as Commissar of War, echoed these sentiments. He also urged tribunals to remember their 'very great educational importance' as they pronounced on actions that ran contrary to the new revolutionary order, defining the new relations, conduct, and discipline required by the workers' state. As such, tribunals needed to think not only about punishment in the trial but how that punishment will appear outside of the courtroom. He despaired at the frequency with which newspapers carried sentences that may have made sense within the context of the case described in court but when removed from this context appeared lenient or absurd, and thus sent the wrong message to the wider audience. For Trotskii, tribunals should have the 'broad masses' in their minds, not just the accused, and they must connect punishment with education, while newspapers should add mitigating circumstances into their reports to make the rationale behind sentences clearer to the reading public. He recognized that the low educational levels of many tribunal officials may be causing problems, but stressed the importance of ensuring that all those who heard or read about the sentence should be deterred from following a similar course of action, encouraged if they had acted correctly, and not 'demoralized' because the sentence made little sense.[21]

Some local officials agreed. Instructions from the chair of the tribunal in Kursk echoed these views when he recognized the power of the legal process to educate the largest number of working people, and when he advised public pronouncements to include a short history of the case and the characteristics of the crime to enable a better understanding of the sentence.[22] Other officials saw the legal process as a 'school' and knew agitation underpinned the work of tribunals;[23] their 'vocation', in the words of one, was to use specific cases to 'teach' the working people a sense of legality.[24] Iu. Iu. Mezhin, the chair of the Main Railway Tribunal, could well have been quoting Lenin when urging the wider publication of sentences locally and the organization of more large trials with public significance in May 1920.[25]

Another official specifically highlighted the importance of 'popularizing' sentences. While admitting the best means of exposing people to revolutionary justice was through attendance at trials, the next best step was to publicize trials as widely as possible, distributing sentences as orders around the military, for instance, or

[21] *The Military Writings and Speeches of Leon Trotsky: How the Revolution Armed*, trans. B. Pearce (5 volumes, London, 1979–81), II, 200–3 (23 April 1919). See also his order on 9 May 1920 (III, 176). Some tribunals were finishing by explaining the 'meaning (*smysl'*)' of the sentence by the end of the year; RGASPI, f. 17, op. 109, d. 245, ll. 2–3ob (report on military tribunals at the South-west Front, August 1920).

[22] GARF, f. R-1005, op. 5, d. 136, l. 98 (published instructions, *c.*1922).

[23] GARF, f. R-3042, op. 1, d. 23, l. 37 (anonymous report on railway tribunals, *c.*1921).

[24] GARF, f. R-1005, op. 3, d. 80, l. 35 (report from the chairman of the tribunal in Vladikavkaz, 9 August 1921).

[25] GARF, f. R-3042, op. 1, d. 2, l. 12 (telegram to all railway tribunals, 3 May 1920).

publishing reports in the press. In the case of banditry, posting sentences on public buildings and spreading them around local villages worked. This publicity must not be in 'official' language, but easily comprehensible, ideally in the form of short notes and articles. The official also recognized that tribunals often lacked the skills to do this, particularly those working quickly in travelling sessions, but he argued that newspapers could intervene to transform brief notes into effective articles. In the longer term, more experienced workers were needed to oversee publicity. He also believed the 'centre' could do more, producing more orders, distributing them more widely, and publishing regular collections of sentences.[26] For this official, the centre and the provinces, and the legal authorities and the media, all needed to work together to ensure revolutionary justice was communicated effectively and its educational potential fulfilled. This was easier said than done, of course, and nowhere is this more apparent than in the primary means of publicity—newspapers.

The Language of Justice

The press was central to revolutionary discourse. Statistics vary, as always, but there were apparently 563 newspapers and 753 journals by late 1918, with circulation increasing tenfold since the October Revolution. *Izvestiia* was the largest paper, with 300,000–400,000 copies printed daily; *Pravda* followed, with 130,000 copies; and several other papers in the two largest cities were close behind.[27] In the military alone, there were around twenty-five army-level and seventy divisional papers.[28] Circulation figures shrank under the pressures of civil war, particularly the absence of paper and printing presses, and *Izvestiia* had fallen to 275,000 copies daily by March 1920, with the majority of provincial papers printing 5,000–10,000 copies and *uezd* papers 3,000.[29] Even major papers like *Pravda* were only able to print two-page editions through much of 1920. Many papers preferred to send copies to institutions, where more people would read them, than to individuals. Nonetheless, there remained 312 national and provincial papers in early 1922, along with 490 *uezd* papers, all with a daily circulation of over 2.6 million.[30] These numbers decreased in 1922 as many papers were forced to become financially self-sufficient, but the press remained the main means of disseminating news and ideology.

[26] RGVA, f. 33988, op. 2, d. 245, ll. 11ob-14ob (report on military tribunals on the Western Front in 1921).

[27] Kenez, *Birth of the Propaganda State*, 44–5.

[28] D. Liventsev, *Voennaia propaganda na RKKF v period grazhdanskoi voiny (1917–1921 gg.)* (Voronezh, 2013), 25–6.

[29] L. Molchanov, *Gazetnaia pressa Rossii v gody revoliutsii i Grazhdanskoi voiny (okt. 1917–1920 gg.)* (Moscow, 2002), 52 (see also 14–28, 52–3).

[30] Kenez, *Birth of the Propaganda State*, 225.

Like all institutions, Narkomiust recognized the importance of publishing from the start. By autumn 1918, it had published a collection of articles, *Revoliutsiia i pravo*; two volumes of the document collection, *Materialy Narodnogo Komissariata Iustitsii*; a collection of decrees; and the first volume of the journal *Proletarskaia revoliutsiia i pravo*. All had print runs of at least several thousand copies.[31] By 1922, further collections of decrees had been published, along with Narkomiust's reports to various official congresses; *Materialy* had reached over a dozen editions; *Proletarskaia revoliutsiia i pravo* was on its fifteenth edition; a new weekly journal, *Ezhenedel'nik sovetskoi iustitsii*, had been launched; and attempts were being made to provide guides to people's courts, summaries of key laws, and other materials to make the new system more accessible.[32] The end of the civil war and the legal reforms of 1922 heralded a growth in legal publications locally but, as with Narkomiust's publications, most seemed aimed at guiding and educating legal officials rather than the wider public. The focus, as one commentator noted, was always on the legal content rather than on popularity or accessibility.[33] It was not until *Rabochii sud* (a journal for professionals in Petrograd) published *Sud idet!* in 1924 that a broader audience was targeted. Cheaper and with a mix of articles on famous historical trials, sensational current cases, and broad legal developments, *Sud idet!* reached print runs that were many times greater than its parent publication. Before then, legal organs were forced to rely on the mainstream press, their greater print runs, and their wider audience.

The problem with the major newspapers, however, was the surfeit of 'news' during the civil war, as many topics—international, national, and local—jostled for attention. In autumn 1918 Lenin urged newspapers to focus less on politics and more on the achievements of building a new life, and on exposing and condemning those opposing progress.[34] Law could have fitted neatly into this, but newspapers showed few signs of responding to Lenin's call. International, military, and party news dominated national newspapers, while local papers added economic concerns. Law was important, but so too was everything else. At the same time, the number of trials was increasing rapidly, far too many to discuss individually, and becoming too common to count as significant 'news'. Few newspapers, struggling for staff, sent journalists to observe anything other than the most high-profile trials.

The onus, therefore, often fell on tribunals to provide material to newspapers and push for its publication. Apparently some military tribunals paid a member of staff to prepare articles for publication and liaise with editors.[35] Most tribunals,

[31] GARF, f. A-353, op. 2, d. 14, ll. 80–80ob (report, 9 September 1918).
[32] *Ezhenedel'nik sovetskoi iustitsii* [hereafter *ESIu*], 22 January 1922, 15.
[33] S. Zaitsev, 'Iuridicheskaia pechat' po SSSR', *ESIu*, 38, 29 September 1923, 877–8.
[34] Lenin, *Collected Works*, XXVIII, 96–8 (*Pravda*, 20 September 1918).
[35] I. Vorob'ev and L. Khlamov, 'Na zashchite revoliutsionnago Petrograde', in *Na strazhe sotsialisticheskoi zakonnosti (50 let voennym tribunalam)* (Moscow, 1968), 130–1.

though, were too overloaded and short-staffed themselves to communicate effectively with the press. And even then there was no guarantee of success. A few letters sent by the Cassation Tribunal to the editorial board of *Izvestiia* in early July 1919 provide a one-sided snapshot of the tensions. The first on 2 July asks *Izvestiia* to publish reports on the meeting of the tribunal on 26 June (the same request is also sent to *Vechernie Izvestiia*). A second on 9 July asks that the details of a particular case are published the next day, while querying when a report of a meeting on 3 July will be published—apparently the tribunal was assured this would appear on 5 July but it had not yet appeared. A final letter on 12 July presses *Izvestiia* to publish an account of a meeting on 10 July as soon as possible.[36] Throughout, there is an expectation on the part of the tribunal that its activities will be reported in *Izvestiia*, but annoyance that this is not being done automatically, or even when requested or promised.

Nevertheless, tensions aside, the main national newspapers, *Izvestiia* and *Pravda*, did provide space for legal issues, publishing decrees and reports from congresses, while legal theorists used their pages to promote revolutionary justice and debate contentious elements, such as the role of advocates and disputes with the Cheka. Tribunals received more coverage than people's courts and both had more than the Cheka. Much the same was true for local newspapers. There was less on legislation unless it had an immediate local impact, such as amnesties, and only the odd article on revolutionary justice broadly, while local departments of justice and congresses were reported on instead of national equivalents. Local tribunal officials sometimes wrote articles addressing specific concerns. M. V. Kozhevnikov, chair of Irkutsk's tribunal and later author of a standard history of Soviet law, linked national concerns about banditry to a local trial of 261 people for resisting Soviet policies.[37] The chairman of the Black Sea military tribunal used an interview to defend the existence of special military courts against arguments that military cases could be heard in civilian courts after hostilities had died down. In Briansk, the tribunal's presidium put its name to a front-page, headline article highlighting the 'epidemic' of theft, bribery, and crimes of office.[38]

Newspapers were also used in other ways by tribunals. In 1918, *Krasnaia gazeta* included an appeal from the then Commissar of Justice, P. I. Stuchka, for people to serve in the new courts,[39] while *Rabochaia Moskva* was used in 1922 to seek public scrutiny of a list of over 800 applicants to serve in the new College of Advocates to check whether anyone was unsuitable for any reason.[40] *Izvestiia Shuiskago soveta*

[36] GARF, f. R-1005, op. 2, d. 3, ll. 80–4 (various correspondence, 2–12 July 1919).

[37] *Vlast' truda* [Irkutsk], 5 February 1921, reprinted in *Sibirskaia vandeia. Dokumenty* (2 volumes, Moscow, 2000–1), I, 543–4.

[38] *Krasnyi Chernomorsko-Azovskii flot*, 12 March 1921, 3–4; *Brianskii rabochii*, 16 September 1922, 1 (copies are in GARF, f. R-1005, op. 1, d. 56, ll. 32–32ob and op. 3, d. 106, l. 3 respectively).

[39] *Krasnaia gazeta. Vechernii vypusk* [Petrograd], 28 February 1918, 4.

[40] *Rabochaia Moskva*, 13 July 1922, 1; 2 August 1922, 2, 7; 23 August 1922, 3.

published front page appeals in July 1918 asking for denunciations of currency traders and speculators, as well as for information on two missing offenders, including a deserter.[41] One paper published a physical description of a wanted person, while another asked for the whereabouts of named individuals.[42] This was a valuable tactic for travelling sessions, in particular, which were organized away from the location of the crime and the trial, with little time to prepare, and needed to gather evidence and publicize forthcoming trials. One session along the Volga, for instance, used local newspapers to call for witnesses, issue summons to the accused, and advertise the time and location of trials.[43] Local papers often carried adverts for forthcoming trials, noting the allegations, the leading figures for the prosecution, and the time and location, usually stressing that entry was free. *Kommunisticheskii trud* advertised one trial as it might a theatrical performance. Under a large banner, 'Today's Court', it outlined the plot, named the villains (thirty-five businessmen) and the heroes (the prosecutors), with the lead prosecutor in pride of place (in large type), the prominent Bolshevik K. B. Radek.[44]

The most common coverage in all newspapers, though, was of the trials themselves. National newspapers carried reports on all tribunals consistently throughout the civil war. In *Izvestiia*, the frequency of articles was high in 1918–19, dropping down in late 1919 and through 1920–1, before rising again in 1922. At their height, there was an article every two or three days, with longer coverage of prominent trials mixed with short notes on other trials. *Pravda* followed a similar trajectory, although its coverage virtually disappeared in 1920 amid numerous two-page issues. It is hard to trace the level of coverage in local newspapers; a sample of various titles for different parts of this period suggests regular coverage in many cases, but fewer articles than *Izvestiia* and some local papers proving far more assiduous than others. Most provided a fair representation of the different crimes targeted by tribunals, although some mass crimes, such as desertion in 1919–20 and bribery in 1922, enjoyed more systematic coverage as part of broader state-driven propaganda campaigns.

Few trials, however, made front-page news, and they were usually placed behind discussions of major policies, military matters, and international affairs. *Izvestiia* placed its report on the very first trial on its sixth page, and this level of priority remained typical across the civil war. In mid- to late 1922 when tribunals enjoyed almost daily coverage, these short articles were consistently placed at the end of *Izvestiia* alongside sport, theatre, art, adverts, and once even a chess problem.[45] Throughout 1919, at the height of the conflict, *Pravda* usually placed

41 *Izvestiia Shuiskago soveta*, 25–8 July, 30 July 1918.

42 *Zaria* [Simbirsk], 7 June 1919, 4; *Boevaia Pravda* [Petrograd], 22 April 1920, 4; 27 April 1920, 4.

43 See the cuttings in GARF, f. R-3042, op. 1, d. 96, ll. 68–70 (undated, but between May and September 1922).

44 *Kommunisticheskii trud* [Moscow], 15 December 1921, 3.

45 *Izvestiia*, 31 December 1922, 5.

its coverage on the final page, also alongside discussions of books or the theatre. The same was true in local papers. Saratov's *Izvestiia* and *Krasnyi Baltiiskii flot*, for instance, also buried their reports at the end amid sport, culture, and theatre adverts.[46]

This sense of unimportance was reinforced by the title, which usually made little attempt to attract the reader. Many newspapers, including *Izvestiia* and *Pravda*, used factual titles for much of their coverage, such as 'The Revolutionary Tribunal' or 'The Affair / Case (*delo*) of [name of the accused]'. As the civil war progressed, subheadings were used inconsistently to provide an indication of the crime, with more emotive language usually reserved for particular criminals, such as 'malicious' deserters or 'counter-revolutionary' priests. The situation became worse as *Pravda* (by late 1918) and then *Izvestiia* (by 1921) placed many reports on tribunals under the title of 'The Legal Department', which implied that law was no different to any other state activity. Some local newspapers headed up their coverage of prominent trials with 'In Moscow', thereby implying these were removed from local concerns, contradicting the state's emphasis on the universal relevance of revolutionary justice.

Against this background, even the simple steps a few newspapers took, usually local ones, stand out. Some were better at promoting the *revolutionary* nature of law, even if only through using titles such as 'The Red Court' or 'Revolutionary Justice'. *Krasnaia gazeta* (Petrograd) used 'Crimes against the Revolution' or 'Crimes against the People', before settling on 'The People's Court' in 1920–1 to report the activities of all courts, although usually tribunals. Presumably it felt this helped convey that all courts represented the will of the people. *Krasnoe znamia* placed the educational remit to the fore, regularly reporting on trials under a title asking rhetorically, 'what does the tribunal punish?'[47] Others deftly transformed coverage of particular trials into broader articles against specific crimes. An article in *Boevaia Pravda*, for instance, turned a case against a soldier who had self-harmed to escape from military duty into a general attack on the practice, repeatedly describing those involved as 'weak' comrades, self-interested, and 'traitors to the revolution'.[48] These small steps indicated what newspapers could do—if they tried—to attract readers to their coverage of law and help fulfil the educational potential of law and tribunals.

A larger problem than uninspiring titles was equally uninspiring content. Historians have commented on the 'dull', 'repetitive', and 'monotonous' content,

[46] See, for example, *Izvestiia Saratovskago soveta rabochikh, soldatskikh i krest'ianskikh deputatov i raionnago ispolnitel'nago komiteta*, 27 March 1918, 4; and *Krasnyi Baltiiskii flot*, 2 October 1920, 4.

[47] *Krasnoe znamia* [Penza], 27 May 1920, 2; 29 May , 1; 24 July , 2; 17 September , 1; 23 November , 2; 21 December , 3. Whether consciously or not, the reports published under this title conveniently covered a whole range of crimes, including a corrupt Cheka official and people's court judge.

[48] *Boevaia Pravda*, 22 November 1919, 4.

and the 'doggedly didactic' tone of the majority of articles during this period.[49] Articles on law tend to fall into the 'dull' category rather than the overly didactic. The rhetorical devices, binary images, and emotive language observed elsewhere are usually absent.[50] To be sure, the coverage promotes the official narrative and is selective in its descriptions of trials. The defence receives less space as the civil war progresses, although their voice remains present, and newspapers almost never critiqued the trial or the sentence. One very rare example came when *Kommunisticheskii trud* reported on a trial in which a former railway tribunal chairman was convicted of exceeding his authority and prohibited from holding public office for five years. This verdict, the paper argued, was too lenient. Others in the case had been sentenced to forced labour and this sentence made it impossible to speak of 'revolutionary legality and a legal proletarian dictatorship'.[51] Overwhelmingly, though, papers conformed to the tribunal's views, even if similar criticism was common in less public circles.

Despite this conformity, though, much of the language remained descriptive and strangely dispassionate, especially when considering some of the public rhetoric surrounding tribunals. The language in *Izvestiia*, for instance, which provided more coverage than *Pravda*, was fairly neutral throughout, with limited use of 'counter-revolution' and other pejorative terms. Some local newspapers were more willing to utilize the language of the class enemy, but the coverage remained less aggressive than might be expected. Therefore, it becomes particularly noticeable when newspapers do depart from this norm, such as when covering the trials resulting from the campaign against church valuables later in the civil war. Here, the language is always uncompromising: the 'princes' of the church are being dragged in front of the court of workers and peasants; the clergy are monarchists, bourgeoisie, and landowners; and they are immoral for refusing to use their wealth to help the hungry. These reports used the pejorative term for priests, *pop*, and talked of a '*popovskii*' counter-revolution.[52]

There may be reasons for these exceptions. Newspapers may have found it easier to use such language when dealing with obvious class enemies than with crimes committed by workers and peasants. It must have also been easier to get caught up in this rhetoric when reporting on large, state-sponsored campaigns such as this one against the clergy or the trial of the Socialist Revolutionaries (SRs) described below (in the final section of this chapter). A bigger factor may have simply been space. These campaigns were allocated far more space. Most trials were covered by a few lines on the crime, the perpetrators, and the sentence; it was difficult to do anything innovative or educational in a paragraph or two. No

[49] Kenez, *Birth of the Propaganda State*, 45, 224; D. Raleigh, *Experiencing Russia's Civil War: Politics, Society and Revolutionary Culture in Saratov, 1917–1922* (Princeton, 2002), 227.

[50] Raleigh, *Experiencing Russia's Civil War*, 53–4.

[51] *Kommunisticheskii trud*, 27 August 1921, 3.

[52] See, for example, *Rabochaia Moskva*, 6 May 1922, 2; 9 May 1922, 1.

explanation could be provided for sentences (assuming the author knew the reasons for a particular sentence) and there was no space to emphasize the messages or lessons from trials. The descriptive nature and the brevity of the vast majority of articles accentuated the dispassionate impression, as did the tendency of many newspapers, such as *Pravda*, to group several short reports of trials together, thereby quickly switching the reader's attention before any messages had been reinforced.

It may be that newspapers hoped the narrative would convey the message, and some have argued that a logical narrative (story) can be a persuasive tool in law, increasing the likelihood that an account is seen as truthful.[53] Yet even then newspapers could have presented this narrative in a more engaging manner. The use of subheadings at the start to describe the nature of the crime (or subject of the story) was employed inconsistently by most newspapers, as were subheadings throughout in longer accounts to distinguish between the elements of the story (such as speeches by different defendants, prosecutors, or witnesses) or the use of bold type to emphasize key points (or messages) in the story. *Izvestiia* started to employ a more informal and chattier approach by spring 1922, often using dialogue to convey the story, which was more engaging, but more explicit educational messages tend to appear only in local newspapers. An article in *Rabochaia Moskva* entitled 'The Soviet Court: Checkmate' took a strong moralistic approach to a workers' dispute and finished with an open call to 'Comrade Readers'—no one can play chess with the Soviet state and doing so will be very dangerous.[54] Another report in an Irkutsk newspaper, *Vlast' truda*, used the final few paragraphs on a trial of 138 peasants for participating in an armed uprising to emphasize that the proletarian court did not waste time when deciding who was correct and who was guilty, and anyone who had not understood beforehand what the worker-peasant government meant in practice should have now left the court as convinced supporters.[55]

Alongside space, the other fundamental problem seems to be authorship. Few articles, like most during this period, have a named author, but, more importantly, few were written on the basis of first-hand observation, apart from the initial trials and occasional high-profile trials. This mattered as observation brought the emotion that made articles more readable and informative. The difference can be seen in *Rabochaia Moskva*. It seemed to have a particular journalist, S. Bei-vich (often simply S. B.), who reported on tribunals. All the reports in this paper tend to be more accessible than those in *Izvestiia* or *Pravda*, with a greater attempt to convey a story and catchier subheadings, but Bei-vich's articles were more

[53] J. Christopher Rideout, 'Stroytelling, Narrative Rationality, and Legal Persuasion', *Legal Writing: The Journal of the Legal Writing Institute*, 14 (2008), 53–86.

[54] *Rabochaia Moskva*, 5 April 1922, 6.

[55] *Vlast' truda* [Irkutsk], 12 February 1921, reprinted in *Sibirskaia vandeia*, I, 583.

effective still. He used a mix of personal detail, emotive language, and drama to convey the real moral messages that leading Bolsheviks no doubt wished to see in all press coverage. Under the title 'The Soviet Court: To Shoot!', for instance, he described a trial in Moscow's tribunal on 2 March 1922. Two defendants were accused of theft from a factory. The first, a 19-year-old youth, was asked if he pleaded guilty and he shamelessly replied 'yes', seeing himself as a hero. The other youth was apparently an entirely different character, 'timid' and 'remorseful'. After exploring their backgrounds, the crime, and building up the tension, the report moved to the verdict. The first defendant, as an unrepentant recidivist, was sentenced to be shot; the second, as a repentant offender, to a year in prison. The audience was shaken, but the message clear: the crime harmed the factory and production, the state has (inevitably) captured the perpetrators, and revolutionary justice has considered all the circumstances. Repeat offenders cannot expect mercy.[56] This structure—story, individuals, drama, and moral tale—was repeated in Bei-vich's articles, with guilt and motivation always mentioned, however briefly.

Bei-vich was unusual, but there were a few other journalists emerging who specialized in legal matters. E. A. Finn, for example, reported on (and later wrote memoirs of) the first trials held by Petrograd's tribunal in late 1917. He worked for *Krasnaia gazeta*, *Rabochii sud*, and *Sud idet!*, as well as contributing articles on legal matters to *Izvestiia*. He later wrote books on legal issues and published a collection of legal speeches.[57] There were also a few legal officials with experience of journalism, such as V. V. Sorokin, a former editor of the 5th Army's newspaper, *Nash put'*, before chairing its military tribunal, or V. Poliakov, who had edited *My stroim* and headed a local union of printers before chairing Kursk's tribunal.[58] This experience is rarely evident in most articles, however, and any evidence of first-hand observation, sometimes in the form of informal 'impressions (*vpechatleniia*)' appended to the usual factual account or brief comments on the state of the perpetrators or mood of the audience, helped transform articles into more emotive and engaging accounts of proceedings.

Of course, the fact that most accounts could have been more engaging does not mean that no one read them or that they did not convey a message. Readers were used to this style of reporting, and the voracious demand for news is well documented. Contemporary diarists all mention seeking out newspapers and their importance as a source of information. A peasant from Vologda province, A. A. Zamarev, recorded his searches for recent newspapers and his despair when

[56] *Rabochaia Moskva*, 5 March 1922, 6.

[57] See his memoirs, E. Finn, 'Antisovetskaia pechat' na skam'e podsudimykh (Zametki sovremennika o tribunalakh po delam pechati)', *Sovetskoe gosudarstvo i pravo*, 2 (1967), 70–5; 'Pervye sovetskie narodnye sudy. Zametki zhurnalista', *Sotsialisticheskaia zakonnost'*, 11 (1967), 65–8; and 'Pervyi revoliutsionnyi tribunal', *Sovetskaia iustitsiia*, 8 (1967), 16–18; 9 (1967), 16–18; 10 (1967), 16–17.

[58] V. Sorokin, 'Na strazhe zavoevanii revoliutsii', *Sovetskaia iustitsiia*, 2 (1958), 33; GARF, f. R-1005, op. 3, d. 137, l. 4 (report to the Supreme Tribunal, 5 May 1922).

these proved futile. He read national and local papers, and welcomed the opening of a 'people's house' nearby with accessible literature.[59] Even the Bolsheviks' critics, quick to dismiss the accuracy of the press, still read papers and obtained their information on trials from press reports.[60] The Bolsheviks used the press to guide people on what was worth thinking about, and law was one of these topics, even if it was often superseded by others. If readers read papers regularly, then even the brief reports charting the activities of tribunals sent out messages about what constituted a criminal act and the shifting priorities of the state, even if the wider context and the rationale for particular punishments was absent.

What went on in a public courtroom also provided more productive material for wider dissemination than what went on behind closed doors at the Cheka. Coverage of the latter was more sporadic and even briefer—just occasional lists of who had been shot and for what—which conveyed a blunt message but could not match even the limited detail on trials. Papers could do more with the debates, speeches, and sentences emerging from revolutionary justice. Articles could, and occasionally did, explore the nature of revolutionary justice, warn against particular acts, and probe into specific crimes, both nationally and locally.

It is also not hard to imagine the flurry of reports on a major trial attracting the attention of all but the most disinterested reader. The same was true of the appearance of a tribunal itself in some areas. The arrival in Orsha of a travelling session of the Gomel' provincial tribunal serves as a good example. Up to this point, the local newspaper, *Nabat*, rarely covered the tribunal in Gomel', over 150 miles away. However, on 16 July 1919 the paper announced the session had arrived in the town a few days previously and would start holding public meetings. From then on, the paper covered the session's activities extensively with almost daily reports on the first or second pages until 27 August, when the session appears to have departed. The coverage alternated between adverts for forthcoming trials and articles on the trials 'from the hall' of the tribunal.[61] All are signed 'B', suggesting a particular reporter was responsible for reporting on the session. Most reports—in line with others—are fairly dry and factual, with the occasional educational message about the dangers of world capitalism, class enemies, or particular crimes.[62] The coverage disappeared after August as the tribunal once again became remote from local concerns, but this month-long, unusually intensive reporting must have educated readers about tribunals, the nature of counter-revolutionary crime, and the role of revolutionary justice.

[59] *Dnevnik Totemskogo krest'ianina A. A. Zamareva. 1906–1922 gg.* (Moscow, 1995), 158, 173, 186, 197, 201.

[60] For example, *Neizdannyi V. G. Korolenko. Dnevniki i zapisnye knizhki. 1919–1921. Tom 2* (Moscow, 2013), 66 (24 May 1919); and N. Okunev, *Dnevnik Moskvicha (1917–1924)* (Paris, 1990), 128 (3 January 1918), 403 (12 December 1920).

[61] The coverage stretches from *Nabat* , 16 July 1919, 2, to 27 August 1919, 2, always on pp. 1–2.

[62] *Nabat*, 23 July 1919, 2; 26 July 1919, 1; 14 August 1919, 1; 25 August 1919, 2.

Nonetheless, the issues with newspapers dominated contemporary discourse. A survey conducted in Voronezh province in 1923 noted problems accessing papers, discontent over content, format, and cost, and difficulties in understanding them. There was too much on the party and too many confusing words. From a legal perspective, a worrying number of people still did not understand what the state meant by even basic terms like 'class enemy', with some believing it was some type of party or simply people who opposed class.[63] Other studies of readers in the 1920s highlighted the dichotomy between the content of papers and what people actually wanted to read.[64] People needed to be not just literate but politically literate to understand new revolutionary language. This, it has been argued, meant newspapers favoured existing and emerging political elites or, at best, the politically active.[65]

It is clear, therefore, that Lenin, Trotskii, and others were correct to worry about how trials were reported. Too many reports were short or bland—perhaps inevitably given the cursory nature of many trials—and little could be learned from a few lines on crimes and sentences. Many reports failed to utilize the drama of the courtroom effectively to draw in readers, and messages were non-existent, unclear, or implied, contrasting sharply with the blunt, explicit language used by Lenin and others in their published speeches and articles.

Images of Justice

Images also turned out to be a problematic means of communicating revolutionary justice. Mass photography was still in the future, few publications were capable of printing photos regularly, and those that survive usually come from specialist publications or depict prominent trials. As a result, few images of 'everyday' tribunals exist. Political posters were printed in huge numbers and displayed throughout urban and rural Russia in a variety of ways, but their focus was on class enemies and counter-revolution more generally. Caricatures and cartoons used similar techniques but also appeared sporadically in the press, rarely focused on law, and then only on a few major trials. Newsreels were starting to demonstrate the potential of film but faced technical barriers, and they were again an option only for a few trials. Nevertheless, all these appeared under state sponsorship and were created to promote a particular image of revolutionary justice, so they still form part of broader attempts to publicize law, even if the actual audience is not always clear.

[63] Ia. Shafir, *Gazeta i derevnia* (Moscow, 1923), 32, 41, 61, 64, 72, 95, 142–5.
[64] J. Brooks, 'Studies of the Reader in the 1920s', *Russian History*, 9, 2–3 (1982), 187–202.
[65] J. Brooks, *Thank You Comrade Stalin! Soviet Public Culture from Revolution to Cold War* (Princeton, 2000), 12–13.

The earliest images came from the first trial— Countess S. V. Panina in Petrograd in December 1917. One photograph shows Panina at the back of the court with the doors guarded by two soldiers. Several people are seated at desks in front of her, while the camera looks over the heads of the audience. Everyone is looking to the left of the photo, presumably at the judges, who are not visible, and there is a certain formality, not least with some people in suits and one (possibly Panina's lawyer) writing notes.[66] Another photograph shows the judges. As seen in Figure 4.2, these well-dressed figures, the majority in 'bourgeois' suits and ties, are sitting behind a table with papers, books, and paperweights, which also conveys a sense of formality.[67] The supposed 'anti-theatrical theatricality' of these early courts, where participants took pains to demolish theatrically the formalities of the old legal system in favour of a new, proletarian justice, is complicated by these images.[68] Some aspects had changed, but other elements convey continuity with 'normal' and formal expectations of legal procedure, no doubt to reinforce the legitimacy and authority of the court.

Most of these images were clearly staged, of course, and none more so than in a trial of clergy in Saratov where the audience have turned to face the camera behind them. But this just reinforces the importance attached to conveying an objective, regulated justice (as represented by papers, books, and a sense of procedure) rather than an arbitrary, subjective justice. The photo from Saratov shows an orderly and structured court with smartly dressed judges and lawyers examining papers.[69] A photo of the department of justice in Cherepovets consisted of young, suited men standing behind a table with books, papers, and a bell.[70] A group portrait of a military tribunal in the Volga consists of two members in suits and others dressed smartly or in uniform, while two hold folders, implying official papers.[71] Some courts are more informal, whether self-consciously or through practical necessity, while some take pains to showcase their revolutionary nature through a portrait of Marx or Lenin or by hanging the red flag.[72] Yet later 'model'

[66] Occidental College Special Collections and College Archives, Bessie Beatty Papers, at http://callimachus.org/digital/collection/p16061coll38/id/134/rec/114 [accessed 12 March 2020]. There are various photos available throughout the civil war of the 'enemy' under guard, thereby emphasizing the punitive element of revolutionary justice, although these are usually obvious class enemies such as Panina; see, for example, the images of arrested clergy in *Sledstvennoe delo Patriarkha Tikhona: Sbornik dokumentov po materialam Tsentral'nogo arkhiva FSB RF* (Moscow, 2000), 416–17.

[67] Occidental College Special Collections and College Archives, Bessie Beatty Papers, at http://callimachus.org/digital/collection/p16061coll38/id/131/rec/158 [12 March 2020].

[68] Cassiday, *Enemy on Trial*, 37.

[69] A. Mramornov (ed.), *Sudebnyi protsess protiv Saratovskogo dukhovenstva v 1918–1919 gg.* (Saratov, 2013), front cover.

[70] GARF, f. A-353, op. 5, d. 18, ll. 203–4 (photograph from 1921).

[71] *Energiia mechty. K 100-letiiu Velikoi rossiiskoi revoliutsii* (Moscow, 2017), 91.

[72] W. Sunderland, *The Baron's Coat: A History of the Russian Empire in War and Revolution* (Ithaca, 2014), 219; A. Galkin, 'Pervyi tribunal (Vospominaniia), *Rabochii sud*, 21 (1927), 1653–4; and the various photos in *Na strazhe sotsialisticheskoi zakonnosti (50 let voennym tribunalam)* (Moscow, 1968), 130, 135, 140, 153.

and 'show' trials, such as those of Admiral Kolchak's ministers in 1920 in Omsk or Metropolitan Veniamin in 1922 in Petrograd, see continuity triumph over change: formal rooms and layouts create more of an impression than the revolutionary symbols above the judges or any banners in the audience.[73]

The most extensive photographic coverage of a trial before 1922 appears to be that of former commissar, P. E. Dybenko, in May 1918. The Photography and Film Committee of the People's Commissariat of Enlightenment (Narkompros) commissioned a record of Soviet life in 1918 that included photos showing Dybenko in court, the judges arriving (looking more informal than in other photos, with two dressed in typical Bolshevik leather jackets), Dybenko speaking, witness testimony, Krylenko addressing the court, and the audience awaiting the verdict.[74] The most intriguing depict the court environment, conveying a formal atmosphere in one respect, with people taking notes, papers scattered across tables, and a suited Krylenko delivering the prosecution's case (Figure 6.1), but also revealing some of the informalities associated with the new courts, not least the audience pushing forward as they strained to hear the verdict (Figure 4.3). In portraying formality and informality alongside continuity and change, photographs aimed to convey that revolutionary justice was just as authoritative as before but now served the interests of a different class.

Dybenko's trial was also unusual as it was the first trial with film footage, apparently commissioned at the same time as the photos. The footage featured in the first edition of the weekly newsreel *Kino-Nedelia* on 20 May 1918, which included the future director, Dziga Vertov, as part of its working collective.[75] The coverage consisted of one and a half minutes (from a total of seven minutes for the edition) shot outside the court.[76] The members of the tribunal were shown—all suited or in long jackets—with a focus on the chairman, Ia. L. Berman. The lawyers (also suited) were introduced, as was the defendant, who entered alongside four others, including two sailors. Dybenko was also seen smoking inside, and there was a short clip of him in the war. The footage was staged, with the individuals stopping as they entered, staring at the camera and joking. There were no shots from inside the courtroom, either because the authorities did not want to film a trial live at this stage (even without sound) or because it was too cumbersome to film in the relatively small courtroom.

[73] See the images in S. Drokov, 'Sud na atamanovskom khutore', *Belaia armiia. Beloe delo*, 7 (2000), 73; and https://humus.livejournal.com/6581735.html [accessed 16 October 2019].

[74] Getty Research Institute, 97.R.36, box 1, photos 114–21. I am very grateful to George Levy for alerting me to their existence. For the background to the collection, see M., Khrustaleva, 'Cursed Days: The Getty Collection of Soviet Photographs from 1918', *Women East-West*, 7, 2 (2018), available at https://files.constantcontact.com/f916d256201/6e22b05a-acb7-46c4-a98a-2e939469d356.pdf [accessed 12 March 2020].

[75] For background details on *Kino-Nedelia* (1918–19), see J. Mackay, *Dziga Vertov: Life and Work. Volume 1: 1896–1921* (Brighton, MA, 2018), 194–7, 210–28.

[76] See https://www.youtube.com/watch?v=sygQ59ySZLs [accessed 12 March 2020]. The coverage is from 3:43 to 5:12, and I am again indebted to George Levy for pointing me towards this film.

Figure 6.1 The prosecutor, N. V. Krylenko, at the trial of P. E. Dybenko, May 1918.
Source: Getty Research Institute, Los Angeles (97.R.36).

All of this was typical for newsreels—Russian or otherwise—during this period. Most focused on topics for around a minute, with short intertitles introducing the characters and scenes briefly, and trials had been covered in this manner before, with those involved in the trial of General V. A. Sukhomlinov for treason in September 1917 captured on film for the revolutionary newsreel *Svobodnaia Rossiia*.[77] The novelty of film, all revolutionaries believed, had the potential to mobilize new audiences. Demanding more newsreels, A. V. Lunacharskii, Commissar of Narkompros, argued that good cinema not only spreads ideas but prompts an emotional response, facilitating engagement and mobilization. According to him, Lenin agreed on cinema's importance, noting that as a 'visual newspaper' it added a sense of reality to ideas,[78] while Trotskii declared that it 'attracts, enlightens, strikes the imagination'.[79] It promised to spread easily comprehensible 'truths' to millions.

Although there were sometimes only 5–10 copies of a newsreel for the entire country due to a chronic shortage of film,[80] more people watched newsreels than

[77] Mackay, *Dziga Vertov*, 205–6, 209–10.

[78] A. Lunacharskii, 'The Tasks of the State Cinema in the RSFSR (1919)' and 'Anatolii Lunacharskii: Conversations with Lenin (1925)', in R. Taylor and I. Christie (eds.), *The Film Factory: Russian and Soviet Cinema in Documents, 1896–1939* (London, 1988), 47, 57.

[79] L. Trotskii, 'Vodka, tserkov' i kinomatograf', *Pravda*, 12 July 1923, 2.

[80] Kenez, *Birth of the Propaganda State*, 109.

conventional films during this period, and they formed a central part of Bolshevik agitation, particularly when combined with short agitational films. Agitational trains and boats all had cinemas, one of which held 800–900 people. One train trip recorded 116,000 attending 97 screenings in summer 1919; another 32,750 viewing 34 screenings. In all, it has been estimated that over 2.2 million attended almost 2,000 film showings in five trains and one boat as they travelled across Russia's provinces in 1918–20, with films prompting applause and debate. Most of the 700,000 who watched films in the 'October Revolution' train in 1919–20 had never seen film before.[81] The same is probably true of soldiers in the Red Army, where the number of cinemas more than doubled from 102 at the end of 1918 to 220 in early 1920.[82]

The format of newsreels, however, while interesting for providing images of those involved, was unable to fulfil the educational role of courts alone. Newsreels were a 'screen newspaper' in a sense, with images of current 'news' designed to educate and mobilize, and were particularly useful for the illiterate. But short intertitles and restricted shots could convey very little about trials. By its very existence the coverage of Dybenko's trial stated that this was 'news', but the intertitles only introduced the participants and were silent on the allegations and the sentence. This either suggested that viewers were expected to know of these individuals already and the purpose of the film was to bring this knowledge to life, or, if not, that the film was to prompt them to search for information.[83] This is not to say that newsreels were only illustrating newspapers—something denied strongly recently[84]—but they were nevertheless expected to work in conjunction with the press, while retaining a distinct form.

The fact that trials were too complex to be conveyed effectively on film may explain why so few were covered in newsreels. One survey has calculated that 63 per cent of the coverage of *Kino-Nedelia* was of political figures, which aimed to provide the party with a human face and make the Bolsheviks appear 'real' to viewers. This focus on leadership and the state also aimed to convey a sense of authority as well as the Bolsheviks as agents of revolutionary progress.[85] By contrast, trials and legal proceedings took up 9 per cent of the coverage, appearing

[81] See V. Karpinskii (ed.), *Agitparpoezda VTsIK* (Moscow, 1920), 18; L. Maksakova, *Agitpoezd 'Oktiabr'skaia revoliutsiia' (1919–1920)* (Moscow, 1956), 14, 30, 32, 171–2; and R. Argenbright, 'The Soviet Agitational Vehicle: State Power on the Social Frontier', *Political Geography*, 17, 3 (1998), 259–62.

[82] V. Kolychev, *Partiino-politicheskaia rabota v krasnoi armii v gody grazhdanskoi voiny 1918–1920* (Moscow, 1979), 145.

[83] As one scholar has noted, all newsreels were at the end of the 'news chain', completing the picture by showing audiences what newspapers had been discussing, with the focus on the visual; L. McKernan, 'Newsreels: Form and Function', in R. Howells and R. Matson (eds.), *Using Visual Evidence* (Maidenhead, 2009), 96.

[84] Mackay, *Dziga Vertov*, 212, 223.

[85] G. Roberts, *Forward Soviet! History and Non-fiction Film in the USSR* (London, 1999), 15–21.

in four newsreels.[86] As well as Dybenko's trial, there were twenty seconds in the third edition on 15 June 1918 on the 'revolutionary tribunal' investigating the murder of two Kadet politicians. Apart from the fact that there was no trial in this instance, the footage was even less informative than for Dybenko, simply showing several people standing in the snow, presumably at the time of the crime in January, and the two accused sailors smoking.[87] This edition also covered a murder case, while the fourteenth edition reported on the opening of Moscow's regional people's court, including its building and composition.

There was also a short agitational film, also involving Vertov, on the trial of the Red Army commander F. K. Mironov, in October 1919. Prefaced by several (for the time) lengthy intertitles explaining Mironov's alleged revolt against Soviet power, the film showed footage of captured soldiers, Mironov's lawyers, Mironov travelling to court, and a large crowd of observers outside, before the key figures entered the courtroom (some acknowledging the camera) followed by the audience (soldiers). Intertitles clarify each stage of the process and the camera enters the court with snapshots of the key figures speaking, unlike the footage from Dybenko's trial. The film finished by stating that Mironov was sentenced to death before being granted mercy by the highest authorities on account of his previous service to the revolution.[88] One scholar has noted that the speakers talk in front of a convenient white background, which aids the quality of the footage and suggests either the filming of the trial was a priority or some of the speeches were later re-enacted for the camera.[89] In any case, this was the longest (at just over eight minutes) and most comprehensive film of a trial to date, and it managed to convey—as far as was possible with the technology—the trial's narrative and complemented the press coverage.

It is probably no coincidence, therefore, that this footage was recycled into Vertov's multireel 'History of the Civil War' in 1921, while the Dybenko coverage did not even make it into his 'Anniversary of the Revolution' in late 1918.[90] There also do not appear to have been any fictional agitational films from 1918 to 1922 on trials, although some stories focused on counter-revolutionary crimes such as desertion, stressing the need to overcome 'darkness' and a 'lack of consciousness'.[91] The difficulties of filming trials—real or fictional—effectively, along with other priorities, may explain why it took several years for film to return to court.

[86] Mackay, *Dziga Vertov*, 213. Forty-three editions of *Kino-Nedelia* were made from May 1918 to June 1919. I have viewed the eighteen editions available online, but a detailed list of the contents of all the editions is in *Sovetskaia kinokhronika, 1918–1925 gg. Annotirovannyi katalog. Chast' 1: Kinozhurnaly* (Moscow, 1965), 9–38.

[87] See https://www.youtube.com/watch?v=q1SijySldBk, 5:42–6:02 [accessed 12 March 2020].

[88] See https://www.youtube.com/watch?v=WBtIRMH6h7g [accessed 12 March 2020].

[89] J. Hicks, *Dziga Vertov: Defining Documentary Film* (London, 2007), 26.

[90] Mackay, *Dziga Vertov*, 228; S. Ishevskaya, 'The Intertitles of Dziga Vertov's *Anniversary of the Revolution*', *Studies in Russian and Soviet Cinema*, 13, 1 (2019), 18–39.

[91] *Sovetskie khudozhestvennye fil'my. Annotirovannyi katalog. Tom I. Nemye fil'my (1918–1935)* (Moscow, 1961), 5–37 (see especially the entry for 'Deserters (1919)' on 9–10).

After *Kino-Nedelia* ended in 1919, Vertov worked on various projects before helping to launch a more ambitious newsreel in 1922—*Kino-Pravda*, literally 'cinema truth'. Twenty-three editions were produced before it finished in 1925.[92] Consciously intended as a cinematic newspaper or film version of *Pravda*, it also served as a vehicle for Vertov and others to experiment with their view that film could be used to reveal a deeper level of insight and 'truth' than other media. By capturing an event on film in a particular way, Vertov argued, the film-maker was determining and ensuring its historical and social value; in short, filming an event emphasized its significance. Attention was paid to the thematic unity of the film, to the 'reality' of life laid bare by the camera in all its forms, and to the intertitles, a necessary evil in the absence of other means of explanation.[93] Poor material conditions, particularly a lack of funding, led Vertov to complain that the state did not assign enough importance to newsreel but, although there is no evidence so far to draw a direct link, *Kino-Pravda* conveniently started just in time to film the largest trial to date (that of the SRs) and, in doing so, significantly extended the existing limited experiences of filming trials (see the final section in this chapter).

As a 'mechanically reproducible art form', enabling an identical message to be spread countless times across Russia's expanse, film was supposed to supersede the unique theatrical performance for agitational purposes.[94] Yet, ironically, the theatre proved more effective in *engaging* the public in revolutionary justice. This was not through 'traditional' plays, although many of those involved in theatre aimed to place its educational capabilities in the service of the socialist revolution.[95] The same was true of circus and puppet shows, both of which used accessible performances to denounce the revolution's enemies.[96] But these all involved the audience *watching* rather than *engaging*, and there is little evidence that any addressed law specifically rather than focusing more broadly on enemies.

Instead, revolutionary justice was addressed directly and engagingly through theatrical agitational trials.[97] Drawing on the pre-revolutionary tradition of moral and didactic plays alongside the inherent theatricality of the courtroom and the

[92] Roberts, *Forward, Soviet*, 21–7. For the contents, see *Sovetskaia kinokhronika*, 41–6. Twenty-two episodes are available at https://vertov.filmmuseum.at/en/film_online/kino-pravda [accessed 12 March 2020].

[93] See various articles in *Kino-Eye: The Writings of Dziga Vertov*, edited by A. Michelson (Berkeley, 1984), 10–11, 32–3, 41.

[94] Cassiday, *Enemy on Trial*, 22–4.

[95] See V. Kerzhentsev, *Tvorcheskii teatr. Puti sotsialisticheskogo teatra* (3rd edition, Moscow, 1919), esp. 75–80.

[96] A. Gérin, *Devastation and Laughter: Satire, Power and Culture in the Early Soviet State, 1920s-1930s* (Toronto, 2018), 77–9; C. Kelly, *Petrushka: The Russian Carnival Puppet Theatre* (Cambridge, 1990), 189–94.

[97] This paragraph draws heavily on the relevant sections of Cassiday, *Enemies on Trial*, esp. 15–19, 51–8; R. Stites, 'Trial as Theatre in the Russian Revolution', *Theatre Research International*, 23, 1 (1998), 7–13; and especially E. Wood, *Performing Justice: Agitation Trials in Early Soviet Russia* (Ithaca, 2005).

idealistic plans of activists for 'living' newspapers,[98] agit-trials took their early Soviet form in the Red Army at some stage during the middle of the civil war. Political commissars sought to mobilize soldiers bored with the usual meetings and lectures and used the courtroom scenario to attract soldiers. 'Trials' dealt with current 'crimes', whether hooliganism, alcoholism, or desertion, with the aim of mobilizing the audience in support. Scripts were published and circulated that covered characters, narratives, and how to set up the court and mimic legal procedure. Much relied on improvisation and local circumstances, though, allowing local actors to adapt characters and to adopt local events as part of the grander narrative. They were cheap and easy to organize, and could focus on any crime. Such trials were advertised as 'courts' and were often barely distinct from real courts in terms of their structure and educational message. By encouraging audience participation, they aimed to break down the barriers between the stage and real life. As the civil war progressed, more 'political' issues were covered, including counter-revolutionary enemies such as the Whites, General P. N. Vrangel' and the Kronstadt rebels.

Hundreds of thousands of spectators probably attended agit-trials during the civil war as a novel form of entertainment,[99] and audiences apparently participated enthusiastically during this initial period. Organizers hoped to foster revolutionary consciousness and a greater legal consciousness, as 'trials' were concerned not just with 'laws' but with the moral and social wrong committed by the crime and the rationale behind an appropriate sentence. In watching and participating in agit-trials, people should learn to 'act Bolshevik'.[100] Observers agreed, invariably reporting a large, engaged, and enthusiastic audience.[101] One agit-trial transformed a passive audience into a 'living, thinking' collective, according to one report.[102] But while there is no doubt that agit-trials provided a more flexible format for exploring revolutionary justice than other means of communication, there is no evidence to suggest that Narkomiust or local legal officials were involved in them. Agit-trials tended to be organized by local party activists with their own concerns that may or may not have coincided with the objectives of those directly involved in the law. Until 1922, moreover, agit-trials focused on abstract concepts or enemies who were never subjected to a real trial (such as Vrangel'). It was only with the trial of the SRs that agit-trials started to re-enact actual trials (see the final section in this chapter).

[98] See V. Burecharskii, *Zhivaia gazeta. Rukovodstvo dlia agitatorov, zhurnalistov i rabotnikov ROSTA* (Kazan', 1920); and Gérin, *Devastation and Laughter*, 86–8.

[99] Cassiday, *Enemies on Trial*, 55.

[100] Wood, *Performing Justice*, 10.

[101] For example, 'Sud nad Leninym', *Pravda*, 22 April 1920, 2; 'Sud nad sovetskoi vlast'iu', *Pravda*, 21 December 1920, 2; 'Sud nad R.K.P.', *Pravda*, 18 February 1921, 2; and the detailed guidance for a trial of Vrangel', 'Instsenirovka agitatsionnykh sudov', *Vestnik agitatsii i propagandy*, 25 November 1920, 25–7.

[102] 'Sud nad Leninym', 2.

Photographs, films, and agit-trials, however, were all dwarfed in scale by the circulation figures of 'political' posters. Across the civil war, as many as 10 million copies of over 3,600 different posters were produced, particularly in the Red Army, but involving 453 different state institutions in 76 different cities and towns.[103] Displayed as flyers posted on the walls of workplaces, reading rooms, and other public spaces, published in journals and even painted on the side of agitational trains, they became the chief means of reaching the illiterate population as well as reinforcing key messages for everyone. Using simple and uncompromising images with minimal reliance on text, these posters visualized the criminals targeted by tribunals, whether former officers, well-fed capitalists and kulaks or bandits, thieves and bribe-takers, and—most importantly—urged proactive attacks to remove their corrosive influence.

Posters focusing specifically on revolutionary justice seem to be rare, though, with the vast majority concentrating on military or other political themes. The best known, entitled 'The People's Court', was created in 1919 by Dmitrii Moor, one of the most famous poster artists, with 125,000 copies printed (Figure 3.11).[104] More allegorical than specific, it portrays a soldier, peasant, and worker forcing a long line of familiar enemies (with short descriptions) into a queue under the banner of 'long live the soviets'. The figures are both symbolic (the bourgeoisie, the capitalists dragging their gold and holding factories, the secret police, and international monarchies) and specific, but, with the exception of V. M. Purishkevich and I. G. Shcheglovitov (who was depicted pushing the laws of the old regime), none of the figures actually faced trial but instead represented threats (General A. I. Denikin and Admiral A. V. Kolchak), former political opponents (A. F. Kerenskii, E. K. Breshko-Breshkovskaia, P. N. Miliukov, and A. I. Guchkov) and demonized figures from the old regime (A. D. Protopopov, I. L. Goremykin, and others). This poster, then, is less a portrayal of courts and more another symbolic representation of the revolutionary regime's power over its enemies and, indeed, of the overthrow of traditional power relations. Still, it was republished elsewhere and reinforced the messages about enemies facing the wrath of revolutionary justice.[105]

The poster—as with so many others—was also a satirical attack on the absurdities of the old world. Taking a variety of forms, from the visual satirical poster,

[103] For various statistics, see S. White, *The Bolshevik Poster* (New Haven, 1988), vi, 40, 43, 91, 109–10.

[104] HIA, Poster collection, RU/SU 63 (https://digitalcollections.hoover.org/objects/25235) [accessed 8 February 2019]; B. Butnik-Siverskii, *Sovetskii plakat epokhi grazhdanskoi voiny 1918–1921* (Moscow, 1960), 205. This print run has been described as 'very large' and 'enormous' in comparison with other posters: White, *Bolshevik Poster*, 94; and V. Bonnell, *Iconography of Power: Soviet Political Posters under Lenin and Stalin* (Berkeley and Los Angeles, 1997), 204. The poster was certainly well known to contemporaries; V. Polonskii, *Russkii revoliutsionnyi plakat* (Moscow, 1925), 73.

[105] Moor contributed to various publications and *Krasnoarmeets*, a journal aimed at soldiers, printed this poster as a detachable and expandable endpiece (10–15 (1919)). This journal itself had a print run later of 1,000 (40–41 (1921), 32).

cartoon, or caricature to textual stories, songs, and poems, satire worked alongside 'serious' texts to increase the emotional response. Although these forms often merged into one another, and were sometimes hard to distinguish from non-satirical images or texts, they all intended to use humour or parody to reveal inconsistencies or threats, and thus to discredit, destroy, and highlight unacceptable behaviour and beliefs. By using humour and pushing the boundaries of reality, artists hoped to fuel emotions like indignation and hatred, while deconstructing and laughing at threats demonstrated superiority over them.[106]

The civil-war period saw several short-lived satirical journals appear in limited print runs, but cartoons and caricatures were also evident in the mainstream press, with *Pravda*, for instance, publishing some, as well as various local newspapers. Indeed, the initial coverage of the Purishkevich Affair in November 1917 was accompanied by a cartoon in *Pravda* depicting the various monarchists, industrialists, officers, and a priest allegedly involved in the plot enjoying a 'Last Supper', toasting a portrait of Nicholas II (Figure 3.1).[107] The exaggerated nature of the cartoon, almost identical to the poster, lent itself to the vivid and emotional depiction of enemies to discredit them. Here, the parody of the last supper mocked the plotters, discrediting and ridiculing them. However, as with posters, depictions of specific trials rather than generalized enemies were rare prior to the trial of the SRs. Moor's 'The People's Court' was essentially satire, inverting the traditional social order by showing the lower classes wielding power over former elites, and creating, as one scholar noted, a parody of former monarchical or religious ceremonies by having them all march along in line to face justice. Similarly, as in a caricature, their features are exaggerated and ridiculed.[108]

The potential of satire was increasingly appreciated as the civil war progressed. In June 1922, the most famous satirical journal, *Krokodil*, emerged. This started life as a weekly supplement of *Rabochii* (later *Rabochaia gazeta*) before transforming into a separate journal later in the year. Like other such journals, it was a 'transmedia' or 'multimedia' production, as different types of media (images, texts, photographs), different genres (journalistic, satirical, literary), and different registers (formal, colloquial) came together and, in the case of a major story, all contributed something distinct to its telling.[109] This constituted a dramatic alternative to the dull and predictable format of the mainstream press. It also covered a vast range of subjects given cohesion by a general desire to unmask the threats to communism. Like *Kino-Pravda*, its emergence conveniently coincided with the trial of the SRs, and its coverage, as will be seen below, provided an example of

[106] See Gérin, *Devastation and Laughter*, 9–13, 33–4. For a brief history of satire in 1917–18, see T. Filippova, 'Satiricheskaia periodicheskaia pechat'', in *Rossiia v 1917 godu. Entsiklopediia* (Moscow, 2017), 860–4.

[107] *Pravda*, 8 November 1917, 3.

[108] Gérin, *Devastation and Laughter*, 50, 127–9, 132, 136.

[109] J. Etty, *Graphic Satire in the Soviet Union: Krokodil's Political Cartoons* (Jackson, 2019), 12, 47, 55–6, 125.

how these journals could extend that provided by the press, combining a variety of methods to spread the educational message of the trial.

Less innovatively, Moor produced a drawing of a specific trial for *Krokodil*, entitled 'The Depot' (Figure 6.2), depicting trains rushing chaotically into a depot (the tribunal) from all directions, making a head-on crash inevitable. Ostensibly this referred to a major trial of 133 railway workers for corruption and bribery at a time when economic concerns were being prioritized during the New Economic Policy (NEP). Yet the caption, 'all roads lead to . . . the revolutionary tribunal', was surely intended to be read as a much broader, menacing message to all criminals that their crimes would have consequences. It also reinforced the content of numerous decrees from this period (especially concerning economic matters), all of which used the threat of a tribunal to compel people to adhere to the regulations.

Although satire could be hard to comprehend, often requiring contextual knowledge, the message in the above forms of art usually remained clearer than elsewhere in the art world. The creation of Narkompros after October 1917 had seen modernist, avant-garde art come to prominence as many artists sought a *revolutionary* form of art suitable for the new world. Yet many of their experiments were incomprehensible to the public and, consequently, distrusted by Bolshevik leaders for their lack of agitational value. Realist depictions of the revolution took a back seat to symbolic representations, even if artists like Boris Kustodiev demonstrated how 'traditional' paintings could provide accessible portrayals of revolutionary events and Bolshevik power.[110] As a result, there were almost no artistic depictions of revolutionary justice and the rare exception illustrated some of the other problems involved. In 1919, Ivan Vladimirov painted a scene showing a landlord and a priest condemned to death by a tribunal (Figure 6.3). Yet the scene was ambiguous. The condemned can be viewed as hateful 'class enemies' or 'dignified victims'. The tribunal is either sweeping away the remnants of the exploitative old world (also represented by a broken violin and religious icon) or an improvised form of arbitrary violence. The requisitioned chairs illustrated the informality of the court, but empty wine bottles and rubbish suggested drunken lawlessness. This ambiguity is unsurprising when considering the artist's own balancing act: anti-Bolshevik at heart, but recognizing their hold on power; needing to avoid censure, but also needing to sell to both sides to survive as the art market collapsed during the civil war.[111]

Whether any of these images were influential is difficult to ascertain. There is little evidence on exactly how photographs were used, never mind how people

[110] For more, see *Revolution: Russian Art, 1917–1932* (London, 2017); and P. Kachurin, *Making Modernism Soviet: The Russian Avant-Garde in the Early Soviet Era, 1918–1928* (Evanston, 2013).

[111] E. Danielson, 'The Imagery of Ivan A. Vladimirov in the Hoover Archives: But is it Art?', *Slavic & East European Information Resources*, 19, 3–4 (2018), 159–74.

Figure 6.2 The Depot (1922).
Source: *Krokodil*, 15 (27), 3 December 1922, 16.

Figure 6.3 A Landlord and a Priest Condemned to Death by the Revolutionary Tribunal (1919).
Source: Painting 10, Ivan Alekseevich Vladimirov paintings, Box 2, Hoover Institution Archives.

reacted to them, and while millions may have watched newsreels, the testimony of their enthusiastic reaction comes from those officials with a vested interest to say as much. Posters were omnipresent across Russia during this period but, again, there is no firm evidence on how people reacted and whether they saw them as anything other than the background to everyday life.[112] While more innovative and engaging than newspapers, satirical journals required too much political literacy and existing knowledge to reach all the population. *Krokodil*, indeed, only intended to target politically aware workers, like its parent paper, *Rabochii*.[113] This was demonstrated when an activist showed later editions to peasant women in Voronezh; they enjoyed the caricatures but did not understand a single one properly. He suggested the images needed to be more like the traditional *lubok* to have a larger impact.[114] Yet, ultimately, the messages in images like Moor's two drawings seem accessible and, when images worked in tandem

[112] For a fascinating study of Soviet theories of the viewer, see M. Arbuthnot, 'The People and the Poster: Theorizing the Soviet Viewer, 1920-1931', *Slavic Review*, 78, 3 (2019), 717-37.
[113] Gérin, *Devastation and Laughter*, 62, 73.
[114] Shafir, *Gazeta i derevnia*, 67, 144. The *lubok* was a simpler form of print, less capable of conveying detailed political messages; see S. Norris, *A War of Images: Russian Popular Prints, Wartime Culture and National Identity, 1812–1945* (DeKalb, 2006).

with texts, as was the case with the newsreels and in *Krokodil*, they must have spread the educational message of courts to a wider audience.

The Trial of the Socialist Revolutionaries

By 1922, there were signs that the various means for publicizing revolutionary justice were coming together more systematically as the emphasis on 'model' and 'show' trials grew. There had been high-profile trials before, of course, but, while there were increasing levels of organization behind these trials, this usually focused on selecting the defendants, formulating the case, and guiding the trial rather than managing the publicity, even if these trials were reported on extensively. A case in point was the trial of Kolchak's ministers in Omsk in May 1920. The published documents reveal that senior officials discussed everything from the investigation, defendants, and lawyers to the location of the trial, the audience, and the sentence. But while the tribunal's chairman, A. G. Goikhbarg, and another judge wrote newspaper articles, there is no evidence of a coordinated publicity campaign.[115]

This had changed by May 1922 as preparations for two unrelated trials gathered pace. The first, the trial of Metropolitan Veniamin in June–July, saw clear concerns about publicity expressed during the preparations. The trial was part of a broader campaign against the Church that had intensified as the state attempted to confiscate church valuables, ostensibly to fund famine-relief measures, and the Church resisted what it saw as arbitrary seizures of holy items. There had been a campaign against the Church more broadly in the press, while the clergy had been one of the revolution's traditional enemies since the October Revolution, but the Bolsheviks feared this campaign had died down, nationally and locally, and felt there was insufficient coverage of the forthcoming trial.[116] Trotskii was tasked by the Politburo to instruct the editors of Moscow's newspapers to pay immediate attention to the trial and, in particular, the 'crimes' of the Church hierarchy. Trotskii promptly dispatched a blistering note to the editors of *Izvestiia*, *Pravda*, and *Rabochaia Moskva* that started by expressing his sheer disbelief over the lack of coverage despite the excellent opportunity provided by the trial to convey the state's anti-religious message. He then ordered the editors to devote significant space to the trial over the following weekend and told them what to argue: that the investigation had revealed a centralized, counter-revolutionary organization that was acting against the people while hidden behind the façade of religious belief;

[115] *Protsess nad Kolchakovskimi ministrami. Mai 1920* (Moscow, 2003), 12–41, 440–2; and *Izvestiia*, 22 June 1920, 1; 25 June 1920, 1; 26 June 1920, 1. Also V. Poznanskii, 'Sud nad ministrami Kolchaka', *Izvestiia Sibirskogo otdeleniia akademii nauk SSSR. Seriia istorii, filologii i filosofii*, 1 (1990), 44–51.

[116] *Arkhivy Kremlia. Politbiuro i tserkov' 1922–1925 gg.* (2 volumes, Moscow, 1997–8), I, 253 (meeting of the presidium of the GPU, 3 May 1922).

and that Church leaders used the Church's wealth to fund an international monarchist plot and associated propaganda rather than to provide aid to starving people. These leaders needed to be brought to justice and, Trotskii added ominously, the editors would also be held to account if these orders were not followed.[117] Needless to say, the three papers all ran articles on the Church and the trial that weekend.[118] Once started, the trial then received extensive publicity and numerous photographs survive.

The second and better known trial of 1922 was that of the SRs in June–August. Just as all elements of the trial process—accusations, defendants, lawyers—were decided by the highest political authorities (see Chapter 4), so too was the publicity. But what was particularly notable was the scale of the coverage and its variety. All the media discussed above were used to create an unprecedented, coordinated agitational campaign. The educational potential of the trial was appreciated from the start—the editor of *Izvestiia*, Iu. M. Steklov, was involved in the initial discussions—but plans for publicizing the trial at home and abroad gathered pace from early May. The commission leading the process agreed on 6 May to instruct the editors of *Pravda*, *Izvestiia*, *Rabochaia Moskva*, and *Rabochii* to start preparing the widest possible campaign on the trial immediately. Senior Bolsheviks like N. I. Bukharin and Radek were tasked with writing articles attacking the international supporters of the SRs, especially their foreign lawyers. The commission advised publishing proclamations on the trial and photos of the victims of SR 'terrorist' acts, mainly M. S. Uritskii and V. Volodarskii but also other civil-war casualties.[119] A subsidiary commission tasked with overseeing the agitational campaign met for the first time on 12 May, discussing publications, print runs, and responsibilities in detail. From then, the publicity campaign was in full swing. Further meetings discussed 'counter-propaganda' abroad, an illustrated volume, special brochures, posters, biographies of Bolshevik victims, and preparing material on the trial for the press.[120]

The level of control stands out. Meetings even discussed suitable slogans to accompany the campaign and these were finalized on 2 June, and some of these—most obviously, slogans targeting foreign advocates, linking the SRs with foreign powers and with terror, and denouncing the SRs as enemies of the proletarian state—are evident throughout the press coverage.[121] But the level of thought also stands out as senior Bolsheviks debated the most effective means of publicity.

[117] *Arkhivy Kremlia*, I, 199 (meeting of the Politburo, 4 May 1922), 254–5 (letter to editors, 4 May 1922).

[118] *Izvestiia*, 6 May 1922, 1; 7 May 1922, 3; *Pravda*, 6 May 1922, 1–2, 4; 7 May 1922, 1–2; and *Rabochaia Moskva*, 6 May 1922, 2; 7 May 1922, 2.

[119] *Sudebnyi protsess nad sotsialistami-revoliutsionerami (iiun'-avgust 1922 g.)* (Moscow, 2002), 396, 728 (protocol of the leadership committee).

[120] *Sudebnyi protsess*, 401–5, 412–18 (various protocols of the agitational committee, 12 May–3 June 1922).

[121] *Sudebnyi protsess*, 414–15 (protocol of the agitational committee).

Trotskii, for instance, was keen to see a more nuanced approach, less of the 'shrieking and cursing' of earlier articles and more on the 'heroic' period in the SRs' history in order to achieve the trial's goals of isolating the leadership, discrediting the party's recent actions, and winning over the rank and file rather than alienating them.[122] All of this, furthermore, was intended to guide Bolshevik party members in their own efforts to publicize the trial. A briefing document on 19 May advised local party committees on the trial's most important goals, while guidance was also published in the party's journal for activists.[123] Party organs mobilized the local press, held lectures, and organized factory meetings and other activities. Efforts to mobilize workers gathered pace in late May with the organization of the 'popular' protests that greeted the arrival in Russia of the foreign defence lawyers.[124]

On 7 June, the day before the trial started, the agitational committee met to discuss how to proceed during the trial. They stressed the need to link agitation to the trial, no doubt feeling that the coverage needed to reflect themes being discussed at that time in the trial and provide evidence for the allegations made in court. The press should comment on the process *and* draw links to counter-revolutionary activities.[125] Yet another commission was created to monitor the progress of the trial; as G. E. Zinov'ev, another prominent Bolshevik, later admitted, such a major trial 'must' represent a 'great step forward' in the 'political enlightenment of the widest masses in the town and the villages'.[126]

The press certainly put an unprecedented amount of effort into covering the trial. Both *Izvestiia* and *Pravda* ran articles on the front or second page of almost every issue from mid-May to mid-August, and the same was true of local papers. And, initially at least, newspapers made an effort to be more innovative and engaging, bringing together various techniques developed over previous years. Most obviously, several articles were grouped together, each conveying a distinct element of the educational message. The coverage in *Izvestiia*, for instance, started with a general article addressed to workers of all countries on the trial of the 'so-called SRs'. Other articles focused on gaining support from the Communist

[122] *Sudebnyi protsess*, 402–3 (telegram from Trotskii to the leadership committee, 13 May 1922).

[123] *Sudebnyi protsess*, 407–8 (telegram); and *Vestnik agitatsii i propagandy*, 4–5, 15 June 1922. Later articles updated agitators on the trial's progress: for example, P. Sh., 'Pervye itogi es-erovskogo protsessa', *Vestnik agitatsii i propagandy*, 6, 1 July 1922, 55–67; various articles in *Vestnik agitatsii i propagandy*, 7, 15 July 1922; its renamed successor, *Kommunisticheskaia revoliutsiia*, 8, 1 August 1922; and, among other articles in this issue, P. Shubin, 'Itogi protsessa', *Kommunisticheskaia revoliutsiia*, 9–10, 1 September 1922, 79–89.

[124] On party organs in the Urals, see F. Faizrakhmanova, 'Agitatsionno-propagandistskaia deiatel'nost' partiinykh organizatsii Urala sredi rabochikh v sviazi s sudebnym protsessom nad rukovodstvom partii pravykh eserov', in V. Kulikov (ed.), *Klassovaia bor'ba na Urale (1917–1932 gody)* (Sverdlovsk, 1974), 58–65.

[125] *Sudebnyi protsess*, 418–20 (protocol of the agitational committee).

[126] G. Zinov'ev, 'Protsess eserov i ubiistvo Volodarskogo', *Pravda*, 20 June 1922, 1.

International, young SR sympathizers, and workers.[127] *Rabochaia Moskva* published articles on the severity of SR activities, their alleged plans for a future government, and the mistaken support of non-party workers for the SRs. Here, again, were complementary but distinct messages: the SRs have harmed the proletarian state, they still pose a threat, and workers should not be deluded by them.[128] *Krasnyi sever* (Vologda), as an example of a provincial newspaper, adopted a similar multipronged attack, but spread over days. Articles made various arguments, from justifying the revolutionary court and linking the SRs to a range of counter-revolutionary activities to labelling them accomplices of imperialism, highlighting workers' support for the accusations, and attacking the foreign lawyers.[129]

This coverage soon formed several consistent lines of attack: the 'terrorist' acts of the SRs against the revolution and the proletarian state; their alleged links with other counter-revolutionary enemies and thus their betrayal of socialism; and the similar abandonment of revolutionary ideals and the workers by foreign socialists sympathetic to the SRs, as revealed by their provision of defence lawyers headed by the Belgian Emile Vandervelde and including the Germans Kurt Rosenfeld and Theodor Liebknecht. All the papers used terms such as 'bourgeois', 'counter-revolution', and 'enemies of the people' as a matter of course.

One attempt made by the press to engage their audience was by making much greater use of satire than before. To be sure, the majority of the coverage remained standard articles, but some papers frequently mixed this with cartoons, caricatures, verse, and other material. *Pravda* was the main national exponent of this method. It had only published cartoons sporadically before, for instance, but now published several on this trial alone, drawn by well-known artists such as Viktor Deni and Boris Efimov. These attacked the foreign lawyers or the leaders of the SRs in emigration, such as V. M. Chernov (usually depicting them as in league with foreign capitalists), or targeted the leading figures among the accused in the trial.[130] *Izvestiia* only published one cartoon, attacking Vandervelde (although this was one more on a trial than ever before).[131] Cartoons were far more frequent in *Rabochaia Moskva*. One of these, unusually, depicted the trial in progress, illustrating the 'flowery eloquence (*tsvety krasnorechiia*)' of one of the defendants, M. I. Gendel'man. Starting by calmly talking about the Bolsheviks' manipulation of the workers' demonstration on 20 June, he becomes ever more hysterical as he starts to contradict himself: the march did not include workers, only communists; there were workers, but they were deceived by the communists and the press; the workers were not deceived at all but knew that communists are 'scoundrels

[127] *Izvestiia*, 19 May 1922, 2. [128] *Rabochaia Moskva*, 19 May 1922, 1.
[129] See *Krasnyi sever* , 20 May–9 June 1922 (usually pages 1 or 2).
[130] See, for example, *Pravda*, 4 March 1922, 1; 4 July 1922, 1; and 12 July 1922, 1.
[131] *Izvestiia*, 14 June 1922, 1.

(*merzavtsy*)' and only went because they were forced. By the end, Gendel'man has worked himself up to such a state that he is losing his glasses as the judge gestures for calm.[132] All this supported the arguments in the texts that the arguments of the SRs were irrational and inconsistent. Mostly, though, cartoons focused more on undermining the SRs than the trial, reinforcing the key message that the SRs cannot be trusted.

The same was true of the other common forms of satire—verses and short stories. *Pravda* had occasionally published poems and satirical verses by the well-known 'proletarian' poet and satirist Dem'ian Bednyi, and now published more; a derisive attack on Vandervelde accompanied its first extensive coverage of the forthcoming trial, for example.[133] These ditties (*chastushki*), satirical or otherwise, were popular before 1917, and their short, sharp, and ephemeral nature proved perfectly suited to conveying revolutionary politics.[134] Though the ditties were often oral, written versions were more common in local papers. Humorous and in colloquial Russian, they were clearly intended to contrast (either as light relief or as an accessible, emotional, and agitational form of argument) with the usual, longer, and more formal articles. *Krasnyi sever* placed an article on 30 May linking the SRs to capitalists and monarchists alongside a short satirical verse and a *fel'eton* (from the French *feuilleton*, a strand of which developed in Russia in the nineteenth century as a short polemical, satirical, and political story) attacking the foreign socialist lawyers.[135] Sometimes, the *fel'eton* transformed into a play or the verse into a song. In all cases, the message was blunt, such as a sarcastic verse/song (readers were told it should rhyme to the tune of another song) published in *Rabochaia Moskva* linking the SRs' advocates to the Romanovs, Denikin, Vrangel', Versailles, and the bankers, and declaring they had left the revolution to welcome the counter-revolution.[136] Only occasionally was their use more subtle, such as when *Izvestiia* placed a verse promoting patriotism for Russia amid its coverage of the trial—an implicit contrast to the treacherous and international machinations of the SRs.[137]

This variety of material was extended further in the illustrated supplement (soon renamed *Krokodil*) to *Rabochii* (Moscow), then *Rabochaia gazeta*. Its weekly coverage combined fact and satire, image and text. The first issue after the start of the trial epitomized its approach. A cartoon criticizing the international socialist movement was on the cover, followed by a colloquial satirical text attacking the SRs and then a 'History of the SR Party' in caricatures depicting the party's steady transformation (in the Bolsheviks' eyes) from revolutionaries to counter-revolutionaries. This message was supported on following pages by a song

[132] *Rabochaia Moskva*, 30 June 1922, 3.

[133] *Pravda*, 14 May 1922, 2; 19 May 1922, 3; 25 May 1922, 1.

[134] I. Raikova, 'Chelovek i revoliutsiia v zerkale chastushki', in *Velikaia rossiiskaia revoliutsiia: obshchestvo, chelovek, kul'tura, povsednevnost'* (2 volumes, Moscow, 2017), II, 176–87.

[135] *Krasnyi sever*, 30 May 1922, 2.

[136] *Rabochaia Moskva*, 10 June 1922, 2.

[137] *Izvestiia*, 24 June 1922, 2–3.

('The bombs of the SRs'), an article, and another cartoon. There were then photographs of judges, lawyers, and key defendants (including brief biographies covering their nefarious activities). An article on Lenin's would-be assassin in 1918, F. E. Kaplan (an SR and thus representing their crimes), and photos of abusive banners at recent demonstrations against the foreign defence lawyers (representing popular support for the trial) led into a break for other news. Later there was another photo of the demonstrations and, after another break, more caricatures (a bourgeois played Vandervelde like a guitar, and Chernov and Martov were depicted as foreign agents). Several satirical verses and caricatures attacking Vandervelde and Chernov completed the coverage.[138] There was less in subsequent issues, but the same multimedia approach. All this constituted a blizzard of messages, presented very differently from the mainstream press, with different formats on the same page and messages reiterated throughout the issue.

The illustrated supplement was unique in its use of photos.[139] The trial was the most photographed so far, with most photos focusing on three themes. There were many shots, first of all, from inside the courtroom, with images of the judges, lawyers, and defendants as well as shots of the room and the audience. This was a means of transporting viewers into the trial itself in a way that texts could never achieve. There were also plenty of images from the demonstration on 20 June, particularly 'popular' banners demanding the death sentence.[140] The illustrated supplement was unusual in also printing broader views to emphasize the scale and significance of the demonstration, with hundreds of people pictured outside the trial and in Red Square. It also published drawings of the march based on the photos to emphasize key messages, including the judges addressing the crowds (thus reflecting the people's will), the scale of the crowds, and large-scale drawings of the banners and effigies.[141] Finally, there were photos of the key protagonists. As always, it is difficult to know how extensively these images were viewed at the time. Some were used as agitational materials, with photos of individuals, for example, appearing as postcards.[142] Others were published by the illustrated supplement and a few other journals. Some were probably intended to go into exhibitions and publications after the trial, but these grand plans were later scaled down.

The final distinctive element of the coverage—after its scale and variety—was the use of workers' letters and petitions. The organizers were keen to demonstrate, on the one hand, that the trial had popular support and, on the other, that it was mobilizing workers. *Izvestiia* and *Pravda* were publishing reports of support from

[138] *Rabochii. Illiustrirovannoe prilozhenie k № 81*, 11 June 1922, 1–10, 12, 14–15.

[139] *Rabochii. Illiustrirovannoe prilozhenie k № 87*, 18 June 1922, 8–9; *Rabochaia gazeta. Illiustrirovannoe prilozhenie k № 99*, 2 July 1922, 7.

[140] For example, photos held by Alamy; search the trial at https://www.alamy.com/ [accessed 24 September 2018].

[141] *Rabochii. Illiustrirovannoe prilozhenie k № 93*, 25 June 1922, 7–9.

[142] *Sudebnyi protsess*, see photos placed before p. 513.

Moscow and the provinces before the trial had even started. When it did begin, letters from the provinces, petitions from workers, and accounts of local meetings—all condemning the SRs, of course—were published almost daily, sometimes under the headings of 'feedback (*otkliki*)' or 'the voice of the workers'. The same was true of local papers, such as *Rabochaia Moskva* or *Krasnyi sever*.

There were two problems once the trial started, though. First, while the coverage of all the above themes continued, the primary focus turned to reporting the key speeches. This was much harder to do engagingly, even if newspapers made more use of subheadings, catchy titles, and bold type than before. Many papers resorted to printing speeches almost verbatim to convey the dense arguments, occasionally supplemented by more personal impressions from observers or commentators. Second, this difficulty was exacerbated by the unexpected length of the trial—two sessions a day, six days a week, for eight weeks rather than the one to three weeks apparently anticipated.[143] Speeches lasted hours, even days, and dealt with complex detail. This placed huge pressure on the publicity effort, and fears quickly emerged that it was not proving effective despite the huge efforts.

These fears crystallized around publicity for the demonstration on 20 June. Plans for a 'spontaneous' demonstration of workers in support of the trial were already well underway on 7 June. A meeting of the agitational commission on 13 June resolved that the coverage should not take the form of 'vulgar abuse' (an implicit critique of the existing coverage) but concrete facts. Editors needed to follow directives precisely and daily information would be sent to them. The meeting also highlighted the *fel'eton*, recognizing the importance of keeping the coverage diverse, entertaining, accessible, and engaging. On 20 June, another meeting admitted that the coverage so far was 'exhausting' and that this could not be maintained. Attendees feared a fall in interest after the demonstration, so they resolved to reduce the coverage to retain interest and build up to a greater focus on the concluding speeches and sentence, which should focus on the factual evidence and the guilt of individuals (rather than generic attacks on the SRs). To achieve this, verbatim reports of proceedings should be curtailed in favour of concise articles, and press coverage should be supplemented by separate collections of documents and small brochures on the activities of the SRs and on the role of the proletarian court.[144]

The press did cover the demonstration extensively, advertising it beforehand, urging people to participate on the day by publishing inflammatory articles and satirical verses, and stressing its significance afterwards.[145] But discontent at the publicity campaign persisted. The agitational commission recorded its dissatisfaction again on 23 June. The coverage was too 'coarse (*grubyi*)', 'polemical', and

[143] M. Jansen, *A Show Trial under Lenin* (The Hague, 1982), 61–2.
[144] *Sudebnyi protsess*, 489–91 (protocols).
[145] *Izvestiia*, 18 June 1922, 2; 20 June 1922, 1; 22 June 1922, 1–3; 23 June 1922, 2; and *Pravda*, 18 June 1922, 3; 20 June 1922, 1–4; 22 June 1922, 2–3; 23 June 1922, 1.

'monotonous'. This tone, the committee argued, 'hurts the ear' and fails to transmit the gravity of the defendants' testimony. The committee went on to criticize how witness statements were presented (they did not emphasize the threat of the SRs sufficiently), citing an article in *Pravda* as an example of bad practice. More generally, reports were simply untidy (with inaccurate or confusing discussions), with another offending article in *Pravda* cited. Such issues were apparently visible in any account of the trial. The committee reminded the press that the trial was crucial in incriminating the SRs in front of the workers and urged reports to remedy these deficiencies immediately.[146]

The committee's concerns were fuelled by reports on the ground. Many thousands of workers attended agitational meetings and signed petitions, but this did not mean uncritical support. Secret police reports disclosed various scenarios (from tightly controlled meetings to spontaneous gatherings) and responses (from dissenting voices to enthusiastic support). When requested, most workers signed petitions, but for a variety of reasons and often mechanically, while a significant number remained doubtful or passive.[147] Apparently 300,000 marched in Moscow on 20 June, 200,000 in Petrograd, and tens of thousands in provincial cities.[148] Many carried banners and effigies of SRs, and a delegation was permitted to address the court. Yet many no doubt attended as it was paid holiday. Even in the trial itself, police agents had to sit among the hand-picked audience to ensure the correct 'popular' responses at key moments.[149]

This passivity might explain why some activists started using agit-trials to re-enact the trial, even before the real trial had started.[150] Party officials in Perm' organized one for local communists and non-party workers in May. The prosecution focused on the SRs' crimes against the revolution and the workers, the defence was met with indignant shouts, and the death sentence was pronounced. An account of the proceedings was sent out across the *uezd* and apparently helped to inform up to eighty meetings and assemblies.[151] An agit-trial was held on successive days in Vologda: at the 'People's Theatre' on 9 June for union and party officials and soldiers; and at the 'People's House' on 10 June for railway workers. A report described how SR leaders and terrorists were accused of

[146] *Sudebnyi protsess*, 491–2 (protocol).

[147] *Sudebnyi protsess*, 63–8 (introduction). See also K. Morozov, *Sudebnyi protsess sotsialistov-revoliutsionerov i tiuremnoe protivostoianie (1922–26)* (Moscow, 2005), 216–20; K. Murphy, *Revolution and Counterrevolution: Class Struggle in a Moscow Metal Factory* (Oxford, 2005), 161–2; S. Pirani, *The Russian Revolution in Retreat, 1920–24: Soviet Workers and the New Communist Elite* (Abingdon, 2008), 147–55; and S. Smith, *Captives of Revolution: The Socialist Revolutionaries and the Bolshevik Dictatorship, 1918–1923* (Pittsburgh, 2011), 253–4.

[148] Morozov, *Sudebnyi protsess*, 235–45; Jansen, *Show Trial*, 144–6.

[149] Morozov, *Sudebnyi protsess*, 443–52; Cassiday, *Enemy on Trial*, 44–6. See also the discussion in Chapter 4.

[150] The first recreations of actual trials as opposed to abstract crimes appear to have started in spring 1922 with the Church trials, but this was a very close second; Wood, *Performing Justice*, 82.

[151] Faizrakhmanova, 'Agitatsionno-propagandistskaia', 61.

murdering representatives of Soviet power, with workers, peasants, and the party as witnesses. The Mensheviks, international capital, the clergy, and the Socialist International were also indicted. Here, the crimes of the SRs were clarified and the audience received a clear sense of the issues. None of those involved had specialist knowledge, but apparently the effect of a courtroom was recreated successfully, with everyone convincing in their parts. The prosecutor managed not only to highlight the terrorism of the SRs but to undermine them ideologically. The court, in short, had apparently achieved its aims.[152] These agit-trials aimed to prepare people for the forthcoming trial, helping them to understand the key issues. Travelling performers and puppet shows acted out parts of the trial on Moscow's streets as it progressed,[153] while agit-trials afterwards helped people appreciate what had happened, thereby publicizing the trial further. Scripts for such trials were even prepared for distribution.[154] Everything involved in such a trial—writing scripts, rehearsing, preparing slogans, and reacting to arguments—enabled people to engage with the educational messages more proactively than simply reading about them.

Ultimately, however, as the Politburo realized on 22 June, the main problem was that the trial had lasted too long, people were simply losing interest, and it should be wrapped up as soon as possible.[155] Yet it proved impossible to do this for another month and a half. In the meantime, the authorities continued to issue orders to the press; the Politburo, for example, ordered papers to run special editions to highlight the crimes of the SRs in July 1917 as the fifth anniversary of the disturbances of the July Days approached.[156] And the press continued its daily coverage; *Izvestiia* even tried to revive interest with a front-page editorial collating the lessons of the trial so far.[157] Yet all newspapers, national and provincial, published fewer articles on the trial after the demonstration.

Against this background—declining coverage and falling interest—it is unsurprising the press struggled to present the trial's finale effectively. The party's internal debates over the sentence (discussed in Chapter 4) did not help. Equally, the material emerging from the trial remained difficult to work with – Krylenko's closing speech, for instance, lasted eighteen hours over two days.[158] Nevertheless, few publications even attempted to convey drama. The illustrated supplement depicted the bourgeoisie reading that the end of the trial was near and dreading the sentence,[159] while Narkomiust's own publication finished its penultimate article with Krylenko's call for the death penalty hanging in the air.[160] Most

[152] *Krasnyi sever*, 8 June 1922, 1; 9 June 1922, 1; 11 June 1922, 2. [153] Jansen, *Show Trial*, 145.
[154] Wood, *Performing Justice*, 83–4. [155] *Sudebnyi protsess*, 282–3 (resolution).
[156] *Sudebnyi protsess*, 283 (resolution, 29 June 1922). These were published on 16 July in *Izvestiia* and *Pravda* to reflect the post-1918 calendar.
[157] *Izvestiia*, 26 July 1922, 1. [158] Smith, *Captives of the Revolution*, 255.
[159] *Rabochaia gazeta. Illiustrirovannoe prilozhenie k № 117*, 23 July 1922, 2.
[160] *ESIu*, 29–30, 10–17 August 1922, 13–17.

papers simply published the closing arguments and the sentence. *Izvestiia* published two articles after the sentence: one on the 'truth' behind the terrorist plots of the SRs and the other on the impact of the sentence on the SRs and the White emigration. *Pravda* had more, mainly through Radek's efforts, but he was focused on influencing the international reaction.[161] This seems an anticlimactic end to an otherwise unprecedented publicity effort and a missed opportunity.

The most innovative attempt to convey the drama of the sentence actually came on film. *Kino-Pravda* had helped its audience visualize the key elements of the press coverage from the start. The first edition on 5 June showed the 'popular' protests against the arrival of the foreign lawyers in Russia.[162] The second episode on 12 June, several days after the start, devoted two-thirds of its content to the trial. The key individuals were pictured as usual, but shots from inside the court were more extensive than before, showing the audience, lawyers, defendants, and judges in a grand room (chandeliers visible), amid a businesslike, if slightly chaotic, atmosphere as people sit at tables, shuffle papers, chat, and work.[163] The authority of the court was evident in the documents visible in the film, everyone standing as the suited judges entered, and the formal speeches. The viewer was transported into the courtroom as far as was possible. There were still inevitable limitations: intertitles remain terse and descriptive—the defendants enter, the judges enter, and so on—and the length meant not everything could be filmed. Observers recall that special lights around the court were switched on at key moments as the cameras started rolling.[164] To fully understand the trial, therefore, viewers still needed text.

Yet under Vertov's increasingly experimental guidance, *Kino-Pravda* did make the most of the new technology to emphasize key points. In the third edition on 22 June, devoted entirely to the trial, the main event was reading the indictment, and the film returned to this several times, which had the effect of conveying the scale of the crimes, as did the different camera angles showing the number of pages in the indictment. The film was also effective in promoting the scale of the demonstration on 20 June, with extended shots of the marchers, close-ups of their banners and effigies, excerpts from the speeches by judges and lawyers, and one intertitle noted the pouring rain, implying the marchers' commitment.[165] The coverage then died down for several editions, suggesting Vertov (like the newspapers) was struggling to find something new to say. It returned with the finale,

[161] *Izvestiia*, 13 August 1922, 1; 19 August, 2; and *Pravda*, 10 August 1922, 1; 16 August, 1; 19 August, 1; 26 August, 1; 27 August, 1; 20 August, 1.

[162] https://vertov.filmmuseum.at/en/film_online/kino-pravda/detail?kinopravda_id=1484826734766, 10:33–11:20 [accessed 12 March 2020].

[163] https://vertov.filmmuseum.at/en/film_online/kino-pravda/detail?kinopravda_id=1484829340598, 4:44–11:00, with 9:02–11:00 in the courtroom [accessed 12 March 2020].

[164] F. Mackenzie, *Russia before Dawn* (London, 1923), 284.

[165] https://vertov.filmmuseum.at/en/film_online/kino-pravda/detail?kinopravda_id=1484829340601, 0–7:39 [accessed 12 March 2020].

this time framed by a story that built tension and permitted the key message—the sentence—to be repeated several times. The edition began with a staged scene in which two 'workers' (one was Vertov's brother) were reading a paper and laying a bet on the fate of the SRs, suggesting the verdict remained in doubt. The closing speeches followed—intertitles conveyed key phrases—before the judges retired to consider the sentence. Vertov was not permitted to film the sentence, so the coverage shifted repeatedly from an expectant audience to the hands of a clock, which moved around to symbolize the passing of time as the judges debated, as did their empty seats. More time passed. People read, smoked, and snoozed. A day was ripped from a calendar, and then another. When the sentence came, people rushed to read papers, excerpts were plastered on billboards, and boys sold papers through tram windows. This too was staged, with Vertov himself in a scene, and the desire to convey public interest is clear. Returning, finally, to the workers who placed the bet enabled the film to reiterate the sentence twice more.[166]

Not everyone was convinced. While generally positive, a review of this edition in *Pravda* criticized the flippant and irrelevant scenes at the start when the 'gentlemen (*dzhentl'men*)' (not workers) debated whether the SRs should be shot and saw the absence of any footage depicting the 'grandiose' nature of the popular demonstrations during the trial (covered in earlier editions) as a 'serious omission'. Although concluding that it was 'interesting and not at all tiring' and technically good, the opening paragraphs suggested the reviewer was not convinced that film had realized its agitational potential.[167] Nevertheless, *Kino-Pravda* covered the trial far more systematically and effectively than earlier attempts, and it was inevitable that this footage would be used again. Most significantly, much of it was compiled into a single twenty-minute film released later in 1922, with only a couple of minutes of new footage of witness testimony in the middle.[168] This film reinforced the trial's message and significance in the months afterwards.

The intention had been to publish the full transcripts of the trial afterwards to further publicize the key messages. This never happened. There may have been a lack of resources, but it seems more likely that the unrepentant attitude of the SRs in court, the mixed reaction to the trial, and the realization that it had gone on for far too long warned against such a massive undertaking. Instead, the Bolsheviks published volumes on the accusations, the sentence, and the prosecutors' closing speeches. None were accessible, composed as they were of long and dense texts. The volume containing the closing speeches, for instance, consists of over 200

[166] https://vertov.filmmuseum.at/en/film_online/kino-pravda/detail?kinopravda_id=1484829340611, 0:10–11:12 [accessed 12 March 2020]. On the filming, see Hicks, *Dziga Vertov*, 29–30.

[167] A. Z., 'Na vechere "Kino-pravdy"', *Pravda*, 2 September 1922, 6. When further criticism emerged later, Vertov claimed his work found success amongst the workers; Roberts, *Forward, Soviet*, 43–5.

[168] 'Sud protsess nad pravymi eserami (1922)', available at https://www.youtube.com/watch?v=wZ9H08saDsY [accessed 12 March 2020].

pages of unbroken text alleviated only by bold type for key phrases and points.[169] It seems unlikely these volumes had a large audience.

Overall, though, the trial of the SRs saw an unprecedented publicity campaign, notable for its scale, the range of media used, and a more creative use of these media than before. The importance of those involved, from senior Bolsheviks to prominent artists, resulted in a coordinated campaign with a clear narrative. It remains difficult to say how far this succeeded in convincing ordinary Russians, but it is clear that the state was dissatisfied even as the trial progressed, with senior Bolsheviks believing the educational messages were still not being conveyed as effectively as possible. Any sign of dissent or passivity indicated a degree of failure. With hindsight, it is not so much that readers would have failed to take away the key messages—these were reiterated so many times in various ways—but that dense print, repetitive content (particularly in the mainstream press), and predictable accusations probably stopped many from reading in the first place. This trial remained a significant step forward for publicizing revolutionary justice, demonstrating the level of state control, the coordination and thediversity that could be achieved, but it must have been an impossible task to find an unequivocally successful formula for publicizing a trial that lasted so long.

After the trial of the SRs had finished, the illustrated supplement published an image (Figure 6.4) of a worker peering out of a tribunal asking a crowd of bourgeoisie and priests who was next. Indeed, what was next? The emergence of 'model' and 'show' trials in 1921–2 led to trials that were not simply as prominent as the trials of Panina, Purishkevich, and others were in 1917–18 but were subject to organized, coordinated, and extensive publicity. It was intended that no one should be able to ignore these trials and their educational message. Even if most trials were not subject to an all-encompassing publicity campaign, the authorities were more alert to their broader educational potential. In Smolensk, N. S. Karzhanskii, a journalist, compiled his daily newspaper reports on the latest trial of the local clergy into an accessible book. With a picture of a snake (a symbol frequently associated with exploitative, bourgeois enemies of the revolution) entwined (or masked) with a cross, the introduction made it clear that the book was intended as a lesson that transcended the specifics of the trial to attack religion as a whole. Clear subheadings, dramatic dialogue, vivid impressions of individuals and developments, and frequent illustrations (even poems) culminated in an account by a former 'unconscious' believer who had transformed into a

[169] *Obvinitel'noe zakliuchenie po delu Tsentral'nogo komiteta i otdel'nykh chlenov inykh organizatsii Partii sotsialistov-revoliutsionerov* (Moscow, 1922); *Protsess P. S.-R.: Prigovor Verkhovnogo revoliutsionnogo tribunala postanovlenie prizidiuma V.Ts.I.K. i vozzvanie Kominterna* (Moscow, 1922); and *Protsess P. S.-R.: Rechi gosudarstvennykh obvinitelei: Lunacharskogo, Pokrovskogo, Krylenko, predstavitelei kominterna: K. Tsetkin, Muna, Bokani.* (Moscow, 1922).

Figure 6.4 'Now that the SRs are finished... Who is next?' (1922).
Source: *Rabochaia gazeta. Illiustrirovannoe prilozhenie k № 135*, 13 August 1922, 16.

'conscious' Soviet citizen after experiencing the trial.[170] Another book aimed to use a trial of Menshevik activists in Kiev in 1920 to demonstrate why the Mensheviks needed to be 'killed' as a party.[171] Still another saw 7,000 copies printed of a 500-page collection of Krylenko's speeches to commemorate five years of the Supreme Tribunal. Taken from thirteen trials, the speeches were selected to represent a wide range of different crimes, from counter-revolutionary organizations and newspapers to economic crimes and corrupt officials. The trial of the SRs was centre stage, emphasizing its status as *the* major trial so far. Key points were highlighted in bold to ensure the reader paid attention, and Krylenko was clear on the volume's educational objectives.[172]

[170] N. Karzhanskii, *Protsess Smolenskikh tserkovnikov. 1–24 avgusta 1922 g.* (Smolensk, 2008 [1922]).

[171] *Partiia men'shevikov i denikinshchina. Protsess Kievskikh men'shevikov (21–23 marta 1920 goda)* (Moscow, 1923).

[172] N. Krylenko, *Za piat' let, 1918–1922gg. Obvinitel'nye rechi po naibolee krupnym protsessam, zaslushannym v Moskovskom i verkhovnom revoliutsionnykh tribunalakh* (Moscow–Petrograd, 1923).

All this anticipated the 'totalizing script' seen in later show trials,[173] and clearly the institutions, practices, and experience needed to organize the trials of the later 1920s and 1930s were forged during this period. Yet this does not disguise the fact that, for much of the civil war, revolutionary justice had a mixed educational record. On the one hand, courts provided better material for dissemination than the organs of revolutionary violence, and this was exploited by newspapers and to a much lesser extent by visual media. Tribunals, in particular, received a significant amount of coverage. On the other hand, much coverage was monotonous and dull, shaped as it was by the material pressures of civil war and the more obvious attraction of other news topics. There was no direct link, moreover, between the clarity of the message and how it was received and understood, or, indeed, whether it was received at all. Occasional snippets of information suggest a mixed response, varying between trials, groups, and media. Some people's lives and mentalities were no doubt shaped by law, in part at least, while others ignored most or all of it as irrelevant to the pressing matter of survival during a civil war. For the Bolsheviks, effectiveness was measured in terms of whether people adhered to the message. In this case, the result is also mixed: they retained and strengthened their hold on power, but crime continued and the Bolsheviks were clearly concerned about the effectiveness of the messages emerging from tribunals at least. Ultimately, if law is to be truly effective in achieving its objectives, people need to have respect for it and confidence in it, and both of these elements were not only lacking among large segments of the population during the civil war but also were issues that Bolsheviks rarely addressed.

[173] Cassiday, *Enemy on Trial*, 6.

Conclusion

In 1923, 10,000 copies were published of a book commemorating the fifth anniversary of the Supreme Court, formerly known as the Supreme Tribunal.[1] Containing articles from current and former commissars of justice, D. I. Kurskii and P. I. Stuchka, as well as leading tribunal officials, it presented an overview of the activities of tribunals during the civil war. The editor, V. V. Sorokin, an experienced military tribunal judge, seemed well aware that the book appeared during a period of transition for Soviet law. Some articles looked back, charting the goals and activities of all three types of tribunals—civilian, military, and transport—through laws, statistics, reports, and memoirs. Other articles looked forward, explaining the new law codes and clarifying legal structures after the reforms in 1922. Taking these articles together, readers were left in no doubt of the significant role that law had played in achieving victory in the civil war and its ongoing importance in building a new socialist state.

The striking images that adorned the text reinforced this message. The front cover contrasted tsarism, where the scales of justice were controlled by the bourgeoisie, with the new proletarian justice, where the heroic worker had discarded his hammer and now, standing alongside copies of the new law codes, wielded a sword over the vanquished bourgeoisie.[2] The strong arm of the law was now weighted firmly in favour of ordinary Russians (Figure 7.1). Another image emphasized the centrality of law in defending the achievements of the October Revolution by placing a worker with a sword against a backdrop of the codes, sandwiched between scenes of industrial and agricultural progress. Yet another saw two swords emerging from the codes to defend this progress from two predatory, capitalist serpents (Figure 7.2). By wielding the sword, these images also depicted law's proactive role as a weapon to fight the revolution's enemies, reiterated in the images of a sword spearing a serpent across the bottom of most pages. The combined motif of defence *and* attack was far from unique during this period—the centrepiece of the Cheka's emblem was a sword and a shield—and this book has made it clear that law was seen as a double-edged sword through this

[1] *Piat' let Verkhovnogo suda, 1918–1923* (Moscow, 1923).

[2] This portrayal fits into the emerging image of the worker in Bolshevik iconography; V. Bonnell, *Iconography of Power: Soviet Political Posters under Lenin and Stalin* (Berkeley and Los Angeles, 1997), 23, 33.

The State versus The People: Revolutionary Justice in Russia's Civil War, 1917–1922. Matthew Rendle, Oxford University Press (2020). © Matthew Rendle.
DOI: 10.1093/oso/9780198840428.001.0001

Figure 7.1 Front cover of *Five years of the Supreme Court*

Source: *Piat' let Verkhovnogo suda, 1918–1923* (Moscow, 1923).

Figure 7.2 Illustration from *Five years of the Supreme Court*
Source: *Piat' let Verkhovnogo suda, 1918–1923* (Moscow, 1923).

transitional period: a means of defending a new, prosperous socialist state on the one hand, and a weapon with which to attack the enemy on the other.

This publication was not the only celebration of law in the weeks and months after the fifth anniversary of the October Revolution. Occasional articles in the national press highlighted the specific role of law,[3] while there were extensive assessments in legal publications. The weekly journal of the Commissariat of Justice (Narkomiust) published a 'jubilee' edition in December 1922 where Stuchka outlined the key arguments that reverberated through all these assessments. The October Revolution had heralded a revolution in law; indeed, it was initially even more revolutionary in deed than word as people acted spontaneously to create new courts and apply revolutionary consciousness to procedures and sentencing. Landmark actions and decrees followed—taking over the old Ministry of Justice, issuing the Decree on Courts, establishing the new courts, and so on. Stuchka conceded there had been problems and mistakes but argued that the achievements of these courts had justified their creation and reminded readers, moreover, that the revolution in law was ongoing.[4]

Other contributors to this jubilee edition and similar articles in other legal journals made comparable arguments. Those in senior positions, like Stuchka, tended to emphasize achievements in terms of issuing decrees and creating new legal structures.[5] Those involved more with the everyday activities of courts talked instead of the immense challenges initially faced by courts and how they had been overcome, reminiscing about the scale of the threats, poor working conditions, and the 'revolutionary proletarian creativity' that had empowered them to emerge victorious from the civil war.[6] All agreed that they had built a strong (*sil'nyi*) and powerful (*moshchnyi*) state organ that had played a decisive role in defending the achievements of the revolution and would continue to do so.

[3] For example, Ia. Brandenburgskii, 'Piat' let sovetskoi iustitsii', *Izvestiia*, 7 November 1922, 7.

[4] Reprinted as P. Stuchka, 'Five Years of Revolution in Law', in W. Rosenberg (ed.), *Bolshevik Visions* (2nd edition, 2 volumes, Ann Arbor, 1990), I, 190–6.

[5] See, for example, 'Iz deiatel'nosti Moskovskogo komissariata po sudebnomu vedomstvu (Beseda s Narkomom Iustitsii tov. Dm. Iv. Kurskim' and N. Krylenko, 'Cherez piat' let', *Ezhenedel'nik Sovetskoi iustitsii* [hereafter *ESIu*], 44–45, 7 December 1922, 4–7.

[6] A. D'iakonov, 'Posle oktiabr'skie eskizy', *ESIu*, 44–45, 7 December 1922, 10–11; and A. Lunin, 'Pered piatoi godovshchinoi', *Proletarskii sud*, 1, October 1922, 21–3.

Subsequent anniversaries saw these arguments refined as officials increasingly portrayed the civil war as a crucial 'formative' experience in the development of Soviet law while romanticizing their 'heroic' struggle during this period, whether working day and night in temperatures so cold that the ink in their pens froze solid or overcoming the absence of written laws and guidance to become the 'revolution's mouthpiece'.[7] The abolition of most tribunals after 1922–3 only reinforced their arguments. After all, they reasoned, exceptional justice had been rationalized by the scale of the threat and by then they were no longer needed; in other words, their own success had rendered tribunals obsolete. What remained was a more structured form of law that retained the capacity to target the revolution's enemies but did so within a clearer framework of law codes, legal procedures, and regular courts.

The first historians of tribunals and revolutionary justice, many of whom had been involved themselves, also took this success for granted, providing largely descriptive accounts that implied the centrality of courts to Bolshevik victory and stressed their 'historic' role.[8] Later Soviet histories used this template, painting a picture of a developing legal system that had successfully targeted the revolution's enemies while moving ever closer to achieving the legal and procedural 'norms' that characterized the post-civil war period.[9] Even the most systematic Soviet work on tribunals, a three-volume study, concluded only that they had played a 'significant' role, completed 'titanic' work, and, despite problems, fulfilled their 'historical mission' to defend the October Revolution.[10] Western studies were not much more insightful; for most, the centralized, repressive tribunal system either represented 'legalized lawlessness' and the subservience of law to violence or was simply the formative period before a semblance of 'legality' re-emerged in the Soviet legal system.[11]

[7] A. Kirzner, 'Shest' let v Sovetskom sude', *Rabochii sud*, 9–10 (1925), 416; B. Arsen'ev, 'Desiat' let raboty v organakh Sovetskoi iustitsii', *Proletarskii sud*, 19–20 (1927), 35–6; and N. Krylenko, 'Pora!', *Revoliutsiia prava*, 4 (1927), 84–91. See also various articles in *ESIu*, 43, 7 November 1927; *Rabochii sud*, 21 (1927); and, on the tenth anniversary of military tribunals, *Vestnik Verkhovnogo Suda SSSR i Prokuratury Verkhovnogo Suda SSSR*, 5–6 (14–15), December 1928. For background, see S. Fitzpatrick, 'The Civil War as a Formative Experience', in A. Gleason, P. Kenez, and R. Stites (eds.), *Bolshevik Culture* (Bloomington, 1985), 57–76.

[8] For example, Ia. Berman, *Ocherki po istorii sudoustroistva RSFSR* (Moscow, 1924), 71; and M. Kozhevnikov, *Istoriia sovetskogo suda 1917–1956 gody* (Moscow, 1957), 114–15.

[9] For example, V. Portnov and G. Smirnova, *Sovetskaia voennaia iustitsiia (1918–1920 gg.)* (Moscow, 1960), 46; V. Portnov and M. Slavin, *Stanovlenie pravosudiia Sovetskoi Rossii (1917–1922 gg.)* (Moscow, 1990), 163; and N. Smirnov, *Vysshie sudy revoliutsii (Tsentral'nye revoliutsionnye tribunaly, 1918–1922gg.)* (Moscow, 1990), 63–4.

[10] Iu. Titov, *Sozdanie sistemy sovetskikh revoliutsionnykh tribunalov* (Moscow, 1983), 100; Iu. Titov, *Razvitie sistemy sovetskikh revoliutsionnykh tribunalov* (Moscow, 1987), 69–70; and Iu. Titov, *Sovetskie revoliutsionnye tribunaly v mirnye gody stroitel'stva sotsializma* (Moscow, 1988), 70–2.

[11] For example, J. Hazard, *Settling Disputes in Soviet Society: The Formative Years of Legal Institutions* (New York, 1960), 477–91; S. Kucherov, *The Organs of Soviet Administration of Justice: Their History and Operation* (Leiden, 1970), 662–74; and R. Pipes, *Legalised Lawlessness: Soviet Revolutionary Justice* (London, 1986), 20.

The conclusions of various studies based on the archives of provincial tribunals in the last two decades have been more intriguing. On the one hand, they have painted a more detailed picture of the repressive role of tribunals based on analyses of cases and sentences, especially their 'significant' participation in campaigns against banditry, desertion, and food-tax violations.[12] On the other, several remind us that courts were heavily involved in all the major activities of the early Soviet state, from the war against internal and external enemies to restoring social order, regulating the economy, and cultural–educational work.[13] One even pointed out the atmosphere of fear fostered by tribunals and their role in fuelling suspicion beyond the obvious physical elimination of class enemies.[14] By being involved in all this, it is implied, the role of tribunals must have been sizeable.

This study has adopted a similar approach by covering all of the activities of tribunals and, through these, their potential impact. It has tried to be, however, more appreciative of the multitude of issues facing tribunals and alert to the main problem that is rarely acknowledged: the difficulty of assessing impact and success when the objectives are varied and evidence patchy during a period of intense conflict.[15] At a basic level, it seems unlikely that tribunals were as successful as many studies have implied. There was a sizeable gap between the *ideal* of cementing state authority, guiding behaviour and thought, and eradicating counter-revolutionary activity, and the *reality* of ongoing political and social conflict alongside rising levels of crime. Yet it is unlikely that the Bolsheviks, Narkomiust, or officials expected tribunals to solve all their problems. Instead, their goals were multifaceted; they were *helping* to extend state authority, control behaviour, punish, and educate, and they were only one of a number of organs active in each of these areas. At another level, the Bolsheviks had emerged victorious by 1922, with major threats defeated and with a stronger central state re-established, even if some local autonomy remained. There was ongoing social unrest, but it was becoming less significant, and the residue of support for other political parties was not sufficient to challenge Bolshevik supremacy. It remains difficult, though, to determine how far tribunals contributed to these achievements as opposed to other approaches and organs.

[12] For example, P. Fedorenko, 'Revoliutsionnye tribunaly Smolenskoi gubernii (dekabr' 1917-1922 gg.)' (*kandidat* dissertation, Smolensk State University, 2006), 188–95; and A. Makutchev, '*Prigovor okonchatel'nyi, obzhalovaniiu ne podlezhit...' Revoliutsionnye tribunaly v Sovetskoi Rossii v gody Grazhdanskoi voiny* (Moscow, 2012), 159–60.

[13] For example, A. Abramovskii, 'Stanovlenie sovetskoi sudebnoi sistemy na Urale v 1917-1918 gg.' (*kandidat* dissertation, Cheliabinsk Institute of the Ural Academy of State Service, 2004), 314; and D. Gor'ev, *Deiatel'nost' revoliutsionnykh tribunalov na Kubani (1918–1922 gg.)* (Armavir, 2011), 135–8.

[14] M. Pivovarov, 'Revoliutsionnye tribunaly v Sibiri (noiabr' 1919 - ianvar' 1923 g.)' (*kandidat* dissertation, Novosibirsk State University, 2007), 186–7.

[15] On the difficulties of measuring the effectiveness of law, see M. Feeley, 'The Concept of Law in Social Science: A Critique and Notes on an Expanded View', *Law and Society Review*, 10, 4 (1976), 497–523.

Much of this difficulty is down to the nature of the evidence. The vast majority comes from tribunals in the form of decrees, case files, trial transcripts, sentences, reports, and broader assessments. This material cannot easily measure state power. There is rarely any material on whether sentences are enacted and with what effect. And, of course, none of it tells us directly how people experienced trials and understood their educational message, or whether tribunals were forging Soviet citizens. This book has tried to work around these inevitable gaps in various ways, but it remains hard to come to firm conclusions, as some have done, that tribunals were the 'most important' instrument of political power for the Bolsheviks or that tribunals failed because they did not deliver the 'real justice' that people desired or foster a popular legal consciousness.[16] It is impossible to pronounce so definitively either way.

Instead, the underlying point emerging from this book is that tribunals do not conform to easy stereotypes.[17] They dealt with huge numbers of cases. There were many instances of inconsistencies and arbitrary behaviour, but also many more cases when tribunals followed recognizable procedures. There were no law codes and a confusing number of decrees, yet many cases were dealt with rationally and effectively. There were plenty of instances of tribunals wielding their punitive power, thereby contributing to—and increasing—the levels of violence that accompanied the civil war. There is more evidence, though, of a wide variety of sentences and acts of 'mercy'. All this makes it harder to judge the impact of tribunals, as they cannot be simply categorized as organs perpetuating arbitrary violence as historians have often done, but they are not a regular form of justice either. As this book has argued, however, this is what made tribunals distinct: as 'fighting' organs engaged in 'battles' on various 'fronts', their form of political justice operated at the intersection of law and violence, offering elements of both to the new state.

This study has explored several of the most important contributions of tribunals, none of which is easy to quantify in terms of success or failure. First and foremost, tribunals acted in conjunction with other state organs to extend and strengthen Bolshevik authority. The myriad of local committees and local party organs conducted the lion's share of the everyday projection of state power. But tribunals helped enforce that power in key ways. As political courts staffed by party members, tribunals were solely concerned with the interests of the state and dealt with those who refused to obey the orders of other state

[16] See, respectively, Pivovarov, 'Revoliutsionnye tribunaly', 187, and C. Story, 'In a Court of Law: The Revolutionary Tribunals in the Russian Civil War, 1917-1921' (PhD dissertation, University of California Santa Cruz, 1998), 185–8.

[17] A point also made in A. Retish, 'Judicial Reforms and Revolutionary Justice: The Establishment of the Court System in Soviet Russia, 1917-22', in C. Read, P. Waldron, and A. Lindenmeyr (eds.), *Russia's Home Front in War and Revolution, 1914–22. Book 4: Reintegration—The Struggle for the State* (Bloomington, 2018), 400–1.

organs. As Chapters 1 and 2 described, tribunals spread across Russia, reaching into the military, transport networks and remoter rural areas. This reach extended that of the other punitive organ—the Cheka—and constituted a different type of force, offering a range of responses and acting as an educational forum. Doing all this within a legal environment, even if flawed, provided a degree of legitimacy to the state's directives. Moreover, as noted in Chapter 3, tribunals regulated the state apparatus itself, devoting immense effort to combatting crimes committed by state officials. This also enhanced legitimacy—seemingly no one was above the law—and it must have contributed to the growing effectiveness of state authority, even if it did seem like a futile battle against a growing epidemic of corruption.

These attempts to regulate the behaviour of state officials were part of the Bolsheviks' larger battle to control definitions of the revolution and thus what constituted counter-revolution. This was the second major contribution of tribunals. As the revolution evolved, and threats ebbed and flowed, so too did counter-revolution change, and this was seen clearly in the courtroom, as Chapters 3 and 4 discussed. In the decrees on tribunals and their sentences, the state clarified what was considered counter-revolutionary at a given time, with the court serving to promote and justify these categorizations. It is hard to tell when the voices of the accused were muted, but it seems likely, as explored in Chapter 5, that many people neither denied the concept or threat of counter-revolution nor disagreed with the need for an exceptional court to combat this threat. Instead, they disputed whether their actions constituted counter-revolution. Courts were the discursive forum where this dialogue between the state and the people took centre stage, particularly as more 'counter-revolutionaries' started coming from the lower social classes as the civil war intensified.

The trial was the focal point of the legal process and formed the third contribution of tribunals: it was where this dialogue occurred, it pronounced the sentence, and it provided the material for the wider educational message. Yet as Chapters 4 and 5 emphasized, the punitive force employed by tribunals was complicated. In many cases, the legal process and public trial produced either a harsh sentence or an arbitrary one, not dissimilar from the private administrative justice imparted by the Cheka. But in many more cases, the use of a variety of sentences, combined with the logical use of mercy, served to further the state's objectives while reflecting the challenges it faced at any given time. This flexibility was at the heart of what tribunals offered the Bolsheviks.

As a final contribution, the legal process and trials provided more potential material for publicity and education than other, less public organs. It is clear from Chapter 6 that the coverage of tribunals in the mainstream press was greater than that afforded to either people's courts or the Cheka, and it ranged from sweeping articles on the purpose of tribunals to short notices of crimes and sentences. The message of revolutionary justice was spread widely beyond the courtroom. There were even signs in the later model and show trials that a multimedia approach could come together with the complementary use of visual and moving images alongside texts. This must have helped raise the awareness and profile of tribunals and reinforce the state's ideology and authority.

It is worth reiterating that tribunals were not as effective in any of these areas as they could have been. For every town, village, regiment, and station visited by a tribunal, there were many more that never saw tribunals throughout the civil war. For every 'crime' investigated competently and trial conducted according to procedure, there was a case where the investigation was rushed and which culminated in an abrupt trial. For every rational sentence, there was an arbitrary judgement, and numerous 'counter-revolutionaries' escaped the reach of the law for every one convicted. Many sentences were never served in full for various reasons. For every sympathetic and receptive audience, there were indifferent and sceptical ones, with some hostile receptions. For every article on tribunals in newspapers, there were more instances when their activities were ignored, under-reported or marginalized. And for every observer or reader influenced by the messages emerging from trials or the wider publicity surrounding them, there must have been plenty who remained disinterested or carried on behaving and thinking as before. In some cases, it is clear that, rather than facilitating political and social order, tribunals—like the Cheka—could exacerbate conflict and violence further, particularly when dealing with contentious, life-and-death matters like desertion and food supply.

The Bolsheviks, however, were aware of these failings. Lenin, for one, never seemed to believe tribunals were sufficiently repressive or fulfilled their educational potential, and debates raged periodically in Narkomiust and among local officials as they searched for ways to make tribunals more effective and efficient. Nevertheless, the Bolsheviks continued to invest in tribunals, because they believed tribunals made a significant contribution during the civil war despite these problems. This contribution may not have been as revolutionary as the Bolsheviks claimed; after all, the simplified class justice championed immediately after the October Revolution steadily morphed into a more complex and traditional system of justice as the civil war progressed. Equally, tribunals and other courts did not succeed in creating an entirely new legal culture, transforming the relationship between law and the state, and how individuals thought and interacted with the law. There was too much continuity in practices and mentalities on both sides. The Bolsheviks instead tried to harness the benefits that law brings to all states for their own ends, whether facilitating political and social control, effective governance, popular support, or greater legitimacy, even if their politics meant these activities were more pervasive, invasive, and punitive than elsewhere. As the Italian Marxist Antonio Gramsci later argued, law is the 'negative' side of any state's civilizing mission, inseparable from the 'positive' educational role of schools and other state activities—it 'urges', 'incites', 'solicits', and, if all else fails, 'punishes'.[18]

The particular benefits of harnessing law for the revolutionary state have been evident throughout this study. The Bolsheviks used law to define, delegitimize, and destroy the remnants of the old regime, whether in the form of individuals, 'exploitative' social groups, or organizations. The flipside of defining the old was to promote the new, and law was used to define revolutionary, and thus acceptable, actions and thoughts. More than this, law helped promote the very concept of change, stressing the *revolutionary* nature of proletarian justice and the importance of being *revolutionary* for enacting real change in society. Defining the revolution, of course, was inseparable from defending it, in this case by categorizing and targeting counter-revolution in all its various forms. The elasticity of the term was deliberate, providing law (and thus the state) with the power and flexibility to react to the evolving nature of the threats facing the Bolsheviks. Furthermore, while the ability of law to influence people directly may be doubted during such a lawless period, crimes and trials highlighted what the Bolsheviks deemed politically significant and provided ideological explanations to guide people's reactions. In doing so, law influenced the nature and direction of the revolution as well as reinforcing the authority and legitimacy of the new state. Finally, the Bolsheviks sought to bring an end to the immediate revolutionary period by using law to mark the parameters and objectives of the new political and social order alongside alleviating conflict and imposing order, even if their broader ambitions would take years of transformation.

Law did not stop playing a role after the civil war. To be sure, with the abolition of the vast majority of tribunals there was no longer an institutionalized framework of organs operating at the intersection of law and violence in civilian life, even if the option of exceptional justice persisted and tribunals continued in the military. As a consequence, a sharper divide returned between law and violence, as represented by Narkomiust and the GPU. Indeed, as the conflict between the two erupted again in 1922, complaints over extrajudicial activities and sentencing without trials echoed the arguments in 1918–19 described in the first two chapters, and these debates rumbled on through the 1920s.[19] Part of this no doubt reflected the general institutional battles for influence and resources that became an enduring feature of the Soviet state. Part of it, though, remained a conflict between law and violence, their respective roles in determining the basis of the Soviet state, and the possibilities of finding a compromise between the two.

[18] See 'The Conception of Law' and 'The State' in Q. Hoare and G. Nowell Smith (eds. and trans.), *Selections from the Prison Notebooks of Antonio Gramsci* (London, 1971), 247, 258.

[19] D. Shearer and V. Khaustov, *Stalin and the Lubianka: A Documentary History of the Political Police and Security Organs in the Soviet Union, 1922–1953* (New Haven, 2015), 36, 39–43 (various documents, 9 October 1922 to 1 July 1927).

Revolutionary justice also left a deeper lasting legacy. As noted, exceptional justice continued in the form of special courts and military tribunals, while show trials remained a favoured method of dealing with politically significant crimes. Judging individuals on all the issues (social background, material circumstances, and mentality) that affected their relations to the state also continued. All this meant that law's role as an instrument of political and social control remained significant, so the institutions and practices discussed in this book undoubtedly provided the framework and experiences that facilitated the show trials, Gulag camps, and terror of later periods, even if none of this was inevitable in 1922.[20]

Harder to judge is the legacy of revolutionary justice on mentalities. On the side of the state, the pervasive fear of counter-revolution so evident in tribunals evolved and transformed after the civil war but never disappeared, and the belief that counter-revolutionary enemies remained at large formed the ideological justification for the drift towards further conflict. This was particularly true of the state's relations with rural Russia, where widespread conflict over desertion, banditry, and food tax saw the heavy use of tribunals and reinforced the Bolsheviks' natural suspicions of the revolutionary credentials of the peasantry. From the peasants' perspective, this conflict quickly alienated them from the state that ostensibly ruled in their name, and no doubt these memories remained when collectivization emerged in the late 1920s. More broadly across society, this study has demonstrated the 'revolving door' of revolutionary justice during this period as lots of people experienced tribunals before their cases were dismissed, their sentences were suspended or amnestied, or their relatively short prison sentences were served and they returned to society.[21] Many of these people, unsurprisingly, held a different conception of their 'crimes' than the state. The impact of these experiences on state–society relations is impossible to assess with any certainty, but it must have added to the tensions and grievances emerging from Russia's brutal civil war.

[20] See S. Barnes, *Death and Redemption: The Gulag and the Shaping of Soviet Society* (Princeton, 2011), 14–15; D. Crowe, 'Late Imperial and Soviet "Show" Trials, 1878-1938', in D. Crowe (ed.), *Stalin's Soviet Justice: 'Show' Trials, War Crimes Trials, and Nuremburg* (London, 2019), 31–77; J. Harris, *The Great Fear: Stalin's Terror of the 1930s* (Oxford, 2016), 31–5; and P. Solomon, *Soviet Criminal Justice under Stalin* (Cambridge, 1996), 448.

[21] This term is borrowed from G. Alexopoulos, 'Amnesty 1945: The Revolving Door of Stalin's Gulag', *Slavic Review*, 64, 2 (2005), 274–306.

Bibliography

Archival Material

Bakhmeteff Archive, Rare Books and Manuscripts Library, Columbia University (BAR)

E. L. Packer Papers
S. V. Panina Papers
I. N. Steinberg Papers

Getty Research Institute, Los Angeles

97.R.36Soviet Photographs from 1918

Gosudarstvennyi arkhiv Rossiiskoi Federatsii, Moscow (GARF)

f. R-336Sledstvennaia komissiia Revoliutsionnogo tribunala pri Petrogradskom Sovete rabochikh, krest'ianskikh i soldatskikh deputatov
f. R-337Revoliutsionnyi tribunal pechati
f. A-353Narodnyi komissariat iustitsii RSFSR
f. R-393Narodnyi komissariat vnutrennikh del RSFSR
f. R-543 Sledstvennaia komissiia Verkhovnogo revoliutsionnogo tribunala pri Vserossiiskom Tsentral'nom Ispolnitel'nom Komitete
f. R-1005Verkhovnyi tribunal pri Vserossiiskom Tsentral'nom Ispolnitel'nom Komitete
f. R-1074Revoliutsionnyi tribunal pri Petrogradskom Sovete rabochikh, krest'ianskikh i soldatskikh deputatov
f. R-1235Vserossiiskii Tsentral'nyi Ispolnitel'nyi Komitet
f. 1788Ministerstvo vnutrennikh del Vremennogo pravitel'stva
f. 1790Ministerstvo iustitsii, 1917
f. 1791Glavnoe upravlenie po delam militsii i po obespecheniiu lichnoi i imushchestvennoi bezopasnosti grazhdan ministerstva vnutrennikh del Vremennogo pravitel'stva
f. R-3042Voenno-transportnaia kollegiia Verkhovnogo suda RSFSR
f. R-5209Mezhduvedomstvennaia komissiia po provedeniiu amnistii soglasno mezhdunarodnym dogovoram, zakliuchennym RSFSR

Hoover Institution Archives, Stanford University (HIA)

L. E. Browne Papers
Poster Collection
I. A. Vladimirov Paintings

Occidental College Special Collections and College Archives, Los Angeles Bessie Beatty Papers

Rossiiskii gosudarstvennyi arkhiv sotsial'no-politicheskoi istorii, Moscow (RGASPI)

f. 17 Tsentral'nyi komitet KPSS
f. 85 G. K. Ordzhonikidze
f. 558 I. V. Stalin

Rossiiskii gosudarstvennyi voennyi arkhiv, Moscow (RGVA)
f. 33987 Sekretariat predsedatelia Revoliutsionnogo voennogo soveta respubliki
f. 33988 Sekretariat zamestitelia predsedatelia Revoliutsionnogo voennogo soveta respubliki

Smolensk Regional Party Archive (SA) [microfilm copies in various libraries]
WKP 2, 6, 130, 206, 273, 282

Tsentral'nyi gosudarstvennyi arkhiv Moskovskoi oblasti, Moscow (TsGAMO)
f. 66 Moskovskii sovet rabochikh, krest'ianskikh i krasnoarmeiskikh Deputatov
f. 4612 Moskovskii gubernskii revoliutsionnyi tribunal
f. 4613 Moskovskii revoliutsionnyi tribunal
f. 4762 Moskovskii okruzhnoi voenno-transportnyi tribunal
f. 4998Otdel iustitsii Mossoveta

YIVO Institute for Jewish Research, New York (YIVO)
RG 366 I. N. Steinberg Papers

Legal Periodicals

Date ranges of issues read
Ezhenedel'nik sovetskoi iustitsii (1922–9) [Moscow]
Materialy Narodnogo Komissariata Iustitsii (1918–22) [Moscow]
Materialy Narodnogo Komissariata Iustitsii. USSR (1919) [Kiev]
Pravo i sud (1924–6) [Saratov]
Pravo i zhizn' (1922–8) [Moscow]
Proletarskaia revoliutsiia i pravo (1918–21) [Moscow]
Proletarskii sud (1922–8) [Moscow]
Rabochii sud (1923–9) [Leningrad]
Revoliutsiia prava (1925, 1927–9) [Moscow]
Revoliutsionnaia zakonnost' (1926) [Moscow]
Sudebnaia praktika (1927) [Moscow]
Sud idet! (1924–31) [Leningrad]
Sovetskoe pravo (1922–30) [Moscow–Leningrad]
Vestnik proletarskogo prava i iuridicheskikh norm (1922) [Tambov]
Vestnik Sovetskoi iustitsii (1923–8) [Kazan'/Khar'kov]
Vestnik Verkhovnogo Suda SSSR i Prokuratury Verkhovnogo Suda SSSR (1925–8) [Moscow]

Newspapers and Periodicals

Date ranges of issues read
Boevaia pravda (1919–20) [Petrograd]
Bor'ba (1918) [Morshansk]
Den' (1917–18) [Petrograd–Moscow]
Izvestiia (1917–22) [Petrograd–Moscow]
Izvestiia gub. ispolnitel'nykh komiteta Vladimirskago gubernskogo i uezdnogo sovetov rabochikh, sold. i krest. Deputatov (1918) [Vladimir]

Izvestiia Kronshtadtskogo soveta rabochikh, matrosskikh i krasnoarmeiskikh deputatov (1919) [Kronstadt]

Izvestiia Kurskago ob"edinennago soveta raboch., soldatsk., i krest'iansk. deputatov (1918) [Kursk]

Izvestiia Morshanskago soveta rabochikh, soldatskikh i krest'ianskikh deputatov (1918) [Morshansk]

Izvestiia narodnogo komissariata po voennym delam (1918–21) [Moscow]

Izvestiia Saratovskago soveta rabochikh, soldatskikh i krest'ianskikh deputatov i raionnago ispolnitel'nago komiteta (1918) [Saratov]

Izvestiia Shuiskago soveta (1918) [Shuia]

Izvestiia Simbirskogo gubernskogo soveta rabochikh i krest'ianskikh deputatov (1919) [Simbirsk]

Izvestiia Syzranskago soveta rabochikh, soldatskikh i krest'ianskikh deputatov (1917–18) [Syzran']

Izvestiia Syzranskago uezdnogo i gorodskogo sovetov i partii kommunistov (1919) [Syzran']

Kommunisticheskii trud (1920–2) [Moscow]

Krasnaia armiia (1918) [Petrograd]

Krasnaia gazeta (1918–22) [Petrograd]

Krasnoarmeets (1919–21) [Moscow]

Krasnoe znamia (1919–21) [Penza]

Krasnyi Baltiiskii flot (1919–20) [Petrograd]

Krasnyi ofitser (1919) [Moscow]

Krasnyi sever (1917–22) [Vologda], at https://www.booksite.ru/krassever/ [accessed 25 July 2019]

Krokodil (1922) [Moscow]

Morshanskaia kommuna (1918) [Morshansk]

Nabat (1919–20) [Orsha]

Novaia zhizn' (1917–18) [Petrograd]

Novyi den' (1918) [Moscow]

Odesskii listok (1917) [Odessa]

Pravda (1917–22) [Moscow]

Put' kommunista (1919–20) [Iukhnov]

Rabochaia i krest'ianskaia krasnaia armiia i flot (1918) [Moscow]

Rabochaia Moskva (1922) [Moscow]

Rabochii. Illiustrirovannoe prilozhenie (1922) [Moscow]

Serp i molot (1919–20) [Novosil']

Soldatskaia Pravda (1917–18) [Petrograd]

Stenograficheskie otchety Moskovskogo Soveta Rabochikh i Krasnoarmeiskikh Deputatov (1919–20) [Moscow]

Syzranskii kommunar (1920–1) [Syzran']

Vecherniia izvestiia Moskovskago soveta rabochikh i krasnoarmeiskikh deputatov (1918) [Moscow]

Vestnik Komissariata vnutrennikh del (1918) [Moscow]

Vestnik Otdela Mestnago Upravleniia Komissariata Vnutrennikh Del (1917–18) [Moscow]

Vlast' sovetov (1918–22) [Moscow]

Vpered! (1917–18) [Petrograd]

Za svobodu! (1918) [Samara]
Zaria (1919–20) [Simbirsk]

Film

Kino-Nedelia (1918–19), various at http://www.youtube.com [accessed 12 March 2020]

Kino-Pravda (1922–5), at https://vertov.filmmuseum.at/en/film_online/kino-pravda [accessed 12 March 2020]

Sovetskaia kinokhronika, 1918–1925 gg. Annotirovannyi katalog. Chast' 1: Kinozhurnaly (Moscow, 1965)

Sovetskie khudozhestvennye fil'my. Annotirovannyi katalog. Tom I. Nemye fil'my (1918–1935) (Moscow, 1961)

Contemporary Documents and Publications

1917 god v Saratovskoi gubernii (Saratov, 1957)
'"27-go fevralia my mogli stat' grazhdanami..." Tiuremnye zapisi V. M. Purishkevicha. Dekabr' 1917-mart 1918 g.', *Istoricheskii arkhiv*, 5–6 (1996), 118–49
Acton, E., and Stableford, T., *The Soviet Union: A Documentary History. Volume I, 1917–40* (Exeter, 2005)
Alimov, P., 'Tri goda Sovetskoi iustitsii v Sibiri', *Zhizn' Sibiri*, 6–7 (1923), 74–86
Amnistiia 1922 goda k V-oi godovshchine Oktiabr'skoi Revoliutsii (Moscow, 1922)
'Antonovshchina'. Krest'ianskoe vosstanie v Tambovskoi oblasti v 1920–1921 gg.: Dokumenty, materialy, vospominaniia (Tambov, 2007)
Arkhiv VChK: Sbornik dokumentov (Moscow, 2007)
Arkhivy Kremlia. Politbiuro i tserkov' 1922–1925 gg. (2 volumes, Moscow, 1997–8)
Belenkin, B. (ed.), *Pervye aresty. 25 oktiabria 1917–4 ianvaria 1918* (Moscow, 2017)
Bergovskaia, I., and Filimonov, V., *Kaluzhskaia sovetskaia respublika: Istoriia v dokumentakh* (Kaluga, 2012)
Bonch-Osmolovskii, A., *Kak i dlia chego bol'sheviki unichtozhili sud* (n.p., n.d.)
Bor'ba za oktiabr'skuiu revoliutsiiu vo Vladimirskoi gubernii (1917–1918gg.) (Vladimir, 1957)
Bor'ba za sovetskuiu vlast' v Abkhazii (Sukhomi, 1957)
Browder, R., and Kerensky, A. (eds.), *The Russian Provisional Government 1917* (3 volumes, Stanford, 1961)
Bukharin, N., and Preobrazhensky, E., *The ABC of Communism* (London, 1919), at https://www.marxists.org/archive/bukharin/works/1920/abc/index.htm [accessed 20 October 2019]
Bunyan, J., and Fisher, H., *The Bolshevik Revolution, 1917–18* (Stanford, 1961)
Burecharskii, V., *Zhivaia gazeta. Rukovodstvo dlia agitatorov, zhurnalistov i rabotnikov ROSTA* (Kazan', 1920)
Butnik-Siverskii, B., *Sovetskii plakat epokhi grazhdanskoi voiny 1918–1921* (Moscow, 1960)
Cain, M., and Hunt, A., *Marx and Engels on Law* (London, 1979)
Chel'tsov-Bebutov, M., *Sotsialisticheskoe pravosoznanie i ugolovnoe pravo revoliutsii* (Khar'kov, 1924)
Chetvertyi Vserossiiskii s"ezd sovetov rabochikh, krest'ianskikh, soldatskikh i kazach'ikh deputatov. Stenograficheskii otchet. Moskva, 1918g. (Moscow, 1919)
Chirikov, E., *Dushevnyi razgovor pro svobodu* (Petrograd, 1917)

Daly, J., and Trofimov, L. (eds.), *Russia in War and Revolution, 1914–1922. A Documentary History* (Indianapolis, 2009)
Danishevskii, K., *Revoliutsionnye voennye tribunaly* (Moscow, 1920)
Dekrety sovetskoi vlasti (18 volumes, Moscow, 1957–2009)
Delo Fani Kaplan ili kto strelial v Lenina (Moscow, 2003)
Delo generala L. G. Kornilova; Avgust 1917g.-iiun' 1918g: Dokumenty (2 volumes, Moscow, 2003)
Delo komanduiushchego Baltiiskim flotom A. M. Shchastnogo (Moscow, 2013)
'Delo L. Martova v revoliutsionnom tribunale', *Obozrenie*, 15 (1985), 45–6
'Delo L. Martova v revoliutsionnom tribunale (okonchanie)', *Obozrenie*, 16 (1985), 43–6
'Delo' Mitropolita Veniamina (Petrograd, 1922 g.) (Moscow, 1991)
Delo provokatora Malinovskogo (Moscow, 1992)
Duranty, W., 'Defy Soviet Court in Treason Trial', *The New York Times*, 10 June 1922, 1
Duranty, W., 'Goad Communists to Fury in Moscow', *The New York Times*, 12 June 1922, 3
Duranty, W., 'Spare 14 Socialists; Hold 12 Hostages', *The New York Times*, 10 August 1922, 4
Dvenadtsat' smertnikov: Sud nad sotsialistami-revoliutsionerami v Moskve (Berlin, 1922)
Emel'ianov, I., *Chto takoe revoliutsionnaia zakonnost' i zachem ona nuzhna* (Moscow, 1926)
Energiia mechty. K 100-letiiu Velikoi rossiiskoi revoliutsii. Vystavka v Gosudarstvennom istoricheskom muzee (Moscow, 2017)
Fainblit, S., *Amnistiia i sudebnyi prigovor* (Moscow–Leningrad, 1928)
'F. E. Dzerzhinskii o revoliutsionnoi zakonnosti', *Istoricheskii arkhiv*, 1 (1958), 3–25
F. E. Dzerzhinskii—predsedatel' VChK-OGPU. 1917–1926 (Moscow, 2007)
Fel'shtinskii, Iu. (ed.), *VChK-GPU. Dokumenty i materialy* (Moscow, 1995)
Filipp Mironov (Tikhii Don v 1917–1921 gg.). Dokumenty i materialy (Moscow, 1997)
Gernet, M., *Sud ili samosud* (Moscow, 1917)
Goikhbarg, A., *Sotsial'noe zakonodatel'stvo sovetskoi respubliki (vvedenie)* (Moscow, 1919)
Goliakov, I. (ed.), *Sbornik dokumentov po istorii ugolovnogo zakonodatel'stva SSSR i RSFSR, 1917–1952 gg.* (Moscow, 1953)
Grazhdanskaia voina v Prikam'e. Mai 1918 - ianvar' 1920 gg. (Perm', 2008)
Hibben, P., 'Moscow's Treason Trial', *The Nation*, 27 September 1922, 299–300
Iakobi, P., *Amnistii 1917 goda* (Petrograd, 1917)
Il'iukhov, A., *Revoliutsiia 1917 goda na Smolenshchine (khronika sobytii)* (Smolensk, 2007)
Istoriia zakonodatel'stva SSSR i RSFSR po ugolovnomu protsessu i organizatsii suda i prokuratury, 1917–1954 (Moscow, 1955)
Ivantsova, O. (ed.), *Sledstvennoe delo bol'shevikov: Materialy Predvaritel'nogo sledstviia o vooruzhennom vystuplenii 3–5 iiulia 1917 g. v g. Petrograde protiv gosudarstvennoi vlasti. Iiul'-oktiabr' 1917. Sbornik dokumentov* (2 volumes, Moscow, 2012)
Iz istorii Vserossiiskoi Chrezvychainoi komissii (1917–1921 gg.) (Moscow, 1958)
'Iz istorii vzaimootnoshenii chrezvychainykh komissii i revoliutsionnykh tribunalov', *Voprosy istorii*, 7 (1990), 155–63
Karpinskii, V. (ed.), *Agitparpoezda VTsIK: ikh istoriia, apparat, metody i formy raboty* (Moscow, 1920)
Karzhanskii, N., *Protsess Smolenskikh tserkovnikov. 1–24 avgusta 1922 g.* (Smolensk, 2008)
Kazanskaia gubernskaia chrezvychainaia komissiia (1917–1922). Sbornik dokumentov i materialov (Kazan', 1989)
Kerzhentsev, V., *Kul'tura i sovetskaia vlast'* (Moscow, 1919)
Kerzhentsev, V., *Tvorcheskii teatr. Puti sotsialisticheskogo teatra* (Moscow, 1919)

'Kniaz' G. E. L'vov v Ekaterinburgskoi tiur'me. Obstoiatel'stva aresta i osvobozhdeniia. Mart-iiun' 1918 g.', *Istoricheskii arkhiv*, 3 (2002), 140–70
Kozhevnikov, M., and Lagovier, N., *Obshchestvennyi obvinitel' (Ocherk o znachenii, pravakh i obiazannostiakh obshchestvennykh obvinitelei)* (Moscow, 1925)
Krasnaia kniga VChK (2 volumes, Moscow, 1990)
Krasnaia Moskva 1917–1920 gg. (Moscow, 1920)
Krest'ianskii front 1918–1922 gg. Sbornik statei i materialov (Moscow, 2013)
Krest'ianskoe dvizhenie v Povolzh'e. 1919–1922 gg.: Dokumenty i materialy (Moscow, 2002)
Kronshtadt 1921. Dokumenty o sobytiiakh v Kronshtadte vesnoi 1921 g. (Moscow, 1997)
Krylenko, N., 'Revoliutsionnye tribunaly', *Vestnik zhizni*, 1 (1918), 81–7
Krylenko, N., 'Revoliutsionnye tribunaly v praktike rossiiskoi proletarskoi revoliutsii', in *Oktiabr'skii perevorot i diktatura proletariata. Sbornik statei* (Moscow, 1919), 250–9
Krylenko, N., *Sudoustroistvo RSFSR (lektsii po teorii i istorii sudoustroistvo)* (Moscow, 1923)
Krylenko, N., *Za piat' let, 1918–1922gg. Obvinitel'nye rechi po naibolee krupnym protsessam, zaslushannym v Moskovskom i verkhovnom revoliutsionnykh tribunalakh* (Moscow–Petrograd, 1923)
Krylenko, N., *Sudebnye rechi (izbrannoe)* (Moscow, 1964)
Kumakov, A., and Simonov, A (eds.), *Proletarskaia revoliutsiia, kakoi my ee ne znaem* (2 volumes, Saratov, 2016)
Kurskii, D., 'Narodnyi sud', *Vestnik zhizni*, 2 (1918), 73–7
Kurskii, D., 'Narodnye sudy', in *Oktiabr'skii perevorot i diktatura proletariata. Sbornik statei* (Moscow, 1919), 241–9
Kurskii, D., *Na putiakh razvitiia sovetskogo prava. Stat'i i rechi. 1919–1926* (Moscow, 1927)
Kurskii, D., *Izbrannoe stat'i i rechi* (2nd edition, Moscow, 1958)
Latsis, M., *Dva goda bor'by na vnutrennem fronte* (Moscow, 1920)
Lenin, V., *Collected Works* (47 volumes, Moscow, 1960–70)
Lenin, V., *Polnoe sobranie sochinenii* (5th edition, 55 volumes, Moscow, 1971-75)
Levye esery i VChK: Sbornik dokumentov (Kazan', 1996)
Lubianka: Organy VChK-OGPU-NKVD-NKGB-MGB-MVD-KGB. 1917–1991. Spravochnik (Moscow, 2003)
Maliantovich, P., *Revoliutsiia i pravosudie (Neskol'ko myslei i vospominanii)* (Moscow, 1918)
Martov, Iu., *Izbrannoe* (Moscow, 2000)
MChK. Iz istorii Moskovskoi chrezvychainoi komissii. Sbornik dokumentov (1918–1921 gg.) (Moscow, 1978)
Meijer, J. (ed.), *The Trotsky Papers 1917–1922* (2 volumes, The Hague, 1964–71)
Michelson, A. (ed.), *Kino-Eye: The Writings of Dziga Vertov* (Berkeley, 1984)
Mramornov, A. (ed.), *Sudebnyi protsess protiv Saratovskogo dukhovenstva v 1918–1919 gg.* (Saratov, 2013)
Novoselov, D., '"Pristupit' nemedlenno k likvidatsii VChK..." Proekt L. B. Kameneva o reformirovanii VChK i sistemy revtribunalov', *Voenno-istoricheskii zhurnal*, 12 (2006), 51–5
Novoselov, D., 'Nesostoiavshaiasia reforma: proekt L'va Kameneva o reformirovanii VChK i sistemy revtribunalov', *Voenno-istoricheskii arkhiv*, 3 (2010), 29–43
Obshchestvo i vlast' (1918–1920). Dokumenty uezdnykh s"ezdov Sovetov Mordovii. Tom I (Saransk, 2010)
Obvinitel'noe zakliuchenie po delu Tsentral'nogo komiteta i otdel'nykh chlenov inykh organizatsii Partii sotsialistov-revoliutsionerov (Moscow, 1922)
Ol'govich, *Velikaia rossiiskaia respublika* (2nd edition, Petrograd, 1917)

Partiia levykh sotsialistov-revoliutsionerov. Dokumenty i materialy (3 volumes, Moscow, 2000–17)

Partiia men'shevikov i denikinshchina. Protsess Kievskikh men'shevikov (21–23 marta 1920 goda) (Moscow, 1923)

Pavlov, P., *O professii iurista* (Moscow, 1917)

'Pervye narodnye revoliutsionnye sudy v Petrograde', *Istoricheskii arkhiv*, 1 (1957), 107–28

Piat' let Verkhovnogo suda, 1918–1923 (Moscow, 1923)

Piatyi Vserossiiskii s"ezd sovetov rabochikh, krest'ianskikh, soldatskikh i kazach'ikh deputatov. Stenograficheskii otchet. Moskva, 4–10 iiulia 1918g. (Moscow, 1918)

Pipes, R. (ed.), *The Unknown Lenin: From the Secret Archive* (New Haven, 1996)

Pis'ma vo vlast'. 1917–1927 (Moscow, 1998)

Pis'ma vo vlast' v epokhu revoliutsii i grazhdanskoi voiny (2nd edition, Novosibirsk, 2015)

Polianskii, N., *Revoliutsiia-torzhestvo prava* (Moscow, 1917)

Polianskii, N., *Pravda i lozh' v ugolovnoi zashchite* (Moscow, 1927)

Polonskii, V., *Russkii revoliutsionnyi plakat* (Moscow, 1925)

Portugalov, G., *Revoliutsionnaia sovest' i sotsialisticheskoe pravosoznanie* (Petrograd, 1922)

Pravoeserovskii politicheskii protsess v Moskve. 8 iiunia-4 avgusta 1922 g. Stenogrammy sudebnykh zasedanii (Volumes 1–2, Moscow, 2011)

Pravookhranitel'nye organy Ufimskoi gubernii v gody revoliutsii i grazhdanskoi voiny (1917–1922): Sbornik dokumentov i materialov. Ch. 2 (Ufa, 2009)

Preobrazhensky, N., 'Proletarian Courts', *Soviet Russia*, V (July–December 1921), 122–4

'Prispelo vremia podviga…' Dokumenty Sviashchennogo Sobora Pravoslavnoi Rossiiskoi Tserkvi 1917–1918 gg. o nachale gonenii na Tserkov' (Moscow, 2012)

Prokuratura i advokatura (Moscow, 1922)

Protokoly zasedanii Soveta Narodnykh Komissarov RSFSR. Noiabr' 1917-mart 1918gg. (Moscow, 2006)

Protsess nad Kolchakovskimi ministrami. Mai 1920 (Moscow, 2003)

Protsess P. S.-R.: Prigovor Verkhovnogo revoliutsionnogo tribunala postanovlenie prizidiuma V.Ts.I.K. i vozzvanie Kominterna (Moscow, 1922)

Protsess P. S.-R.: Rechi gosudarstvennykh obvinitelei: Lunacharskogo, Pokrovskogo, Krylenko, predstavitelei kominterna: K. Tsetkin, Muna, Bokani. (Moscow, 1922)

Reisner, M., *Pravo i revoliutsiia* (Petrograd, 1917)

Revvoensovet Respubliki. Protokoly. 1918–1919 gg. (Moscow, 1997)

Revvoensovet Respubliki. Protokoly. 1920–1923 gg. (Moscow, 2000)

Rivlin, E., *Sovetskaia advokatura* (Moscow, 1926)

Rodin, D., 'Revoliutsionnye tribunaly v 1920-1922 gg.', *Vestnik statistiki*, 8, 1–3 (1923), 155–89

Rosenberg, W. (ed.), *Bolshevik Visions: First Phase of the Cultural Revolution in Soviet Russia* (2nd edition, 2 volumes, Ann Arbor, 1990)

Rozenberg, V., *Svobodnyi narod* (2nd edition, Moscow, 1917)

RSFSR. Narodnyi Komissariat Iustitsii. Otchet IX Vserossiiskomu s"ezdu sovetov (Moscow, 1921)

RSFSR. Tiuremnoe delo v 1921 godu. Otchet Narodnogo Komissariata Iustitsii po Tsentral'nomu Ispravitel'no-Trudovomu Otdelu IX-mu Vserossiiskomu S"ezdu Sovetov R., Kr., i K. D. (Moscow, 1921)

'"Rukovodstvuias' obstoiatel'stvami dela i veleniiami revoliutsionnoi sovesti": Dokumenty Tsentral'nogo gosudarstvennogo arkhiva Moskovskoi oblasti o deiatel'nosti Moskovskogo revoliutsionnogo tribunala. 1917–1922 gg.', in *Almanakh 'Rossiia. XX vek'*, at https://www.alexanderyakovlev.org/almanah/inside/almanah-intro/72272 [accessed 12 March 2020]

'Rukovodstvuias' revoliutsionnoi sovest'iu...' Sbornik dokumentov po istorii Altaiskoi gubChK 1919–1922 (Barnaul, 2006)
Safonov, D., *Mezhdu imperiei i respublikoi sovetov: mestnye vlasti na iuzhnom Urale v 1917–1918 gg.* (Orenburg, 2008)
Sbornik tsirkuliarov plenuma verkhovnogo tribunala VTsIK za 1921 god (Moscow, 1922)
Shafir, Ia., *Gazeta i derevnia* (Moscow, 1923)
Shchegolev, P. (ed.), *Padenie tsarskogo rezhima* (7 volumes, Leningrad, 1924–7)
Shearer, D., and Khaustov, V., *Stalin and the Lubianka: A Documentary History of the Political Police and Security Organs in the Soviet Union, 1922–1953* (New Haven, 2015)
Shestoi vserossiiskii chrezvychainyi s"ezd sovetov rab., kr., kaz. i krasnoarm. deput.: stenograficheskii otchet. 6–9 noiabria 1918 g. (Moscow, 1919)
Sibirskaia vandeia. Dokumenty (2 volumes, Moscow, 2000–1)
Sledstvennoe delo Patriarkha Tikhona: Sbornik dokumentov po materialam Tsentral'nogo arkhiva FSB RF (Moscow, 2000)
Sovetskaia derevnia glazami VChK-OGPU-NKVD, 1918–1939 (4 volumes, Moscow, 1998–2003)
Sovetskaia prokuratura: Sbornik dokumentov (Moscow, 1981)
Sovetskaia prokuratura: Sbornik vazhneishikh dokumentov (Moscow, 1972)
Stalin, I., *Trudy. Tom 8 (aprel'-iiun' 1918)* (Moscow, 2016)
Statistika amnistirovannykh v oznamenovanie desiatiletiia Oktiabr'skoi revoliutsii (Moscow, 1928)
Storella, C., and Sokolov, A., *The Voice of the People: Letters from the Soviet Village, 1918–1932* (New Haven, 2013)
Stuchka, P., *Izbrannye proizvedeniia po Marksistsko-Leninskoi teorii prava* (Riga, 1964)
Stuchka, P., 'Revoliutsionnaia bor'ba ili bor'ba s kontrrevoliutsiei (1919)', reprinted in P. Stuchka, *Za Sovetskuiu vlast' v Latvii, 1918–20: Sbornik statei* (Riga, 1964), 477–80
Stuchka, P., *Selected Writings on Soviet Law and Marxism*, ed. R. Sharlet, P. Maggs, and P. Beirne (Armonk and London, 1988)
Sudebnye organy Sibiri v 1920-e – 1930-e gody. Sbornik dokumentov (Novosibirsk, 2013)
Sudebnye rechi sovetskikh obvinitelei (Moscow, 1965)
Sudebnyi protsess nad sotsialistami-revoliutsionerami (iiun'-avgust 1922 g.) (Moscow, 2002)
Takticheskii tsentr. Dokumenty i materialy (Moscow, 2012)
Tarle, E. (ed.), *Revoliutsionnyi tribunal v epokhu velikoi Frantsuzskoi revoliutsii* (2 volumes, Moscow, 1918–19)
Taylor, R., and Christie, I. (eds.), *The Film Factory: Russian and Soviet Cinema in Documents, 1896–1939* (London, 1988)
The Military Writings and Speeches of Leon Trotsky: How the Revolution Armed, trans. B. Pearce (5 volumes, London, 1979–81)
The Twelve Who Are to Die: The Trial of the Socialist-Revolutionists in Moscow (Berlin, 1922)
Trainin, A., *Amnistiia k desiatoi godovshchine. Osnovnye nachala tekst i kommentarii* (Moscow, 1927)
Trotskii, L., *Sochineniia* (21 volumes, Moscow–Leningrad, 1925–7)
Trudy tsentral'nyi statisticheskogo upravleniia. Tom VIII. Vypusk 2. Statisticheskii ezhegodnik 1918–1920 gg. Vypusk vtoroi (Moscow, 1922)
Trudy tsentral'nyi statisticheskogo upravleniia. Tom VIII. Vypusk 6. Statisticheskii ezhegodnik 1922 i 1923 g. Vypusk vtoroi (Moscow, 1925)
Ugolovno-protsessual'nyi kodeks R. S. F. S. R. utv. V. Ts. I. K. 25 Maia 1922g. s alfavitno-postateinym ukazetelam i oglavleniem (Moscow, 1922)

Ugolovnyi kodeks R.S.F.S.R s predisloviem i alfavitno-postateinym ukazetelam (Moscow, 1922)

Uprochenie sovetskoi vlasti v Moskve i Moskovskoi gubernii (Moscow, 1958)

V-ii, S., *Revoliutsionnyi tribunal (Krasnyi sud)* (Rostov-on-Don, 1919)

Veger, V., *Distsiplina i etika zashchitnika* (Moscow, 1925)

Velikaia oktiabr'skaia sotsialisticheskaia revoliutsiia na Ukraine. Fevral' 1917-aprel' 1918. Sbornik dokumentov i materialov v trekh tomakh (3 volumes, Kiev, 1957)

V. I. Lenin i VChK: Sbornik dokumentov, 1917–1922gg. (2nd edition, Moscow, 1987)

Vnutrennie voiska sovetskoi respubliki (1917–1922 gg.) (Moscow, 1972)

Vostryshev, M., *Povsednevnaia zhizn' Rossii v zasedaniiakh mirovogo suda i revtribunala. 1860-1920-e gody* (Moscow, 2004)

Wade, R. (ed.), *Documents of Soviet History. Vol. I: The Triumph of Bolshevism, 1917–1919* (Gulf Breeze, 1991)

'Zagovor monarkhicheskoi organizatsii V. M. Purishkevicha', *Krasnyi arkhiv*, 26 (1928), 169–85

Zile, Z. (ed.), *Ideas and Forces in Soviet Legal History: A Reader on the Soviet State and Law* (Oxford, 1992)

Memoirs, Diaries, and Letters

Agabekov, G., *ChK za rabotoi* (Berlin, 1983)

Beatty, B., *The Red Heart of Russia* (New York, 1918)

Bryant, L., *Six Red Months in Russia* (London and West Nyack, 1982)

Chebotkov, A., 'Na zale revoliutsii', in N. Aref'ev (ed.), *Vo imia pravosudiia: sbornik statei i ocherkov o sovetskom sude* (Kuibyshev, 1982), 23–4

Chuvatin, A., 'Delo uchastnikov belogvardeiskogo desantnogo otriada', in *Voennye tribunaly—organy sotsialisticheskogo pravosudiia* (Moscow, 1958), 242–6

Chuvatin, A., 'Pervye tribunaly', in *Voennye tribunaly—organy sotsialisticheskogo pravosudiia* (Moscow, 1958), 53–62

Dan, F., *Two Years of Wandering. A Menshevik Leader in Lenin's Russia* (London, 2016)

Dmitriev, N., 'Revoliutsionnyi voennyi tribunal divizii v 1919-1920 godakh', in *Voennye tribunaly—organy sotsialisticheskogo pravosudiia* (Moscow, 1958), 70–2

Dmitriev, Iu., 'Revoliutsionnyi tribunal', in K. Atarov (ed.), *Pavel Postyshev: Vospominaniia, vystuplenie, pis'ma* (Moscow, 1987), 344–8

Dnevnik Totemskogo krest'ianina A. A. Zamareva. 1906–1922 gg. (Moscow, 1995)

Emmons, T. (ed.), *Time of Troubles: The Diary of Iurii Vladimirovich Got'e* (London, 1988)

Finn, E., 'Antisovetskaia pechat' na skam'e podsudimykh (Zametki sovremennika o tribunalakh po delam pechati)', *Sovetskoe gosudarstvo i pravo*, 2 (1967), 70–5

Finn, E., 'Pervye sovetskie narodnye sudy. Zametki zhurnalista', *Sotsialisticheskaia zakonnost'*, 11 (1967), 65–8

Finn, E., 'Pervyi revoliutsionnyi tribunal', *Sovetskaia iustitsiia*, 8 (1967), 16–18; 9 (1967), 16–18; 10 (1967), 16–17

Gershun, B., 'Vospominaniia advokata', *Novyi zhurnal*, 43 (1955), 134–52

Glushchenko, I., 'Na Tsaritsynskom fronte', in *Na strazhe sotsialisticheskoi zakonnosti (50 let voennym tribunalam)* (Moscow, 1968), 179–80

Golder, F., *War, Revolution and Peace in Russia: The Passages of Frank Golder, 1914–1927* (Stanford, 1992)

Gurevich, Ia., 'Delo grafini S. V. Paninoi v revoliutsionnom tribunale', *Russkoe bogatstvo*, 11–12 (1917), 283–98

Hullinger, E., *The Reforging of Russia* (London, 1925)

Kamenskii, F., 'Pervyi tribunal v Petrograde. Zametki zhurnalista', *Sotsialisticheskaia zakonnost'*, 4 (1967), 20–3; 5 (1967), 19–22
Karabchevskii, N., *Chto glaza moi videli* (2 volumes, Berlin, 1921)
Kayurov, V., 'The First People's Court', *Sputnik*, 7 (1967), 84–5
Kedrov, M., *Za Sovetskoi sever: Lichnye vospominaniia i materialy o pervykh etapakh grazhdanskoi voiny, 1918 g.* (Leningrad, 1927)
Kobiakov, S., '"Krasnyi sud": Vpechatleniia zashchitnika v revoliutsionnykh tribunalakh', *Arkhiv Russkoi revoliutsii*, 7 (1922), 246–75
Kozlovskii, M., 'Vospominaniia predsedatelia pervoi sledstvennoi komissii petrogradskogo soveta rabochikh i soldatskikh deputatov M. Iu. Kozlovskogo', *Sotsialisticheskaia zakonnost'*, 4 (1967), 17–18
Mackenzie, F., *Russia before Dawn* (London, 1923)
Maier, N., 'Sluzhba v komissariate iustitsii i narodnom sude', *Arkhiv Russkoi revoloiutsii*, 8 (1923), 56–109
Martynov, M., 'Pervyi revoliutsionnyi sud', in N. Aref'ev (ed.), *Vo imia pravosudiia: sbornik statei i ocherkov o sovetskom sude* (Kuibyshev, 1982), 18–22
Morozov, D., 'Strazh revoliutsii', in I. Kirillov and A. Tarasenko (eds.), *Grozovye gody: Vospominaniia starykh kommunistov* (Ivanovo, 1961), 258–66
Muller, L., 'Deiatel'nost' revoliutsionnogo tribunala', in G. Vendrikh (ed.), *Kak my borolis' za vlast' sovetov v Irkutskoi gubernii (vospominaniia aktivnykh uchastnikov Velikoi Oktiabr'skoi sotsialisticheskoi revoliutsii* (Irkutsk, 1957), 141–50
Neizdannyi V. G. Korolenko. Dnevniki i zapisnye knizhki. 1919–1921. Tom 2 (Moscow, 2013)
Okunev, N., *Dnevnik Moskvicha (1917–1924)* (Paris, 1990)
Pavlov, V., 'Moi vospominaniia o "Krestakh"', *Krasnaia letopis'*, 2–3 (1922), 144–9
Peshekhonov, A., *Pochemu ia ne emigriroval?* (Berlin, 1923)
Postyshev, P., *Iz proshlogo* (2nd edition, Moscow, 1958)
Reed, J., 'How the Russian Revolution Works', *The Liberator*, 1, 6 (1918), 16–21
Romanovskii, S., 'Sluzhenie rodine', in *Voennye tribunaly—organy sotsialisticheskogo pravosudiia* (Moscow, 1958), 80–9
Rozenshtein, M., 'V Blagushe-Lefortovskom raione', in N. Ovsiannikov (ed.), *Oktiabr'skoe vosstanie v Moskve* (Moscow, 1922), 101–16
Shakibaev, S., *Chrezvychainaia komissiia* (Alma Ata, 1978)
Sheremeteva, O., *Dnevnik i vospominaniia* (Moscow, 2005)
Shteinberg, I., *Ot fevralia po oktiabr' 1917 g.* (Berlin, 1919)
Shteinberg, I., *Nravstvennyi lik revoliutsii* (Berlin, 1923)
Sisson, E., *One Hundred Red Days: A Personal Chronicle of the Bolshevik Revolution* (Westport, 1977)
Smirnov, D., *Zapiski chekista* (2nd edition, Minsk, 1972)
Sorokin, V., 'Na strazhe zavoevanii revoliutsii', *Sovetskaia iustitsiia*, 2 (1958), 33–4
Sorokin, V., 'Stranichki proshlogo', in *Voennye tribunaly—organy sotsialisticheskogo pravosudiia* (Moscow, 1958), 63–9
Steinberg, I., *Als ich Volkskommissar war. Episoden aus der russischen Oktoberrevolution* (Munich, 1929)
Steinberg, I., *In the Workshop of Revolution* (London, 1955)
Tagantsev, N., 'Iz moikh vospominanii', in *1917 god v sud'bakh Rossii i mira. Fevral'skaia revoliutsiia: Ot novykh istochnikov k novomu osmysleniiu* (Moscow, 1997), 245–9
Tagantsev, N., 'Iz moikh vospominanii', in *1917 god v sud'bakh Rossii i mira. Oktiabr'skaia revoliutsiia: Ot novykh istochnikov k novomu osmysleniiu* (Moscow, 1998), 315–20

Tyrkova-Williams, A., *From Liberty to Brest-Litovsk: The First Year of the Russian Revolution* (London, 1919)
Ustiuzhaninov, A., 'V voennye gody', in *Voennye tribunaly—organy sotsialisticheskogo pravosudiia* (Moscow, 1958), 90–3
Utevskii, B., *Vospominaniia iurista* (Moscow, 1989)
Vinberg, F., *V plenu u 'obez'ian' (zapiski 'kontr-revoliutsionera')* (Kiev, 1918)
Volgina, E., 'Iz revoliutsionnogo proshlogo', *Voprosy istorii KPSS*, 5 (1959), 174–83
Volzhskaia, E., 'Odna iz pervykh', *Sovetskaia iustitsiia*, 21 (1967), 24–6
Williams, A., *Through the Russian Revolution* (London, 1923)
Williams, A., *Journey into Revolution: Petrograd, 1917–1918* (Chicago, 1969)
Zavadskii, S., *Na puti k revoliutsii 1905–1918* (Moscow, 2017)
Zvezdov, A., 'V period podgotovki Oktiabr'skoi revoliutsii', in *V boiakh za vlast' sovetov (vospominanii uchastnikov sotsialisticheskii revoliutsii i grazhdanskoi voine v Omske i Omskoi oblasti)* (Omsk, 1957), 38–43

Secondary Sources

Ablazhei, N., and Komissarova, E., 'Amnistiia riadovykh belogvardeitsev i ikh reemigratsiia iz Kitaia v 1920-e gg.', *Gumanitarnye nauki v Sibiri*, 2 (2007), 49–52
Abramov, V., 'Formirovanie i deiatel'nost' revoliutsionnykh voennykh zheleznodorozhnykh tribunalov na territorii Penzenskoi gubernii na pervom etape svoego sushchestvovaniia (1920–1921 gg.', in O. Petrunina (ed.), *XXI vek: itogi proshlogo i problemy nastoiashchego. Vyp. 4. Ch. 1* (Penza, 2003), 135–43
Abramov, V., 'Kadrovyi sostav Penzenskogo gubernskogo revoliutsionnogo tribunala (1918–1922 gody)', in *Aktual'nye problemy istoricheskoi nauki: Mezhvuzovskii sbornik nauchnykh trudov molodykh uchenykh. Vypusk I* (Penza, 2003), 177–88
Abramov, V., 'Sozdanie i deiatel'nost' mestnykh revoliutsionnykh tribunalov (1918–1922 gg.) (po materialam Penzenskoi gubernii)' (*kandidat* dissertation, Penza State Pedagogical University, 2004)
Abramovskii, A., 'Stanovlenie sovetskoi sudebnoi sistemy na Urale v 1917-1918 gg.' (*kandidat* dissertation, Cheliabinsk Institute of the Ural Academy of State Service, 2004)
Adams, W., 'Capital Punishment in Imperial and Soviet Law', *The American Journal of Comparative Law*, 18, 3 (1970), 575–94
Adler, N. (ed.), *Understanding the Age of Transitional Justice* (New Brunswick, 2018)
Aleshkina, E., *Mestnoe pravotvorchestvo v period sozdaniia sovetskogo gosudarstva* (Voronezh, 1977)
Alexopoulos, G., 'The Ritual Lament: A Narrative of Appeal in the 1920s and 1930s', *Russian History*, 24, 1–2 (1997), 117–29
Alexopoulos, G., 'Victim Talk: Defense Testimony and Denunciation under Stalin', *Law & Social Inquiry*, 24, 3 (1999), 637–54
Alexopoulos, G., *Soviet Amnesty Tales: Stories of Redemption, 1920s-1960s* (Washington, 2004)
Alexopoulos, G., 'Amnesty 1945: The Revolving Door of Stalin's Gulag', *Slavic Review*, 64, 2 (2005), 274–306
Allo, A., 'The "Show" in the "Show Trial": Contextualizing the Politicization of the Courtroom', *Barry Law Review*, 15 (2010), 41–72
Ansheles, I., *Ustroistvo sovetskogo suda* (Moscow, 1925)
Antonova, L., 'Sudy, rozhdennye revoliutiei', *Sovetskaia iustitsiia*, 21 (1967), 10–13

Antonova, L., 'Velikaia Oktiabr'skaia revoliutsiia i sozdanie narodnykh sudov, 1917-1918 gg.', *Iuridicheskaia Rossiia* (2008), at http://law.edu.ru/doc/document.asp?docID=1133185 [accessed 12 March 2020]

Arbuthnot, M., 'The People and the Poster: Theorizing the Soviet Viewer, 1920-1931', *Slavic Review*, 78, 3 (2019), 717–37

Aref'ev, N., 'U istokov pravosudiia', in N. Aref'ev (ed.), *Vo imia pravosudiia: sbornik statei i ocherkov o sovetskom sude* (Kuibyshev, 1982), 8–17

Argenbright, R., 'The Russian Railroad System and the Founding of the Communist State: 1917-1922' (PhD dissertation, University of California, Berkeley, 1990)

Argenbright, R., 'Honour Among Communists: 'The Glorious Name of Trotsky's Train', *Revolutionary Russia*, 11, 1 (1998), 45–66

Argenbright, R., 'The Soviet Agitational Vehicle: State Power on the Social Frontier', *Political Geography*, 17, 3 (1998), 253–72

Argenbright, R., 'Marking NEP's Slippery Path: The Krasnoshchekov Show Trial', *The Russian Review*, 61, 2 (2002), 249–75

Argenbright, R., 'Soviet Agitational Vehicles: Bolsheviks in Strange Places', in M. Bassin, C. Ely, and M. Stockdale (eds.), *Space, Place and Power in Modern Russia: Essays in the New Spatial History* (DeKalb, 2010), 142–63

Argenbright, R., 'Vanguard of "Socialist Colonization"? The Krasnyi Vostok Expedition of 1920', *Central Asian Survey*, 30, 3–4 (2011), 437–54

Aronson, G., 'Stalinskii protsess protiv Martova', *Sotsialisticheskii vestnik*, 7–8 (1939), 84–9

Astaf'ev, N., Vishniakov, V., and Fin'ko, O., *Politicheskaia amnistiia* (Moscow, 1999)

Attwell, J., 'The Russian Jury', *Slavonic and East European Review*, 53, 130 (1975), 44–61

Baberowski, J., 'Law, the Judicial System and the Legal Profession', in D. Lieven (ed.), *The Cambridge History of Russia. Volume II: Imperial Russia, 1689–1917* (Cambridge, 2006), 344–68

Bækken, H., *Law and Power in Russia: Making Sense of Quasi-Legal Practices* (Abingdon, 2019)

Baker, M., *Peasants, Power, and Place: Revolution in the Villages of Kharkiv Province, 1914–1921* (Cambridge, MA, 2016)

Bakulin, V., and Vychugzhanina, A., 'Organy chrezvychainoi iustitsii Viatskoi gubernii v 1918-1922 gg.', *Vestnik Viatskogo gosudarstvennogo gumanitarnogo universiteta*, 2 (5) (2011), 90–9

Ball, M., 'The Play's the Thing: An Unscientific Reflection on Courts Under the Rubric of Theater', *Stanford Law Review*, 28, 1 (1975), 81–115

Ball, M., 'All the Law's A Stage', *Law and Literature*, 11, 2 (1999), 215–21

Balmasov, S., *Krasnyi terror na vostoke Rossii v 1918–1922 gg.* (Moscow, 2006)

Barnes, S., *Death and Redemption: The Gulag and the Shaping of Soviet Society* (Princeton, 2011)

Baxi, U., '"The State's Emissary": The Place of the Law in Subaltern Studies', in P. Chatterjee and G. Panday (eds.), *Subaltern Studies VII: Writings on South Asian History and Society* (New Delhi, 1992), 247–64

Becker, E., 'Judicial Reform and the Role of Medical Expertise in Late Imperial Russian Courts', *Law and History Review*, 17, 1 (1999), 1–26

Beer, D., *Renovating Russia: The Human Sciences and the Fate of Liberal Modernity, 1880–1930* (Ithaca, 2008)

Beirne, P. (ed.), *Revolution in Law: Contributions to the Development of Soviet Legal Theory, 1917–1938* (Armonk, 1990)

Belenkin, B., 'Repressivnye praktiki bol'shevistskoi vlasti na rannem etape (25 oktiabria 1917 – 4 ianvaria 1918)', in *Uroki Oktiabria i praktiki sovetskoi sistemy 1920–1950-e gody* (Moscow, 2018), 712–27

Berg, G. van den, 'Elements of Continuity in Soviet Constitutional Law', in W. Butler (ed.), *Russian Law: Historical and Political Perspectives* (Leyden, 1977), 215–34

Berg, G.van den, 'Special Courts in the USSR: Their Nature and Activities', *Review of Socialist Law*, 3 (1982), 237–50

Berg, G.van den, 'The Soviet Union and the Death Penalty', *Soviet Studies*, 35, 2 (1983), 154–74

Berg, G.van den, 'Special Courts: Lessons from History', *Review of Socialist Law*, 10 (1984), 63–76

Berman, H., *Justice in the USSR* (Cambridge, MA, 1963)

Berman, H., *Law and Revolution: The Formation of the Western Legal Tradition* (Cambridge, MA, 1983)

Berman, H., 'The Rule of Law and the Law-Based State (*Rechtstaat*). With Special Reference to the Soviet Union', in D. Barry (ed.), *Toward the 'Rule of Law' in Russia? Political and Legal Reform in the Transitional Period* (Armonk, 1992), 43–60

Berman, Ia., *Ocherki po istorii sudoustroistva RSFSR* (Moscow, 1924)

Beznasiuk, A., and Zviagintsev, V., *Tribunal. Arbat, 37 (dela i liudi)* (Moscow, 2006)

Bhat, G., 'The Consensual Dimension of Late Imperial Russian Criminal Procedure: The Example of Trial by Jury', in P. Solomon (ed.), *Reforming Justice in Russia, 1864–1996: Power, Culture and the Limits of Legal Order* (Armonk, 1997), 61–81

Bhat, G., 'The Rule of *Zakon*: The Criminal Cassation Department and Legality in Late Imperial Russia, 1866-94', *The Russian Review*, 72, 4 (2013), 622–46

Bialkowski, Z., 'The Transformation of Academic Criminal Jurisprudence into Criminology in Late Imperial Russia' (PhD dissertation, University of California, Berkeley, 2007)

Bilenko, S., and Kostenetskii, A., 'Dokumenty TsGAOR SSR ob organizatsii i deiatel'nosti revoliutsionno-voennykh tribunalov na transporte (1920–1923 gg.)', *Sovetskie arkhivy*, 2 (1989), 53–6

Bilsky, L., 'Political Trials', in N. Smelser and P. Baltes (eds.), *International Encyclopedia of the Social and Behavioural Sciences. Volume 17* (Oxford, 2001), 11712–7

Blokhintsev, A., 'Imenem revtribunala...', in *Komissary ognennykh let. Bortsy za valst' Sovetov na rodine V. I. Lenina* (Ul'ianovsk, 1977), 108–12

Bogoliubov, S. (ed.), *Zakonotvorchestvo 1917 goda: uchebno-nauchnoe posobie* (Moscow, 2017)

Bonnell, V., *Iconography of Power: Soviet Political Posters under Lenin and Stalin* (Berkeley and Los Angeles, 1997)

Boobbyer, P., *Conscience, Dissent and Reform in Soviet Russia* (Abingdon, 2005)

Borisoglebskii, V., 'Voennye tribunaly – organy sotsialisticheskogo pravosudiia', in *Voennye tribunaly—organy sotsialisticheskogo pravosudiia* (Moscow, 1958), 32–49

Borisoglebskii, V., 'Voennye tribunaly – organy sotsialisticheskogo pravosudiia', *Biulleten' Verkhovnogo Suda SSSR*, 6 (1958), 20–9

Borisova, T., 'Zakon "v godinu tiazhkikh ispytanii": sobranie uzakonenii i rasporiazhenii pravitel'stva v 1917-1918 gg.', *Istoricheskie zapiski*, 5 (2002), 129–65

Borisova, T., 'Revoliutsionnoe zakonodatel'stvo v 1917-1918gg.: Vybor iazyka', *Novoe literaturnoe obozrenie*, 108 (2011), at http://magazines.russ.ru/nlo%20/2011/108/bo10.html [accessed 12 March 2020]

Borisova, T., 'The Legitimacy of the Bolshevik Order, 1917-1918: Language Usage in Revolutionary Russian Law', *Review of Central and East European Law*, 37, 4 (2012), 395–419

Borisova, T., 'The Emergence of the Legality Tradition in Russia, 1800-1918' (PhD dissertation, University of Turku, 2016)

Borisova, T., 'The Institutional Resilience of Russian Law through 1905-1917 Revolutions', *Russian Law Journal*, 5, 4 (2017), 108–28

Borisova, T., and Burbank, J., 'Russia's Legal Trajectories', *Kritika*, 19, 3 (2018), 469–508

Borisova, T., and Siro, J., 'Law between Revolution and Tradition: Russian and Finnish Revolutionary Legal Acts, 1917-18', *Comparative Legal History*, 2, 1 (2014), 84–113

Bortnevski, V., 'White Administration and White Terror (The Denikin Period)', *The Russian Review*, 52, 3 (1993), 354–66

Bosiacki, A., *Utopia, Władza, Prawo. Doktryna i koncepcje prawne 'bolszewickiej' Rosji, 1917–1921* (Warsaw, 1999)

Bosiacki, A., 'From Utopia to a Lawless State: Russian Marxism and Russian Revolutions as a Totalitarian Project', in Ł. Adamski and B. Gajos (eds.), *Circles of the Russian Revolution: Internal and International Consequences of the Year 1917 in Russia* (Abingdon, 2019), 40–59

Bowring, B., *Law, Rights and Ideology in Russia: Landmarks in the Destiny of a Great Power* (Abingdon, 2013)

Brazevich, S., 'Istoricheskaia sotsiologiia revoliutsionnogo nasiliia: kontsentratsionnye lageria kak organizovannaia forma politicheskikh repressii v sovetskoi rossii v 1918-1922 gg.', in *Uroki Oktiabria i praktiki sovetskoi sistemy 1920-1950-e gody* (Moscow, 2018), 728–37

Brewer, A., '"Iz poslushaniia ego velichestva ne vykhodim, a ostat'sia nesoglasny": The Perceptions of Law, Justice and a "Just Authority" in the Petitions of Russian Peasants in the Second Half of the Eighteenth Century', *Cahiers du Monde russe*, 53, 1 (2012), 41–64

Brooks, J., 'Studies of the Reader in the 1920s', *Russian History*, 9, 2–3 (1982), 187–202

Brooks, J., *Thank You Comrade Stalin! Soviet Public Culture from Revolution to Cold War* (Princeton, 2000)

Brovkin, V., *The Mensheviks after October: Socialist Opposition and the Rise of the Bolshevik Dictatorship* (Ithaca and London, 1987)

Bukov, V., *Ot Rossiiskogo suda prisiazhnykh k proletarskomu pravosudiiu: U istokov totalitarizma* (Moscow, 1997)

Buldakov, V., *Krasnaia smuta: Priroda i posledstviia revoliutsionnogo nasiliia* (2nd edition, Moscow, 2010)

Burbank, J., 'A Question of Dignity: Peasant Legal Culture in Late Imperial Russia', *Continuity and Change*, 10, 3 (1995), 391–404

Burbank, J., 'Lenin and the Law in Revolutionary Russia', *Slavic Review*, 54, 1 (1995), 23–44

Burbank, J., 'Legal Culture, Citizenship, and Peasant Jurisprudence: Perspectives from the Early Twentieth Century', in P. Solomon (ed.), *Reforming Justice in Russia, 1864–1996: Power, Culture and the Limits of Legal Order* (Armonk, 1997), 82–106

Burbank, J., *Russian Peasants Go To Court: Legal Culture in the Countryside, 1905–1917* (Bloomington and Indianapolis, 2004)

Burbank, J., 'Mercy, Punishment, and Law: The Qualities of Justice at Township Courts', *Kritika*, 7, 1 (2006), 23–60

Burns, R., *A Theory of the Trial* (Princeton, 1999)

Butler, W., *Soviet Law* (2nd edition, London, 1988)

Butler, W., *Russian Law* (3rd edition, Oxford, 2009)

Butler, W., Maggs, P., and Quigley, J. (eds.), *Law after Revolution* (New York, 1988)

Bybee, K., and Narasimhan, A., 'Courts and Judges: The Legitimacy Imperative and the Importance of Appearances', in A. Sarat and P. Ewick (eds.), *The Handbook of Law and Society* (Chichester, 2015), 118–33

Carlen, P., *Magistrates' Justice* (London, 1976)

Carter, A., 'The Bolshevist Substitute for a Judicial System', *Illinois Law Review*, 16, 5 (1922), 345–60

Cassiday, J., *The Enemy on Trial: Early Soviet Courts on Stage and Screen* (DeKalb, 2000)

Charnyi, S., 'Revoliutsionnye voennye tribunaly na transporte. 1918-1923' (2014), at http://polit.ru/article/2014/05/11/revtrib/ [accessed 20 October 2019]

Chekunov, N., *Sudebnaia reforma 1922 goda* (St Petersburg, 2004)

Cherdakov, O., 'Mesto i rol' prokuratury v pravookhranitel'noi sisteme sovetskogo gosudarstva v period ego stanovleniia i razvitiia', *Gosudarstvo i pravo*, 12 (2003), 86–91

Cherkasova, N., 'Stanovlenie institute zashchity v sovetskom sude (1917–1921 gg.), in *Iz istorii sovetskogo gosudarstva i prava* (Moscow, 1989), 77–95

Chigrin, M., 'Dolzhnostnye prestupleniia sotrudnikov pravookhranitel'nykh organov v 1918-1919 gg. (po materialam Simbirskogo gubernskogo revoliutsionnogo tribunala)', *Izvestiia Samarskogo nauchnogo tsentra Rossiiskoi akademii nauk*, 20, 3 (2) (2018), 315–20

Chistiakov, D., 'Organizatsiia kodifikatsionnykh rabot v pervye gody sovetskoi vlasti (1917-1923)', *Sovetskoe gosudarstvo i pravo*, 5 (1956), 10–22

Chuvatin, A., 'Iz proshlogo revoliutsionnykh voennykh tribunalov', *Sovetskaia iustitsiia*, 2 (1958), 30–2

Clover, C., 'Law and the Order of Popular Culture', in A. Sarat and T. Kearns (eds.), *Law in the Domains of Culture* (Ann Arbor, 1998), 97–119

Collins, R., *Violence: A Micro-Sociological Study* (Princeton and Oxford, 2008)

Conquest, R. (ed.), *Justice and the Legal System in the USSR* (London, 1968)

Conway, M., and Gerwarth, R., 'Revolution and Counter-Revolution', in D. Bloxham and R. Gerwarth (eds.), *Political Violence in Twentieth-Century Europe* (Cambridge, 2011), 140–75

Cook, L., 'Collegiality in the People's Commissariats', 1917–1920', *Revolutionary Russia*, 26, 1 (2013), 1–31

Cotterrell, R., *Law's Community: Legal Theory in Sociological Perspective* (Oxford, 1995)

Cotterrell, R., *Law, Culture and Society: Legal Ideas in the Mirror of Social Theory* (Aldershot, 2006)

Cover, R., 'Violence and the Word', *The Yale Law Journal*, 95, 8 (1986), 1601–29

Crowe, D., 'Late Imperial and Soviet "Show" Trials, 1878-1938', in D. Crowe (ed.), *Stalin's Soviet Justice: 'Show' Trials, War Crimes Trials, and Nuremburg* (London, 2019), 31–77

Daly, J., '"Storming the Last Citadel": The Bolshevik Assault on the Church, 1922', in V. Brovkin (ed.), *The Bolsheviks in Russian Society* (New Haven, 1997), 235–68

Daly, J., 'Criminal Punishment and Europeanization in Late Imperial Russia', *Jahrbücher für Geschichte Osteuropas*, 47, 3 (2000), 341–62

Daly, J., 'Political Crime in Late Imperial Russia', *The Journal of Modern History*, 74, 1 (2002), 62–100

Daly, J., *Crime and Punishment in Russia: A Comparative History from Peter the Great to Vladimir Putin* (London, 2018)

Damaška, M., *The Faces of Justice and State Authority: A Comparative Approach to the Legal Process* (New Haven, 1986)

Danielson, E., 'The Imagery of Ivan A. Vladimirov in the Hoover Archives: But is it Art?', *Slavic & East European Information Resources*, 19, 3–4 (2018), 159–74
Demichev, A., and Khachaturov, R. (eds.), *Pamiatniki rossiiskogo prava. V 35 t. T. 21. Pamiatniki prava Vremennogo pravitel'stva* (Moscow, 2016)
Demichev, A., and Khachaturov, R. (eds.), *Pamiatniki rossiiskogo prava. V 35 t. T. 23. Pervye dekrety sovetskoi vlasti* (Moscow, 2016)
Dewey, H., and Kleimola, A., 'The Petition (čelobitnaja) as an Old Russian Literary Genre', *The Slavic and East European Journal*, 14, 3 (1970), 284–301
Dmitrienko, N., '"Delo Tomskikh tserkovnikov" 1922 g.', in M. Plotnikov (ed.), *Sotsial'no-politicheskoe razvitie Sibiri (XIX-XX vv.)* (Tomsk, 1993), 71–81
Douds, L., *Inside Lenin's Government: Ideology, Power and Practice in the Early Soviet State* (London, 2018)
Drokov, S., 'Sud na atamanovskom khutore', *Belaia armiia. Beloe delo*, 7 (2000), 64–80
Dubkov, E., 'Pervye revoliutsionnye tribunaly na Severe', *Sovetskaia iustitsiia*, 21 (1967), 16–17
Duff, A., Farmer, L., Marshall, S., and Tadros, V. (eds.), *The Trial on Trial: Volume 1. Truth and Due Process* (Oxford and Portland, 2004)
Duff, A., Farmer, L., Marshall, S., and Tadros, V. (eds.), *The Trial on Trial: Volume 2. Judgment and Calling to Account* (Oxford and Portland, 2006)
Duff, A., Farmer, L., Marshall, S., and Tadros, V., *The Trial on Trial: Volume 3. Towards a Normative Theory of the Criminal Trial* (Oxford and Portland, 2007)
Duff, A., and Garland, D. (eds.), *A Reader on Punishment* (Oxford, 2004)
Durmanov, N., *Osvobozhdenie ot nakazaniia po sovetskomu pravu* (Moscow, 1957)
Efimov, M., and Zhdanov, D., 'Na krasnom Baltiiskom flote', in *Na strazhe sotsialisticheskoi zakonnosti (50 let voennym tribunalam)* (Moscow, 1968), 134–42
Efremova, N., 'Sozdanie novogo sovetskogo suda (1917-1918 gg.)', in *Iz istorii sovetskogo gosudarstva i prava* (Moscow, 1989), 62–76
Eklof, B., and Saburova, T., *A Generation of Revolutionaries. Nikolai Charushkin and Russian Populism from the Great Reforms to Perestroika* (Bloomington, 2017)
Elie, M., and Hardy, J. '"Letting the Beasts out of the Cage": Parole in the Post-Soviet Gulag, 1953-1973', *Europe-Asia Studies*, 67, 4 (2015), 579–605
Elster, J., *Closing the Books: Transitional Justice in Historical Perspective* (Cambridge, 2004)
Elwood, C., *The Non-Geometric Lenin: Essays in the Development of the Bolshevik Party, 1910–1914* (London, 2011)
Emel'ianova, I., *Revoliutsionnoe pravosoznanie i pravotvorchestvo narodnykh mass v period ot fevralia k oktiabriu 1917 goda: po materialam Kazanskoi gubernii* (Kazan, 1967)
Engelstein, L., 'Combined Underdevelopment: Discipline and the Law in Imperial and Soviet Russia', *The American Historical Review*, 98, 2 (1993), 338–53
Engelstein, L., *Russia in Flames: War, Revolution, Civil War, 1914–1921* (New York, 2017)
Ershova, E., 'Pervyi protsess petrogradskogo revtribunala v 1917 godu: Po materialiam zhurnala "Russkoe bogatstvo" i drugie istochnikam', in *Neizvestnyi stranitsy istorii Verkhnevolzh'ia*' (Tver, 1994), 88–102
Etty, J., *Graphic Satire in the Soviet Union: Krokodil's Political Cartoons* (Jackson, 2019)
Fairfax-Cholmeley, A., 'Reassessing Revolutionary Justice: Suspects, the Paris Revolutionary Tribunal and the Terror in France, 1793-4' (PhD dissertation, Queen Mary University of London, 2011)
Fairfax-Cholmeley, A., 'Mapping the Terror: The Paris Revolutionary Tribunal and the Development of a National System of "Revolutionary Justice" in France, 1793-94', *European History Quarterly*, 44, 1 (2014), 5–32

Fairfax-Cholmeley, A., 'Creating and Resisting the Terror: The Paris Revolutionary Tribunal, March-June 1793', *French History*, 32, 2 (2018), 203–25

Faizrakhmanova, F., 'Agitatsionno-propagandistskaia deiatel'nost' partiinykh organizatsii Urala sredi rabochikh v sviazi s sudebnym protsessom nad rukovodstvom partii pravykh eserov', in V. Kulikov (ed.), *Klassovaia bor'ba na Urale (1917–1932 gody)* (Sverdlovsk, 1974), 58–65

Farfel', A., *Bor'ba narodnykh mass protiv kontrrevoliutsionnoi iustitsii Vremennogo pravitel'stva* (Minsk, 1969)

Farmer, L., 'Trials', in A. Sarat, M. Anderson, and C. Frank (eds.), *Law and the Humanities: An Introduction* (Cambridge, 2010), 455–77

Fedorenko, P., 'Iz istorii Revvoentribunala (RVT) Zapadnogo Fronta v gody grazhdanskoi voiny', in V. Shuliakov (ed.), *Smolensk i Gnezdovo v istorii slavianskogo mira* (Smolensk, 2005), 149–55

Fedorenko, P., 'Revoliutsionnye tribunaly Smolenskoi gubernii (dekabr' 1917–1922 gg.)' (*kandidat* dissertation, Smolensk State University, 2006)

Fedorenko, P., 'Revoliutsionnye tribunaly Smolenskoi gubernii kak organy politicheskikh repressii (1918-1922 gody)', in E. Kodin (ed.), *Istoriia stalinizma: repressirovannaia rossiiskaia provintsiia* (Moscow, 2011), 134–42

Feeley, M., 'The Concept of Law in Social Science: A Critique and Notes on an Expanded View', *Law and Society Review*, 10, 4 (1976), 497–523

Feeley, M., *The Process is the Punishment: Handling Cases in a Lower Criminal Court* (New York, 1992)

Figes, O., *Peasant Russia, Civil War: The Volga Countryside in Revolution, 1917–1921* (Oxford, 1989)

Figes, O., 'The Red Army and Mass Mobilization during the Russian Civil War, 1918-1920', *Past and Present*, 129 (1990), 168–211

Filippova, T., 'Satiricheskaia periodicheskaia pechat'', in *Rossiia v 1917 godu. Entsiklopediia* (Moscow, 2017), 860–4

Fitzpatrick, S., 'The Civil War as a Formative Experience', in A. Gleason, P. Kenez, and R. Stites (eds.), *Bolshevik Culture* (Bloomington, 1985), 57–76

Fitzpatrick, S., 'Supplicants and Citizens: Public Letter Writing in Soviet Russia in the 1930s', *Slavic Review*, 55, 1 (1996), 78–105

Foucault, M., *Discipline and Punish: The Birth of the Prison* (London, 1977)

Fraiman, A., *Forpost sotsialisticheskoi revoliutsii. Petrograd v pervye mesiatsy sovetskoi vlasti* (Leningrad, 1969)

Fraiman, A., 'Dekret Soveta Narodnykh Komissarov o revoliutsionnom tribunale pechati', *Vspomogatel'nye istoricheskie distsipliny*, 4 (1972), 15–29

Frame, M., 'Crime, Society and "Revolutionary Conscience" during the Russian Civil War: Evidence from the Militia Files', *Crime, Histoire & Sociétés/Crime, History & Societies*, 17, 1 (2013), 129–50

Frame, M., 'State Expansion and the Criminal Investigation Militia during the Russian Civil War', *History*, 98, 331 (2013), 406–27

Frame, M., 'Concepts of Policing during the Russian Revolution, 1917-1918', *Europe-Asia Studies*, 68, 10 (2016), 1654–71

Frank, S., *Crime, Cultural Conflict, and Justice in Rural Russia, 1856–1914* (Berkeley, 1999)

Freeman, M., *Necessary Evils: Amnesty and the Search for Justice* (Cambridge, 2009)

Friedman, L., *The Legal System: A Social Science Perspective* (New York, 1975)

Friedman, L., 'The Place of Legal Culture in the Sociology of Law', in M. Freeman (ed.), *Law and Society* (Oxford, 2006), 185–99

Frierson, C., 'Crime and Punishment in the Russian Village: Rural Concepts of Criminality at the End of the Nineteenth Century', *Slavic Review*, 46, 1 (1987), 55–69

Frierson, C., '"I Must Always Answer to the Law..." Rules and Responses in the Reformed Volost' Court', *The Slavonic and East European Review*, 75, 2 (1997), 308–34

Garland, D., *Punishment and Modern Society: A Study in Social Theory* (Oxford, 1990)

Gaudin, C., *Ruling Peasants: Village and State in Late Imperial Russia* (DeKalb, 2007)

Geertz, C., 'Local Knowledge: Fact and Law in Comparative Perspective', in C. Geertz, *Local Knowledge* (New York, 1983), 167–234

Geifman, A., 'The Origins of Soviet State Terrorism, 1917-21', in M. Levitt and T. Novikova (eds.), *Times of Trouble: Violence in Russian Literature and Culture* (Madison, 2007), 152–62

Geisinger, A., 'A Travelling Revolutionary Tribunal of 1921', *Journal of the American Historical Society of Germans from Russia*, 6, 1 (1983), 23–5

Gérin, A., *Devastation and Laughter: Satire, Power, and Culture in the Early Soviet State, 1920s-1930s* (Toronto, 2018)

Gernet, M., *Prestupnost' za granitsei i v SSSR* (Moscow, 1931)

Gerson, L., *The Secret Police in Lenin's Russia* (Philadelphia, 1976)

Gertsenzon, A., *Bor'ba s prestupnost'iu v RSFSR* (Moscow, 1928)

Gertsenzon, A., 'Gubernskie revoliutsionnye tribunaly, narodnye sudy i tovarishcheskie sudy v 1918-1920 gg. (Materialy k istorii sovetskoi ugolovnoi politiki)', *Sovetskoe gosudarstvo*, 6 (1933), 57–72

Gertsenzon, A., 'Iz istorii sovetskogo ugolovnogo prava', *Uchenye Trudy. Vsesoiuznyi institute iuridicheskikh nauk ministerstva iustitsii SSSR. Vypusk X* (Moscow, 1947), 88–151

Gertsenzon, A., *Ugolovnoe pravo i sotsiologiia (Problemy sotsiologii ugolovnogo prava i ugolovnoi politiki)* (Moscow, 1970)

Getzler, I., *Martov: A Political Biography of a Russian Social Democrat* (Cambridge, 1967)

Gilley, C., *The 'Change of Signposts' in the Ukrainian Emigration* (Stuttgart, 2009)

Gimpel'son, E., *Sovety v gody inostrannoi interventsii i grazhdanskoi voiny* (Moscow, 1968)

Gimpel'son, E., *Sovetskie upravlentsy 1917–1920 gg.* (Moscow, 1998)

Ginsburg, T., and Moustafa, T. (eds.), *Rule By Law: The Politics of Courts in Authoritarian Regimes* (Cambridge, 2008)

Gizatulin, Sh., *Prestupnost' v Rossiiskoi provintsii i bor'ba s nei v Oktiabre 1917–1922 gg. (na materialakh Samarskoi gubernii)* (Samara, 2012)

Golder, B., and Fitzpatrick, P., *Foucault's Law* (Abingdon, 2009)

Golinkov, D., 'Pervye sudebnye protsessy v revoliutsionnom tribunale', *Sovetskaia iustitsiia*, 21 (1963), 18–20

Golinkov, D., 'Delo o monarkhicheskom zagovore Vladimira Purishkevicha', *Sovetskaia iustitsiia*, 20 (1965), 22–3

Golinkov, D., 'Kto byl organizatorom iunkerskogo vosstaniia v oktiabre 1917 goda', *Voprosy istorii*, 3 (1966), 202–5

Golinkov, D., 'Pervaia sovetskaia sledstvennaia komissiia', *Sotsialisticheskaia zakonnost'*, 4 (1967), 18–20

Golinkov, D., 'Sudebnyi protsess po delu "Takticheskogo tsentra"', *Sovetskaia iustitsiia*, 15 (1967), 15–16

Golinkov, D., *Krushenie antisovetskogo podpol'ia v SSSR* (3rd edition, 2 volumes: Moscow, 1980)

Golubtsov, S., *Moskovskoe dukhovenstvo v preddvernii i nachale gonenii 1917–1922 gg.* (Moscow, 1999)

Gorecki, J. (ed.), *Sociology and Jurisprudence of Leon Petrażycki* (Urbana, 1975)

Gor'ev, D., 'Sovetskoe sudebnoe stroitel'stvo na Kubani v 1918 godov', *Kul'turnaia zhizn' Iuga Rossii*, 5 (34) (2009), 110–11

Gor'ev, D., 'Vosstanovlenie revoliutsionnykh tribunalov na territorii Kubano-Chernomorskoi oblasti v nachale 20-x godov XX veka', *Izvestiia vysshikh uchebnykh zavedenii. Severo-Kavkazskii region. Obshchestvennye nauki*, 3 (2010), 46–50

Gor'ev, D., *Deiatel'nost' revoliutsionnykh tribunalov na Kubani (1918–1922 gg.)* (Armavir, 2011)

Gornyi, A., 'Iz istorii sovetskoi voennoi prokuratury', *Sotsialisticheskaia zakonnost'*, 5 (1972), 21–6

Gorodetskii, E., *Rozhdenie sovetskogo gosudarstva 1917–1918* (Moscow, 1987)

Gorokhovskii, N., *Stanovlenie i pravovoi status voennykh tribunalov v Srednem Povolzh'e (noiabr' 1917 g. – 1922 g.)* (Tol'iatti, 2004)

Greene, R., *Bodies Like Bright Stars: Saints and Relics in Orthodox Russia* (DeKalb, 2010)

Griffiths, J., 'What is Legal Pluralism?', *Journal of Legal Pluralism*, 24 (1986), 1–55

Gusev, L., *Sovetskaia voennaia iustitsiia v gody inostrannoi voennoi interventsii i grazhdanskoi voiny (1918–1920 gg.)* (dissertation autoreferat, Moscow, 1950)

Hagenloh, P., '"Mass Operations under Lenin and Stalin', in J. Harris (ed.), *The Anatomy of Terror: Political Violence under Stalin* (Oxford, 2013), 163–75

Halfin, I., *Intimate Enemies: Demonizing the Bolshevik Opposition, 1918–1928* (Pittsburgh, 2007)

Harding, N., *Lenin's Political Thought* (2 volumes, London, 1977–80)

Hasegawa, T., 'Crime and Police in Revolutionary Petrograd, March 1917-March 1918: Social History of the Russian Revolution Revisited', *Acta Slavica Iaponica*, 13 (1995), 1–41

Hasegawa, T., *Crime and Punishment in the Russian Revolution: Mob Justice and Police in Petrograd* (Cambridge, MA, 2017)

Hay, D., 'Property, Authority and the Criminal Law', in D. Hay et al., *Albion's Fatal Tree: Crime and Society in Eighteenth-Century England* (London, 1975), 17–63

Hazard, J., 'Law and Tradition in the New Russia', *Oxford Slavonic Papers*, 4 (1953), 132–50

Hazard, J., 'What Soviet Amnesty Means', *Foreign Policy Bulletin*, 32, 16 (1953), 1–2

Hazard, J., *Settling Disputes in Soviet Society: The Formative Years of Legal Institutions* (New York, 1960)

Hazard, J., 'The Courts and the Legal System', in C. Black (ed.), *The Transformation of Russian Society. Aspects of Social Change since 1861* (Cambridge, MA, 1967), 145–64

Hazard, J., 'Soviet Law: The Bridge Years, 1917-1920', in W. Butler (ed.), *Russian Law: Historical and Political Perspectives* (Leyden, 1977), 235–57

Hazard, J., *Recollections of a Pioneering Sovietologist* (New York, 1987)

Healey, D., *Bolshevik Sexual Forensics: Diagnosing Disorder in the Clinic and Courtroom, 1917–1939* (DeKalb, 2009)

Hesse, C., 'The Law of the Terror', *Modern Languages Notes*, 114, 4 (1999), 702–18

Hickey, M., 'Moderate Socialists and the Politics of Crime in Revolutionary Smolensk', *Canadian-American Slavonic Studies*, 35, 2–3 (2001), 189–215

Hicks, J., *Dziga Vertov: Defining Documentary Film* (London, 2007)

Hirst, P., 'Marx and Engels on Law, Crime and Morality', *Economy and Society*, 1, 1 (1972), 28–56

Hoare, Q., and Nowell Smith, G. (eds. and trans.), *Selections from the Prison Notebooks of Antonio Gramsci* (London, 1971)

Hoffmann, D., *Cultivating the Masses: Modern State Practices and Soviet Socialism, 1914–1939* (Ithaca, 2011)
Holquist, P., 'Anti-Soviet *Svodki* from the Civil War: Surveillance as a Shared Feature of Russian Political Culture', *The Russian Review*, 56, 3 (1997), 445–50
Holquist, P., '"Information is the Alpha and Omega of Our Work": Bolshevik Surveillance in its Pan-European Context', *The Journal of Modern History*, 96, 3 (1997), 415–50
Holquist, P., *Making War, Forging Revolution: Russia's Continuum of Crisis, 1914–1921* (Cambridge, MA, 2002)
Holquist, P., 'State Violence as Technique: The Logic of Violence in Soviet Totalitarianism', in A. Weiner (ed.), *Landscaping the Human Garden* (Stanford, 2003), 19–45
Holquist, P., 'Violent Russia, Deadly Marxism? Russia in the Epoch of Violence, 1905-1921', *Kritika*, 4, 3 (2003), 627–52
Humphreys, S., 'Law as Discourse', *History and Anthropology*, 1, 2 (1985), 241–64
Huskey, E., *Russian Lawyers and the Soviet State: The Origins and Development of the Soviet Bar, 1917–1939* (Princeton, 1986)
Huskey, E., 'A Framework for the Analysis of Soviet Law', *The Russian Review*, 50, 1 (1991), 53–70
Huskey, E., 'From Legal Nihilism to *Pravovoe Gosudarstvo*: Soviet Legal Development, 1917-1990', in D. Barry (ed.), *Toward the 'Rule of Law' in Russia? Political and Legal Reform in the Transitional Period* (Armonk, 1992), 23–42
Iarov, S., 'Na zare sovetskogo sledstviia: Ideologiia i praktika 1918-1919', *Minuvshee*, 18 (1995), 315–37
Iarov, S., *Chelovek pered litsom vlasti. 1917–1920-e gg.* (Moscow, 2014)
Ingraham, B., *Political Crime in Europe: A Comparative Study of France, Germany, and England* (Berkeley, 1979)
Ioffe, G., 'Respublika kumov'ev kak proshla pervaia repetitsiia stalinskikh protsessov', *Rodina*, 8 (1990), 12–18
Isaev, I., 'Revoliutsionnaia psikhologiia i revoliutsionnaia zakonnost' (opyt 1917 g.)', in P. Volobuev (ed.), *Revoliutsiia i chelovek: sotsial'no-psikhologicheskii aspekt* (Moscow, 1996), 28–39
Isaev, V., Mikheev, D., and Ugrovatov, A., *Mezhdu politikoi i pravom: sudy Sibiri v 1920-e-1930-e gg.* (Novosibirsk, 2014)
Ishevskaya, S., 'The Intertitles of Dziga Vertov's *Anniversary of the Revolution*', *Studies in Russian and Soviet Cinema*, 13, 1 (2019), 18–39
Ivanov, A., *Vladimir Purishkevich—opyt biografii pravogo politika (1870–1920)* (Moscow–St Petersburg, 2011)
Ivanov, A., 'Konkurenty bol'shevikov sprava: Monarkhicheskaia organizatsiia V. M. Purishkevicha v 1917 g.', in *Velikaia rossiiskaia revoliutsiia 1917. 100 let izucheniia* (Moscow, 2017), 213–19
Ivanov, V., 'Organizatsiia suda i prokuratury: Puti sozdaniia novogo revoliutsionnogo suda', in O. Ioffe (ed.), *Sorok let sovetskogo prava, 1917–1957* (2 volumes, Leningrad, 1957), I, 561–98
Ivanov, V., 'U istokov sovetskogo ugolovnogo zakonodatel'stva', *Sovetskaia iustitsiia*, 3 (1967), 11–13
Ivanova, G., *Labor Camp Socialism: The Gulag in the Soviet Totaliterian System* (Armonk, 2000)
Jakobson, M., *Origins of the Gulag: The Soviet Prison Camp System, 1917–1934* (Lexington, 1993)

Jansen, M., *A Show Trial under Lenin: The Trial of the Socialist Revolutionaries, Moscow 1922* (The Hague, 1982)

Jansen, M., 'The Bar During the First Years of the Soviet Regime: N. K. Murav'ev', *Revolutionary Russia*, 3, 2 (1990), 211–23

Juviler, P., *Revolutionary Law and Order: Politics and Social Change in the USSR* (New York, 1976)

K., 'Revoliutsionnye tribunaly', *Sovetskaia iustitsiia*, 21 (1937), 38–44

Kachurin, P., *Making Modernism Soviet: The Russian Avant-Garde in the Early Soviet Era, 1918–1928* (Evanston, 2013)

Kail', M., *Vlast' i pravoslavnye veruiushchie v Rossiiskoi provintsii nachala 1920-x godov* (Smolensk, 2008)

Kail', M., *Pravoslavnaia tserkov' i veruiushchie Smolenskoi eparkhii v gody revoliutsii i grazhdanskoi voiny* (Moscow, 2010)

Kail', M., 'Sudebnye protsessy nad provintsial'nym dukhovenstvom i veruiushchimi 1918–1922 godov: kharakter, granitsy i stepen' repressivnogo vozdeistviia', in E. Kodin (ed.), *Istoriia stalinizma: repressirovannaia rossiiskaia provintsiia* (Moscow, 2011), 338–49

Kalashnikova, N., *Istoriia sovetskoi kassatsii po ugolovnym delam* (Moscow, 1959)

Kalyvas, S., *The Logic of Violence in Civil War* (Cambridge, 2006)

Kalyvas, S., Shapiro, I., and Masoud, T. (eds.), *Order, Conflict and Violence* (Cambridge, 2008)

Kamalova, G., and Maiorov, V., *Sovetskaia pravookhranitel'naia sistema Urala v period ee stanovleniia (1921–1929 gg.)* (Cheliabinsk, 2010)

Karev, D., *Sovetskoe sudoustroistvo* (Moscow, 1951)

Karsch, S., *Die bolschewistische Machtergreifung im Gouvernement Voronež (1917–1919)* (Stuttgart, 2006)

Kashevarov, A., *Pravoslavnaia Rossiiskaia tserkov' i sovetskoe gosudarstvo (1917–1922)* (Moscow, 2005)

Kelly, C., *Petrushka: The Russian Carnival Puppet Theatre* (Cambridge, 1990)

Kelly, C., '"How to Write to the Newspaper": Language and Power at the Birth of the Soviet Public Language', in N. Vakhtin and B. Firsov (eds.), *Public Debate in Russia: Matters of (Dis)order* (Edinburgh, 2016), 101–26

Kenez, P., 'Lenin and the Freedom of the Press', in A. Gleason, P. Kenez, and R. Stites (eds.), *Bolshevik Culture* (Bloomington, 1985), 131–50

Kenez, P., *The Birth of the Propaganda State: Soviet Methods of Mass Mobilization, 1917–1929* (Cambridge, 1985)

Khachaturov, R., 'K voprosu o vosstanovlenii sovetskogo sudebnogo apparata v Vostochnoi Sibiri (1920 g.)', *Voprosy teorii i istorii gosudarstva i prava. Trudy Irkutskogo gosudarstvennogo universiteta im. A. A. Zhdanova. Tom 58, seriia iuridicheskaia, vypusk 9, chast' pervaia* (Irkutsk, 1969), 110–32

Khachaturov, R., 'Sozdanie revoliutsionnykh tribunalov v gorode Irkutske', *Voprosy teorii i istorii gosudarstva i prava. Trudy Irkutskogo gosudarstvennogo universiteta im. A. A. Zhdanova. Tom 45, seriia iuridicheskaia, vypusk 8, chast' 1* (Irkutsk, 1971), 88–94

Khachaturov, R., 'Sozdanie revoliutsionnykh tribunalov v vostochnoi sibiri', *Voprosy teorii prava i gosudarstvennogo stroitel'stva* (Tomsk, 1978), 95–9

Khachaturov, R., and Shuvalova, V., 'Sozdanie sovetskikh sudov v Irkutske', *Sovetskaia iustitsiia*, 21 (1967), 14–15

Khrustaleva, M., 'Cursed Days: The Getty Collection of Soviet Photographs from 1918', *AWSS Association for Women in Slavic Studies. Women East-West*, 7, 2 (2018), at https://

files.constantcontact.com/f916d256201/6e22b05a-acb7-46c4-a98a-2e939469d356.pdf [accessed 16 November 2018]

Kirchheimer, O., *Political Justice: The Use of Legal Procedure for Political Ends* (Princeton, 1961)

Kirchheimer, O., 'Politics and Justice', in F. Burin and K. Shell (eds.), *Politics, Law and Social Change* (New York, 1969), 408–27

Kirmse, S., '"Law and Society" in Imperial Russia', *InterDisciplines*, 2 (2012), 103–34

Kirmse, S., *The Lawful Empire: Legal Change and Cultural Diversity in Late Imperial Russia* (Cambridge 2019)

Kirmse, S. (ed.), *One Law for All? Western Models and Local Practices in (Post-)Imperial Contexts* (Frankfurt. 2012)

Kivelson, V., 'Muscovite "Citizenship": Rights without Freedom', *The Journal of Modern History*, 74, 3 (2002), 465–89

Klevtsov, A., 'Ob otnoshenii kommunistov k advokature v 1920-e gody', in Iu. Pilipenko and S. Volodina (eds.), *Advokatura. Gosudarstvo. Obshchestvo* (Moscow, 2006), 367–72

Klimenko, V., *Bor'ba s kontrrevoliutsiei v Moskve, 1917–20* (Moscow, 1978)

Klimenko, V., *Moskva. Revoliutsiia. Pravoporiadok. Stolichnaia pravookhranitel'naia sistema: vozniknovenie, razvitie, bor'ba v kontse 1917–1920 gg.* (Moscow, 2010)

Klimenko, V., *Oktiabr' i revoliutsionnoe nasilie (1917–1920 gg.)* (Moscow, 2010)

Kliukin, A., 'Sudebnye organy Tambovskoi gubernii v 1920-1928 gg.' (*kandidat* dissertation, Tambov State Technical University, 2006)

Knepper, P., *Writing the History of Crime* (London, 2016)

Kollmann, N., 'The Quality of Mercy in Early Modern Legal Practice', *Kritika*, 7, 1 (2006), 5–22

Kollmann, N., *Crime and Punishment in Early Modern Russia* (Cambridge, 2012)

Kolotkov, M., 'Revoliutsionnye tribunaly sovetskoi Rossii v 1917–1922 gg.: Organizatsionnoe stroitel'stvo i pravovaia deiatel'nost' (na primere Kurskoi gubernii)', *Aktual'nye problemy Rossiiskogo prava*, 4 (9) (2008), 68–74

Kolychev, V., *Partiino-politicheskaia rabota v krasnoi armii v gody grazhdanskoi voiny 1918–1920* (Moscow, 1979)

Kossov, I., 'Stanovlenie narodnykh sudov i Narkom iustitsii RSFSR' (*kandidat* dissertation, Russian State Humanities University, 2006)

Kostrova, O., 'Sudebnye preobrazovaniia v Rossii v 1917–1922 gg. (na primere Nizhegorodskoi gubernii) (*kandidat* dissertation, Moscow Humanitarian-Economics Institute—Nizhnii Novgorod Branch, 2008)

Kowalsky, S., *Deviant Women: Female Crime and Criminality in Revolutionary Russia, 1880–1930* (DeKalb, 2009)

Kozhevnikov, M., 'Komissariaty po sudebnomu vedomstvu – otdely iustitsii', *Sovetskaia iustitsiia*, 21 (1937), 33–7

Kozhevnikov, M., *Sovetskaia advokatura* (Moscow, 1939)

Kozhevnikov, M., 'Organy, vypolniavshie funktsii sovetskoi prokuratury do ee uchrezhdeniia (1917-22 gg.)', *Uchenye zapiski. Trudy Iuridicheskogo fakul'teta*, 144 (1949), 37–84

Kozhevnikov, M., *Istoriia sovetskogo suda 1917–1956 gody* (Moscow, 1957)

Kozlova, K., and Orlov, V., 'Pervoe zasedanie narodnogo revtribunala', *Voprosy istorii*, 10 (1977), 211–15

Krapp, P., 'Amnesty: Between An Ethics of Forgiveness and the Politics of Forgetting', *German Law Journal*, 6, 1 (2005), 185–95

Krasil'nikov, S., *Sovetskie sudebnye politicheskie protsessy v 1920–1930-e gg.* (Novosibirsk, 2014)

Krestiannikov, E., 'Along the Routes of Justice: Judicial Circuit Riding in Western Siberia during the Late Imperial Period', *Kritika*, 20, 2 (2019), 315–44
Krylenko, N., *Revolutionary Law* (Moscow, 1933)
Krylenko, N., 'Vozniknovenie i pervye mesiatsy raboty revoliutsionnykh tribunalov' in N. Krylenko (ed.), *Problemy ugolovnoi politiki* (4 volumes, Moscow, 1935–7), III, 30–54
Krylenko, N., 'Oktiabr' i sud', *Sovetskaia iustitsiia*, 21 (1937), 5–10
Krylov, I., *Sudebnaia ekspertiza v ugolovnom protsesse* (Leningrad, 1963)
Kuchemko, I., *Ukreplenie sotsialisticheskoi zakonnosti v Sibiri v pervye gody NEPa (1921–1923)* (Novosibirsk, 1981)
Kucherov, S., *Courts, Lawyers and Trials under the Last Three Tsars* (New York, 1953)
Kucherov, S., *The Organs of Soviet Administration of Justice: Their History and Operation* (Leiden, 1970)
Kudriavtsev, V., and Trusov, A., *Politicheskaia iustitsiia v SSSR* (Moscow, 1990)
Kuritsyn, V., 'Sledstvie i sudebyi protsess po delu o miatezhe "levykh" eserov', *Sovetskoe gosudarstvo i pravo*, 8 (1968), 144–8
Kuritsyn, V., 'Stanovlenie sovetskoi advokatury', *Sovetskoe gosudarstvo i pravo*, 7 (1971), 113–18
Kuritsyn, V., *Perekhod k nepu i revoliutsionnaia zakonnost'* (Moscow, 1972)
Kuritsyn, V., *Stanovlenie sotsialisticheskii zakonnosti* (Moscow, 1983)
Kuromiya, H., *Stalin* (Harlow, 2005)
Kutsova, E., *Sovetskaia kassatsiia kak garantiia zakonnosti i pravosudii* (Moscow, 1957)
Kvashis, V., *Gumanizm sovetskogo ugolovnogo prava* (Moscow, 1969)
Landis, E., *Bandits and Partisans: The Antonov Movement in the Russian Civil War* (Pittsburgh, 2008)
Lapenna, I., 'Lenin, Law and Legality', in L. Schapiro and P. Reddaway (eds.), *Lenin. The Man, The Theorist, The Leader: A Reappraisal* (New York, 1967), 235–64
Laputin, V., 'Voennye sudy na strazhe sotsialisticheskoi zakonnosti', in L. Smirnov, V. Kulikov, and B. Nikiforov (eds.), *Verkovnyi sud SSSR* (Moscow, 1974), 110–22
Lauchlan, I., 'Chekist *Mentalité* and the Origins of the Great Terror', in J. Harris (ed.), *The Anatmony of Terror: Political Violence under Stalin* (Oxford, 2013), 13–28
Leggett, G., 'The Cheka and a Crisis of Communist Conscience', *Survey*, 25, 3 (1980), 122–37
Leggett, G., *The Cheka: Lenin's Political Police* (revised edition, Oxford, 1986)
Lenoe, M., *Closer to the Masses: Stalinist Culture, Social Revolution, and Soviet Newspapers* (Cambridge, MA, 2004)
Leont'ev, Ia., and Rublev, D., 'Marusia Nikiforova pered Revtribunalom: istoriia odnogo pokazatel'nogo protsessa', in A. Posadskii (ed.), *'Atamanshchina' i 'partizanshchina' v Grazhdanskoi voine: ideologiia, voennoe uchastie, kadry. Sbornik statei i materialov* (Moscow, 2015), 40–60
Levinson, S., 'Law as Literature', *Texas Law Review*, 60, 3 (1982), 373–403
Levin-Stankevich, B., 'Cassation, Judicial Interpretation and the Development of Civil and Criminal Law in Russia, 1864-1917: The Institutional Consequences of the 1864 Court Reform in Russia' (PhD dissertation, State University of New York, Buffalo, 1984)
Levshin, K., *Dezertirstvo v Krasnoi armii v gody Grazhdanskoi voiny (po materialam Severo-Zapada Rossii)* (St Petersburg, 2016)
Leyda, J., *Kino: A History of the Russian and Soviet Film* (3rd edition, London, 1983)
Lezov, I., 'Sudebnoe stroitel'stvo na mestakh v pervye mesiatsy sovetskoi vlasti', *Vestnik Moskovskogo universiteta. Seriia 11. Pravo*, 1 (1998), 115–22
Liakas, A., 'Pervye proletarskie sudy', *Sotsialisticheskaia zakonnost'*, 7 (1967), 17–19

Lih, L., 'Melodrama and the Myth of the Soviet Union', in L. McReynolds and J. Neuberger (eds.), *Imitations of Life: Two Centuries of Melodrama in Russia* (Durham, NC, 2002), 178–207

Lih, L., *Lenin* (London, 2011)

Likhachev, P., 'Sorokoletie voennykh tribunalov', *Sotsialisticheskaia zakonnost'*, 12 (1958), 7–11

Lindenmeyr, A., 'The First Soviet Political Trial: Countess Sofia Panina before the Petrograd Revolutionary Tribunal', *The Russian Review*, 60, 4 (2001), 505–25

Lindenmeyr, A., *Citizen Countess: Sofia Panina and the Fate of Revolutionary Russia* (Madison, 2019)

Litvin, A., *Krasnyi i belyi terror v Rossii. 1918–1922 gg.* (Moscow, 2004)

Liventsev, D. V., *Voennaia propaganda na RKKF v period grazhdanskoi voiny (1917–1921 gg.)* (Voronezh, 2013)

Livshin, A., *Nastroeniia i politicheskie emotsii v Sovetskoi Rossii: 1917–1932 gg.* (Moscow, 2010)

Lomov, V., and Lomov, N., *Organy predvaritel'nogo sledstviia Sovetskoi Rossii v period grazhdanskoi voiny (seredina 1918 g.-1920 g.)* (Volgograd, 2003)

Lovell, S., 'Stenography and the Public Sphere in Modern Russia', *Cahiers du Monde russe*, 56, 2–3 (2015), 291–325

Luneev, V., 'Politicheskaia prestupnost', *Gosudarstvo i pravo*, 7 (1994), 107–21

Luneev, V., 'Politicheskaia prestupnost' v Rossii: Proshloe i nastoiashchee', *Obshchestvennye nauki i sovremennost'*, 5 (1999), 66–79

McAuley, M., *Bread and Justice: State and Society in Petrograd, 1917–1922* (Oxford, 1991)

McDonald, T., *Face to the Village: The Riazan Countryside under Soviet Rule, 1921–1930* (Toronto, 2011)

Mackay, J., *Dziga Vertov: Life and Work. Volume 1: 1896–1921* (Brighton, MA, 2018)

McKernan, L., 'Newsreels: Form and Function', in R. Howells and R. Matson (eds.), *Using Visual Evidence* (Maidenhead, 2009), 95–106

McKnight, B., *The Quality of Mercy: Amnesties and Traditional Chinese Justice* (Honolulu, 1981)

McReynolds, L., *Murder Most Russian: True Crime and Punishment in Late Imperial Russia* (Ithaca, 2013)

Maksakova, L., *Agitpoezd 'Oktiabr'skaia revoliutsiia' (1919–1920)* (Moscow, 1956)

Maksimova, O., *Zakonotvorchestvo v Sovetskoi Rossii v 1917–1922 godakh* (Moscow, 2011)

Makutchev, A., *'Prigovor okonchatel'nyi, obzhalovaniiu ne podlezhit...' Revoliutsionnye tribunaly v Sovetskoi Rossii v gody Grazhdanskoi voiny* (Moscow, 2012)

Malkevich, T., 'K istorii pervykh dekretov o sovetskom sude', *Sovetskoe gosudarstvo i pravo*, 7 (1940), 94–107; 8–9 (1940), 164–79

Malykh, I., 'Sozdanie i deiatel'nost' revoliutsionnykh tribunalov na Iuzhnom Urale v 1919–1921 godakh (istoricheskii aspekt)' (*kandidat* dissertation, Cheliabinsk Institute of the Ural's Academy of State Service, 2010)

Mason, L., 'The "Burden of Proof": Criminal Justice and the Renewal of Oral Culture during the French Revolution', *The Journal of Modern History*, 76, 1 (2004), 29–61

Mawani, R., 'Law's Archive', *Annual Review of Law and Social Science*, 8 (2012), 337–65

Mawdsley, E., 'The Case of Captain Shchastny', *Sbornik: Newsletter of the Study Group on the Russian Revolution*, 3 (1977), 22–33

Mawdsley, E., *The Russian Revolution and the Baltic Fleet* (Basingstoke, 1978)

Mawdsley, E., *The Russian Civil War* (revised edition, Edinburgh, 2000)

Maximoff, G., *The Guillotine at Work. Vol. I: The Leninist Counter-revolution* (Sanday, 1979)

Meierhenrich, J., and Pendas, D., '"The Justice of My Cause is Clear, but There's Politics to Fear": Political Trials in Theory and History', in J. Meierhenrich, and D. Pendas (eds.), *Political Trials in Theory and History* (Cambridge, 2017), 1-64

Melancon, M., 'Revolutionary Culture in the Early Soviet Republic: Communist Executive Committees versus the Cheka, Fall 1918', *Jahrbücher für Geschichte Osteuropas*, 57, 1 (2009), 1–22

Melgounov, S., *The Red Terror in Russia* (Westport, 1975)

Merryman, J., *The Civil Law Tradition: An Introduction to the Legal Systems of Western Europe and Latin America* (2nd edition, Stanford, 1985)

Mironova, T., 'Revoliutsionnyi tribunal pechati petrogradskogo soveta', in G. Sobolev (ed.), *Piterskie rabochie v bor'be s kontrrevoliutsiei v 1917-1918gg.* (Moscow, 1986), 166–70

Miroshnichenko, I., 'Polozhenie o voennykh sledovateliakh ot 30 sentiabria 1919 g. i ego znachenie v razvitii instituta predvaritel'nogo sledstviia v sovetskom ugolovnom protsesse', *Vestnik Moskovskogo universiteta. Seriia XII. Pravo*, 1 (1967), 46–54

Miroshnichenko, I., 'Predvaritel'noe sledstvie v organakh sovetskoi voennoi iustitsii v gody grazhdanskoi voiny i interventsii (1918–1921 gg.), *Vestnik Moskovskogo universiteta. Seriia XII. Pravo*, 4 (1968), 26–36

Miroshnichenko, I., 'Revoliutsionnye voennye tribunaly v grazhdanskuiu voinu (1918-1920 gody)', in *Na strazhe sotsialisticheskoi zakonnosti (50 let voennym tribunalam)* (Moscow, 1968), 109–18

Miroshnichenko, I., *Vozniknovenie i razvitie revoliutsionnykh voennykh tribunalov (1918–1920 gg.)* (dissertation autoreferat, Moscow, 1968)

Mishunin, P., 'Iz istorii pervogo dekreta o sude', *Voprosy istorii*, 4 (1949), 9–21

Mishunin, P., *Ocherki po istorii sovetskogo ugolovnogo prava, 1917–1918 gg.* (Moscow, 1954)

Molchanov, L., *Gazetnaia pressa Rossii v gody revoliutsii i Grazhdanskoi voiny (okt. 1917–1920 gg.)* (Moscow, 2002)

Molodtsygin, M., *Krasnaia armiia: Rozhdenie i stanovlenie. 1917–1920 gg.* (Moscow, 1997)

Moore, S., *Law as Process: An Anthropological Approach* (London, 1978)

Morozov, K., *Sudebnyi protsess sotsialistov-revoliutsionerov i tiuremnoe protivostoianie (1922–1926): etika i taktika protivoborstva* (Moscow, 2005)

Morozov, K., 'Aktory sudebnogo protsessa sotsialistov-revoliutsionerov 1922 g. v kontekste ego istoricheskogo znacheniia', in *Sudebnye politicheskie protsessy v SSSR i kommunisticheskikh stranakh Evropy* (Novosibirsk, 2011), 10–23

Morozova, O., *Antropologiia grazhdanskoi voiny* (Rostov-on-Don, 2012)

Moustafa, T., 'Law and Courts in Authoritarian Regimes', *Annual Review of Law and Social Science*, 10 (2014), 281–99

Mozokhin, O., *Pravo na repressii: Vnesudebnye polnomochiia organov gosudarstvennoi bezopasnosti (1918–1953)* (Moscow, 2006)

Mramornov, A., 'Sudebnyi protsess protiv pravoslavnogo dukhoventsva v Saratove v 1918-1919 godakh', *Otechestvennaia istoriia*, 4 (2008), 97–104

Mukhamedov, R., Chigrin, M., and Nikitin, A., 'Kontrrevoliutsionnye prestupleniia v sudebnoi praktike Simbirskogo gubernskogo revoliutsionnogo tribunala v 1918-1920 godakh', *Nauchnyi dialog*, 5 (2019), 348–64

Muranov, A., and Zviagintsev, V., *Sud nad sud'iami (osobaia papka Ul'rikha)* (Kazan', 1993)

Murav, H., *Russia's Legal Fictions* (Ann Arbor, 1998)

Muravyeva, M., 'The Culture of Complaint: Approaches to Complaining in Russia – An Overview', *Laboratorium*, 6, 3 (2014), 93–104

Murphy, K., *Revolution and Counterrevolution: Class Struggle in a Moscow Metal Factory* (Oxford, 2005)

Musaev, B., *Prestupnost' v Petrograde v 1917–1921gg. i bor'ba s nei* (St Petersburg, 2001)

Nader, L., *The Life of the Law: Anthropological Projects* (Berkeley, 2002)

Naimushin, M., *Deiatel'nost' revoliutsionnykh tribunalov i organov VChK v Avtonomnoi oblasti Komi (Zyrian) (1918–1921 gg.)* (Syktyvkar, 1996)

Narskii, I., *Zhizn' v katastrofe: Budni naseleniia Urala v 1917–1922 gg.* (Moscow, 2001)

Na strazhe sotsialisticheskoi zakonnosti (50 let voennym tribunalam) (Moscow, 1968)

Nasybullin, F., 'Sudebnaia reforma 1922 g. i ee osushchestvlenie v Tatarii', in *Razvitie politiko-pravovoi sistemy sotsializma (istoriia i sovremennost')* (Sverdlovsk, 1988), 64–70

Nazarenko, K., *Flot, revoliutsiia i vlast' v Rossii: 1917–1921* (Moscow, 2011)

Nelken, D., 'Defining and Using the Concept of Legal Culture', in E. Örücü and D. Nelken (eds.), *Comparative Law: A Handbook* (Oxford, 2007), 109–32

Nethercott, F., *Russian Legal Culture Before and After Communism: Criminal Justice, Politics, and the Public Sphere* (Abingdon, 2007)

Neuberger, J., 'Popular Legal Cultures: The St Petersburg *Mirovoi sud*', in B. Eklof, J. Bushnell, and L. Zakharova (eds.), *Russia's Great Reforms, 1855–1881* (Bloomington, 1994), 231–46

Neuberger, J., '"Shysters" or Public Servants? Uncertified Lawyers and Legal Aid for the Poor in Late Imperial Russia', *Russian History*, 1–4 (1996), 295–310

Newman, D., 'Criminal Strategies and Institutional Concerns in the Soviet Legal System: An Analysis of Criminal Appeals in Moscow Province, 1921-1928' (PhD dissertation, University of California Los Angeles, 2013)

Newman, D., 'Cassation of Criminal Cases from Moscow Province Courts and Tribunals, 1921-1928', *The Soviet and Post-Soviet Review*, 41, 2 (2014), 146–68

Newman, K., *Law and Economic Organization: A Comparative Study of Preindustrial Societies* (Cambridge, 1983)

Newton, S., *Law and the Making of the Soviet World: The Red Demiurge* (Abingdon, 2015)

Nikolaev, A., 'Vremennye sudy v Petrograde (mart-iiul' 1917 g.): vzlet i padenie', in *Epokha voin i revoliutsii: 1914–1922* (St Petersburg, 2017), 87–99

Norris, S., *A War of Images: Russian Popular Prints, Wartime Culture and National Identity, 1812–1945* (DeKalb, 2006)

Novikova, L., 'Russia's Red Revolutionary and White Terror, 1917-1921: A Provincial Perspective', *Europe-Asia Studies*, 65, 9 (2013), 1755–70

Novitskaia, T., 'Pravosoznanie trudiashchikhsia mass i bor'ba s samosudami v pervyi god sovetskoi vlasti', *Vestnik Moskovskogo universiteta. Seriia 11. Pravo*, 1 (1982), 40–5

Novitskaia, T., *Grazhdanskii kodeks RSFSR 1922 goda* (Moscow, 2012)

Novoselov, D., 'Krizis VChK v kontse 1918 – nachale 1919 godov', *Otechestvennaia istoriia*, 6 (2005), 66–77

Oda, H., 'The Emergence of *Pravovoe Gosudarstvo (Rechsstaat)* in Russia', *Review of Central and East European Law*, 25, 3 (1999), 373–434

Okorokov, A., *Oktiabr' i krakh russkoi burzhuaznoi pressy* (Moscow, 1970)

Oleinik, I., *Organy iustitsii sovetskoi Rossii v 1917–1936 gg.* (Ivanovo, 2003)

Olikov, S., *Dezertirstvo v krasnoi armii i bor'ba s nim* (Moscow, 1926)

Orlov, I., and Markosian, G., *Vziatka i bor'ba s nei v gody nepa* (Moscow, 2011)

Orlov, V., 'Iz istorii stanovleniia sotsialisticheskoi zakonnosti', *Istoriia SSSR*, 6 (1975), 113–24

Ovechkin, V., 'Dezertirstvo iz Krasnoi armii v gody grazhdanskoi voiny', *Voprosy istorii*, 3 (2003), 108–15

Palat, M., 'Regulating Conflict through the Petition', in M. Palat (ed.), *Social Identities in Revolutionary Russia* (Basingstoke, 2001), 86–112

Palmer, N., Clark, P., and Granville, D. (eds.), *Critical Perspectives in Transitional Justice* (Cambridge, 2012)

Papazian, E., *Manufacturing Truth: The Documentary Moment in Early Soviet Culture* (DeKalb, 2009)

Pashentsev, D., and Bogoliubov, S. (eds.), *Pravovye osnovy rossiiskikh revoliutsionnykh preobrazovanii 1917 goda* (Moscow, 2019)

Pavlov, D., 'Tribunal'nyi etap sovetskoi sudebnoi sistemy. 1917–1922 gg.', *Voprosy istorii*, 6 (2007), 3–16

Pavlov, V., and Uzdin, M (eds.), *Istoriia zheleznodorozhnogo transporta Rossii i Sovetskogo Soiuza* (2 volumes, St Petersburg, 1994–7)

Pendas, D., 'Testimony', in M. Dobson and B. Ziemann (eds.), *Reading Primary Sources: The Interpretation of Texts from Nineteenth- and Twentieth-Century History* (London, 2009), 226–42

Penter, T., 'Öffentlichkeit und Rechtsprechung unter der frühen Sowjetmacht. Der Prozeß gegen den "Južnyj Rabočij" in Odessa 1918', *Jahrbücher für Geschichte Osteuropas*, 50, 4 (2002), 558–76

Penzin, G., 'Oktiabr' i stanovlenie apparata okhrany revoliutsionnogo poriadka i zakonnosti v Sibiri (konets 1917-nachalo 1920 gg.)', in *Ustanovlenie i uprochenie sovetskoi vlasti v Sibiri (1918–1925 gg.). Novosibirskii gosudarstvennyi pedagogicheskii institut. Nauchnye trudy. Vypusk 102* (Novosibirsk, 1974), 3–16

Pertsev, V., '"Imenem revoliutsii!": Iz istorii sozdaniia i deiatel'nosti Voronezhskogo gubernskogo revoliutsionnogo tribunala v 1917-1923 gg.', *Vestnik Voronezhskogo gosudarstvennogo universiteta. Seriia: Istoriia, politologiia, sotsiologiia*, 1 (2008), 28–43

Petrochenkov, A., 'Stanovlenie i razvitie sistemy voennykh sudov (voennykh tribunalov) v Rossii', *Rossiiskaia iustitsiia*, 1 (2009), 57–61

Petukhov, G., *Sovetskii sud i stanovlenie revoliutsionnoi zakonnosti v gosudarstvennom upravlenii* (Kiev–Odessa, 1982)

Petukhov, N., *Istoriia voennykh sudov Rossii* (Moscow, 2005)

P'ianova, O., 'Normativno-pravovye polozheniia organizatsii revoliutsionnykh tribunalov v pervyi period razvitiia sovetskogo gosudarstva i prava', in A. Kiselev (ed.), *Problemy istorii v stat'iakh i tezisakh molodykh uchenykh* (Omsk, 2002), 80–9

P'ianova, O., 'Revoliutsionnye tribunaly Zapadnoi Sibiri (konets 1917 – nachalo 1923 gg.)' (*kandidat* dissertation, Omsk State Pedagogical University, 2002)

P'ianova, O., 'Normativno-pravovye osnovy vossozdaniia revoliutsionnykh tribunalov Zapadnoi Sibiri. Sentiabr' 1919 g. – iiun' 1921 g.', in I. Vetrenko (ed.), *Sotsial'no znachimye problemy sovremennogo obshchestva* (Omsk, 2005), 10–20

Pinnow, K., 'From All Sides: Interdisciplinary Knowledge, Scientific Collaboration, and the Soviet Criminological Laboratories of the 1920s', *Slavic Review*, 76, 1 (2017), 122–46

Pipes, R., *Legalised Lawlessness: Soviet Revolutionary Justice* (London, 1986)

Pipes, R., 'Lenin's Gulag', *International Journal of Political Science and Development*, 2 (6) (2014), 140–6

Pirani, S., *The Russian Revolution in Retreat, 1920–24: Soviet Workers and the New Communist Elite* (Abingdon, 2008)

Pivovarov, M., 'Struktura i kadrovyi sostav revoliutsionnykh tribunalov v Sibiri (konets 1919 - nachalo 1923 g.)', in I. Kuznetsov (ed.), *Sibir': problemy istorii povsednevnosti XVII-XX vv.* (Novosibirsk, 2005), 114–25

Pivovarov, M., 'Uchastie revoliutsionnykh tribunalov Sibiri v prodovol'stvennoi kampanii 1920-1921 gg.', *Gumanitarnye nauki v Sibiri*, 2 (2005), 88–91

Pivovarov, M., 'Revoliutsionnye tribunaly v Sibiri (noiabr' 1919 - ianvar' 1923 g.)' (*kandidat* dissertation, Novosibirsk State University, 2007)

Plekhanov, A., *Dzerzhinskii. Pervyi chekist Rossii* (Moscow, 2007)

Plotniek, A., *Petr Stuchka i istoki sovetskoi pravovoi mysli, 1917–1925* (Riga, 1970)

Plotnikov, I., *Kniaz' G. E. L'vov: Zhizn' i deiatel'nost', tiuremnoe zakliuchenie v Ekaterinburge, obstoiatel'stva osvobozhdeniia* (Ekaterinburg, 2011)

Polianskii, N., 'Revoliutsionnye tribunaly', *Pravo i zhizn'*, 8–10 (1927), 67–79

Polianskii, N., 'Obshchestvennoe obvinenie v sovetskom zakonodatel'stve', *Sotsialisticheskaia zakonnost'*, 11 (1937), 57–66

Pomeranz, W., 'Justice from Underground: The History of the Underground *Advokatura*', *The Russian Review*, 52, 3 (1993), 321–40

Pomeranz, W., 'Legal Assistance in Tsarist Russia: The St Petersburg Consultation Bureaus', *Wisconsin International Law Journal*, 14, 3 (1996), 586–610

Pomeranz, W., 'The Practice of Law and the Promise of Law: The *Advokatura* and the Civil Process in Tsarist Russia', *Kritika*, 16, 2 (2015), 235–62

Pomeranz, W., *Law and the Russian State: Russia's Legal Evolution from Peter the Great to Vladimir Putin* (London, 2018)

Pomeranz, W., 'The Provisional Government and the Law-Based State', in C. Read, P. Waldron, and A. Lindenmeyr (eds.), *Russia's Home Front in War and Revolution, 1914–22. Book 4: Reintegration—The Struggle for the State* (Bloomington, 2018), 111–37

Popkins, G., 'Code versus Custom? Norms and Tactics in Peasant Volost Court Appeals, 1889-1917', *The Russian Review*, 59, 3 (2000), 408–24

Popkins, G., 'Peasant Experiences of the Late Tsarist State: District Congresses of Land Captains, Provincial Boards and the Legal Appeals Process, 1891-1917', *Slavonic and East European Review*, 78, 1 (2000), 90–114

Portelli, A., 'The Oral Shape of the Law: The "April 7 Case"', in A. Portelli, *The Death of Luigi Trastulli and Other Stories: Form and Meaning in Oral History* (Albany, 1991), 241–69

Portnov, V., 'Revoliutsionnye tribunaly v pervye gody sovetskoi vlasti (1917–1920 gg.), *Sovetskaia iustitsiia*, 22 (1966), 18–19

Portnov, V., 'Organizatsiia ugolovnogo pravosudiia RSFSR (1917-1922 gg.)', *Vestnik Moskovskogo universiteta. Seriia XII. Pravo*, 6 (1972), 47–54

Portnov, V., 'V. I. Lenin i stanovlenie revoliutsionnoi zakonnosti v pervye gody Sovetskoi vlasti (1917-1920 gg.)', *Istoriia SSSR*, 2 (1980), 46–55

Portnov, V., 'Revoliutsionnaia zakonnost' v pervye gody Sovetskoi vlasti (1917–1920)', in *Pravovye problemy istorii gosudarstvennykh uchrezhdenii* (Sverdlovsk, 1983), 3–16

Portnov, V., 'Velikii oktiabr' i sozdanie osnov pravosudiia v sovetskoi Rossii', *Vestnik Moskovskogo universiteta. Seriia 11. Pravo*, 6 (1987), 22–30

Portnov, V., and Slavin, M., *Pravovye osnovy stroitel'stva Krasnoi Armii, 1918-1920gg.* (Moscow, 1985)

Portnov, V., and Slavin, M., *Stanovlenie pravosudiia Sovetskoi Rossii (1917–1922 gg.)* (Moscow, 1990)

Portnov, V., and Smirnova, G., *Sovetskaia voennaia iustitsiia (1918–1920 gg.)* (Moscow, 1960)

Pozdniakova, A., 'Dolzhnostnye prestupleniia sotrudnikov pravookhranitel'nykh organov v 1918-1919 gg. (po materialam Viatskogo gubernskogo revoliutsionnogo tribunal)', *Vestnik Viatskogo gosudarstvennogo gumanitarnogo universiteta*, 4 (5) (2012), 79–84

Pozdniakova, A., 'Deiatel'nost' Viatskogo gubernskogo revoliutsionnogo tribunala v 1918–1922 gg. kak faktor stabilizatsii vlasti bol'shevikov v regione' (dissertation autoreferat, *kandidat* dissertation, Viatka State Humanitarian University, 2015)

Poznanskii, A., 'Advokat - aktivnyi propagandist sovetskogo prava', *Sotsialisticheskaia zakonnost'*, 2 (1958), 65–6

Poznanskii, V., 'Sud nad ministrami Kolchaka', *Izvestiia Sibirskogo otdeleniia akademii nauk SSSR. Seriia istorii, filologii i filosofii*, 1 (1990), 44–51

Pronin, V., 'Organizatsiia i deiatel'nost' pervykh sudov Rossiiskoi Federatsii', *Sovetskaia iustitsiia*, 9 (1957), 27–30

Quenoy, P.du, 'Perfecting the Show Trial: The Case of Baron von Ungern-Sternberg', *Revolutionary Russia*, 19, 1 (2006), 79–93

Quigley, J., *Soviet Legal Innovation and the Law of the Western World* (Cambridge, 2007)

Rabinovich, P., 'Bor'ba za sovetskuiu sotsialisticheskuiu zakonnost' v RSFSR (1917–1920 gg.)', *Pravovedenie*, 5 (1967), 122–31

Rabinowitch, A., 'The Shchastny File: Trotsky and the Case of the Hero of the Baltic Fleet', *The Russian Review*, 58, 4 (1999), 615–34

Rabinowitch, A., *The Bolsheviks in Power: The First Year of Soviet Rule in Petrograd* (Bloomington and Indianapolis, 2007)

Raikova, I., 'Chelovek i revoliutsiia v zerkale chastushki', in *Velikaia rossiiskaia revoliutsiia: obshchestvo, chelovek, kul'tura, povsednevnost'* (2 volumes, Moscow, 2017), II, 176–87

Rakhunov, R., 'Istoriia sozdaniia odnogo dekreta', *Sovetskaia iustitsiia*, 8 (1967), 17–18

Rakhunov, R., 'Rol' V. I. Lenina v sozdanii sovetskogo suda', *Sotsialisticheskaia zakonnost'*, 2 (1969), 3–8

Raleigh, D., *Experiencing Russia's Civil War: Politics, Society and Revolutionary Culture in Saratov, 1917–1922* (Princeton, 2002)

Rasskazov, L., *Karatel'nye organy v protsesse formirovaniia i funktsionirovaniia administrativno-komandnoi sistemy v Sovetskom gosudarstve (1917–1941gg.)* (Ufa, 1994)

Rasulev, A., *Sozdanie i razvitie sovetskogo suda v Uzbekistane* (Tashkent, 1958)

Rat'kovskii, I., *Krasnyi terror i deiatel'nost' VChK v 1918 godu* (St Petersburg, 2006)

Rawson, D., 'The Death Penalty in Late Tsarist Russia: An Investigation of Judicial Procedures', *Russian History*, 11, 1 (1984), 29–52

Read, C., *War and Revolution in Russia, 1914–22* (Basingstoke, 2013)

Regel'son, L., *Tragediia Russkoi tserkvi* (Moscow, 2007)

Rendle, M., 'Revolutionary Tribunals and the Origins of Terror in Early Soviet Russia', *Historical Research*, 84, 226 (2011), 693–721

Rendle, M., 'The Problem of the 'Local' in Revolutionary Russia: Moscow Province, 1914-1922', in S. Badcock, L. Novikova, and A. Retish (eds.), *Russia's Home Front in War and Revolution, 1914–22. Book 1. Russia's Revolution in Regional Perspective* (Bloomington, 2015), 19–44

Rendle, M., 'How Revolutionary was Revolutionary Justice? Legal Culture in Russia Across the Revolutionary Divide', in M. Neumann and A. Willimott (eds.), *Rethinking the Russian Revolution as Historical Divide: Tradition, Rupture, and Modernity* (London, 2017), 46–66

Resis, A., 'Lenin on Freedom of the Press', *The Russian Review*, 36, 3 (1977), 274–96

Retish, A., 'Peasant Identities in Russia's Turmoil: Status, Gender, and Ethnicity in Viatka Province, 1914-1921' (PhD dissertation, Ohio State University, 2003)

Retish, A., *Russia's Peasants in Revolution and Civil War* (Cambridge, 2008)
Retish, A., 'Controlling Revolution: Understandings of Violence through the Rural Soviet Courts, 1917-1923', *Europe-Asia Studies*, 65, 9 (2013), 1789–806
Retish, A., 'Breaking Free from the Prison Walls: Penal Reforms and Prison Life in Revolutionary Russia', *Historical Research*, 90, 247 (2017), 134–50
Retish, A., 'Poisk spravedlivosti v revoliutsii: mestnaia sudebnaia Sistema Viatskoi gubernii v 1917-1922 gg.', in *Epokha voin i revoliutsii: 1914–1922* (St Petersburg, 2017), 100–11
Retish, A., 'Judicial Reforms and Revolutionary Justice: The Establishment of the Court System in Soviet Russia, 1917-22', in C. Read, P. Waldron, and A. Lindenmeyr (eds.), *Russia's Home Front in War and Revolution, 1914–22. Book 4: Reintegration—The Struggle for the State* (Bloomington, 2018), 371–401
Revolution: Russian Art, 1917–1932 (London, 2017)
Rideout, J. C., 'Storytelling, Narrative Rationality, and Legal Persuasion', *Legal Writing: The Journal of the Legal Writing Institute*, 14 (2008), 53–86
Rivlin, A., 'Pervye zakonodatel'nye akty o sovetskom sude na Ukraine', *Sovetskoe gosudarstvo i pravo*, 11 (1949), 57–65
Robbins, R., *Overtaken by the Night: One Russian's Journey through Peace, War, Revolution & Terror* (Pittsburgh, 2017)
Roberts, G., *Forward Soviet! History and Non-fiction Film in the USSR* (London, 1999)
Romashkin, P., *Amnistiia i pomilovanie v SSSR* (Moscow, 1959)
Rosen, L., *Law as Culture: An Invitation* (Princeton, 2006)
Rosenberg, W., 'Paramilitary Violence in Russia's Civil Wars, 1918-1920', in R. Gerwarth and J. Horne (eds.), *War in Peace: Paramilitary Violence in Europe after the Great War* (Oxford, 2013), 21–39
Rozental', I., 'Purishkevich – izvestnyi i neizvestnyi (k voprosu ob evoliutsii pravogo radikalizma v Rossii)', in *Problemy politicheskoi i ekonomicheskoi istorii Rossii* (Moscow, 1998), 284–303
Rozhneva, Zh., 'Sudebnye protsessy predstavitelei "istoricheskoi kontrrevoliutsii" v 1920-e gg. na territorii Zapadnoi Sibiri', in *Sudebnye politicheskie protsessy v SSSR i kommunisticheskikh stranakh Evropy* (Novosibirsk, 2011), 23–33
Rudnev, D., and Tsybov, S., *Sledovatel' Verkhovnogo tribunala* (Tallin, 1971)
Ryan, J., *Lenin's Terror: The Ideological Origins of Early Soviet State Violence* (London and New York, 2012)
Ryan, J., 'Cleansing NEP Russia: State Violence against the Russian Orthodox Church in 1922', *Europe-Asia Studies*, 65, 9 (2013), 1807–26
Ryan, J., 'The Sacralization of Violence: Bolshevik Justifiations for Violence and Terror during the Civil War', *Slavic Review*, 74, 4 (2015), 808–31
Ryan, J., '"They know not what they do?" Bolshevik Understandings of the Agency of the Perpertrator, 1918-1930', *Historical Research*, 90, 247 (2017), 151–71
Ryan, J., '"War against War": The Significance of the Great War in the Thought of V. I. Lenin on Violence, 1914-21', in C. Read, P. Waldron, and A. Lindenmeyr (eds.), *Russia's Home Front in War and Revolution, 1914–22. Book 4: Reintegration—The Struggle for the State* (Bloomington, 2018), 257–78
Sakwa, R., *Soviet Communists in Power: A Study of Moscow during the Civil War, 1918–1921* (Basingstoke, 1988)
Sanborn, J., *Drafting the Russian Nation: Military Conscription, Total War, and Mass Politics, 1905–1925* (DeKalb, 2003)
Sapargaliev, M., *Ocherk po istorii sovetskogo suda v Kazakhstane (1918–1920 gg.)* (Alma Ata, 1955)

Sarat, A. (ed.), *Law, Violence, and the Possibility of Justice* (Princeton, 2001)
Sarat, A., and Kearns, T., 'A Journey Through Forgetting: Toward a Jurisprudence of Violence', in A. Sarat and T. Kearns (eds.), *The Fate of Law* (Ann Arbor, 1991), 209–74
Sarat, A., and Kearns, T., 'Beyond the Great Divide: Forms of Legal Scholarship and Everyday Life', in A. Sarat and T. Kearns (eds.), *Law in Everyday Life* (Ann Arbor, 1993), 21–61
Sarat, A., and Kearns, T. (eds.), *Law's Violence* (Ann Arbor, 1993)
Sartori, P., 'What Went Wrong? The Failure of Soviet Policy on *Sharī'a* Courts in Turkestan, 1917-1923', *Die Welt des Islams*, 50 (2010), 397–43
Schapiro, L., 'The Importance of Law in the Study of Politics and History', in L. Schapiro, *Russian Studies*, ed. E. Dahrendorf (London, 1986), 29–44
Schmidt, B., and Schröder, I. (eds.), *Anthropology of Violence and Conflict* (Abingdon, 2001)
Schramm, J-M., 'Testimony, Witnessing', in A. Sarat, M. Anderson, and C. Frank (eds.), *Law and the Humanities: An Introduction* (Cambridge, 2010), 478–95
Schröder, I., and Schmidt, B. (eds.), *Anthropology of Violence and Conflict* (Abingdon, 2001)
Scott, J., *Domination and the Arts of Resistance: Hidden Transcripts* (New Haven, 1990)
Semiderkin, N., 'Sozdanie pervogo sovetskogo kodeksa', *Vestnik Moskovskogo universiteta. Seriia 11. Pravo*, 6 (1987), 38–46
Service, R., *Stalin* (London, 2004)
Shalamov, M., *Istoriia sovetskoi advokatury* (Moscow, 1939)
Shapiro, M., *Courts: A Comparative and Political Analysis* (Chicago, 1981)
Shapiro, M., 'Courts in Authoritarian Regimes', in T. Ginsburg and T. Moustafa (eds.), *Rule By Law: The Politics of Courts in Authoritarian Regimes* (Cambridge, 2008), 326–35
Shapko, V., *V. I. Lenin—sozdatel' sotsialisticheskoi zakonnosti* (Moscow, 1965)
Shatkovskaia, T., *Pravovaia mental'nost' Rossiiskikh krest'ian vtoroi poloviny XIX veka: opyt iuridicheskoi antropometrii* (Rostov-on-Don, 2000)
Shelley, L., 'Soviet Criminology after the Revolution', *The Journal of Criminal Law and Criminology*, 70, 3 (1979), 391–6
Shelley, L., 'Soviet Criminology: Its Birth and Demise, 1917-1936', *Slavic Review*, 38, 4 (1979), 614–28
Shishkin, V., 'Ishimskii sudebnyi protsess (22-28 fevralia 1921 g.)', in I. Kuryshev (ed.), *Krest'ianstvo vostochnykh regionov Rossii i Kazakhstana v revoliutsiiakh i grazhdanskoi voine (1905–1921gg.)* (Ishim, 2006), 187–201
Shishov, O., 'Smertnaia kazn' v istorii Sovetskogo gosudarstva', in S. Kelina (ed.), *Smertnaia kazn': za i protiv* (Moscow, 1989), 97–130
Shklar, J., *Legalism: Law, Morals, and Political Trials* (new edition, Cambridge, MA, 1986)
Shoemaker, K., 'Punishment', in A. Sarat, M. Anderson, and C. Frank (eds.), *Law and the Humanities: An Introduction* (Cambridge, 2010), 517–29
Shorokhova, A., 'Vozniknovenie i deiatel'nost' revoliutsionnogo tribunala v BashSSR', in A. Piletskii (ed.), *Problemy teorii i iuridicheskoi praktiki v Rossii* (Samara, 2006), 187–91
Shorokhova, A., 'Stanovlenie i razvitie sovetskogo suda v Bashkirii' (*kandidat* dissertation, Bashkir State University, 2007)
Shub, D., 'The Trial of the SRs', *The Russian Review*, 23, 4 (1964), 362–9
Siegelbaum, L., 'Defining and Ignoring Labor Discipline in the Early Soviet Period: The Comrades-Disciplinary Courts, 1918-1922', *Slavic Review*, 51, 4 (1992), 705–30
Siegelbaum, L., 'Narratives of Appeal and the Appeal of Narratives: Labor Discipline and its Contestation in the Early Soviet Period', *Russian History*, 24 (1997), 65–87

Silbey, S., 'Legal Culture and Cultures of Legality', in J. Hall, L. Grindstaff, and M-C Lo (eds.), *Handbook of Cultural Sociology* (London, 2010), 470–9

Simonett, J., 'The Trial as One of the Performing Arts', *American Bar Association Journal*, 52, 12 (1966), 1145–7

Simonian, M., *Zhizn' dlia revoliutsii* (Moscow, 1962)

Sipeikin, A., *Politika sovetskoi vlasti v otnoshenii Russkoi pravoslavnoi tserkvi v 1917–1921 godakh (na materialakh Tverskoi gubernii)* (Tver', 2007)

Skorkin, K., *Na strazhe zavoevanii Revoliutsii. Istoriia NKVD-VChK-GPU RSFSR. 1917–1923* (Moscow, 2011)

Smele, J., *The 'Russian' Civil Wars, 1916–1926: Ten Years That Shook the World* (London, 2015)

Smirnov, N., *Vysshie sudy revoliutsii (Tsentral'nye revoliutsionnye tribunaly, 1918–1922gg.)* (Moscow, 1990)

Smirnov, N., *Repressirovannoe pravosudie* (Moscow, 2001)

Smirnov, V. and Usmanov, R., *Istoriia advokatury Srednego Urala* (Ekaterinburg, 1999)

Smith, S., *Captives of Revolution: The Socialist Revolutionaries and the Bolshevik Dictatorship, 1918–1923* (Pittsburgh, 2011)

Smith, S. A. 'Year One in Petrograd', *New Left Review*, 52 (July–August 2008), 151–60

Smith, S. A., 'Introduction: Reflections on Villains, Victims and Violence', *Europe-Asia Studies*, 65, 9 (2013), 1691–9

Smith, S. A., *Russia in Revolution: An Empire in Crisis, 1890 to 1928* (Oxford, 2017)

Smith, S. A., 'Violence in the Russian Revolution and Civil War, 1914-20', in Ł. Adamski and B. Gajos (eds.), *Circles of the Russian Revolution: Internal and International Consequences of the Year 1917 in Russia* (Abingdon, 2019), 25–39

Smykalin, A., 'Oktiabr'skaia revoliutsiia i sozdanie pervykh sovetskikh kodeksov', in *Razvitie politiko-pravovoi sistemy sotsializma (istoriia i sovremennost')* (Sverdlovsk, 1988), 33–43

Smykalin, A., 'Sozdanie sovetskoi sudebnoi sistemy', *Rossiiskaia iustitsiia*, 2 (2002), 39–42

Smykalin, A., 'Sudebnaia reforma 1922 goda', *Rossiiskaia iustitsiia*, 4 (2002), 39–42

Sokolov, K., 'Deiatel'nost' repressivnykh organov Tverskoi gubernii v 1918–1920 godakh', in *Neizvestnyi stranitsy istorii Verkhnevolzh'ia* (Tver', 1994), 102–13

Solomon, P., 'Soviet Penal Policy, 1917-1934: A Reinterpretation', *Slavic Review*, 39, 2 (1980), 195–217

Solomon, P., 'Criminalization and Decriminalization in Soviet Criminal Policy', *Law and Society Review*, 16, 1 (1981–2), 9–44

Solomon, P., *Soviet Criminal Justice under Stalin* (Cambridge, 1996)

Solomon, P. (ed.), *Reforming Justice in Russia, 1864–1996: Power, Culture and the Limits of Legal Order* (Armonk, 1997)

Solomon, P., 'Courts and Judges in Authoritarian Regimes', *World Politics*, 60, 1 (2007), 122–45

Solomon, P., 'Judicial Power in Authoritarian States: The Russian Experience', in T. Ginsburg and T. Moustafa (eds.), *Rule By Law: The Politics of Courts in Authoritarian Regimes* (Cambridge, 2008), 261–82

Solomon, P., 'Understanding the History of Soviet Criminal Justice: The Contribution of Archives and Other Sources', *The Russian Review*, 74, 2 (2015), 401–18

Sorokin, P., 'The New Soviet Codes and Soviet Justice', *Michigan Law Review*, 23, 1 (1924–25), 38–52

Stan, L. (ed.), *Transitional Justice in Eastern Europe and the Former Soviet Union: Reckoning with the Communist Past* (Abingdon, 2009)

Starr, J. and Collier, J. (eds.), *History and Power in the Study of Law: New Directions in Legal Anthropology* (Ithaca, 1989)
Sternik, I., 'Bor'ba za revoliutsionnuiu zakonnost' v pervye gody Sovetskoi vlasti', *Sovetskaia iustitsiia*, 4 (1957), 32–5
Sternik, I., 'V. I. Lenin i pervye sudebnye dekrety', *Sovetskoe gosudarstvo i pravo*, 4 (1976), 112–14
Stites, R., *Revolutionary Dreams: Utopian Vision and Experimental Life in the Russian Revolution* (Oxford, 1989)
Stites, R., 'Trial as Theatre in the Russian Revolution', *Theatre Research International*, 23, 1 (1998), 7–13
Story, C., 'In a Court of Law: The Revolutionary Tribunals in the Russian Civil War, 1917-1921' (PhD dissertation, University of California Santa Cruz, 1998)
Strange, C. (ed.), *Qualities of Mercy: Justice, Punishment and Discretion* (Vancouver, 1996)
Stremovskii, V., *Uchastniki predvaritel'nogo sledstviia v sovetskom ugolovnom protsesse* (Rostov-on-Don, 1966)
Strogovich, M., *Voennye tribunaly sovetskogo gosudarstvo* (Moscow, 1942)
Stuchka, P., *Revoliutsionnaia rol' Sovetskogo prava* (3rd edition: Moscow, 1934)
Sudakova, T., 'Sozdanie i deiatel'nost' Otdeleniia Verkhovnogo tribunala VTsIK v Gorskoi ASSR (1921–1923 gg.): Istoricheskii aspekt' (*kandidat* dissertation, North Ossetian State University, 2009)
Sulaimanova, Kh., 'Istoricheskii ocherk o sozdanii sovetskikh sudov v Uzbekistane', *Sovetskoe gosudarstvo i pravo*, 3 (1949), 61–9
Sulaimanova, Kh., *Sobranie sochinenii. Tom I* (Tashkent, 1967)
Sunderland, W., *The Baron's Coat: A History of the Russian Empire in War and Revolution* (Ithaca, 2014)
Suny, R., *Red Flag Unfurled: History, Historians and the Russian Revolution* (London, 2017)
Swain, G., *Russia's Civil War* (Stroud, 2000)
Tager, A., 'Osnovyne problemy kassatsii v sovetskom ugolovnom protsesse', in N. Krylenko (ed.), *Problemy ugolovnoi politiki* (4 volumes, Moscow, 1935–7), IV, 67–86
Tager, A., 'Sovetskaia advokatura za 20 let', *Sotsialisticheskaia zakonnost'*, 11 (1937), 67–82
Tashbekova, I., and Kolotkov, M., 'Organizatsionno-pravovaia deiatel'nost' revoliutsionnykh tribunalov v sovetskoi Rossii v 1917–1922 gg.', *Aktual'nye problemy Rossiiskogo prava*, 1 (10) (2009), 62–9
Taylor, R., 'A Medium for the Masses: Agitation in the Soviet Civil War', *Soviet Studies*, 22, 4 (1971), 562–74
Teitel, R., *Transitional Justice* (Oxford, 2000)
Tepliakov, A., *Protsedura: ispolnenie smertnykh prigovorov v 1920–1930-x godakh* (Moscow, 2007)
Terliuk, I., '*Komunistichna revoliutsiia zgori' v Ukraini: z istorii stanovlennia ta zakriplennia v Ukraini radians'koi derzhavnosti i prava (1917–1920-ti rr.)* (L'viv, 2010)
Timasheff, N., 'The Impact of the Penal Law of Imperial Russia on Soviet Penal Law', *American Slavic and East European Review*, 12, 4 (1953), 441–62
Tissier, M., 'Local Laws and the Workings of Legal Knowledge in Late Imperial Russia', *Ab Imperio*, 4 (2012), 211–44
Tissier, M., 'Legal Literature 'for the People' and the Use of Language (Late Nineteenth and Early Twenteith Century)', in N. Vakhtin and B. Firsov (eds.), *Public Debate in Russia: Matters of (Dis)order* (Edinburgh, 2016), 85–100
Titkov, V., 'Organizatsionno-pravovye osnovy sovetskogo pravosudiia (1917-1929 gg.)' (*kandidat* dissertation, Vladimir Judicial Institute, 2008)

Titlinov, B., *Tserkov' vo vremia revoliutsii* (Petrograd, 1924)

Titov, Iu., 'Sudebnye organy v bor'be s kontrrevoliutsiei v vosstanovitel'nyi period', *Sotsialisticheskaia zakonnost'*, 9 (1967), 9–12

Titov, Iu., 'Pervye shagi gubernskikh sudov po sudebnoi reforme 1922 goda', *Vestnik Moskovskogo universiteta. Seriia XII. Pravo*, 1 (1974), 12–18

Titov, Iu., *Sozdanie sistemy sovetskikh revoliutsionnykh tribunalov* (Moscow, 1983)

Titov, Iu., 'Razvitie sistemy sovetskikh revoliutsionnykh tribunalov kak organov bor'by s naibolee opasnymi prestupleniiami', in Iu. Titov (ed.), *Voprosy istorii ugolovnogo prava i ugolovnoi politiki* (Moscow, 1986), 74–146

Titov, Iu., *Razvitie sistemy sovetskikh revoliutsionnykh tribunalov* (Moscow, 1987)

Titov, Iu., 'Revoliutsionnye tribunaly v bor'be s tserkovnoi kontrrevoliutsiei', in I. Isaev and O. Omel'chenko (eds.), *Istoriko-pravovye voprosy vzaimootnoshenii gosudarstva i tserkvi v istorii Rossii* (Moscow, 1988), 147–68

Titov, Iu., *Sovetskie revoliutsionnye tribunaly v mirnye gody stroitel'stva sotsializma* (Moscow, 1988)

Titov, Iu., 'Pervye normativnye akty o sovetskikh revoliutsionnykh tribunalakh', *Sovetskoe gosudarstvo i pravo*, 1 (1990), 119–24

Tokarev, Iu., 'Dokumenty narodnykh sudov (1917–1922 gg.)', in S. Valk (ed.), *Voprosy istoriografii i istochnikovedeniia istorii SSSR* (Moscow–Leningrad, 1963), 143–75

Tokarev, Iu., *Narodnoe pravotvorchestvo nakanune Velikoi Oktiabr'skoi sotsialisticheskoi revoliutsii* (Moscow, 1965)

Tret'iakovich, A., 'Stanovlenie sistemy sovetskogo pravosudiia (1917-1918 gg.)', *Istoriia gosudarstva i prava*, 9 (2006), 36–7

Tsivian, Y., *Early Cinema in Russia and its Cultural Reception* (Chicago, 1998)

Tuan, Y., *Space and Place: The Perspective of Experience* (London, 1977)

Turin, V., 'Ot kollegii pravozastupnikov do advokatury', *Sovetskaia iustitsiia*, 9 (1957), 38–40

Turin, V., 'Pervye shagi sovetskoi advokatury', *Sovetskaia iustitsiia*, 8 (1962), 18–19

Ul'ianova, L., 'Pervye shagi v sozdanii sovetskoi advokatury', *Vestnik Moskovskogo universiteta. Seriia XII. Pravo*, 1 (1971), 69–72

Urilov, I., *Iu. O. Martov: Politik i istorik* (Moscow, 1997)

Ushakov, I., 'Sozdanie pervogo narodnogo suda v Petrograde', *Sovetskoe gosudarstvo i pravo*, 1 (1957), 3–12

Utevskii, B., *Dosrochnoe osvobozhdenie i amnistiia* (Moscow, 1927)

Varfolomeev, Iu., *Rassledovanie deiatel'nosti praviashchego klassa Rossiiskoi imperii chrezvychainoi sledstvennoi komissiei vremennogo pravitel'stva* (Saratov, 2011)

Vasilenko, V., 'Bil'shovits'ki amnistii pochatku 1920-x rr. iak zasib borot'bi proti povstans'kogo rukhu', *Z arkhiviv VUChK-GPU-NKVD-KGB*, 1 (2011), 89–155, at http://history.org.ua/JournALL/gpu/gpu_2011_1/5.pdf [accessed 7 August 2017]

Vasilyev, P., 'Beyond Dispassion: Emotions and Judicial Decision-Making in Modern Europe', *Rechtsgeschichte—Legal History*, 25 (2017), 277–85, at https://pdfs.semanticscholar.org/e657/2f0e53778837cee2171f1bb0b0cdd1ac8062.pdf [accessed 17 October 2017]

Vasilyev, P., 'Revolutionary Conscience, Remorse and Resentment: Emotions and Early Soviet Criminal Law, 1917-22', *Historical Research*, 90, 247 (2017), 117–33

Vasilyev, P., 'Sex and Drugs and Revolutionary Justice: Negotiating "Female Criminality" in the Early Soviet Courtroom', *Journal of Social Policy Studies*, 16, 2 (2018), 341–54, at https://jsps.hse.ru/article/view/7833/8628 [accessed 20 October 2019]

Velikorodnova, A., '"Revoliutsionnaia zakonnost'" revtribunala', in *Pravookhranitel'nye organy Iuzhnogo Urala: istoriia i sovremennost'* (Orenburg, 2000), 119–22
Velikorodnova, A., 'Revoliutsionnye tribunaly kak predshestvenniki sovetskikh sudov', *Nauka XXI veka: Problemy i perspektivy: Materialy XXIV prepodavatel'skoi i XLII studencheskoi nauchno-prakticheskoi konferentsii OGPU. 4–5 aprelia 2002 g. Ch 5: Sektsii filosofii, istorii, sotsial'no-politicheskikh i ekonomicheskikh teorii* (Orenburg, 2002), 124–8
Vereshchagina, A., *Ugolovnaia iustitsiia mezhrevoliutsionnogo perioda (fevral'-oktiabr' 1917 goda)* (Moscow, 2016)
Verhoeven, C., 'Court Files', in M. Dobson and B. Ziemann (eds.), *Reading Primary Sources: The Interpretation of Texts from Nineteenth- and Twentieth-Century History* (London, 2009), 90–105
Vetrova, Z., 'Bor'ba s kontrrevoliutsionnoi pechat'iu v Petrograde v oktiabre-dekabre 1917g. (istoriografiia i istoriia)', in G. Sobolev (ed.), *Piterskie rabochie v bor'be s kontrrevoliutsiei v 1917–1918 gg.* (Moscow, 1986), 160–6
V. I. Lenin o demokratii i zakonnosti (Moscow, 1970)
V. I. Lenin o zakonnosti i pravosudii. Voprosy bor'by s prestupnost'iu. Vyp. 11 (Moscow, 1970)
Vladimirov, K., 'Red East: Soviet Central Asia in the 1920s', *Journal of Eurasian Studies*, 1 (2010), 127–33
Wagner, W., 'Tsarist Legal Policies at the End of the Nineteenth Century: A Study in Inconsistencies', *Slavonic and East European Review*, 54, 3 (1976), 371–94
Walzer, M., *Regicide and Revolution: Speeches at the Trial of Louis XVI* (new edition, New York, 1992)
Werth, N., 'A State against its People: Violence, Repression, and Terror in the Soviet Union', in S. Courtois et al. (eds.), *The Black Book of Communism: Crimes, Terror, Repression* (Cambridge, MA, 1999), 33–268
White, S., *The Bolshevik Poster* (New Haven, 1988)
Williams, M., Nagy, R., and Elster, J. (eds.), *Transitional Justice* (New York, 2012)
Wimberg, E., '"Replacing the Shackles": Soviet Penal Theory, Policy and Practice, 1917-1930' (PhD dissertation, University of Pittsburgh, 1996)
Winnie, L., 'The French Revolutionary Trials', in J. Meierhenrich and D. Pendas (eds.), *Political Trials in Theory and History* (Cambridge, 2017), 134–56
Wirtschafter, E., 'Russian Legal Culture and the Rule of Law', *Kritika*, 7, 1 (2006), 61–70
Witte, J., 'Violence in Lenin's Thought and Practice: The Spark and the Conflagration', *Terrorism and Political Violence*, 5, 3 (1993), 135–203
Wolfe, B., *Three Who Made a Revolution* (2 volumes, New York, 1964)
Wood, E., *Performing Justice: Agitation Trials in Early Soviet Russia* (Ithaca, 2005)
Wright, A., 'Stemming the Flow: The Red Army Anti-Desertion Campaign in Soviet Karelia (1919)', *Revolutionary Russia*, 25, 2 (2012), 141–62
Wright, A., 'The Establishment of Bolshevik Power on the Russian Periphery: Soviet Karelia, 1918-1919' (PhD dissertation, University of Glasgow, 2012)
Zalogina, O., 'Voprosy gosudarstva i prava v resheniiakh VI vserossiiskogo chrezvychainogo s"ezda sovetov', in *Iz istorii sovetskogo gosudarstva i prava* (Moscow, 1989), 36–45
Zelitch, J., *Soviet Administration of Criminal Law* (Philadelphia, 1931)
Zhil'tsov, S., *Smertnaia kazn' v istorii Rossii* (Moscow, 2002)
Zviagintsev, V., 'Pervyi smertnyi prigovor', *Chelovek i zakon*, 3–4 (1991), 112–47

Index

Note: Figures are indicated by an italic "*f*", respectively, following the page number.

Geographical references refer to tribunals operating in that location, publications from that location, and events taking place in that location.

Personal names are included for Bolsheviks, legal officials and other significant individuals, but not for those mentioned in case files unless there is more than one reference.

For the benefit of digital users, indexed terms that span two pages (e.g., 52–53) may, on occasion, appear on only one of those pages.